Outlook traveller
getaways»

weekend
breaks from Chennai

First Edition 2007
Copyright © Outlook Publishing (India) Private Limited, New Delhi. All Rights Reserved
Price: Rs 295
ISBN 81-89449-07-9

DISCLAIMER
No part of this book may be reproduced, stored in a retrieval system or transmitted in any form or means electronic, mechanical, photocopying, recording or otherwise, without prior written permission of Outlook Publishing (India) Private Limited. Brief text quotations with use of photographs are exempted for book review purposes only

As every effort is made to provide accurate and up-to-date information in this publication as far as possible, we would appreciate if readers would call our attention to any errors that may occur. Some details, however, such as telephone and fax numbers or email ids, room tariffs and addresses and other travel related information are liable to change. The publishers cannot accept responsibility for any consequences arising from the use of information provided in this book. However, we would be happy to receive suggestions and corrections for inclusion in the next edition. Please write to: The Editor, Outlook Traveller Getaways, AB-10, Safdarjung Enclave, New Delhi-110029

outlooktraveller.com
For updates, packages, news and new destinations, log on to our website
www.outlooktraveller.com

FROM THE EDITOR-IN-CHIEF

www.outlooktraveller.com

Editorial
EDITOR-IN-CHIEF Vinod Mehta
PRESIDENT & PUBLISHER
Maheshwer Peri
EDITOR Manju Rastogi
DEPUTY EDITOR Lesley A. Esteves
ASSOCIATE EDITOR Deepa A
CONSULTING EDITORS Ranee Sahaney,
Nagraj Adve

Research
INFO AND RESEARCH COORDINATORS
Rani G. Kalra, Julia Dutta, Mridula Bhalla,
A. Prabhavati
RESEARCHER-WRITER Prerna Singh
RESEARCHERS Geeta Tuteja,
Rajini Vasanth

Design
CONSULTING ART DIRECTOR
Runu Saxena
SENIOR DESIGNER Deepak Suri
DESIGNERS Rahul Sharma, Ashish
Rozario, Ronald Joseph, Deepika Agrawal
GRAPHIC DESIGNERS Rajesh K.G.,
Suraj Wadhwa
DTP COORDINATOR Ganesh Shah

Photography
PHOTO EDITORS Asmita Rangari,
Sanjay Sharma
PHOTOGRAPHER Bharat Aggarwal
PHOTO COORDINATORS Simrita Takhtar,
Priyali Saxena, Priyam Dhar, Kuldeep Kalia

Production
GENERAL MANAGER Anup Dwivedi
REGIONAL MANAGER Rakesh Mishra
ASSOCIATE MANAGERS Shashank Dixit,
Shekhar Pandey

Business Office
NATIONAL MANAGER Anand Dutt
NORTH Hiramoni Sarma, Arti Marwah,
Niraj Dubey
CIRCULATION Sudipto Mookherjee

Printed and published by
MAHESHWER PERI
on behalf of Outlook Publishing (India)
Private Limited from AB-10, Safdarjung
Enclave, New Delhi-110029

Printed at Infomedia India Ltd
A Wing, Ruby House, JK Sawant Marg
Dadar (West) Mumbai-400028

Dear Reader,

This guide book brings our award-winning weekend breaks series to Chennai readers, with 52 getaways spread across the four southern states.

For the past few months we have been steeped in the wealth of Tamil Nadu's heritage, in the ancient temples of southern Andhra, in the tiger lands of Tipu Sultan's realm in south Karnataka and in the kaleidoscopic colours of the very blessed state of Kerala. We stood awed before Lord Venkateshwara's abode in Tirumala, went birdwatching at Vedanthangal, gazed fascinated from elephant back at the lush expanses of Nagarhole and sank back to relax in the healing hands of the Ayurveda masters in Kumarakom. And we played, angled, trekked and worshipped along the banks of that most beautiful of rivers, the Cauvery.

So rich is the realm of this sacred river that no less than three Unesco World Heritage sites lie within its delta. We rode a coracle below the point where the Cauvery makes her dramatic entry into Tamil Nadu from Karnataka. We sampled the fragrant Ponni rice that grows only along her banks. And we bathed in her waters at 4.30 am under the all-knowing gaze of Lord Ranganathaswamy in Srirangam.

Chennai is well placed to make a holiday out of every weekend for it boasts the hi-tech East Coast Road, which has made Pondy a mere 3 hours drive away; it's Koyambedu Terminus — the largest in Asia — affords Chennai a multitude of comfortable overnight connections to the far-out Nilgiris, south-central Tamil Nadu and to south Andhra. Even more comfortable overnight trains cut the distance to the glorious backwaters of Kerala.

Here are your 52 reasons to make good use of your 52 weekends. May your journeys of discovery be as incredible as ours.

VINOD MEHTA
Editor-in-Chief

contents

TAMIL NADU

Mahabalipuram	**14**
Thirukaikundram	18
Kanchipuram	**21**
Sriperumbudur	27
Vedanthangal Bird Sanctuary	**28**
Pondicherry	**32**
Arikamedu	Auroville	44
Thiruvannamalai	**46**
Sattanur Dam	Gingee Fort	51
Yelagiri Hills	**52**
Jalagamparai Waterfalls	56
Chidambaram	**57**
Tranquebar	**64**
Karaikal	69
Kumbakonam	**70**
Nachiar Kovil	Thiruvidaimarudur	75
Darasuram	Swamimalai	76
Gangaikondacholapuram	78
Tiruchirapalli	**81**
Thirupattur	92
Hogenakkal Falls	**94**
Thanjavur	**99**
Thiruvaiyaru	108
Nagapattinam	**112**
Thiruvarur	117
Yercaud	**120**
Kamarajar Valley	**124**
Chettinad	**132**
Avudayarkovil	140
Palani	**144**
Madurai	**151**
Alanganallur	Pazhamudircholai	164
Azhagar Kovil	166
Kodaikanal	**169**
Beri-Jam Lake	176
Indira Gandhi Wildlife Sanctuary	**178**

THE NILGIRIS	
Coonoor	186
Kotagiri	190
Ooty	192
Bellikkal	206
Red Hills	210
Parson's Valley	215
Mudumalai Wildlife Sanctuary	219

ANDHRA PRADESH	
Tirumala-Tirupati	231
Srikalahasti	243
Lepakshi	247
Horsley Hills	250

KARNATAKA	
Healing in Bangalore	256
Bannerghatta National Park	264
Nandi Hills	271
Bheemeshwari	274
Sangam	Mekedatu	Kokrebellur Pelicanry	278
Shivanasamudram	279
Srirangapatna	283

RECLAIM YOUR LIFE.

TATA Safari

Mysore	289
Biligiri Rangaswamy Hills	302
Nagarhole National Park	306
Sravanabelagola	313

KERALA

Palakkad	**322**
Malampuzha	332
Nelliyampathy	**334**
Kollengode	338
Thrissur	**340**
Guruvayur	**347**
Periyar Tiger Reserve	**354**
Gavi	Peermade	370
Kottayam	**372**
Mannanam	Ettumanur	380
Panachikkad Temple	Changanassery	382
Kozhikode	**385**
Kochi	**400**
Kumarakom	**420**
Vythiri	**430**
Salim Ali Bird Sanctuary	**436**
Alappuzha	**445**

SPECIALS

Days in the forest Mannavanur-Berijam Trek	462
Treks in the Nilgiris	466
Jallikattu, Alanganallur	471
Melattur Mela Keeping the faith	472
Nilgiri Mountain Railway	474

INFORMATION

Travel Helplines	478
Tourist Offices	481
Access at a Glance	482
Train Reckoner To...	484
Train Reckoner From...	486

Travel Agents	488
Accommodation Listings	492
Go There For...	530
Index	532

ROUTE/ TOURIST GUIDES

Tamil Nadu	12
Kanchipuram City	20
Tiruchirapalli City	80
Madurai City	152
Kodaikanal City	168
The Nilgiris	184
Mudumalai	220
Andhra Pradesh	228
Tirumala City	230
Karnataka	254
Mysore City	290
Kerala	320
Periyar Tiger Reserve	356
Kozhikode City	384
Kochi-Ernakulam City	398
Salim Ali Bird Sanctuary	438

HOW TO USE THIS BOOK

How the book is organised
This book features weekend getaways spread over five regions in South India: Tamil Nadu, the Nilgiri Hills in Tamil Nadu, Andhra Pradesh, Karnataka and Kerala

Route/ tourist guide
Each region opens with a topographical route/ tourist guide showing
♦ recommended route with approximate distances
♦ national highways, state and district roads
♦ symbols for facilities in towns/ cities and on highways, such as petrol pumps, garages, chemists and tourist attractions
The route guides are intended for general orientation only. In addition, some of the larger destinations and wildlife parks have tourist guides

Info box
Each destination opens with distance from Chennai, and journey time by road, rail and air (if any). The best mode of travel is placed first keeping in view the connectivity, mobility and time taken to get there. The suggested route is briefly charted for your convenience

Fast Facts
Indicates the best time to go keeping in view the climate/ season. Also lists the tourist offices at the destination, nearby hub towns and in Chennai, plus the STD code for the area

Access at a Glance is a quick reckoner to distances and travel time from Chennai (page 482) to help you make the best choice of both destination and transport Our **Train Reckoner** presents the best trains out of Chennai (page 484) to your destination, and back to Chennai (page 486). However, always check the latest rail timings on the website indianrailways.gov.in for current information

Car A comfortable drive just under 8 hrs along the excellent 308-km national highways stretch till Dharmapuri. Exit west from Chennai onto NH4 (Bangalore Road) to Ranipettai via Sriperumbudur and Kaveripakkam. Turn left on NH46 to Krishnagiri via Vellore, Ambur, Vaniyambadi and Bargur. Stop for a bite at Hotel Tamil Nadu in Krishnagiri. Join NH7 and turn south to Dharmapuri. Follow the state road west past the villages of Indur, Nagadasapattinam and Pennagaram to Wodapati at the base of the falls, 47 km from Dharmapuri

Getting There
Provides details on rail, road, bus and air routes, whichever exists. **Air** mentions nearest airport, airlines that service it, the distance and time taken to reach the destination from there and approximate taxi fare. **Rail** mentions nearest railhead, distance from the destination and best rail options to and from Chennai. **Car** charts the route including direction, NH numbers, distances and vital turning points. **Bus** mentions details of services, where available, from the Koyambedu bus terminus in Chennai to each destination

8 | CHENNAI WEEKEND BREAKS

HOW TO USE THIS BOOK

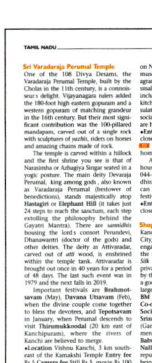

USP Box
Most destinations have a short feature that highlights some unique aspect, a twist in the tale, an interesting detour, or a nugget from history

Where to Stay
For the better-known destinations with numerous hotels, only a representative listing has been given, with phone numbers and tariffs (lowest and highest). Note that the facilities listed are not exhaustive. Our **Accommodation Listings** from pages 492 to 527 lists more hotels for several destinations. The listings given here are purely representative and should not be construed as recommendations either by the author or the publisher. A more subjective view may be present in the accompanying article on your destination

Where to Eat
This section highlights the culinary experience that each destination offers, and mentions some restaurants with their preferred offerings, plus popular eateries

Tourist Offices (page 481) lists state tourism offices in Chennai. **Travel Agents** (page 488) lists select agents in Chennai, Bangalore, Mysore, Trichy, Ooty and other big destinations

Feedback
We hope you found this book useful. We welcome your comments and suggestions as to how we can make it more so. Please do fill in the Feedback Form at the back of the book so that we can incorporate the best suggestions in the next edition. Also, you will receive email updates on special offers, travel features and news from our website www.outlooktraveller.com

Route/ Tourist Guide Legends

V	Distance in km		National Park/ WLS	⋈	Bridge		Masjid/ Mosque
65	NH Number		Bird Sanctuary		Gate/ Pol		Dargah
	National Highway	▲	Camping		Water Body		Cave
	Road	🍴	Restaurant		Clock Tower		Taxi Stand
	State Boundary	✈	Airport		Post Office		Parking
	Route		Railway Station		Bank		Waterfall
	Train Route		Bus Terminal		Hospital	R	Range Office
	Trek Route		Petrol Pump		Tourist/ Info Centre		TV Tower
●	Destination		FRH	▲	Peak Height		
◎	Other Places		Hotel		Temple		
⊙	Arounds		Boat Jetty		Church		

CHENNAI WEEKEND BREAKS | 9

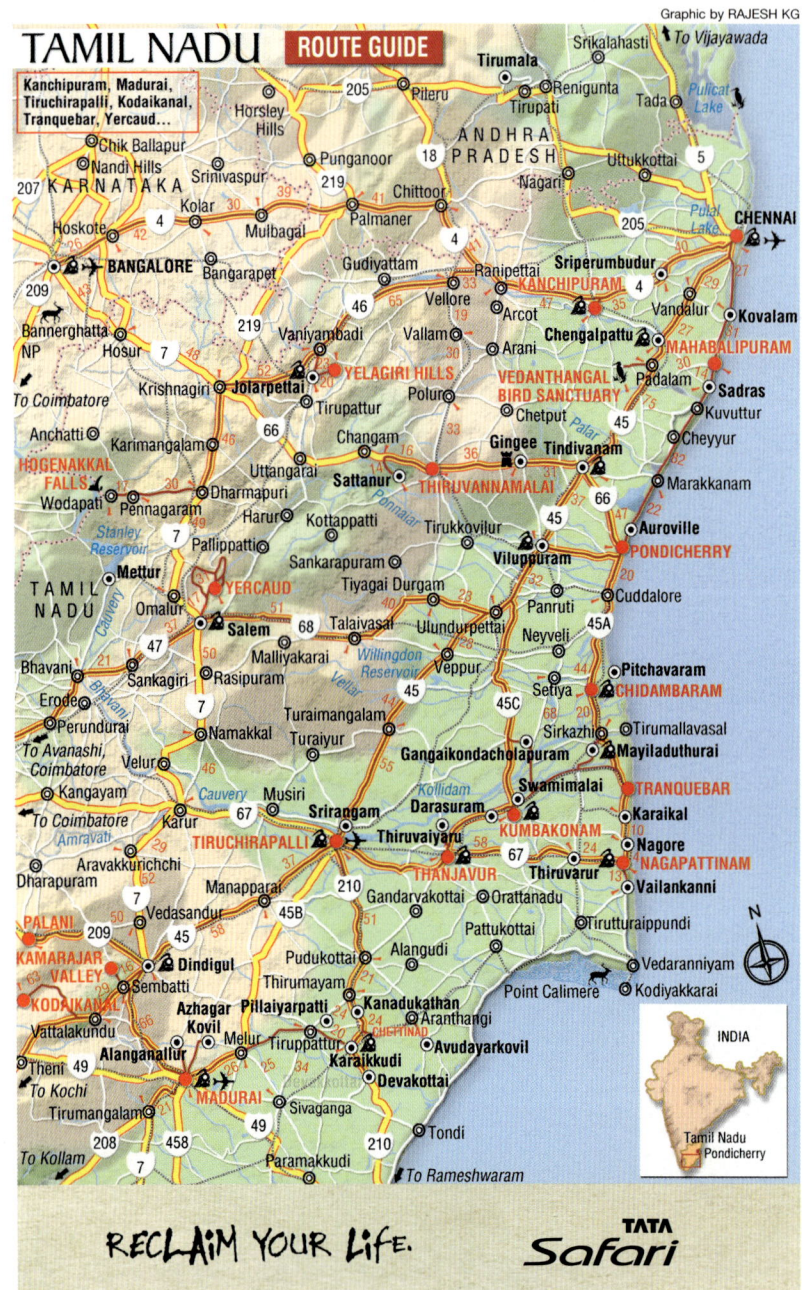

Tamil Nadu

Follow the East Coast Road to the historic port towns of India's very own Gold Coast, gateways to heritage-rich realms by the sacred Cauvery

Riding past exquisite sculpture in a town where monuments sprout like vegetation

MAHABALIPURAM
HERITAGE VILLAGE BY THE SEA

State Tamil Nadu
Location On the Coromandel Coast in Kanchipuram District of north-west Tamil Nadu
Distance 58 km S of Chennai JOURNEY TIME **By road** 1½ hrs
Route East Coast Road (SH49) to Mahabalipuram via Thiruvanmiyur, Uthandi, Padur, Kelambakkam and Tirupporur (*see route guide on page 12*)

■ BY VAISHNA ROY

One very good reason for driving down to the temple town of Mahabalipuram is the drive itself. Come down the hi-tech East Coast Road. On your left are glimpses of surf breaking on endless coastline, interspersed with stretches of casuarina groves and all along the road, food courts, amusement parks and art villages. Mahabalipuram, also called Mammallapuram, is an ancient seaport named after Mammala or Narasimha Varman I, the Pallava ruler who set up his capital here and established a centre of sculpture and art.

Its history dates to the early 5th century when it was a thriving port. Mahabalipuram contains India's oldest examples of Dravidian buildings and sculpted rock-panels. The striking feature of the sculpture here is that it is all monolithic — giant works carved from single rocks. The fabulous and ancient carvings make the town an acknowledged UNESCO World Heritage site.

ORIENTATION

The exit road from the **East Coast Road** (ECR) joins **East Raja Street**, that runs right into the heart of Mahabs (as the town is popularly known), marked by the **Bus Stand**. The **Shore Temple Road** leads east from the bus stand to the Shore Temple and main Mahabalipuram Beach. The Perumal Temple, Krishna's Butterball and Arjuna's Penance are among a number of sights clustered along a short walk west of the bus stand. East Raja Street south of the bus stand becomes **West Raja Street** and leads to the ASI Museum, the Mahishasuramardini Cave, Shiva and Adivaraha temples, and further south to the sculptor's village and the Pancha Ratham.

Resorts, guest houses, restaurants and curio shops are all north of the bus stand, on lanes leading east to the beach off East Raja Street, and are clustered around **Othavadai Street** and **Othavadai Cross** in particular. The big seaside resorts are further north from here, off the ECR. The **Tamil Nadu Hotel** and **Tourist Office** are in this stretch.

◆**Vehicle entry fee** Car Rs 25, bus Rs 50

THINGS TO SEE AND DO

This soporific seaside temple town is a place where you don't have to worry about turning the wrong corner. Caves, sculptures, temples and ruins sprout like vegetation — there are more than 40 carved monuments. Lit after dusk, these monuments assume a magnificent aura.

The Shore Temple

The temple, Mahabalipuram's signature symbol, lies on the shore, its silhouette beautiful against the changing colours of the sky. At times the waves can sweep right into the temple. In fact, the sea has claimed many parts of the magnificent temple, made of charcolite, and that it has survived these centuries is miracle enough. A dyke has now been built around the temple to preserve it. The Shore Temple is dedicated to Shiva with his consort Parvati and sons, Vinayaka and Karthikeya. Here too you will find the **Sthala Shayana Perumal** — the only place where Vishnu is seen reclining on the floor — which has to be seen in segments through various doors in the central shrine. Pillars of the temple bear the Pallava emblem, roaring lions. On weekends, the temple is lit up after sunset, making for a spectacular sight.

The temple is said to be one of seven that existed here in 600 CE. Explorers believe one of the other six has been uncovered by the tsunami of 2005, in the waters off Mahabalipuram.

◆**Entry fee** Indians Rs 10, foreigners Rs 250, ticket valid for two monuments on one day (Shore Temple and Pancha Rathams) **Timings** 9 am-5.30 pm, open daily **Camera fee** Still free, video Rs 25 **Illumination timings** Sunset to 8 pm

Arjuna and the Pandavas

In the middle of town is **Arjuna's Penance**, the world's largest bas-relief panel. Arjuna is said to have meditated upon Shiva here. Measuring 27m by 9m, this gargantuan rock has over a hundred carved figures. It is slashed by a naturally formed perpendicular fissure that has been creatively included in the depiction of River Ganga's descent to Earth.

→ FAST FACTS

When to go
November to March
Tourist offices
● Dept of Tourism, Govt of TN
Kovalam Road, Mahabalipuram
Tel: 044-27442232
● TTDC
Tourism Complex, FF
No. 2 Wallajah Road, Chennai
Tel: 044-25367850-54
Website: tamilnadutourism.org
STD code 044

TAMIL NADU

A resort off the ECR, north of Mahabs

→ GETTING THERE

Rail Nearest railhead: Chengalpattu (Tel: 044-27423444; 31 km/ 1 hr). However, rail is an inconvenient option
Car Exit south onto the East Coast Road from Thiruvanmiyur, past Kativakkam, Neelankarai, Panayur and Uthandi, then on to the bridge over the Muttukadu backwaters, continuing straight past Kovalam Junction and on to Crocodile Bank and Pattipulam. Shortly, beachside resorts on your left announce the approaching left exit off the ECR into Mahabalipuram. Watch out for it after the TTDC petrol bunk
Bus Buses leave every 30 mins between 5.30 am and 10.30 pm for Mahabalipuram from Chennai's Metropolitan Bus Terminus (Tel: 044-24794705-09) at Koyambedu. Tickets start at Rs 30

On the right stands **A Family of Monkeys**, sculpted on a single piece of rock. A stone's throw from here is **Krishna's Butterball**, a natural rock formation — a boulder resting on the tip of a slope, completely defying gravity.

Southwards from Arjuna's Penance is the **Krishna Mandapam** (with scenes of Lord Krishna lifting Mount Govardhan hewn in the rock) and **Pancha Pandava Mandapam** (carved with vaults and short pillars). Above the cave stands the small **Ulaganatha** (world's hero) **Temple** for Shiva, on a granite mandapam built in the 8th century. The temple offers a view of the entire town.

South-west of these structures are three cave temples. Striking amongst them is the **Mahishasuramardini Cave Temple** with sculpted celestial beings and battling demons.

Amidst boulders and thickets stands the **Adivaraha Cave Temple** with sculpted panels of Pallava kings and queens. To the north-west is the **Tirumurthi Cave Temple**, dedicated to the triumvirate of Brahma, Vishnu and Shiva. Further south is **Ganesha Ratham**, a two-storeyed rock-cut temple.
♦**Timings for all sights** 9 am-5.30 pm

Pancha Ratham
This is a cluster of six unfinished structures, each built of a single rock and unique in shape among Indian temples, on the road to Kalpakkam, 1 km south of Mahabalipuram. They represent the *rathas* (chariots) of the five Pandavas. The sixth chariot is that of Draupadi, wife to all of them. Typical of the 7th century Pallava style, the chariots are in axial alignment. Work stopped after the death of Narasimha Varman in 668 CE.
♦**Entry fee** See 'Shore Temple' on page 15
Timings 9 am-5.30 pm

Tiger Cave
This cave of sculptures, framed within a large boulder, is a 7th century shrine dedicated to Goddess Durga, and is a

beautiful example of the same art that has made the Shore Temple so famous. There are many reasons for the name. One school of thought has it that the crown of carved *yazhi* heads that decorates the mandapam here was mistakenly considered to be carved tiger heads. The shrine was also intended as an open-air theatre, where dance performances were once held for the royal family. Today, it's a popular picnic spot, off the ECR, 5 km north of Mahabs.

Mahabalipuram Dance Festival

The month-long festival is held against the enchanting backdrop of the monuments every year from Dec 25-Jan 31, and showcases Bharatanatyam, Kuchipudi, Kathakali and various folk dances, performed by renowned artistes from across India. Every night has a new performance. For schedules and tickets, contact the Tourist Office (Tel: 044-27442232; *see 'Fast Facts' on page 15*).

Shopping

Mahabs has its distinct touristy quarters, lined with shops selling everything from exquisite sculpture to summer wear and shell artefacts, hammocks and Kashmiri rugs. Browse and pick up a couple of souvenir sculptures in black stone, granite, soft and grey soapstone (Rs 100 upwards). For serious carvings though, visit the rows of sculpture workshops that line the streets of Mahabs. For, the town is today an established school of sculpture, with artists coming here from around the world to apprentice with the town's famous sculptors. Here, you will find giant elephants and horses, gods and goddesses carved in the trademark Pallava style. Also check out the government-run **Poompuhar**.

WHERE TO STAY

Off ECR

GRT Temple Bay and Beach Resort (Tel: 044-27443636; Tariff: Rs 6,000-12,000) offers 72 rooms, a restaurant, Ayurvedic massage, a health club, swimming pool and best of all, private access to the beach. **Hotel Golden Sun and Beach Resort** (Tel: 27442245-46; Tariff: Rs 1,300-2,800) offers 58 rooms, a restaurant, swimming pool and Ayurvedic massage. **Mamalla Beach Resort** (Tel: 27442375/ 475; Tariff: Rs 1,045-1,750) is a compact resort offering 35 rooms, a restaurant and swimming pool. All three are on Kovalam Road. **Ideal Beach Resort** (Tel: 27442240; Tariff: Rs 1,850-6,000) in Devaneri is among the best options, with 45 rooms, a swimming pool and Ayurvedic massages. Tamil Nadu Tourism's (TTDC) **Hotel Tamil Nadu** (Tel: 27442361-63; Tariff: Rs 1,350) is a resort complex on the beach. It has a swimming pool and bar.

CHENNAI KI GURU
Prachi, Hotel Advisor at Travelguru. Has tips on Chennai which get you away from the tourist spots and help you enjoy the city like the locals.

Choose from our network of over 4000 hotels in India. Serviced apartments, budget hotels, luxury resorts, palaces, business accommodations, houseboats and more.

1-800-22-4878
022-4030-4878
www.travelguru.com

India's Largest Hotel Network

Playing on an off-duty catamaran on Mahabalipuram Beach

In Town
Sterling Mahabalipuram Beach Resorts (Tel: 27442287; Tariff: Rs 2,200-5,000) on Shore Temple Road is a 5-star hotel with 26 rooms and two suites, a multi-cuisine restaurant, a bar, a swimming pool and Ayurvedic massage. **Hotel Mammala Bhavan** (Tel: 27442250/ 60; Tariff: Rs 300-420) has budget non-AC rooms on South Mada Street. The newer **Mammala Heritage** (Tel: 27442060/ 260/ 360; Tariff: Rs 1,050-1,500) on East Raja Street has both AC and non-AC rooms.

Of the many budget options clustered along Othavadai Street, **Tina Blue View Lodge** (Tel: 27442319; Tariff: Rs 200-500) is very popular. It offers 15 rooms and Ayurvedic massage.

For more hotels and details, see Mahabalipuram Accommodation Listings on page 520

WHERE TO EAT

When you are hungry in Mahabalipuram, head straight to Othavadai Street. Try the tiger prawns at the popular **Moonrakers'** (Tel: 044-27442115) or at its sister concern **The Blue Elephant** (Tel: 27442811), right opposite the street. **Le Palais Croisette** serves good German Bakery-style chocolate cakes, cinnamon rolls and coffee. **Nautilus** is a French café two doors down from Moonrakers. Towards the shore, **Tina Blue View Lodge** (Tel: 27442319) is favoured for its pancakes served on its rooftop terrace restaurant. **Dreamland**, right opposite, is popular for seafood pasta and excellent filter coffee. A few small restaurants on the beach offer seafood and beer. **Ananda Bhavan** serves a good South Indian thali.

In addition, all the luxury hotels have good multi-cuisine dining options.

AROUND MAHABALIPURAM

Thirukaikundram (16 km)
Thirukaikundram, or Pakshitirtham, is famous for its **Shiva Temple** perched atop a hill and reached by 550 steps, where two eagles come to feed every afternoon. Legend has it that they are the same two eagles from time immemorial. The town is on SH58 to Chengalpattu. ∎

Inputs by Sudha G. Tilak and Lalitha Sridhar

Holidays will never be the same again.

Escape from your stress and routine. Head to MGM Beach Resorts, ECR, Chennai. Pay a visit!

MGM BEACH RESORTS

East Coast Road, Muttukadu, Chennai - 603 112.
Ph: +91 - 44 - 2747 2435 / 6 / 7. Email: reservations@mgm-hotels.com
Sales Office: Ph: 044-28476234 / 4210 7272. Mobile: 98407 03865 / 98407 03814. Email: sales@mgm.co.in

Perfect setting for Birthdays, Anniversaries, Get-togethers

TAMIL NADU

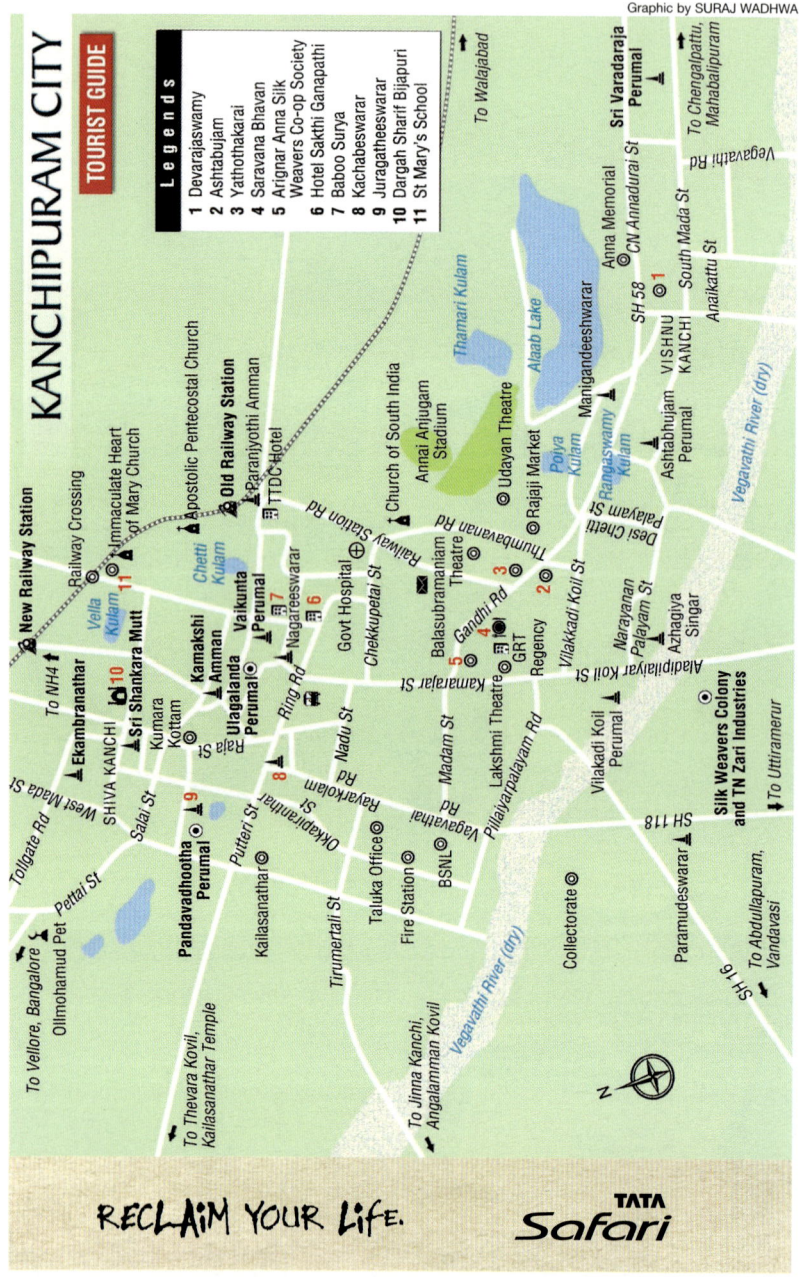

20 | CHENNAI WEEKEND BREAKS

Photographs by G SIVAPERUMAL

Shri Varadaraja Perumal procession during Brahmotsavam festivities

KANCHIPURAM

NAGARESHU KANCHI — A CITY LIKE NO OTHER

State Tamil Nadu
Location This famous temple and sari town, on the banks of the now dry Vegavathi River, forms a heritage-rich triangle with Chennai and Mahabalipuram in north-east Tamil Nadu, and lies just off NH4 that connects Chennai to Bangalore
Distance 75 km SW of Chennai **JOURNEY TIME By road** 1½ hrs
Route NH4 to Vedal via Thiruverkadu, Poonamallee, Sunguvarchatiram and Sriperumbudur; SH58 to Kanchipuram (*see route guide on page 12*)

■ BY SUDHA G. TILAK
AND JAYA MADHAVAN

Kamakshi, one who has eyes full of love, inspires the same feeling in those who come to see her. *Nagareshu Kanchi*! (A city like Kanchi!), it was said. A thousand temples in one place had to be without parallel. Even with less than a tenth left now, Kanchipuram remains one of India's seven *mokshapuris* — sacred cities that guarantee salvation, and the only one in South India. It is also called the Varanasi of the South. Each temple has a story, and each lane, bylane and street has at least one temple.

Kanchipuram's temples showcase some of the best in Dravidian architecture, an amalgam of styles introduced by the city's many rulers — the Pallavas, Cholas, Vijayanagara kings and Nayaks. In between the city also had to reckon with many invasions, when some of the stunning temples were used as garrisons. It was the British who introduced sericulture to Kanchipuram's weaving community. The legendary 'Kancheevaram' saris have since kept the city's name glowing like the shimmer of silk.

CHENNAI WEEKEND BREAKS | 21

ORIENTATION

Kanchi is situated 5 km south of NH4. The **railway station** is 1 km ahead of the town, and the **bus stand** lies exactly midway between Shiva Kanchi to the north and Vishnu Kanchi to the south. The area with more Shiva temples, including the **Ekambranathar** and **Kailasanatha** temples, is called **Shiva Kanchi** or **Big Kanchipuram** and the southern area, including the **Varadaraja Perumal Temple**, is known as **Vishnu Kanchi** or **Little Kanchipuram**. Hire an auto to get around the city.

THINGS TO SEE AND DO

Though Vishnu Kanchi is said to have more Vishnu temples, it is Shiva Kanchi (the best place to start your tour), that has the largest number of important temples, both Shaivite and Vaishnavite. The Kanchi Kamakoti Peetham, the mutt set up by saint-philosopher Adi Sankara, is also here. So are hundreds of looms that spin the fabled Kancheevaram sari.

→ FAST FACTS

When to go Sept-Feb, when it's cooler but time a visit also to catch the Panguni Uthiram festival (Mar-Apr)
Tourist offices
● TTDC ❶
Hotel Tamil Nadu, opp Old Railway Station, Kamatchi Amman Sannathi Street, Kanchipuram
Tel: 27222553-54; Fax: 27222552
● TTDC ❶❺
No. 2, Wallajah Road, Chennai
Tel: 044-25367850-54
Website: tamilnadutourism.org
STD code 044

Kamakshi Amman Temple

There are a number of Shiva temples in Kanchipuram, but none of them have a *sannidhi* (sub-shrine) for Parvati. At Kanchi, Kamakshi is the appointed consort for all the Shiva temples. The name Kamakshi is often interpreted as one with eyes of desire. In fact, the letter *Ka* stands for Saraswati and *Ma* for Lakshmi, and *Akshi* means eye. Kamakshi is hence an embodiment of the aspects of Parvati, Lakshmi and Saraswati.

Beneath the gold-plated vimanam is the sanctum, situated within the Gayatri Mandapam, supported by 24 pillars synchronising with the 24 letters of the Gayatri Mantra. Inside sits Kamakshi, resplendent with four hands holding noose, staff, sugarcane bow and flower arrows. If you crane your neck, you can catch a glimpse of the Tapas Kamakshi on her right, poised on one foot in penance to win Shiva. On her left is the Bilakasam, a huge gap in the floor (not visible from outside the sanctum) from where Kamakshi is said to have emerged as a shaft of light. It is believed that Adi Sankara, who holds second place of importance in this shrine, attained samadhi by merging with the goddess within. To the right of the deity are Kalvar and Soundarya Lakshmi and to the left are Varahi, Santhana Ganapathy and Arupalakshmi.

The **Pancha Tirtham** or Pancha Gangai, the tank on the west side of the temple, is believed to contain water from the five faces of Shiva. Beside it is the shrine of Lord Vishnu in three postures: sitting, standing and reclining. Two demons guard the entrance and it is locked. You can see the seated Vishnu from outside. An exhibition on Adi Sankara's life is on display in the **Vasantha Mandapam**, in the outer prakaram.

Pujas are performed five times a day. **Sankara Jayanthi** is celebrated for 10 days in the Tamil month of Chithirai (Apr-May). During **Navaratri**, the entire temple is illuminated and cultural shows are conducted. Every evening the goddess is dressed in a different *alankaram* and, wearing rare and special jewels, is taken out in a **procession**.

◆**Location** Shiva Kanchi, 1¹/₂ km south of the railway station, 1¹/₂ km north of the main bus stand **Timings** 6 am-noon, 4-8.30 pm (4-9.30 pm on Fridays) **Temple Tel** 044-27222609

TIP Men must remove their shirts to enter the Gayatri Mandapam. Cameras and mobile phones are permitted only in the outer prakaram

Ekambranathar Temple

Originally built by the Pallavas and the Cholas, the Ekambranathar Temple marks the site at which Shiva is worshipped in the form of earth. According to legend, the lingam was fashioned by Parvati herself when she was cursed to be born on earth. When the River Vegavathi tried to wash it away, Parvati embraced it to protect it. Touched by the gesture, Shiva descended to marry her. The divine wedding happened beneath a mango tree, earning Shiva the name Ekambranathar, *eka* meaning one and *amra* meaning mango. The tree (believed to be around 3,000 years old) is said to bear four different kinds of mangoes, sweet, sour, bitter and tangy, one for each Veda.

Vishnu is worshipped as Nilathunda (piece of moon) or Chandrakanda Perumal. During the churning of the ocean, the story goes, Vishnu was unable to bear the poisonous heat that emanated and prayed to Ekambranathar for relief. Shiva allowed the cool rays of the moon on his forehead to fall upon Vishnu, healing him. Covering an area of 23 acres, the temple has five prakarams, a 'thousand'-pillared hall (with only 100 pillars) and a rajagopuram rising to more than 160 ft. The huge temple tank, the **Shivagangai Tirtham**, is situated at the northern end.

Six services are offered daily. The 13-day **Brahmotsavam** celebration for Panguni Uthiram is grand, with the **Adigara Nandi** (silver bull) procession and the

SHALINI SARAN/ INDIAPICTURE

The idli with imagination

Once there was a simple, soft idli. It then decided to dress up. A dash of mustard, a sprinkling of pepper, some juliennes of ginger teamed up with clunky asafoetida and saucy curry leaves. Even the plump centre was gone. Out came a cylinder, sliced neatly. Very trim and proper. The name, says cookbook author Sabita Radhakrishna, happened probably because this idli is considerably embellished — like the colourful saris from Kanchipuram.

But wait, you cannot easily find a plate of the famous 'Kancheevaram idlis' in Kanchi itself. The waiters at the many eateries we tried shrugged when we asked for the rebel idlis. Only select hotels serve them, and on select days. **Sridhar Café** serves them on Thursdays (3-5 pm), **Hotel Chakra** near Theradi, Gandhi Road, on Tuesdays (1-6 pm), and **Saravana Lunch Home** on Sunday evenings. **Varadaraja Perumal Temple** (Tel: 044-27269773) serves a limited number of Kanchipuram idlis as prasad, but they go very fast. One can, however, pay Rs 100 (in person or by MO) and give two days' notice to get a huge Kanchipuram idli, one foot in diameter, made exclusively for you in the temple kitchen. The idli is offered to Lord Varadaraja before it is given to you.

wedding of Shiva and Parvati, when couples assemble to get married or re-tie their mangalsutra as an auspicious act.
♦**Location** Shiva Kanchi, 2 km south-west of Kamakshi Temple **Timings** 6 am-12.30 pm, 4-8.30 pm **Temple Tel** 044-27222084 **Email** kanchiekambaranathar@sancharnet.in

Kailasanatha Temple
The Pallava King Narasimhavarman II (700-728 CE) built the temple, outshining his father Narasimhavarman I's achievements at Mahabalipuram (*see page 14*). Listed as the oldest structure in Kanchipuram, it is intriguing for its quietude, lack of ostentation and sequestered location. The walls sculpted with images of Shiva, Parvati and watchful lions on the top conceal more than 50 tiny meditation chambers.

→ GETTING THERE

Rail Kanchipuram Station (Tel: 044-27223149). From Chennai there are three fast passenger trains at 7.15 am, 5.50 and 7 pm, but the trip is easier by road
Car Kanchipuram is a short, smooth drive from Chennai. Take Poonamallee High Road (NH4 to Bangalore) past Koyambedu to Thiruverkadu, Poonamallee, Sunguvarchatiram and Sriperumbudur till Vedal. A short distance after Vedal, turn left onto SH58 to Kanchi, 5 km away. A taxi for a two-day trip to Kanchi will cost Rs 2,500
Bus Buses leave every 15 mins from 4.30 am to 10.30 pm, from Chennai's Metropolitan Bus Terminus (Tel: 044-24794705) at Koyambedu. Private buses ply this route en route to Vandavasi, Cheyyar and Thiruvannamalai. These can be boarded at Guindy or Koyambedu

The temple is built out of soft sandstone. There are no entrance gopurams, only the vimanam above the sanctum. The interiors reveal traces of the once colourful frescoes. Devotees can get within 6 ft of the resplendent ebony-black, 16-faceted lingam.

This sparsely visited temple comes alive during **Shivaratri**, with huge crowds jostling to get a glimpse of the 6-foot lingam.
♦**Location** In Shiva Kanchi, 4 km south-west of the Kamakshi Temple **Timings** 6 am-noon, 4-7 pm
TIP Non-Hindus are allowed only in the outer prakaram and cannot go beyond the first enclosure in the inner prakaram

Sankara Mutt
The Sankara Mutt, established by Adi Sankara, enshrines the *brindavana* (samadhi) of Paramacharya Sri Chandrasekhara Saraswati, which is open for worship. Mobile phones and cameras are restricted near the samadhi.
♦**Location** 2 km north-west of Kamakshi Temple **Timings** 6 am-noon, 4-8 pm

Sri Varadaraja Perumal Temple
One of the 108 Divya Desams, the Varadaraja Perumal Temple, built by the Cholas in the 11th century, is a connoisseur's delight. Vijayanagara rulers added the 180-foot high eastern gopuram and a western gopuram of matching grandeur in the 16th century. But their most significant contribution was the 100-pillared mandapam, carved out of a single rock with sculptures of *yazhis*, riders on horses and amazing chains made of rock.

The temple is carved within a hillock and the first shrine you see is that of Narasimha or Azhagiya Singar seated in a yogic posture. The main deity Devaraja Perumal, 'king among gods', also known as Varadaraja Perumal (bestower of benedictions), stands majestically atop **Hastagiri** or **Elephant Hill** (it takes just 24 steps to reach the sanctum, each step extolling the philosophy behind the

The Silk Route

Moderately heavy and easy to maintain, the Kancheevaram sari is synonymous with the city where it's woven. Many families preserve them as heirlooms.

The thread is dyed and sun-dried. The maximum length on a traditional loom is an 18-yard warp. This means that, typically, no more than three saris can be identical. It takes 20 days to weave one sari. Border designs such as the *annapakshi* (a mythical bird), *yazhi* (the fierce, ornate lion), the mango, the elephant and the temple gopuram are eternal favourites. The *buttas* are small woven dots that embellish the body of the fabric. For those who can afford it, there is the stunning *vaira oosi* ('diamond needles' — one thread of silk and one thread of zari woven alternately to make a sari that is part colour and part gold). The **Ekambaranathan sari** and the **Avudaiyar sari** are inspired by the sculptures in the temples by the same name.

Pure gold zari (*jarikai* in Tamil) was used till the turn of the century. The silver zari (made of gold-electroplated silver wire) used now is procured from Surat. You will also get the cheaper 'tested zari' (copper electroplated with silver and coated with gold). Remember, the heavier the sari, the better the quality.

Buy (Rs 2,000 upwards), and bequeath.

Lalitha Sridhar

Gayatri Mantra). There are *sannidhis* housing the lord's consort Perundevi, Dhanawantri (doctor of the gods) and other deities. The deity as Attivaradar, carved out of *atti* wood, is enshrined within the temple tank. Attivaradar is brought out once in 40 years for a period of 48 days. The last such event was in 1979 and the next falls in 2019.

Important festivals are **Brahmotsavam** (May), **Davana Utsavam** (Feb), when the divine couple come together to bless the devotees, and **Tepotsavam** in January, when Perumal descends to visit **Thirumukkoodal** (20 km east of Kanchipuram), where the rivers of Kanchi are believed to merge.

♦**Location** Vishnu Kanchi, 3 km southeast of the Kamakshi Temple **Entry fee** Rs 5 **Camera fee** Still Rs 5, movie Rs 100 **Timings** 6.30 am-noon, 3.30-8 pm **Temple Tel** 044-27269773 **Email** devadirajan_2004@sancharnet.in **Website** kanchivaradarajar.com

TIP Non-Hindus not allowed beyond the flagstaff

A painting in the Museum of Folk Art, which is set in a 400-year-old traditional house

Museum watch

The **Kanchi Kudil** (dwelling of Kanchi), on Nainar Pillai Street, is a novel heritage museum, located in a 100-year-old agrarian house. The house is divided into small cubicles of different living areas, including a fully equipped traditional kitchen. Framed write-ups that encapsulate the history of Kanchipuram, its social mores and traditional way of life, are hung on the walls for a quick scan.

♦**Entry fee** Rs 10 **Timings** 9.30 am-6 pm, closed on public holidays

TIP For group bookings inclusive of home cooked meals call 044-27227680

A 400-year-old traditional house houses the **Museum of Folk Art** (Tel: 044-27220112/ 0450) on Brahma Mandhiram, 6 Lingappan Street. Here one can view interesting everyday and festive exhibits.

♦**Entry fee** Rs 10 **Timings** 9.30 am-5 pm, closed on public holidays

Shopping

Kanchipuram, also known as the Silk City, houses more than 5,000 families engaged in weaving and selling some of the finest silks in the country (*see 'The Silk Route' on page* 25). The sellers are private merchants and cooperatives run by the state government. Gandhi Road is a good place to buy silk saris, some of the larger shops being **Prakash Silk Sarees**, **BM Fabrics**, **BM Silk Saris**, **Kamatchi Co-optex** and **Thiruvallur Co-operative Society**. **Varadaram Retailer** and **Srinivasa Silk** on TK Nambi Street (Gandhi Road Extension) are wholesale merchants and offer a good range. **AS Babu Shah** in Sheikpet, Nadu Street, and **Nalli Silks** on Nellukkara Street are reputed silk houses. You can see saris being made at Pillayar Palayam, $2^{1}/_{2}$ km west of the main bus stand.

WHERE TO STAY

Though low on aesthetics, the functional **Hotel Tamil Nadu** (Chennai Tel: 044-27222553-54; Tariff: Rs 350-550) on Rail Road is liveable. The branch of **MM Hotels** (Tel: 27227235/ 45; Tariff: Rs 550-1,100), run by Chennai-based Saravana

Bhavan, on Nellukkara Street is the next best choice. It offers a good location, quick meals and working ACs. The 3-star **GRT Regency** (Tel: 27225250; Tariff: Rs 1,250-2,250) on Gandhi Road was a pleasant surprise. The rooms were clean and luxurious. Other stay options include the 3-star **Heritage Inn** (Tel: 27227780/ 817; Tariff: Rs 490-800), on Nadu Street, that has room service and running hot water, and is walking distance from the railway station, bus stand and the Kanchi Mutt. Also try **Hotel Jaybala International** (Tel: 27224348; Tariff: Rs 150-1,090) on Gandhi Road.

For more hotels and details, see Kanchipuram Accommodation Listings on page 517

WHERE TO EAT

The best bets in Kanchi would be **Hotel Saravana Bhavan** (Tel: 044-27222505) and **Saravana Lunch Home** (at Gandhi Road and near the bus stand), as popular for tasty food as for hygiene. **Hotel Abirami** on Kamarazar Street and **Hotel Sakthi Ganapathi** (Tel: 27225652; opens at 5 am) opposite the bus stand serve excellent breakfast. **Sridhar Café** (Tel: 27223888) on Gandhi Road is as good. Also try the **India Coffee House** (Tel: 27225644) near Theradi. **Adayar Ananda Bhavan** at Nellukkara Street serves great fast food items, snacks and sweets. GRT **Regency** (Tel: 27225250) has separate veg and non-veg restaurants.

> TIP *See 'The idli with imagination' on page 23 to get your share of the famous Kanchipuram or kovil idlis*

AROUND KANCHIPURAM

Sriperumbudur (35 km)
This town, back on the Chennai-Bangalore NH4 towards Chennai, houses the immaculate **memorial** to the former Indian prime minister, Rajiv Gandhi, who was assassinated here in 1991. The town is the birthplace of Sri Ramanuja (born 1017), foremost exponent of the philosophy of Vishishtadwaita (a blend of philosophies of Dvaita and Advaita). Sri Ramanuja is believed to have been an incarnation of Ananta, the primordial serpent. He questioned the practice of untouchability and invested the lower castes with the sacred thread. At the **Adikesava Perumal Temple**, Ramanuja occupies a place of importance as significant as the main deity and his consort Ethiraja Nadavalli. The temple is more than 2,000 years old.

The grand **Brahmotsavam**, also known as **Bhasyakara Chaitrotsavam**, is in April; Ramanuja is then dressed like a king and is taken out on a white horse alongside elephants, camels and horses.
♦**Timings** 6.30 am-noon, 4-8.30 pm ■

DELHI KI GURU
Deepti, Hotel Advisor at Travelguru. Well acquainted with NCR, she knows the shortest route to N.E.P.Z from Connaught Place.

Choose from our network of over 4000 hotels in India. Serviced apartments, budget hotels, luxury resorts, palaces, business accommodations, houseboats and more.

1-800-22-4878
022-4030-4878
www.travelguru.com

India's Largest Hotel Network

TAMIL NADU

KR GANESH/ WILDERFILE

VEDANTHANGAL BIRD SANCTUARY

THE BIRD PARADISE

State Tamil Nadu
Location Spread across 73 acres of a tank-fed lake, dotted by islands of mangroves, evergreen scrub and thorn forest, close to Padalam in Kanchipuram District
Distance 86 km SW of Chennai JOURNEY TIME *By road* $1^3/_4$ hrs
Route NH45 to Padalam Junction via Tambaram, Vandalur Zoo and Chengal-pattu; district road to Vedanthangal Bird Sanctuary (see *route guide on page 12*)

■ BY LAKSHMI INDRASIMHAN

Usually, getting to bird sanctuaries in Tamil Nadu involves a lot of teeth-rattling road time, but pleasantly, the drive to Vedanthangal is nothing like that. A quick afternoon's drive along the newly polished NH45 from Chennai gets you to the oldest water bird sanctuary in the country, also a delightful retreat from the grime and the noise of the city.

As we enter the Vedanthangal Bird Sanctuary, through a gate guarded by monkeys, no less, there is the thrum of satisfied birds eating, swimming, diving, homemaking and squawking. They seem to be happy doing what they are doing, enjoying their last few days of rest before starting on the long flights home. They are accustomed to visitors, and some of the birds venture quite close to the tourists. Beyond the islands full of mangroves, they perch on the trees that line the banks and reach out to the water.

Atop a watchtower in Karikili; A darter spreads its wings (right)

VEDANTHANGAL

TAMIL NADU

The Barringtonia mangroves of the sanctuary create a floating habitat for a variety of migratory birds. We walk along a shaded stone pathway around the mangroves to view the birds on our left. On the other side are extensive chartreuse paddy fields and a gorgeous sunset — luckily, we are visiting at the right time. The setting is so beautiful that I feel the sanctuary extends beyond its watery boundaries. We try to guess the number of birds by counting how many there are in the trees. It proves a futile exercise, as the mangroves extend far into the distance and the horizon seems to rustle with white wings. Official reports claim there are anything between 10,000 and 20,000 birds per season, resting, sheltering and breeding on what are apparently 2,000 partially submerged trees.

We climb a watchtower and watch a trio of painted storks gather twigs to build their nests. Their delicate balancing act on the thinnest of branches reminds me of the gravity-defying scenes in a martial arts flick, where a dexterous fight takes place atop bamboo reeds. The painted storks are by far the most expressive species in the sanctuary, with milky wings that rise to fuschia at the tips. That said, there is considerable pleasure watching birds that are not involved in any balancing act, but are merely resting.

We notice many villagers in the sanctuary; they wield considerable influence in the running of the sanctuary. Village boundaries and that of the reserve meld together, and in fact, the 73-acre sanctuary and its surroundings were only deemed a protected zone after the complaints of villagers about the intemperate hunting of the birds by the British. It is a suitably impressive history for a park that is a great example of a well-managed protected area.

At dusk, you can watch young goatherds returning home with their flocks or the brightly painted oxen preparing to doze off — all an integral part of the typical evening scene in villages. The pace of life suddenly seems slower, and coupled with the pacifying landscape and the harmonious coexistence of humans and nature that we see around us, life's harsher realities seem a world away — if only for the time you actually spend in the park.

Vedanthangal is great for people of all ages looking for the romance of the countryside and the excitement of wildlife, but with little of the attendant difficulties of early morning treks or crouching in the underbrush. The sanctuary is a bit like a park, open to

E HANUMANTHA RAO/WILDERFILE

→ FAST FACTS

When to go The sanctuary season is November to March. Breeding season lasts from October/ November to March, peaking in Dec-Jan when about 30,000 birds nest here

Tourist office
- Wildlife Warden's Office
DMS Campus, Teynampet
Chennai-600006; Tel: 044-24321471
Email: wlwchennai@nic.in
STD code 044

TAMIL NADU

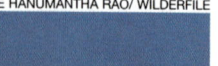

A painted stork watches over its young in the haven of Vedanthangal

everyone for a lazy evening stroll, but with very many birds flocking around. And in the fading golden light, it seems much more than the sum of its parts.

ORIENTATION

Take **NH45** from Chennai to the nearest township, **Chengalpattu**. From here, continue to the **Padalam Junction** (Padalam Town is 12 km from the sanctuary). Turning right from here, drive for about 20 mins and you'll pass the **Forest Rest House** (FRH); drive on for another kilometre to reach the **sanctuary gate**, the adjoining **ticket booth** and the car park. There is an **interpretation centre**, where a knowledgeable ticket collector will also act as your guide. **Guides** can be hired at the sanctuary as well.

The birds can be viewed from the stone paved path that follows the lake's **western embankment**. Most facilities have been designed with the tourist in mind and are very well-maintained. There are granite benches along the way for you to rest and various **watchtowers** that offer good views of the sanctuary, though I don't think the binoculars affixed to the towers were working when we were there. For good measure, there are even bathrooms at the sanctuary!

♦**Sanctuary entry fee** Adults Rs 5, children Rs 2 **Camera fee** Rs 50 **Parking fee** Rs 10 **Timings** 5.30 am-6 pm

THINGS TO SEE AND DO

Said to be the oldest water sanctuary in India, the Vedanthangal Bird Sanctuary was granted legal protection in 1798 and recognised as a sanctuary in 1936. The 1962 Madras Forest Act accorded it the status of a reserve forest and, subsequently, the 1972 Wildlife Protection Act pronounced it a wildlife sanctuary. Spread over 30 hectares, the ecosystem of the tank is made up of islands of Barringtonia mangroves, evergreen scrub and thorn forest. You can spend long hours just watching the birds go about their daily routine and not get bored at all. Children, in particular, will find a visit to this bird sanctuary an engrossing one.

Birdwatching

Follow the paved path, dotted with several watchtowers and benches, to survey the birds nesting in the tank area and their counterparts in the surrounding fields and scrub. Amongst the many different bird species here, look for white ibis, Asian spoonbill, grey heron, grey pelican, rosy pelican, night heron and cormorant. Both in the sanctuary areas and outside (especially in the surrounding fields and grasslands), you are bound to spot the Eurasian thick-knee, cuckoo shrike and yellow-wattled lapwing, apart from several other Indian species.

TIP Take binoculars, a bird book and a zoom lens camera along

WHERE TO STAY AND EAT

The **Forest Rest House** (Vedanthangal Tel: 044-27500006; Chennai Tel: 044-24321471; Tariff: Rs 300-400), 1 km from the sanctuary gate, has 4 clean, well-maintained rooms (2 AC and 2 non-AC). Meals are available on request. There is even a playground for kids. Reservations can be done through the Wildlife Warden's office in Chennai (*see 'Fast Facts' on page 29*). There is a cluster of tea shops right outside the main gate. There are also a few gift shops here, and vendors selling guavas, tender coconuts and delicious watermelons.

→ GETTING THERE

Rail Nearest railhead: Chengalpattu (044-27423444; 30 km/ 45 mins), with numerous passenger connections from Chennai. A taxi to Vedanthangal costs Rs 300-500, but given the short distance, rail is an inconvenient option
Car Take NH45, exiting via Pallavaram, Tambaram and Vandalur Zoo to Chengalpattu via Guduvancheri and Singaperumalkovil. Continue 19 km south down NH45 till Padalam Junction. Turn right here to access the sanctuary road. Vedanthangal is 11 km away
Bus Buses are available from Chennai, but it's best to have your own vehicle

For more details, see Vedanthangal Accommodation Listings on page 527

AROUND VEDANTHANGAL

Karikili Bird Sanctuary (9 km)
Just 9 km west on Uttaramerur Road, this is another great retreat for birdwatchers. Leave Vedanthangal early to enjoy the wonderful morning scenery. For details, contact Selvam at 044-27500006. ■

Choose from our network of over 4000 hotels in India. Serviced apartments, budget hotels, luxury resorts, palaces, business accommodations, houseboats and more.

1-800-22-4878
022-4030-4878
www.travelguru.com

India's Largest Hotel Network

Early morning fresh market at Sri Aurobindo Ashram in the French Quarter

PONDICHERRY
THE FRENCH CONNECTION

Union territory of Pondicherry
Location Just north of the mouth of the Gingee River on the Coromandel Coast, 20 km north of Cuddalore
Distance 162 km S of Chennai JOURNEY TIME **By road** 3 hrs
Route East Coast Road to Pondicherry via Kelambakkam, Tirupporur, Mahabalipuram, Sadras, Kuvuttur, Marakkanam and Kalapet (*see route guide on page 12*)

■ BY CHARU SONI

They like to call it the French Riviera. But Pondicherry has no Cote d'Azure style resorts, no energising art, craft or fashion events, water sports or golden-sand beaches. Life is slow, almost staid. Therein lies its charm.

Planned to a geometric grid by its erstwhile French rulers, with a grand canal dividing the town into the Tamil side, once known as Ville Noir (Black Town) where teaming masses made their home and the European side or Ville Blanche (White Town) where the foreign expatriates and the French diplomatic corps have carved out a base, the town's status quo remains largely unchanged. Except that it's the grandees of local government who now sprawl across Ville Blanche. Also new are the Aurobindo Ashram's offsprings — the spiritual newcomers to the city.

During the French rule, spanning 281 years, the colonisers kept to their side of the town, keeping the masses out. In 1761, the British drove the French out. The city became a mere shadow of its former glamorous self. Simple and severe structures replaced lavish villas, grandiose churches, clubs and hotels. And it is this Pondicherry that we have inherited.

ORIENTATION

Pondicherry is an easy city to navigate. The streets are neatly labelled and numbered. The entire city lies within a neat, circular oblong. **Anna Salai** and **Goubert Avenue** (Beach Road) are the eastern and western sides of the oblong, respectively. **South Boulevard** (Subbaiah Salai) and **North Boulevard** (SV Patel Road) are its southern and northern sides. **Lal Bahadur Shastri Street** and **Jawaharlal Nehru Street** are arterial roads linking Anna Salai to Goubert Avenue. **MG Road** and **Ambour Salai** link the North and South boulevards. The beach, Aurobindo Ashram, most sights, and a majority of its better hotels and restaurants lie within the wide streets of the **French Quarter**, south of the canal. Immediately north of the canal is the **Tamil/ Hindu Quarter** which extends up till Anna Salai. The **Muslim Quarter** is a small square in south Pondy.

The **Bus Stand** is just north of the great oval, beyond the **Botanical Gardens** on LBS Street. There is a **taxi stand** outside the bus stand (a day's sightseeing costs Rs 1,200 approx).

THINGS TO SEE AND DO

You can take in all the sights with this book in hand, or opt for organised tours. Pondicherry Tourism offers a good half-day tour of key sites (1.30 pm-5 pm; Rs 90 per person; boarding from Autocare office near Ashram main gate). Aurobindo Ashram organises a worthwhile Pondicherry Tour (8.30 am and 2 pm; Rs 60 per person; boarding as above). INTACH's (62, Aurobindo Estate; Tel: 0413- 2227324) guided tour (Rs 500 for 6) needs at least a day's advance booking. They can help you secure permission to visit Ananda Rangapillai, Pondicherry's most celebrated *dubash*'s (colonial agent) home, located in the Tamil Quarter.

Beach Road, French Quarter

All the pretty streets of Pondicherry are concentrated on this side of the town. The wind-swept Beach Road, also known as Goubert Avenue, is lined with a host of late-18th and early-19th century buildings. These include the **Ashram Press**, the **Town Hall** (the former Hotel de Ville), the **War Memorial**, the circular 88-foot tall **lighthouse** (now the Central Excise Officer's residence), **Selva Mansion** with a vintage car perpetually parked in its garage and the yellow-plastered **French Consulate General** (the former House of the Navy Admiral).

Running parallel to all these stately mercantile and gubernatorial buildings (characterised by high boundary walls, colonnaded porticoes, balustrades, balconies and columns capped with ornate capitals) is the promenade where the city's denizens come for a leisurely stroll in the evenings. Most of the action then is centred round **Le Café** (the former Custom House that adjoined the wooden pier whose stumps are still

→ FAST FACTS

When to go July to February is best. Great in the rains, pleasant in winter
Tourist offices
● PTDC ❶ ❺
40, Goubert Avenue, Beach Road
Pondicherry. Tel: 0413-2339497
Website: tourism.pon.nic.in
● Department of Tourism ❶
Govt of Pondicherry (*address as above*)
Tel: 2334575
● PTDC ❶
Tourism Complex, No. 2, Wallajah Road, Chennai. Tel: 044-2330532
Email: tourismpondy@sify.com
STD code 0413

PONDICHERRY

Evening on Goubert Avenue, the promenade that runs along Pondicherry's beach

visible in the distance) and the star-shaped podium bearing eight magnificent **granite pillars** and a **statue** of a marching **Gandhi**. This was where French governor Joseph Francois Dupleix's (1742-54) statue stood till it got relegated to the tiny children's park at the southern end of the promenade.

Walking the streets

Rue Dumas, the oldest street in the city, is where the first French settlers lived. Cutting it at its first intersection from the South Boulevard end is the **Rue du Bazar St Laurent** — a quiet street that delivered daily provisions to the settlement. Today, Rue Dumas is home to the **Hotel de Pondicherry**, run out of a 19th-century villa, the immaculately maintained **Ecole Francaise d'Extreme Orient** (School of Oriental Studies), the forlorn statue of **Joan of Arc** standing in the middle of an unkempt garden and the serene **Notre Dame des Anges Church** with an entrance from **Rue Surcouf**.

The next street **Rue Romain Rolland** fronts **Hotel de L'Orient**, the **Cluny Embroidery Centre**, some boutiques and an art gallery. The 18th century house, occupied by the Cluny Centre, is unique for its arched doorway surmounted by stone baskets overflowing with fruits — one of few remains (other than the **Capuchin Tower** on Rue Romain Rolland) of the Pondicherry that Dupleix built.

Mission Street

This busy commercial street, which falls on the Tamil side of the grand canal, is home to the biggest church in Pondy, the **Church of the Immaculate Conception**, more popularly referred to as the **Cathedral**. This stately late-Renaissance structure was rebuilt in 1791 on the site of the church burnt by the British. Peek into the **Archbishop's residence** sitting just next to it to have a look at the symmetrical arched porticoes.

TIP On Sunday, you can either visit the Cathedral to witness a mass in Tamil or the Notre Dame des Anges Church on Rue Surcouf for a mass in French

Sri Aurobindo Ashram

Situated almost immediately behind the Raj Niwas, the pearl grey-and-white Ashram buildings are the most orderly part of the city. Most of the quarters here are closed to the public with the exception of **Sri Aurobindo Ashram** where the mortal remains of the philosopher Sri Aurobindo Ghosh and his spiritual partner, The Mother, are interred. The Mother was a French woman who met Sri Aurobindo in 1914. She came to Pondy in 1920 and never left. Together they evolved a system of spiritual upliftment called 'Integral Yoga'. After Sri Aurobindo attained samadhi in 1950, it was under her guidance that several centres of excellence like the Ashram School, Auroville, cottage industries and the Sri Aurobindo International Centre for Education, among other institutions, were established.

The grand villa in which the Ashram is situated was originally the **residence of Dupleix** (built in 1749). A visit to the Ashram is a strictly solemn affair conducted in pin-drop silence. The rooms where The Mother and Sri Aurobindo lived, on the upper floor, are open to public viewing only on certain days of the year, referred to as **Darshan Days**. Visitors are not allowed to make any offerings, not even flowers.

♦**Location** A short distance from Beach Road, on Rue De La Marine **Timings** 8 am-noon, 2-6 pm **Darshan Days** Jan 1, Feb 21, Feb 29, Apr 24, Aug 15, Nov 17, Nov 24 and Dec 5. If you visit the Ashram on your birthday then an exception is made and darshan allowed **Aurobindo Ashram Tel** 0413-2233649

Manakula Vinayakar Temple

No other temple has such an amazingly large number of reliefs and paintings of Vinayakar. Legend has it that saint Murrandi Siddhar found a Vinayakar in a *kulam* (pond) surrounded by *manal* (sand) near the beach. Thus, the deity came to be called Manakula Vinayakar. The Mother is quoted to have said that it was the deity here who helped Sri Aurobindo and her get funds when they needed money for setting up the ashram.

♦**Location** 200m west of the Aurobindo Ashram **Timings** 5.45 am-12.30 pm, 4-9.30 pm **Special darshan ticket** Rs 10. **Temple Tel** 2336544

Bharathi Park

This park marks the town square, where the French financial and administrative buildings were concentrated. The **Raj Niwas** (governor's mansion), was a hotel meant especially for the members of the French East India Company, next to which stands the **Museum** and the **Romain Rolland Library**. The **Museum** is worth a peep-in, not only for its garden villa architecture, but also for its exhibits that include a **pousse-pousse** carriage (which the owner steered and a servant pushed), a sedan chair, coins and a collection of Chola bronzes. But most interesting of all is the archaeological exposition, which includes finds from the ancient site of Arikamedu (*see page 44*).

Choose from our network of over 4000 hotels in India. Serviced apartments, budget hotels, luxury resorts, palaces, business accomodations, houseboats and more.

Hotel	Rating
Hotel Corbelli	Budget
Hotel Sunway	3 ★
Le Dupleix	4 ★

MTNL/BSNL Toll Free No.
1–800–22–4878
022-4030-4878
www.travelguru.com

India's Largest Hotel Network

The person featured above is an actual Travelguru employee

PONDICHERRY

Bharathi Park — Pondy's town square

→ GETTING THERE

Rail Pondicherry has a metre gauge station (Tel: 0413-2336684) connected to Viluppuram on broad gauge, which is a better railhead (38 km/ 45 mins). Even then, for the return journey, there is no convenient connection for a weekend trip, so it's best to travel by road
Car A smooth and pleasurable drive down the wide East Coast Road that links Chennai to Pondicherry. Exit from Tiruvanmiyur and follow the ECR till Pondy via Muttukadu, Tirupporur, Kuvuttur, Marakkanam and Kalapettai
Bus State buses leave every 30 mins from Chennai's Metropolitan Bus Terminus (Tel: 044-24794705) at Koyambedu. Among many private operators, **Praveen Travels'** (Chennai Tel: 044-28193538) services leave Koyambedu at 4.30 and 6 pm (Rs 150-200)

◆**Entry fee** Rs 2 **Timings** 10 am-5 pm, Mondays and public holidays closed

The other side of the Raj Niwas is the **Ashram Dining Hall** where you can get a bite of organically grown food and the **Cercle de Pondicherry**, a private club that was established in 1899 as a pleasure house for the French nobles. Right next door is the **Legislative Assembly** building. Across the square is the commercial face of Pondicherry, which includes the bustling **Chambre de Commerce**, the seedy looking **Hotel Qualithe** (said to be the oldest surviving hotel in the city) and the UCO Bank. The square is dominated by the **Ayi Mandapam** arch.

Vedapureswarar Temple
The presiding deity of this small and beautiful temple is a majestic *swayambhu* lingam facing east. The rajagopuram features stucco relief sculptures. There is a giant Nandi, and altars to Vinayaka and Murugan. The lord's consort, Thirupurasundari, is resplendent.
◆**Location** $1/2$ km west of the Ashram, at the intersection of Iswaran Koil Street and MG Road **Timings** 6 am-noon, 4-9.30 pm **Temple Tel** 2336686

Varadaraja Perumal Temple
Similar in structure to Vedapureswarar Temple and managed by the same trust, the deities of this quiet Vaishnavite shrine are Vishnu as Varadaraja Perumal and Lakshmi as Thayar.
◆**Location** Next to the Vedapureswarar Temple **Timings** 6.30-11.45 am, 4.15-9.15 pm **Temple Tel** 2224340

The Tamil Quarter
In this part of the town, the streets get narrow, the houses smaller and the temples bigger. Though there are a few traditional houses still left untouched (look for the façades bearing the *thalvaram*, a street verandah with a slanting roof supported by wooden pillars), most others have metamorphosed into ugly

Make Your Stay Memorable in Pondicherry.

Surabi
The Vegetarian Restaurant

L' Héritage
The Multi-cuisine Restaurant

Ecstasy
The Cocktail Lounge

Situated in the heart of the city. Seventy centrally air-conditioned well appointed rooms and suites. Facilities include direct dialing, Wi-Fi internet connectivity, LCD TV with satellite channels, round the clock room service, same day laundry, doctor on call, Kerala ayurvedic rejuvenation, ethnic swimming pool, beauty care salone, gymnasium etc., to make your stay memorable in Pondicherry.

L' Habitat
The mini banquet

Rendez-vous
The conference and banquet halls

tantra
poolside lounge

www.anandhainn.com
s.v. patel road, pondicherry-605 001. india.
tel: 91 413 : 22 33 000 / 2330711-14. fax: 91 413 : 233 1241
email: checkin@anandhainn.com

PONDICHERRY

A truck shifts sand against a dramatic sunset sky in Pondicherry

urban dwellings. Amid it all hides a unique specimen of Franco-Tamil architecture — the **Mansion of Ananda Rangapillai**, built in 1738.

Ananda Rangapillai (1709-1761) was one of the most successful and celebrated agents (*dubash*) of the Compagnie. The mansion (still home to the family), which stands on a street bearing his name, faces the market that was once the centre of all business activity in the city. It has a Tamil ground floor and a European first floor with a courtyard (*koudam*) in its middle. The Tamil section is carved out of deep red-coloured teak, circled with copper, whereas the European section bears iron and plaster balustrades, pillars with Doric capitals and French windows!

♦**Entry** By appointment through Intach (Aurobindo Estate; Tel: 0413-2227324)

Pondicherry suburbs

The city's overcrowded and busy suburbs are home to a few churches built during the French era. **St Andrew's Church** in **Orlypet** was built by *dubash* Pierre Canagrayan. Burnt down by the British, it was rebuilt in 1830. Today, only the foundation stone is what remains of the original structure. Another church worth a visit for its co-option of Hindu practices is the **Notre Dame de Lourdes** (consecrated in 1877) in **Villianur**, some 9 km from the town centre. The small church houses a tank where people make offerings (*theppa thiruvizha*) before entering the church barefooted, just as they would in a temple.

♦**Timings** 6 am-noon and 4-9 pm

For perfect sunsets and enjoyable boating, head for the **Chunambar Boat House** (7 km; Rs 125 per person for a 1-hr sea cruise, minimum 10 people).

SHOPPING

The **Grand Bazaar** on the bustling Jawaharlal Nehru Street is the primary shopping area in Pondicherry. **Auroshikha** (Tel: 0413-2200329, 2201701; Website: auroshikha.com) on Rue de la Marine has high quality, non-toxic scented candles and agarbattis besides handmade paper stationery and other interesting gift items, all quite expensive. **Boutique d' Auroville** on Mission Street sells Aurobindo Ashram publications and CDs. **Sri Aurobindo Handmade Paper** on SV Patel Road sells handmade stationery, files, cards and marble-paper items. **Fleurs en Flacon**, on Rue Saint Gilles near the Aurobindo

A Timberland for $2?

A Marlboro for $3?

A Diesel for $4?

A whole wardrobe of international labels for under $9?

No. 33A, Ambalathadayar Madam St, Pondicherry - 605 001. Ph: 2342075.
1st Floor, Ispahani Centre, 123/124 Nungambakkam High Road,
Chennai - 600 034. Ph: 28332111.

The French Roll

On a walk along the streets of Pondy, you may see people playing with heavy metal balls on a cleared piece of earth. This is Pétanque. It is all about getting as close to the "pig" as possible! A *cochonnet* (a wooden ball) is thrown into position and teams battle to land their *boules* (metal balls weighing about 800 gm) as close as possible to the "pig" to win.

A team may have three or four players with two balls each. The team that wins the toss draws a circle and throws the *cochonnet* a distance of 6-10m. With both their feet inside the circle the rest of the *pétanquers* (players) throw their *boules* knocking the opponent's *boule* away and placing their own closest to the *cochonnet*. Every team has *pointeurs* (good at placing the *boule*) and *tireurs* (good at knocking off the opponent's *boule*). The game is played for 13 points in France but 15 in

Pondicherry. At the outset it may seem very simple, but the game demands a high level of proficiency. A player should be able to calculate the trajectory, the right amount of backspin and choose between the lighter and heavier *boule* for the intended effect. In Pondicherry the game is often played in the evenings. The relaxed pace favours a greater level of socialising for players and spectators.

Gopinath S

Ashram, sells curios, painted handkerchiefs and perfumes. **Cottage Industries**, located next to the Head Post Office, sells incense sticks and cones, incense holders, potpourri and seeds of flowering plants. If you are interested in antiques and sculptures, try the various **art outlets** that dot the road to Auroville (shops are open only in the evenings). For incense sticks, small figurines made from fibre, wood or metal, cute marble stands and other souvenirs, check out the roadside shops in front of Manakula Vinayakar Temple.

WHERE TO STAY

Pondicherry offers a few heritage stay options besides large and busy hotels that offer budget accommodation. **The Promenade** (Tel: 0413-2227750; Tariff: Rs 3,250-7,500) is a stylish sea-facing hotel in the French Quarter, with 35 rooms. Its sister property, **Le Dupleix** (Tel: 2226999; Tariff: Rs 2,850-5,500) is a heritage hotel, with 14 rooms near the town square.

Famous for its brilliant theatre productions, **Adishakti's** (Tel: 2622287; Tariff: Rs 1,300-1,500) charms are impossible to ignore. Stay at the gorgeous guesthouse just to soak in the buzz that pervades the three-acre campus. Or stay longer, take martial arts lessons, and avail of the services of the kalaripayattu guru for massages.

Hotel Mass (Tel: 2204001; Tariff: Rs 1,500-5,000) is among the largest and best hotels here, with 78 rooms on Maraimalai Adigal Salai.

Then there is the **Villa Helena** (Tel: 2226789; Tariff: Rs 2,000-2,500), set in a 19th century French garden house on Rue Suffren. **Hotel de L'Oriente** (Tel: 2343067-68; Tariff: Rs 2,000-5,000), a Neemrana property on Rue Romain Rolland, is a beautifully restored building with a grand staircase, French windows and four-poster beds. **Hotel de Pondicherry** (Tel: 2227409; Tariff: Rs 1,500-2,800) on Rue Dumas is another carefully renovated mansion, offering Ayurvedic massages and visits to local craftsmen.

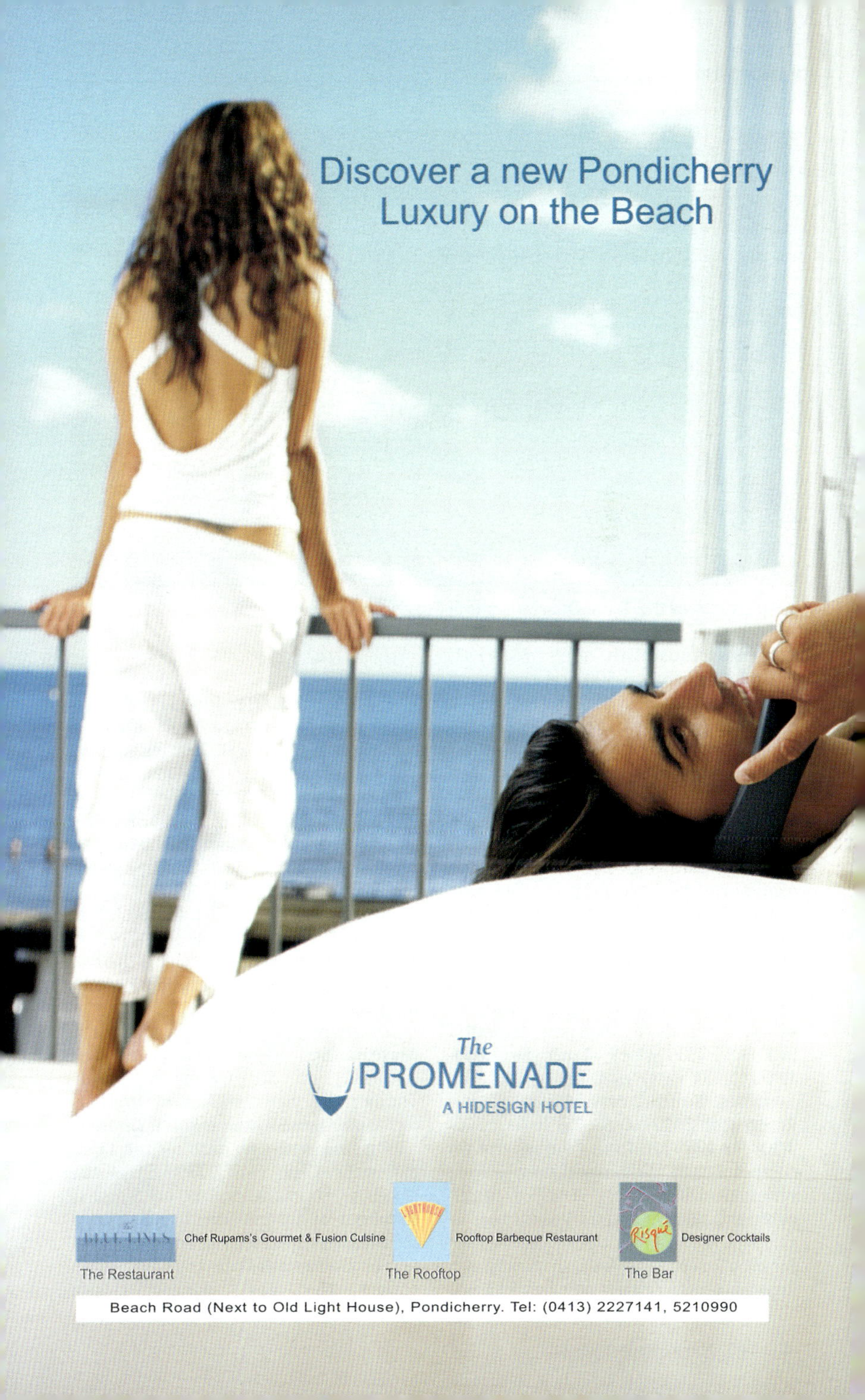
Discover a new Pondicherry
Luxury on the Beach
The
PROMENADE
A HIDESIGN HOTEL
Chef Rupams's Gourmet & Fusion Culsine
The Restaurant
LIGHTHOUSE
Rooftop Barbeque Restaurant
The Rooftop
Risqué
Designer Cocktails
The Bar
Beach Road (Next to Old Light House), Pondicherry. Tel: (0413) 2227141, 5210990

PONDICHERRY

GOPINATH S

Busy streets of the Tamil Quarter's shopping centres by night

Rendezvous Inn (Tel: 2339132, 2330238; Tariff: Rs 5,500), on the corner of Rue Suffren and Rue Bussy, has 6 rooms and enjoys a homely ambience with Vincent and Jessica Mathais cooking up French and Western specialities for their guests.

For a cheaper stay either head for the **Ashram Park Guest House** (Tel: 2233644; Tariff: Rs 400-1,000) or the Ashram-run heritage property, **Sea Side Guest House** (Tel: 2331713; Tariff: Rs 600-900). Both are situated on Beach Road and follow a strict no smoking, no drinking regimen. Larger hotels are **Ram International** (Tel: 2337230; Tariff: Rs 425-825) on Anna Salai and **Anandha Inn** (Tel: 2330711-19; Tariff: Rs 1,850-3,900) on SV Patel Salai.

Hotel Pondicherry Ashok Beach Resort (Tel: 2655160-63; Tariff: Rs 2,800-3,200) is $19^1/_2$ km from Pondicherry on Kalapet Beach. The resort has a wide verandah with beach views, a multi-cuisine restaurant and a pleasant bar.

For more hotels and details, see Pondicherry Accommodation Listings on pages 513-514

WHERE TO EAT

The French Quarter hotels offer an interesting variety of European, often a la carte French cuisine, at their restaurants. The **Carte Blanche** (Tel: 0413-2343067) restaurant at Hotel de L'Oriente specialises in enjoyable, though not very authentic, Creole cuisine. **The Bistro** (Tel: 2227409) at Hotel de Pondicherry also offers some French dishes.

Rendezvous Inn (Tel: 2339132) at 30, Rue Suffren offers French, Indian and Chinese specialities. Ask for the fish in white wine, the *coq au vin* (chicken in red wine) and the paella.

Less expensive fare can be had at the **Ajantha Sea View Restaurant** (Tel: 2349032) on 50, Goubert Avenue. Though the view is pleasant from its rooftop restaurant, the menu is limited.

On fine evenings, head for the Tapas bar at **Le Club** (Tel: 2339745) at the Hotel de Pondicherry, but on Sundays shepherd family and friends to **Satsanga** for their lavish Sunday brunch.

For Continental breakfast and black coffee, the **Park Guest House**

PONDICHERRY

Matrimandir, dedicated to the universal mother, at Auroville

Restaurant on Beach Road is a good option; it comes with an excellent view of the sea. **Honey Dew** nearby is the perfect place to stop by for a limited range of nice, inexpensive desserts.

Those with a weakness for Chettinad cuisine can head for the quaint traditional Tamil house converted into the restaurant **Appachi** (Tel: 2220613) on 9 Rue Rangapillai. Streets like **SV Patel Salai** and **Anna Salai** are replete with regular Tamil tiffin rooms.

Hotel Jayaram's veg restaurant on Kamaraj Road is a good bet for decent food and excellent filter coffee. Another good place for tasty food and swift service is **Hotel Saravana Bhavan**, located on MM Adigal Road.

AROUND PONDICHERRY

Arikamedu (6 km)
Arikamedu, just 15 mins away, is situated at the estuary of the River Ariyankuppam. Excavations carried out here have found signs of intermittent settlement from 2nd BCE to 12 CE. Besides, there are the ghostly ruins of a seminary known as the Mission House, built in the 17th century.

While walking on the ancient mounds of the estuary, you can still come across glass remains from the Roman amphorae, pottery shards and beads. Also visible near the bend of the river are ancient bunds.

Auroville (14 km)
The 'universal city' of Auroville was inaugurated on February 28, 1968 by The Mother (*see page 35*). Take the old Chennai Road (not ECR), with a right detour to Matrimandir after 8 km. Auroville was meant to be a place which "no nation could claim as its own, where all human beings ... could live freely as citizens of the world". Tourists are not welcome except at the **Matrimandir** dedicated to the 'universal mother'. Inside the globe, at its very top, is a **white room** with a **crystal orb**, which emits blue light.

TIP Tourists can only view Matrimandir from outside, between 10 am and 4 pm. Have lunch at the **New Creation Corner** (ask for directions at the Matrimandir Information Kiosk; Tel: 0413-2622204/ 68) which offers delicious Indian and Continental fare besides exotic juices ∎

Inputs by Deepa Kandaswamy

HOTEL MASS PONDICHERRY

Redefining Hospitality...

Maraimalai Adigal Salai, Puducherry - 605 001.
Ph.: +91 - 413 - 4207001 (11 Lines)
Fax: +91 - 413 - 4207012
E-mail: reservations@hotelmass.com
Website: www.hotelmass.com

TAMIL NADU

SAIBAL DAS

Selling jasmine flower offerings to pilgrims near Arunachaleswara Temple

THIRUVANNAMALAI
ARUNACHALA — FIRE MOUNTAIN

State Tamil Nadu
Location At the foot of the holy Arunchala Hill, the ancient temple town of Thiruvannamalai towers over the plains of Thiruvannamalai (North Arcot) District in north Tamil Nadu
Distance 198 km SW of Chennai **JOURNEY TIME** *By road* 4$1/2$ hrs
Route NH45 to Tindivanam via Vandalur, Chengalpattu and Madurantakam; NH66 to Thiruvannamalai via Vallam, Gingee and Alampundi (*see route guide on page 12*)

■ BY SUMATHI CHANDRU

If Mount Kailash is where Shiva resides, Arunachala Hill in Thiruvannamalai is Shiva himself. At the foothill of the oldest rock formation in the subcontinent is one of the grandest, most revered temples in India. A Panchabhoota Shivasthala, Shiva presides as fire in Thiruvannamalai. The magnificent temple to Arunachaleswara, with the hill as its backdrop, rises from the plains, a soaring vision of the natural and the divine. Another indelible impression is the one seen from the heights of Skandashramam, somewhere halfway up the Arunachala Hill. It was home for six years to the great seer Ramana Maharishi, whose ashram and samadhi, also at the foot of the hill, continue to draw the devout to Thiruvannamalai, showing the way to higher truths.

As the breeze whispers and rustles through the trees in this quiet, high retreat, it is easy to see why the saint chose to be here.

THIRUVANNAMALAI

LEGENDS AND MYTHOLOGY

So long ago that time was beyond measure, in the first *kalpa*, Shiva revealed himself as a lingam, says the Shiva Purana. As Vishnu and Brahma were engaged in a terrible war, each keen on proving his supremacy, Shiva appeared as an effulgent column of fire between them. Blazing incomparably, with neither beginning nor end in sight, the flames dazzled the two gods, who set forth to find its ends, agreeing to concede defeat to the one who did so first.

Brahma became a swan and flew towards the top of the column of fire, while Vishnu became a boar who ploughed his way to its base. Time ceased to have meaning as they flew and dived, tiring eventually, but the column of fire showed no signs of ending. Vishnu returned to the battlefield, fearful and exhausted. Brahma continued his upward flight without end.

Shiva observed their nonplussed arrogance and as he shook with laughter, the ketaki flowers on his head fell down the endless column, in a ceaseless downward spiral. Brahma saw them and asked the flowers from whose head they had fallen, and from where...? They told him they had been falling forever. Resorting to a trick, Brahma decided to lie that he had seen the beginning of the column and requested the ketaki flowers to pretend they had witnessed his success. Chastened, Vishnu accepted Brahma's supremacy but as he did so, a resounding Om shook the universe and Shiva, the god of gods, stood before them. He spared Vishnu for his honesty and declared that the blue god would be worshipped as much as Shiva himself. The lying Brahma, decreed Shiva, would never be worshipped in a temple thence. The column of fire was manifest as the Arunachala (*aruna* = red, *achala* = immovable) Hill, the Agni Sthalam, where Shiva is worshipped as fire. But the ketaki never adorned Shiva again.

THINGS TO SEE AND DO

The Arunachaleswara Temple, the Ramana Ashram and the Skandashramam, and other sights near here, will easily occupy visitors for two full days. Many devotees, however, plan a longer stay at the sylvan Ramana Ashram.

When Ramana Maharishi, then a young boy who was drawn by a primordial longing to see Arunachaleswara, first alighted at Thiruvannamalai Station on September 1, 1896, and headed straight to the temple, he said to the lord,
"O God, obedient to Thy call,
Here have I come, deserting all."

Many followed him, and he never left.

Arunachaleswara Temple

On the banks of **Shiva Gangai Tirtham**, the temple is dedicated to Subrahmanya, which is also called the **Valaikaappu Mandapam**, for the goddess here is adorned with bangles (*valai*) once a year in a festival held in the month of Aadi (Jun-Jul). The temple has four outer gopurams and five inner gopurams, all painted off-white. The complex is the second largest in India, after Srirangam (*see page 84*). It was in a pillar of this temple that Subrahmanya appeared before Saint Arunagirinathar. There is a

→ FAST FACTS

When to go Nov-Feb is most pleasant
Tourist office
● TTDC ❶ ❺
No. 2, Wallajah Road, Chennai
Tel: 044-25367850-54
Fax: 25361385; Email: ttdc@vsnl.com
Website: tamilnadutourism.org
STD code 04175

CHENNAI WEEKEND BREAKS | 47

TAMIL NADU

→ GETTING THERE

Rail Nearest railhead: Tindivanam (67 km/ 1½ hrs), with numerous daily connections to Chennai. However, a road journey from Chennai is a much more convenient option
Car A fast drive of 4-5 hrs on NH45. Stop en route for a darshan at the ancient Rama Temple at Madurantakam, right besides a beautiful *eri* (lake). The drive to Thiruvannamalai is through verdant Tamil Nadu countryside full of green-gold fields, innumerable tamarind trees, mud houses with thatched roofs, piles of drying hay and bundles of freshly harvested sugarcane
Bus Thiruvannamalai is well connected by bus from Chennai's Metropolitan Bus Terminus (Tel: 044-24794705) at Koyambedu. A bus leaves every 10 minutes (express service Rs 62; point-to-point Rs 55)

special sannidhi for this saint-poet, composer of the lyrical *Thiruppugazh* (songs in praise of Subrahmanya).

The young Ramana meditated in a dark recess at the temple, the **Patala Lingam Sannidhi**, unmindful of insects and scorpions, which bit him in the damp pit leading to oozing sores on his thighs and legs. Seshadri Swamigal cared for him at such times.

Devotees undertake the sacred *girivalam*, circumambulation of the Arunachala Hill, and thus Shiva himself, especially on Pournami (full moon day). Crowds of pilgrims chant Shiva's name. Maharishi Ramana was known to take even two to three days to return from the walk, which he also undertook sometimes as an overnight *pradakshina*. The path passes by several small temples. A darshan of the Ashta Lingam (Yama, Niruthi, Varuna, Vayu, Kubera, Easanya and Indra) is had on the way. Once part of the teeming throng, there is no room to exit, for the path becomes so crowded. *Girivalam* will take about 4-5 hrs, and is performed even on non-Pournami days.

The first puja of the year begins with the worship of the temple's cow and elephant. There are six main pujas during the day, the first being at 5.30 am. Special darshan tickets cost Rs 100 (a queue that moves faster). Among the 90 festivals celebrated throughout the year, the most important are the **Uttarayana Festival** (Jan) and the **Tiruvoodal Festival** (Jan-Feb), which commemorates Saint Sundarar's efforts to reconcile a quarrelling Shiva and Shakti. It is staged in what is still called the Tiruvoodal Street, an enactment in which temple priests play an important role. **Maha Shivaratri** (Feb) is also important, and the story of Brahma, Vishnu and other deities offering homage to Shiva as the column of fire is re-enacted then *(see Legends and Mythology on page 47)*. The **Karthigai Deepam Festival**, also called Annamalai Deepam (Nov-Dec), is particularly extraordinary at Thiruvannamalai. After sunset, an enormous fire is lit on the crest of Arunachala Hill, with a 30-m long wick dipped in 2,000 litres of ghee. Considered supremely sacred, it is seen and venerated for miles around and telecast live on television. It has been documented as the earliest festival of South India and its antiquity has also been traced to the oldest available Tamil work, *Tolkappiyam*, which studies have dated in the region of 2000-2500 BCE.

♦**Location** Centre of town, 2 km from bus stand **Timings** 5.30 am-12.30 pm, 3.30-9.30 pm **Temple Tel** 04175-252438
TIP Cameras and mobiles not allowed

Ramana Ashram
Ramana Maharishi is perhaps unique in our time for he perfectly embodied the

ultimate truth of self-realisation. The Sage of Arunachala spoke very little and wrote even less but his teachings are widely documented. He preferred to communicate in silence, a silence so deep and powerful that it attracted ardent seekers from all over the world. Bhagvan, as he was lovingly called by his devotees, was accessible to everyone 24 hrs a day. His sense of equality was absolute. The peace and radiance of his presence was a direct pointer to the natural state within the heart of all beings. In 1950, shortly before he shed the body, the Maharishi remarked, "They say that I am going but where can I go. I am here." True to his word, he continues to be a tangible presence in Ramana Ashram, a flourishing haven of peace. There is a samadhi with a serene statue of Ramana where worship is offered. Devotees meditate in the prayer hall here. There are no rigid rules or schedule of activities and the homely environment leaves visitors free to pursue individual spiritual practices. A stay here is a highly recommended experience.

South Indian breakfast (7 am), satvik lunch (11.45 am) and a light dinner (7.45 pm) are served free to all visitors in a large, brightly lit dining hall. The bookshop at the ashram has an excellent selection of publications on Ramana Maharishi's life and teachings. For a stay at the ashram, bookings have to be made at least two months in advance, and even earlier if a visit is planned around Dec-Jan, when Ramana Jayanthi, the Maharishi's birthday, is celebrated with a great gathering of his devotees, elaborate pujas and open-house feasts. Tidy and comfortable rooms are available. Write to The President, Sri Ramanasramam, Thiruvannamalai, Tamil Nadu-606603; Tel: 04175-237292; Website: ramana-maharishi.org.

◆**Location** 2 km from Arunachaleswara Temple, adjacent to Seshadri Swamigal Ashram, on Chengam Road **Timings** Open through the day

PARVIN SINGH

Nandi statue, Arunachaleswara Temple

Skandashramam

This lovely tree-shaded hermitage, halfway up the Arunachala Hill, overlooks the temple and town. Ramana Maharishi lived and meditated here in a cave-hut from 1916 to 1922, and his mother attained *mukti* here. Accessed from Ramana Ashram, it takes 30 to 45 mins to climb here. The atmosphere at Skandashramam is so serene that many pilgrims meditate here. Devotees carry footwear in plastic bags if they wish to return directly to the town, otherwise footwear may be left at the Ramana Ashram. It is inappropriate to step with shod feet on the sacred Arunachala Hill. The Maharishi's spartan, limestone-washed cottage is surrounded by an oasis of green and has its own stream

TAMIL NADU

Catamarans dry beside Sattanur Dam on the Thenpennai River

gurgling by. You get a spectacular view of the temple from here. The **Virupaksha Cave**, named after the saint from Karnataka who lived here from 1899 to 1916, can be seen while descending. Even closer to the foothill is the **Mamara Guhai** (cave under the mango tree), where Bhagvan Ramana stayed for a while.

♦**Location** Half-way up the Arunachala Hill **Timings** 6-11.30 am, 4-7.30 pm

Seshadri Swamigal Ashram

Caregiver and contemporary of Ramana Maharishi, Seshadri Swamigal was a compassionate holy man, loved in spite of his eccentric ways. He attained samadhi in 1929. The ashram gives us a feeling of being in a hermitage. The fountains and trees add to the peaceful atmosphere. Bhajans fill the air on Monday evenings (7-8 pm).

♦**Location** 2 km from Arunachaleswara Temple, next to Ramana Ashram, on Chengam Road **Timings** 6 am-1 pm, 4-9.30 pm **Temple Tel** 236999

WHERE TO STAY

A stay at the **Ramana Ashram** *(see page 48)* is without comparison, but only serious seekers of the ashram's spiritual experience are encouraged to stay, although nobody is turned away. The **Seshadri Swamigal Ashram** (Tel: 04175-236999; Minimum donation: Rs 150, Rs 500 for AC rooms) provides simple, clean rooms at short notice. They have a decent vegetarian hotel here. **Hotel Arunachala** (Tel: 228300; Tariff: Rs 250-900), near the temple, is one of the most popular hotels. It is a deserved reputation given its location, neat rooms and friendly staff. **Hotel Ganesh International** (Tel: 226701-2; Tariff: Rs 125-900), on Periya Theru (Big Street) offers similar accommodation. Opt for the 'deluxe' rooms at **Hotel Ramakrishna** (Tel: 250005-06; Tariff: Rs 231-880), on Polur Road, about a kilometre away from the temple.

For details, see Thiruvannamalai Accommodation Listings on pages 525-526

THIRUVANNAMALAI

WHERE TO EAT

Again, **Hotel Arunachala's** restaurant scores in popularity. The idlis are soft and the 'roast' (extra crisp dosais) hot off the tava. Lunch is Andhra-style meals. A decent range of hot, hygienic South Indian meals can be had at the hotel attached to **Seshadri Swamigal Ashram**. There are many 'lunch home'-style eateries around the temple, with varying degrees of hygiene. A meal at **Ramana Ashram** is a must and many prefer to have the satvik food, served without charge, at the ashram for all their meals.

AROUND THIRUVANNAMALAI

Sattanur Dam (30 km)
A must-visit is a trip to the scenic Sattanur Dam, just off NH66 towards Krishnagiri, where the brimming waters of the Thenpennai River lap the peaceful shore. Taxis from Thiruvannamalai charge Rs 500 for the round-trip. The road can get lonely so ensure there's adequate daylight left for the trip.

Gingee Fort (36 km)
The deserted Gingee Fort (also Senji or Shinjee, 800 ft) rises majestically above the road to Thiruvannamalai, tempting visitors to make the climb to the crumbling ruins. The fort stretches over three hills (Rajgiri, Krishnagiri and Chandrayan Durg) that look as if they were a humongous pile of loose boulders. The origins of Gingee are traced to the shepherd chief Ananda Kone who's said to have established a small fortress here in 1200 CE.

Entry to the fort is through a gateway that leads into a narrow gorge (no more than two horses abreast) opposite the Kalyana Mahal, a six-storeyed palace. Inside the fort stand granaries, ammunition holds, temples, quarters for the soldiers, tanks for elephants and horses and domed-roof structures.

Atop, some 700 ft above, is a small wooden bridge, that connects to the citadel. The view from here opens to vast fields and the tiny Gingee town below. To reach the top you have to climb innumerable steep stone steps and several strong and narrow granite gateways. Half way to the summit is the **Kamala Khanni Ammal shrine**, behind which is a beautiful mural painted on the cliff face. In front of the shrine is a rectangular platform surrounded by trishuls tied with red cloth. Human and animal sacrifices are said to have been performed here. The temple predates the fort.

Gingee Fort is back towards Tindivanam on NH66. Taxi charges approx Rs 700 (1 hr) for a drop.
♦**Entry fee** Indians Rs 20, foreigners Rs 100 **Timings** 9 am-5 pm, Tuesdays closed **Camera fee** Still Rs 50, video Rs 250 ■

TAMIL NADU

The curving ghat road from Jolarpettai winds its way up to Yelagiri

YELAGIRI HILLS
A HALF-HORSE TOWN

State Tamil Nadu
Location The Yelagiri and neighbouring Javadhi Hills tower above Jolarpettai in north Tamil Nadu, offering commanding views of the plains of southern Andhra Pradesh
Distance 253 km SW of Chennai **JOURNEY TIME** *By road* 5 hrs *By rail* 3 hrs + 45 mins by road
Route NH4 to Ranipettai via Poonamallee, Sriperumbudur and Kaveripakkam; NH46 to Vaniyambadi via Vellore, Vadapudupatu, Kommeswaram, Ambur and Vinnamangalam; state road to Yelagiri Hills via Ponnari and Jolarpettai (*see route guide on page 12*)

■ BY BRINDA VASUDEVAN
AND VAISHNA ROY

If doing nothing in peace and quiet in cool climes is your idea of a perfect weekend, Yelagiri would fit the bill perfectly. It's a half-horse town dignified by one main road, which has teashops, liquor shops, and a couple of 'fancy' stores. That's it. There's precious little to 'do'. Therein lies Yelagiri's charm.

Yelagiri is actually a cluster of small villages, spread over a couple of hills. There's little or no sightseeing, no shopping, no touts, and no souvenir hunting. And no sign of the hordes of tourists who have managed to ruin hill stations like Ooty. Of course, there are the typical things, some of dubious value, which the government has put in place for tourists. The lake is beautiful enough, and the desultory boating fits

YELAGIRI HILLS

right in with the mood. The so-called garden around the lake is neither Mughal in splendour nor cosily charming, it's simply there. And, yes, there's the mandatory children's park.

Yelagiri's charm lies in its moderation — the hills around are gentle, the lake is just large enough to stroll around, the weather is uniformly pleasant, even during May and June. A typical day here might go something like this: good breakfast, a gentle walk. Lots of rest, then lunch. More rest. Another gentle walk. Dinner. Lots more rest. Blissful day.

→ FAST FACTS

When to go November to February
Tourist office
● TTDC ❶ ⓑ
No. 2, Wallajah Road, Chennai
Tel: 044-25367850-54
Fax: 25361385; Email: ttdc@vsnl.com
Website: tamilnadutourism.org
STD code 04179

THINGS TO SEE AND DO

During the day, sit by the lake with a book, or just stretch out under a tree and count the leaves as they fall. Come the evening, watch the sun set over the hills. If you actually want to do something, take a bus to the nearby villages — autos and buses are available for moving around in Yelagiri — or trek through the wooded slopes. Or visit some of the temples the locals recommend.

Punganoor Lake

Tourism in Yelagiri revolves around this smallish, artificial lake. You can take a serene ride on the lake by rowboat or pedal boat; mercifully, noisy, polluting motor boats have not yet caught on.

Having done that, you could stroll across to the other side of the lake, where there's a 'hanging view point', a platform on top of a tree, from where you get a bird's eye view of the lake and its surroundings. There's the garden around the lake, with slides and other games for the smaller kids.

Velavan Temple

This is a temple dedicated to Lord Murugan atop the hillock, with a gigantic statue of **Gadothgajan** in front. Local festivals are conducted here during the Tamil month of Adi (Jul-Aug). Incidentally, the temple is also a perfect viewing point for impressive vistas of the Yelagiri Hills.

JAIPUR KA GURU
Zafar, Hotel Advisor at Travelguru, knows where to head for the finest tie-n-dye bandhani sarees.

Choose from our network of over 4000 hotels in India. Serviced apartments, budget hotels, luxury resorts, palaces, business accommodations, houseboats and more.

1-800-22-4878
022-4030-4878
www.travelguru.com

India's Largest Hotel Network

iCONTRACT.TG.07.3248

CHENNAI WEEKEND BREAKS | 53

TAMIL NADU

V MUTHURAMAN

Government Silk Farm

It involves a longish walk along mulberry plantations and might involve climbing over a couple of fences, but if you manage to get a friendly official to show you around, the sericulture tour is very interesting. To get to the silk farm, located at Mangalam, head to Yelagiri's bus stand at Athanavur. From here, it's a straight road (5 km) to Mangalam.

Swamimalai Hill

Perhaps the most strenuous activity over the weekend would be a trek up the Swamimalai, at 4,338 ft, the highest point in Yelagiri. It could be a goodish 2-hr climb, interspersed with breaks to catch your breath. The climb may be taxing, but it's worth it because you get a breathtaking view of the valley from the top. This hill has some good trekking routes through dense reserved forests. These, though, are pretty busy on weekends. The best time for treks to Swamimalai is November to January, when it's deliciously cool.

WHERE TO STAY AND EAT

Hotel Hills (Tel: 04179-245301-03; Tariff: Rs 1,000-3,000) is a 5-min walk from the lake, offering clean and comfortable

Headless shrine

If you love contrasts, stop off at Vellore en route to Yelagiri. It's worth the halt simply to wander around the old fort. Built some time in the 1500s by the Vijayanagara kings, the fort is now maintained by the Archaeological Survey of India. And it's in excellent condition; the grand ramparts are solid, and the wide moat and huge gates can still keep invaders at bay.

The **Jalagandeeswarar Temple**, situated within the fort (*see photo*), is famous for its craftsmanship. In fact, several experts are convinced that the sculptures in this temple surpass even those of the stupendous Meenakshi Temple at Madurai (*see page 155*).

The lingam at the temple is supposed to have been placed above an underground stream. Legend has it that during the wars with the Adil Shahis of Bijapur, the reigning Vijayanagara king, fearing a Bijapuri victory, hid the deity to prevent destruction. But he hid it too well, and the lingam was never found. In fact, even today locals often refer to the temple as *daivam illada kovil* (temple with no deity).

4-bedded rooms, bonfires on the spacious lawns, plenty of outdoor games and a kiddies' park, apart from all the necessary mod-cons. **Zeenat's Taj Garden Resort** (Tel: 245231/ 245445; Tariff: Rs 900-1,800) is a great place to stay. It has 3, 5 and 6-bedded family cottages, with 25 rooms in all, spread over 11 acres, and arranges taxis, sightseeing and trekking in the hills around. Kids will be entertained by their many indoor and outdoor games, or busy themselves in the playground. They also have a restaurant with fixed timings serving South and North Indian buffet meals to guests only at Rs 300 a day.

Hotel Yelagiri (Tel: 245236; Tariff: Rs 500-600) is at Athanavur, not far from the boathouse. Vijay Kumar, the manager, arranges sightseeing all around Yelagiri, plus treks up to Swamimalai, Jalagamparai Falls and to the Nilavoor Mariamman Temple. The best lodging that can be had here are the deluxe suites. The hotel also offers a 25-bedded dorm at Rs 800 for the whole dorm.

Hotel Nigress (Tel: 245264; Tariff: Rs 850-950) has six cottages offering hill views. The hotel has a park for kids plus a large garden, offers room service and arranges sightseeing and taxis.

For details, see Yelagiri Hills Accommodation Listings on page 527

WHERE TO EAT

The best restaurant in town is **Diana** at Hotel Hills. Non-guests can eat here on weekends, but do reserve a table first. The **Garden Restaurant** at Hotel Nigress serves up a variety from North and South Indian to Chinese and Continental. Try the biryani. Southie, northie and Chinese can be had 24 hours a day at **Hotel Yelagiri**.

AROUND YELAGIRI

Jalagamparai Waterfalls (44 km)
The Attaru River flows through the Yelagiri Hills, resulting in a lovely waterfall about an hour's trek from Yelagiri. It's a very popular spot. Adjacent to the falls is a Murugan temple, constructed in the shape of a lingam. You can also drive to Jalagamparai via Jolarpettai and Tirupattur. At Tirupattur, take the road opposite Sacred Heart College for the falls. This last stretch is 10 km. You can also drive to Mangalam, park your car and trek 4 km (one way) to the falls. Hotels arrange guides for the trek for approx Rs 300 both ways. The best time to do this would be post-monsoon when the falls are at their best. The worst time is between the summer months of April and June, when they're bone-dry. ■

→ GETTING THERE

Rail Nearest railhead: Jolarpettai (20 km/ 3/4 hr) **Best option TO** Kovai Express (dep: Chennai Central 6.15 am; arr: Jolarpettai 9.13 am) Taxis up to Yelagiri will cost Rs 400-500 approx **Best option FROM** Kovai Express (dep: Jolarpettai 5.50 pm; arr: Perambur 8.44 pm, Chennai Central 9.20 pm) **Car** A comfortable drive just under 5 hrs along the 233-km stretch till Jolarpettai. Take NH4 to Ranipettai via Sriperumbudur and Kaveripakkam, then NH46 to Vaniyambadi via Vellore and Ambur. Watch out for the Old RTO office on the right side of the road, approximately 3 km out of Vaniyambadi. Opposite the Old RTO office, turn left to Jolarpettai via Ponnari. Yelagiri is a lovely drive up a winding ghat road from here
Bus Leave every hour (Rs 140-170) for Jolarpettai (en route Tiruppattur) from Chennai's Metropolitan Bus Terminus (Tel: 044-24794705) at Koyambedu

CHIDAMBARAM

V MUTHURAMAN

The temple to Nataraja reflected in the still waters of the tank in the foreground

CHIDAMBARAM
THILLAI — TEMPLE OF THE COSMIC DANCER

State Tamil Nadu
Location Chidambaram, originally known as Thillai, is just 16 km from the mangrove forests of Pitchavaram that open out to the Bay of Bengal. These forests are the only place where Thillai trees (commonly known as the blinding tree, *Excoecaria agallocha*) are found now
Distance 226 km S of Chennai **JOURNEY TIME** *By road* 5 hrs
Route East Coast Road to Pondicherry via Mahabalipuram and Marakkanam; NH45A to Chidambaram via Cuddalore and Alapakkam (*see route guide on page 12*)

■ BY JANAKI VENKATARAMAN

Like in many of the greatest temple towns in India, Chidambaram lends itself better to glossy photographs in coffee table books, somehow removed from the everydayness of its rather dusty streets. There was a time very long ago, when town planners ensured that the temple, which remains central to any pilgrim destination even today, towered above everything else, a lofty inspiration for its residents and visitors. Today, the 40 magnificent acres of gopurams, tanks and prakarams of the temple to Nataraja at Chidambaram lie within a maze of misplaced urbanisation. But this Panchabhoota Shivasthala, one of the five great temples where Shiva presides as a primordial element — here, he is worshipped as ether or space — is hardly going to be obscured by a few anonymous buildings. It is a treasure so glorious and generous that it is easily found.

TAMIL NADU

LEGENDS AND MYTHOLOGY

Chidambaram has another name as well: Puliyur or Vyaghrapuri, after Sage Vyaghrapadhar, who, along with sages Patanjali and Jaimini, is said to have done many years of penance. When Shiva appeared before them, they asked him for only one boon: that they should see his *ananda thandavam* (blissful dance) in Thillai. Shiva agreed and set a date for his performance. The day was a Thursday in the Tamil month of Thyy (Jan-Feb) with the asterism of Poosam. All the gods and sages gathered in Thillai to watch the *thandavam*. And how did Nataraja (*natanam* means dance) dance for them? Wrote the poet Muthu-thandava, "Shaking a tiny drum with his right hand, the other bestowing grace, holding fire in one left hand, while the other pointed to his bent leg trampling on Apasmara, his matted locks swirling in all directions, the Ganga and crescent moon adorning his flying hair... thus danced the Lord of the Universe, his dance of joy." When Shiva finished dancing, the sages asked another boon of him — that he should perform his *thandavam* eternally in this sthala. Shiva agreed and told them that they too would be with him when he danced in Thillai. So it is believed that in Thillai, not only is Shiva in an eternal state of *ananda thandavam*, but also all the gods and the sages, with him, worshipping him. When you worship Nataraja, you worship them too.

THINGS TO SEE AND DO

It takes at least half a day to thoroughly see and enjoy the temple of Nataraja and Govindaraja Perumal (in the same complex). While in Chidambaram, one can also visit the Thillai Kali Temple, less than half a kilometre east. Further east of Chidambaram is Pitchavaram, where boating in the backwaters is popular.

Nataraja Temple

It is often said in Tamil that when the word 'temple' is uttered without any name attached to it, it can only be one temple: that of Nataraja at Chidambaram, so perfect is this temple, in its deity, in its architecture, in its concept, and its ambience. *Chith* means 'knowledge' and *ambaram* 'vast, immeasurable space'. Chidambaram is thus the kshetra of boundless knowledge.

The deity is Nataraja, who dances to the *pranava* (primordial) sound of Om. There are 10 sacred tanks in Chidambaram but of these, the temple tank, **Sivaganga**, which lies between the sanctums of Nataraja and his consort Sivakamasundari, is the holiest.

The temple of Thillaikoothar or Nataraja is presided over by four looming towers, the tallest of which, the west gopuram, rises to 135 ft and is topped by 13 copper *kalasams* (pot-like finials). On both sides of the rajagopuram are sculptures depicting various legends as well as dancers in Bharatanatyam *karanas* (poses). The temple, as we see it now, was built in the 11th century by King Vikrama Chola. The form of Shiva as Nataraja is a sculptural innovation of the later Chola period. The gilded tiles of the

→ FAST FACTS

When to go Any time of the year
Tourist offices
- Tourist Information Centre ●
Railway Feeder Road, Chidambaram
Tel: 04144-238739
- TTDC ● ●
No. 2, Wallajah Road, Chennai
Tel: 044-25367850-54
Website: tamilnadutourism.org
STD code 04144

CHIDAMBARAM

Sculptures on the temple of Thillaikoothar depict various legends

roof of the Nataraja sanctum, which looks as if it is woven, is a striking feature of this temple.

The temple has four prakarams and five *sabhais* or halls. Entering by the southern tower, one visits the shrine of the gigantic idol of Mukkuruni Vinayaka (8 ft tall), who is said to be potent in answering prayers. Among other shrines in the outer prakaram is that of Goddess Sivakamasundari. In the goddess' shrine is a sanctum for a rare deity, Chitragupta, Yama's clerk, who keeps account of the good and bad deeds of people. The walls of the shrine are covered with paintings of scenes from the *Devi Mahatmiyam* (the story of the goddess), but most of these have been damaged. Look out for the granite pillar, which has been carved as intricately as if it were wood.

The sanctum of Nataraja, the **Chithambalam**, is in the first prakaram. The *vimanam* of the sanctum, with its gilded tiles, glows impressively. The front portion of the sanctum is known as Kanakasabhai and the inner sanctum, where the deities are kept, the Chithsabhai. Every feature of the structure of the Chithambalam has significance. The Kanakasabhai rests on 64 wooden rafters, which represent the 64 arts. The 21,600 tiles, which form the roof, are said to indicate the number of breaths a human draws in a day; the 72,000 nails used to hammer down the tiles are said to indicate the *nadis* (veins and nerve endings, feeling which Ayurvedic doctors diagnose ailments) in a human body; the nine golden *kalasams* refer to the nine Shaktis, the nine natural energies. Inside the Kanakasabhai, which is at an elevation, the 18 pillars indicate the 18 Puranas; the five silver steps refer to the *panchakshara* (the Shiva mantra); the 96 silver interstices indicate the 96 Shaivite cults; the five pillars of the Chithsabhai denote the five senses. Of the 10 pillars of the Brahma Peetham (the base on which Nataraja and Sivakamasundari stand), the lower six denote the six Shastras and the other four indicate the four Vedas. The dance of numbers is evident everywhere here.

While the elegant *panchaloha* idols of Nataraja and Sivakamasundari are kept in the Chithsabhai, it is a small *sphatika*

TAMIL NADU

Fresh steamed idlis on West Car Street

→ GETTING THERE

Rail Chidambaram Station is poorly connected to Chennai with just the Sethu Express, which departs at the inconvenient time of 1 pm from Tambaram, reaching Chidambaram at 6.33 pm. For a weekend trip, it's better to go by road

Car Chidambaram is a smooth 5½-hr drive from Chennai down the lovely East Coast Road till Pondicherry via Tirupporur, Sadras and Marakkanam. Continue south of Pondy onto NH45A to Chidambaram via Ariyankuppam, Cuddalore and Alapakkam

Bus State buses (Rs 140) leave every half hour and private buses (Rs 140) every four hours from Chennai's Metropolitan Bus Terminus (Tel: 044-24794705) at Koyambedu

(crystal) lingam, in its gold casket, which is worshipped with *abhishekham*. No electrical lighting is used in the Kanakasabhai or Chithsabhai. Only large brass and silver lamps are lit with ghee (no oil) to illumine the sanctum.

To the left of the Chithsabhai is a curtained-off space. Behind the curtain lies the Chidambara Rahasyam or the 'Secret of Chidambaram'. At the time of the aarti, the curtain is whisked aside briefly and one sees a flash of a garland of gold *vilva* leaves against the far wall (there is said to be a *chakra* on that wall) and while the eyes are still getting used to the play of light and darkness, the curtain is whisked back. The Chidambara Rahasyam is explained as the worship of god as formless space.

Go early and try to catch the early morning worship of the *spatika* lingam. It is a lovely experience.

The prakaram of Nataraja contains a surprise in the form of a large shrine for Vishnu, the **Govindaraja Perumal Temple**. Here Vishnu reclines on Adisesha and is attended on by his consorts, Sridevi and Bhudevi. Of special importance are the two large copper *tiruvadigal* (Vishnu's feet) that are installed in the prakaram. Devotees touch their heads to the feet in a moment of complete surrender. When one stands in the prakaram, facing the Nataraja sanctum, one can also see the east-facing sanctum of Govindaraja — it is a unique feature of the Chidambaram Temple that both the Shiva and Vishnu sanctums can be seen from the same point.

The temple is looked after by the Dikshitars, hereditary priests who are exclusively dedicated to the Nataraja Temple. Said to have come to Chidambaram with Nataraja himself, they once numbered 3,000 and consider the lord as one of their clan. Now, there are 350 families of Dikshitars in Chidambaram and the primary occupation of the men of every family is priestly duty at the temple.

◆**Location** 1 km west of the railway station **Timings** 6 am-noon, 4.30-10 pm **Puja timings** 9 and 11 am, noon, 6, 8 and 10 pm; at each puja, *abhishekham* is performed for the *sphatika* lingam

TIP There's a Rs 50 per person fee for going up to the Kanakasabhai and seeing the Chidambara Rahasyam

Festivals

The Nataraja Temple celebrates three major festivals in a year. Great crowds gather for the 10-day **Ani** (Jun-Jul) **Tirumanjanam**. On each day, the *panchamurtis* (Shiva, Parvati, Vinayaka, Murugan and Chandikeswarar) are taken in a procession on the four streets surrounding the temple, in silver and golden vehicles. On the ninth day of this festival, the deities are taken out in their chariots (*ther*). In Margazhi (Dec-Jan), another 10-day festival is held around the asterism of Tiruvathirai, the star of Nataraja. During the **Maha Shivaratri Festival** in Masi (Feb-Mar), many famous dancers perform in the five-day **Natyanjali classical dance festival**.

TIP Photography or videography is strictly prohibited beyond the outer prakarams. Everyone, including non-Hindus, is allowed up to the Kanakasabhai — *no one*, but the priest, is allowed into the Chithsabhai. Men wishing to enter the Kanakasabhai must go bare-chested

Thillai Kali Amman Temple

Located on the northern edge of Chidambaram, this very popular Shakti sthala is said to have been built by King Kopperunjingan (1229-1278). Once when Shiva and Shakti competed with each other in dancing, Shiva struck a fabulous pose, lifting his leg high. Shakti could not match that pose because of modesty, and so lost the contest. By the rules of the contest, the loser had to leave Thillai and reside outside. So Shakti moved to a location at the edge of the kshetra and a Kali Temple came up there. Thillai Kali is credited with curative powers and showers health and prosperity on those who worship her.

◆**Location** $1/2$ km east of the Nataraja Temple **Timings** 6 am-noon, 4-9 pm

Pitchavaram Backwaters

Do make a trip to the mangrove backwaters of Pitchavaram (16 km east of Chidambaram). TTDC runs the **Arignar Anna Tourist Complex** (Tel: 04144-249536) here, which offers boating facilities (Rs 25 per person per hour; 8 am-5 pm) and a restaurant. The mangrove forests here are a botanist's delight, with many rare trees and plants, and birds that migrate seasonally. The coastline here was less affected by the tsunami of December 2004 because of Pitchavaram's thick mangroves.

KERALA KA GURU
Cyrus, Hotel Advisor at Travelguru, knows 'God's Own Country' like his backyard, and the place to get the tastiest Chicken Stew and Appam.

Choose from our network of over 4000 hotels in India. Serviced apartments, budget hotels, luxury resorts, palaces, business accommodations, houseboats and more.

1–800–22–4878
022-4030-4878
www.travelguru.com

India's Largest Hotel Network

TAMIL NADU

The mangrove forests of Pitchavaram are a botanist's — and tourist's — delight

WHERE TO STAY

Chidambaram has a mix of basic but acceptable hotels and a number of low-priced lodges. **Hotel Ritz** (Tel: 04144-223312-14; Tariff: Rs 263-1,362) is on VGP Street. The rooms and bathrooms are decent. It has a multi-cuisine restaurant and friendly staff. Also on VGP Street is **Hotel Saradharam** (Tel: 221336-40; Tariff: Rs 499-Rs 1,800), which is plush to look at and has reasonably clean rooms and bathrooms. They have three restaurants, all of which are popular with the locals. On the East Car Street is **Hotel Akshaya** (Tel: 220191-92; Tariff: Rs 350-Rs 850), which has basic amenities, friendly staff and a multi-cuisine restaurant. Apart from these hotels, there are a number of lodges near the main bus terminus, which are safe but not very clean. Book in advance at the bigger hotels as there is sometimes a rush of either pilgrims, or people visiting the Annamalai University.

For more hotels and details, see Chidambaram Accommodation Listings on page 515

WHERE TO EAT

If you want hygienic surroundings and decent food, your best bets are the restaurants in the hotels. **Pallavi**, **Anu Pallavi** and **Geetanjali**, in Hotel Saradharam (Tel: 04144-221336), are very popular. While the first two serve both vegetarian and non-vegetarian food, Geetanjali serves pure vegetarian. Their vegetarian thalis and tandoor dishes are much sought after. **Aswini Restaurant** in Hotel Akshaya (Tel: 220191) is also recommended. They offer multi-cuisine food but their strength is their regular South Indian fare. Among the smaller eateries, **Udipi Krishna Hotel** in East Car Street, and **Krishna Bhavan**, on West Car Street, are popular and serve basic but tasty South Indian food such as idli, dosai, pongal, vadai, uthappam and rava dosai. *Yelai sappadu* (three course rice meal on a banana leaf) is served only during the lunch hours. There are a number of other such eateries on both these streets, and a quick look will enable you to make sure they are reasonably clean. ■

Opens Early. Shuts Late.

In&Out Convenience Stores from Bharat Petroleum.
Now shop and do much more while you fuel.

At select Bharat Petroleum pumps

Groceries • ATM • Money Transfer • Music • Beverages • Chocolates • Ice-creams • Snacks • Ready-to-eat • Frozen Foods

Photographs by G SIVAPERUMAL

The 17th century Dansborg Fort — a lone Danish legacy

TRANQUEBAR
FOOTNOTE OF HISTORY

State Tamil Nadu
Location Tranquebar, or more properly Tharangambadi, lies just north of the mouth of the Cauvery where she flows into the Bay of Bengal, on the Coromandel Coast
Distance 279 km S of Chennai **JOURNEY TIME** *By road* 6 hrs
Route East Coast Road to Pondicherry via Muttukadu, Mahabalipuram, Sadras and Marakkanam; NH45A to Tranquebar via Cuddalore, Alapakkam, Chidambaram and Sirkazhi (*see route guide on page 12*)

■ BY VAISHNA ROY

When I first visited Tranquebar more than six years ago, I remember how startled I was at these solid Danish remains by the sea shore. I certainly didn't remember any of it from my history books, and to find that a relatively unknown group of Nords had lived and built and fought here, and left behind this architectural legacy not six hours from Chennai, was a delicious discovery.

Six years ago, Tranquebar was truly a ghost city — abandoned colonial structures in a walled town just outside the pale of a sleepy Tamil village. Today, there's a buzz about the place — buildings have been restored, visitors have multiplied, the fort looks freshly painted. In fact, on Sunday, what with the crowds of day-trippers and the ice-cream man, we could well have been on a beach in Chennai.

The sleepy town is stirring to life as a tourist spot mainly because of the Danes themselves. Deeply interested in this exotic piece of their past, they come in droves, gazing at the ramparts their ancestors built or looking for names in the graveyard. They have a Tranquebar Association, which works with the Archaeological Survey of India in renovation projects. Interestingly, their work extends beyond the fortified 'white' city into the village as well. A Danish couple owns an old Tamil house here, where they spend some weeks each summer. The Danish Bestseller Foundation has bought and refurbished a set of five traditional houses on Goldsmith Street, and an NGO has already leased one of these. Plus, the Delhi-based Neemrana Hotels is revamping as many as three buildings here for use as resorts.

In a somewhat ghoulish way, the tsunami is also responsible for the rash of development work. Dozens of schools, computer training centres, and tailoring classes have sprung up. There are NGO offices everywhere. On my last visit, about two dozen catamarans lay scattered on the beach. Today, there are barely three, lost in the crowd of flashy new fishing boats that have taken over the sand. Meanwhile, the fort and the temple ruins have been taken over by the picnickers, their voices and plastic packets blowing across in the sea breeze.

Obviously what I'm seeing is the beginning of the end of the tranquil fishing village. Soon, it might be a full-fledged beach resort, with restaurants serving gobi manchurian and German bakeries run by Nepalese boys. That should bring the crowds in. Today, the only people coming are history and solitude buffs. Oh yes, and the picnickers.

Ironically, the beginning of all this was a clever fraud. The Danish king Christian IV, tricked by a fortune-hunter into believing Ceylon had signed a treaty assigning trading rights to the Danes, sent off a convoy to the Indian Ocean. After much chaos, the ships finally ended up at Tarangambadi, or The Place of the Dancing Waves, on the Coromandel Coast. Admiral Ove Giedde, leader of the expedition, negotiated a trade agreement with Raghunatha Nayak, King of Tanjore, and laid the foundations for this Danish outpost in the early 1600s. Sold in 1845 to the British, it continued its long trading tradition, and now of course it's beginning to be occupied by travellers, the new colonialists.

Thankfully, unlike many heritage buildings that end up bang in the middle of a city, with their attendant grime and itinerant residents, Tranquebar is in miraculous isolation and

→ FAST FACTS

When to go Avoid blazing May and June, and wet December and January. Ideally, try to go in February-March.
Tourist offices
● TTDC ❶
Tourist Information Centre
24 King Street, Tharangambadi
District Nagapattinam
Tel: 04365-289034-36, 288065
● Information Counter ❶
Dept of Tourism, Govt Tourist Home, Bharathaiar Road, near Bus Stand, Kolipathu, Karaikal
Tel: 04368-222621, 222177
● TTDC ❶❻
No. 2, Wallajah Road, Chennai
Tel: 044-25367850-54
Email: ttdc@vsnl.com
Website: tamilnadutourism.org
STD code 04365

spectacularly located, thus making it easier to work with. It shares this stretch of the Coromandel with places like Pondicherry, Karaikal, Poompuhar, and Chidambaram, all brimful with history and culture. Perhaps what we are seeing is the beginning of a new awareness of the rich heritage this stretch of coastline holds. And hopefully some sensitive showcasing. The beginning seems auspicious enough. Neemrana Resorts has done a painstaking and tasteful job of restoring the old collector's bungalow.

THINGS TO SEE AND DO

Nothing quite prepares you for that dramatic first sight. You drive in through an arch, a sort of gone-to-seed Arc de Triomphe, into a street lined on either side by aged buildings, and the road then widens out and there all of a sudden in front of you is the blindingly blue sea and on the sand to your right is the **Dansborg Fort**. Dull mustard in colour, solid, square, and very European in the middle of a blazing South Indian landscape.

◆**Entry fee** Indians Rs 5, foreigners Rs 50
Timings 10 am-5.30 pm

The street is **King Street** or *Kongensgade*, and was once the main street of this 17th-century Danish settlement in Tranquebar or Tharangambadi, to give it its correct Tamil name. On my left, diagonally opposite the fort is the **Danish Governor's House**, a beautiful colonial bungalow that's falling to pieces in front of our eyes. Drive past it and at the top of the road, sitting incongruously intact in this city of ruins is the **Bungalow on the Beach**, now restored as a resort (*see 'Where to Stay' on page 68*). Once the residence of the Danish Governor's ADC and later the British Collector's, it is positioned stunningly, commanding a sweep of sea, sand and the fort.

From the verandah of the resort, the fort looks solitary, somewhat lonely, somewhat dwarfed by the sweep of the sea and the stretching sands. It's hard to believe that for the Danes this fort in a remote fishing village in South India was second in size only to Elsinore, their gloomy Hamlet's castle. And hard to visualise that this was the capital of the trade that existed here for about 250 years starting 1620.

The time to venture out is early mornings and early evenings, when the sun loses its ferocity. To the fort, for walks on the beach, into the village to see the newly renovated Tamil homes. The rest of the time is spent on the lovely large balcony, enjoying the quiet, the view, and the moonlight on the waves. The newly restored Tamil homes with their characteristic inner courtyards, low doors and pillared corridors look beautiful, tempting enough to make one want to move in,

→ GETTING THERE

Rail Nearest railhead: Mayiladuthurai Station (40 km/ 1 hr), but connections with Chennai are not convenient for a weekend break

Car Tranquebar is a smooth drive from Chennai. Exit Chennai from Thiruvanmiyur to catch the East Coast Road to Pondicherry via Mahabalipuram and Marakkanam. The ECR continues south from here as NH45A to Tharangambadi (Tranquebar) via Cuddalore, Alapakkam, Chidambaram and Sirkazhi

Bus Two TNSETC buses leave at 8 pm and 9 pm for Tharangambadi (Tranquebar) from Chennai's Metropolitan Bus Terminus (Tel: 044-24794705) at Koyambedu, arriving 10 hrs later in the early morning at Tranquebar

The tiny Masilamani Nathar Temple on the Tharangambadi seashore

especially when you walk into the backyard. From here you can see the breakers crashing in and a lone blue sail far out in the sea.

On this, my second visit, I find two things remain the same — one is the little museum inside the fort, as sad, dingy and poorly displayed as it was on my first trip. Can't the government hand these things over to qualified and passionate museologists? The second is the ruined **Pandya Temple** on the edge of the sea — as elegant and stoical as ever, although leaning a little more into the waves, some more of its cornices and friezes sacrificed to the inexorable water. This small, compact Masilamani Nathar temple dates back to 1305 and is credited to the then ruler Maravarma Kulasekara Pandyan. On closer inspection, I realise it is not as untouched as I had thought. There are signs of renovation — a brash new roof, daubs of whitewash — and from wishing that it would be restored I think it was better off left abandoned.

What has enjoyed a better fate is the Evangelical Lutheran **New Jerusalem Church** on King Street. Built in 1718 by Bartolomeus Ziegenbalg, the first Protestant missionary to arrive in India, it was restored recently and stands exactly as it did almost 300 years ago. Ziegenbalg is credited with setting up Tamil Nadu's first printing press, writing the first Tamil translation of the Bible, and even with the first Tamil-English dictionary. His grave is in front of the church altar, while the cemetery outside is another interesting walk down history. A little further down is the **Church of Zion**, founded in 1701 and also restored recently.

At **Tirukkadaiyur**, 10 minutes from Tranquebar, is a beautiful 11th century Chola temple dedicated to the legend

TAMIL NADU

The Evangelical Lutheran New Jerusalem Church on the Kongensgade

of Shiva and Markandaya, his devotee. Destined to die at 16, on the appointed date Markandaya ran and tied himself to the linga. Unfazed, Yama threw his noose around both Markandeya and the linga. Angered, Shiva captured Yama under his left foot. He let him go later, but since this is the place where death was temporarily defeated, to this date married couples celebrate a spouse's 60th or 80th birthday with a visit to this temple.

WHERE TO STAY AND EAT

Tranquebar has just two options. **Bungalow on the Beach** (Tel: 04364-288065, 289034-36; Tariff: Rs 4,000-5,000) is the Neemrana resort in the erstwhile and beautifully restored collector's house. My tall, cool room is made for lazy weekends, with its billowing blue curtains that seem to bring the sea inside. The French window opens out to a balcony, where we sip tea watching the fishing boats bobbing on the horizon.

The eight rooms, each named after a Danish ship that visited Tranquebar, are straight out of the 18th century — tall shuttered wooden doors and windows, peaking ceilings and period furniture. Outside, the halls and corridors are lined with fascinating old maps, pictures and more delicious period furniture.

The resort has a fixed menu for each day, with one French/Continental selection and one Indian. The soups are excellent but the Continental food way too bland for my taste. The Indian fare is better but the desserts disappoint.

Tamil Nadu Hotel (Tel: 288065, 289034-36; Tariff: Rs 150-600), right next door near the old Post Office, is a much more prosaic building but nothing can spoil the view outside and the rates make up for the lack of poetry. With clean, spacious air-conditioned rooms and dorms (seven beds), this is also run by Neemrana although owned by the government. It serves good reliable South Indian food.

You could try the smaller restaurants in the city for local fare, but the options are minimal and iffy.

For details, see Tranquebar Accommodation Listings on page 526

AROUND TRANQUEBAR

Karaikal (15 km)
Part of the Union Territory of Pondicherry (*see page 32*), Karaikal, like Pondicherry, is a lazy hamlet built to a geometric grid holding tentatively to its French antecedents. Its main thoroughfare, Bharathiar Road, is lined with shops selling everything a small town may need. It's also a preferred halt for those wishing to go to the Navgraha Sthalas or Thirunallaru, the abode of Lord Saturn, barely 5 km west of Karaikal. Within the town is the 1891 **Church of Our Lady of Angels**, the 19th-century **Mastan Syed Dawood Dargah** and the ancient **temple of Karaikal Ammai**.

The temple has an interesting story that is traced back to the 7th century CE Bhakti movement in Tamil Nadu, which also establishes the antiquity of the town. The tale recalls how a rich merchant's pious wife, Punithavanthi, fed mangoes meant for her husband to a hungry sadhu. Angry at being slighted in this manner, the husband chided his wife. Terrified, Punithavanthi prayed to Lord Shiva, who answered her prayer by bestowing upon her a basket of celestial mangoes. To this day, during the annual Mangani festival (Jun-Jul) when the procession bearing the goddess passes through Karaikal, people throw mangoes at the goddess! Karaikal is south of Tranquebar, towards Nagore, on NH45A.

Also visit the **Jadayupureeswar Temple** at TR Pattinam, 5 km south of Karaikal on NH45A, dedicated to the mythical bird Jatayu from the Ramayana. A small shrine right of the main sanctum hosts the small blackened statue of the brave avian avatar, who is believed to have fallen here after a desperate fight to free Sita from Ravana.

♦**Entry** Free **Timings** 6 am-noon, 6-9 pm, open all days

Stop for a bite at the Karaikal Tourism Department-run **Garden Restaurant** located in an old sprawling colonial bungalow on Beach Road. Watch out for the still functioning old **lighthouse** that looms over the property. **Karaikal Beach** nearby comes alive in the evenings when families come to enjoy the sea and its cool breeze. Stop by the makeshift stalls to sample some unique Tamil variations of Chinese dishes.

Nagore (25 km)
See page 114 ■

M BALAN/ SOUTHINDIAPICTURE

Sarangapani Temple — the biggest in Kumbakonam

KUMBAKONAM
CELESTIAL POT OF NECTAR

State Tamil Nadu
Location The second largest town in Thanjavur is centred around not one but a clutch of major temples; the Cauvery flows to the north and the Arasalar to the south
Distance 303 km SW of Chennai **JOURNEY TIME By rail** 9 hrs **By road** $7^1/_2$ hrs
Route East Coast Road to Pondicherry via Mahabalipuram and Marakkanam; NH45A to Sirkazhi via Cuddalore and Chidambaram; SH64 to Kumbakonam via Vaithiswarankoil and Mayiladuthurai (*see route guide on page 12*)

■ BY JANAKI VENKATARAMAN

Kumbakonam, or 'the town of the celestial pot', is known for many things: the liveliness of its inhabitants and the colourfulness of their speech, its finely worked brass vessels and its heavenly 'degree' coffee. That makes for two Kumbakonams really, the mindscape and the pilgrim centre. For to speak of Kumbakonam minus its temples is like speaking of Varanasi minus the Ganga. This foremost temple town is perhaps the most special destination in the Cauvery Delta. What other name can fit a town that has no less than 80 temples, most of them ancient, all of them significant? Plus the tirthams: the Cauvery and Arasalar rivers flow on either side, and then there is the Mahamaham Tank, holier even than the holiest of rivers. In the Tamil months of Margazhi (Dec-Jan) and Thyy (Jan-Feb), the mist rises from the rivers and wraps itself like fine muslin around the swathes of green fields and the towering temple gopurams. The lilting voices of groups of women singing songs in praise of Vishnu and Shiva soar softly as the inky sky shades over, and the morning wakes up to Kumbakonam.

KUMBAKONAM

LEGENDS AND MYTHOLOGY

Kumbakonam is said to be the very site where, after the Great Deluge and just before the advent of Kaliyuga, the celestial pot of nectar containing the seeds of all life to come, came to rest. It was here that Shiva, as hunter, chose to shoot an arrow at the pot and break it, so that its contents may spill and life could begin again. *Kumbam* is 'pot' and *konam* is 'crooked' — the pot that broke crookedly when Shiva's arrow hit it. There are two landmarks in Kumbakonam, which underline the legend behind the town's name: the Adi Kumbeswarar Temple to Shiva, who broke the *kumbam*; and the Mahamaham Tank, where the nectar from the pot fell.

THINGS TO SEE AND DO

Ruins of Chola palaces can still be sighted around the town. The temples they built are still very much in evidence. Two days are adequate to cover the major temples in Kumbakonam. Autos are the best way to travel within and around Kumbakonam. Taxis cost approx Rs 1,200 per day.
TIP At the temples listed below, still and video cameras can be used only in the outer prakarams, and non-Hindus are not allowed near the main sanctums

Adi Kumbeswarar Temple

Built by the early Cholas, possibly before the 7th century CE, this Thevaram temple has been extensively renovated and added to by the later Cholas, the Nayaks and the Marathas. While the temple has a well called the **Kura Tirtham** (*kura* means well), it is the Mahamaham Tank, about 2 km southeast of the temple, which is most sacred.

The sculptural wealth of this temple is amazing. There is no mandapam, pillar or ceiling which is not ornamented. There are sculptures depicting scenes from the Puranas and the 12 zodiac signs, among others. Some years ago, an underground tunnel was discovered in the temple, near the sanctum of Lord Kumbeswarar. Among other things, a stone *nadaswaram* (wind instrument) was found there. This can actually be played, so finely has it been carved.

The lingam in the Kumbeswarar sanctum is a *swayambhu* and is slightly lopsided in shape. The idol is never bathed but only coated with *punugu* (the oily, scented secretion of the civet cat). As a further protection, it is encased in silver. Kumbeswarar is said to grant happiness and prosperity in this world, and liberation in the next, to all his true devotees.

The **sanctum of Goddess Mangalambigai** is grand. The 4-foot tall idol, sheathed in gold, stands on a gold *peetham* (base), said to be energised by 72 crore mantras. Its walls and ceiling are covered with vegetable dye paintings and gem encrusted Tanjore work. Another shrine is that of **Jurahareswarar** ('he who destroys fevers'). Devotees pray to him to cure fever.

The temple's annual **float festival** is held in Panguni (Mar-Apr) at the Mahamaham Tank. The **annual procession** takes place in Chittirai (Apr-May).

→ FAST FACTS

When to go It is hot and humid in the summer (Apr-Jun) but many of the temple festivals take place in summer. Dec-Mar, just after the rains, when the Cauvery looks enchanting, is best
Tourist office
● TTDC ❶ ⓑ
No. 2, Wallajah Road, Chennai
Tel: 044-25367850-54
Fax: 25361385; Email: ttdc@vsnl.com
Website: tamilnadutourism.org
STD code 0435

♦**Location** 2 km north-west of the Mahamaham Tank **Timings** 6 am-12.30 pm, 4-8.30 pm **Puja timings** 7 and 9 am, noon, 5, 7 and 8.30 pm

Mahamaham Tank

The 3-acre spread of the Mahamaham Tank is not a perfect rectangle. Instead, the north and south banks curve slightly so that, from an aerial view, the tank faintly resembles the pot that broke here and made the tank sacred. There are **19 tirthams** (wells) within the tank. On its banks are shrines for 16 lingams.

The Ganga, and Yamuna and other holy rivers, legend has it, come to bathe in the tank and rid themselves of the accumulated sins of so many people bathing in them. In the **Kasi Viswanathar Temple** on the north bank of the Mahamaham Tank stand the idols of the nine river goddesses. The lingam in this temple is said to have been made with sand and nectar by Shiva himself.

The tank is the venue for the **Mahamaham Festival**, considered equivalent to the sacred Maha Kumbha Melas. This sacred event occurs once in 12 years in the Tamil month of Maasi; Feb-Mar. The last Mahamaham Festival was held in March 2004, when some 4-5 million devotees converged on the town to bathe in the tank. Annually, the Maasi Maham is celebrated with nine days of festivities, including a **Theppotsavam** (float festival).

♦**Location** 2 km south-east of Adi Kumbeswarar Temple **Tank timings** 24 hours **Temple timings** 7 am-12.30 pm, 4.30-9 pm

Sarangapani Temple

This is the biggest temple in Kumbakonam. The 44-m tall, 11-tiered tower of this temple is striking. One of the 108 Divya Desams, this temple is third in the line of the most important Vaishnavite sthalas, the first two being Srirangam and Tirupati. The temple has five prakarams and its water tank is called **Portamarai Kulam** (pond of the golden lotus). The main sanctum is shaped like a chariot with 12 sculpted columns. Equally noteworthy is the stone trelliswork here.

Goddess Mahalakshmi as Komalavalli Thayar is said to have married Lord Vishnu as Sarangapani ('he who holds the Sarangam, Vishnu's bow'), in one of their many avatars, in this sthala. As the goddess came to this kshetra before Sarangapani and waited for her consort here, it is her shrine that must be visited before devotees go on to the sanctum of Sarangapani.

♦**Location** Just a large tank, the Hema Pushkarni, separates this temple from

---

→ GETTING THERE

Rail Kumbakonam Station **Best option TO** Rockfort Express (dep: Chennai Egmore 10.30 pm, Mambalam 10.40 pm, Tambaram 11 pm; arr: Kumbakonam 7.30 am) **Best option FROM** Rockfort Express (dep: Kumbakonam 7.30 pm; arr: Tambaram 4.16 am, Mambalam 4.34 am, Chennai Egmore 5.15 am)

Car Kumbakonam is a smooth drive from Chennai, though $7^1/_2$ hrs is on the longish side for a weekend break. Exit Chennai from Thiruvanmiyur to catch the East Coast Road to Pondicherry via Mahabalipuram and Marakkanam. The ECR continues south from here as NH45A to Sirkazhi via Cuddalore and Chidambaram. Turn right onto the state highway to Kumbakonam via Vaithiswarankoil, Mayiladuthurai, Aduthurai and Tiruvidaimarudur

Bus Many buses (Rs 95-120) leave for Kumbakonam from Chennai starting 5 am. from Chennai's Metropolitan Bus Terminus (Tel: 044-24794705) at Koyambedu. The last bus leaves at 10.30 pm

that of Adi Kumbeswarar **Timings** 7 am-12.30 pm, 4.30-9 pm **Website** sarangapanitemple.org

More to see

Do take time off to see **the house of Srinivasa Ramanujan** (on Sarangapani Sannidhi Street; 10 am-5 pm), a memorial to the mathematical genius.

A **bath in the Cauvery**, especially early in the morning, is very refreshing. There are many ghats along the banks, but the most preferred are the **Sarkarai Padithurai** (ghat) and the **Bhagavatha Padithurai**, both off Kamakshi Josier Street. The best time of the year for a dip is between December and March. The morning and evening pujas (9 am and 6 pm) at the **Kanchi Kamakoti Peetham Mutt**, situated by the banks of the Cauvery on Mutt Street, always attract devotees. This mutt was the headquarters of the *peetham* until about 100 years ago.

SHOPPING

Kumbakonam is famous for heavy stainless steel and brass vessels. In the Kumbeswarar Sannidhi corridor, you can get fine quality stainless steel vessels from **MVM Stores**. For brass vessels, go to either **RS and Co**, or **Karpaga Vilas Stores**, on Big Street, close to the Kumbeswarar Temple. You can bargain for sturdy iron griddles and vegetable cutters, and *panchaloha* icons and bells from Swamimalai. For silk saris, there is the reliable **Swaminatha Iyer Stores**, also on Big Street (prices start at Rs 1,500). On the same street is **Gopaldoss Jewellery**, a trusted shop for diamonds, gold and silver. There are also many silk weavers on Gandhi Adigal Salai. All the shops mentioned here are closed on Sundays.

WHERE TO STAY

Kumbakonam offers a reasonable choice of hotels and all are centrally located, within a kilometre's radius of the Adi Kumbeswarar Temple. **Hotel Rayas** (Tel: 0435-2423170-72; Tariff: Rs 550-1,750) on the Head Post Office Road, has basic facilities, friendly staff and a North Indian restaurant. **Hotel Green Park** (Tel: 2402852-53; Tariff: Rs 582-1,500), on Lakshmi Vilas Street, near Vijaya Theatre, is very clean and has a good multi-cuisine restaurant. The hotel arranges tours to various temples and is

DINODIA PHOTO LIBRARY

What's brewing?

The Kumbakonam 'degree coffee' is made with the finest coffee seeds, is slow roasted, and distilled in brass filters. The 'degree' refers to both the purity of the milk as well as the heat at which the ingredients are mixed. The flavour of the coffee is ensured by always keeping the decoction warm, in a double boiler. The milk should be freshly boiled and must not simmer. One more thing: coffee is never as aromatic as when the decoction is extracted from a brass filter. Kumbakonam degree coffee comes in a tumbler and *dabara*, a shallower vessel into which the scalding hot coffee is swished from a height in long, swift streams, so that when the steaming beverage finally rests in front of you, it is frothy and fragrant. Most of the eateries mentioned in *Where to Eat* (*see page 74*) will serve it at Rs 5-7 per tumbler.

TAMIL NADU

The holiest of holy Mahamaham Tank, venue of a great festival held every 12 years

very helpful with information about transportation and route maps. It also offers cab services for pilgrimages around Kumbakonam to even those who do not stay in the hotel.

Hotel Adithya (Tel: 2421794-95; Tariff: Rs 498-1,200) on Tanjore Main Road, offers basic amenities. It has a multi-cuisine veg restaurant. **Hotel Kasi International** (Tel: 2431055/ 255; Tariff: Rs 400-800) on Town High School Road, offers clean rooms and a veg restaurant.

Paradise Resort (Tel: 2416469, 3291354; Tariff: Rs 2,450), on the Tanjore Main Road, has a Chettinad-style décor with 18 aesthetically designed rooms. Their treetop restaurant serves vegetarian Chettinad dishes.

For more hotels and details, see Kumbakonam Accommodation Listings on page 519

WHERE TO EAT

There are a number of small restaurants serving basic South Indian vegetarian food in the main bazaar area, around the Kumbeswarar Temple. **Adithya** (Tel: 0435-2421794-95), opposite Sarangapani Temple, is a good option, as is **Archana**, on Big Street. **Hotel Saravana**, opposite Gandhi Park, serves good veg thalis. **Hotel Venkataramana**, opposite Gandhi Park, is a great favourite. South Indian veg meals and tiffin are served on banana leaves on long tables in a huge, airy hall. In a nearby lane is the **Mami Mess**, an eatery run from home. Food is served on banana leaves spread on the floor. The lady of the house serves the meal and the ambience is homely. Both Venkataramana and Mami are closed on Sundays.

For multi-cuisine food, the restaurant in **Hotel Green Park** (Tel: 2402852) is a good choice. **Pallavi Tiffin Centre**, a roadside eatery near the Sarangapani Temple is hugely popular with the locals and serves everything from ghee roast dosais to soft idlis to *koththu* paranthas. Also the *kuzhi paniyaram* and *appam* with stew at **Paradise Resort** (Tel: 2416469).

TIP While in Kumbakonam, do not forget to taste the 'degree' coffee (*see 'What's brewing' on page 73*)

TAMIL NADU

AROUND KUMBAKONAM

Nachiar Kovil (10 km SE)
A special feature of this temple to Srinivasa and his consort Vanjulavalli Thayar, is the impressive idol of Kal (stone) Garudan (kite), the mount of Vishnu, who is seen here with large wingspans and a strong body. Twice during the year (on the fourth day of Panguni/ Mar-Apr, and on the fourth day of Margazhi/ Dec-Jan), the Kal Garudan is taken out of his shrine to serve as Srinivasa's mount during processions. It takes four men to carry the Garudan out of his sanctum. As they carry him out he seems to become heavier and they need eight men, then 16 and so on until 64 men are required to carry him out of the temple and 128 to move him in the procession. His weight seems to decrease in the same proportion on the return journey until only four men are required to carry him back into his sanctum. Huge crowds turn out to see this phenomenon.
♦**Location** By the banks of the Arasalar
Timings 7.30 am-12.30 pm, 4.30-9 pm
Temple Tel 0435-2467167, 2466459
Website kalkarudabhagavan.com

Thiruvidaimarudur

The revered Shiva sthala of Thiruvidaimarudur (*thiru* = holy, *idai* = middle, *marudu* = marudu trees, also known as Madhyarjunam, is said to be over 1,200 years old. It was renovated by Varaguna Pandian (9th century CE) and Kulothunga I (11th century). The deity here is Marudavaanar or Mahalingeswarar and his consort is Brihatsundaragujambal. This kshetra in the middle region, between Varanasi and Rameswaram, is considered as holy as the other two. It is believed that Shiva himself laid down the protocol of Saivite worship here. The six daily worship services, the mantras and rituals, the hand and finger gestures of the priests, and the procedures for making offerings, followed in Shiva temples to this day are said to have been formulated by Shiva himself at this temple.

On a niche high up in the wall to the left of the second entrance is a strange looking stone figure. It looks human but without any specific features, its limbs curling back against its body, its head bowed — the very picture of mental depression. This is the Brahmahatti, the spirit that clings to people who have committed heinous crimes. It is said a Chola king once killed a Brahmin inadvertently, thereby bringing the Brahmahatti *dosham* (sin) on himself. He got rid of it only by entering the sanctum of Mahalingeswarar. Something similar happened to a Pandya king too. And he too was rid of the Brahmahatti as he crossed the second entrance to the sanctum of Shiva. Fearing, however, that the Brahmahatti would cling to him

TAMIL NADU

V MUTHURAMAN

The spacious Nageswarar Temple

again if he came that way once more, the king left by another exit. Even today, all visitors are advised to never re-cross the second entrance, where the Brahmahatti waits. Mentally disturbed people and those who are said to be 'possessed' are brought to this temple to be cured.

♦**Location** 8 km north-east of Kumbakonam **Timings** 6 am-noon, 4-9 pm **Temple Tel** 0435-2461946

Darasuram (4 km)

The magnificent **Airavateeswara Temple** here was built in the 12th century by King Raja Raja II, with subsequent additions by the Nayak kings. Legend has it that Indra's elephant Airavata worshipped Shiva at this spot and the lord took on the name of his devotee. Declared a UNESCO World Heritage Site (one of the three within this region, the other two being Thanjavur's Brihadeeswara Temple (*see page 101*), and Gangaikondacholapuram (*see page 78*), the Airavateeswara Temple is being maintained by ASI

though it comes under the patronage of the Thanjavur royal family. This is a temple in which one needs to spend at least a few hours to take in the sheer wealth of sculptural detail and the amazing beauty of the stone-work.

Among the many highlights of this extraordinary temple are: the lovely vimanam; the hall of the main sanctum, which has been built at a height and is shaped like a chariot supported by wheels on one side and horses and elephants on the other; the detail in the sculpture on the pillars in the main hall, which depict scenes from the Puranas as well as from the lives of the people of the 12th century. The steps leading to the top of the *bali peetham* (sacrificial stone) have been made of a kind of stone which reproduces musical notes if you roll a stone down them.

♦**Location** 4 km west of Kumbakonam
♦**Timings** 6 am-noon, 4-8 pm

TIP Photography is allowed inside the main mandapams. Non-Hindus are allowed quite close to the sanctum

Swamimalai (8 km)

Lord Subrahmanya chose to have one of his six sacred hill homes at Swamimalai. The **Swaminatha Swamy Temple** was built by the early Chola kings. The **Cauvery** flows just 150m south of the temple. There are ghats for bathing here. A man-made hill of stone has been erected for Subrahmanya's sanctum, to which 60 steps lead up from the ground level. It is customary to break a coconut on the first step before beginning the climb. On the gopuram are scenes sculpted from the Skanda Purana. The sacred well, the **Vajra Tirtham**, is said to cure many diseases.

The idol of Swaminatha in the main sanctum is majestic. Six feet high and beautifully proportioned, the statue holds the *dandayutham* (staff or club) in the right hand, while the left hand rests lightly on the thigh. Every Thursday, the idol is adorned in a royal costume.

Opens Early. Shuts Late.

In&Out Convenience Stores from Bharat Petroleum.
Now shop and do much more while you fuel.

**Groceries • ATM • Money Transfer • Music • Beverages • Chocolates
• Ice-creams • Snacks • Ready-to-eat • Frozen Foods**

TAMIL NADU

A mural depicting hunters on the ceiling of a Shiva temple near Kumbakonam

The most important festivals of the temple are the 10-day **Brahmotsavam** in Chittirai (Apr-Mar), the 10-day **Skanda Sashti Festival** in Aippasi (Oct-Nov), the 10-day **Karthigai** in Karthigai (Nov-Dec), and the **Thyy Poosam Festival** in Thyy (Jan-Feb). Swamimalai is a *prarthanai sthala* and devotees throng here year round to fulfil vows and make offerings.
♦**Location** In the busy bazaar street in the middle of Swamimalai **Timings** 6 am-1 pm; 4-9 pm **Puja timings** (Abhishekham) 7.30, 9, 11 am and 12.30 and 5 pm **Temple Tel** 0435-2454421
TIP Cameras and video cameras are allowed in the outer prakarams but not near the sanctums. Non-Hindus are allowed up to the main sanctum

Stay here at **Sterling Swamimalai** (Tel: 0435-2480044/ 385; Tariff: Rs 2,250-4,000; *see page 524 for details*), in the village of Thimmakudy near Swamimalai (2 km east towards Kumbakonam). Built around a 19th century *agraharam* (Brahmin street) house, the hotel has every modern convenience in a rural ambience. There are facilities for Ayurvedic oil massages and steam baths, traditional games, rides in bullock carts, cutcheries (classical music concerts) and folk art performances, and meals in the *mutram* (central courtyard) of the ancient house. For meals, the **Sterling Resort restaurant** is open to non-guests too.

Gangaikondacholapuram (36 km W)
The nondescript village of Gangaikondacholapuram is home to the magnificent ruins of the **Brihadeesvara Temple**, a UNESCO World Heritage Site. King Rajendra Chola I (1012-1044 CE) built this temple to celebrate his conquest of lands up to present-day Bangladesh. From this triumphant journey, he brought back the waters of the sacred Ganga and poured it into the absolutely enomous tank here, then named Chola Ganga and now referred to as Ponneri. He assumed the title Gangaikondachola and constructed the great temple at Gangaikondacholapuram (the Chola land where the Ganga was brought/ conquered). The temple is almost an exact replica of the Big Temple of Thanjavur (*see page 101*).
♦**Timings** 7 am-noon, 4-9 pm ■

Balancing life.

A wellness experience that encompasses Ayurveda, Yoga and Meditation. To take you back to your pure self, in sync with the nature that surrounds you. Setting you free. To discover life and all its simple joys all over again. The cgh earth wellness experience. Offered at all our resorts under the supervision of a team of highly qualified Ayurvedic physicians, Yoga experts and spiritual mentors. An experience that transcends the ordinary. An experience that brings in total harmony of the body, mind and soul.

cgh earth wellness experiences
Bangaram Island | Brunton Boatyard | Casino Hotel | Coconut Lagoon
Kalari Kovilakom | Marari Beach | Spice Village | SwaSwara | Visalam

experience hotels

Central Reservations: Casino Building Cochin Kerala India Phone: +91-484-3011711 Fax: 2668001
Email: contact@cghearth.com www.cghearth.com

TAMIL NADU

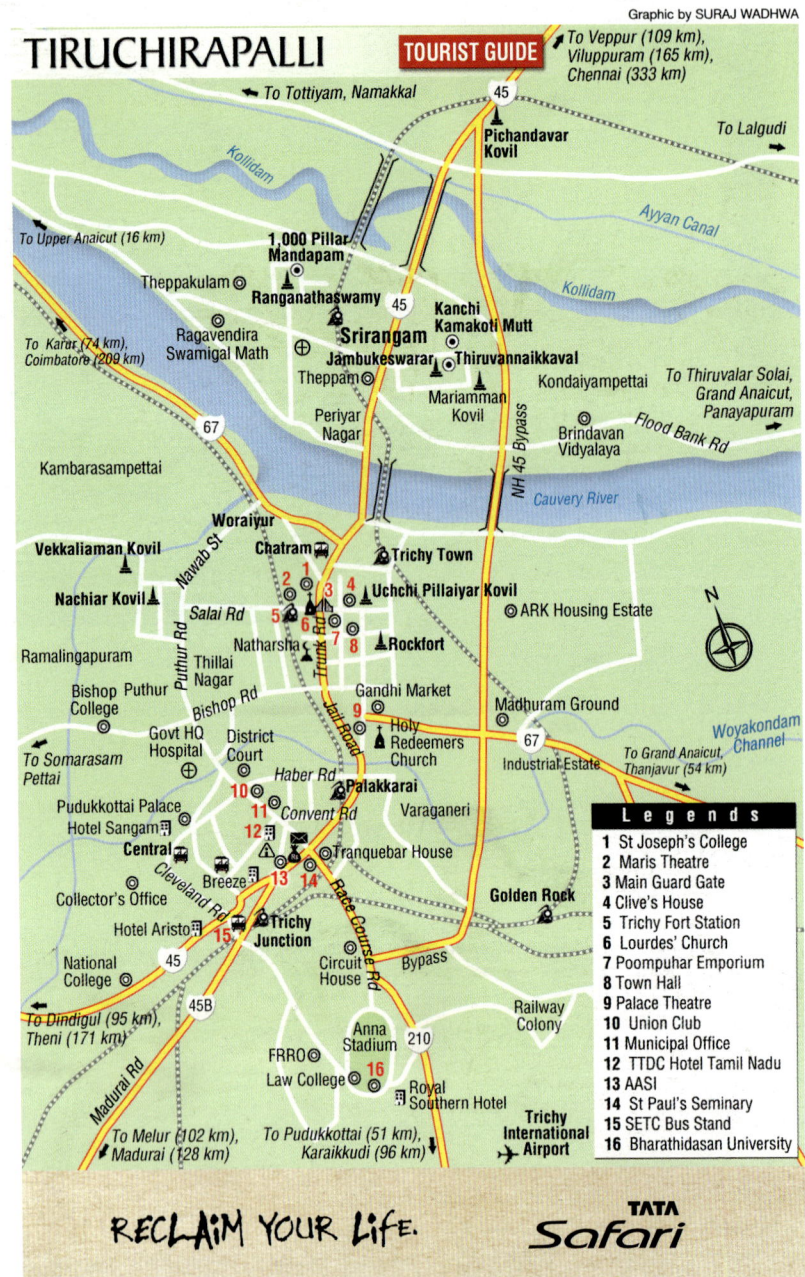

TIRUCHIRAPALLI

Photographs by G SIVAPERUMAL

View of Trichy City from the Malaikottai, or Rockfort, Temple

TIRUCHIRAPALLI
HEAVENS ON EARTH

State Tamil Nadu
Location At the confluence of the Cauvery with its Kollidam tributary, Tiruchirapalli or simply Trichy, is central to Tamil Nadu, both in terms of location and connectivity; its landscape is dominated by massive rocks jutting into the sky, earning it the name Rock City
Distance 327 km SW of Chennai JOURNEY TIME **By rail** 7 hrs **By road** 8 hrs **By air** 50 mins
Route NH45 to Trichy via Vandalur, Tindivanam, Viluppuram, Ulundurpettai, Turaimangalam and Srirangam (*see route guide on page 12*)

■ BY DEEPA KANDASWAMY

The bustling city of Trichy, an affectionate acronym for Tiruchirapalli, wears its accolades lightly. Visible for miles, a gargantuan 83-m high rock, part of a 3,500-million-year-old hill chain that is older than the Himalaya and adorns the city like a broken necklace, is home to a remarkable fort-temple. The Ranganathaswamy Temple on the nearby island of Srirangam is a seven-walled complex spread over 156 acres, making it a small town in itself, the only one of its kind in the world. The temple's 236-foot high rajagopuram is the tallest in the world. It is the holiest of Vaishnava temples. Yet Srirangam is also a supremely sacred Shaivite tirth as well, site of the Panchabhoota Shivasthala of Thiruvannaikaval.

The Natharsha Dargah here is one of the oldest mosques in India and the Varma Kalai, the ancient martial art that was the precursor to Kerala's Kalaripayattu, traces its orgin to Trichy. Patanjali, father of yoga, lived, wrote the Yoga Sutras, taught his three disciples,

TAMIL NADU

and attained samadhi here. In Trichy is the only temple that has separate *sannidhis* for Brahma, Vishnu and Shiva, and their consorts. Shaivism and Vaishnavism made peace in this city, where every sculpture in every temple tells a story, but as quietly as the Cauvery.

The city was ruled variously by the early Cholas, then the Pallavas, who lost it to the Pandyas before the Cholas re-asserted themselves in the 10th century CE, and built a fort on the gigantic rock in the centre of town. Tiruchirapalli came to be called Malaikottai (Rockfort).

LEGENDS AND MYTHOLOGY

Vibhishana, brother of Ravana, was carrying the Ranga Vimana (idol of Lord Ranganatha), which he had secured from Rama at the lord's coronation ceremony in Ayodhya. He wished to take it to Lanka. He stopped at the spot where the Cauvery meets its tributary, the Kollidam, as he had to perform his daily prayer. He knew that if he placed the vimanam on the ground, it would take root there. Vibhishana handed it to a boy playing nearby, agreeing to the condition that he would come when called thrice. The child called his name as many times in quick succession and before Vibhishana could hurry back, set the vimanam upon the sand and took to his heels. Vibhishana rapped him on his head but destiny prevailed. Sri Ranganathaswamy never left what then became Srirangam, site of the largest temple complex in India. The deity still faces south, towards Lanka. The hill the boy ran to, where he revealed himself to be Vinayaka, became the Uchchi Pillaiyar Kovil. The indentation on the idol is said to testify to Vibhishana's fury.

ORIENTATION

The town's main landmarks are the Central and the Chatram bus stands. **Central Bus Stand** is next to the railway station in south Trichy. **Chatram Bus Stand** is 1/2 km west of Rockfort in north Trichy. The area around the Central Bus Stand, commonly referred to as **Cantonment**, is Trichy's business/administrative zone. The area around Chatram, often referred to as **Main Guard Gate** or the **Bazaar area**, is the commercial zone of Trichy. Buses ply from both bus stands to all the temples, including the 600-acre island of **Srirangam**, set upon the Cauvery and 7 km north of Trichy. Autos and taxis are ideal for getting around. There are **Tourist Info Counters** at the railway station and airport, apart from the tourist offices in the city (*see 'Fast Facts' at left*).

→ FAST FACTS

When to go Any time of the year. It rains in November. December-March is particularly pleasant
Tourist offices
● Department of Tourism
Govt of Tamil Nadu, Near Central Bus Stand, Cantonment, Trichy
Tel: 0431-2460136
● TTDC
McDonald's Road, Trichy
Tel: 0431-2414346
● TTDC
No. 2, Wallajah Road, Chennai
Tel: 044-25367850-54
Website: tamilnadutourism.org
STD code 0431

THINGS TO SEE AND DO

Malaikottai (Rockfort) and Thiruverumbur are both rock temples; it's best to see one in the early hours of the day and the other late in the evening as the rocky terrain here heats up fast. Srirangam will need a day in itself. Many of the temples

Jambukeswarar Temple, where Shiva presides as the primordial element of water

in Trichy are ASI-protected monuments. Since all the temples close in the afternoons, shopping and other sightseeing may be done then.

Malaikottai/ Rockfort Temple

Over 2,500 years old, the early Cholas built the exterior of this fort-temple in stages. The three main *sannidhis* (altars) are that of Maanika Vinayakar at the entrance, Thayumanavarswamy midway and Uchchi Pillaiyar at the top, with several smaller sites of interest en route.

At the foot of the hill is the beautiful **Maanika Vinayakar Temple**. Apart from the three main altars at Malaikottai, 258 steps up is a **cave temple to Shiva**, built by the Pallava king Mahendra Varma between 600 and 630 CE. It is a two-storeyed architectural marvel of great tranquillity featuring exquisite carvings.

The oldest of the three *sannidhis*, said to date to before the Ramayana, is that of Shiva as **Thayumanavar**, which is midway up Malaikottai. It is said that the *swayambhu* lingam here was worshipped as Sevandhi (after marigold, the flower offered to the lord) Naadhar. Below Thayumanavar Temple are two **cave shrines**, which have beautiful Pallava sculptures dating to the 6th and 7th centuries CE, the imprint of Vibhishana's footprint (*see 'Legends and Mythology' on facing page*), and an underground *sannidhi* to Ayyanar, the village guardian deity.

After climbing 417 steps to the top, we reach the **Uchchi Pillaiyar Kovil** to which the lad Vinayaka ran. Its golden vimanam gleams in the sun. The view of Trichy from here is panoramic.

Every pournami, the *utsavars* of all three temples are taken around the rock in the streets below. The **temple car festival of Chithirai** (Apr-May), the **Aadi Pooram Festival** (Jul-Aug) and the **Theppam** (float) **Festival** in Panguni (May-Jun) are famous.

♦**Location** 1/2 km east of the Chatram Bus Stand **Timings** Maanika Vinayakar Temple: 6 am-noon, 4-9 pm (10 pm Fri); Thayumanavar Temple: 6 am-12.5 pm, 4-8 pm; Uchchi Pillaiyar Kovil: 6 am-8 pm **Temple Tel** 0431-2704621 **Website** thiruchyrockfort.org

TIP Non-Hindus are not allowed in the Uchchi Pillaiyar Kovil

TAMIL NADU

Erumbeswarar Temple, Thiruverumbur

Built on another gigantic 150-foot high rock, this temple has been a protected heritage site since 1914 and is referred to as Dakshin Kailash. This is the only place Mallik Ghafur could not capture when he invaded Trichy. The sculptures from the mandapam he destroyed were saved and the temple thus has two idols of each: Shiva as Dakshinamurthy, Vinayakar and Chandikeswarar, the deity who is turned away in deep meditation and is said to have Shiva's ear, one of only two gods who have Eswar (Shiva) suffixed to his name (the other being Saniswarar [Sani Bhagvan]). You can make out both Shiva and Parvati in the lingam. Since only *punugu* (secretion of the civet cat) can be applied on the lingam, no *abhishekam* is performed on it. At the entrance is a huge temple tank. The third prakaram is around the rock itself. In the first prakaram is an intricately carved 12-pillared mahamandapam. The luminous lingam, lit from behind, faces east.

♦**Location** 10 km east of Rockfort on the Trichy-Thanjavur Highway **Timings** 6 am-noon, 4-8 pm

Marigold offerings for the gods

PRASHANT PANJIAR

Ranganathaswamy, Srirangam

When Vaishnavites simply say 'kovil' (temple), they refer to the Ranganathaswamy Temple in Srirangam, for such is its unqualified glory. The most important of the 108 Divya Desams, the seven prakarams here are with reference to the seven *chakras* (nodal energy points) in the human body, at the centre of which the *atma* (soul) resides. Similarly, within the seven prakarams resides the atma of the universe: Vishnu.

The Ranganathaswamy Temple Complex, the largest in India, is a 156-acre world in itself. The sacred and mesmerisingly beautiful idol of Lord Ranganatha, Vishnu in Ananthashayanam (eternal repose) is 21 ft long, and its antiquity is not known. The southern 236-foot high (78m) rajagopuram of the Ranganathaswamy Temple is the tallest in the world.

The eight monolithic pillars in the **Sesharayar Mandapam**, to the south of the fourth prakaram, have life-like relief sculptures of warriors on horses. Opposite here, only 953 pillars of the **Thousand Pillar Mandapam** still stand.

For the complete pilgrimage experience, start as early as 4.30 am. Have a cleansing bath in the **Cauvery** at the **Amma Mandapam** (1 km south-east of the temple). Enter the temple via the **Ranga Vaasal** in the fourth prakaram (the outer fifth, sixth and seventh prakarams are dotted with houses, shops and small temples. Head straight for the main *sannidhi*. To witness the glorious **Vishwaroopa Darshanam Puja**, one needs to be at the main sanctum by 5.45 am (special entrance ticket for this puja Rs 50; at other times Rs 20). Music is played to wake up the lord. The deity is resting on Adishesha, the divine serpent, and at his feet is Vibhishana, Ravana's brother. By 6.15 am, the temple elephant and a cow are brought to face each other at the entrance to the sanctum, so that the lord may see them first thing in the morning.

TIRUCHIRAPALLI

Ranganathaswamy Temple Complex — the largest in India — at Srirangam

Head to the museum counter in the fourth prakaram to purchase a ticket (Re 1) for the **view tower**, located next to the **temple museum** (Rs 20; open 9 am-1 pm, 2-6 pm). Enjoy a splendid view of the entire complex.

The **samadhi of Sri Ramanujacharya** (1071-1137) is opposite here. The Vaishnavite saint-philosopher lived in Srirangam and wandered over the Indian subcontinent propagating Vaishnavism. He wrote the masterly *Sri Bhashyam*, which is considered the final word on Brahma Sutra.

Now head for the third prakaram with its magnificent mandapam, which has 212 intricately sculpted pillars. Here is the **Chandra Pushkarni Tirth**, around which are several *sannidhis*, and a room that houses the deities' palanquins, chariots and jewels.

The second prakaram can be entered via the **Aryabhatta Gopuram**, which has a huge sculpture of Garuda atop. There are several mandapams here but no *sannidhis*. The first prakaram, called the **Raja Mahendran Prakaram**, is mostly covered. The **Thayar Sannidhi**, sanctum of the lord's consort, Goddess Ranganayaki, is enchanting.

The 21-day **Vaikuntha Ekadashi** that takes place in Marghazi (Dec-Jan), is an unparalleled celebration at Srirangam. The grandly attired *utsavar* idol of Lord Ranganatha sets forth in a magnificent procession through the **Swargavaasal** (the door to heaven; seen to the north of the second prakaram), which remains closed all through the year otherwise. This sight is believed to guarantee passage to heaven for the devotees. On Vaikuntha Ekadashi, Ranganathaswamy is mortal king of earth for a day. He grants audience in the **Thousand Pillar Hall** in the fourth prakaram and returns to his sanctum only late in the night. Lakhs throng the temple from dawn to midnight.

♦**Location** 4 km north of Chatram Bus Stand and 9 km north of the Central Bus Stand **Timings** 7 am-1 pm, 2-6 pm; the sanctum remains closed for rituals from 8 am-9 am, 1-2 pm and 6-7 pm **Temple Tel** 2432246 **Email** srirangamtemple@sancharnet.in **Website** srirangam.org

TIP Non-Hindus aren't allowed into the main sanctums

TAMIL NADU

The southern rajagopuram of Ranganathaswamy Temple is the tallest in the world

Jambukeswarar Temple, Thiruvanaikkaval

Cross the **Cauvery** to approach the sacred Jambukeswarar Temple in peaceful, green Thiruvanaikkaval, the Srimath Tirtha, and one among the Panchabhoota Shivasthalas, where Lord Shiva presides as the primordial element of water. The lord's consort, Akhilandeswari, is believed to have consecrated the *appu* (water) lingam from the waters of the Cauvery to attain knowledge. She was initially considered an *ugra devathai* (fiery goddess). Hearing this, Saint Adi Sankara was saddened. He thus consecrated two Srichakras on the goddess' ears, turning her into a peaceful deity. Adi Sankara sang the famous *Soundaryalahiri* here, inscribed in Tamil outside the goddess' *sannidhi*. She remains Shiva's student, a *kanya*, giving Thiruvanaikkaval the name of Gnanakshetram (kshetra of knowledge). Thus, there is no tradition of Thiru Kalyanam (enactment of the divine wedding) in this temple.

Called Naavarka in ancient times, this area was a forest of *nagapazham* or jambu trees (*Eugenia jambolana*/ jamun) and the lingam is located under one, fulfilling a promise made by Lord Shiva to Sage Jambumadhavan. According to legend, two devotees of Shiva were cursed to be born as an elephant and a spider. Each morning, the elephant would bathe in the Cauvery, bring flowers and fruits for the lord, clean the altar and offer worship. Later, the spider would build a web so drying leaves wouldn't fall on the lingam, and offer worship. The web was destroyed by the elephant every morning and rebuilt by the spider each evening. One day, the spider spotted the elephant destroying its web. Angered, it entered the elephant's ear, killing it, and dying in the process. The elephant (*aanai*) attained moksha, and Naavarka was renamed Thiru Aanaika (*thiru* being a respectful, sacred prefix), eventually Thiruvanaikkaval. The spider was reborn as a Chola king.

An interesting tale is narrated about his birth. The royal astrologer told his parents, Subhadeva and Kamalavati, that they would be blessed with a male successor of great fame if the birth took place at a particular time, but that any time other than this would have dire consequences. As the queen went into labour earlier than the prescribed time, she bade her attendants tie her legs and hang her upside down, delaying birth. She achieved her objective but the baby was born with reddened eyes, earning the name 'chen kannan' (the one with red eyes), going on to be the famous King Kochenkannan Chola, who built this temple over 2,500 years back. However, blessed with memories of his previous birth, he had the temple built in such a way (an architectural fact to this day) that elephants can never enter the main sanctum, or even have darshan from afar.

Spread over 18.65 acres, the temple complex includes five prakarams, several mandapams and unique sculptures. Succeeding Chola, Nayak, Pandya and Pallava rulers added to the temple. There is a splendid 32-foot high, 8,000-foot long **Thiruneetran** (sacred ash) **Madhil** (wall) in the fifth prakaram. Another unique aspect is that the lingam in the main sanctum is not visible from outside. A small door with nine slots called *navadwaram* (*nava* = nine, *dwaram* = doors) blocks it. A side entrance is available (special entrance fee Rs 10). It is believed that if the lingam is viewed through all the nine holes, it is equivalent to bathing in the **nine tirthas** that the temple has.

The French Army occupied this complex for two days while it fought the British in the 2nd Carnatic War.

The **Uchikaala Puja** (11 am-12.30 pm), when the head priest dresses up as the goddess and leaves from the Akhilandeswari Sannidhi to re-enact the consecration of the *appu* lingam in the main sanctum, must not be missed.

◆**Location** Also in Srirangam, 1 km away from the Ranganathaswamy Temple **Timings** 6 am-8.45 pm; 6 am-9 pm on Fri, Sun and festival days **Temple Tel** 2230257 **Email** tvkoil@sancharnet.in **Website** thiruvanaikkavaltemple.org

TIP Non-Hindus not allowed inside the main sanctum of Jambukeswarar

Uthamar Kovil

One of the 108 Divya Desams, Janaka, father of Sita, is the legendary builder of this temple. According to legend, King Dasaratha and his queens performed a yagna here to Shiva and sought progeny, after which Rama and his brothers were born. The Dasaratha lingam shrine is believed to testify to this visit. The inner sanctum of Vishnu is similar to the one at Srirangam except it also has Brahma in the body of Vishnu. Uthamar Kovil is believed to be the birthplace of Brahma, and the area used to be known as Brahmapuri. In this temple, the Trinity

→ GETTING THERE

Air Trichy International Airport (Tel: 0431-2340551; 8 km south of the city centre), connected to Chennai by a daily flight each from Kingfisher Airlines and Air Deccan. Indian Airlines has a flight every day except Friday. Taxi to town costs approx Rs 100-150

Rail Tiruchirapalli Station **Best option TO** Rockfort Express (dep: Chennai Egmore 10.30 pm, Mambalam 10.40 pm, Tambaram 11 pm; arr: Srirangam 4.04 am, Tiruchirapalli Town 4.14 am, Ponmalai Golden Rock 4.24 am, Tiruchchirapali 5.15 am) **Best option FROM** Rockfort Express (dep: Tiruchirapalli 10 pm, Ponmalai Golden Rock 10.10 pm, Tiruchchirapali Town 10.20 pm, Srirangam 10.30 pm; arr: Tambaram 4.16 am, Mambalam 4.34 am, Chennai Egmore 5.15 am). Nellai and Pandyan are equally good options

TIP The Rockfort Express halts for only one minute at all suburban stations of Chennai and Trichy; Madras-Mangalore Express is also a good option, departing Egmore at 10 pm and arriving at Tiruchirapalli at 4.45 am, where it halts for 30 mins

Car NH45 is the smooth, direct link between the state capital and Trichy. Exit Chennai via Tambaram onto NH45 past Vandalur Zoo, and on to Trichy via Chengalpattu, Madurantakam, Tindivanam, Vikravandi, Viluppuram, Ulundurpettai, Veppur, Turaimangalam, Padalur and Srirangam

Bus Buses leave every 5 minutes for Trichy from Chennai's Metropolitan Bus Terminus (Tel: 044-24794705) at Koyambedu. Private buses also leave from just outside the Koyambedu terminal and charge Rs 350-400

of Hindu deities have separate *sannidhis* as do their consorts and hence the name — Uthamar or Supreme. It is also known as Pichandavar Kovil.

♦**Location** 7 km north-west of Rockfort on Trichy-Salem Road **Timings** 7 am-noon, 4.30-8 pm **Temple Tel** 2591466

TIP For the ideal darshan, arrive at 5 pm

Vekkaliamman Temple, Woraiyur

The revered goddess here, a form of Shakti, presides from a sanctum that has no vimanam and is exposed to the sky. The crown on the deity seems to glow. Uniquely, devotees leave letters (Rs 5) with prayers and complaints for the deity in the sanctum. Each Friday, the goddess is adorned with golden *kavasam* or shield (10-11 am), and with sandalwood paste every evening.

♦**Location** 3 km west of Rockfort and 3 km north of the Central Bus Stand **Special entrance ticket** Rs 25 **Timings** 5.30 am-9 pm **Temple Tel** 2761869 **Website** vekkaaliammantemple.org

More to see

Near the Rockfort Temple tank is the **house of Robert Clive**, now turned into a hostel, a historical building. To the west of the tank is the neo-Gothic cathedral of **Our Lady of Lourdes** (open 8 am-5 pm), built in 1840. South-west of Rockfort is **St John's Church** (open 9 am-5 pm), an ornate, French-style building till the louvered doors are opened and the church turns into a pavilion! The **Trichy Museum** (near Super Bazaar; Tel: 2708809; open 9.30 am-5 pm on all days except Fridays; entry fee adults Rs 5 adults, children Rs 3, foreigners Rs 100) is a treasure trove of ancient and rare sculptures, paintings, vessels, coins, and some fossils from the Palaeolithic Era. South of the Rockfort tank is the **Natharsha Dargah**, one of the oldest in India, the final resting place of Baba Natharvalli who came to Trichy in 958 CE and lived here for 68 years, performing miracles and curing people.

Your royal host in Trichy

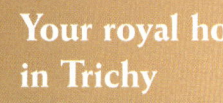
Sangam Hotels

Collector's Office Road,
Trichy- 620 001, India
Phone: 91 431-2414 700,
Fax: 91 431-246 418

For central reservations:
Sangam Hotels, Collector's Office Road, Trichy- 620 001, India
Phone: 91 431-2414 700, Fax: 91 431-246 418
E mail: hotelsangam@vsnl.com; reservation@hotelsangam.com
Website : www.hotelsangam.com

Sushma/SAN.07.03

TAMIL NADU

Offerings of garlands and flowers on sale at the Jambukeswarar Temple

A must-see is the engineering wonder and **only functioning stone dam in the world**, the 300-m long **Kallanai** (*kallu* = stone, *anai* = dam) or **Grand Anaicut** (20 km north-east of Trichy, built by Karikala Chola in the 2nd century CE to stop floods in the Cauvery. It makes an ideal picnic spot, complete with a park. **Mukkombu** (15 km north-west, on the Salem Road) is another picnic spot; the Cauvery splits into three tributaries here.

SHOPPING

Burma Bazaar (closed Wednesdays) and **NSB Road** (near Rockfort) are bustling markets with everything from handicrafts to hi-tech gadgets. The latter has the oldest clothing stores such as **Saradas** and **Thaila Silks**, famous for inexpensive, quality shopping. For wholesale rates, head for the biggest markets, which stretch around **Big Bazaar Street** and **Allimaal Street**, the wholesale trading centre for all of Tamil Nadu. A gem cutting and jewellery retail centre, the **Diamond Bazaar Street** lies adjoining. The shops in and around the Ranganathaswamy Temple in Srirangam are famous for *paavai* (crafted like a girl holding a lamp) and *pradosham villakkus* (lamps, here in brass). Bargaining is recommended. George Orwell and Arthur Conan Doyle wrote of the unmatched **'Trichinopoly' cigar**. Shops in luxury hotels stock them across India; buy them cheap from the factory outlets in the Srinivasa Nagar area.

WHERE TO STAY

Trichy has accommodation available across budgets. The majority of hotels are located in and around the Central Bus Stand/ Cantonment area due to its proximity to the railway station. Some of the 3- and 4-star hotels in this area, which have spacious rooms, pools, gyms and multi-cuisine restaurants are: **Jenny's Residency**, now called **Breeze Residency** (Tel: 0431-2414414-19; Tariff Rs 750-3,500) on MacDonald's Road, **Hotel Femina** (Tel: 2414501; Tariff Rs 650-2,500) on Williams Road, **Hotel Royal Southern** (Tel: 2421303-07; Tariff:

The Prefered Business Class Hotel at TRICHY

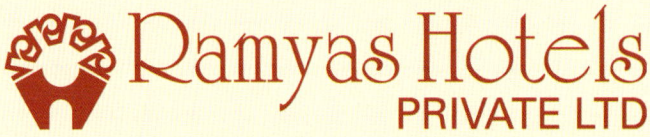

Ramyas Hotels
PRIVATE LTD

13-D/2, Williams Road, Thiruchirappalli, Tamilnadu, India. Pin : 620 001.
Ph: 2414646 / 4747, 4000400. Fax: 0431-2414852.
E-mail : ramyashotel@gmail.com   www.ramyas.com

Rs 1,800-3,000) on Race Course Road and **Hotel Sangam** (Tel: 2414480/ 700; Tariff: Rs 2,400-5,500) on Collector's Office Road, which has well-maintained rooms and a good restaurant and coffee shop.

Some of the good mid-range hotels in the Cantonment area, which provide both non-AC and AC accommodation and have large, spacious rooms with clean, well-maintained bathrooms are **Hotel Ramyas** (Tel: 2414646/ 747; Tariff: Rs 450-2,100) on Williams Road and **Hotel Tamil Nadu** (Tel: 2414346/ 78; Tariff: Rs 325-850) on MacDonald's Road.

Good places to stay near the Chatram Bus Stand/ bazaar area are **Hotel Gajapriya** (Tel: 2414411-15; Tariff: Rs 315-2,250), **Hotel Mayas** (Tel: 2705712; Tariff: Rs 500-1,700) on Karur Road, which has a good ambience and clean, large rooms, and **Hotel Chitra** (Tel: 2711086-89; Tariff: Rs 425-1,200) on Chintamani Street, near the Karur Bypass Road, which too has neat rooms.

Sculpted pillar at Ranganathaswamy

For more hotels and details, see Tiruchirapalli Accommodation Listings on page 526

WHERE TO EAT

Hotel Femina (Tel: 0431-2414501) provides a good South Indian breakfast; their *venn pongal* is especially good. The **Food Court** located next to it serves fast food like chaat, samosas, pav bhaji and pizza. **Sangeetha Restaurant**, on the ground floor of Hotel Aanand (Tel: 2415545), serves tasty vegetarian thalis. For dessert, Continental, Chinese, Italian and North Indian food, **Hotel Sangam** (Tel: 2414480) and **Hotel Royal Southern** (Tel: 2421303) are recommended but are slightly pricey. For particularly good filter coffee, stop at **Vasantha Bhavan** in Hotel Abirami, close to the Rockfort Temple tank or **Hotel Abirami** (Tel: 2415001), near the Central Bus Stand. Vasantha Bhavan also serves piping hot idli, dosa and poori varieties. **Sri Krishna Sweets** in Thiruverumbur is famous for pure ghee melt-in-the-mouth Mysore pak; their piping vadas and samosas are popular.

AROUND TRICHY

Thirupattur (26 km)
Ask for the way to the **Brahma Temple**, although the presiding deity is Shiva as Brahmapureeswarar. It is believed that Brahma himself consecrated the 12 Shivalingams in this temple. Shiva's consort is the radiant Brahmanayaki. Posing in padmasana, the monolithic idol of Brahma is very finely carved, and is probably the largest in India — $6^1/_2$ ft wide and 6 ft high. Left of this sannidhi is the *jeeva samadhi* of **Patanjali**, the father of yoga. Pretty lotuses bloom in the almost over 2,500-year-old temple tank, the **Brahma Tirth**.

♦**Location** On NH45 towards Chennai, 10 km from Samayapuram is Siruganaur. Turn off the highway here to travel 4 km to the temple **Timings** 7 am-noon, 4.30-7.30 pm **Temple Tel** 2650439 ∎

TAMIL NADU

Photographs by SRIKANTH KOLARI

HOGENAKKAL FALLS
CAUVERY'S PLAYGROUND

State Tamil Nadu
Location The spectacular Hogenakkal Falls mark the dramatic descent of the Cauvery River down the Melagiri Hills into Tamil Nadu from Karnataka, 47 km west of Dharmapuri on NH7
Distance 355 km SW of Chennai **JOURNEY TIME By road** 8 hrs
Route NH4 to Ranipettai via Poonamallee, Sriperumbudur and Kaveripakkam; NH46 to Krishnagiri via Vellore, Ambur, Vaniyambadi and Bargur; NH7 to Dharmapuri via Karimangalam; state road to Wodapati at the base of Hogenakkal Falls via Pennagaram (see route guide on page 12)

■ **BY VIVEK NARAYANAN**

Hogenakkal is a jewel, no doubt, but something of a rough and grimy jewel at first swipe. The town itself is an acquired taste, not quite as charming, as pretty, as well-serviced, or not even, unfortunately, as remote, rural and as untouched as you might wish it to be. On the one hand, although it is technically inside a protected forest reserve, you can find all kinds of plastic refuse littered almost mockingly right around the various 'No Plastic Allowed in Hogenakkal' signs, next to the big booming, zooming minivans. On the other hand, it seems nothing at all for phone reception (whether in STD booths or in cellphones!) to vanish for days on end, with enquiries earning only diffident half-shrugs. This is the kind of town where travellers rarely stay for more than one night because, after that, there are few advertised options for things to do; this is the kind of town that resigns itself to people passing through.

Parisal rides near the Bathing Falls

And yet (and this is a very big "and yet") you might find all your reservations slipping away as you approach Hogenakkal's central drama, its *raison d'etre* — the falls, and the great, winding Cauvery River they draw from. The falls are not any one spot but a winding labyrinth of high, narrow canyons through which the river snakes, and from which the river thunderingly falls in a number of places, with greater or lesser height, more or less force. It's a source of endless surprise how quick and easy it is to wind around a canyon and enter into beauty, forgetting the town entirely.

Just beyond the falls, and accessible by your little boat, lies the rugged forest with the river widening and flowing through it, and little fishing villages that seem to have as little use for tourists as tourists do for them.

THINGS TO SEE AND DO

There is a standard itinerary one follows at Hogenakkal, and it almost always begins with a visit to the **Hanging Bridge** and the **Bathing Falls**. These can be found a couple of minutes from the town centre, after negotiating a couple of small parks and a small market complex of stalls that sell, among other things, swimming shorts and Hogenakkal's delicious fried fish. Go past the bathers on the ghats; to the right you'll find the steps that go down to the Bathing Falls; go left to reach the bridge.

The Bathing Falls are divided into two sections, one for men and a more secluded one for women. There are bars to keep you from falling off the cliff. A bath here is one of the must-do highlights of Hogenakkal. The water is supposed to have various healing properties, having first passed through thick, medicinal forests. Indeed, there is nothing quite like the calm high one feels on emerging from a good water-pounding here. Before you go in, just above the stairs, several men (none for women,

it seems) will accost you with offers of a supposedly 'Ayurvedic' **oil massage**. Do it if you really enjoy being manhandled with gingelly oil — but you'd probably get a safer massage just by lingering a little longer under the forcefully drubbing water, showing it your back, neck and each of your limbs in turn. If you care about the environment, don't use soap under the falls. Go early in the morning to avoid the crowds. Go often.

The Hanging Bridge is a very short suspension bridge that links the more populous Hogenakkal side to the scrubby, unpopulated forest where, although there are signs discouraging you from doing so, no one will stop you from wandering around a little bit. You pay Rs 3 to get on, and you do it mostly for a vaguely daring view of the falls. There is a place along the bridge from where the view is supposed to be the most ideal; try inching along to find it, or perhaps ask one of the locals to show you the exact spot.

→ FAST FACTS

When to go If high drama and raging water is what you're after, go between June and August. Although that is also the height of the tourist season, the rest of the year the place will be less crowded, the river water will be much shallower and the falls less thrilling

Tourist offices
- TTDC ❶
Tamil Nadu Tourism Hotel
Pennagaram, via Hogenakkal
Tel: 04342-256447
- TTDC ❶❺
No. 2, Wallajah Road, Chennai
Tel: 044-25367850-54
Website: tamilnadutourism.org
STD code 04342

TAMIL NADU

The handiest boat

Let us now make the effort to call them *parisals* — for that is what they are called in South India. You would find equivalents in Vietnam and in Wales, where they have an excitable society dedicated to them and where, yes, they are known as coracles. However, they certainly did not come to us from Wales. The Portuguese traveller Domingo Paes admired them at Hampi in the 16th century and historians date them to a thousand years or more in the rough accounting of pre-colonial time. This little craft surely did not take too much trouble to invent; but it has lasted all this while because of its remarkable resilience, comfort and sheer handiness. A *parisal* is not very easy to navigate, and is best kept for placid waters or going downstream; yet, because of its shallowness it is virtually impossible to sink, even in the face of powerful waterfalls. You can easily fit four or five people in a *parisal*, and have enough room to lie back and stretch your legs out.

In Hogenakkal and neighbouring villages along the Cauvery, you see them everywhere: propped up against houses, rolled along by little kids, swinging precariously from the backs of scooters. Locals use them for fishing and occasionally, by turning them upside down and placing them over stakes, as very shady roadside shelters. The *parisals* in Hogenakkal are mostly made by boat-builders in the nearby town of Uttamalai, and in bamboo season, you can see them at work. Want to take one home? Expect to pay about Rs 2,000, not including the little paddle.

Parisal ride

Without a doubt, this is the main reason to come to Hogenakkal. Boatmen also serve as guides here, and if you linger anywhere for a moment or two, they will find you. Starting from just near the Bathing Falls, the boatman takes the *parisal* (see 'The handiest boat' above) down steps cut into the canyon, and very soon you have negotiated what seems like far from the sound and litter of the town, weaving through the waterways, seeing the spots where, for instance, a song from the Mani Ratnam movie *Roja* was shot, getting intentionally drenched or sprayed under a number of little falls, looking with awe at a couple of big ones, seeing tiny rainbows form before your eyes, perhaps bathing again at a secluded fall, then negotiating to wider, calmer waters and a bank where you lunch on fish and relax for a little while before heading back. If you ask the boatman, he might take you for a little walk through the forest, perhaps show you a small 'forest temple' dedicated to the folk goddess Mariamman, or take you a little further down the waterway.

Officially speaking, you pay Rs 10 per person in forest tolls and then, the government rates dictate that you pay Rs 40 per person for each hour in the *parisal*. In practice, this is just an index. While the toll remains standard, the rates for the ride are subject to bargaining and may vary widely depending on a number of factors. If you want to stay on and lunch properly at the far bank, you'll pay more. In the high season, when the water is deep and unpredictable, insist that the boatman doesn't take on more than about four passengers per *parisal*.

Parisal ride from Billigundu

One draw back to the ride just around the falls is that it can sometimes get rather crowded. For a much rarer and more fascinating experience, pay double the amount and ask the boatman to take you on a long ride through the forest, starting upstream of the falls, in the nearby town of Billigundu. He won't be able to take the shaky *parisal* upstream, so first he will have to transport the craft to the bank at Billigundu on the top of a bus. Billigundu is a small village deep in this forest with a small, **old** and famous **church** and also a surprisingly large and impressive **new church**. From here, you'll take in some 8 km of secluded river and forest before you hit the falls, and you'll be much happier at the end of it all.

Crocodile Park

There's not all that much to see in this little park on the other side of Hogenakkal town, but if you have an hour to kill, it's definitely worth incorporating. What you get are about six pens packed with crocodiles. They look almost cute in the way that only crocodiles can, lounging over each other and sleeping (which, for a crocodile, means playing dead) with their jaws locked open. They're part of a Forest Department initiative to save the Cauvery crocodile by recovering the eggs and rearing them in captivity.

◆**Entry fee** Rs 2 **Timings** 7 am-5 pm

→ GETTING THERE

Car A comfortable drive just under 8 hrs along the excellent 308-km national highways stretch till Dharmapuri. Exit west from Chennai onto NH4 (Bangalore Road) to Ranipettai via Sriperumbudur and Kaveripakkam. Turn left on NH46 to Krishnagiri via Vellore, Ambur, Vaniyambadi and Bargur. Stop for a bite at Hotel Tamil Nadu in Krishnagiri. Join NH7 and turn south to Dharmapuri. Follow the state road west past the villages of Indur, Nagadasapattinam and Pennagaram to Wodapati at the base of the falls, 47 km from Dharmapuri

Bus Buses leave every hour to Dharmapuri from Chennai's bus terminus (Tel: 044-24794705) at Koyambedu. From Dharmapuri, you can get an auto, taxi or local bus to Hogenakkal

WHERE TO STAY AND EAT

Restaurants and eating joints in Hogenakkal are basic; but one must-try is fried fish from the roadside stands, deliciously and tartly spicy. The common fish are *kotla* and *viral*; in the

TAMIL NADU

high season you'll get the big guys, like *keluthi* and *rog*.

TTDC's **Hotel Tamil Nadu** (Tel: 04342-256447), spitting distance from the falls and the Hanging Bridge, is the fanciest, most reliable place in town. Don't expect the world! It's a bit dark and gloomy and, as the manager will somewhat defiantly remind you, it's "not a star hotel". The place is geared for people who don't stay more than one night — if you do, you'll have to beg and plead to have the sheets changed. If you book a deluxe AC room, you might, in reality, have to choose between a room with a nice AC and a small bathroom without a working geyser, or a room with a nice bathroom and a sluggish AC (be sure to choose the latter). Still, be assured that during movie shoots the big stars always stay here and nowhere else. (Even if the lesser producers are sometimes put up in the private hotels.)

Apart from Hotel Tamil Nadu, no other hotel in town will show you a tariff card. The price of a room always varies and is bargained for. In peak season, you would pay up to Rs 600 for an AC double with four beds; or between Rs 200-250 for a more common non-AC room. If you just need a place to put your stuff and doss for a couple of hours, ask if the hotel has 12-hr rates, which many do.

Among the private hotels, you would do no better than the **Sri Priya Lodge** in the centre of town. The staff and owner are the friendliest, the rooms are simple but have high ceilings and are airy.

The **CM Hotel** is the tallest hotel in town (the communication tower stands on top of it) and boasts that it is the only "starred hotel". However it seems a bit shady and the person at the reception refused to show us a room or even discuss ball-park tariffs. One wonders what is going on here.

For details, see Hogenakkal Accommodation Listings on page 516

AROUND HOGENAKKAL

Mettur Dam, the nearest well-known attraction, is a 65-km drive away, but ask the locals to show you the trail up Hogenakkal's surrounding **Melagiri Hills**; walk up for a couple of hours and you will be able to see the dam from there.

Going or coming between Hogenakkal and Dharmapuri, you might make quick stops just off the main road at various towns to see the **Aiyanar temples**. The Aiyanars, historically, are the traditional security-guard deities for Tamilian towns, but the temples in this stretch have especially lovely and mammoth Aiyanar statues, 10 to 15 ft high, modernised to include statues of policemen as secondary helpers to the deities. Two of the most impressive Aiyanars can be found in **Nagadasapattinam** (28 km from Hogenakkal back towards Dharmapuri) and **B Agraharam** (26 km from Hogenakkal, take a right from the town centre). ■

Freshly fried spicy kotla and viral fish

An array of thalayatti bommai — Thanjavur's colourful head nodding dolls

THANJAVUR

PERIYA KOVIL — AN EMPEROR'S VISION

State Tamil Nadu
Location Thanjavur, the most important town of Chola Nadu — the fertile Cauvery Delta — is located where the river, flowing east from Trichy, branches into four streams, the Vadavar, Vettar, Vennar and Kudamurutti, before re-emerging as the Cauvery at Thiruvaiyaru
Distance 339 km SW of Chennai JOURNEY TIME **By rail** 7^1/$_2$ hrs **By road** 8 hrs **By air** 50 mins + 1^1/$_2$ hrs by road
Route East Coast Road to Pondicherry via Mahabalipuram and Marakkanam; NH45A to Sirkazhi via Cuddalore and Chidambaram; SH64 to Kumbakonam via Mayiladuthurai; NH45C to Thanjavur via Papanasam (*see route guide on page 12*)

■ **BY JANAKI VENKATARAMAN**

They call it *manji soozh Thanjai* — the mist enveloped town. Out of fondness, one imagines. Or for the rhyme. For, you cannot come across a flatter countryside. So where can the mist come from? From the river, natives explain, amazed that you have to ask.

In Margazhi and Thyy, the Tamil months that correspond to December, January and February, a soft mist rises from the Cauvery at dawn. It swirls around the paddy fields and mango groves, slips through the tamarind orchards and wraps itself like fine muslin around the lofty temple towers and palaces. For a short span of time, the town looks as magnificent and mysterious as its history warrants. Then the sun comes out, the mist vanishes and Thanjavur puts on its everyday face, dusty and

TAMIL NADU

crowded. Still, glimpses of past grandeur flicker through, like the ripples that lap the shores of the Cauvery when it rains.

It was a demon who gave life to Thanjavur with his dying breath. When the *rakshasa* Thanjan lay torn asunder by Lord Vishnu, he begged, "Let there be a great and joyous city on this spot by the Cauvery where you have chosen to slay me, O Compassionate Lord, so that all who see it may remember my name." And so it was. Thanjai also means 'refuge' in Tamil.

The town and the delta region surrounding it have indeed been a haven for the many who come here. Not for nothing was Thanjavur called the 'granary of the South'. Thanjavur was once the capital of a kingdom so fertile that elephants rather than horses or oxen were used to thrash the abundant paddy. Rich harvests, a lush countryside and a full flowing, divine river made for a contented people who had the leisure and the inclination for engaging in all the fine things of life: culture, religion, architecture and literature. Visitors will be surprised by the glimpses of ancient buildings almost on every street or, at the very least, ruins that are more magnificent than the latest buildings man claims to be proud of. At once stately and gracious, Thanjavur soars grandly above the dust of humdrum modernity, resonating with the generosity of the Chola, Nayak and Maratha rulers who reigned here in a manner so powerful that they almost do so to this day. Even the characters of successive conquerors seemed to change once they had assumed power — they became gentler and more responsible rulers, visionary builders and patrons of the arts. Thanjai did that to people. This is the town where even the autorickshaw driver will speak knowledgeably about both politics and classical music — he is heir to a culture, which, for hundreds of years, nourished and celebrated literature and the arts. Talk to him, or simply listen to stones speak.

The tragedy of Thanjavur is also the drying up of the Cauvery, whose waters are now the subject of an unresolved dispute with the upper riparian state of Karnataka. The Cauvery is not just a river, it is an inherent element in the lives of the delta people, and the subject of much lyrical writing. Many of the villages that once resounded with the strains of the *nadaswaram* (wind instrument) and the *jathis* (rhythmic footwork) of Bharatanatyam dancers, have turned into ghost hamlets. But when it rains, like it did last year, the sparkling waters of the Cauvery seem to breathe life into Chola Nadu's magnificent past.

> ### → FAST FACTS
>
> **When to go** It rains in November and early December. But soon after, when the fields are emerald green and the winter mild, is the best time to go. Try and visit during Pongal festivities (mid-Jan)
>
> **Tourist offices**
> - Dept of Tourism ❶❷
> Govt of TN, Tourism Complex
> Gandhiji Road, Thanjavur
> Tel: 04362-231421/ 231325
> - TTDC ❶❷
> Tourism Complex, Wallajah Road, Chennai. Tel: 044-25367850-54
> Email: ttdc@vsnl.com
> Website: tamilnadutourism.org
>
> **STD code** 04362

ORIENTATION

Thanjavur is one of the biggest towns in the Cauvery Delta. **Thanjavur Junction** (railway station) is slightly to the south of the centre of town. The arterial **Gandhiji Road** connects the station to the **Express Bus Terminus**, 4 km north. This is

THANJAVUR

The massive Brihadeesvara Temple looks awesome even from a distance

known as the **Old Bus Stand**, at which state transport express and local buses halt. There is another major bus terminus, the **New Bus Stand**, which is around 6 km from the railway station on the **Trichy Road**. Long distance buses, which are not express services and halt at many places en route, stop here. Most hotels are situated within a 3-km radius from the famous **Big Temple**. Autos charge Rs 25-30 from the Old Bus Terminus to the hotels or the Big Temple, and upwards of Rs 50 from the Railway Station or the New Bus Stand. You can also hire an auto for the whole day (from, say, 8 am to 4 pm) for Rs 250-300 (petrol is extra).

THINGS TO SEE AND DO

The Cauvery Delta region is full of temples. There is really no village here which does not have a shrine, and no shrine that does not have an interesting legend to tell. It is said that there are at least 24 temples of antiquity in Thanjavur Town itself. Yet, when one says Thanjavur, the temple that comes instantly to mind is the Big Temple, that colossal edifice built by Rajaraja Chola, greatest of the Chola kings, in the early 11th century.

Brihadeesvara Temple

True to its more popular name, the Periya (big) Kovil (temple), everything about the shrine to Brihadeesvara is BIG. Being part of the historical Sivaganga Fort, the temple is surrounded by a (now dry) moat, and with its enormous entrance arch, looks awesome even from a distance. With a sandstone-coloured finish, this is a peaceful temple that looks both grand and understated. Do pause at the entrance to be blessed by the temple elephant. For a token coin, you will receive a moist blessing on the top of your head.

Built by the Chola emperor, Rajaraja Chola, the construction of this magnificent temple began in 1003 CE, and was completed in 1009 CE. The Brihadeesvara Temple sprawls across an expanse of 33,000 sq ft. Unlike in most South Indian temples, the entrance tower is shorter and less ornate than the one over the sanctum. The latter is 13-tiered and 197 ft tall. The single block of granite that perches atop this tower weighs 80 tonnes. In an unparalleled feat of engineering, a 4-mile long ramp was built to roll the cupola into place. Fascinatingly, the shadow of the cupola never falls on the ground. Facing the main sanctum, in its own stone mandapam, is a splendid 12-foot tall monolithic **idol of Nandi**. The lingam in the main sanctum is also 12 ft high with a circumference of 54 ft.

The **shrine of Goddess Brihan Nayaki** (*brihan* = big), to the north of the sanctum, is noteworthy not only for the beauty of the idol but also for the exquisite stone frescoes on the walls outside the sanctum. Also here is the **shrine of Saint Karuvurar**, who consecrated the temple, which has been built to resemble a cave. The **Murugan shrine** nearby is built like a chariot, with intricate stone carving. Unlike in other Shiva shrines, the Navagrahas (the nine planetary gods) are not depicted in their usual forms, but as lingams. They are seen in the outer corridor. Altogether the Big Temple houses 252 Shivalingams. It is said that if you circumambulate the temple four times, that is equal to circumambulating one lingam 1,008 times!

Declared a UNESCO World Heritage Site in 1987, the Big Temple, which, after its initial years of glory, had fallen into a period of neglect, is now pleasingly renovated with landscaped gardens. In the southern, outer corridor, is a small ASI **museum**, displaying pieces of sculpture. This temple is the first in a set of three similar Shiva temples built by successive Chola kings, the other two being at Gangaikondacholapuram (*see page 78*) and Darasuram (*see page 76*). The latter are also UNESCO World Heritage Sites and all three take your breath away by their sheer size, and the complexities of their architecture and sculpture.

Twice-monthly **Pradosham** pujas draw hundreds of devotees, and the milk *abhishekham* done for the Nandi and lingam is a magnificent sight to behold.

The temple celebrates **Maha Shivaratri** in Masi (Feb-Mar), **Navaratri** in Purattasi (Sep-Oct) and **Rajarajan** in Aippasi (Nov-Dec) with fervour.

♦**Location** Within Sivaganga Fort, 4 km west of railway station **Timings** 7.30 am-noon, 4-8 pm **Temple Tel** 04362-223384 **Web** thanjavurpalacedevasthanam.org
TIP Non-Hindus are allowed only up to the sanctum

Strings of harmony

If you ever wanted to buy a **veena**, the stringed musical instrument that is akin to the sitar, Thanjavur is the place for the genuine item with a heavenly twang. Just approach any one of the 50-odd veena makers in Thanjavur. Many of them are located in the streets off Therku Veedhi. Over 50-year-old Balan, who lives in Nanayakkara Chetti Street, off Therku Veedhi, is pretty savvy as veena makers go. Asked about his craft, he whips out a CD to display how a veena is made. Shaped from jackfruit timber, fitted with rosewood or teak frets, keys and fine steel strings and, finally, embellished with lovely ivory carving (cheap plastic stickers have now taken the place of the exquisite inlay work done before). Veenas cost anything from Rs 3,500-5,000.

G SIVAPERUMAL

THANJAVUR

The Palace Museum exhibits the personal collection of Thanjavur's erstwhile royals

Mariamman Temple

Goddess Mariamman, a manifestation of Shakti, was worshipped here in the form of an anthill for a long time. It was only in the 18th century that a temple was built here. The seven-tiered gopuram came up only two years ago. It is still maintained by the descendants of the royal family of Thanjavur. This Shakti temple is credited with curative and healing powers. Devotees come here to pray for relief from measles, chicken pox and skin sores. The goddess is also called Muthu Mariamman because of the belief that drops of moisture, like pearls (*muthu*), appear on the face and head of the idol from time to time.

No *abhishekam* is performed on the idol. It is coated instead with *punugu*, the oily, perfumed, secretion of the civet cat.
♦**Location** 5 km from the Brihadeesvara Temple, in Punnaianallur **Timings** 6 am-9 pm **Temple Tel** 267740 **Website** thanjavurpalacedevasthanam.org

Bangaru Kamakshi Amman Temple

The idol in the temple to Goddess Bangaru (gold) Kamakshi is really made of gold, and is said to have been shifted to Thanjavur during the invasion of Kanchipuram (*see page 21*), where it originally was.
♦**Location** 2 km north-west of the Big Temple **Timings** 6 am-noon, 4-9 pm

A fort, a church and a palace

The Brihadeeswara Temple is encircled by the 16th century **Sivaganga Fort**, modified by the Marathas in the 17th century. The 35-acre fort includes the temple complex, the Schwartz Church, the Royal Palace along with two museums, and the **Sivaganga Tank** and **Park** to its north, close to the junction of the west and south ramparts of the fort. The fort's ramparts are mostly intact; the moat exists sans water.

The **palace** must have been wonderful once upon a time. Today, the walls have crumbled, the interiors are damp, the durbar looks tacky and the tunnels have all caved in. Visit it for three reasons: the **Rajaraja Museum** and the **Art Gallery**, both of which have a stunning collection of rare Chola bronzes and granite sculptures. The **Saraswati Mahal Library**, close by, is known for its precious collection of palm leaf manuscripts.

TAMIL NADU

Steaming hot idlis made from the flavourful Ponni rice of the Cauvery delta

Known as Saraswati Bhandar earlier, the library evolved into its present size under the patronage of Sarabhoji II. Today, it boasts of a staggering collection of 44,000 palm leaf manuscripts (including colour plates from a book on Chinese torture!) besides paintings and writing equipment. The adjacent bookshop sells Mahal publications.

♦**Rajaraja Museum entry fee** Indians Rs 5, children Rs 3; foreigners Rs 50 and 25, respectively **Timings** 10 am-5 pm, open all days **Camera fee** Rs 30 **Art Gallery entry fee** Indians Rs 5, children Rs 2, foreigners Rs 20 **Timings** 9 am-1 pm and 3-6 pm **Cameras** Still Rs 30, video Rs 200 **Art Gallery Tel** 239823

♦**Library timings** 10 am-1 pm, 1.30-5.30 pm, Wednesdays closed

The ornamental balconies of the six-storey **Sharajah Madi** (open 10 am-5.45 pm; entry fee: adults Rs 5, children Rs 2), in the eastern part of the palace, offer a panoramic view of Thanjavur Town.

The small **Palace Museum** within the complex exhibits the personal collection of the royal family: arms, vessels, clothes, paintings and so on. The descendants of Sarabhoji II still live in a section of the palace. Tours to the present royal quarters are organised by Babaji Rajah Bhonsle Chattrapathy (Tel: 04362-231486), 13th in the Maratha line of royalty.

Raja Sarabhoji II was a liberal man, as is evidenced by the **Schwartz Church**, just north of the Shivaganga Tank. The church, now protected by the ASI, was built in 1779 by the king, for the Danish missionary Rev Christian Fredriech Schwartz. The rosewood pulpit from which Schwartz preached still stands, as does the rosewood pew where the king liked to sit and pray.

SHOPPING

Thanjavur paintings (Rs 1,800 to upwards of Rs 2 lakh), which use semi-precious stones and gold foil to create highly skilled representations of deities in a style unique to the region, make a fine purchase. More a craft than an art, the practice of this richly ornamented representation of Hindu deities has now large-

THANJAVUR

ly moved to Chennai. While new Tanjore paintings look a little garish, genuine antiques look gracefully pigmented and ornamented. The Palace Museum has quite a collection. You will also find Tanjore 'plates' (brass plates with silver inlay work), bronze and panchaloha icons, brass lamps, bells and puja accessories here. Genuinely antique Tanjore paintings are rare, and can be found only in ancestral homes or abroad. We now get newly painted pieces, and some that are given an 'antique finish'. A couple of well-known private antique dealers are: **VR Govindarajan** at Kuthiraikatti Street, Karanthai, and **N Arumugam** (Tel: 04362-271687) at 1861, West Main Street, Thanjavur. Both these dealers operate out of their homes. For reasonable prices and good quality, go to **Poompuhar** on Gandhiji Road, or the antique shops on South Keezha Veedhi.

Thanjavur is most renowned for the veena (Rs 3,500-5,000, *see 'Strings of harmony' on page 102*), Goddess Saraswati's divine instrument. The colourful Thanjavur *thalayatti bommais* (head nodding dolls; Rs 50 upwards) are also famous. Made of either clay or papier mache, these rounded dolls usually come in pairs and are weighted at the bottom in such a way that they rock with the gentlest breeze. A variation is the dancing doll, which, by the use of a spring, keeps shaking her head like a Bharatanatyam dancer. These dolls are available near the Mariamman Temple at Punaianallur or in carts outside the Big Temple.

WHERE TO STAY

Thanjavur has a good choice of hotels to suit all budgets, and most are placed within a 3-km radius of the Big Temple. Book well in advance if you a plan a trip around the Thyagaraja Aradhanai (*see Thiruvaiyaru on page 108*). **Hotel Parisutham** (Tel: 04362-231801, 231844; Tariff: Rs 4,500-6,500) on Grand Anicut Canal Road offers lovely rooms and excellent service. **Hotel Sangam** (Tel: 239451-56; Tariff: Rs 2,100-4,600), on Trichy Road, is a good choice in terms of cleanliness, good service and decent food. **Hotel Oriental Towers** (Tel: 230724/ 30; Tariff: Rs 600-3,000), on Srinivasan Pillai Road, is also well maintained, and has both veg and non-veg restaurants.

Hotel Gnanam (Tel: 278501-08; Tariff: Rs 900-2,250) on Anna Salai, **Hotel Temple Tower** (Tel: 276333-34; Tariff: Rs 450-2,000) on SM Road, **Hotel Ideal Riverview Resort** (Tel: 250833; Tariff: Rs 2,600-3,500) on Palli Agraharam, Karanthai and Tamil Nadu Tourism's **Hotel Tamil Nadu** (Tel: 231421, 231024; Tariff: Rs 300-1,000) on Gandhiji Road, are all decent mid-range hotels. Not all these hotels provide running hot water but it is arranged

JAIPUR KA GURU
Zafar, Hotel Advisor at Travelguru, knows where to head for the finest tie-n-dye bandhani sarees.

Choose from our network of over 4000 hotels in India. Serviced apartments, budget hotels, luxury resorts, palaces, business accommodations, houseboats and more.

1-800-22-4878
022-4030-4878
www.travelguru.com

India's Largest Hotel Network

when requested. Coffee is usually not available before 6.30 am and, breakfast, not before 8 am. If you need to leave early, it's much better to walk out of the hotel to the nearest roadside coffee stall, which will sell filter coffee and a basic breakfast (idli, pongal) as early as 5 am.

For more hotels and details, see Thanjavur Accommodation Listings on pages 524-526

→ GETTING THERE

Air Nearest airport: Trichy International Airport (Tel: 0431-2340551; 54 km/ 1½ hrs). Kingfisher Airlines and Air Deccan have a daily flight each from Chennai. Indian has four flights a week. Return taxi fare for Thanjavur is Rs 1,700-1,800
Rail Thanjavur Station **Best Option TO** Rockfort Express (dep: Chennai Egmore 10.30 pm, Mambalam 10.40 pm, Tambaram 11 pm; arr: Thanjavur 6.15 am) **Best option FROM** Rockfort Express (dep: Thanjavur 8.30 pm; arr: Tambaram 4.16 am, Mambalam 4.34 am, Chennai Egmore 5.15 am)
Car Follow the East Coast Road from Chennai till Pondicherry. Continue south along NH45A till Sirkazhi via Cuddalore and Chidambaram, where you must turn right towards Vaithiswarankoil and continue on to Thanjavur via Mayiladuthurai, Kumbakonam and Papanasam
TIP Don't follow the traditional route to Thanjavur along NH45 to Ulundurpettai, then NH45C to Thanjavur via Vriddhachalam, as it sees a lot more traffic
Bus Many express buses connect Chennai to Thanjavur's Bus Stand (Tel: 04362-230950). Non-AC night buses (Rs 180) leave Chennai's Metropolitan Bus Terminus (Tel: 044-24794705) at Koyambedu between 8 and 10.30 pm

WHERE TO EAT

Thanjavurians are finicky about food. Even at the most obscure eatery the food will be wholesome and tasty. A note of caution: while most hotels claim a multi-cuisine profile, it's best to bank on the South Indian thalis, with steaming hot Ponni rice (from the Cauvery delta — the river is also called Ponni, 'the golden one') and *thayir saadam* (curd rice), a bland foil, often served with a seasoning of mustard and curry leaves, that can be called the most indispensable dish of Thanjavurians. A host of pickles like the maangai *thokku* — spicy grated mango — are unique to the region; there are also preserves like salted, sun-dried and fried cluster beans, lady's finger, mild chillies and a variety of berries to go with the curd rice. The idlis are always soft 'like jasmine', and the coffee aromatic. Thanjavur's roasted cashew nuts are favourite snacks. Fried and coated with pepper, they are crunchy and full of flavour (Rs 230-250 per kg).

Try the regular banana leaf vegetarian meal at **Venkata Lodge**, Gandhiji Road, to the east of the Big Temple. One of the oldest eateries in the town (est: 1926), its popular snacks, served only around 4 pm, include wheat halwa, pakoras and bhajjis.

If you want a certain level of hygiene and a peaceful ambience, it's better to eat at one of the restaurants in the higher-end hotels. **Hotel Parisutham's** (Tel: 04362-231801) two restaurants, **La Repas** (for non-veg) and **Geetham** (for veg) are both highly recommended. Geetham's 10-dish vegetarian thali is great value for money at Rs 150. There is no dearth of small, independent eateries in Thanjavur. **Padma Hotel**, **Vasantha Vihar**, **Ananda Bhavan** (all on Gandhiji Road), **Geetha Hotel**, **Ganesh Bhavan** (near the railway station) and **Karthik Hotel** (Tel: 278662-63) near the Old Bus Stand are all decent vegetarian eateries, which serve very authentic and tasty South Indian food.

Indulge in the sheer splendour

Trichy Road,
Thanjavur - 613 007, India
Phone: 91 4362-239451
Fax: 91 4362-236695

For central reservations:
Sangam Hotels, Collector's Office Road, Trichy- 620 001, India
Phone: 91 431-2414 700, Fax: 91 431-246 418
E mail: hotelsangam@vsnl.com; reservation@hotelsangam.com
Website : www.hotelsangam.com

Sushma/SAN.07.03

TAMIL NADU

A slower pace on the gaily painted, quiet backstreets of Thanjavur

Gnanam (Tel: 278501-08), opposite the bus-stand, is also a good bet. While the food is tasty, these eateries cannot boast of good standards of hygiene.

AROUND THANJAVUR

Thiruvaiyaru (13 km)
Thiruvaiyaru is a small, quiet town. However, its modesty belies its importance as a pilgrim centre. On the highway from Thanjavur, you pass five bridges — over the Vadavar, Vettar, Vennar, Kudamurutti and Cauvery, the five rivers from which Thiruvaiyaru gets its name (*thiru* = sacred; *ai* = five; *aaru* = river). The presiding deity of the Shiva temple here, Panchanatheesvarar (in Tamil, Ayyarappan — both mean the same thing, 'the Lord of the Five Rivers') also gets his name from them.

Thiruvaiyaru is considered as holy as Varanasi and bathing in the Cauvery here is as guaranteed to rid devotees of sins as bathing in the Ganga.

The **Panchanatheesvarar Temple** sprawls over a 14-acre campus and is both grand and serene. Beyond the temple are lush paddy fields and groves. The lingam in the main sanctum and the idols of Goddess Dharmasamvardhini (Aramvalartha Nayaki in Tamil — both mean, 'She who nurtures dharma'), Vinayaka, Muruga and Nandi, are said to have been found underground by a king whose chariot wheels got embedded in the ground where the temple now stands. A wise minister advised the king to dig around the wheels and there came into view not only the idols but also a living *siddha* (a realised being) who was in deep meditation, his locks spread across the pit like banyan roots. The stunned king fell at his feet. The yogi blessed him and commanded him to build the temple for Aiyarappar at the same spot. Inscriptions and architectural details point to the temple having been built in the early Chola period.

Of special importance is the **shrine of Shiva as Alkondesar**, opposite the southern entrance. Legend goes that it was here that Shiva killed Yama, god of death, for daring to lay hands on a young devotee of his. Outside the shrine, *kungiliyam* (benzoin) burns in a holder night

One Revolution Ahead

WHO SAYS YOU CAN'T PLEASE ALL THE PEOPLE ALL THE TIME?

GOODYEAR IS THE ONLY TYRE APPROVED BY EVERY CAR MANUFACTURER IN INDIA.

Goodyear tyres come with more than just comfort and safety. They come with the trust of every car manufacturer in India.

Our tyres have withstood the toughest tests and have emerged winners every time. With supreme technology that ensures a smoother drive on any terrain, Goodyear is not just the preferred choice but the only choice of millions, the world over.

For more information call
1800-11-6767

Visit us at www.goodyear.co.in or SMS GY to 56767.

Goodyear is a registered trademark of Goodyear Tire and Rubber Co. The names and logos of actual companies mentioned herein may be their respective trademarks.

TAMIL NADU

DR. MS MAYILVAHNAN/ SOUTHINDIAPICTURE

Brihadeesvara Temple — a UNESCO World Heritage Site — within Sivaganga Fort

and day, the belief being that the smoke protects people from the fear of death.

The temple tank, **Surya Pushkarni**, is large. It was from bathing in this tank that the ageing and frail saint, Tirunavukkarasar, rose to see a vision of Shiva on Mount Kailash. The temple celebrates this event in a festival in Adi (Jul-Aug).

♦**Location** About a kilometre from the main bazaar street in the middle of the town **Timings** 6 am-noon, 4-9 pm **Temple Tel** 04362-260332

TIP Non-Hindus are not allowed into the sanctum. Still and video cameras can only be used in the outer prakarams

The 18th century saint-composer, Sri Thyagaraja, whose life was characterised by the ceaseless and divine music that flowed from him, was a resident of Thiruvaiyaru. His samadhi on the banks of the Cauvery is one of the reasons why people visit the place today.

Thyagaraja's family lived all his life in a house in Thirumanjana Veedhi (a kilometre south of the samadhi), given to the family by the Maratha royal family of Thanjavur. It is preserved for the public to visit even today (a good time to visit is around 11 am; the house is not kept open right through the day). The worship of Rama became the keynote of the boy's life, and he composed his first *kriti*, *Namo namo Raghavaya...* when he was 13, spontaneously, while worshipping the deity. Bhakti and music thereafter became his only interests in life. Thyagaraja composed more than 800 songs on Rama alone, apart from kritis praising other deities, including Aiyarappar. The **samadhi of Thyagaraja** is housed in a small shrine in the middle of a shady stretch of land on the banks of the river. The view from here, of the river, the ghats (there are 24 in the town), and the many mansions built along the river by the Marathas, is very pretty.

Every year the death anniversary of Saint Thyagaraja is commemorated on Bahula Panchami (mid-Jan) at his samadhi with a music festival, the **Thyagaraja Aradhanai**. The best known Carnatic musicians join lesser known voices in singing the pancharatna kritis, the five compositions that are considered Thyagaraja's gems or ratnas.

♦**Location** 2 km north of the Panchanatheesvarar Temple **Timings** 7 am-noon, 4-8.30 pm

Swamimalai (31 km), **Darasuram** (34 km), **Kumbakonam** (38 km)
See page 70 ■

Waiting for pal abhishekham at the Kayarohanaswamy Temple

Photographs by GANESHMUTHU

NAGAPATTINAM
NAGAI: CITY OF SERPENTS

State Tamil Nadu
Location A port-town lying between the meeting of the Cauvery and Kollidam rivers with the Bay of Bengal, the coastline of its district (also called Nagapattinam) stretches 180 km
Distance 308 km S of Chennai **JOURNEY TIME** **By rail** 9 hrs **By road** 7½ hrs
Route East Coast Road to Pondicherry via Mahabalipuram and Marakkanam; NH45A to Nagapattinam via Cuddalore, Alapakkam, Chidambaram, Sirkazhi, Tranquebar, Karaikal and Nagore (*see route guide on page 12*)

■ BY JANAKI VENKATARAMAN

The sun rises and, like the warp and weft of a double-coloured fabric, the ocean turns orange-blue with the surge of each faraway wave. By the shore, warm, white foam washes weather-beaten *kattumarams* (catamarans), and the smell of rotting fish hangs heavily in the air with more than a hint of sadness. Nagai, as the tranquil seaside setting of this ageless picture is fondly called, has never been the same since the tsunami of December 26, 2004. The debris of destroyed boats and houses still litters the beach. What is less obvious is the devastating toll on human life, in many cases shattered beyond 'rehabilitation'. But evidence of Nagai's resilience is everywhere.

On the highway from Sirkazhi to Nagapattinam is the famous Nagore Dargah (*see page 114*). All along the way, long lines of pilgrims can often be seen on a *padayatra* (pilgrimage by foot) to the church at Vailankanni (*see page 115*). Dressed in saffron and wearing prayer beads, they look very much like the Hindu Ayyappa devotees. This is one place where people accept the rituals and shrines of all faiths as their own. As Nagai hobbles back to its old, confident self, it is clear the prayers of its peoples are not going unanswered.

THINGS TO SEE AND DO

The **Kayarohanaswamy Temple** is central to the town. The **railway station** is about ³/₄ km to the east, the **main bus stand** a similar distance to the northeast. Most of the hotels are on **Collectorate Road**, which is around 2 km from the railway station. It takes a day to see the temples in Nagapattinam and another to cover nearby tourist and pilgrim spots, of which there are many. Autos and taxis are easily available. In the major temples below, still and video cameras are not allowed beyond the outer prakaram, and non-Hindus are not allowed into the main sanctums.

Kayarohanaswamy Temple

This spacious Chola temple was built before the 8th century CE. It has three rajagopurams and two wide prakarams (the outer prakaram was used for accommodating tsunami survivors for four months after the calamity — the temple fed them right through that time).

In the sanctum of Kayarohanar is a rare addition. On the wall behind the lingam is a bas relief sculpture of Uma Maheswarar, as he appeared in Pundarigar's vision. Devotees with Naga *dosham* (an astrological anomaly that is considered inauspicious) in their horoscopes worship Kayarohanar to be rid of it. Goddess Neelayadakshi ('she of the dark blue eyes') is even better known than her consort. Her idol is known to be so beautifully adorned that one needs 'a thousand eyes' to take it all in. This temple is also a sthala for Sani Bhagvan.

The 18-day Vaikasi (May-Jun) **Brahmotsavam** attracts big crowds. The 10-day Adi (Jul-Aug) **Pooram Festival** is special to the goddess, and includes a three-day float festival. In Ani (Jun-Jul), the temple conducts the **Adibhakta Nayanar Festival** to commemorate the attainment of *mukti* by a fisherman who became a saint. Nagai fisherfolk take part in this festival in a big way.

♦Timings 6 am-noon, 4.30-9.30 pm
Temple Tel 04365-242844

Soundararaja Perumal Temple

One of the 108 Divya Desams, this temple is remarkable for the sheer beauty of the idol of Vishnu. Over 6 ft tall and elegantly sculpted, the deity is so pleasing to look upon that, as it happened with the legendary Prince Dhruva, you might forget to ask for a boon. Built by the Cholas, the temple was renovated by the Nayak kings. The *utsavar* idols require special mention for their grace and radiance.

→ FAST FACTS

When to go Any time of the year. It is hot in April-June but many of the temple festivals take place in summer. December-March, just after the rains, is best

Tourist offices
● Information and PR Officer ❶
State Collectorate, Nagapattinam
Tel: 04365-253040
● Information and PR Officer ❶
State Collectorate, Thiruvarur
Tel: 04366-221352
● TTDC ❶ ❺
No. 2, Wallajah Road, Chennai
Tel: 044-25367850-54
Website: tamilnadutourism.org
STD code 04365

◆**Location** West of Kayarohanaswamy Temple **Timings** 7.30 am-noon, 5.30-9 pm **Temple Tel** 04365-221374

Nellukadai Mariamman Temple

The folk goddess Mariamman often transcends her folk image to be identified as a form of Shakti or Parvati. The Nellukadai Mariamman of Nagapattinam is one such deity. Her temple was built and is still being maintained by a single family, that runs a *nellukadai*, or paddy trading shop.

The goddess is believed to cure ailments, and grant health and prosperity to her devotees. It is believed that if a chronically sick child is given in 'adoption' to the goddess, the child regains its health.

◆**Location** In the bazaar near the railway station **Timings** 6 am-1 pm, 5-9 pm

→ GETTING THERE

Rail Nagapattinam Station **Best option TO** Tambaram-Nagore Express (dep: Tambaram 7.45 pm; arr: Nagapattinam 4.27 am) **Best option FROM** Kamban Express (dep: Nagapattinam 22.15 pm; arr: Tambaram 7.45 am)

Car Nagapattinam is a smooth drive from Chennai. Exit Chennai from Thiruvanmiyur to catch the East Coast Road to Pondicherry via Mahabalipuram and Marakkanam. The ECR continues south from here as NH45A to Nagapattinam via Cuddalore, Alapakkam, Chidambaram, Sirkazhi, Tranquebar, Karaikal and Nagore

Bus TNSETC buses leave every hour and private buses leave from 9.30 pm-11 pm for Nagapattinam from Chennai's Metropolitan Bus Terminus (Tel: 044-24794705) at Koyambedu

Nagore Dargah

The Nagore Dargah, the final resting place of Meeran Sahib Abdul Qadir Shahul Hamid Badshah, is an oasis of calm, 4 km north of Nagapattinam. All that we know of Meeran Sahib is from the 1898 Tamil epic *Kanjul Karamat*, written by Gulam Qadir Navalar, the most accessible version of which is AR Syed Haja Mohideen's 1963 book *Karunaikkadal* (Sea of Compassion). Meeran Sahib was born in Manikapur, Ayodhya district, on the tenth day of the month of Jumaad-ul-Akhir in the year 910, as per the Islamic calendar, estimated to be in the early 1500s according to the Gregorian calendar. He was born to the devout couple, Syed Hasan Kuthus and Saeeda Fathima. During his lifetime, Meeran Sahib travelled far and wide, inspiring piety and faith with his faultless living and miraculous acts. He once cured Achutappa Naicker, one of the Nayak kings of Thanjavur, of what was believed to be a witchcraft-induced affliction. In return, when offered riches, Meeran Sahib refused them, asking instead to be allowed a small piece of land when he should require it. It is this piece of land that is now the site of the Nagore dargah. The most architecturally striking features of the Dargah are the five whitewashed minarets, built by different potentates during different periods. The oldest of the minarets is the 77-foot high Sahib Minara, which was built by Ebrahim Khan of Gingee (*see page 51*) in 1645-46.

The entrance to the dargah is lined with shops and beyond them is the dargah itself. The main place of prayer is the *rawla* or tomb, which consists of an anteroom and a room that encloses the actual tomb of the saint. This room has an ornamented double door, which keeps the tomb hidden from view. In front of this door is a golden box containing the wooden slippers used by Meeran Sahib. A narrow, perfumed passage runs around the room and is

Nagore Dargah, final resting place of Meeran Sahib Abdul Qadir Shahul Hamid Badshah

used by devotees to circumambulate the tomb. This part of the dargah is open only to men and boys; a token Rs 2 entry fee is charged. A dip in a tank near the dargah, the **Peer Kulam**, is believed to cure many diseases.

Nagore can be seen in a half-day trip (taxi Rs 200) from Nagapattinam.

♦**Location** $^1/_2$ km east of NH45A **Timings** The dargah itself is never closed. The ornamented door to the tomb is opened only at specific times. Every morning, it is kept open from 4.20-7 am, which was the time during which Meeran Sahib passed away. In the evenings, it is opened at dusk (the actual time varies everyday) and is kept open till 9 pm (up to 10 pm on Thursdays). On Fridays, the door also opens from noon-2 pm **Dargah Tel** 04365-250194

Vailankanni Church

The whitewashed splendour of the **Shrine Basilica of Vailankanni**, on the coast 13 km south of Nagapattinam, leaves a lasting impression on any visitor. Hailed as the Lourdes of the East, Vailankanni is where Mary, mother of Jesus Christ, is believed to have appeared twice. The first instance was roughly 400 years ago, when Vailankanni was a mere hamlet of no consequence. A poor shepherd boy carrying milk to a rich man in Nagapattinam rested a while in the shade of a banyan tree. A lady of exceeding beauty, with a child in her arms, asked him for some milk to feed her child. He did so. After she had fed the child, both the mother and baby smiled at him and disappeared. When the boy reached his master's house, later than expected, he apologised and explained. However, when the lid of the milk pot was lifted, it was brimming with milk. The master realised that a miracle had taken place, and went and prostrated himself at the spot where it had happened. The story of the miracle spread and soon, the pond was called Madha Kulam, or Our Lady's Tank, as it is still called today.

The second appearance of Mary was a few years later. A poor widow and her lame son lived in Vailankanni. Every morning, the widow would carry her son to a place called Nadu Thittu, which was a platform near a banyan tree. There he would sell buttermilk to weary travellers. One very hot day, when the boy had no customers, a lady with a child appeared suddenly before him. Both she and her child were indescribably beautiful, and were dressed in garments of the purest white. She asked for some buttermilk and fed it to her child. Then, she asked the boy to go to a certain Catholic man in Nagapattinam, tell him what had happened, and ask him to build a shrine to her at that spot. When the boy protested that he couldn't walk, she told him to get up and go. The boy was miraculously cured, and ran all the way to Nagapattinam. When he reached his destination, the Catholic man readily believed him: he too had been visited by Mary in his dream the previous night. The people of the village then joined hands to erect a thatched chapel to Mary, calling her Arokia Madha, or Our Lady of Health.

Shrine Basilica of Vailankanni

In the early 17th century, a Portuguese ship sailing from Macau to Colombo was beset by a fierce gale, and was tossed about on the waves. The sailors beseeched Mary to save them. Instantly, the sea was calmed. When the sailors came ashore at Vailankanni, they offered thanks to Mary in the thatched shrine. This happened on September 8, the Feast of the Day of the Birth of the Virgin Mary. The sailors built a brick and mortar chapel to Mary.

The Shrine Basilica of Our Lady of Good Health is a sprawling, very spacious complex that dominates the little town of Vailankanni. There are four major structures within the complex: the **Shrine Basilica** itself, the chapel near **Madha Kulam**, the chapel at **Nadu Thittu** and the **Museum of Offerings**.

♦**Location** Dominating the landscape of the beachfront **Timings** 5.40 am-9 pm **Shrine office** Rev Fr P Xavier, Rector, Shrine Basilica, Vailankanni-611111 **Tel** 04365-263423, 263530 **Website** vailankannichurch.org

Devotees take home blessed oil and water from the Madha Kulam for their healing powers and offer silver and gold versions of favours received as thanksgiving. An astonishing display of such items is on display in the **Museum of Offerings**. Within the complex are many facilities for pilgrims, including a canteen, numerous soft drinks stalls, souvenir stalls, toilets, rooms to stay, a hospital and a dispensary. Hundreds of thousands of pilgrims gather to celebrate the birthday of Mary during the Feast of Our Lady of Good Health (Aug 29-Sep 8).

Taxis from and to Nagapattinam charge Rs 650, and Vailankanni is also well connected by buses.

WHERE TO STAY AND EAT

Nagapattinam offers a fair choice of hotels to suit middle-level budgets. **Hotel Subham Park** (Tel: 04365-251000; Tariff: Rs 450-690), near the Collectorate,

NAGAPATTINAM

Juice stall on the streets leading to the Kayarohanaswamy Temple

Nagore Road, is basic but clean and has separate veg and non-veg restaurants. **Hotel Sea Horse** (Tel: 247047; Tariff: Rs 175-800), on Public Office Road, offers the basics and multi-cuisine restaurants.

Hotel Tamizhagam (Tel: 221010; Mobile: 09442081752; Tariff: Rs 450-1,200), on Thoni Thurai Road, is bang on the beach, but don't expect a great view.

Apart from the restaurants in the above hotels, there are a number of inexpensive eateries on Public Office Road, which offer basic South Indian meals and tiffin. **Uma Food Corner** (only 5.30-10.30 pm), on the same road, runs a bakery and has a drive-in restaurant that specialises in Chinese and tandoor dishes.

For details, see Nagapattinam Accommodation Listings on page 522

AROUND NAGAPATTINAM

Thiruvarur (24 km)
Night has fallen and cool shadows barely quiver in the silver moonlight that reigns over the spacious, magnificent **temple to Thyagarajaswamy** in Thiruvarur.

The legend of how Thyagarajaswamy came to this sthala is an interesting one. Long ago, the legendary king Muchukunda Chola helped the king of the devas, Indra, in defeating an asura named Valan. Grateful, Indra told Muchukunda to ask him for a gift. Muchukunda, who was an ardent devotee of Shiva, asked for the idol of Thyagesar that Indra worshipped. Indra, who was extremely loathe to part with the idol, made six similar idols and placed all of them in a row, and told Muchukundan that if he could spot the real idol among the seven, he could have it. Muchukunda was helped by Shiva to spot the real idol and a very impressed Indra gave Muchukunda all the seven idols. These seven idols were installed by Muchukunda Chola in seven sthalas in the Cauvery Delta, known as the the *sapthavidanga* sthalas. The original idol has been placed in the temple in Thiruvarur, just as Shiva had

TAMIL NADU

The 25-acre Kamalalayam Tank of the huge Thyagarajaswamy Temple, Thiruvarur

demanded of Muchukunda. In all these temples, Shiva is seen as Thyagaraja, the benign, royal ascetic deity placed in a niche in the corridor surrounding the main sanctum.

As befits a deity whose compassion encompasses the universe, everything about the temple at Thiruvarur is generously proportioned: the temple itself, its towers, its tank and its *ther*. Although the temple is popularly known as that of Thyagaraja, that name refers only to the majestic *panchaloha* idol of Shiva in its own sanctum. The stone lingam in the main sanctum is called Vanmeeganathar. The well-proportioned (110 ft x 60 ft) entrance to this magnificent temple is crowned by a five-tiered gopuram (120 ft), which abruptly diminishes in size and is thus quite different in appearance from that of other grand temples. This is only one of the seven towers of the Thyagarajaswamy Temple, which define Thiruvarur's skyline.

The temple spreads over a generous 20 acres. The captivating **Kamalalayam Tank** (temple of the lotus or *kamalam*) lies to its west, a full 25 acres of rippling waters fed by perennial underground wells. The *sannidhi* to Kamalambal, after whom the vast tank is named, is in the third or outermost prakaram. She remains unmarried to Shiva despite her fervent penance. She is said to grant intelligence, education and finally, enlightenment, to her devotees.

The Thyagarajaswamy *sannidhi* is in the innermost prakaram of the temple. The pillars of the mandapam outside the sanctum are richly carved. The idol of Thyagarajaswamy is majesty personified. The resplendently attired and ornamented idol is so completely covered that devotees only see the face of the deity. The Nandi in the Thyagaraja sanctum is unusual in that he is in a standing posture. The legend behind this is that once Thyagarajaswamy was in such a hurry that he did not wait for Nandi to get up from his seated position to carry him and began walking. Ever since Nandi is said to have resolved that he would always stand in Thyagesar's presence, so as to be available as his mount always.

Thyagaraja is the patron of dance and music. Perhaps it was no coincidence that the *trimurtis* (three divinities) of Carnatic music, saint-composers Thyagaraja, Shyama Shastri and Muthuswamy Dikshitar, were all born in Thiruvarur.

To the north of the Thyagarajaswamy sanctum is the *sannidhi* of **Vanmeeganathar** or Putridankonda Peruman ('he who lives in the anthill'). Here, Shiva rose from the mud of a termite hill to destroy Vishnu's sudden pride. The *sannidhi* to Runavimochanar (*runa* means debt and this lingam rids the devotee of the debt of rebirth) is to the west of the Thyagarajaswamy sanctum. It is a popular and happy belief, however, that the deity helps debtors to be freed of their financial burdens. The *sannidhi* of Thyagarajaswamy's consort, **Neelothpalambal** (*neelothpalam* means 'blue lily'), is in the second prakaram. Next to the goddess stands another woman, perhaps a friend, on whose shoulder sits the baby Subrahmanya. One hand of the goddess is placed very lovingly on her son's head. This is an unusual arrangement, rarely seen.

Thiruvarur celebrates **nitya pradosham**. The daily pradosham hour falls just before dusk and coincides with the evening puja at 6 pm, which, in the Thiruvarur temple, is conducted elaborately with *abhishekam*, and all the *upacharam* (rituals of courtesy, like offering mirror, fan and light to the deity). It is a puja well worth watching.

♦**Location** Centre of town, less than $1/2$ km from main bus stand **Timings** 6 am-noon, 4-9 pm **Temple Tel** 04366-242343

At the centre of the Kamalalayam Tank is the *maragatha* (emerald) lingam *sannidhi* of **Naganathaswamy**. The temple opens only at 5 pm every day. Small motor boats run by the Tourism Department take pilgrims to the shrine (Rs 10 per person per trip). The tank is open from 8 am and the boats can take you around the tank for fun, even if the temple is not open. The annual float festival (Teppotsavam) of Kalyanasundarar (the *panchaloha* idol of Thyagarajaswamy) is celebrated in Vaikasi (May-Jun) in the Kamalalayam Tank for three days in a row. Every day, the decorated and lit up float travels around the tank three times. Apart from the priests and the musicians, the float carries some 600 devotees on each trip!

A visit to the **erstwhile homes of the musical trinity** Thyagaraja (on Vadakku Veedhi), Shyama Shastri (on Mettu Theru) and Muthuswamy Dikshitar (on Raja Street) is a must for lovers of Carnatic music. All these streets lie within a kilometre of the temple (autorickshaws will take you on a tour to all three for around Rs 40). ■

With Vidya Sigamany and Navin Sigamany in Nagore and Vailankanni

TAMIL NADU

DR. MS MAYILVAHNAN/ SOUTHINDIAPICTURE

All the action in Yercaud is centred on its picturesque Big Lake

YERCAUD
IN CLIVE'S FOOTSTEPS

State Tamil Nadu
Location Yercaud is 4,500 ft above sea level in the orange- and coffee-flavoured Shevaroy Hills of north-central Tamil Nadu
Distance 350 km SW of Chennai **JOURNEY TIME By rail** 7 hrs + 1 hr by road **By road** 6½ hrs
Route NH45 to Ulundurpettai via Tambaram, Chengalpattu, Tindivanam, Vikravandi and Viluppuram; NH68 to Salem via Tiyagai Durgam, Kallakkurichi, Talaivasal, Attur and Valappadi; state road to Yercaud (*see route guide on page 12*)

■ BY KG KUMAR

Yercaud is easily India's cheapest hill station destination. Make that 'least expensive', for so rich is Yercaud in its natural charm and its potential for bountiful discovery that to label it 'cheap' would be truly insulting. It's sometimes referred to as the "poor man's Ooty", but "smart man's Ooty" would be nearer the mark.

'Yercaud' is how the Brits got around the tongue-twister 'Yericaud', Tamil for 'lake-forest'. This little hill station lies in the Shevaroy Hills, part of the Eastern Ghats. Unlike the more lush Western Ghats, the Eastern Ghats are generally dry, and feature short and rocky hills, and Yercaud is thus a wonderful aberration.

Spread over just 383 sq km, Yercaud is small enough not to tire you, and yet spread out in mysterious little ways to give you a sense of serenity. Less crowded than Ooty or Kodaikanal, Yercaud is where you go to when you

TAMIL NADU — YERCAUD

simply wish to apply salve to your soul. Or, simply to recollect, along with the poet, emotions in tranquility amidst sunflowers, dahlias and roses.

THINGS TO SEE AND DO

The 31-km uphill drive from the town of Salem takes about an hour. You will have to negotiate 20 fairly smooth hairpin bends. As you approach Yercaud, you can't miss the coffee plantations and orange groves. Check into your hotel, slip into your sneakers and set out to explore this quiet homage to lake and forest.

Big Lake, Small Boat

The main attraction is the **Big Lake**, where much of the action takes place. But this being laid back Yercaud, the action is decidedly low-key and restful. Like boating. You can hire 2- or 4-seater pedal boats and 4-seater rowboats. Near the lake is **Anna Park**, with a well-groomed garden. It's crowded in May, when a week-long summer festival takes place. But if you or your kids fancy flower shows, dog shows, boating races and fairs, that's a good time to go. Also check out the **Small Lake**, fed by seven wells, situated close to town.

Ladies and Gents

Lady's Seat overlooks the winding ghat road and offers a spectacular view of Salem. Try reaching this vantage point at night, after dinner. The walk won't just help digest your meal; gazing at the twinkling lights of Salem town in the distance to the left will also put you in a lovely, tranquil mood. For those interested in a closer view, there's a mounted telescope. Swing it to your extreme right to see the **Mettur Dam** on the **Cauvery River**. Great shots of the river can be had from this spot in the late afternoon, when the sun's rays are reflected in its waters.

Close to Lady's Seat is a **silk farm** and **Pagoda Point**, a viewing point that's sometimes called **Gent's Seat**, in some corny sense of gender equality.

Shevaroy Temple and Bear's Cave

Situated atop Servaroyan Hill, the Shevaroy Temple is the highest point in Yercaud, 5,326 ft above sea level. The temple is dedicated to the local deity Servaran and his consort Kaveriamma. Local tribals celebrate their annual festival here each May. On the way to the temple, near the **Norton Bungalow** (one of the oldest in Yercaud), is **Bear's Cave**, believed to have been the entrance to an escape tunnel of a long gone raja. Today, the cave is covered over with vegetation and rocks. Though it is on private property, the public can still visit it.

Killiyur Falls

This 300-foot-high waterfall is situated amidst picturesque surroundings. The water comes via a stream all the way from the Big Lake.

→ FAST FACTS

When to go The only season that could be described as 'off' is July-August. The rest of the year, Yercaud enjoys pleasant weather. Winter tends to be slightly chilly, but never cold enough for heavy woollens

Tourist offices
- Dept of Tourism ❶
Govt of Tamil Nadu, Hotel Tamil Nadu (near Big Lake), Yercaud
Tel: 04281-222273, 223334-36
- TTDC ❶❻
No. 2, Wallajah Road, Chennai
Tel: 044-25367850-54
Fax: 25361385; Email: ttdc@vsnl.com
Website: tamilnadutourism.org
STD code 04281

TAMIL NADU

DR. MS MAYILVAHNAN/ SOUTHINDIAPICTURE

Church at Montfort School

Botanical Garden
The Botanical Garden is home to hundreds of plants, including rarities like the pitcher plant. You will also find specimens of the famous *kurinji* flower, which blooms once in 12 years across the Western and Eastern Ghats in South India. The garden has an **orchidarium**, reputed to be India's third largest, after the ones in Kolkata and Shillong. It houses over a hundred species of orchids, of which about 30 are exclusive. In fact, it has an orchid or three found nowhere else in the world. Plant-lovers mustn't give this a miss.

Montfort School
Your kids may not enjoy the idea of being dragged off to see a specimen of what they have escaped from, but the famous 86-year-old Montfort School (Tel: 04281-222160, 222328) is well worth a visit for its old-world granite-and-wood architecture, sprawling grounds and majestic church. Perhaps the kids can be enticed by the prospect of exploring the school's small menagerie, open to the public only on Sundays. But you must call in advance and take permission from the school authorities.

The Grange
This imposing castle-like building in Yercaud was built by a former British Collector of Salem, MD Cockburn. However, the Grange is famous not for its founder but for a distinguished guest from Madras who frequently took weekend breaks in Yercaud.

Robert Clive worked as a clerk in the East India Company's office in Madras. Clive lived and worked at Fort St George, just off the bay which brought only some respite every afternoon from a heat the Englishman could barely tolerate. It is said that Clive grew so miserable and homesick that he tried to kill himself, but the gun failed to fire.

Perhaps those breaks up in cool Yercaud had something to do with Clive's eventual recovery from being perennially depressed to becoming commander of the British forces. What we do know for sure is that he went on to win India for the Empire in the historic Battle of Plassey. Which goes to show what wonders rejuvenating weekend breaks can do for your career.

Fun for the kids
There's boating on the Big Lake and picnics to be had in cool glades and near waterfalls. Hotel Shevaroys has the **Magic Mountain** building with computer games and dashing cars for kids. It's open to all for a fee.

WHERE TO STAY

Hotel Shevaroys (Tel: 04281-222383-86; Tariff: Rs 625-2,025), on the main road above the lake, is the classiest hotel in Yercaud. It arranges a pick-up from Salem, should you need it. In case you

YERCAUD

are taking the kids along, **Sterling Days Inn Resort** (Tel: 222700/ 06/ 08; Tariff: Rs 1,750-2,700), near Lady's Seat, has indoor games, plus a discotheque.

Green Fort Inn (Tel: 222767; Tariff: Rs 600), on Pagoda Point Road, has 8 cottages. **Hotel Shoba** (Tel: 222409; Tariff: Rs 250-400), behind the telephone exchange, arranges for such things as a taxi or a doctor, but has no restaurant. **Silver Holiday Cottages** (Tel: 222541, 222656; Tariff: Rs 400-600), opposite the lake at Lake Point has 23 rooms.

Hotel Tamil Nadu (Tel: 223334-36, 222273; Tariff: Rs 300-700), near the lake, offers boating on the lake, and has a park for kids. **The House of Peace** (Tel: 222401; Tariff: Rs 350 per person per day, meals included) on Ram Road is among the most affordable places in Yercaud. Besides regular facilities, this hotel has a prayer hall. **Hotel Select** (Tel: 222525; Tariff: Rs 300-500) is near the bus stand. They also have two 10-bedded dormitories (Rs 900).

For more options and details, see Yercaud Accommodation Listings on page 527

WHERE TO EAT

All the hotels have restaurants serving Southie food. **Sterling Days Inn Resort** has a multi-cuisine restaurant. Non-veg gourmets don't miss **Hotel Shevaroys'** Malabar chicken curry and tandoori fish tikka. **Hotel Select** has a restaurant that also serves South Indian. **Silver Holiday Cottages** can arrange buffets in case your group is large. Call ahead to have a meal here. ∎

→ GETTING THERE

Rail Nearest railhead: Salem Junction (31 km/ 1 hr) **Best option TO** Yercaud Express (dep: Chennai Central 10.30 pm; arr: Salem Junction 5.15 am) Take a cab to Yercaud for Rs 600 (one way), or a bus for Rs 11 **Best option FROM** Yercaud Express (dep: Salem Junction 10 pm; arr: Chennai Central 4.30 am) **Car** From Chennai, follow NH45 to Ulundurpettai via Chengalpattu, Tindivanam and Viluppuram, then NH68 to Salem via Kallakkurichi and Attur. From Salem take the ghat road up to Yercaud **Bus** Take the evening state bus (Rs 220) from Chennai's Metropolitan Bus Terminus (Tel: 044-24794705) at Koyambedu, or an overnight private bus (Rs 325). Buses leave every 20 mins from Salem to Yercaud

Choose from our network of over 4000 hotels in India. Serviced apartments, budget hotels, luxury resorts, palaces, business accomodations, houseboats and more.

Hotel	Rating
Yashoda Home Stay	Budget
Lake Forest Hotel	3 ★
Hotel Grand Palace	3 ★

MTNL/BSNL Toll Free No.
1-800-22-4878
022-4030-4878
www.travelguru.com

travelguru™
India's Largest Hotel Network

TAMIL NADU

KAMARAJAR VALLEY
DRIVE INTO YOUR DREAMS

State Tamil Nadu
Location In the foothills of the Kannivadi Hills, which join the Palani Range in west-central Tamil Nadu, 25 km from Dindigul
Distance 447 km SW of Chennai JOURNEY TIME **By rail** 7 hrs + 45 mins by road **By air** 1 hr + 2½ hrs by road
Route NH45 to Sembatti via Vandalur, Chengalpattu, Tindivanam, Viluppuram, Ulundurpettai, Veppur, Trichy, Manapparai, Vadamadurai and Dindigul; state road to Kamarajar Valley via Athoor Village (*see route guide on page 12*)

■ BY SHOBHA WARRIER

The highway from Chennai passes picturesque country on the long drive to Sembatti. It is just superb in parts. At other places, you are forced to slow down and travel precariously, often in the wrong lane. Further, like elsewhere on Indian highways, you are accompanied by overloaded lorries, bullock carts, darting pedestrians, and level crossings that stay closed till the cows come home — all of which serve to reinforce the desperate desire to escape.

KAMARAJAR VALLEY

Having survived such terrors of the road and done the long drive, you would love the smell of the countryside as you turn off onto the smaller roads after Dindigul. The road gets narrower and rougher and the last part takes you back to basics; parts of it are macadamised, and parts rutted by bullock carts.

But then, technology has no place in a setting as rustic and beautiful as the Kamarajar Valley, with its beautiful reservoir that supplies neighbouring Dindigul. Ringed by the Kannivadi and Palani hills, surrounded by coffee, pepper and cardamom estates and home to a lake watered by two sprightly hill streams — the Kallalar and Kodavan — this valley holds a peace you've only ever known in your dreams. Roll down the windows and breathe in deep. Pull into your home stay by Kamarajar Lake and switch off the city.

→ FAST FACTS

When to go December to February is the best season. It can be quite warm in April and May. The heat lessens from June as the monsoon starts. The Palani Hills start pushing up from the earth abruptly at Kamarajar Valley and extend westwards for 50 km. Some of the cooler air wafts down. Yet, being on the leeward side, there is little rain and it will still be warm till October when the North-East monsoon blows from the east. The rains stop by November end and the air is cool till end of February
STD code 0451

Kamarajar Lake

TAMIL NADU

Photographs by PRANAV PURUSHOTHAM

An evening at Holland House with the Palani Hills in the background

THINGS TO SEE AND DO

The Kamarajar Valley is for those who want to be away from it all without letting go of creature comforts. The home stays here offer the perfect environment for this — greenery on all sides, oodles of peace and a lake that is quiet as the night. And surprisingly, no mosquitoes at all!

The atmosphere of the 'resorts' are a great help too. You feel at home as the proprietors treat you as part of their extended family — which includes dogs, cats, cows and any other guests who may be staying there at the time. The environment is made even more conducive for lazing around by comfortable temperatures most of the year.

Away from civilisation, there is no dust in the atmosphere, the air is relatively dry, and on cloudless and moonless nights you can see all the stars you never saw in the metropolis, against a pitch black sky. With the lake alongside, the place is teeming with waterfowl and other birds. Listen to the birds in the bushes and around the lake. There were scores of weaver birds weaving their nests even in the gardens of the home stays. We did hear peacocks call, and later saw three of them cross the road during our evening stroll.

Take a walk

The home stays (all three of them) are located on the northern banks of Kamarajar Lake, an artificial lake created by the Kallalar and Kodavan rivers, which are basically the run-off from the steep hills that form a huge arc to the west and north. Kamarajar Lake provides drinking water for nearby Dindigul. You could take a walk around its 6-km circumference when the water level is relatively low, avoiding soft marshy ground. It shouldn't take more than two hours of leisurely ambling. This may not be possible between November and March when the lake is fuller.

The home stays will say you can take a swim as there aren't crocs in the lake, but please DON'T. The lake supplies drinking water and it's also against the law as a warning posted in Tamil at the weir will tell you.

Sadayandi Cave Temple

This is a small shrine at the dam, which you would have passed on your way to the home stay bungalows. Goat sacrifices are still performed here occasionally. Climbing up the steep rock face at the temple, you can reach the Sadayandi Cave Temple cut into the monolith. The climb takes about 20 minutes.

Take a hike

Literally. Walk further up the road you took past Athoor to the valley. It reduces to a footpath and climbs more than a thousand metres into the hills. The sparser vegetation of the plains becomes dense and the path takes you past mango groves and then through forests to a beautiful waterfall. This can take anywhere between 4 and 6 hours and is certainly not for the weak-kneed. The round trip will take up a whole day, so do carry food and water along.

You can also trek through the hillside up to a less-travelled road that goes to Kodaikanal (a third route in addition to the ones from Kodaikanal Road and Palani). Walk up along the road, which climbs along what are essentially the first hills of the Palani Range of the Western Ghats, affording magnificent views of the plains and valleys. You could also wander into the farms alongside. There are mango and jackfruit orchards, limes and lemons abound, and there are lots of estates that grow coffee and pepper. Be careful as you explore these estates as they have no boundary walls and stretch to the edge where terra firma abruptly drops down several hundred metres into the valley. Make sure it is not below your feet.

The trips can last as long as you want, since you can stop at any of the hamlets en route and take a bus to come down to Athoor. The home stays also provide guides for these treks.

Mounds of plump jackfruit in Athoor

Choose from our network of over 4000 hotels in India. Serviced apartments, budget hotels, luxury resorts, palaces, business accommodations, houseboats and more.

1-800-22-4878
022-4030-4878
www.travelguru.com

India's Largest Hotel Network

TAMIL NADU

→ GETTING THERE

Air Nearest airport: Madurai (100 km/ 2½ hrs), connected by 10 flights daily to Chennai, by Paramount Airways, Indian, Air Deccan, Kingfisher Airlines and Jet Airways. Taxi to Athoor costs about Rs 1,200, but the going is slow because you have to drive all the way through Madurai City first
Rail Dindigul Junction (25 km/ 45 mins) **Best option TO** Pandian Express (dep: Chennai Egmore 9.30 pm; arr: Dindigul Junction 4.30 am). A taxi from Dindigul costs Rs 350 **Best option FROM** Nellai Express (dep: Dindigul Junction 10.20 pm; arr: Tambaram 5.19 am, Mambalam 5.34 am, Chennai Egmore 6.10 am)
TIP Kanyakumari Express has almost matching timings for the return journey, among other good alternatives
Car The long 11-hr drive to Kamaraj Valley from Chennai cannot be attempted for a short weekend getaway. For a longer vacation, follow NH45 past Chengalpattu, Tindivanam, Viluppuram, Ulundurpettai, Trichy, Manapparai and Dindigul. Drive on down NH45 for about 3 km, ignoring the exits into Dindigul and the road to Palani, and turn right on the road to Sempatti. Just after the bus stand in Sempatti is a roundabout with a road going right to Palani/ Coimbatore. Don't take it, but after another 1 km, turn right at the small temple to Athoor. A sign here says 'Attur'. Follow this road for about 4 km to Athoor Village. Turn right after the Catholic Church and a further 5 km takes you to the Sadayandi Temple and the dam. The guest houses are 2 km further down the road, by now almost a dirt track

Athoor Village

Athoor is always part of itineraries offered by the home stays, and is popular with their foreign guests. You can skip it because Athoor is indeed just like any other Indian village. It has a post-office, a branch of Canara Bank, a temple, a mosque, a Catholic church, tea shops and a noisy vegetable market. But you can buy good tea at the bazaar.

WHERE TO STAY AND EAT

The Kamarajar Valley has become an attractive retreat thanks to the three home stays there, which border the lake just below the scarp of the hills. It doesn't get any more rustic and away-from-it-all than in these homes. Birds and butterflies flit about their gardens. Brahmini kites, owls and peacocks are frequent visitors. All three are operated by European expatriates who first came here in connection with children sponsored by them at Boys Town in Athoor, a hostelry for poor schoolboys run by an NGO. It is absolutely essential to obtain advance booking, though there may be vacancies during non-peak season (April to November). Group discounts are available. Peak season is December to March.

All the guest houses arrange pick-ups and drops from and to Dindigul Station, either by taxi or on two-wheelers. Other common facilities include bicycles on hire, small libraries, guides for treks and birdwatching, and two-wheeler trips to viewpoints or places nearby like Palani, Madurai or Kodaikanal.

Lakeside Guest House (Tel: 0451-3298132; Tariff: Rs 1,500, including meals) is run by Joe Homan, an Englishman who's been in and out of India for the last 40 years. Twelve years ago, while searching for a place to spend his retirement, he found the Kamarajar Lake and valley, bought 5 acres just 100m away from its banks and has stayed put ever since. Those acres are now

TAMIL NADU

Thrills on wheels

Two of the pleasures one must not forgo here are trekking in the wilderness and taking a motorbike ride along the scenic roads in the Kamarajar Valley. We set out on the trip with Gé, who runs Double Dutch Resorts. We first trekked up a nearby hill along a small and verdant path up to a point on the ghat road where Palraj, one of the staff at the guest house, was waiting on his Enfield Diesel.

As we went up the hill, Gé showed us the sights, pointing out the flora that dots the surface of the hill. The journey was tiring in the beginning as it was warm in the valley, but it became progressively more refreshing as we trudged up the hill and the mercury fell a few degrees. After trekking for a good two hours, we reached the point on the road where Palraj was waiting.

Palraj told us that the road we were taking would lead to Kodaikanal if we went all the way. This was one of the three routes to the famous hill station and, thankfully, was the one less patronised, enabling us to take in the unspoiled natural beauty all around.

The most spectacular sight is that of the plains stretching along for miles, viewed from a lookout point deep within a coffee plantation. It is a sight that will be etched in my mind forever, as will be the journey through the thickly wooded estates to the points.

Trips are Rs 4 per km, so typical rates are Rs 70 to Sempatti and Rs 150 to Dindigul.

---

landscaped and at the centre of it all sits the sprawling guest house. You can stay in the main house in five double rooms, or in any of six cottages on the grounds.

Apart from arranging visits to watch elephants logging, and to coffee and pepper estates, as well as walking, trekking and birdwatching sorties, Lakeside takes care of all the basics from laundry to room service and onward travel bookings. The food here is mostly Continental, and Indian meals are low on spices. If you aren't staying here, call ahead and book a table.

Holland House (Tel: 2556763; Tariff: Rs 1,100-2,260), aka Double Dutch Resorts, is run by a Dutch couple Gemma and Gè Mol, who built it nine years ago. Stay in the three deluxe rooms in Villa Flamboyant that's near the water, or in the cheaper rooms within the main building that is Holland House. Food is extra (Rs 150-300 a meal), and they arrange massages on request. Kamarajar Lake is on the southern border of the garden, and there's no fence.

Another Englishman, Dr Christopher Lucas, has been running **Cardamom House** (Tel: 2556765-66; Tariff: Rs 3,600-4,400) for more than four years. Dr Lucas spent most of his life in India, building his own retirement dream close to the foothills of the Kannivadi Hills. They offer sightseeing tours, birdwatching, yoga, meditation, and swimming in the lake. Indian and Continental food, served in the large verandah or on the roof, is charged extra, at approximately Rs 650 per person per day. If you aren't staying here, please call ahead for meals. Cardamom House, like the other home stays, offers an eco-friendly vacation.

For details, see Kamarajar Valley Accommodation Listings on page 516 ■

V MUTHURAMAN

Preparing for Pongal festivities in a heritage Chettiar nattukottai

CHETTINAD
PAST CONTINUOUS

State Tamil Nadu
Location Chettinad is a closely knit cluster of villages dotting the scrubby flatlands around the town of Karaikkudi, in the semi-arid Sivaganga district of south-central Tamil Nadu. Karaikkudi is 80 km east of Madurai and 96 km south of Trichy
Distance Karaikkudi, the nominal capital of Chettinad, is 444 km SW of Chennai **JOURNEY TIME By road** $8^1/_2$ hrs **By rail** $8^1/_2$ hrs + 2 hrs by road **By air** 1 hr + 2 hrs by road
Route East Coast Road to Pondicherry via Mahabalipuram and Marakkanam; NH45A to Sirkazhi via Cuddalore and Chidambaram; SH27 to Pudukottai via Kumbakonam, Thanjavur and Gandarvakottai; NH210 to Karaikkudi via Thirumayam (*see route guide on page 12*)

■ BY AMBIKA MENON AND LALITHA SRIDHAR WITH VIDYA SIGAMANY AND NAVIN SIGAMANY

Karaikkudi can lay claim to being the hub of the 75 surviving clusters of villages broadly referred to as Chettinad (a delicious memory associated with, mostly and unfortunately, only chicken; a forgivable misconception this story seeks to dispel).

Dusty streets lead you through Karaikkudi to what were surely among the most immaculately tended garden paths and mansions this side of the subcontinent. Everywhere there is muted evidence of adversities overcome by grit, daring and imagination.

Chettinad culture is without parallel. Wood is worked in massive doorways that showcase the most dexterous carvings. Gold and silver jewellery is

CHETTINAD

sublime in form and generous in volume. Refined crafts give the arid region a stunning foil. Native looms add splendid colour to the arid land. Business acumen has left an unparalleled legacy of arts patronage and sustained philanthropy. Grand mansions and beautiful temples rise like mirages, only they are very real. The cuisine is so ambrosial that its popularity has already made it the fourth compulsory victim in every joint which simultaneously serves Chinese-Mughlai-South Indian. Here is a heritage that is facing a terrible decline, but continues to reflect the gumption typical to the natives of this territory, the community that lent its name to its homeland: the Chettiars.

As early as the 11th and 12th centuries, the Chettiars followed the shipping routes of the Pandyas. They journeyed across the seas, expanding their networks even as they supplied provisions to the royal ships. Trade in salt, silks, teak, spices, timber and precious gemstones prospered. Enterprise and initiative made them the leading merchant capitalists of South India. Proximity to the royals brought them land rights in and around Pudukottai and Sivaganga. They became the *Nagarathars* (town-dwellers, also meaning sophisticated, a nomenclature used interchangeably with 'Chettiar') and their magnificent homes came to be called the *nattukottais* (literally, land fortresses).

Following the fortunes of the East India Company, they established branches in Ceylon, Malaya, Indonesia, Vietnam, Singapore and Burma. Political changes in these nations led to a devastating turn of fortunes. Massive investments were obliterated overnight. Chettiar men returned, deep in debt, to sell everything in their homes, from jewellery to iron objects, by the kilo. It was the beginning of a downward spiral that, sadly and irrevocably, continues to this date.

While most of the community is now living in the shadow of its rich past, others have re-invented themselves in industrialised or technology-driven businesses, elsewhere. They have left behind a unique heritage in various states of dilapidation, hiding such beauty that it makes every visitor a discoverer. Chettinad is a place where to take a step forward is to find yourself going back in time.

ORIENTATION

Staying in **Karaikkudi** or Kanadukathan is quite ideal, both in terms of facilities for visitors, and access to sites to see. Karaikkudi is a small, easily navigated town. The **bus stand** is a 10-min walk away (or Rs 30 by auto) from the centre of town, where the hotels are located; the **railway station** is about 3 km away. **Pillaiyarpatti** is about 12 km north of Karaikkudi. It is easy to get there by bus; frequent services are available from the Karaikkudi Bus Stand. By cab (Rs 350 return), it takes about half an hour each way. The beautiful mansions of **Pallathur** and **Kanadukathan** are 14 km north-east and 12 km north of Karaikkudi respectively. They too are best reached by taxis. Autos run only within the town.

→ FAST FACTS

When to go Summers (Apr-Jun) are very hot. November (when it rains) to February is pleasantly cool
Tourist office
● TTDC ℹ️🛏️
No. 2, Wallajah Road, Chennai
Tel: 044-25367850-54
Email: ttdc@vsnl.com
Website: tamilnadutourism.org
STD code Karaikkudi 04565

THINGS TO SEE AND DO

No one in Chettinad anticipated tourists. Today, however, some Chettinad mansions have opened their doors to travellers. Over two days, do a tour of the magnificent mansions (even the ones that are falling apart are awe-inspiring) in the region around Karaikkudi. Visit the temples at Pillaiyarpatti and Avudayarkovil, shop for crafts and learn about a highly evolved culture. If all the Chettiar clan temples are to be seen, another day would be needed.

MAGNIFICENT MANSIONS

Many of the Chettiar mansions are so majestically built that they straddle more than one block, or sprawl across two parallel streets, each having a 'main' entrance. They are sometimes even bestowed with two postal addresses!

Two or three storeys tall, set back from the thoroughfare by imposing gates, they have sloping red-tiled roofs, most in a state of disrepair. The façades are typically embellished with extravagant statues and impressive gargoyles, featuring an unusual but not unpleasant medley of the Hindu gods and goddesses alongside European figurines. The grand door opens to a huge home designed around two, sometimes three, sunlit courtyards. In keeping with old-world tradition of hospitality, the front door is open throughout the day, closed only when the family retires for the night.

This floor plan also allows you to see right to the other end of the building in one sweep of the eye. The interiors and rooms face inward into courtyards. Relax awhile on the *thinnai*, the pillared platform abutting the main door. This was where the men of the house would enjoy a tumbler of coffee; it is also where a wayfarer would be allowed to sleep in days when the fastest mode of transport was a bullock cart. It's a good vantage point to take in the splendid aesthetics of Chettiar homes — granite and marble pillars, polished and carved Burmese teak, superb decorative tiles, Thanjavur art and paintings, and crystal chandeliers. Structure and proportion are in perfect balance. How did they get it all so right?

The interiors use traditional *athangudi* tiles (named after the village that has been traditionally making them, 15 km from Karaikkudi) — natural dyes shaded indigo and green, sometimes crimson. The walls are plastered in a mixture of powdered shells, lime, jaggery and spices, including *gallnut* (myrobalan). It keeps the interior of the house cool in the hot and humid summers and lasts a lifetime, often more. The muted shine comes from egg white!

A **guided tour** of the Chettinad mansions that have opened their doors to the public is possible only through

→ GETTING THERE

Air Nearest airport: Madurai (80 km/ 2 hrs), with numerous daily connections from Chennai. Taxis to Karaikkudi charge Rs 1,400

Rail Karaikkudi Junction is linked to Tambaram by only the Sethu Express, which arrives at the inconvenient hour of 1.55 am. It's best to travel to Madurai (*see page 158 for train connections*) and take a taxi from there

Car An 8½-hr drive from Chennai, first along the ECR till Pondy, then NH45A to Sirkazhi. Turn right to Thanjavur via Kumbakonam. At Thanjavur, turn left to Pudukkottai via Gandarvakkottai, and continue south down NH210 to Karaikkudi via Tirumayam

Bus KPN Travels (Tel: 044-24791525) or Praveen Travels (Tel: 28193538) offer luxury bus services to Karaikkudi from Koyambedu in Chennai (Rs 340-430)

CHETTINAD

TAMIL NADU

Exquisite interiors of a grand Chettinad mansion

the hotels in this region (*see 'Where to Stay' on page 139*). Guests of the boutique hotel, **The Bangala** in Karaikkudi, get the best guided tours of the Chettiar *nattukottais*.

AMM Nattukottai, Pallathur

The AMM Nattukottai of the Murugappa Group in Pallathur (on Aranthangi Road) is a private yet collective residence. In keeping with the times, the family has built bungalows behind the old *nattukottai*, in the same architectural style, for each of the sons. This village is home to a **Vairavar Temple**. It's known for its **musical pillars**, each of them producing a different note of the *saptaswaram*, the septave of Indian music. Do observe the sculptures, especially the horses and elephants.

Pallathur is 12 km north of Karaikkudi on NH210, via Kottaiyur, towards Trichy.

M.Rm.Rm. House, Kanadukathan

There is much to see at the M.Rm.Rm. House at Kanadukathan. In an effort to increase awareness and revive the region's fortunes, the low-profile owner of this stunning mansion has turned the first floor of her home into a museum. It is here that you will find a sumptuously laid out corridor full of everyday pages from a colourful Chettiar history: travelling kitchens, crafts, fabrics, paintings and, most of all, explanations.

Noted architect Benny Kuriakose has documented the plan of the entire house and the original drawings are on display. The techniques of weaving *kottans* (palm leaf baskets) and egg plastering of walls is also explained. Browse through Kuriakose' coffee table book on Chettiar heritage, co-authored by historian S Muthiah. You can buy a lovely sketchbook of line drawings that showcase the house. Also on sale are exquisite *kottans* in the most tasteful colours.

Kanadukathan is 14 km north of Karaikkudi on NH210, via Kottaiyur and Palathur, towards Trichy.

♦**Permission** Guests of The Bangala need no prior permission. Others may e-mail the M.Rm.Rm. Cultural Foundation at vvisalam@vsnl.com or chettinad_culture@vsnl.net

Home fires

Clichés can be most unsettling. Before I left for Karaikkudi, I was generously burdened with advice that seemed to stem from a wealth of knowledge on Chettinad food. That it was much too fiery, and so to take along plenty of Digene; that it was much too oily, and so to walk around frenetically between meals; that it included dubious meats, and so to always check whether the chicken was really chicken and not crow. One friend even gave me what must surely be the most unique suggestion ever to be dispensed before a food trip: "Don't eat too much."

As it turned out, I was only too glad to disregard all their suggestions, but very particularly that last one. At The Bangala in Karaikkudi, I was put through a crash course in authentic Chettinad cuisine, at the end of which I was convinced that it is not too fiery or oily, that its meats are honest and true, and that above all, one should always, always eat too much.

The Bangala is a classic Chettinad home converted into a comfortably minimalist retreat. "We pride ourselves on our kitchen, on showing people what real Chettinad food is like," says Mrs Vishalakshi Ramaswamy, one of the two chatelaines of The Bangala. "And it isn't at all like people imagine it to be, nor what restaurants all over Tamil Nadu have suddenly started serving."

She says this at breakfast on the first day, over what has got to be the most definitive proof of her statement — the *paniyaram*. Made of a blended batter of rice and pulses, the humble *paniyaram* is the base for an endless succession of fantastic culinary riffs. Fried in hot oil, to be served with an onion-tomato-chilli chutney as tiny, flat *vellai paniyarams* for breakfast; combined with black pepper, onion and curry leaves, steamed with oil in moulds, and served with sambhar as *kuzhi paniyaram* for tiffin; shaped into little balls along with mustard seeds, onion and coconut, and fried till golden brown as masala *cheeyam*; made of five different rice types as *anjarusi paniyaram*.

In its most visually fascinating form, the batter is squeezed out of a single hole in a hollowed coconut shell, a rapid finger movement flicking white globules into hot oil to form little fried nuggets of *paniyaram*. These are then dunked in a mixture of sweetened milk and coconut milk, flavoured with elaichi, and served as the light-as-air *paal paniyaram*. "Begin with the *paal paniyaram*," advises Mrs Ramaswamy. "It's always good to have a sweet beginning to your endeavour." Frankly, it's also always good to have *paal paniyaram*.

A little while later, I speak to America Natesan, a chef so delightfully named because his employer, a Mr Alagappa Chettiar working for the United Nations, took him along to New York. Between 1964 and 1968, America Natesan did his bit for world peace, turning out *badam halwa* that, according to some conspiracy theorists, ensured that the Six-Day War lasted only six days. Forty years later, he's still cooking — he has to rush off, after our conversation, to supervise a festive lunch.

America Natesan is the ideal teacher. He fills me in on the fundamentals — how a meal will never have more than three fried items, how colour is so important that coriander chutneys will sometimes be made solely for their greenness, how the number of side dishes in a Chettinad meal will always be an odd number, and how at really big lunches that number can go as high as 13. But Chettinad's famed magic with meat operates throughout my stay at The Bangala. There is a fillet of pan-fried seer fish, soft as butter and spiced to perfection. There are chicken gravies — full and even-tempered the first day, sharp and hot

V MUTHURAMAN

CHETTINAD

TAMIL NADU

V MUTHURAMAN

A host of cooks prepare traditional Chettinad delicacies; Drying meat (left)

the next. There is a fine prawn masala and an even better quail masala, chewy and dense with smoky flavour. There is a mutton pulao, the meat so soft it almost blends into its ghee-filled habitat of rice.

The typical Chettinad meal is strikingly similar to meals all over South India, but with distinctive little variations of its own. It will begin with a fragrant Chettinad soup, often made with drumsticks and touched with cinnamon and bay leaves. It will proceed through rice and *kozhambu*, a thickened, tangy stew that takes on the character of its chief ingredient — red and full-bodied with tomato, dark and fierce with black peppercorns, light and sunny with buttermilk. Specific to Chettinad is the *yelan kozhambu*, a thin concoction made of beans and coriander in dal water.

The *kozhambu* safely stowed, the meal will then meander through possibly sambhar and certainly rasam and curds. Running in parallel throughout is America Natesan's motif of odd-numbered side dishes — a *kootu*, a *pachidi* (a sort of raita, but made with vegetables), a masal of potato or yam, a *thovattal* of fried vegetables tempered with coconut, and very incongruously,

a cutlet, crumbed and fried on the outside and soft meat or potato on the inside. Just in case you'd run out of choice by the time curd rice rolled around, there are pickles — the classic South Indian mango pickle, as well as the more unique, incredibly salty pork pickle. To make sure that guests don't go hungry for the next couple of years, wedding lunches will also include a side platter, or *varkanam*, of mixed rices — lemon, coconut, sweetened milk, sugar- and quick-fried fritters called *bajjis*.

Where dessert could possibly go after that is a mystery. But go it does. It could be *paal paniyaram* or *carrot halwa* or the sticky-sweet *akkara vadisal*. To be honest, I wouldn't actually know. After tasting America Natesan's *badam halwa* on the first day, I insisted on repeating that for every meal thereafter. On our final encounter, I looked at her, glistening with ghee and sparkling with saffron. She looked at me. I have never been good with farewells, and on this occasion, it would diminish my masculinity in no way to admit that I had tears in my eyes.

TIP *See 'Where to Eat' on page 140 for more places to eat Chettinad food in Chettinad*

Samanth Subramaniam

TAMIL NADU

The Pillaiyarpatti Kovil is commonly believed to be the oldest temple to Ganesha

Right next door is the knighted **Raja of Chettinad's Nattukottai**. Endowed with towering portraits set in a high-ceiling entrance hall, this mansion actually has a lift, the only one in Chettinad. It's a grand, colonial-style family home. There are huge portraits and sepia-tinted photographs on the walls.

♦**Timings** 9.30 am to 4.30 pm, closed when royalty is in residence **Permission** Approach the caretaker

Devakottai

Drive down to Devakottai, 17 km south of Karaikkudi on NH210, the region's second largest town and its commercial centre. It has many *nattukottais*. The **Periya Minor's veedu** (Tamil for house) is extraordinary: sumptuously carved pillars, century-old Italian floor tiles and a Spanish tiled roof.

CHETTIAR TEMPLES

All Chettiars belong to one or other of the nine idyllically-set, largely deserted clan temples, or **Nagara Kovils** (temples of the Nagarathars), at Ilayathangudi, Mathur (opened only during clan celebrations), Vairavan Kovil, Pillaiyar-patti (*see below*), Iranikovil, Nemam, Iluppaikkudi, Soorakkudi and Velangudi. Being devout Shaivites, most of their temples are dedicated to Shiva, Parvati and Ganesha. The Chettiar temples, open to all, are located within a 25-km radius of Karaikkudi, and can be reached easily by taxi.

Karpaga Vinayakar Temple

Carved out of the rock that forms the backdrop to the temple as well, the **Pillaiyarpatti Kovil** (Pillaiyaru = Ganesha, *patti* = village) is commonly believed to be the oldest temple to Ganesha, dating back to the 5th century CE. The main *sannidhi* (altar) is dedicated to Ganesha as Karpaga Vinayakar. The figure of Ganesha with its two arms, right-turning trunk and a plain, unadorned head-dress points to its hoary nature. There are other *sannidhis* in the temple, to Shiva and Shakti. There is something very comforting about being in this ancient, lively, hugely popular temple.

On the monthly Chathurtis (the fourth day after Amavasya and Purnima), the deity is taken out in a procession. The grandest celebration of all is Ganesh Chathurti (Aug-Sep), when thousands of people visit the temple. As Ganesha is the god of auspicious beginnings, both the Tamil (Apr 14) and Gregorian New Year attract huge crowds. The most special form of worship is the **Ganapati Homam** (a notice of 10 days-1 month is required), an elaborate yagna with special incantations for Ganesha.

♦**Location** Pillaiyarpatti is 12 km northwest of Karaikkuddi via Kovilur **Timings** 5.30 am-1 pm, 4.30-8 pm **Temple Tel** 04577-264241

TIP Cameras and cell phones are not allowed inside

SHOPPING

Karaikkudi is a treasure trove for antique hunters. **Antique shops** abound and the range of wares presented, mainly taken from old Chettiar homes, is mind-boggling. Knick-knacks and instruments, pictures and photo-frames, toys and tools from different parts of the world can be found here. Prices are highly variable and bargaining works. **Muneswaran Street** has a sprinkling of antique stores. **Kattu Raja**, on Palaniappa Chettiar Street, is also recommended.

Every Monday a lively open-air *chandai* (market) comes to life next to **The Bangala** (*see alongside*), which also has a craft-shop stocked with lovely buys, though definitely pricey. It stocks some beautiful collectibles in painted wood, fabrics, metal and palm leaf. Look out for **kottans**. This dying leisure craft of Chettiar women has been revived by the **M.Rm.Rm Foundation** (Chennai Tel: 044-24614313). Harvested palm leaves are dried in the summer, cut, hand-dyed in splendid colours and painstakingly woven (a 5-sq inch basket/ box would cost about Rs 50). The **M.Rm.Rm.House** in **Kanadukathan** (*see page 135*) also stocks them. The **Chettinad sari**, in heavy textured cotton using a unique two-ply yarn called *eerily*, and noted for its wide borders, checks and stripes in striking colour combinations of yellow, orange, red and black, can be bought from **RMR** on MM Street, Karaikkudi. Or get these straight from the loom at **Mahalakshmi** nearby, where they are also custom-made.

WHERE TO STAY

In Karaikkudi
The Bangala (Tel: 04565-220221, 250221; Tariff: Rs 3,200), a local corruption of 'bungalow', is a 75-year-old colonial-style heritage home that still maintains the original sprawling garden and tennis courts. The renovated structure has 12 AC rooms with modern bathrooms. This is the best place to stay. The Bangala arranges excellent guided

tours of Karaikkudi and other villages in Chettinad. Groups of around 50 can avail of a day halt and lunch.

In the following hotels, where rooms cost about as much as a meal at The Bangala does, visitors can expect reasonably clean and well-maintained amenities though there is not much to distinguish one from the other: **Hotel Subhalakshmi Palace** (Tel: 235200-06; Tariff: Rs 447-2,700) on Sekkalai Road, **Golden Singar Hotel** (Tel: 235521-23; Tariff: Rs 410-715) on 100 Feet Road, **Hotel Malar** (Tel: 239601-05; Tariff: Rs 425-750) on Madurai Main Road, and **Hotel Udhayam** (Tel: 233142, 234068; Tariff: Rs 199-1,350) in Krishna Arcade.

In Kanadukathan

Eleven of the 126 rooms in the grand **Chettinadu Mansion** (Tel: 273080; Mobile: 09443495598; Tariff: Rs 4,000-6,000), behind the raja's palace, have been renovated to accommodate guests. The ambience is magnificent. They also offer guided tours. Several Tamil movies have been shot at this *nattukottai*.

Kanadukathan also houses **Visalam** (Tel: 273354-57; Website: cghearth.com; Tariff: Rs 4,500), a 72-year-old *nattukottai* restored to its original state, with 15 rooms equipped with all mod cons. The hotel, run by the CGH Earth group, offers traditional Chettinad meals, such as curried raw mangoes, lamb soup, peppery chicken and fried murrel fish.

For more hotels and details, see Chettinad Accommodation Listings on pages 514-515

WHERE TO EAT

If you're staying at a *nattukotai*, you must taste the home recipes of authentic Chettinad cuisine (*see 'Home Fires' on page 136*), made usually on advance notice. This is possible at **The Bangala** (Tel: 04565-220221; Rs 800 per non veg meal for a party of 4 or less, Rs 600 per meal for 6 or more people) and the **Chettinadu**

Traditional bridal necklace

Mansion (Tel: 273080; lunch and dinner Rs 400 per person, breakfast Rs 200). The owners of The Bangala take pride in personally supervising their tables and engaging guests in a unique voyage of culinary discovery.

Street-side restaurants also serve spicy rasams and *varuvals* (fries). The best vegetarian food can be had at **Meenakshi Bhavan** (Tel: 234433, Krishna Arcade, Sekkalai Road), while for non-vegetarians, **Friends** on Church 1st Street, down the road from Hotel Subhalakshmi Palace, offers authentic Chettinad-style food. **Sri Hotel Saravana** (Tel: 232290), next to Golden Singar Hotel on 100 Feet Road, also serves good veg food. Restaurants attached to lodges or budget hotels are usually veg and do a decent job of Chettinad veg dishes. **Subhalakshmi Palace** (Tel: 235200-06) and **Udhayam** have vegetarian restaurants, while **Hotel Malar** (Tel: 239601) has both veg and non-veg restaurants, and a bar.

AROUND KARAIKKUDI

Avudayarkovil (50 km)
To say that the **Athmanathaswamy Temple** is grand would be an understatement — the splendour of its carvings and architecture is a feast for one's eyes. Each pillar of the hall seen as one enters the south-facing temple is richly carved with elegant figures from the Hindu pantheon.

May we suggest a place for your next break

Bullock cart rides, that put the pace of the city to pity

Ask for an authentic Chettinad recipe demonstration

A little pool and fitness center to keep you trim

Getting there:
1½ hours by road from Trichy or Madurai

Chettinadu Mansion
Genetically Chettinad

For enquiries: info@deshadan.com www.chettinadmansion.com Mobile: 098463 44305

S.A.R.M. House, Behind Raja's Palace, Kanadukathan, Sivaganga Dist. Tamil Nadu, South INDIA. Ph: 0091-4565-273080. Mobile : 094434 95598

Dry fish seller at Karaikkudi's colourful weekly chandai

The **Thyagaraja Mandapam** in the open, third prakaram holds many sculptural masterpieces — the most noticeable ones being the sculptures of Kama and Rati and the statue of Manikkavachagar — one of the best-known Nayanmars and, prior to that, prime minister of a Pandyan king. Behind the Thyagaraja Mandapam, and attached to it, is the **Oonjal Mandapam**, also adorned with many sculptures.

To the south of the prakaram is the **Thillai Mandapam**, also rich with sculptures, including ones depicting Manikkavachagar as a minister and then ascetic. Leading off from this mandapam is the second prakaram, which is unused, bat-infested and not usually entered, except by the most adventurous.

In the first and **innermost prakaram**, there are three main sannidhis. The central one to Shiva as Athmanathar has no lingam and only the base, the *avudayar*, is seen. When there is no physical lingam, where then is the question of performing abhishekam? At Avudayarkovil, this is got around in a unique way. The main offering to the deity is rice, greens and bitter gourd cooked together. In front of the sanctum, there is a stone platform, on which piping hot rice and vegetables are spread out. The steam rising from this is the abhishekam for Shiva is seen as the formless Athmanathaswamy! This *neive-dyam* (offering to the gods) is a unique form of worship in Avudayarkovil.

Also within the first prakaram is the shrine to Parvati as Yogambigai, also formless. The depiction of her footprint is pointed out by the officiating priest. To the east of this *sannidhi*, and directly behind Athmanathar's sanctum is a canopy with a striking sculpture of a tree wrought in stone. At its base is a small sculpture of Manikkavachagar receiving the words of Shiva.

♦**Timings** 6.30 am-9 pm

From Karaikkudi, drive north along NH210 towards Trichy and at Kottaiyun, turn right towards Aranthangi via Puduvayal, then south to Avudayarkovil. ■

Here, the past and the present
come together, to form a world of peace.

Long, narrow, almost empty streets. On either side of them stand massive, beautifully built homes alive with never-ending stories of a bygone era. A bullock cart laden with hay ambles by. Vendors sit in corners, vegetables spread colourfully on the ground. A tailor works on his ancient sewing machine. A cow strolls along languidly. The modern world seems far, far away... This is Chettinad, a land frozen in time. And tucked away in its heart is a home that opens up a new world of experiences of the land. Welcome home to Visalam.

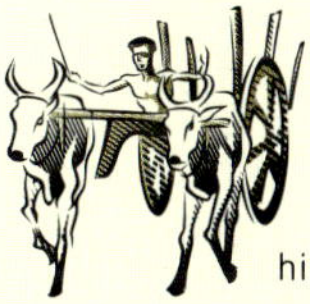

Visalam
a cgh earth experience

Central Reservations: Casino Building Cochin Kerala India Phone: +91-484-3011711 Fax: 2668001
Email: contact@cghearth.com www.cghearth.com

PRASHANT PANJIAR

The tram service to the Murugan Temple, for those daunted by the 659 steps

PALANI

GNANATIRTHAM — PILGRIMAGE FOR KNOWLEDGE

State Tamil Nadu
Location Part of the Western Ghats, en route to Kodaikanal from Madurai, Palani — abode of Subrahmanya — is located 618 ft above sea level in Dindigul District
Distance 479 km SW of Chennai **JOURNEY TIME By rail** 7 hrs + $1\frac{1}{2}$ hrs by road **By air** 1 hr + 3 hrs by road
Route NH45 to Dindigul via Tindivanam, Viluppuram, Ulundurpettai, Veppur, Trichy, Manapparai and Vadamadurai; NH209 to Palani via Oddanchatram (see *route guide on page 12*)

■ BY DEEPA KANDASWAMY

Shanmugha, Karthikeya, Skanda, Guhan, Kumara, Saravana, Dhandayuthapani, Sachidananda, Velan, Arumugam, Subrahmanya — these are among the several names of Subrahmanya, the younger son of Shiva and Parvati. Subrahmanya, which in Tamil means one with eternal beauty, youth and charm, is a deeply adored deity in southern India, and there isn't a Shaivite temple in the South without a separate *sannidhi* dedicated to Subrahmanya. The Tamil people have claimed him for their own, and the six sacred hill homes (*see 'Aarupadai Veedu' on page 148*) dedicated to him are all located in Tamil Nadu. As we drive up to Palani, the lush green hills cool the atmosphere and begin one's spiritual renewal even before one arrives. The hills are the best place to unwind and rejuvenate the body, mind and soul. It appears that Lord Subrahmanya agrees.

LEGENDS AND MYTHOLOGY

Palani or Pazhani traces its name to Pazhamnee, which in turn came from *pazham* (fruit) and *nee* (you). Legend has it that the divine Sage Narada, who was visiting Shiva and Parvati, did not wish to meet them empty-handed, even though they were all-powerful. Therefore, he took with him a pomegranate (considered the fruit of wisdom) given to him by Brahma. Finding Shiva and Parvati along with their two young children, Vinayaka and Subrahmanya, he was in a quandary as to which child to give it to, so handed the fruit to Lord Shiva himself. Since both Vinayaka and Subrahmanya wanted it, Shiva told them he would give it to the son who finished going around the world first. While Subrahmanya climbed on his peacock and literally undertook the task of circling the world at great speed, Vinayaka circumambulated his parents once saying they were the world anyway. Vinayaka got the pomegranate. When Subrahmanya returned to find the fruit had been given to Vinayaka, he was terribly upset, and left for Thiruavinankudi, now located at the foothills of Palani. Parvati consoled her son by saying, *gnana pazham nee* (you are the fruit of wisdom), so why do you require a wisdom fruit? Palani resonates with her words every time the name is uttered.

In another legend, when Rishi Agastya performed penance at Kailash, Shiva and Parvati appeared on two separate hills, the Sivagiri and Shaktigiri, and allowed Agastya to take it to Podhigai, a hillock in ancient Pandyanadu, his abode in the South. Agastya bade his disciple Idumban to bring the hills. Idumban carried them with ease, by slinging them over his shoulders like a *kavadi*, now the terms of reference for a stick decorated with an arch and slung with pots of offerings. Idumban paused to rest at Thiruavinankudi but he could not lift the hills once he had placed them down. A small child, the frustrated Subrahmanya, who was angry as he had lost the contest, was standing on Sivagiri. When Idumban asked the child to move, the boy refused saying it was his father's home. Furious, Idumban fought with the child, and was killed. Realising the child was Lord Subrahmanya, Idumban's wife Idumbi prayed to him, and Subrahmanya resurrected the slain Idumban, who asked for forgiveness and made two wishes, both of which were granted. The first wish was that whoever carried a *kavadi* resembling the two hills he had carried, would be blessed. Secondly, he was to remain the chief sentinel for all those who wished to see the lord. Shaktigiri later came to be known as Idumban Hill while Sivagiri, where Subrahmanya stood, came to be called the Palani Hill. Even today, thousands of devout pilgrims undertake an annual pilgrimage, many hoisting the wooden *kavadi*, walking barefoot for days from villages as far as Chettinad and beyond, an arduous journey sustained only with food and drink given by generous villagers who wait for them along the way, to reach Palani on the auspicious Thyy Poosam (end-Jan).

→ FAST FACTS

When to go Any time of the year. Nov-Feb are the most pleasant
Tourist offices
- TTDC ⓘ
Opp Winch Temple, West Giri Station Palani. Tel: 241156
- TTDC ⓘⓑ
No. 2, Wallajah Road, Chennai
Tel: 044-25367850-54
Website: tamilnadutourism.org
STD code 04545

TAMIL NADU

ARCHITECTURE AND ANTIQUITY

The Dhandayuthapani Swamy Temple located atop the Sivagiri Hill was built by King Cheraman Perumal in the 9th century CE, and expanded over the centuries by the Nayaks, Pandiyas, Kongu Cholas, and the kings of Mysore and Vijayanagar. The sanctum, however, dates back over 5,000 years to the time of Siddhar Bhogar, who crafted the idol here. It is a beautiful temple with elaborately carved pillars, stone mandapams and paintings. The altar has a golden vimanam, an unusual pyramidal structure topped with an octagonal cupola atop which is a gold flagpost. No one knows the antiquity of the Thiruavinankudi Temple at the foot of the hill, except that it predates the Dhandayuthapani Temple. It is probably one of the earliest shrines to Subrahmanya.

ORIENTATION

The **Thiruavinankudi Temple** is located at the foot of the **Palani Hill**, on top of which is the **Dhandayuthapani Temple**. The main entrance is on the eastern side. All vehicles are allowed up to this point. It is customary to visit the Thiruavinankudi Temple first before heading for the Dhandayuthapani Temple. Autos and taxis are available from the **bus stand** and hotels up to the Thiruavinankudi Temple.

The hill temple can be accessed in four ways — climbing the **693 steps** carved out of rock, the **elephant path** where pilgrims climb a paved path as opposed to steps, the **rope car** (which takes 2-2½ mins to reach the top), and the **winch** (which takes about 8 mins). The rope car is not only a short ride but convenient for the elderly, for pregnant women, those with disabilities, the sick, and children. The climb uphill can be tough during summer. The **rope car station** (Timings: 7 am-12.30 pm, 1.30-5 pm; fee: Rs 15 each way) is situated near the **taxi stand** at the foothill, and the **winch station** (5 am-9 pm; fee: Rs 10 each way) is exactly opposite. The ropeway carries only four people to a car and makes for a comfortable ride, unlike the winch, which accommodates more people on a longer, jerky ride.

◆**Vehicle entry toll fee** Rs 20

→ GETTING THERE

Air Nearest airport: Coimbatore (105 km/ 3 hrs), connected to Chennai by 10 daily flights by Paramount Airlines, Indian, Air Deccan, Jet Airways and Kingfisher Airlines. Taxi costs approx Rs 2,800 to Palani

Rail Nearest railhead: Dindigul Junction (57 km/ 1½ hrs) **Best option TO** Pandian Express (dep: Chennai Egmore 9.30 pm; arr: Dindigul Junction 4.30 am). A taxi from Dindigul to Palani costs Rs 1,000 **Best option FROM** Nellai Express (dep: Dindigul Junction 10.20 pm; arr: Tambaram 5.19 am, Mambalam 5.34 am, Chennai Egmore 6.10 am)

TIP Kanyakumari Express has almost matching timings for the return journey

Car The long 12-hr drive to Palani from Chennai cannot be attempted for a weekend trip. For a longer vacation, follow NH45 past Chengalpattu, Tindivanam, Viluppuram, Ulundurpettai, Trichy, Manapparai and Dindigul. Turn right on NH209 to Palani via Oddanchatram. The last 27 km from Oddanchatram is a ghat drive

Bus Two TNSETC Buses (Rs 270) leave at 8 pm for Palani from Chennai's Metropolitan Bus Terminus (Tel: 044-24794705) at Koyambedu. Private services leave at 8 pm (Rs 330). Both arrive at Palani 10 hours later in the early morning. The roads are well maintained, which makes the journey pleasant

Campers take an early morning stroll in the misty forests of the Palani Hills

THINGS TO SEE AND DO

One can be in and out of this town in a day but at least two days are definitely recommended to imbibe the spiritual experience of being in Palani.

Thiruavinankudi Temple

This is the third Aarupadai Veedu (*see Aarupadai Veedu on page 148*) of Subrahmanya. The presiding deity is Velayutha Swamy. It is a beautiful rock temple with a remarkable main altar — probably the only one that has the sacred idol of Lord Subrahmanya as a child perched on the peacock with his *vel* (sacred spear). Here, the *vel* is studded with diamonds. Subrahmanya is said to being holding court here, resolving disputes of deities and devotees alike. The temple has three prakarams — two inside and one outside, around the Palani Hill, which is common to both this temple and the one atop the hill. It has a magnificent six-tiered rajagopuram with colourful stucco sculptures and a large temple tank. There are small altars to other deities and paintings, which were added later on. An interesting spot in the temple is the small altar just outside the sanctum with stone sculptures that explain how the Thiruavinankudi Temple got its name (*Thiru* = Lakshmi, *Aa* = Kamadenu, *Inan* = Surya, *Ku* = Bhoomadevi, *Di* = Agni meditated here). Devotees perform *girivalam* (circumambulation of the hill), considered to be the third prakaram, before heading for the Dhandayuthapani Temple.

The *utsavar* deity is taken around in *girivalam* during the Krithigai asterism each month between 7 and 7.30 pm.

There is a bathing ghat in the Shanmuga River (3 km west of Palani Town), said to have purifying powers. People throng here on eclipses and new moon days; rites for deceased ancestors are also performed in a particular area. *Kavadi* bearers have a bath here before marching to the temple. Buses ply between the town and the ghat.

There are five information offices run by the temple management (which is

Aarupadai Veedu: Six abodes of Subrahmanya

Aaru means six and *padai veedu* refers to the place where soldiers camp during war (*padai* = army; *veedu* = home). Why are the six significant temples of Subrahmanya called this? One reason is that Sangam poet Nakkerar wrote of these six sthalas as the primary temples of Subrahmanya in an epic called *Thirumurugatrupadai*. He begins with Thiruparamkundram (*see page 157*), and lists the other five in this order: Thiruchendur, Palani, Swamimalai (*see page 76*), Thiruthani and Pazhamudhircholai (*see page 164*). It is said that the six temples also refer to the six faces (meaning dimensions or *gunas*) of Subrahmanya. But why call a temple a *padai veedu*? It arises from the belief that every human being is at constant war with the evil forces within him and Subrahmanya leads the forces of good against them. His temples are the places where we rest from the unceasing war within ourselves.

All the six Aarupadai Veedu sthalas are built on top of hills, said to be Subrahmanya's favourite landscape. It is said that there are specific benefits to praying at each of these sthalas. If you pray to him in Thiruparamkundram, where he married Indra's daughter, Devasena, he gives you wealth; at Thiruchendur, where he destroyed the asura Soora-

padman, he gives you courage; at Palani where, annoyed with his parents, he became a child sanyasi, it is *punya* or good karma; at Swamimalai, where he became his father's guru, it is enlightenment; at Thiruthani, where he rested after the war with Soorapadman, it is the arrival of auspicious things in your life; and at Pazhamudhircholai, where he married Valli, he gives without qualification whatever is worth having in this life.

Janaki Venkatraman

common to all temples listed here). They are located in the following places: Giri Street, Winch Station (Tel: 04545-224229), the bus stand, railway station and temple office. All these offices are open 8 am-8 pm all days of the week. For further enquiries, contact Joint Commissioner/ Executive Officer, Arulmigu Dhandayuthapani Swami Devasthanam Office, Adivaram, Palani-624601; Tel: 242236; Fax: 241417; Email: lord muruga@eth.net; Website: palani.org
♦**Location** At the foot of the Palani Hill
Timings 7.30 am-8.30 pm
TIP Special darshan ticket Rs 150; festival days ticket Rs 300

Dhandayuthapani Swamy Temple
The idol here is the only one of its kind known to mankind. It has been shaped from *navabhashanam*, an amalgam of nine minerals, the secret behind the combination of which is no longer known. Its composition has healing properties. Sage Bhogar is credited with crafting and installing it here over 5,000 years ago. The *vigraham* (idol) is also unique for it is a standing Subrahmanya with a clean-shaven head, dressed in a loincloth like a sanyasi, bearing a staff and not the *vel*, the lord's sacred spear.

In the south-west corner of the first prakaram is the samadhi of Sage Bhogar.

There is a small altar where the walls are painted with a pictorial depiction of how Sage Bhogar came to live here and how he made the idol of Dhandayuthapani. An underground tunnel connects this shrine to the main sanctum. This temple has three prakarams, with two atop the hill. While the outer prakaram takes you around the whole temple, the inner prakaram is smaller. The third prakaram is at the bottom of the hill, which is 2.4 km, in keeping with the circumference of the hill.

There are several smaller altars and the side near the shrines to Shiva and Parvati, opposite the **Vaathiya Mandapam** (meant for performing arts), is said to be the peak of the hill. There are both male and female *dwarapalikas*, magnificently carved in stone. Lord Dhandayuthapani dazzles in different *alankarams*, dressed as a sanyasi, hunter, child, astrologer, raja, and in fragrant white flowers like the jasmine, during the six different pujas of the day. As we rested and absorbed the experience, we took in a panoramic view of Palani from the hilltop before heading down.

The main events on the festival calendar of the two temples are **Krithigai** (Nov-Dec), **Thyy Poosam** (Jan-Feb), **Panguni Uthiram** (Mar-Apr), **Agni Nakshatiram** in Vaikasi (May-Jun) and the six-day **Skanda Shasti** celebrations in the month of Aipasi (Oct-Nov), which is the only time the *utsavar* deity of Dhandayutha Swamy descends from the hill to re-enact the destruction of four asuras in the four corners of the *giri veethi* (path around the hill), culminating in the *soorasamharam* (slaying of the demon Surapadman).

TIP Special entrance tickets Rs 10, Rs 20 (festival time); watch out for the monkeys when you are in queue to enter the main sanctum

♦**Location** On Palani Hill **Timings** 6 am-8 pm; 4 am-midnight on festive occasions; the temple remains closed for four days every two years when renovation and painting is done (usually in late Sep or early Oct) **Temple Tel** 04545-242236

Saravana Poigai
Traditionally, devotees bathe here before entering the temple. There are separate bathing areas for men and women.
♦**Location** 100m north-east of the Thiruavinankudi Temple

Periyayudayar Temple
On the eastern banks of the **Shanmugha River**, a gentle, unpolluted breeze and birdsong serenade this ancient temple in the mornings and evenings. Shiva is seen as Brihadeesvara, or Periyayudayar (he who is great) in the form of a *swayambhu* lingam. Only male gods are found in this temple; among them is a

Choose from our network of over 4000 hotels in India.
Serviced apartments, budget hotels, luxury resorts, palaces, business accommodations, houseboats and more.

1-800-22-4878
022-4030-4878
www.travelguru.com

India's Largest Hotel Network

stately image of Dakshinamurti, a rare sculpture that features Shiva in the Rudra tandava pose.
◆**Location** 5 km west of foothill of Palani Hill **Timings** Same as Palani temples

Periya Nayaki Amman Temple
The presiding goddess is the guardian deity of Palani. It is believed that the idol was shifted here from the Periyayudayar Temple when it was attacked. The rajagopuram was built by the Vijayanagar kings but remains incomplete for unknown reasons.
◆**Location** 2 km west of Palani Hill

WHERE TO STAY AND EAT

There are no upmarket hotels in Palani, and the accommodation that is available is arrayed around the hill itself, not far from the temple. All accommodation costs are double during the festival seasons. The **Dhandayuthapani Nilayam** (Tel: 04545-242325; Tariff: Rs 200-1,000) is maintained by the temple management itself, and is located at the foothill. The rooms and loos are clean. **Hotel Tamil Nadu** (Tel: 241156; Tariff: Rs 275-495), located on the main Giri Street near the Winch Station, offers AC and non-AC rooms. The linen is fresh but the loos are not well maintained. **Hotel Subam** (Tel: 242672, 241410; Tariff: Rs 175-1,200), located to the north of Giri Street, at the foothill, has well-maintained AC and non-AC rooms and loos. Some of the larger rooms can accommodate four people.

For meals there really isn't much choice but basic South Indian food can be found at **Hotel Annapoorna** on North Giri Street. **Hotel Tamil Nadu** offers South Indian meals though the ambience leaves a lot to be desired. There are eateries near the bus stand and station but they don't look too inviting.

A couple of wilderness resorts in the surrounding hills offer the best accommodation. **Elephant Valley** (Tel: 230399, 655751; Tariff: Rs 2,300-3,850) is a stylish eco lodge and organic farm with cottages set across a 100-acre nature reserve. Treks, nature walks and horse rides are at hand for exploring the hills around. It's great for elephant spotting. To get there from Palani, drive towards Perumal Malai and 2 km before you reach, take a right to Ganesh Puram. Elephant Valley is located at the end of this road.

The road leading to **Bison Wells Lodge** (Tel: 04542-240566; Tariff: Rs: 650-1,450), 30 km from Palani towards Kodaikanal, takes you through some very scenic countryside. The lodge is very compact and you are totally removed from all creature comforts. There is an English-speaking cook who dishes out delicious Indian, Chinese and Western meals, cooked on a wood fire, and makes sure that you are well fed throughout your stay.

For more hotels and details, see Palani Accommodation Listings on page 529 ■
Inputs by Sathya Narayan

Posters of gods and leaders on sale

PRASHANT PANJIAR

Bullfight at the famous Jallikattu festival of Alanganallur

V MUTHURAMAN

MADURAI

MEENAKSHI ON MY MIND

State Tamil Nadu
Location A gently sloping land 330 ft above sea level that lies on either side of the mostly dry Vaigai River, Madurai, in central Tamil Nadu and the second largest city in the state, is centred around the Meenakshi Temple
Distance 461 km SW of Chennai JOURNEY TIME *By rail* $8^1/_2$ hrs *By air* 1 hr *By road* $8^1/_2$ hrs
Route NH45 to Trichy via Vandalur, Chengalpattu, Tindivanam, Vikravandi, Viluppuram, Ulundurpettai, Veppur and Srirangam; NH45B to Madurai via Viralimalai, Tovarankurichchi, Kottampatti and Melur (*see route guide on page 12*)

CHENNAI WEEKEND BREAKS | 151

TAMIL NADU

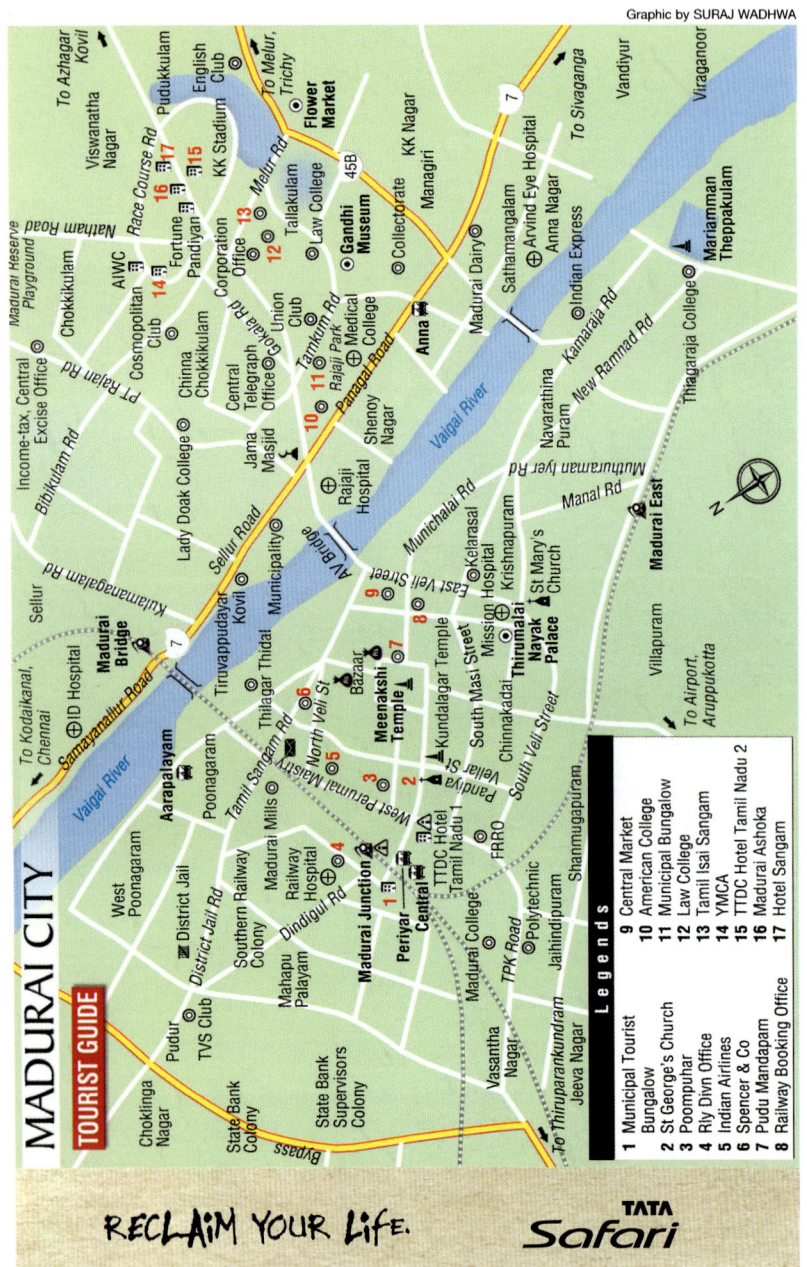

MADURAI

■ BY LALITHA SRIDHAR AND DEEPA KANDASWAMY

Even though Madurai displays all the qualities of a historical Indian city — messy traffic, ugly 'development' and a perpetual tug of war between the old and the new — you will not be thinking about any of that as you stand in a queue, unmindful of humming ventilators and oppressive heat, to catch a glimpse of Meenakshi. Instead, you will find it difficult not to be moved by your tryst with the timeless. Is Madurai Meenakshi or is Meenakshi Madurai? The answer to both questions is yes. One thing every visitor must do is to stand in the shadow of the almost 160-foot tall gopuram of the temple to Meenakshi and lose all sense of time. Then, it isn't hard to understand why Lord Shiva chose this place to perform his 64 *Thiruvilaiyadals* (divine games, often mischievous, that the lord played on gods and mortals), why Goddess Meenakshi chose to marry him here or why their son Subrahmanya also chose Madurai as the venue for his wedding. Sheltered in the cool shadows of this awesome tribute to a primordial divinity, it's even easier to remember why Meenakshi will always remain on your mind, not only while in Madurai but long after you have left her legendary city. There, in the colourful figures of a thousand gods, you'll find concept, structure, measure and aesthetic — as well as the most illogical urge to abandon reason. Imagine stonework not muted by age nor defiled by grease. Imagine ideals as lofty as towering granite. There you have it. Standing in a queue can be a productive exercise!

LEGENDS AND MYTHOLOGY

Initially, this area was forest. According to one legend, having committed a sin, Indra, the king of the devas, wandered the three worlds till he came upon a *swayambhu* lingam under a *kadamba*

Paying salutations to the Sun

TAMIL NADU

(*Anthocephalus cadamba*, commonly known as Indian oak) tree and worshipped it. His sins forgiven, he built a temple to Shiva, covering the deity with a vimanam he brought from the heavens. Eons later, a merchant passing by found this shrine in the forest. He informed King Kulasekara Pandyan, who in turn built a city around the temple and shifted his capital here. A delighted Shiva dropped *madhur* or nectar all over it and from then on the Pandya stronghold came to be called 'Madhurapuri', which over time came to be known as Madurai.

Kulasekara Pandyan's heir, Malayadwaja Pandyan and his queen, Kanchanamala, were childless and thus unhappy. At the sacrificial altar of their intense prayers, a girl-child appeared miraculously. Alas, she was not the son they desired and worse, she had three breasts. They named her Taatakai. She grew up to be a beautiful maiden with eyes like a fish (*meen* translates as fish and *aksham* as eyes, therefore, Meenakshi). She was a warrior of unparalleled valour too. Meenakshi conquered many lands till, one day, she reached Mount Kailash. Here she met Lord Shiva and lo, her third breast disappeared. The god of gods promised to wed her at Madurai as Sundareshwarar (the Shiva of Beauty). Vishnu gave the bride away in a celestial wedding like none other. Meenakshi and Sundareshwarar (also called Sundara Pandyan) ruled Madurai for many happy years. Here too was born their son, Subrahmanya. They stayed on as presiding deities and still watch over the city.

Madurai is also the splendid setting of the great Sangam epic, *Silapaddikaram*.

ORIENTATION

The **Meenakshi Amman Temple** is central to Madurai's topography and mindscape. Its majestic gopurams are visible from afar in spite of the clutter of urban construction that has overtaken the city. Virtually all the main streets in Madurai run roughly parallel to the walls of the great temple. Since most hotels are located around it, the temple is usually at a walkable distance from the hotel itself. The largely dry **Vaigai River**, which looks beautiful after good rains, flows diagonally across Madurai (north-west to south-east), cleaving it into two halves. The **railway station** is 2 km west of the Meenakshi Temple. There are several bus stands in Madurai. Enquire at your hotel to find out which one you should go to for a particular onward journey. Autos are the best way to get around. For the important temples around Madurai, hiring a vehicle would be ideal though buses are available too.

THINGS TO SEE AND DO

Every second address in Madurai is a hotel and every second person a visitor, or so it seems. It is possible to be in and out of Madurai in two days but three days are definitely better. The Meenakshi

→ FAST FACTS

When to go October-March. Catch the festivities of Pongal in January.
Summers (May-Jun) are exceedingly hot
Tourist offices
- Dept of Tourism, Govt of TN ⓘ
1, West Veli Street, Madurai
Tel: 0452-2334757
- TTDC Tourist Info Counter ⓘ
Madurai Railway Station; Tel: 2342888
- TTDC ⓘⓑ
No. 2, Wallajah Road, Chennai
Tel: 044-25367850-54
Fax: 25361385; Email: ttdc@vsnl.com
Website: tamilnadutourism.org
STD code 0452

The Thousand Pillar Hall and Museum in the Meenakshi Amman Temple

Temple alone needs repeated visits for there is too much to see at one go.

Meenakshi Amman Temple

Give yourself a good 3 hrs at the very least to appreciate this temple and its surrounding structures, rightly rated as among the best in South India. On any given day, you will be one among the expected 20,000 visitors who come here.

The divine family — Sundareshwarar, Meenakshi, Vinayakar and Subrahmanya (Murugan) — smile down from the 13th century rajagopuram as we enter via an entrance to the left. Ahead is the **Ashta Shakti Mandapam**, the entrance to which is flanked by two altars with gigantic sculptures of Vallabha Ganapati and Subrahmanya. On the walls are paintings and sculptures depicting scenes from the *Thiruvilaiyadal*. If you notice closely, there is even a picture of Mahatma Gandhi worshipping the goddess! It was probably added after he came here in 1946. Further ahead is the **Meenakshi Naickan Mandapam**, which has six rows of richly sculpted pillars and many flower shops.

We made our way to the Thousand Pillar Hall, towards the **Servaikar Mandapam**. On its left is the **Thirukalyana Mandapam** (the divine wedding hall). Then we come to the **Mangayarkarasi Mandapam**. This is a relatively new mandapam. It contains many statues, including those of former rulers.

At the entrance to the **Thousand Pillar Hall and Museum** is a statue of the temple's architect, Ariyanatha Mudaliar, seated upon a horse. Ask the person who checks tickets at the entrance to play tunes on the **musical pillar** as you need a rod to do this.

♦**Thousand Pillar Hall and Museum entry fee** Adults Rs 5, children Rs 3, **Cameras** Still Rs 25, video Rs 250 **Timings** 7.30 am-5.30 pm

We then cross the splendid, 7-tiered **Chithirai Gopuram** to enter the **Mudali Pillai Mandapam**. It has pictures from the Puranas on the walls and beautiful sculptures of Mohini (Vishnu in the form of a beautiful woman), Bikshandar (Shiva in the form of a beggar), and a monolithic statue of Kadanthai Mudaliar, who built this mandapam and many more.

TAMIL NADU

GAJANANA VAZE/ SOUTHINDIAPICTURE

Next we come in view of the **Pottramarai Kulam** (the golden lotus tank). Surrounded by spacious corridors on all four sides, with paintings depicting scenes from the *Thiruvilaiyadal* and various Puranas, this small tank has a giant lotus crafted in gold. There are pillars in the north corridor that have figures of the local merchant who discovered this shrine, of Kulasekara Pandyan, who built the city, and poets of the golden period in the famous Sangam Age of Tamil literature. To the west of the temple tank is the **Oonjal** (swing) **Mandapam**, the ceiling of which has paintings of the six abodes (Aarupadai Veedu) of Subrahmanya. Adjacent to this is the **Kilikoondu** (*kili* = parrot, *koondu* = cage) **Mandapam**, named so because parrots used to be kept in cages here. This is one of the grandest mandapams in the temple.

Finally we enter the **shrine of Goddess Meenakshi**. At the entrance is a three-tiered gopuram. There are several altars to other deities within this shrine. The *palli arai*, the celestial bedroom of Goddess Meenakshi and Lord Sundareshwarar, is here. We worship the goddess, who is standing gracefully, resplendent and radiant, the very image of beauty and mercy.

We now make our way to **Sundareshwarar's Sannidhi** (altar). The stunning 8-foot tall image of **Mukkuruni Vinayakar** in its outer prakaram left us entranced. It's unbelievable that this huge idol was accidentally discovered while digging for the temple tank during the Thirumalai Nayak reign. As we stand in line to worship the main deity in the sanctum of Lord Sundareshwarar, to our right is the **silver sannidhi of Nataraja** who is 8 ft tall. A bookshelf in this *sannidhi* contains the *Naanmarai* (the four Vedas).

As we leave, we pass the **Kambathadi Mandapam**, another fabulous structure

Blessings from a temple elephant

TAMIL NADU

with sculptures of Shiva and Vishnu in their different manifestations. Also here is a **massive pillar** that depicts the **divine wedding** of Meenakshi and Sundareshwarar.

Our hearts and minds are full. It is a strange mix of having seen a lot and, at the same time, not having seen enough. There is one prayer in our hearts as we leave: that we should come again.

◆**Location** 2 km east from railway station **Special entrance tickets** Indians Rs 15, foreigners Rs 50 **Timings** 6 am-12.30 pm, 4-9.30 pm **Puja timings** Meenakshi Amman Sannidhi: 6 am, 12.30 pm, 4 pm and 9.30 pm; Sundareshwarar Sannidhi: 6 am, 12.30 pm, 4 pm and 9.30 pm **Temple Tel** 0452-2344360

TIP Non-Hindus not allowed into the main sanctums. All pujas last 40 mins

Festivals at the Meenakshi Temple

Chithirai Thiruvizha, a 12-day festivity in April-May, celebrates the coronation of Meenakshi and her marriage to Shiva and concludes with a magnificent temple car procession. The **Vaikasi Utsavam** is a 10-day celebration in the months of May-June. Darshan during the **Oonjal** (swing) **Festival**, another 10-day celebration in the months of June-July, is considered especially auspicious as the *utsavar* idols of both Meenakshi and Sundareshwarar are placed on the golden swing and the divine couple are seen together. Some say they were seen thus as they held court when they reigned over Madurai. The **Aavani Moolam Festival** (Aug-Sep) is an 18-day celebration, which includes the coronation ceremony of Sundareshwarar and features the re-enactment of the *Thiruvilaiyadal*. The **Kollata Vizha** (Oct-Nov) is another unique seven-day celebration, which includes a procession of the goddess on all days and that of the divine couple on the seventh day. The **Theppotsavam** (Jan-Feb) begins with a procession of the deities and culminates in a **float festival** of all the major deities at the Mariamman Theppakulam (*see page 158*).

Thiruparamkundram

This town on the outskirts of Madurai is famous for its shrine to Subrahmanya and Paramagirinathar (Shiva) and is one of the most sacred temples in Tamil Nadu. Dedicated to Muruga, it's visited by thousands throughout the year. Here Subrahmanya is married to Devasenai, daughter of Indra.

The **temple** is at the foot of a sheer rock face. Panels depicting Shiva's dance of bliss, accompanied by a celestial orchestra and an admiring audience are seen outside the sanctum, in magnificent works of art dating back to the Pandya period. The *abhishekam* (ceremonial bath) is offered only to the silver spear held by the presiding deity. Nestled against the hill is the **Saravanapoigai Tank**, lined

HOTEL KA GURU RECOMMENDS IN
MADURAI

Choose from our network of over 4000 hotels in India. Serviced apartments, budget hotels, luxury resorts, palaces, business accomodations, houseboats and more.

Hotel	Rating
Madurai Residency	Budget
Hotel Germanus	3 ★
Hotel Sangam	3 ★

MTNL/BSNL Toll Free No.
1–800–22–4878
022-4030-4878
www.travelguru.com

travel**guru**™
India's Largest Hotel Network

The person featured above is an actual Travelguru employee

TAMIL NADU

→ GETTING THERE

Air Madurai Airport (Tel: 0452-2690433; 10 km from city centre), connected by 10 flights daily to Chennai, by Paramount Airways, Indian, Air Deccan, Kingfisher Airlines and Jet Airways
Rail Madurai Junction **Best option TO** Pandian Express (dep: Chennai Egmore 9.30 pm, Tambaram 9.55 pm; arr: Madurai Junction 6.15 am) **Best option FROM** Pandian Express (dep: Madurai Junction 8.45 pm; arr: Tambaram 4.54 am, Mambalam 5.14 am; Chennai Egmore 5.45 am)
TIP Nellai Express departing Chennai Egmore at 9.30 pm, arriving Madurai at 5.20 am is an equally good option; trains stop for only one minute at suburban stations in Chennai
Car It's a smooth drive down NH45 past Tindivanam, Viluppuram, Veppur and Turaimangalam towards Trichy. After Padalur, 16 km ahead of Turaimangalam, keep a watch out for the NH45 Bypass, which gets you past Srirangam and Trichy in a jiffy. It begins soon after the tiny Pichandar Kovil Temple on your left hand side. The Bypass joins NH45B just south of Trichy Junction, and continues on to Madurai via Viralimalai and Melur
Bus Or go for the AC air-cushioned or sleeper coaches (Rs 350 approx) that run every 15 mins in the night from Chennai's Metropolitan Bus Terminus (Tel: 044-24794705) at Koyambedu. Many private operators ply video and sleeper coaches from Chennai to Madurai. Good operators are Praveen Travels (Chennai Tel: 044-28193538, Madurai Tel: 0452-2336820; Rs 360-500) and KPN Travels (Chennai Tel: 044-24791525, Madurai Tel: 0452-2331941)

with beautiful steps. For the annual Meenakshi Kalyanam Chittirai Thiruvizha, the entire city of Madurai serenades the journey of Muruga, from Thirupparamkunram to Madurai.
♦**Timings** 5.30 am-1 pm, 4 am-8.30 pm Related info **Special darshan ticket** Rs 10 **Temple Tel** 0452-2482248

More to see

The **Thirumalai Nayak Palace** ($1^1/_2$ km south-east of Meenakshi Temple; open 9 am-5 pm on all days; entry fee Rs 10) is a beautiful structure with a massive courtyard surrounded by corridors lined with sculpted pillars that rise 40 ft high, the venue of an enjoyable **Sound and Light Show** (English 7.15 pm, Tamil 8.15 pm; Rs 10; Tel: 0452-2338992). There is also an interesting **museum** inside.

The **Mariamman Theppakulam** (5 km south-east of Meenakshi Temple) is a huge tank built by Thirumalai Nayak in 1636. At the centre of the tank is a small temple to Mariamman, a manifestation of Shakti. Float festivals of the Meenakshi Temple, Azhagar Kovil and Thiruparamkundram Temple are held together here, in a tradition introduced by Thirumalai Nayak. Almost a perfect square measuring 1,000 ft on the north and south, and 950 ft on the east and west, the reservoir is the largest construction of its kind in South India. It is a pleasant place in which to spend some time.

Visit the **Gandhi Museum**, 5 km east of Meenakshi Temple, across the bridge over the Vaigai River, housed in the 300-year-old palace of Rani Mangammal, which has many interesting displays, including the cloth that the Mahatma was wearing when he was shot (the stains of blood are to be seen).
♦**Museum camera fee** Rs 50 **Timings** 6 am-1 pm, 2-6 pm **Tel** 2531060

SHOPPING

Madurai is famous for its brightly coloured, tie-and-dyed cotton Sungudi

Cosmopolitan elegance & comfort

Sangam Hotels

Alagarkoil Road,
Madurai- 625 002, India
Phone: 91 452-2537531,
Fax: 91 452-2537530

For central reservations:
Sangam Hotels, Collector's Office Road, Trichy- 620 001, India
Phone: 91 431-2414 700, Fax: 91 431-246 418
E mail: hotelsangam@vsnl.com; reservation@hotelsangam.com
Website : www.hotelsangam.com

TAMIL NADU

NAMIT ARORA/ PHOTOINDIA

Temple priests catch up on the news on West Chithirai Street

saris. But the collections at the locally popular **Ranee Sarees** and **Alankar Textiles** (both at South Masi Street) are definitely inadequate when compared to the grand range available in Chennai. Browse through the shops on West and North Chithirai streets around Meenakshi Temple and in Town Hall Road, near College House Restaurant. You'll find souvenirs of decorated elephants made of wood and Sungudi (tie and dye) saris.

Tamil Nadu State Handlooms Emporium, on West Chithirai Street, is a good place to shop for saris and cloth material. Again, the Chennai branch is miles ahead. At the temple curio shops, look out for earthen golu dolls — papier mache or painted earthen idols of Hindu gods and goddesses. The workmanship of an artist identified as SG (look for initials behind the idol) is noteworthy. Check out the **Temple Boutique Shop** on North Chithirai Street or **Subiksham**, on West Chithirai Street for antiques, handicrafts, jewellery, Sungudi saris, sculptures and woodwork panels.

Don't miss the huge Madurai **flower market**. It's a bustling hub of activity from 4-11 am. If you are willing to brave the slush, parked trucks, chaos and gusty trading, you will discover virtual hills of the famous Madurai *malli* (jasmine).

WHERE TO STAY

There are so many hotels in Madurai that hoardings welcome visitors to the 'Temple City of Hotels'! The **Taj Garden Retreat** (Tel: 0452-2371601-10; Tariff: Rs 3,700-5,800), on TPK Road, is 4 km away from the Meenakshi Temple and has a panoramic view of both the temple and the city. It also offers a swimming pool, tennis court, gym and Ayurvedic massage. The ITC Welcomgroup's **Fortune Pandiyan Hotel** (Tel: 2537090; Tariff: Rs 2,500-7,500), near the Race Course Road, is where Jayalalithaa and Karunanidhi stay when they come to Madurai. **Hotel Germanos** (Tel: 2382001, 4356999; Tariff: Rs 2,000-4,500; they offer 24 hrs checkout) and **Hotel Sangam** (Tel: 2537531-37; Tariff: Rs 2,400-6,500) are both among the upmarket options, somewhat away from the city centre.

 HOTEL GERMANUS
 MEENAKSHI TEMPLE
 TWIN ROOM
 KING LEISURE ROOM
 ROOF TOP RESTAURANT
 HEALTH CLUB
 UTSAV - RESTAURANT
 COFFEE SHOP

Hotel Germanus
Madurai

Arasaradi, Madurai-10. Tamilnadu. India.
Tel: 0452- 4356999, Fax: 91-452-4356969.
Website: www.hotelgermanus.com,
Email: germanus@eth.net

TAMIL NADU

Arrays of alluring bangles for sale on North Chithirai Street, near the temple

All hotels that follow offer both AC and non-AC deluxe rooms and have well-maintained facilities. **Hotel North Gate** (Tel: 2523030, 4383030; Tariff: Rs 650-1,600) is 3 km east of Meenakshi Temple, opposite American College. West Perumal Maistry Street, where virtually every building appears to be a hotel, is also conveniently close to the railway station and walking distance from the temple. Among the many options here are **Hotel Supreme** (Tel: 2343151-53; Tariff: Rs 560-1,950) and **Hotel Chentoor** (Tel: 2350490, 3042222; Tariff: Rs 605-1,100). This is the only city with two of Tamil Nadu Tourism's Hotel Tamil Nadus. The first **Hotel Tamil Nadu** (Tel: 2337471; Tariff: Rs 250-850) is close to the temple on West Veli Street; they have a family room with six beds too. The other **Hotel Tamil Nadu** (Tel: 2537461; Tariff: Rs 325-1,250), which is 10 km away from the city centre and Meenakshi Temple, is on Azhagar Kovil Road.

For more hotels and details, see Madurai Accommodation Listings on pages 519-520

WHERE TO EAT

Madurai offers a variety of eateries for all budgets. **Madurai Residency** (Tel: 2343140) on West Marret Street has a nice variety of South Indian dishes for breakfast; the rava khichdi, vadas and chutneys are fabulous. For tasty onion rava dosais, puris, North Indian food and dessert items, **Meenakshi Bhavan** (Tel: 2342456) on Town Hall Road is a good option. Head for their AC Hall for a better ambience. **Murugan Idli Kadai** at the Melamaasi Veedhi serves good idlis. They also serve no less than four varieties of ultra-spicy chutney accompaniments. **College House Annai Meenakshi**, on TPK Road, has the friendliest, quickest service. The filter coffee here and at **KPS** on TPK Road must be tried. **Arya Bhavan** (Tel: 2340577) on Melamaasi Veedhi is also very popular: it has two joints, which operate 'By Day' and 'By Night', the latter open the night through.

At **Sriram Mess**, near the Madurai Theosophical Society, you get decent, home-style Tamilian *yelai sappadu* (rice

SOMETIMES THE ONLY ELBOW ROOM THAT WILL DO IS A 1,00,000 FEET IN EVERY DIRECTION.

The Tata Safari Dicor comes to you with the best in class torque of 300 Nm & 115 PS and is designed to conquer just about any terrain thrown at it. Test drive one today, start reclaiming your life.

THE TATA SAFARI

Direct Injection Common Rail Engine

MAKE YOUR OWN ROAD

DUAL AIR BAGS | ABS AND EBD | LEATHER UPHOLSTERY | REVERSE GUIDE SYSTEM | DVD/MP3 SYSTEM WITH DUAL LCD SCREENS

TATA MOTORS Model shown is the Tata Safari Dicor VX version. Features may vary across variants. Visit us at www.safaridicor.com

For assistance call 18-00-225552 (MTNL/BSNL) toll free, or 022-66601050. Regional Office: West: 022-66561600, East: 033-22262784, North: 0124-2805141, South: 080-66620500.

TAMIL NADU

Mounds of lotus buds and fresh Madurai malli at the busy flower market

meal served on banana leaf). There are some **Gujarati Bhojanalayas** too and the one near the west gopuram of Meenakshi Temple is recommended. The Surya rooftop restaurant at **Supreme Hotel** (Tel: 2343151), West Perumal Maistry Street, offers a genuinely splendid view of the Meenakshi Temple towers; enjoy it after dark when the gopurams are lit up and seem to glow from a distance. They also have a bar. **Mahal Hotel** is very famous for its non-veg biryanis. The South Indian thali meals at **Hotel Tamil Nadu** (Tel: 2537461-66), on Azhagar Kovil Road, come with very tasty *vathal kozhambu*, rasam and enormous appalams.

Don't miss the many **Pazhamu-dircholai** fruit juice shops at every second junction: they serve the most delicious fresh juices and milkshakes. Some of their exotic variations include tulsi and red banana.

AROUND MADURAI

Alanganallur (15 km)
The fabled and ferocious *jallikattu* bullfights are held during Pongal in the villages around Madurai. The one in Alanganallur is the most popular.

TIP *See page 471 to read all about the jallikattu at Alanganallur*

Pazhamudircholai (21 km NE)
According to legend, the wise saint-poetess Avvai was travelling to Madurai when she stopped to rest under a tree here. A small boy asked the elderly Avvai if she would like to eat some fruit. When Avvai said yes, he climbed up the *naaval* (black mountain plum) tree and then asked her if she wanted a hot fruit or a cold fruit. Amused by what she considered a silly question, she replied she wanted a cold fruit. The boy proceeded to shake the branches of the tree so that only the ripe fruit fell on the ground. Avvai picked a fruit and blew on it to remove the sand stuck to the fruit. It was at this time that the boy asked, "Grandma, are you blowing on the fruit because it is hot? I thought you didn't want a hot fruit!" Staggered by the truth in the boy's words and realising that his question had been not silly at all, she felt humbled. She told the boy that despite

HOTEL Supreme

Your Home away from Home

Address

110, West Perumal Maistry Street,
Madurai - 625 001,
Tamil Nadu (INDIA).

Phone : +91 452 2343151 (3 lines), 3012222
Fax : +91 452 2342637
Website : www.supremehotels.com
E-Mail : hsupreme@airtelbroadband.in
hotelsupreme@gmail.com

Welcome to Hotel Supreme

As Madurai is famous for Shree Meenakshi Amman Temple, so is Hotel Supreme for its unique hospitality and unlimited services!

Hotel Supreme was established in 1988 and is a pioneer in the Hotel industry in Madurai for it's unique establishments and services. It has the very First Roof Top Restaurant, the only hi-tech Spaceship Bar in the City and offers facilities a tourist or a businessman would expect during his stay, all under one Roof!

As you walk out from the Railway Station.... look up! You can see our Roof Top Restaurant. Our Hotel is just a 5 minutes walk from the Railway Station and only 12 kms. from the Airport. It is situated in a thriving commercial zone and is just 2 kms. away from the great Meenakshi Temple. It's reputed to be the best in south Indian Hospitality, Vegetarian food of International class and most polite services, which make Supreme a traveller's cradle.

Our hotel offers spacious and well-appointed accommodations, beautiful campus setting, a full service restaurant and lounge, and all the amenities you would expect from a premier hotel.

Facilities

- Room service
- Laundry
- Travel desk
- Hi-Tech Bar (Apollo '96)
- Money changer
- Ample car parking space
- Doctor on call
- A/C Restaurant
- Roof Top Restaurant
- Free safety lockers
- Satellite TV
- All major credit cards accepted
- Banquet Halls
- Business center with Internet / Fax / Telephone / Photocopiers

TAMIL NADU

Many flavours of a banana leaf meal

being called wise by many scholars from various kingdoms, she still had a lot to learn. It was then the small boy transformed himself into Subrahmanya.

This is how Pazhamudircholai (*pazham* = fruit, *udir* = shake, *cholai* = garden) or the garden where the lord shook the fruits, got its name. It is a symbolic reference to re-examine one's premise before concluding something is right or wrong. This simple temple has a three-tiered gopuram at the top of which are gold *kalasas* (pots). In the main altar, Subrahmanya stands with both his consorts, Valli and Devasenai. A short climb from the temple is a stone platform, the **Pandavar Padukkai** where the Pandavas are believed to have rested while here. The trail up is rather steep.

♦**Location** On Azhagar Kovil Road
Timings 6 am-8 pm

Azhagar Kovil (21 km NE)

In the scenic foothills of the Azhagar Malai or Cholai Malai is this important temple to Vishnu, reached after a pleasant drive (toll ticket Rs 50) to a lush, forested hill on which, locals say, bisons can be spotted at night. A steep climb of 120 steps to the top leads to the **Rakayi Amman Temple**. Inside this temple, at the centre, is the **Noopurangangai**, a sacred fountain of water whose source is unknown.

The architecture of the Azhagar Kovil, which has four gopurams and three prakarams, is unique. Two forts with a total spread of 100 acres surround the temple, which is located at the centre. The outer fort was built in the 16th century, while the inner fort is believed to be over 2,000 years old and is said to have been under the control of Queen Ulubi who later married Arjuna, the Pandava archer. A reference to this fort and temple is made in the Mahabharata. Ulubi belonged to the serpent community of Nagas who lived here. There are several serpent statues in the hill above the temple.

Among the many amazing sculptures that are found in this temple are the fearsome *yazhis* in the Ariyan Mandapam, past the flagstaff. The main idol of Vishnu as Azhagar is beautiful. The shrine to his consort, Sundarvalli Thayar, is in the first prakaram. There are steps here to climb down and touch the floor of the inner sanctum. It is believed that if the devotee puts both his hands on the floor and prays, his wish will come true. If visiting Madurai in summer, do take in the 10-day **Chithirai Pournami Festival** (Apr-May) at Azhagar Kovil, when the deity is taken in a procession on the fourth day for a bath in the Vaigai, by the banks of which he stays for five days before returning.

♦**Timings** 6 am-12.30 pm, 4-7.30 pm **Special darshan ticket** Rs 10 **Temple Tel** 0452-2470228 (6 am-12.30 pm, 4-7.30 pm, Saturdays closed

TIP Non-Hindus are not allowed inside the main *sannidhi* ■

In the lap of Nature

The Kurumba Village Resort is a rare aromatic arena; far from spicing with mere words, we have established the self-sufficing cottages amidst a SPICE haven where nutmeg, cloves and pepper abound.

INHOUSE ACTIVITIES — Swimming Pool | Table Tennis | Pool Table | Badminton | Board Games | Library | Carrom Board

OUTDOOR ACTIVITIES — Golf | Trekking | Water Park | Tea Estate Tour | Boating | Visit to Ooty | Visit to Coonoor

Kurumba Village Resort
Nilgiris

Ooty Mettupalayam Road, Hill Grove Post, Kurumbadi, Nilgiris, Tamil Nadu.
Ph: +91 9443998886, +91 423 2004850/1/2
E-mail: nilgiris@kurumbavillageresort.com
website: www.kurumbavillageresort.com

TAMIL NADU

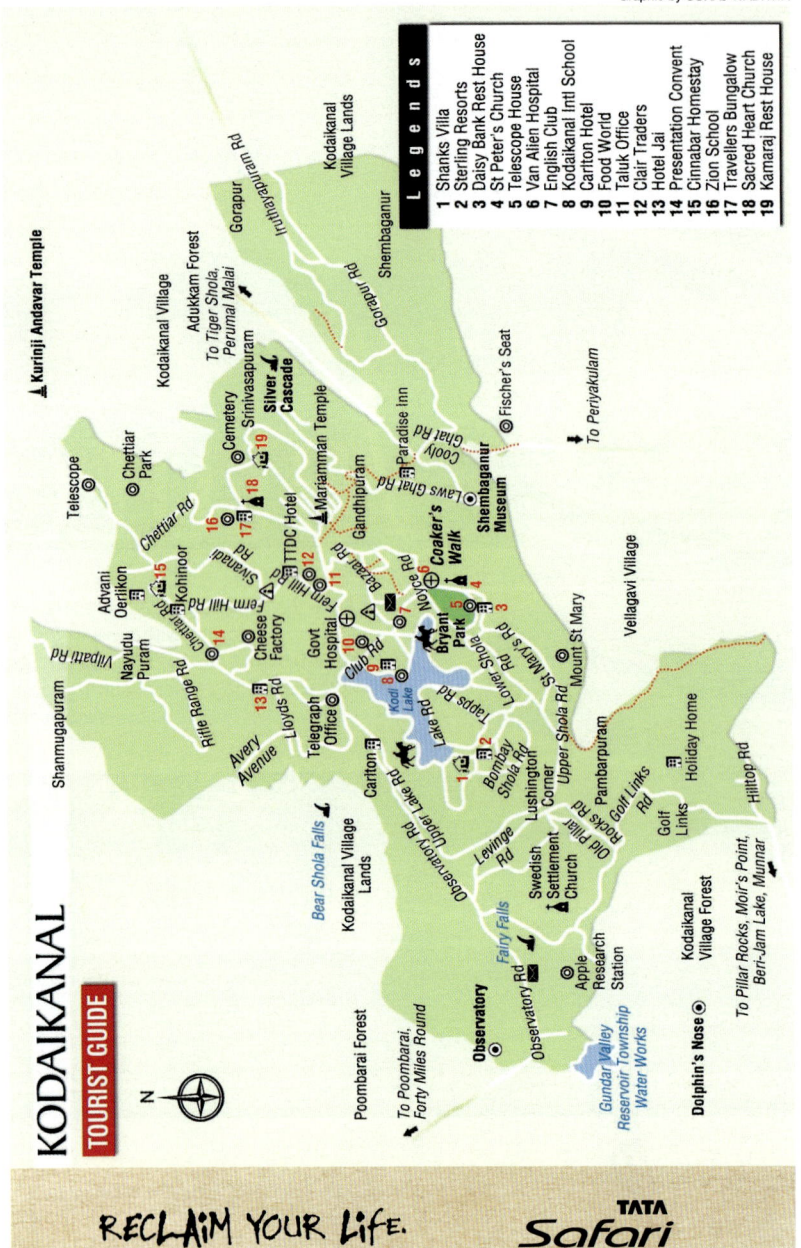

168 | CHENNAI WEEKEND BREAKS

Photographs by PRASHANT PANJIAR

Evening mist descends on Kodi Lake

KODAIKANAL

MISTY MOUNTAIN HOP

State Tamil Nadu
Location On the southern ridge of the Palani Hills in the Western Ghats, 6,854 ft above sea level, bordering Kerala on the west
Distance 521 km SW of Chennai JOURNEY TIME **By rail** 7$\frac{1}{2}$ hrs + 2$\frac{1}{2}$ hrs by road **By air** 1 hr + 3$\frac{1}{2}$ hrs by road
Route NH45 to Vattalakundu via Chengalpattu, Tindivanam, Viluppuram, Ulundurpettai, Veppur, Trichy, Manapparai, Vadamadurai, Dindigul and Sembatti; ghat road to Kodaikanal via Pannikadu (*see route guide on page 12*)

■ BY ROHINI MOHAN
WITH ANURAG MALLICK

On the winding drive from Koda Road Station to Kodi at around 5 am, I try not to make a list of things to do. A list means structure, which means asking someone for directions, and that means going where everyone's been and is still hanging around. Instead, I talk to the driver. "So many tourists spoiling your town, no?" By the end of the 3-hr drive, I'm armed with ideas and a determination that will keep me away from anything that has an attached shopping street. Or a bellboy.

I decide to have a Kodaikanal holiday that isn't ditto my dad's of 25 years ago. Since then, I hear, honeymooners and rowdy boy gangs have taken over. But surely there must be more to Kodi than a repetitive line of rocks giving different views of blinding white mist. Surely it isn't already explored out.

TAMIL NADU

A stroll down Coaker's Walk affords views of the Pambar River and Madurai city

Most of the tourist entertainment in town is centred around the starfish-shaped lake, which forms Kodi's nucleus. Honeymooners take the customary boat-ride, kids scream for horse-rides and parents negotiate with taxi drivers for a day-trip of Kodi's 16-Sights Tour. The town is a small maze of churches, hotels, restaurants, touts and home-made signs advertising home-made chocolates. But look beyond the façade and you'll find another dimension to Kodi.

Look behind the rocks the guide's pointing at; demand to turn left when he turns right; look at the little cottages hidden by the mammoth holiday home. It takes a gritty kind of tourist to outfox the local travel guide. But when you manage, you'll find a door into Kodi that is only for special guests.

But first, promise you won't stone the monkeys. Or etch your eternal love or turbulent lust for someone on a tree.

All right; now we're ready.

THINGS TO SEE AND DO

If it wasn't for the oppressive heat of Madurai, Kodaikanal might have remained an undiscovered gem. Set up as a sanatorium in 1845 by the American Madura Mission, Kodi holds the unique distinction of being the only hill station in India to be established by Americans.

It's ideal if you have your own vehicle, otherwise a taxi or hired bicycles are good options to explore Kodi. Walking unfolds the beauty of Kodi at a more leisurely pace. To a birdwatcher, the region offers many species including endemics like the Kodi White-bellied Shortwing. Trekkers have an option of 17 routes of varying lengths and levels of difficulty, as outlined in a pamphlet called *Sholas For Survival*, available at the District Forest Office (Tel: 04542-240287).

The nature trail

First tick off the regular sights. No sightseeing tour of Kodi can commence without the customary amble down **Coaker's Walk** (entry fee Rs 5), a hill-edged boulevard on the steep southeastern mountainside. Equipped with an **observatory**, the 1-km walk offers panoramic views of Dolphin's Nose, the Pambar River, and of Madurai city.

Bryant Park is a botanical garden set up by a British forest officer. The road meanders past **Green Valley View** (romanticised as Suicide Point because of its sheer drop) and winds 7 km to Kodi's most popular attraction, **Pillar Rocks** — a 400-foot high vertical column of three rocks. Guna Caves is the local name for **Devil's Kitchen**, a deep bat-infested chamber between the three rocks. It was dubbed Guna Caves after it was turned into a romantic kidnapper's lair for a Tamil movie. Loud teenagers stand outside the fencing around the cave, screaming angstful "Abiramiiiii!"s (name of kidnapped in said movie). Inside Devil's Kitchen, the air's muggy, the walls smooth, with little shelves that look perfect for a perch. My guide chucks a pebble that's instantly swallowed by the darkness. We hear the plonk only after about 10 seconds, and a crash of wings flapping. This is the kind of place that teaches you the importance of firm footing.

The road forks at Devil's Kitchen, with a left taking you to the nearby villages of Poombarai, Mannavunar and Kavunji, while a right forms a radial circuit, depositing you back in Kodi near the lake. About 1½ km from the lake are the **Bear Shola Falls**, a watering hole for bears where you are more likely to find excited tourists looking for bears. While **Bambar**, **Glen** and **Fairy Falls** are lesser attractions, Kodi's most popular waterfall is **Silver Cascade**. Situated 7 km outside town, the falls were formed by the backwaters of Kodi Lake.

→ FAST FACTS

When to go All year round, except for late monsoon in November-December
Tourist offices
● Tamil Nadu Tourism ❶ ⓑ
Rest House Complex, near Bus Stand Kodaikanal. Tel: 04542-241338-40
● TTDC ❶ ⓑ
No. 2, Wallajah Road, Chennai
Tel: 044-25367850-54
Website: tamilnadutourism.org
STD code 04542

Joey's forest trek

Joey's house is in the forest, 45-min drive from Kodi. For Rs 250 (includes superb veg lunch cooked with ingredients from his wild farm), he'll take you trekking through the jungle — you'll walk where elephant or bison have. Call Cinnabar (Mobile: 09842145220; *see 'Where to Stay on page 174*) to book your trek.

Getting high

Three kilometres from Kodi Lake is the **Kurinji Andavar Temple**, dedicated to Murugan. Every 12 years, the purple-blue Kurinji flowers carpet the slopes

HOTEL KA GURU RECOMMENDS IN **KODAIKANAL**

Choose from our network of over 4000 hotels in India. Serviced apartments, budget hotels, luxury resorts, palaces, business accomodations, houseboats and more.

Hotel	Rating
Hill Top Tower	Budget
Kodai Resort	3 ★
Kodai International	4 ★

MTNL/BSNL Toll Free No.
1-800-22-4878
022-4030-4878
www.travelguru.com

India's Largest Hotel Network

The person featured above is an actual Travelguru employee

here, which offers spectacular views of Palani Hills, the plains and **Vaigai Dam**.

Another vantage point is **Perumal Peak**, 12 km from Kodi, and the highest peak in the Kodi Hills at 7,874 ft.

Lakeside attractions

The Kodi Lake has been a centre of activity from the time it was dammed in 1867. A walk around the lake (6 km) takes about an hour and a half. The flat road that runs around the lake is an ideal cycling track. Boats, available in perverse single/ double, pedal/ row/ shikara and half-hourly/ hourly combinations can be hired at nominal rates from the **Kodaikanal Boat and Rowing Club** (Tel: 241315), as well as from the Tourist Department. **Pony rides** vary from Rs 50 for a half round of the lake to Rs 100 for a full round. Hire a bicycle and ride the 6-km circumference.

♦**Tickets** Shikaras Rs 10 for 30 mins, other boats Rs 100

Higher learning

The **Shembaganur Museum**, 6 km away, is maintained by the Sacred Heart College, a theological seminary. It was founded in 1895 and houses stuffed birds, rare butterflies, a 300-strong orchid collection, and relics and artefacts of the Paliyan tribes who once lived in these hills.

Take your kids to the **Astrophysical Observatory** (Tel: 240587-89, 240640-44) which stands on the highest point in the area and houses a small **museum** and one of the world's oldest extant telescopes, open to visitors everyday, but only in season.

→ GETTING THERE

Air Nearest airport: Madurai (122 km/ 3½ hrs), connected by 10 flights daily to Chennai, by Paramount Airways, Indian, Air Deccan, Kingfisher Airlines and Jet Airways. Taxi to Kodaikanal costs Rs 1,600

Rail Nearest railhead: Kodaikanal Road (80 km/ 2 hrs) **Best option TO** Pandian Express (dep: Chennai Egmore 9.30 pm, Tambaram 9.55 pm; arr: Kodaikanal Road 5.06 am). Taxi to Kodi costs Rs 1,200. You can also get buses at Rs 30 a ticket **Best option FROM** Pandian Express (dep: Kodaikanal Road 9.25 pm; arr: Tambaram 4.54 am, Mambalam 5.14 am, Chennai Egmore 5.45 am)

Car The long 12-hr drive to Kodi from Chennai is best not attempted for a weekend trip. For a longer vacation, follow NH45 past Tindivanam, Viluppuram, Ulundurpettai, Trichy, Manapparai, Dindigul and Sembatti to Vattalakundu. Shortly after, the ascent to Kodi begins, via Pannikadu. The Silver Cascade Waterfall heralds your arrival to the outskirts of Kodi

Bus Two TNSETC Buses (Rs 325) leave at 6 pm for Kodaikanal from Chennai's Metropolitan Bus Terminus (Tel: 044-24794705) at Koyambedu. Two private services leave at 8 pm. Both arrive at Kodi 12 hours later in the early morning

SHOPPING

The Australian Blue Gum in the Kodi region accounts for much of the eucalyptus oil found on Kodi's streets. Do drop by at **Cottage Crafts** (Tel: 04542-242102) on Hospital Road, run by Corsock (Co-ordinating Council for Social Concerns in Kodi). A **Tibetan Market**, situated on the steep decline from Seven Roads Junction near the Petrol Bunk, offers bargains. The **Potter's Shed** (Tel: 243968) has a shop near the Seven Roads junction. Go spin the wheel at their workshop at Rs 10 per head to spin the wheel, or Rs 160 for donation. The **Art Gallery** (Tel: 246360) is spot on

J'S HERITAGE
Kodaikanal
Hotel & Resort

THE PRINCESS OF HILLS, with its enchanting beauty in the misty mountains is the home of J's Heritage. The group has been in the hospitality industry for over 3 generations. J's Heritage specializes in value for money package tours to various destinations in South India.

Good tours at honest prices.

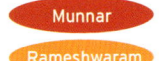

...and more

J's heritage tours of South India.
Corporate getaways, student tours and family picnics.

Visit us at : www.jsheritage.com

J's Heritage Hotel, P.T.Road, Near Seven Road Junction, Kodaikanal, Tamilnadu-624101
J's Heritage Resort, Chettiar Park Road, Kodaikanal, Tamilnadu-624101
Ph: 04542-241323. M: 9443340693. Fax - 04542 - 243730
Banglore no:- 9844049596, 9243102343. Chennai no:- 9841016741
mdu_jaherit@sancharnet.in | jaherit@md5.vsnl.net.in

for penniless idlers. A dramatic lotus theme quilt hangs on one of the walls. Variously sized canvases fill the two small rooms. Adam Khan, Cristina, J Nath, Richard Pike. Not very local-sounding, but the creator of every piece has a home in Kodi, and each work of art is a sketch of the everyday life of the town. You can get contact numbers of artists from here and visit them at their studios. A great place to start is at J Nath's (Tel: 240923) or Adam Khan's (Tel: 240019).

Spend a morning at **Jaysh Quilts** (Tel: 240921, 09894246401) learning quilting for Rs 300 from Jayshree, the architect of the lotus motif quilt in The Art Gallery. You could also buy some of the handmade quilts, priced at around Rs 12,000 (full size). In a house next to hers, five women carefully sew the intricately designed quilts. They came to Jayshree from broken homes, and now they've together built their lives around the income and warmth the quilts bring.

WHERE TO STAY

After a steady stream of visitors for over a century, Kodi has a wide range of accommodation options catering to diverse profiles and tastes. Prices rise abnormally during the main tourist season (May-June) and it's a good idea to book your room beforehand.

Carlton Hotel (Tel: 04542-240056; Tariff: Rs 6,500) is on the lake, and has great views. The bungalow-style **Hotel Valley View Inn** is behind the bus stand, on Post Office Road (Tel: 240181, Tariff: Rs 1,590). Or try **Cinnabar** (Tel: 240220, 09842145220; Tariff: Rs 2,500), a bed-and-breakfast run by a delightful family and happily a good distance from the overcrowded Kodi Lake area. It has two great rooms, and mostly European food, all home-grown on their organic farm.

Equipped with the best view in town, the stone-house **Greenlands Youth Hostel** (Tel: 240899; Tariff: Rs 800-1,600) off Coaker's Walk faces the valley, is comparatively cheap and extremely quiet. **Green Acres** (Tel: 242384; Tariff: Rs 1,350-4,990) near the lake has a spacious garden. **Hill Country Holiday Resorts** (Tel: 240953; Tariff: Rs 2,500-3,900), with 57 cottages on Pallangi Road, boasts a home theatre and plenty of games to keep kids busy. Other good options include **Lily's Valley** (Tel: 240558; Tariff: Rs 1,125-2,250), with 20 cottages on Sivanandi Road, the massive **Sterling Resorts** (Tel: 242380; Tariff: Rs 2,100-3,000) with 104 rooms on Gymkhana Road and **Summer Migrations** (Tel: 241943; Tariff: Rs 2,500-4,500) in Lourdupuram. A good budget option is **Roseflower Resort** (Tel: 244954; Tariff: Rs 1,500), right opposite the TTDC office.

For more hotels and details, see Kodaikanal Accommodation Listings on pages 517-519

The protected Berijam Lake

SANJIV VALSAN

HOTEL DE L' ORIENT, PUDUCHERRY. 18th CENTURY

ENTER THE ROMANCE OF THE LAST SIX CENTURIES:

No one, (but Neemrana), offers you the Rennaissance of historic lifestyles lived out in India. Try out 16th century Portugese, 17th century Danish, 18th century French and 19th century British styles. Now, essentially all integrated into our eclectic Indian potpourri! So choose your century as you choose your south- Indian destination.

LE COLONIAL, KOCHI. 16th CENTURY

BUNGALOW on the BEACH, THRANGAMBADI. 17th CENTURY

WALLWOOD GARDEN, COONOOR. 19th CENTURY

GARDEN HILLS ESTATE, COORG. 19th CENTURY

VILLA POTTIPATI, BANGALURU. 19th CENTURY

In north-India, Neemrana can take you even further – back to the 14th and 15th centuries. Where the architecture of the Delhi Sultans, the Rajputs, Mughals, the British and the Marwari also awaits you for a very memorable holiday, conference or wedding experience

Try any of the 12 Neemrana Hotels. Six of them are within a weekend's jump from Chennai

NEEMRANA non-hotel **HOTELS**

A-58, Nizamuddin East
New Delhi -110013 INDIA
Tel:91-11-24356145, 41825001 Fax: 91-11-2435 1112

In Mumbai
Tel 91-22-24322495 Fax 91-22-24313936
Email:neemranahotelsmumbai@gmail.com

click: www.neemranahotels.com , email: sales@neemranahotels.com

TAMIL NADU

WHERE TO EAT

Kodi offers excellent dining in a motley bunch of eateries, most of them located on Hospital Road. The busy market area near the bus stand is littered with cheap shops selling an assortment of *bhajjis*, *parottas* and South Indian staple. For a more elaborate spread, try the lavish evening buffet at **The Carlton**.

A first-floor establishment on Hospital Road, **Tibetan Brothers** (Tel: 04542-244638) is one honest joint in an overpriced town. You can stuff yourself silly with cheap westernised Tibetan food amid portraits of Potala Palace, Dalai Lama and thangkas. Their momos, thukpas and Amdo fuyong are excellent.

The popular **Silver Inn** is a great place to hang out, sip tea and watch the flow of tourists go by. They offer fresh-baked pizza and a wide array of Continental non-veg fare.

Hotel Punjab is easily the best value-for-money place in town for butter chicken, naan and tandoori dishes.

Kodi's streetside eats: Roasted corn and spicy chilli bhajjis (below)

Eco-Nut stocks health food and home-made goodies. It is just the place to shop if you don't want to stir from your cottage. You can pick up ready-to-eat stuff like fresh brown bread, whole wheat bread, cheese, muffins, jams, peanut butter and a variety of chocolates. Eco-Nut also stocks brown rice, red rice, pure honey, herbal tea and organic dried fruits.

Grab a muffin and a hot chocolate at **Pastry Corner** near Seven Roads Junction, where you can hobnob with Kodi's old and famous. Prasanna and his sister have run this cosy little bakery for years, dishing out heavenly chikoo and peach ice-cream, pizza and puffs. At **Bharat Bakery** near Presentation Convent, you can see just-perfect ginger biscuits being made. Buy a lot. **Fay's Confectionery** (Tel: 241209) is also legendary for its pastries and cakes.

Almost same quality chocolates will be sold everywhere in the town. Don't leave without sampling some of the sweeter pleasures like strawberries, plums, pears, cherries, butter-fruit, jamuns, apples, peaches and *malai pazham*, a variety of banana only available in Kodaikanal.

AROUND KODAIKANAL

Beri-Jam Lake (23 km)
A beautiful reservoir amid dense forests of acacia and pine, Beri-Jam is a protected area, reached after a scenic trek. The combined pressure of reckless camping in a reserve forest, threat of wildlife and mushroom-pickers has resulted in regulated entry. Only 10 permits are given every day, so get your permit the minute the District Forest Office (Tel: 04542-240287) opens, which is at 10 am. It is well worth the trouble. Leave early as staying overnight at Beri-Jam is prohibited, largely because of the threat from wildlife.

TIP *Read more about the trek to Beri-Jam Lake on page 462*

> God lies in the details,
> waiting to be discovered.

It is this simple belief that inspired us to create experience-holidays centred on strong core values of respect for the environment and the community. Holiday packages that take you beyond the beaches, backwaters, hill stations and historic cities, to capture the quintessence of the land. Packages that celebrate the **simple joys of life**, the sheer luxury of simplicity and the magic that lies in everyday wonders. To offer a string of experiences that are unbelievably pure, unexpected and inspiring.

cgh earth experience holidays

| Coconut Holidays | Beach & Backwater Holidays | Island Holidays |
| Adventure Holidays | Wellness Holidays | Rice & Curry Holidays |

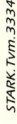

Central Reservations: Casino Building Cochin Kerala India Phone: +91-484-3011711 Fax: 2668001
Email: contact@cghearth.com www.cghearth.com

TAMIL NADU

Leopard rests on a rock; Bonnet macaque has lunch (right)

INDIRA GANDHI WILDLIFE SANCTUARY
ON TOP OF THE WORLD

State Tamil Nadu
Location Indira Gandhi WLS sits astride the Annamalai Hills on the Tamil Nadu-Kerala border, just south of the Palakkad Gap, in Coimbatore District
Distance 597 km SW of Chennai JOURNEY TIME *By rail* 8 hrs + 2 hrs by road *By air* 55 mins + 2 hrs by road
Route NH45 to Ulundurpettai via Tambaram, Chengalpattu, Tindivanam, Vikravandi and Viluppuram; NH68 to Salem via Tiyagai Durgam, Kallakkurichi, Talaivasal, Attur and Valappadi; NH47 to Coimbatore via Bhavani, Perundurai and Avanashi; NH209 to Pollachi; SH19 to Top Slip via Sethumadai (*see route guides on pages 12 and 320*)

■ BY MALVIKA ONIAL

As we walked along a misty trail through the forest, I heard a 'swoosh' and looked up to see a black and white form led on by an arrow of yellow across the tree canopy. It was the magnificent great pied hornbill. With its wide wings spread out, this 3-foot large bird with a yellow bill appeared like a character out of an ancient epic.

The great pied hornbill is just one of the many treasures of the Indira Gandhi WLS, which is home to a number of species such as the tiger, the leopard, the elephant, and the gaur as well as primates that include the bonnet-tailed macaque, the common langur, the Nilgiri langur and the lion-tailed macaque. The last two are on the list of endangered animals, but almost as if on cue to dispel the notion of its vulnerability, a big male Nilgiri langur

INDIRA GANDHI WILDLIFE SANCTUARY

leaped into a tree behind the forest canteen where we had sat down for lunch. A giant squirrel squeaked in a bamboo thicket nearby, seemingly keeping the langur company.

The first morning at Top Slip, I woke up to hear the rambling fluty song of the Malabar whistling thrush. Given to bursts of whistling varied tunes like its cousin the Himalayan or blue whistling thrush, it is sometimes fondly referred to as the 'whistling schoolboy'. However, unlike the Himalayan symphony, the Malabar whistling thrush sounds uncannily like a person whistling and can easily mislead you into thinking you have human company!

Armed with binoculars and raincoats, we set off on our morning trail with Baby, a local nature guide with the Forest Department. Having made my trip right in the middle of the monsoon, I was not expecting too much: neither very good visibility through sheets of rain nor an opportunity to spot all the animals on the sanctuary checklist (except perhaps the leeches!). The incessant rain, however, failed to dampen the spirits of the birds and animals. Racket-tailed drongos announced their presence with good cheer, calling from the treetops and flying across. We also saw the Malabar trogon, the heart-spotted and white-bellied woodpecker, the fairy bluebird, and the other winged wonder that's the southern birdwing, India's largest butterfly.

After the walk, we hopped on to the Forest Department bus that takes tourists on morning and evening rides of the forest. This bus ride gives one a good chance to view the landscape and to sight large mammals such as gaur and elephants. It is also the best opportunity to spot the lion-tailed macaque. These animals are usually found in small groups and are active during the day.

The bus ride also includes a visit to the Forest Department's elephant camp. We arrived just in time to watch the mahouts bring out the elephants' 'evening tea' and joined in to offer them their goodies — huge lumps of flour and jaggery, which the animals eagerly accepted with their probing trunks.

On our way back to the rest house, we were rewarded with a majestic sight. A handsome male gaur with a dark

→ FAST FACTS

When to go Jun-Sep is the best season to spot wildlife. You can see animals again in November and December. The sanctuary is shut from Feb 15-Apr 15

Wildlife/ Forest Dept office
● Wildlife Warden, 176, Meenakalai Salai, Pollachi, Coimbatore-642001
Tel: 04259-225356
● TTDC ❶ ❺
No. 2, Wallajah Road, Chennai
Tel: 044-25367850-54
Website: tamilnadutourism.org
STD code Pollachi 04259

SARAVANA KUMAR/ WILDERFILE

TAMIL NADU

→ GETTING THERE

Air Nearest airport: Coimbatore Airport (76 km/ 2 hrs), connected to Chennai by 10 daily flights. Taxi fare to Indira Gandhi WLS is Rs 800 approx
Rail Nearest railhead: Coimbatore Junction **Best option TO** Nilagiri Express (dep: Chennai Central 9 pm; arr: Coimbatore Junction 5 am. Take a bus to Top Slip from Coimbatore or hire a 4WD and negotiate the price **Best option FROM** Nilagiri Express (dep: Coimbatore 8.55 pm; arr: Chennai Central 5.10 am)
Car A long drive that cannot be attempted over a weekend break. For longer vacations, follow NH45 past Tindivanam and Villupuram to Ulundurpettai. Turn right onto NH68 to Salem via Talaivasal and Attur. Join NH47 till Coimbatore via Bhavani and Avanashi. Turn south along NH209 to Pollachi. The sanctuary gate is 36 km from Pollachi via Sethumadai
Bus Overnight buses leave every 30 mins between 8 pm till early morning for both Coimbatore and Pollachi from Chennai's Metropolitan Bus Terminus (Tel: 044-24794705) at Koyambedu

brown coat and striking white socks stepped out cautiously into a clearing in the forest. The adult male gaur is an imposing creature that can reach up to a height of 7 ft and weigh up to a thousand kilos. But choosing to ignore the busload of eager tourists, it started to nonchalantly graze before disappearing into the forest. Well, another glimpse of this magnificent animal is reason enough to return to the sanctuary.

ABOUT INDIRA GANDHI WLS

The Indira Gandhi Sanctuary lies in the Western Ghats, just south of the Palghat Gap. Previously known as the Annamalai WLS, it spans an area of 958 sq km. The area consists of hilly tracts, its vegetation varying according to change in altitude. As the height increases, grasslands and shola forests replace the rainforests.

Notified as a sanctuary in 1976, it falls in Pollachi, Udumalpet and Valparai taluks in Coimbatore District. About 108 sq km of grasslands was declared as a National Park in 1989, and is known as the Grass Hill National Park. The sanctuary is an important watershed area for Coimbatore and Erode districts. The perennial rivers that originate here feed major reservoirs like Parambikulam, Aliyar, Thirumurthi, Upper Aliyar, Kadambarai, Sholayar and Amaravathy.

With its rich flora and fauna, the sanctuary is considered one of the most promising sites for long term conservation of several rare, endemic and endangered species of animals and plants. It boasts of over 2,000 species of plants, of which about 400 are of medicinal value. The Karian Shola area has been identified as a Medicinal Plant Conservation Area.

The Valparai Plateau, with its tea estates, is in the middle of the sanctuary. Conservationists have expressed worries about the rapid increase in the number of tea plantations; these plantations have destroyed the natural habitat of birds that can survive only in the rainforest.

DR. MS MAYILVAHNAN/ SOUTHINDIAPICTURE

INDIRA GANDHI WILDLIFE SANCTUARY

Rolling vistas near the Kerala border; Elephant safari at Top Slip (left)

ORIENTATION

The Indira Gandhi WLS forms part of a larger conservation area and runs contiguous with the Parambikulam WLS (to its west), and the Eravikulam NP and the Chinnar WLS to its south. **Top Slip**, its main tourist area, is located in the north-west corner. Its name was derived from a practice followed during the time of British rule, when the timber harvested from the forest was slipped down a canal from the hills to the plains below.

The **Ulandi Range** is in the same area as Top Slip, while the **Valparai Tea Estate** is to the south-west of the sanctuary. The **Grass Hill NP** is to the south of the sanctuary. Beyond that is **Amaravathy** (south-east corner of the park). **Aliyar** is to the north-west of the sanctuary. **Forest Rest Houses** are spread across all corners of the park, though a cluster is to be found in the Top Slip area.

Located at an altitude of 2,430 ft, the Top Slip tourism zone is best approached by bus or taxi from **Pollachi**, 40 km south of Coimbatore. Obtain your entry and accommodation permits en route from the Wildlife Warden's office at Pollachi; alternatively, if you are making just a day-trip to Top Slip, get your permit at the **checkpost** at the sanctuary entrance at **Sethumadai**. The 36-km long journey from Pollachi to Top Slip is through a picturesque setting of villages, fields and coconut plantations, which eventually give way to forested hilly tracts.

◆**Sanctuary entry fee** Rs 15 **Cameras** Still Rs 25 per day, video Rs 150 per day **Guide fee** Rs 100 for 3 hrs

THINGS TO SEE AND DO

The sanctuary has a lot to offer visitors. If you are on a 3- to 4-day trip, you can explore the sanctuary on foot, on elephant back or on the tourist bus. It's a good idea to take along binoculars, field guides about plants, mammals and birds, basic medicines, dull-coloured clothing including some warm clothes (it can get quite cold in the morning and night) and a torch. If you are making a trip in the monsoon, be prepared for leeches (carry a little rock salt to wean the leeches off).

The Nilgiri tahr

The Nilgiri tahr (*Hemitragus/ Nilgiritragus hylocrius*), as well as the two other tahr species in the world (Himalayan tahr and Arabian tahr), are members of the Bovidae family of cloven-hoofed mammals that include cattle, goats, sheep and antelope. The Nilgiri tahr is a stocky creature with a short, coarse coat and a bristly mane a few centimetres long. Males are bigger than the females — a fully grown adult male stands about 100 cm at the shoulder and can weigh up to 100 kg. Both sexes have horns curving backwards. In the males, the horns can grow to about 40 cm in length. The adult males have an overall deep brown colour except for their grizzled white lower backs and sides.

The Nilgiri tahr is found only in the Western Ghats in South India, usually at altitudes of over 4,000 ft in the grassy highlands along the crest of the hill range. Believed to have been found over much of

ATUL SHARMA
Too shy for the camera

the Western Ghats, today it is found only in certain areas in the Nilgiri Hills (such as the Eravikulam NP adjoining Indira Gandhi WLS), Annamalai Hills and in some other pockets in Tamil Nadu and Kerala. Tea plantations have destroyed the tahr habitat. Poaching has also contributed to a reduction in their numbers.

Elephant safaris

To explore the sanctuary at a leisurely pace, opt for an elephant safari. You can book your ride at the Tourist Reception Centre at Top Slip. The safari starts from the reception centre twice a day, mornings and afternoons and lasts about 2 hrs. On elephant back, not only do you have a vantage point but some animals such as the otherwise wary sambar may also allow you to approach them closer. There are no elephant rides in the monsoon.

◆**Timings** 10.30 am-1.30 pm, 2.30-4 pm
Safari fee Rs 100 per person

Trekking tours

If you are keen on trekking in the sanctuary, it is compulsory to be accompanied by a guide. They're locals and charge about Rs 100 for a 3-hr long trek. If there are more than four in your group, you will need to hire one more guide. The treks can be booked at the reception centre and can be planned for early mornings or afternoons, between 6 am and 6 pm. The treks are particularly recommended for those interested in getting a glimpse of the sanctuary's wonderful bird life.

◆**Permit fee** Rs 150-300 per person

Don't miss the bus

Bus rides into the sanctuary leave in the mornings and afternoons from the reception centre. The bus fare is Rs 25 per person and the ride lasts for about 2-3 hrs and includes a visit to the Forest Department elephant camp.

◆**Timings** 6.15 am, 11.30 am, 3.15 pm

WHERE TO STAY

There are a number of **Forest Rest Houses** (FRHs) in the sanctuary; some of them have hot water and provision for meals, while others have only basic facilities. For booking any of the FRHs or

INDIRA GANDHI WILDLIFE SANCTUARY

trekking sheds, get in touch with the Wildlife Warden; it's advisable to book accommodation in advance over the phone (*see 'Fast Facts' on page 179*). There is quite a crowd in the weekends.

In Sethumadai
At the entry point of the sanctuary is a **FRH** (Tariff: Rs 250) with only two suites. The caretaker can prepare food; it has attached baths. **The Banyan Tree** (Tel: 04253-244490, Mobile: 09486037669; Tariff: Rs 4,300, inclusive of meals) is a homestay option with four suites. They organise sightseeing and trekking tours.

In Top Slip
FRHs in and around Top Slip include: the **Chital Lodge** (Tariff: Rs 300), which has two suites, the services of a cook and attached baths; **Wood House** (Tariff: Rs 300), with two suites, canteen, attached bath and hot water; **Ambuli Illam** (Tariff: Rs 300), with four suites and a canteen; **Bison Lodge** (Tariff: Rs 250), with four suites and attached bath; and **Hornbill Rest House** (Tariff: Rs 250), with canteen and hot and cold water. Also in Top Slip area is a **dormitory** with 36 beds (Rs 20 per bed). It has a canteen.

Further ahead of Top Slip, in the Manambolly Range, is a **trekking shed** (Tariff: Rs 250) with two rooms, but a permit is needed from the wildlife warden. It's near the Sholayar Power Project. The caretaker can arrange food. There is no electricity at the shed.

For more details, see Indira Gandhi WLS Accommodation Listings on page 516

WHERE TO EAT

If you are staying at any of the FRHs in the Ulandi Range, you can have your meals at the **Top Slip canteen** that's run by the Staff Welfare Association. They offer hot meals at specified times — as it is the only place to eat in Top Slip, book your meal in advance and turn up on time. Simple veg food, consisting of sambhar with rice, rasam, vegetable stew, parathas with korma, dosa and idli-sambhar, is served. You can also buy snacks (biscuits, savoury snacks), cold drinks and bottled water at the canteen. The **Ambuli Illam Rest House** is 2 km away from the reception centre but has its own restaurant, so you don't have to walk it to the Top Slip canteen.

AROUND TOP SLIP

Aliyar Monkey Falls
Over 40 km from Top Slip are the Aliyar Monkey Falls, quite popular with visitors. You can even trek in the Upper Aliyar Region. To get here, one needs to go via Pollachi, from where a taxi will charge you Rs 350. ■

Choose from our network of over 4000 hotels in India. Serviced apartments, budget hotels, luxury resorts, palaces, business accommodations, houseboats and more.

1-800-22-4878
022-4030-4878
www.travelguru.com

India's Largest Hotel Network

The Nilgiris

The colonial era hill stations of the lush Nilgiris, cradled by lakes, downs, plantations and looming blue hills, remain favourite weekend getaways

THE NILGIRIS

Photographs by PRASHANT PANJIAR

The 'take-all-you-can' view from Kodanad

COONOOR
IN THE SHADE OF DODDA BETTA

State Tamil Nadu
Location On a ridge near the highest point in the Nilgiri Range, 17 km short of Ooty
Distance 571 km JOURNEY TIME *By rail* $9^{1}/_{4}$ hrs + 1 hr by road *By air* 55 mins + 2 hrs by road
Route NH45 to Ulundurpettai via Tambaram, Chengalpattu, Tindivanam, Vikravandi and Viluppuram; NH68 to Salem via Tiyagai Durgam, Kallakkurichi, Talaivasal, Attur and Valappadi; NH47 to Avanashi via Perundurai; SH to Mettupalaiyam via Annur; NH67 to Coonoor (*see route guide on pages 12 and 184*)

■ BY SHEILA KUMAR

While just about every hamlet in the Blue Mountains vies for the title of 'Queen of the Nilgiris', mist-wrapped Coonoor in season, when the emerald green of the tea bushes is sharply offset by blood-red poinsettia, purple morning glory and golden sunflowers, is truly a regal sight.

The white man left this hill station years ago but touches of the Raj remain all over Coonoor: in honeysuckle-fronted cottages named 'The Gables' and 'Gorse View', which sit pretty on the side of winding pine-hedged lanes; in areas called Bedford and Elk Hill; in the yew trees that line drives, in the privet hedgerows; and in the headstones of the graveyards where many a Mr Smith, Colonel Hughes and Miss Jones rest in peace.

Ultimately, Coonoor's relaxed pace is its main asset. It's a pace that slowly winds itself around you and before you know it, you are relaxed, too. Tomorrow is another day and can, therefore, wait.

THINGS TO SEE AND DO

Chug along the roads towards the hill tops, find a place to stop and gaze, and all too soon you'll find a soft mist wreathing itself around the hills, the trees and around you. Once you are in Upper Coonoor, take leisurely trips to the nearby tourist gawp-spots. Trek in and around the forests of the Blue Mountains, or sholas as they are known. And, of course, down endless cups of Nilgiris tea.

Sim's Park

Quite the best thing Coonoor has on offer is Sim's Park. It was laid way back in 1874 in a deep ravine, with winding footpaths, pergolas, gazebos, a lily pond, and a dense shola skirting it. Its marvellous trees — a thousand species, including Burma teak, *rudraksh*, mahogany, birch, Spanish cherry, and a lone conifer — were brought in from places as far as Australia, the Canary Islands, Mexico, Patagonia, the Cape of Good Hope, China and Venezuela. Its rose garden is quite something when in season. A Fruit and Vegetable Show is held here annually in May.

Droog Fort

Once used by Tipu Sultan as an outpost, Droog Fort is 15 km from Coonoor. To get there, you have to trudge 4 km through the Nonsuch Tea Estate. Unfortunately, of the fort only a wall has survived. However, located some 6,000 ft above the plains, it offers an awesome view.

More to see

About 8 km from Coonoor, **Lamb's Rock** commands a grand view of the Coimbatore plains. Take along your food and drink and just loll. **Dolphin's Nose** is a

→ FAST FACTS

When to go Coonoor comes into season from April to June and then briefly from September to October. In season, the climate is extremely salubrious and the foliage is out in full glory. Winters are chilly, but beautiful if you can stand the cold. Do remember to carry your woollens

Tourist offices
● Department of Tourism ℹ
Govt of Tamil Nadu, Wenlock Road, Ooty. Tel: 0423-2443977
● TTDC ℹ
No. 2, Wallajah Road, Chennai
Tel: 044-25367850-54
Website: tamilnadutourism.org
STD code 0423

Choose from our network of over 4000 hotels in India. Serviced apartments, budget hotels, luxury resorts, palaces, business accomodations, houseboats and more.

Hotel	Rating
MGM Hillworth Resort	3 ★
Velan Hotel Ritz	3 ★

MTNL/BSNL Toll Free No.
1-800-22-4878
022-4030-4878
www.travelguru.com

India's Largest Hotel Network

The person featured above is an actual Travelguru employee

THE NILGIRIS

→ GETTING THERE

Air Nearest airport: Coimbatore (79 km/ 2 hrs), connected to Chennai by 10 daily flights from Paramount Airlines, Indian, Air Deccan, Jet Airways and Kingfisher Airlines. Taxi to Coonoor costs about Rs 2,000
Rail Nearest railhead: Mettupalaiyam Tel: 2442246 (34 km/ 1 hr) **Best option TO** Nilagiri Express (dep: Chennai Central 9 pm; arr: Mettupalaiyam 6.15 am) Cab to Coonoor costs Rs 1,000 approx **Best option FROM** Nilagiri Express (dep: Mettupalaiyam 7.45 pm; arr: Chennai Central 5.10 am)
TIP Take the Nilgiri Mountain Railway from Mettupalaiyam to Coonoor Station (see page 474)
Car The 571-km drive from Chennai to Coonoor cannot be attempted for a weekend break, especially with the excellent Nilagiri Express connecting Chennai to the Blue Hills. For longer vacations, follow NH45 to Ulundurpettai via Chengalpattu, Tindivanam and Viluppuram. Turn right on NH68 to Salem via Tiyagai Durgam, Kallakkurichi, Talaivasal, Attur and Valappad. Follow NH47 to Avanashi via Perundurai, then turn right on the state road to Mettupalaiyam via Annur and follow NH67 as it winds its way up to Coonoor
Bus TNSETC's daily overnight Ooty bus (dep: 7.15 pm, Rs 305) from Chennai's Metropolitan Bus Terminus (Tel: 044- 24794705) at Koyambedu, stops at Coonoor. **KPN Travels** (044- 24796688) is a good private operator serving this route from Koyambedu (overnight service 6.30 pm, Rs 430). Buses take 13½ hrs to reach Coonoor, and you get there early morning

huge rock that resembles — what else? — a dolphin's nose. About 10 km from Coonoor, this is a popular picnic spot. On a clear day, you can glimpse **Catherine Falls** from atop the nose. **Law's Falls** is another popular picnic spot, 7 km from Coonoor, on the Mettupalaiyam Road.

Wellington

This army township houses the prestigious **Defence Services Staff College**. Wellington's **Golf Course** is hugely popular, not just with those who traipse its manicured greens wielding their irons; hordes of South Indian film crews also periodically descend to shoot their films' mandatory song sequences. Just beyond the golf course lies the **Hidden Valley**, a great trekking route. A relic of the Raj worth visiting is **St George's Church**, its brick red steeple standing out amidst the surrounding green.

WHERE TO STAY AND EAT

The Taj Garden Retreat (Tel: 0423- 2230021/ 42; Tariff: Rs 5,500-7,500) is a gracious colonial bungalow famous for its beautiful gardens. It offers a panoramic view, games, trekking, golf and fishing on request.

The Neemrana Group's heritage, colonial-era property **Wallwood Garden** (Tel: 2230584; Tariff: Rs 1,500-2,250) is set in what was once known as Blair Athol, in Upper Coonoor, built over a 100 years ago by a Scottish Major General. It offers eight beautiful suites in a quiet setting, 2 mins walk from Sim's Park.

Velan Hotel (Tel: 2230084; Tariff: Rs 1,600-2,500) is a popular option with deluxe rooms and suites. **The Blue Hills** on Mount Road (Tel: 2230174/ 892; Tariff: Rs 800-1,200) has 31 rooms, and offers laundry and travel services. **Coral Gable Holiday Home** (Tel: 2232561; Tariff: Rs 800) on Coonoor Club Road is a small, compact hotel with six doubles on offer. The **YWCA Guest House** (Tel: 2234426; Tariff: Rs 200-400) in

In the lap of Nature

The Kurumba Village Resort is a rare aromatic arena; far from spicing with mere words, we have established the self-sufficing cottages amidst a SPICE haven where nutmeg, cloves and pepper abound.

INHOUSE ACTIVITIES Swimming Pool | Table Tennis | Pool Table | Badminton | Board Games | Library | Carrom Board

OUTDOOR ACTIVITIES Golf | Trekking | Water Park | Tea Estate Tour | Boating | Visit to Ooty | Visit to Coonoor

Kurumba Village Resort
Nilgiris

Ooty Mettupalayam Road, Hill Grove Post, Kurumbadi, Nilgiris, Tamil Nadu.
Ph: +91 9443998886, +91 423 2004850/1/2
E-mail: nilgiris@kurumbavillageresort.com
website: www.kurumbavillageresort.com

THE NILGIRIS

Remnants of the Raj dot Coonoor

Wyoming, Upper Coonoor, with spacious and clean single and double rooms, is a good budget option.

Riga Residency (Tel: 0423-2234401/05; Tariff: Rs 1,500-1,800) is a good option next to the Defence Services Staff College in Wellington, with 42 rooms, laundry, a travel desk and room service.

The **Kurumba Village Resort** (Website: kurumbavillageresort.com) in Kurumbadi Village, Upper Burliar, is 12 km from Coonoor Station. It offers well-equipped cottages set amongst nutmeg, clove and pepper gardens, lined with jacaranda, jackfruit and rosewood trees. The resort offers golf, trekking and tea estate tours, among other activities.

The fare at local restaurants is nothing to write home about. There are women who make, bottle and sell **fruit nectars**, mulberry, passion fruit, strawberry, peach and pear, which are absolutely ambrosial. Just ask your hotel about how to get your hands on these. Jams and preserves are another local favourite, easily available at local stores.

Do call ahead and make reservations to dine at Taj Garden Retreat's **Dining Room**, for Indian, Chinese, Continental and breathtaking views of the undulating Nilgiris. The restaurant in Hotel Blue Hills serves Chinese and Indian food; the **Blue Lagoon Bar** here stays open till 10.30 pm.

Riga Residency's **Tycoon Restaurant** is open 24 hours. **Hotel Mahalaxmi** has a 24-hr Chinese restaurant.

For details, see Coonoor Accommodation Listings on pages 515-516

AROUND COONOOR

Kotagiri (19 km)
'Jesus Comes Quickly' hisses a naughty message on the lovely road that snakes past the **Dodda Betta Range** that provides Kotagiri, the Nilgiris' oldest hill station (6,503 ft), with some of its shade and a lot of its mist. This is tea territory and you can't miss the fragrance of the morning cuppa being readied in the factories that dot the sloping hills. There is little to do in Kotagiri town itself, except maybe trekking inside the **Longwood Shola** preserve and playing spot-the-animals. Or getting a nice rub at **Ayurprastha** (04266-272077), run by the Ayurvedic Trust from what used to be a palace. Prior bookings, done in Coimbatore (Tel: 0422-2313188), are a must.

But the spectacular 220°, take-all-you-can view offered by the **Kodanad Viewpoint** (18 km from Kotagiri) is a great reason to go all the way. On a clear day, tens of blue hills and miles of sprawling plains come into focus. And, like in an atlas, the **Moyar River** winds its way, spilling a bit of green on both its sides.

The viewpoint is nestled beside one of the most beautiful 1,000 acres of tea gardens — **Kodanad Estate**. You can stop at the entrance of the estates to pick up farm-fresh tea, which still fetches more than other tea grown in the Nilgiris. ■

Inputs by Palini R. Swamy in Kotagiri

Now open

MGM Hotels and Resorts

Coonoor.
Holiday in the hills

MGM
HILL WORTH RESORTS
COONOOR

Mount Pleasant Road, **Coonoor.** Tamilnadu.

Ph: **+91-423-2207995**   Mobile: **+91-9894857092**

Sales Office: **Chennai** - Ph: **+91-44-28476234 / 42107272**

Email: hillworth@mgm.co.in

Perfect setting for honey mooners, family re-union day

PRASHANT PANJIAR

The Blue Hills unfold as the toy train curves into Ooty

OOTY

QUEEN OF THE NILGIRI HILLS

State Tamil Nadu
Location The Queen of the Blue Mountains sits at 7,440 ft at the centre of the Nilgiri Range
Distance 588 km SW of Chennai **JOURNEY TIME By rail** $9^{1}/_{4}$ hrs + $1^{1}/_{2}$ hrs by road **By air** 55 mins + $2^{1}/_{2}$ hrs by road
Route NH45 to Ulundurpettai via Tindivanam and Viluppuram; NH68 to Salem via Talaivasal and Attur; NH47 to Avanashi via Perundurai; SH to Mettupalaiyam via Annur; NH67 to Ooty via Coonoor and Wellington (see route guides on pages 12 and 184)

■ BY LATHA ANANTHARAMAN

The signs now read Udhagamandalam, or Udhagai for short, but in the mouths of everyone in Tamil Nadu, this town will always be Ooty. Whether or not we have been there, Ooty is a part of our daily lives. Every carrot and cabbage in the market, every packet of cardamom, is said to come from there. On a January day in Chennai, some monkey-capped elder is bound to say, "It feels like Ooty today." For Ooty is synonymous with cold. And in one sense we've all been to the hill stations. We've all grown up on scenes of swirling mists and a heroine and hero running up hill and down dale. In fact, high altitudes seem to be requisite for high living and romance in the movies.

Films are on the tip of the tongue in Ooty. Many travel companies offer a Filmi Chakkar, a tour of places in which scenes have been shot, but on any drive at all in and around Ooty, the guide or driver slips into this mode, pointing out the meadow on which MGR sang out in search of love in *Anbe Vaa* more than 40 years ago, or the junction at which a modern heroine posted a letter in front of the Hindustan Photo Films factory and then crossed the road to board a bus. At the lookout over the stunning Ketty Valley, as visitors catch sight of the diminutive train track emerging from the slopes, young and old unanimously murmur "Chayya chayya".

And does the reality fall short? On the contrary, it soars well beyond what we've seen on 70mm. Yes, the queen of hill stations is grey at the temples, and her jowls spill over her collar. Slopes terraced with carrots and cabbages, still called English vegetables, are giving way to terraced houses, even multi-storeyed flats. The town in the valley is a mess of muddy roads now, in the rains. But the beauties of Ooty still lie just around the bend.

Ooty, the 'Scotland of the East', is one of the most popular holiday destinations in South India. In season, it's all about a crush of tourists on bad roads and shopkeepers out to fleece you. But there's a secret to getting the best out of a trip to Ooty and it is this: go off-season. The low season is far from desolate here. Every comfort is still on offer, with the blessed addition of elbow room and a slow pace. Be sporting about the rain. All it takes is an umbrella and a change of socks to taste the endless charms of these high hills on your own terms. This Ooty is a series of piquant montages: the sun lighting up one hill even as the other beside remains shrouded in green velvet; ponies contentedly chomping grass by the kerbside; the sharp fragrance of ghostly pines lining a mist-laden road; acacias in full bloom; the bright gold of witches' broom dotting every hill; the aroma of hot filter coffee and even hotter sambar.

THINGS TO SEE AND DO

South India's most popular hill station has plenty of attractions, both on and off the beaten path. Walks and rides around the hills are probably the best way to enjoy a holiday here. On the easy climb up Elk Hill, bluespike, orange dots of lantana, hanging trumpets of datura, and the lesser and greater glories of ipomoea are enchanting, with or without wildflower book in hand. Garden flowers hang over walls and creep under fences to join their wild cousins.

Horse riders get a superb meander through the roads around town, under dark, mossy trees and over meadows. Along some lanes women gather eucalyptus leaves to make aromatic oils. The scent of eucalyptus and pine is sharp in the morning air. Some of these rides skirt villages that are home to the Nilgiris' tribal communities, the best known of which are the Toda.

Gardens

An abiding delight are the **Botanical Gardens** (Tel: 0423-2442545), spread over 65 acres on the slopes just north of Charing Cross. Alarming crowds mill about the ticket counters, but the grounds inside are spacious. These gardens were laid out in 1847 on a lavish scale. Species of a temperate climate,

→ FAST FACTS

When to go April to June and again in September and October. But do go in March when the flowers are just beginning to bloom. Or late October and November when the cold is invigorating, but not unbearable

Tourist offices
- Govt of Tamil Nadu Tourist Office Wenlock Road, Ooty-643001
Tel: 0423–2443977
- TTDC ❶ ❺
No. 2, Wallajah Road, Chennai
Tel: 044-25367850-54
Website: tamilnadutourism.org
STD code 0423

THE NILGIRIS

Traditional Raj-era buildings in the 'Scotland of the East'

maple, oak, laurel and azalea, are planted here alongside fleshier tropicals and rich collections of climbing, creeping and pendant flowers. But the main attraction here is the fossilised tree trunk — all of 20 million years old. There are also mini Italian and Japanese gardens. A **Summer Festival** is held here each year in May, with a grand **Flower Show** taking centre-stage.

♦**Entry fee** Adults Rs 5, children Rs 3 **Timings** 7.30 am-6 pm

The **Rose Garden**, atop a hill off Etiennes Road, is all of 10 acres and in winter, when the 1,919 varieties (!) of roses of all hues, pink, red, orange, pale green, even black, are out, a stroll in this heavenly, scented garden is an unforgettable experience.

♦**Entry fee** Adults Rs 10, children Rs 5 **Timings** 8.30 am-6.30 pm

Ooty Lake

This 2½-km long lake with wooded banks to the west of the town, was artificially created in 1824 by John Sullivan, Collector of Coimbatore, who dammed up some streams to ensure water supply for the hill station of his ambitions, a settlement in a wholesome environment in which hot and bothered Englishmen could recharge themselves. Amenities in the shape of pavements and ice cream kiosks and activities like boating and pony rides have recently been added to the lake by the Tourism Department, but that is not nearly as lamentable as it sounds. The **boat house** on the lake is well removed from the bustle of the town and offers pleasanter views than its cramped entrance would suggest.

♦**Boating fee** Rs 30 per person **Timings** 8.30 am-6.30 pm

Raj remains

The colonial remnants of Ooty are well assimilated into daily life. Mansions have been absorbed into college campuses and Spencer's & Co is now an NIIT centre. Nineteenth-century architecture persists in clusters, notably near the **Collector's Office**, where the **Union Church**, the State Bank of India, and the Oriental Building housing **Higginbotham's** bookshop form a good circuit for those who like to look at old buildings.

The most picturesque of these is **St Stephen's Church** (built in 1829), the oldest church in the Nilgiris, with modest Gothic arches, yielding cane pews, and pretty clerestory windows. The churchyard rises in steps behind the building, offering distant views and atmosphere in spades. Ivy-covered tombstones evoke rustling crinolines, stiff-backed colonels and Victorian sentiment, along with Victorian rates of child mortality. Tiny tombs are inscribed with sorrowful verses, "Suffer the children to come to me" or, most heartbreaking, "Thy will be done." Much of the Raj lies in those graves.

Other churches of Ooty

Union Church and **Holy Trinity Church**, Gothic and Tudor in appearance, with magnificent stained glass windows, intricately carved pews, plaques detailing the British battalions who attended the services there, and tranquil cemeteries, are worth a dekko. **St Thomas Church** commands a compelling view of Ooty Lake. The **Kandal Church** houses a Relic of the True Cross on which Christ was crucified. Special Novena Prayers and Holy Masses are offered every Friday at this shrine and the annual feast is held on May 3rd.

Adventure

There are a number of planned trekking routes from Ooty. Climb up the highest peak in the Blue Mountains at 8,606 ft — **Dodda Betta**, or Big Mountain — a mere 10 km from Ooty. Dodda Betta commands the juncture of the Western and Eastern Ghats, offering vistas of the Nilgiri range that are unmatched. Come here to find the magnificent scale that drew plains people so far from home in the 19th century. In clear weather, you can see Ooty town, Ketty Valley, Coonoor and the cantonment of Wellington, Avalanche Dam and Mukurthi. A blank whiteness in the rainy season often dissolves into sudden clarity, so it is worth waiting at the top. If the mist is unremitting, the walk up to the peak has its own charms, warmed with a paper cone of boiled peanuts or hot mixture, the chitchit of whiteyes in the shrubs, and the sight of grey tits, tame as sparrows, picking up fallen nuts.

The Tourism Department arranges **hang-gliding** courses from March to May every year, plus the stream and lakes of the Nilgiris are an **angler's delight**, stocked as they are with good trout, carp and trench.

Picnic spots

Wenlock Downs, Ooty's most popular picnic spot, is a vast expanse (a mind-boggling 20,000 acres) of undulating

Choose from our network of over 4000 hotels in India. Serviced apartments, budget hotels, luxury resorts, palaces, business accomodations, houseboats and more.

Hotel	Rating
Hotel Darshan	Budget
Ooty Villa Park	3 ★
Holiday Inn Gem Park	4 ★

MTNL/BSNL Toll Free No.
1-800-22-4878
022-4030-4878
www.travelguru.com

India's Largest Hotel Network

THE NILGIRIS

DINODIA PHOTO LIBRARY

In the Cairn Hill Shola

Sholas, significant repositories of diversity, are tropical montane forests found in the southwestern Ghats above 5,900 ft. Shola trees are stunted and gnarled by the windy conditions of high plateaus. The best places to experience shola forests are the Nilgiri and Palani Hills (see page 144), and the High Range at Kodaikanal (see page 168).

In the Nilgiris an accessible walking site is the Cairn Hill Shola, outside Ooty. This forest is a designated Important Bird Area site; several species are found here including the black and orange flycatcher, white-bellied shortwing and Nilgiri laughing thrush. Access is easy (bus or auto), and the area is marked with a Forest Department signboard. Starting above Bryant Park, several unmarked roads lead through the shola. Many of the best sholas in the Palanis are off-limits; however, Bombay Shola, within city limits, is lovely for a walk. The Cairn Hill and Bombay Shola walks are 2-4 hrs; many of the several longer walks go through reserve forests. The Forest Department requires written permission for these.

The Nilgiri Wildlife and Environment Association is very helpful for trekking information: write to them c/o District Forest Office, Nilgiris South Division, Mount Stewart Hill, Ooty, Nilgiris District, Tamil Nadu 643001. Tel: 0423-2444083

landscape, which used to be the ground for the Ooty Hunt. Today, the downs encompass the **Gymkhana Club**, the Government Sheep Farm and the Hindustan Photo Films Company; a great walk along grassy knolls and quiet roads. Other picnic spots include the **Ninth Mile** and **Sandy Nallah**, a popular spot for film shoots, and where Ajay Devgan set up a fairy tale castle for *Raju Chacha* a few years ago.

Cairn Hill is situated about 3 km on the road to Avalanchi and really is one of the last original walks. The entrance road to the hill is flanked by dense cypress trees, a serenity that is only complemented by soft birdsong. An excellent picnic spot. **Avalanche** is a beautiful lake hedged by a shola and overrun with avifauna. The place got its name after an avalanche struck it in 1823. This is one great spot for trout fishing. Rods are available on hire from the trout hatchery at Avalanche.

SHOPPING

Ooty is also famous for its tea, home-made chocolates, aromatic oils and spices. Home-made chocolates in every flavour you can imagine and some you haven't yet dreamed up can be found in every other shop on Ooty's Commercial Road. However, connoisseurs will tell you there's just one stop for chocolates in all of the Nilgiris, at the unpretentious **King Star Confectionery** (Tel: 0423-2445785) on Hospital Road. Manned by enthusiastic staff who will insist you try out their newest flavours, King Star stocks a variety of flavoured chocolates and fudges. By evening, most of the top favourites (coconut crunch, mints, rum and raisin) are sold out.

The TN state handicrafts centre, **Poompuhar** occupies its own building on Coonoor Road (NH67), and is a must visit for local handicrafts. **Higginbothams** (Tel: 2442546), the famous bookshop, is on Commercial Road.

Experience The Imperial Splendor

Glyngarth Villa

Set amidst the serene Blue mountains, in the south of India is the unparalleled "Queen of Hill Stations", Ooty. Here, touching the heavenly clouds the magnificient "Glyngarth Villa" surrounded by boundless tranquillity and splendour. Wake up to the chirping of birds, the rustling of leaves, and let the fresh mountain air soothe your heart and soul. The Villa is situated in four acres of greenery and woods. It has 5 deluxe double bedrooms with modern suite bathrooms and 24 hours hot water.

Location : OOTY
(110 kms from Coimbatore & 320 kms from Bangalore)

Paradise ... ever since 1850

Golf Club Road, Finger Post, Ootacamund,
The Nilgiris - 643001, India.
Ph: 91-423-2445754, 91-423-2445115.
M : 9843070095
glyngarth@sify.com, glyngarth@rediffmail.com.
www.glyngarthvilla.com

For Reservations at Bangalore Contact

Footloose Yatra Consultants
Ph : 080-25357117, 25357116, 25352424
tourplans@footlooseyatra.com.

THE NILGIRIS

→ GETTING THERE

Air Nearest airport: Coimbatore (96 km/ 2$^1/_2$ hrs), connected to Chennai by 10 daily flights by Paramount Airlines, Indian, Air Deccan, Jet Airways and Kingfisher Airlines. Taxi to Ooty costs Rs 1,200 approx

Rail Nearest railhead: Mettupailayam Tel: 2442246 (51 km/ 1$^1/_2$ hrs) **Best option TO** Nilagiri Express (dep: Chennai Central 9 pm; arr: Mettupalaiyam 6.15 am) Cab to Ooty costs Rs 500 approx **Best option FROM** Nilagiri Express (dep: Mettupalaiyam 7.45 pm; arr: Chennai Central 5.10 am)

TIP Ride the Mountain Railway (see page 474) to Ooty from Mettupalayam

Car The 588-km drive from Chennai to Ooty cannot be attempted for a weekend break, especially with the excellent Nilgiri Express connecting Chennai to the Blue Hills. For longer vacations, follow NH45 to Ulundurpettai via Chengalpattu, Tindivanam and Viluppuram. Turn right on NH68 to Salem via Tiyagai Durgam, Kallakkurichi, Talaivasal, Attur and Valappad. Follow NH47 to Avanashi via Perundurai, then turn right on the state road to Mettupalaiyam via Annur and follow NH67 as it curves up to Ooty via Coonoor and Wellington

Bus TNSETC has a daily overnight service (dep: 7.15 pm, Rs 305) to Ooty from Chennai's Metropolitan Bus Terminus (Tel: 044-24794705) at Koyambedu. KPN Travels (044-24796688, 24797998) is a good private operator serving this route from Koyambedu (overnight service 6.30 pm, Rs 430). Buses take 14 hrs to reach Ooty. Early next morning you are greeted by the misty Blue Hills

Shops such as **Mohan's** near the Collector's Office sell Toda embroidered shawls and linens, as do women at an arched hut just inside the entrance to the Botanical Gardens. Tribal products also include aromatic oils and honey. Tea, spices and biryani ingredients, such as nutmeg flower and lichen, are sold at many shops along Commercial Road and at the Super Market in Charing Cross, along with home-made chocolates (Rs 30-55 for 100g).

The **Big Shop** (Tel: 2444136) on Commercial Road is the haunt of those who like to collect jewellery and artefacts of unusual shape and design. Their in-house jewellers copy out the traditional Toda silver jewellery in gold. **K. Mahaveerchand** (Tel: 2443359) in the somewhat crowded Main Bazaar area has Toda silver.

WHERE TO STAY

Nothing of 'snooty Ooty' seems to remain. Nostalgia seekers who head out to the stately hotels that once hosted home-grown and foreign royals and now cater to movie stars will find that luxury and high living thrive, but without the off-putting smell of exclusivity. The hill station in season is a mad crush, so make reservations well in time. Ooty's hoteliers are uniformly courteous. Hotels do not all start their high and low seasons on the same dates, so double-check rates for the dates you want.

The town has many opulent hotels. At Taj's **Savoy Hotel** (Tel: 0423-2444142-47; Tariff: Rs 5,500-10,800) on Sylk's Road, north-west of the town, you can enjoy a luxury hill holiday in any kind of weather, thanks to games rooms, billiards, movies, a gym, deep verandahs from which to look out on a lovely garden, and well-maintained, stylish rooms. The **Fernhill Palace** (Tel: 2443912/ 15; Tariff: Rs 8,500-20,000) is part of a large property southwest of the town owned by the Wodeyars of Mysore.

A getaway that nature designed herself

In the heart of the Mudumalai Forest, on the banks of a natural mountain stream is an exotic wildlife gateway : **Casa Deep Woods.**

600 trees grace the five acres at Casa Deep Woods. And not a single tree was cut as the gateway took shape. Rather the well-furnished cottage were built around the trees.

Casa's SPA offers a spectrum of Ayurvedic wellness treatments.

Everyday in Casa is funfilled. You can enjoy wild life spotting, trekking, jeep safari, night jeep trails, nature walks, elephant rides, bornfire barbeque. Besides these we have a recreation room with indoor games, volley ball and badminton court.

For reservations :
Bangalore - Tel : 080-25570148 / 25301794
Mob : 9844525151/9448486194
Resort : Mudumalai Forest, Foot hills of Ooty
Nilgiri dist., Tamilnadu. Ph : 0423 2526391/35
Email : casaholidays@airtelbroadband.in web : www.indianjungle.com

THE NILGIRIS

PROF VINAYA KUMAR/ SOUTHINDIAPICTURE

One among many chapels stands guard over the lush hills of Ooty

Regency Villa (Tel: 2443098; Tariff: Rs 1,900-2,200), part of the Fernhill property, offers unparalleled palatial authenticity at an unbelievable price. Its deluxe rooms (Rs 1,800 low season, Rs 2,000 high season) are in a building more than 140 years old. The cottages (Rs 1,600 low season, Rs 1,700 high season) are less royal but still feel like a Sharmila Tagore movie. Ignore the worn upholstery and patchy walls and you can have an affordable, nostalgic Ooty holiday.

The biggest hotel in town, the **Howard Johnson Monarch** (Tel: 2444408/ 18; Tariff: Rs 2,500-5,000) on Havelock Road near the Botanical Gardens, offers the Coy Boy bar and disco, a laser disc theatre and lots of games for kids, with a special Kids Corner to boot. **The Willow Hill** (Tel: 2444037; Tariff: Rs 900-1,700), also on Havelock Road, is a charming hotel, more like an inn.

In the mid range, **Hotel Nahar Nilgiris** (Tel: 2442173, 2443685; Tariff: Rs 2,250-3,750) in Charing Cross has modern, comfortable rooms. Also in Charing Cross, the budget **Hotel Durga** (Tel: 2443837/ 2443598; Tariff: Rs 999-1,300) has, in addition to an 1895 photo panorama of Ooty in the lobby, rooms that are much cleaner than those of its similarly priced neighbour, TTDC's **Hotel Tamil Nadu** (Tel: 2444370; Tariff: Rs 425-1,425).

Reflections Guest House (Tel: 2443834/ 5800; Tariff: Rs 600-800) is particularly well located, walkable from Ooty Station and bang on the north shore of Ooty Lake. **Hotel Lakeview** (Tel: 2443580-82; Tariff: Rs 1,200-1,500) also has good views of the lake, from beyond the western shore. South of the lake, Karnataka Tourism's **Mayura Sudarshan** (Tel: 2443828; Tariff: Rs 450-650) is well-located 2 km inside the Botanical Gardens at Fernhill. This area has quite a few good options, including **Sterling Days Inn** (Tel: 2441073-74; Tariff: Rs 2,500-5,000) further up the hill, which boasts a disco, gift and grocery shops, games rooms, massage centre, Internet access, trekking and a host of activities.

THE NILGIRIS

Baskets of fresh Nilgiri's produce add their colour to the Ooty bazaar

Holiday Inn Gem Park (Tel: 2441761-62; Tariff: Rs 6,000-20,000) on Sheddon Road, is well-equipped with a disco, temperature-controlled swimming pool, central heating and a health club, and offers beautiful valley views.

South of Havelock on Church Hill Road are the budget dorms of Tamil Nadu Tourism's **Youth Hostel** (Tel: 2443665; Tariff: Rs 140-1,000). Everyone, whether staying at **Hotel Villa Park** (Tel: 2442434-35; Tariff: Rs 1,200-2,800) earlier known as Dasaprakash, of Mysore fame, or not, should come here for an unbeatable South Indian thali.

For more hotels and details, see Ooty Accommodation Listings on pages 522-524

WHERE TO EAT

Ooty has several Chinese restaurants, most of them serving indifferent fare, but **Shinkows** (Tel: 0423-2442811), opposite the elegant brick building of the Nilgiri Library, continues to occupy top place. **Kurinji** on Commercial Road serves up delicious South Indian fast food... crisp dosas, spicy vadas and steaming sambar. Do try the Nilgiri speciality, the *varki* from **West Coast Bakery** (Tel: 2443050) on Commercial Road. The *varki* is a cross between a *chakli* and a biscuit, crisp, flaky and melt-in-the-mouth delicious. All over town, even the shabbiest tea stalls sell good cardamom and masala chai.

Then there are the hotel restaurants. Nilgiri Woodland's **Toda Arch** has a multi-cuisine menu, as does Ooty Gate's **Aroma Delights**. But do call ahead if you want to eat at the latter. Other multi-cuisine options are Sterling Fernhill's **Gulmohar Restaurant**, Hotel Lakeview's **Supper Club**, Hotel Khem's **Memory Lane** and the cafés at **Hotel Mount View**, **Blue Hill International** and **The Willow Hill**. Drop by at the latter's restaurant for great views over candle-lit dinner if you aren't staying there.

Holiday Inn Gem Park has the speciality **Jade Garden** Chinese Restaurant and the 24-hr **Toda Café**, a multi-cuisine option. Hotel Nahar Nilgiris

Why should a beach experience be called SwaSwara?

Because this is a journey that takes you beyond the sun, sand and the sea, to the soul of the beach. A journey through Yoga, Meditation and Ayurveda. A journey through a series of simple experiences that opens up a whole **new way of living**. Everything here furthers your journey. A special dome for meditation. Twenty-four traditional Konkan villas made from local materials to live in. Fresh tropical fruits, vegetables and fish to relish. Coconut groves, farms, paddy fields... every detail here pays tribute to nature, the environment and the community. Making you one with the elements. And leading you to SwaSwara - your inner vibration, the music of your soul.

SwaSwara
a cgh earth experience

Central Reservations: Casino Building Cochin Kerala India Phone: +91-484-3011711 Fax: 2668001
Email: contact@cghearth.com www.cghearth.com

THE NILGIRIS

Tourists take a laidback ride on the artificially-created Ooty Lake

also has two options, **Chandan Veg Restaurant** serving Chinese and North Indian, and a **Garden Snack Bar** for tiffin. TTDC's **Hotel Tamil Nadu** and KSTDC's **Mayura Sudarshan** both serve South and North Indian fare. The former has a bar. The latter also serves Chinese.

Garden Restaurant, Nahar Hotel's pleasant coffee shop, is especially known for its idlis, served with four kinds of chutney. Nilgiri Woodlands' **Toda Arch** is colonial in style, with wood floors, embroidered drapes, and posies of wildflowers, and good veg offerings. A hearty Punjabi thali can be had in **Dhabba Express** on Coonoor Road, a shed paved with terracotta and hung with hurricane lanterns, with mosquitoes and flies battling for airspace. Or skip the aeronautics and go to the Villa Park's high-priced but spotless and unpretentious **Almora**, for a range of North Indian, Chinese and Continental veg dishes. Its North Indian thali is filling, with the unorthodox but welcome addition of rasam. The same hotel's **Krishna Bhavan**, also veg, serves tiffins all day.

AROUND OOTY

Coonoor (17 km)
See page 186

Parson's Valley (19 km)
See page 215

Pykara Lake (21 km)
Pykara's dense sholas, Toda settlements, shallow downs and of course the blue, still waters of the lake, make it a lovely getaway from your getaway. Apart from quiet walks through the lush surrounds, Pykara has a **boathouse** and **restaurant** maintained by Tamil Nadu Tourism. To get to Pykara from Ooty, head west towards Gudalur on NH67, and turn right 3 km later to Pykara.
◆**Boating fees** Paddle boat Rs 100 for $1/2$ hr, row boat Rs 120 for 4 people for 20 mins, motor boat deluxe (4 people) Rs 400 for 20 mins **Timings** 9 am to 6 pm Tel: 2254105

Red Hills (28 km)
See page 210

THE NILGIRIS

SRIKANTH KOLARI

Welcoming lawns of Bellikkal Estate, set in complete isolation high up in the Nilgiris

BELLIKKAL
HAIRPIN BENDS TO HEAVEN

State Tamil Nadu
Location Bellikkal is a Nilgiri village on the edge of the Sigur Plateau, 16 km north of Ooty
Distance 604 km SW of Chennai JOURNEY TIME **By rail** $9^{1}/_{4}$ hrs + 2 hrs by road **By air** 55 mins + 3 hrs by road
Route NH45 to Ulundurpettai via Chengalpattu, Tindivanam and Viluppuram; NH68 to Salem via Talaivasal and Attur; NH47 to Avanashi via Perundurai; SH to Mettupalaiyam via Annur; NH67 to Ooty via Coonoor and Wellington; ghat road to Bellikkal via Marlimund Lake (*see route guides on pages 12 and 184*)

■ BY SUNAAD RAGHURAM

Loosen your purse strings until your purse sags earthwards, hire a helicopter, fasten your seat belts, take off into the blue yonder and savour the hypnotising sights of the forest-clad Nilgiri mountains down below. Or, simply visit Silver Stones Estate at Bellikkal. Complete isolation at 5,500 ft, just 16 km from Ooty en route to the Kalhatti Ghats, whose curves can give the world's best belly dancer a run for her money. The estate is perched like a lofty eagle adjoining the villages of Akuni and Hulhatti on the northern fringe of the smoky Nilgiri Hills. The 50 acres of absolute wilderness culminate at a point from where you can see nerve-tingling vistas. The forests of Mudumalai and Bandipur spread out down below, with their trees resembling the knotted wool of a million sheep grazing together in the distance. The Moyar River that slithers its way through a deep chasm leaves behind a trail of dense shrubbery along its wake that appears like closely worked embroidery. The dam across it looks much like a toy meant for the amusement of the gods!

From that height, the Sigur Plateau unwraps itself like a fantabulous leaf stretching out in the open. And towards evening, the light and shade effect brought about by the setting sun, punctuated by glinting shafts beaming down from the sky on the innumerable valleys and mountains around, makes for a show that is purely in the realm of the divine.

THINGS TO SEE AND DO

Bellikkal is the place for long ambles along the ghats, or a quiet afternoon by Bellikkal Lake. This is not the place to carry your tuxedo to. Pack some outdoorsy clothes that'll blend in with the surroundings and some good walking shoes. This is an unseen and relatively unexplored section of the over-exploited Nilgiris. Go into the wilds here and you'll literally have a different view of nature.

Wet and wild...

Walk down to **Bison Valley**, that takes its name from the innumerable gaur (Indian bison) that roam around the Sigur area. If you have binocular vision to assist you, you'll delight in the sight of herds of gaur moving around languorously, feeding in the lush

→ FAST FACTS

When to go The only time of the year that's not good for Bellikkal is the rains in October and November, when the curves on the ghat roads become dangerously slippery. The rest of the year is always a great time

Tourist offices
• Govt of Tamil Nadu Tourist Office ℹ
Wenlock Road, Ooty
Tel: 0423-2443977
• TTDC ℹ 🅑
No. 2, Wallajah Road, Chennai
Tel: 044-25368358, 25389857
Fax: 25361385; Email: ttdc@vsnl.com
Website: tamilnadutourism.org
STD code 0423

Picture perfect hill stream

PRASHANT PANJIAR

THE NILGIRIS

→ GETTING THERE

Air Nearest airport: Coimbatore (112 km/ 3 hrs), connected to Chennai by 10 daily flights by Paramount Airlines, Indian, Air Deccan, Jet Airways and Kingfisher Airlines. Taxi to Bellikkal costs Rs 1,800 approx

Rail Nearest railhead: Mettupalaiyam (67 km/ 2 hrs) **Best option TO** Nilagiri Express (dep: Chennai Central 9 pm; arr: Mettupalaiyam 6.15 am) Cab to Bellikkal costs Rs 1,600 approx **Best option FROM** Nilagiri Express (dep: Mettupalaiyam 7.45 pm; arr: Chennai Central 5.10 am)

TIP Ride the Nilgiri Mountain Railway's Udhagamandalam-Mettupalaiyam Passenger (see page 474) past tiny mountain stations to Ooty from Mettupalaiyam on the narrow gauge

Car Bellikal is a long 588-km drive from Chennai that should not be attempted on a weekend break. For longer vacations, follow NH45 to Ulundurpettai via Chengalpattu, Tindivanam and Villupuram. Turn right on NH68 to Salem via Tiyagai Durgam, Kallakkurichi, Talaivasal, Attur and Valappad. Follow NH47 to Avanashi via Perundurai, then turn right on the state road to Mettupalaiyam via Annur and follow NH67 as it curves up to Ooty via Coonoor and Wellington. At Ooty, turn right to Bellikkal via Marlimund Lake

Bus TNSETC has a daily overnight service (dep: 7.15 pm, Rs 305) to Ooty from Chennai's Metropolitan Bus Terminus (Tel: 044-24794705) at Koyambedu. KPN Travels (Tel: 24797998, 24796688) is a good private operator serving this route from Koyambedu (overnight service 6.30 pm, Rs 430). Buses reach Ooty in the early morning

undergrowth. The silver **Kalhatti Falls** shimmer and glint as they cascade down a valley. And from this height and range, the waters seem to come down dreamily in slow motion. The Nilgiri peaks at Bellikkal beckon the intrepid trekker. And if you climb one of them through a series of thin trails passing through the foliage, you'll be astounded by the remarkable splendour of the vast and varied landscape, and the views that accompany the walk. You'll feel on top of the world.

Bellikkal's other attraction is the *kurinji* bush, covered with purplish blue flowers of delicate beauty. When in full bloom, they lend a bluish haze to the area. But these bushes bloom only once in 12 years.

To be in Bellikkal during the monsoon is a truly romantic experience, one that will remain etched in memory. For when it rains, the whole area takes on a hazy magnificence. With umbrella in hand, make your way to the **vantage point** at the end of the estate and just gasp, gawk and drool at the sight in front of you. The mountains that gently wrap the verdant valleys in green gossamer look like they are being showered with a billion tiny, speckled diamonds. And somewhere in the distance, up on a delicate branch, a babbler ruffles itself into a cute, brown ball and shakes itself dry.

Such dazzling sights of nature are not the only things here. The wildlife enthusiast will have no complaints of any kind. Imagine seeing a herd of elephants or gaur or sambar or chital grazing in such complete solitude within the folds of the valleys below that they look almost unreal, as if lodged like terracotta figures on a cardboard model of a forest painted green! Sloth bears and panthers abound too; their droppings at numerous spots around the estate grounds· point to their nocturnal perambulations. And then there are the birds...

... and quiet too

And then there is **Bellikkal Lake** up on the estate, cocooned within the foliage. And as you part the leaves of a small tree near it, you'll see ducks waddling around in the waters. Diving under the surface every now and then, in search of food, they look a picture of quietude. The birdsong in the trees envelope your being with the same effect as the soothing musical strains created by a cultured assemblage of musicians. Control your angling instincts here. Though there's fish in the water, angling is forbidden at Bellikkal Lake. Go into the wilds here and you'll surely have a different view of nature. Both literally and figuratively speaking!

WHERE TO STAY AND EAT

Pannalal and Mridula Chordia's **Silver Stones Estate** (Coonoor Tel: 0423-2230357, Mobile: 09486635445; Tariff: Rs 1,250 per person per day) is in the lap of these unseen parts of the Nilgiris, surrounded by nature at her best. They proudly offer no electricity, no TV, no telephone. In the mountains, you have no need for such mod cons. What they do have in abundance is spring water.

Stay is at an old haveli-like structure within the estate, that was built at the time of the Raj. Food is wholesome South Indian vegetarian. For breakfast,

Cow goes on a tea break

tuck into fresh rolls and croissants with tea. Sandwiches and picnic baskets to take along on treks, or for a romantic lunch by the lake, are packed on request. The Chordias also offer lunch and tea for groups of 10-15 people who want to come up from Ooty for a day and take a break from their break.

For details, see Bellikkal Accommodation Listings on page 514 ■

Photographs by SRIKANTH KOLARI

Panoramic view of Emerald Lake in the southern Nilgiri Biosphere Reserve

RED HILLS
THE ROAD LESS TRAVELLED

State Tamil Nadu
Location The Red Hills area is in an ecologically fragile zone of the Nilgiri Biosphere Reserve where no more development is allowed, 28 km south of Ooty
Distance 600 km SW of Chennai **JOURNEY TIME** *By rail* $9^{1}/_{4}$ hrs + $2^{1}/_{2}$ hrs by road *By air* 55 mins + $3^{1}/_{2}$ hrs by road
Route NH45 to Ulundurpettai via Chengalpattu, Tindivanam and Villupuram; NH68 to Salem via Talaivasal and Attur; NH47 to Avanashi via Perundurai; SH to Mettupalaiyam via Annur; NH67 to Ooty via Coonoor and Wellington; Muthurai Road to Red Hills via Palada, Ithalar and Emerald (*see route guides on pages 12 and 184*)

■ BY SUNAAD RAGHURAM

The narrow Muthorai Road leads out of Ooty to the villages of Palada, Ithalar and Emerald, all surrounded by acres of cabbage and carrot, and further to an area called Red Hills. Take this road out of the clamour of Ooty to put the magic back into jaded Nilgiri holidays. For here, you'll be transported back to the time of the British, with the landscape giving you enough evidence as to why the mandarins of Team Britannica so loved the Blue Mountains.

It is here in Red Hills that the forests are magnificent and vast, the foliage dense, and the air crisp and pure. Lush, eye-soothing greenery covers whole areas right into the horizon. Small rivulets in the hills and the valleys shimmer like silver strings in the sunlight as they cascade down the slopes; the trees are bent low, heavy with their bounty of mouth-watering fruits; and a million flowers bloom in such fantastic hues all around that they make the heart cry out in sheer ecstasy. Somewhere in the long distance, atop a hillock with an ambling road going up the slope, a house with a slanting, tiled roof spews wisps of white smoke from a chimney that joins the cotton-soft clouds, stitching fleeting patterns of art. Wild rabbits prance around in joyous celebration and multi-coloured birds streak across the cobalt sky leaving behind vivid trails.

A great change from the clamour of Ooty, the wildness of Mudumalai and laidback Coonoor. Best of all, Red Hills offers a permanent guarantee of natural beauty, since no further development is possible under the law in the ecologically fragile area of the sensitive Upper Bhavani Sanctuary nearby.

Ringed by an almost never ending array of mountains clothed in olive green finery, Red Hills, so named by the British in remembrance of a similar area in England, is where tranquility meets calm to produce a sense that is soothing and soul-enriching.

THINGS TO SEE AND DO

Eight lakes form the finest beauty spots on the face of Red Hills. You can take a tour of these, all within a 25-km radius of Red Hills. A gentle walk along their shores, with myriad birdsongs as accompaniment, is a great afternoon spent. You can also fish for carp and trout in the lakes while you relax and take in the scenery.

But the best thing to do in Red Hills is to just take a long, unhurried, amble

→ FAST FACTS

When to go The resort is normally closed between June and August for the monsoon. But if you insist that you are the type who loves the rain, then you can head there after calling up the place. It is open through the rest of the year. Summers are wonderfully pleasant and winters cold

Tourist offices
● Dept of Tourism, Govt of TN ⓘ
Wenlock Road, Ooty-643001
Tel: 0423-2443977
● TTDC ⓘ ⓑ
No. 2, Wallajah Road, Chennai
Tel: 044-25367850-54
Fax: 25361385; Email: ttdc@vsnl.com
Website: tamilnadutourism.org
STD code 0423

GOA KA GURU
Rahul, Hotel Advisor at Travelguru. A born adventurer, he has explored Goa's beaches, markets and villages like no one else.

Choose from our network of over 4000 hotels in India. Serviced apartments, budget hotels, luxury resorts, palaces, business accommodations, houseboats and more.

1-800-22-4878
022-4030-4878
www.travelguru.com

travelguru™
India's Largest Hotel Network

iCONTRACT.TG.07.3248

→ GETTING THERE

Air Nearest airport: Coimbatore (124 km/ 3^1/$_2$ hrs), connected to Chennai by 10 daily flights by Paramount Airlines, Indian, Air Deccan, Jet Airways and Kingfisher Airlines. Taxi to Red Hills costs Rs 1,800 approx; from Ooty, taxi charges Rs 800-1,000 approx
Rail Nearest railhead: Mettupalaiyam (79 km/ 2^1/$_2$ hrs) **Best option TO** Nilagiri Express (dep: Chennai Central 9 pm; arr: Mettupalaiyam 6.15 am). Cab to Red Hills costs Rs 1,500-1,600 approx **Best option FROM** Nilagiri Express (dep: Mettupalaiyam 7.45 pm; arr: Chennai Central 5.10 am)
Car Red Hills is a long 600-km drive from Chennai that cannot be attempted for a weekend break. For longer vacations, follow NH45 to Ulundurpettai via Tindivanam and Villupuram. Turn right on NH68 to Salem via Talaivasal and Attur. Follow NH47 to Avanashi via Perundurai, then turn right on the state road to Mettupalaiyam via Annur and follow NH67 as it curves up to Ooty via Coonoor. Take the Muthorai Road past Ooty's Good Shepherd International School. Follow the road past Palada, Ithalar and Emerald (total 20 km from Ooty). About 5 km after Emerald, the road forks. The left goes to Avalanche, you take the right fork to Red Hills
Bus TNSETC has a daily overnight service (dep: 7.15 pm, Rs 305) to Ooty from Chennai's Metropolitan Bus Terminus (Tel: 044-24794705) at Koyambedu. KPN Travels (044-24797998, 24796688) is a good private operator serving this route from Koyambedu (overnight service 6.30 pm, Rs 430). Buses take 14 hrs to reach Ooty, but you get there early morning

amidst the wilderness through the pencil thin pathways that go all around the valleys with the mountain air caressing your face and the greenery inviting you to embrace it with the passion of a lovelorn beloved.

Lake district

The area is dotted by eight lakes, aquamarine in colour and distilled in purity — Emerald, Avalanche, Upper Bhavani (40 km), Parson's Valley Lake (12 km), Porthimund (15 km) and Western Catchment 1, 2 and 3 (40 km). From atop the lofty perches around Red Hills, they appear as impossibly odd-shaped mirrors reflecting the clouds. The occasional glint of the sun is magnified on their surface, as the waters break into fine ripples.

The area receives heavy rainfall every year — 100 inches in just two months between June and August — that fills up the lakes. The light green shrubs of tea gardens roll into the slopes that reach out for the sky. The cool air invigorates the senses and adds a spring to your gait. Towards evening, the winds blowing from across the peaks and through the trees make you long for the warmth of a cosy fireplace.

Avalanche

About 13 km from **Emerald** (7 km from Red Hills by the metalled road to Ooty) is the village of Avalanche where live one of the oldest tribes of the Nilgiris, the Todas. Basically cattle rearers, they would barter ghee and butter for grains in the olden days. And while visiting them, if you happen to see an elderly man placing his foot ritualistically on the head of a woman, don't be appalled. That is how Toda elders bless their young. Avalanche also has a **trout hatchery** that is over a 100 years old.

Then there are the **hydroelectric power stations** at Emerald and Avalanche built in the 1950s to visit.
Note Red Hills Nature Resort arranges all visits and permissions

Red HILLS

Emerald
Nilgiris, Tamil Nadu
91-423-2595755, 2595753, 2595754
(0)9842259554
Email : vijayredhill@yahoo.co.in

THE NILGIRIS

Nature resort in the midst of a sprawling 250-acre tea garden at Red Hills

WHERE TO STAY AND EAT

In the Red Hills area, the one and only post of 'modern' civilisation is **Red Hills Nature Resort** (Tel: 0423-2595755, 09842259544; Tariff: Rs 3,000-4,000 for two, including meals), the home of the Vijaykumars. Situated dramatically on the top of a hillock at 7,000 ft, the whitewashed, gabled bungalow, dating back to 1875, spells aristocracy all the way. It lords over Emerald Lake and the hills beyond, even as the sprawling 250-acre tea garden encircling it lends a rare sense of old world remoteness.

The rectangular shaped lawn to one side of the building is a well-kept baize, and on its fringes grow lilies, chrysanthemums, primulas, petunias, geraniums and the rare canterbury bells, alstromarie and agapantas. The green lawn and the colourful garden are an amazing contrast to the greyishness of a portion of the mountain that is rocky and looms large right behind the bungalow.

Breakfast, lunch and dinner are like family get-togethers at a well laid out dining table in the main bungalow itself. The veggies that go with the meals and also the fruits for dessert are, without doubt, completely organic, having been grown on the estate. I especially remember the succulent pineapple with fresh cream. The unique tenderness of the carrots and the long beans amply testify to that fact. Ask for their special Badaga chicken and beans. There is a fairly well-stocked bar of the fix-it-yourself variety. But you can also carry along your own poison. If you like the tea here, you can buy some from the resort, which stocks excellent tea from the Nonsuch Tea Estate near Ooty.

The Vijaykumars arrange licences for fishing, guides for trekking and sightseeing, and also organise ayurvedic massages and mountain biking. And lastly, if you're alone and wish to hike up one of the mountains or take a stroll through the tea gardens at leisure, you'll surely have some good company — Prince, the friendly German shepherd or Blackie, the vivacious little Daschund.

For details, see Red Hills Accommodation Listings on page 524 ∎

Dam on the Parson's Valley stream in Mukurthi National Park

Photographs by SRIKANTH KOLARI

PARSON'S VALLEY
HAVEN IN A SANCTUARY

State Tamil Nadu
Location Parson's Valley lies within the Mukurthi National Park in the south-west Nilgiris, 19 km from Ooty
Distance 607 km SW of Chennai JOURNEY TIME **By rail** $9^{1}/_{4}$ hrs + 2 hrs by road **By air** 55 mins + 3 hrs by road
Route NH45 to Ulundurpettai via Chengalpattu, Tindivanam, Vikravandi and Viluppuram; NH68 to Salem via Tiyagai Durgam, Kallakkurichi, Talaivasal, Attur and Valappadi; NH47 to Avanashi via Perundurai; SH to Mettupalaiyam via Annur; NH67 to Ooty via Coonoor; ghat road to Parson's Valley (*see route guides on pages 12 and 184*)

■ BY PONNI ARASU

The Mukurthi Peak towers over the Mukurthi National Park, located in the south-eastern corner of the Nilgiri Plateau. Among the least-visited sanctuaries in southern India, Mukurthi holds thick pine and shola forests, dotted with jewel-like lakes. One of these, formed by the Parson's Dam on the Parson's Valley stream, hosts an old colonial hunting house near its shore, that has only recently been opened to tourists.

Located at 7,000 feet and surrounded by the Mukurthi Reserve Forest, the air around Parson's Dam and the Western Catchment Lake is bracing and clean, with a lingering smell of pines. No sign of human beings for miles around; only acres of pine and rhododendron forests snaking with hiking trails, sparkling streams and falls, and interspersed with

THE NILGIRIS

Grasslands of the Western Catchment Area Reserve Forest

open grasslands. This haven, it's difficult to believe, is just under 20 km away from busy Ooty. The pleasurable drive in from Ooty can entail, apart from soothing canopies shading the road, the occasional peacock, sambar or monkey on the side of the road. You may even encounter elephants crossing the road, especially around sunset.

Parson's Valley is as non-touristy as it can get in the Nilgiris. Come if solitude amidst untainted nature calls you.

THINGS TO SEE AND DO

Walk, hike, trek. Pause. Listen to the twittering of the birds. Meet a startled deer at a burbling stream. For visits and treks to Mukurthi Peak and the Mukurthi National Park, advance notice is a must, for the camp has to arrange permission from the Wildlife Warden's office at Ooty (*see 'Fast Facts' on facing page*). Mukurthi, with its extensive shola forests, is ideal country for the Nilgiri tahr. But the creature the park is most renowned for protecting is the humble water buffalo!

Short Treks

Spot wild buffaloes and sambar deer drinking their fill at the Parson's Valley Stream, next to **Hodgson's Camp**. Cross the stream and a short, half hour trek away is the **Sand Mound**, a large area of open grassland surrounded by a verdant pine forest. Here you can sight monkeys and birds, and, if you are lucky, a leopard passing through the forest close by. A brook runs through the rolling downs, and this is the ideal spot for some quiet time in the forest under the open skies. Inspect the 'dilli' tree (as the locals call it), with its beautiful red flowers. These are the commonest trees in the area after pines.

A longer trek from Hodgson's Camp, which will take about four hours back and forth, is to the **Mukurthi Earth Dam**. This dam is a charming spot in the middle of the forest, but the highlight is the trek itself. If you take the route through the Parson's Valley Forest Bridge, stop at the small waterfall right next to the bridge for a breath and a breathtaking view of the grand, oddly shaped Mukurthi Peak. Continue along the forest bridge through the Pykara Main Road, which was once used by the royals of Mysore travelling on horseback, and, till 15 years ago, by the locals for their daily commute. The Earth Dam was one of the first places where rainbow trout fish were released by the British into the Mukurthi River and these, a delicacy in the area, now breed here. On your way back to the camp, climb the **Stone Mound**, a small peak, for a gorgeous view of the Nilgiri Hills.

Day Treks

You can pack food and water and follow the trail to **Kuru Mund** and **Mudi Mund**, which are on the other side of Mukurthi Peak. The **Mukurthi Amman Temple** near the Mukurthi Dam is revered by the local tribes. **Porthi Mund** is another dam on the way to the Western Catchment Area Reserve Forest, with a picturesque view of the hills. The pretty **Emerald Dam** has been aptly named for the colour of its waters. The camp arranges day treks to all these places.

Western Catchment Area Reserve Forest

A drive inside the Western Catchment Area Reserve Forest is an unforgettable, unmissable experience. Special permission from the Forest Department can be obtained at a nominal fee, arranged easily by the Hodgson Camp, if informed in advance. Thickly forested, it is home to the Nilgiri tahr. Sambar deer and Nilgiri langur are also found aplenty here, and there is a high likelihood of catching a glimpse of a leopard.

Driving through the thick wild forests interspersed with the vast grasslands, you might come upon ruins of the houses where lived the men and women who

→ **FAST FACTS**

When to go Between March and June for the pleasant weather and to enjoy the forest when it is in full bloom
Tourist offices
● Wildlife Warden ❶
Mount Stuart Hill
Udhgamandalam (Ooty)-643001
Tel: 0423-2444098
● Govt of Tamil Nadu Tourist Office ❶
Wenlock Road, Ooty-643001
Tel: 0423-2443977
● TTDC ❶ ⓑ
No. 2, Wallajah Road, Chennai
Tel: 044-25367850-54
Website: tamilnadutourism.org
STD code 04232

THE NILGIRIS

→ GETTING THERE

Air Nearest airport: Coimbatore (115 km/ 3 hrs), connected to Chennai by 10 daily flights by Paramount Airlines, Indian, Air Deccan, Jet Airways and Kingfisher Airlines. Taxi to Parson's Valley costs Rs 2,300 approx
Rail Nearest railhead: Mettupalaiyam Tel: 2442246 (70 km/ 2 hrs) **Best option TO** Nilagiri Express (dep: Chennai Central 9 pm; arr: Mettupalaiyam 6.15 am). Taxi to Parson's Valley costs Rs 800 approx
Best option FROM Nilagiri Express (dep: Mettupalaiyam 7.45 pm; arr: Chennai Central 5.10 am)
Car Parson's Valley is a long drive from Chennai and should not be attempted for a weekend break. For longer vacations, follow the route till Ooty (see page 198). Continue down NH67 from Ooty towards Gudalur, and watch out for The Hill Petrol Bunk, about 10 km ahead of Ooty. Turn left and drive 20 km till you reach the Parson's Valley Dam Bridge (where Mani Ratnam's film *Roja*'s last scene was shot). Park your vehicle by the bridge, cross and do the 2-km walk to Hodgson's Camp. Vehicles are barred from crossing the bridge without special permission from the Electricity Board. If you have informed the camp in time and have permission, the winding road route to the camp involves a 4 km downhill drive
Bus TNSETC has a daily overnight service (dep: 7.15 pm) to Ooty from Koyambedu (Tel: 044-24794705). KPN Travels (044-24797998, 24796688) is a good private operator (overnight service 6.30 pm). Buses reach Ooty early next morning. Taxi to Parson's Valley from Ooty costs Rs 800 approx

built, half a century ago, the roads we travel on today. The view from the top of any of the hills within the Catchment Area is stunning. You will see beautiful rhodo and pine forests, mountains, several small streams, a large waterfall, and there, beyond those hills — Kerala!

WHERE TO STAY AND EAT

The fence enclosing **Hodgson's Camp** (Bangalore Reservations Tel: 080-26722750, Mobile: 09845442224; Tariff: Rs 950) marks the only privately owned land within the Mukurthi Reserve Forest, and the only accommodation at Parson's Valley. The acres on which Hodgson's Camp now stands were originally owned by a Britisher, Mr. Hodgson. When leaving India to return to England, Hodgson donated the land, complete with a little hut he had built, to the Nilgiris Game Association, a well-known hunting club for Englishmen at the time. The club charged Rs 2 per night to stay in the hut and Re 1 for people to camp in their own tent!

The land was then taken over by the Forest Department under the British. Post-Independence, in 1964, the land changed hands again, when Mr Lakkiah Gowda bought it in a public auction. His grandchildren today run Hodgson's Camp for tourists. Fishing and hunting are now, of course, strictly forbidden.

Hodgson's original hut has been converted into two comfortable cottages. You can also stay at the 25-bed dorm or pitch tent in the grounds. Wholesome home-cooked meals are provided, made from veggies grown in the campsite. The pleasant old man who shows you around the forest, Durairaj, once worked for the Forest Department, and seems to know every inch of the forests around. Safety as well as exciting information are assured if he accompanies you on treks.

For details, see Parson's Valley Accommodation Listing on page 524 ■

A wild elephant roams through the Mudumalai forest

MUDUMALAI WILDLIFE SANCTUARY
IN THE FOOTHILLS OF THE BLUE MOUNTAINS

State Tamil Nadu
Location On the Karnataka-Tamil Nadu border, along the Mysore-Ooty Highway, within the Nilgiri Biosphere Reserve. Mudumalai is contiguous with Bandipur National Park, separated only by the Moyar River from Karnataka
Distance 661 km SW of Chennai **JOURNEY TIME** *By rail* $9^1/_4$ hrs + 3 hrs by road ***By air*** 55 mins + 4 hrs by road
Route NH45 to Ulundurpettai via Tindivanam and Viluppuram; NH68 to Salem via Tiyagai Durgam, Kallakkurichi, Attur and Valappadi; NH47 to Avanashi via Perundurai; SH to Mettupalaiyam via Annur; NH67 to Gudalur via Coonoor and Ooty; Mysore Highway to Theppakadu, Mudumalai's main forest base (*see route guides on pages 12 and 184*)

■ BY RAMAN KUMAR

My eyes feast on the forest scene as we manoeuvre our jeep on the *kuchcha* tracks of the Bandipur National Park. There are trees with light barks, rolling hills and streams gurgling past rocks. There are chattering mynas, drongos and babblers. A herd of cheetal graze in a grassy patch and, above them, in the trees, a langur troop munches on something. Our guide and driver for the day, Ganga Singh, points to the dirt track and says, "Look, tiger tracks! No wonder there aren't too many cheetal here this morning." A bit further on we see more signs of animals: porcupines, sambar and elephants, all have walked this same dusty path a few hours ago.

Our guide suddenly stops the jeep. I notice some movement between the pillar-like trunks of teak trees. A brownish-black mass is the source of our attention. An elephant? But as the massive animal emerges from cover, I discover that it's a handsome gaur. Sinewy and standing tall at 6 ft, the beast sports a glistening coat, white stockinged legs and an impressive set of horns. It is said that the gaur are the largest wild oxen in the world — and having seen this huge bull, I cannot doubt it! We spot the rest of the herd, which has over a dozen members, mostly females.

The forest seems to be full of gaur and we spot many during the drive. We encounter a herd comprising at least a hundred animals, all of them having congregated to graze on the flush of fresh grass triggered by the monsoon. There's more gaur action as two bulls lock their horns, and the sound of their clashing horns echo through the valley.

Ganga Singh brings the jeep to a stop near the Moyar Gorge. We walk down a small track to the viewpoint. It's windy, but the day has been clear so far. The viewpoint offers a panoramic view of the gorge and surrounding forests. In the background are the Nilgiri Hills, or the Blue Mountains, appearing in a series of successive rows. The gorge cuts through these hills, and at some places is nearly a thousand feet deep. Through this gorge, the Moyar River, now in its rain-filled rush, thunders away.

Stunned by the view into silence, we sit absorbing the surroundings. The hills are now green, but that's the colour of the monsoon. In other months, they are usually clothed in brown, with kaleidoscopic splashes of green and bright hues, the patterns and colours decided by the plants in bloom — it's red in January and February, white and yellow in March and April, and multi-coloured outfits for post-monsoon months.

In the evening, we go for a safari in the Mudumalai National Park, which

Graphic by SURAJ WADHWA

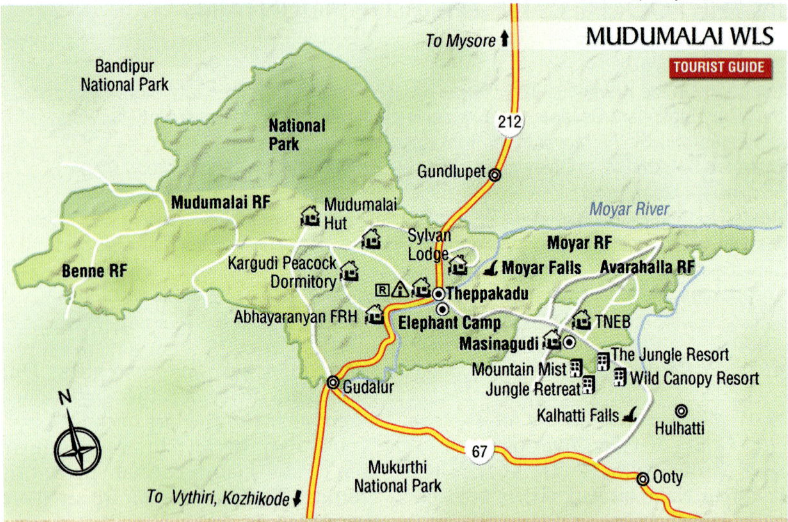

MUDUMALAI WLS
TOURIST GUIDE

RECLAIM YOUR LIFE.

TATA Safari

adjoins Bandipur. The safari bus, operated by the Forest Department, winds through the forest and comes to a halt in front of a tall stone watchtower. Our present run-through-the-jungle was not so rewarding in terms of wildlife sightings, but when the bus comes to a halt at the Moyar Watchtower, all complaints are forgotten.

The tower, built like a lighthouse, stands deep inside the forest on the very edge of a cliff overlooking the Moyar Gorge. The gorge is so deep that I can barely see the river but as I follow my gaze upstream, the view suddenly takes my breath away. The Moyar River, swollen with monsoon water, plummets down hundreds of feet into the gorge, disappearing in its own spray. On the other side, I see the forest canopy spreading like a green carpet, on which flit orioles, cuckoos and bulbuls. A pair of giant squirrels adds a bit of rufous to the predominantly green landscape.

During the following day's safari, we see a magnificent young male elephant with tusks that almost reach up to his toes. He stands in a bamboo clump just beside the road. Lifting his head and trunk to reach the tender bamboo tips, he continues to eat, unmindful of our presence. Since elephants occur in transient populations, there is some chance that tourists might have to return without seeing any pachyderms, even in this high-density elephant zone. Even in the places where elephants live, tuskers, the prime targets of ivory poachers, are very rare. I am fortunate to see this magnificent tusker, and that too at such a close range!

My lucky run continues that evening. As the bus negotiates a curve, we catch sight of one of the most accomplished hunters of the forest — wild dogs. We spot four of them relaxing after perhaps a successful pack hunt.

On my third and final day, I decide to skip the safaris and instead go for a trek (discontinued since then) inside

→ FAST FACTS

When to go Anytime between Apr and Jan is a good time to visit both Bandipur and Mudumalai (it's best from Sep to Dec). Though the parks are open throughout the year, they could be closed during Feb-Apr on account of heavy forest fires

Wildlife/ Forest Dept offices
- Reception Range Office ❶
Theppakadu, Mudumalai
Tel: 0423-2526235
- Wildlife Warden ❶
Mount Stuart Hill
Udhagamandalam (Ooty)-643001
Tel: 0423-2444098
- Govt of Tamil Nadu Tourist Office ❶
Wenlock Road, Ooty-643001
Tel: 2443977
- TTDC ❶ ⓑ
No. 2, Wallajah Road, Chennai
Tel: 044-25367850-54
Website: tamilnadutourism.org
STD code 0423

Bandipur. I choose to explore some promising birding areas over a long trek to a hilltop. Even as my seasoned guide, a local hailing from the indigenous Kuruba tribe, leads me on the trail, deep resonant whoops of langurs announce our presence to everyone for miles around. Though we don't see too many mammals on the trek, the birds don't seem too bothered by our declared presence. Partridges, peacocks, hoopoes, bulbuls, babblers, bee-eaters, doves, noisy parakeets and mynas — all are busy courting and calling. The forest pulsates with the activity of breeding birds in the monsoon. Peacocks strut around with their brilliant, long trains of tail feathers, trying to impress peahens.

THE NILGIRIS

Denizens of Mudumalai (clock wise from top left): **A pair of cheetal deer; Hanuman langurs; Malabar Giant Squirrel; White-socked gaur**

Parakeets fight vociferously over possession of nest holes. Hornbills attend to their incubating mates tucked in tree holes. A hardworking pair of swallows makes endless trips back and forth with food to feed their hungry chicks. The forest is alive! A few hours, a few days spent here are far too few to imbibe its essence. But the city drill beckons and, with a heavy heart, I head back to my cottage to pack my bags. I know I will return, soon.

ABOUT BANDIPUR-MUDUMALAI PARKS

Along the Mysore-Ooty Highway, at the foothills of the Nilgiri mountains, lies some of India's best elephant country. Administered separately, the Bandipur National Park (Karnataka) and the Mudumalai Wildlife Sanctuary (Tamil Nadu) are but components of a single spectacular ecological continuum that also includes Nagarhole (in Karnataka) and Wayanad (in Kerala). Bandipur and Mudumalai are located in the lower reaches of the Nilgiri Biosphere Reserve, which is part of the Western Ghats biodiversity hotspot. This area was once the hunting ground of the Wodeyar royals.

The Mudumalai Sanctuary was set up in 1940, becoming the first sanctuary in Southern India. Covering a stretch of 60 sq km initially, the sanctuary was expanded to 295 sq km by 1956 and thereafter to its present size of 321 sq km. Today both Bandipur and Mudumalai see a huge influx of tourists. Villages located around these protected areas add to the pressure on the forests.

This area receives two monsoons: the south-west (Jun-Sep) and the north-east (Oct-Nov). A brief, cool dry season (Dec-Jan) is followed by summer (Feb-May). This region has a moderate climate all year round and can be visited in any season. Wildlife sightings are fewer in summer compared to other seasons. Unlike temperate forests, these tropical deciduous forests are leafless in summer.

ORIENTATION

The **Reception Range Forest Office** at **Theppakadu** (Tel: 0423-2526235), the entry point into Mudumalai WLS has an **Information Centre**. No trekking is permitted in Mudumalai; neither does the department offer any jeep safaris. Private vehicles are prohibited from entering the Park. Instead, the Forest Department arranges **mini-bus safaris** into the Park, which can be booked at the Theppakadu Reception Range Office. Several **Forest Rest Houses** are scattered across the park. Tour operators in nearby **Masinagudi Town** arrange **birdwatching** and **treks** in the **reserve forest**.

♦**Park entry fee** Indians Rs 35 **Cameras** Still Rs 25, video Rs 150 **Park timings** 7-9 am, 3-6 pm

THINGS TO SEE AND DO

Mudumalai is oriented towards tourism; the Forest Department has well-organised trekking routes inside the parks, and organises safaris as well.

Interpretation centres

Mudumalai boasts of a well-planned information centre, which is located close to the Forest Office at **Theppakadu**, and offers visitors excellent information on the wildlife of this region. The themes are well laid-out, and there are some excellent photographs of wildlife here. Simple but thoughtfully done, the centre also provides information about animal censuses and research done in this area. In addition to these interpretation centres, the Forest Office in Bandipur has a few books and information booklets on sale for visitors.

Jungle safaris

Rides into the parks on specially laid-out dirt roads called 'game roads', which usually pass close to grazing areas, salt licks and water holes offer excellent views of wildlife. Most of the common wildlife (deer, gaur, elephant and langur) can be seen at close range. At Mudumalai and Bandipur, the respective Forest Departments offer hour-long mini-bus safaris inside the park. Though they get crowded during peak holiday seasons, these mini-buses offer ample opportunities to view wildlife.

At Mudumalai, there are no Forest Department jeep safaris and private jeep safaris too are not allowed in the park.

♦**Mudumalai mini-bus safari fee** Rs 35 per head **Timings** 7-9 am, 3-6 pm

Elephant rides

Mudumalai's **Theppakadu Elephant Camp** is one of the biggest elephant camps in South India. As many as 25 elephants are housed here. The camp has elephants that work in the forest, logging timber, and do other forest activities. The evening feeding shows at this camp are crowd pullers. Camp viewings may be closed for short periods

MUMBAI KA GURU
Hari, Hotel Advisor at Travelguru was born and raised in Mumbai. Use his tips and you will fully enjoy the city that never sleeps.

Choose from our network of over 4000 hotels in India. Serviced apartments, budget hotels, luxury resorts, palaces, business accommodations, houseboats and more.

1-800-22-4878
022-4030-4878
www.travelguru.com

India's Largest Hotel Network

THE NILGIRIS

→ GETTING THERE

Air Nearest airport: Coimbatore (169 km/ 4 hrs), connected to Chennai by 10 daily flights by Paramount Airlines, Indian, Air Deccan, Jet Airways and Kingfisher Airlines. Taxi to Mudumalai costs Rs 2,000 approx

Rail Nearest railhead: Mettupalaiyam (Tel: 2442246; 124 km/ 3 hrs) **Best option TO** Nilagiri Express (dep: Chennai Central 9 pm; arr: Mettupalaiyam 6.15 am). Cab to Mudumalai costs Rs 500 approx. **Best option FROM** Nilgiri Express (dep: Mettupalaiyam 7.45 pm; arr: Chennai Central 5.10 am)

Car The 661-km drive from Chennai to Mudumalai must not be attempted for a weekend break. For longer vacations, follow NH45 to Ulundurpettai via Chengalpattu, Tindivanam and Viluppuram. Turn right on NH68 to Salem via Tiyagai Durgam, Kallakkurichi, Talaivasal, Attur and Valappad. Follow NH47 to Avanashi via Perundurai, then turn right on the state road to Mettupalaiyam via Annur and follow NH67 as it curves up to Gudalur via Coonoor and Ooty. Turn right onto the Mysore Highway for Theppakadu, the gateway to Mudumalai. You can also drive to Mudumalai from Ooty via Masinagudi and Bokkapuram Temple

Bus TNSETC has a daily overnight service (dep: 7.15 pm, Rs 305) to Ooty from Chennai's Metropolitan Bus Terminus (Tel: 044-24794705) at Koyambedu. KPN Travels (044-24797998, 24796688) is a good private operator serving this route from Chennai (overnight service 6.30 pm, Rs 430). Buses take 14 hrs to reach Ooty, but you get there early morning. Taxi costs about Rs 1,200 approx to Mudumalai from Ooty

for the public. However, enquiries can be made at the Forest Office in Theppakadu to check the status during your visit.
♦**Camp timings** 7-8 am, 4-5 pm

Moyar Gorge

The Moyar River meanders out of the Nilgiris and emerges in the dry jungles of Bandipur-Mudumalai, where it passes through a spectacular formation of hills referred to as the Moyar Gorge or 'Mysore Ditch'. On the Mudumalai side, bus safaris (upon request) can take you to see the gorge. A watchtower offers a spectacular view of the gorge and the **Moyar Falls**.

Sigur Plateau

The Sigur Plateau harbours extensive scrub and bamboo forests. With the Nilgiris looming right above this plateau, there are some incredible views to be had at the **Bison Valley Viewpoint** on the Mysore-Ooty Road and the **Moyar Falls** in Mudumalai. There are plenty of accommodation options here with a number of resorts located in and around Masinagudi Town (*see Where to Stay below*). It is excellent birding and walking country, though a guide would be required to keep a watch for elephants. The 32-km long forest road to Ooty starts from here. Jeeps can be hired from Masinagudi (7 km from Theppakadu and 26 km from Bandipur) for Rs 700 a day, plus diesel.

Masinagudi tour operators such as **Jungle Retreat** (Tel: 0423-2526430) and **Nature Safari Tours and Treks** (Tel: 2526340, 09443205361) offer customised packages for trips around the Reserve Forest, which include transport and services of a naturalist.

WHERE TO STAY AND EAT

As huge numbers of tourists visit Mudumalai, there is a range of stay options to suit all budgets. The Forest Department lodges predictably have the

THE NILGIRIS

The tiny hill train to the blue mountains passing through patchwork fields

best location. The **Theppakadu Log House** (Tariff: Rs 330-560), near the Moyar River, has two double-bedded and one four-bedded suite. **Sylvan Lodge** (Tariff: Rs 330), also by the Moyar River, just 4 km from Theppakadu, has four double rooms. These two are the best options but there are others, all offering food and hot water. At Abhayaranyam, 3 km from Theppakadu, is another **FRH** (Tel: 0423-2444098; Tariff: Rs 330), which has 2 rooms with attached baths. The caretaker can arrange food. The **FRH Annexe** here has 2 rooms and costs Rs 180 a night. At Kargudi, nearby, is the **Peacock Dormitory**, run by the Forest Department. It has 3 dorms (2 with 20 beds each and one with 10 beds). The **Cuckoo FRH** here has 1 room and costs Rs 180 a night. Bookings for all these can be made at the Wildlife Warden's Office in Ooty (*see Fast Facts on page 221*). You will, however, have to confirm reservations through a personal visit here.

Private resorts cluster around Masinagudi, a village about 12 km from Mudumalai. Options here include **Jungle Retreat** (Tel: 0423-2526469-70; Tariff: Rs 420-3,938) in Bokkapuram Village, 11 km from the Park, has deluxe and regular cottages, a dorm with 30 beds (Rs 400 per bed) and a swimming pool. The Mathais, who own the resort also arrange camping, trekking and birdwatching trips in the Reserve Forest (outside the park) with the services of a naturalist. **Jungle Hut** (Tel: 2526240/ 463; Tariff: Rs 2,387-4,700), run by another family member, also offers similar services. The resort, also in Bokkapuram Village, has 12 rooms and a swimming pool. The **Monarch Safari Park** (Tel: 2526250/ 343; Tariff: Rs Rs 1,100-2,000) has a restaurant with a multi-cuisine menu. The **Bamboo Banks Farm** homestay (Tel: 2526211, 09443205371; Tariff: Rs 1,125-2,000) offers safaris and treks. **New Mountania Rest House** (Tel: 2526267/ 337; Tariff: Rs 1,000-3,500), which arranges birdwatching and **Green Park Resort** (Tel: 2526486; Tariff: Rs 1,000-2,500), which arranges treks, are other good options.

For more hotels and details see Mudumalai Accommodation Listings on page 521 ■
Inputs by Soumya Prasad

ANDHRA PRADESH

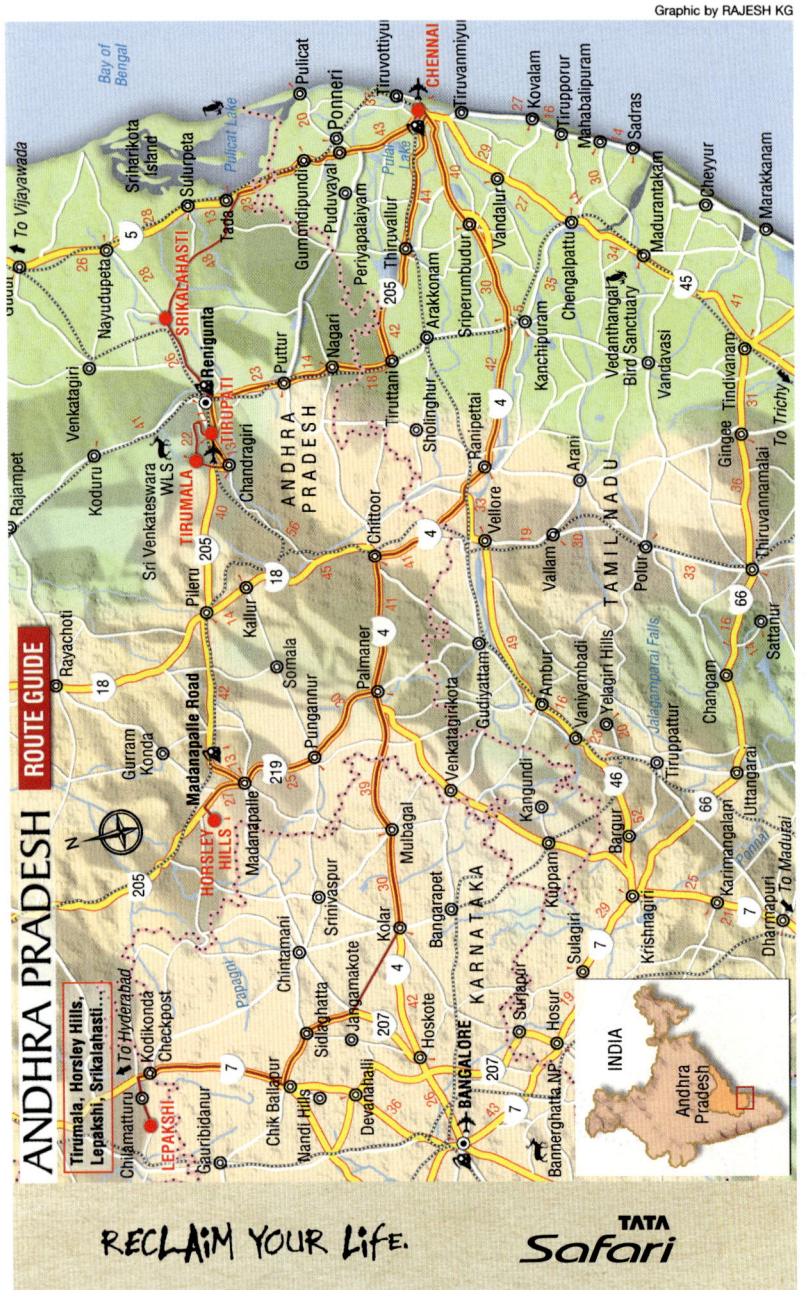

Andhra Pradesh

Visit a little-known hill station and rediscover our long forgotten heritage under the benevolent gaze of the Lord of the Seven Hills

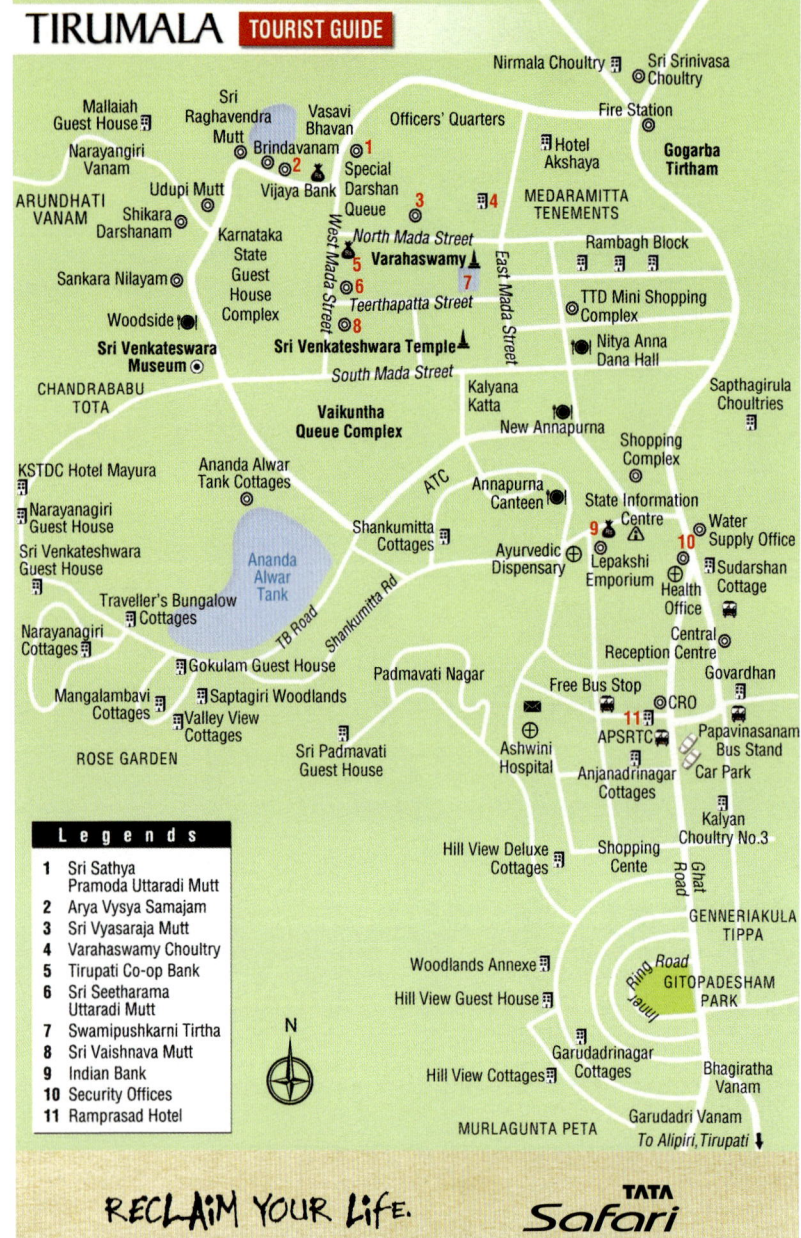

Sri Venkateshwara Temple atop Venkatadri Hill at Tirumala

H SATISH

TIRUMALA-TIRUPATI
VENKATESHWARA: LORD OF THE SEVEN HILLS

State Andhra Pradesh
Location On the picturesque Saptagiri (seven hills) Range, at an altitude of 3,083 ft, in the Chittoor District of southern Andhra
Distances Tirupati is 152 km and Tirumala 174 km NW of Chennai JOURNEY TIME **By road** $3^1/_2$ hrs to Tirupati and $4^1/_2$ hrs to Tirumala **By rail** 2 hrs + 20 mins by road
Route NH205 to Tirupati via Thiruvallur, Thiruttani, Puttur, Vadamala and Renigunta; Ghat Road to Tirumala (*see route guide on page 228*)

■ BY VIMALA MURTHY AND DBN MURTHY

'Venkatadri samam sthanam brahmande naasthi kinchana.'

There is no place in the entire universe equal to Venkatadri. It is a conclusion all devotees of Balaji — and they number in tens of thousands every day — will agree with unanimously. A visit to Tirupati is many things and each of them makes this foremost-among-kshetras remain unparalleled. First, all of us who come here know that it is not possible to predict how long it will take for a darshan of the lord. The queue stretches ahead and behind us, and we know it is endless for there will always be more pilgrims joining the line. We are all links joined by that invisible adhesive: faith. Second, although the hours of waiting are etched interminably in the immediate memory of the trip, they inevitably blur in the weeks that follow. What remains is that enchantingly brief, completely inadequate glimpse of the lord. Is it any wonder that we return time and again, joining that queue and ensuring it remains unending?

ANDHRA PRADESH

Third, the mystique of Tirupati somehow transcends the superlatives that are commonly used to describe it. The statistics are quite amazing (see 'Divining Tirupati' on page 238) but strangely irrelevant. How does it matter that Tirupati is arguably the richest, most visited temple in India? We all know that is not what brings us here. Fourth, as one walks around Tirumala, a township of the floating faithful, the very air is rich with anticipation. It is this wealth that makes Tirupati what it is.

Fifth, as a native of Tirupati says, "I have many friends and acquaintances asking me if I can help them in getting a darshan of Lord Venkateshwara. I tell them all the same thing — I will do what I can but I am really not of any help. It is He who decides. I speak from experience." And like all the other numbers that cannot be counted, this list of what makes Tirupati foremost shall remain without end too. Each of us can add to it with our own experience, which will be unique in its own way. There is, however, one thing that unites us uniformly, inevitably, joyously, absolutely. "Did you get a good darshan?" we are asked after we return. We always say without any doubt, we did.

→ FAST FACTS

When to go Early December is relatively less crowded. There is heavy rush during school vacations and public holidays. New Year's Day and the 10-day Brahmotsavam (Oct) draw the maximum visitors

Sudarshan Ticket Centres
- TTD Information Centre, T Nagar, Chennai. Tel: 044-42129498, 28573835
- TTD Srinivasam Complex, Tirupati Tel: 087-2264537
- TTD choultries, Tirupati. Tel: 2264732

Tourist offices
- Tirumala Tirupati Devasthanam Central Reception Office, Tirumala ⓘ
Tel: 0877-2263883
Website: ttdonline.com
- PRO, TTD ⓘ
Srinivasam Complex, Kapilatirtham Road, Tirupati. Tel: 0877-2264501
- APTDC Tourist Info Centre ⓘⓑ
Room No. 516, Sri Devi Complex Tilak Road, Tirupati
Tel: 0877-2255385, 2289120
- APTDC Tourist Info Counter ⓘⓑ
Punnami Hotel, Srinivasam Complex, Tirupati. Tel: 2289123
- APTDC ⓘⓑ
31/14 Burkit Road, T Nagar, Chennai
Tel: 044-24353373, 65439987
Email: aptdc@satyamnet.in
- TTDC ⓘⓑ
No. 2, Wallajah Road, Chennai
Tel: 044-25367850-54
Website: tamilnadutourism.org
STD code 0877

LEGENDS AND MYTHOLOGY

According to a legend narrated in the Bhavishyottara Purana, Sage Narada once went to the banks of the holy Ganga, where many sages had gathered to perform a sacrifice. When Narada wished to know which among the three chief divinities, Brahma, Vishnu and Shiva, would get the offerings of the sacrifice, the nonplussed rishis appointed Sage Bhrigu to solve their problem. Bhrigu visited Brahmaloka first, but he was ignored by Brahma. He then went to Shiva, who was so engrossed in Parvati that he took no notice of the holy man either. When Bhrigu went to Vaikuntha, Vishnu too, preoccupied with Lakshmi, did not pay attention to him. The enraged Bhrigu kicked Vishnu on his chest, where Lakshmi resided. However, Vishnu, far from getting angry, massaged Bhrigu's foot and

TIRUMALA-TIRUPATI

Photographs by GANESHMUTHU

Burning pure incense offerings for the Lord of the Seven Hills

enquired if the limb was hurt. Appeased, Bhrigu returned and told the other sages that Vishnu deserved their offerings the most.

But Lakshmi, angered by the entire episode, left for Kolhapur (Maharashtra). Vishnu, unable to bear the separation, wandered in search of her, before choosing to reside inside an anthill on the banks of the Swamipushkarni, on the Venkatadri Hill seen today. He later married Akasharaja's daughter, the beautiful Padmavati, an incarnation of Lakshmi. Since Lakshmi had left him, he had no money for his own wedding, and he borrowed what he needed from Kubera. Devotees making offerings at Tirumala believe they are helping the lord repay his debt, and that he in turn will help them. Padmavati is worshipped in a separate temple, in Tiruchanur or Alamelumangapuram (*see page 239*).

The Brahma Purana says that Tirupati is the place Vishnu chose as an alternative to Vaikuntha, his heavenly home. The seven peaks of the Saptagiri Range, of which Tirumala is a part, are said to represent the seven hoods of Adisesha, Vishnu's celestial serpent. They are Seshadri, Neeladri, Garudadri, Anjanadri, Vrishabhadri, Narayanadri and Venkatadri; Tirumala is on the seventh hill, Venkatadri. Going to Tirupati is considered equal to visiting Vaikuntha.

ARCHITECTURE AND ANTIQUITY

There has been long and serious debate on the origins of the deity. Writes Nanditha Krishna in her book *Balaji-Venkateshwara: Lord of Tirumala-Tirupati, An Introduction*, "Hindu deities are generally identified by their attributes, vehicles and distinguishing marks. Venkatesha has no attributes. The original stone image has a crescent mark on the forehead and holds nothing, the jewelled conch and discus being later detachable additions." Nanditha Krishna points to some distinctly Shaivite features such as the matted locks, snake-shaped ornaments and the cobra slung over the right arm. The drapery of the lord resembles a sari and the ceremonial bath is performed only on a Friday with sandal paste and turmeric (women's cosmetics), to the chanting of Sri (Lakshmi) Sukta. There are also several clues pointing to

ANDHRA PRADESH

the deity being Skanda or Murugan, such as the temple's location on a hill and the hunting festival mentioned in ancient Tamil literature. It was Sri Ramanujacharya (1017-1137) who is believed to have established the temple as a Vaishnava kshetra. Regardless of the debate and its direction, even the Alwars, though staunch Vaishnavites, saw both Shiva and Vishnu in the image.

The earliest recorded reference to the temple is by Tamil scholar Tholkappiar in the 2nd century BCE, who referred to the Tirumala Hill as the northern boundary of the Tamil world. Tamil Sangam literature, dated between 2nd and 8th centuries CE, also has many references to the temple and deity. The ancient name of this holy site was Vengadam, derived from the Sanskrit word Venkata, which means 'destroyer of sins'.

ORIENTATION

Tirumala and Tirupati are not the same though they are often referred to synonymously. Tirumala, where the temple to Lord Venkateshwara is located, is 22 km uphill a picturesque, well-maintained forest road interspersed with hairpin bends. The foot of this holy Venkatadri Hill is called Alipiri, from Adi-padi, or 'first step'. The town of Tirupati is 3 km away from Alipiri.

The clean and well-maintained temple town of **Tirumala** is entered via an ornate arch. Soon thereafter is a huge representation of Krishna preaching the Bhagvad Gita to Arjuna. The pathway used by the *padayatris* (pilgrims who arrive on foot) joins the main road near here. The **bus stand** is to the left. The queue lines for tokenholders (paid and free) begin to form in the **queue complex** behind the temple. Then, the labyrinthine queues snake up to the **wooden Mukhadwara** (main entrance) of the temple. In front of the sanctum hall, the **three queues** — Sudarshana tickets, Archananantara Darshanam tickets and the Dharmadarshanam/ Sarvadarshan (ie, free) — merge together. Confined as he is inside the waiting rooms and railings of the queue complex, it is impossible for the devotee to imagine or understand the structure or geography of the temple complex. The queue, however, is a necessary evil, given the sheer numbers who come to worship here. The **bazaar** is a short distance in front of the main gate, and the guest houses are to the north-east and south-east of the temple.

A continuous **free shuttle bus service** is available, which covers places to be seen while in Tirumala. Buses can be boarded from anywhere, to anywhere, and also facilitate commuting from guest houses to the temple.

♦**Packages** APTDC (Chennai Tel: 044-24353373) offers a daily 1-day Chennai-Tirumala tour by AC Volvo coach covering Tirumala, Tiruchanur and Srikalahasti (Rs 1,110 per person). The bus leaves from the APTDC office at Burkit Road (*see 'Fast Facts' on page 232*) at 6.30 pm and arrives in Chennai the next day at 5 pm

THINGS TO SEE AND DO

Darshan of Lord Venkateshwara, the predominant concern of every devotee, could take anywhere between 2 and 5 hrs on normal days. On special days, it could easily be double this time, or more. A waiting time of over 24 hrs is not unheard of. Devotees in the Sarvadarshan (free) queue come to Tirumala prepared for a much longer wait, which can stretch up to three days. Provisions are made for drinking water, soft drinks, coffee/ tea, and toilets, for those waiting in the queue lines. At least one full day with a night halt is essential to appreciate Tirumala and explore the various places of interest on the hill. Another half-day is required to visit temples around Tirupati.

TIRUMALA-TIRUPATI

Traditional folk dances mark the many festivals celebrated at Tirumala

Sri Venkateshwara Temple, Tirumala

The inevitable truth is that devotees spend more time in the queue than in the temple, although considerable effort has been taken by the devasthanam authorities to improve matters. Those with the Sudarshana and Archananantara Darshanam (AAD) tickets (*see below*) are given a time at which they must report at Vaikunthadwaras 1 and 2 respectively. It must be said that the Sarvadarshan queue is not only for those who wish to have darshan without paying a fee, it is also for the bravest. A leading paediatrician we knew would insist on taking his place in the Sarvadarshan queue on his annual pilgrimage to Tirupati. It was, he believed, a good way to remind oneself of equality in the eyes of god. Regardless of which queue one stands in, reserves of patience are found and spent. It is a time ideal for spiritual introspection, though many we know admit to only feeling exasperation.

As the golden doors of the sanctum come within view, a great surge of anticipation sweeps through the waiting devotees, suddenly and collectively. It is a gust of fresh air flooding the huddle of anxious minds, brushing away the debris of doubts. Like a barely comprehended miracle, the aching feet, knees, necks, and thoughts, are replaced with incredible, overwhelming hope. 'Govinda, Govinda!' exults the chorused chant, rising like a heavenward prayer. And heaven is so close at hand.

Entering via the **Mukhadwara**, crowned with seven brass finials, there is the vague impression of a hall decorated with shimmering chandeliers, another of the bedecked temple elephants. Like the scrolling screen of hurried replays are the different mantapams — the **Krishnaraya Mantapam**, the **Ranganayaka Mantapam**, the **Tirumalaraya Mantapam** — each symbolic of the devotion of the patrons after whom they are named. In the Tirumalaraya Mantapam is the Tulabharam, a life-size weighing scale upon which devotees make offerings of sugar, rice, jaggery, money and many other things (the kings of long ago gave gold and jewels) equivalent to their own weight. An **altar to Varadarajaswamy** is close at hand, as is an **idol of Garuda**. The *dhwajasthamba* is breathtakingly huge,

ANDHRA PRADESH

and near it stand idols of Todaramallu, a Muslim chieftain who safeguarded the temple from invaders, alongside his mother and wife. At the entrance to the sanctum, 3-m high metal statues of Jaya and Vijaya, the *dwarapalikas* of Vaikuntha, stand eternal guard. They herald the moment, that most precious moment of darshan. The crush of the crowd is a rage now, seething and mindless. The queues have joined and all are not only equal, they are almost physically one. Your feet are not yours, your hands don't belong anymore. What is more, it doesn't matter. The mind has surrendered to the vision ahead. **Lord Venkateshwara** stands before us.

He towers, resplendent and absolute, in the sanctum lit dimly with oil lamps. He is exactly how you imagined him to be from the countless pictures that you have already seen. The unique *alankaram* (adornment), the *vastras* (clothes) and the *abharanas* (jewels) are all there, a blur of the real and the recollected. Above all, the beautifully proportioned 8-foot tall black stone idol wears a divine smile. The half-closed eyes, and a large part of the forehead are covered with the white *namam*, made, we discover later, of a paste of *pacchekarpura* (borneole flakes) with a red streak of *kasturi* (musk) in the middle, and the mark of butter upon the chin. The lord has four diamond-studded hands. He carries the *chakra* in one and the conch in the other. The left lower hand touches the hip, and the right one is held in the gesture of *vaikuntha-hasta* (boon-bestowal). The ears are adorned with the enormous *makara-kundalas* (crocodile-shaped ear-rings). On the head is his famous diamond-studded crown. Later, you realise it was the aroma of camphor and burning oil which lent such intimacy and immediacy to the life-size image of the lord.

One doesn't need to know Telugu to grasp the meaning of the urgent, irritable, multiple *'Jarakandi! Jarakandi!'*. Yes, yes, we are moving away. With eyes still focused upon that last glimpse of the lord, and the body still being propelled by seen and unseen forces, it is time to stumble out. I find my feet.

Everything else that follows is plainly euphoric: steps falter aimlessly, as if liberated from any purpose. A platform on the side gallery offers a better view of the golden gopuram. A small replica of

→ GETTING THERE

Air Tirupati Airport currently has no connections with Chennai
Rail Nearest railhead: Renigunta Junction (11 km/ 20 mins) **Best option TO** Kacheguda Express (dep: Egmore: 5 pm; arr: Renigunta 8 pm). Taxi to Tirupati costs Rs 150-200 and to Tirumala Rs 450-500.
Best option FROM Chennai Express (dep: Renigunta 5.15 pm; arr: Perambur 6.58 pm, Chennai Central 7.35 pm)
TIP There are faster options (going), but Kacheguda is best for joining the darshan queue early Saturday morning. Saptagiri Express is an equally good option for the return journey
Car The drive to Tirupati is a very pleasant 3 hrs from Chennai, via Tiruvallur, Thiruttani, Puttur and Renigunta. The drive up the winding ghat road to Tirumala takes another hour, and you must pay a toll of Rs 350 for each private car
Bus APSRTC and TNSETC buses leave every 15 mins for Tirupati's Saptagiri Main Bus Stand from Chennai's Metropolitan Bus Terminus (Tel: 044-24794705) at Koyambedu. Tirumala is well connected to Tirupati by APSRTC buses (Rs 22 one-way, 45 mins).
TIP Buses by operators other than APSRTC and vans carrying more than 15 people are not allowed up the hill road

TIRUMALA-TIRUPATI

Pilgrims take a much-needed rest after darshan at TTD's amenities complex

the main idol, **Vimana Venkateshwara**, is worshipped, for one is not to leave the temple without his darshan. In the outer parikrama is a niche with idols of Angada, Sugreeva, Anjaneya, Anantha, Vishwaksena and Garuda. There are counters selling cassettes and gold coins too. The *hundi*, a tall canvas bag with a huge drum below, accepts all offerings, whether in cash or kind. Counting is done once a day in a special store-room, which can be seen from the outside, through glass. The prasadam, served to everyone in a fast-moving line, is quite out of this world. Whether *sakkare pongal* (sweet pongal), ven pongal (white, salted pongal), *puliyogare* (tamarind rice) or *daddhyonnam/ thayir sadam* (curd rice), the servings are generous and the embellishments (ghee, cardamom, cashew nuts, butter, raisins and so on) the richest anywhere. In fact, the cashew nuts seem to equal the grains of rice in the pongal preparations. Suddenly, you realise how hungry you were. All of this is but a sigh, a comma after the full stop.

◆**Timings** 3 am-11.30 pm; darshan for queued devotees commences at 6 am

TIP Non-Hindus entering the temple for darshan of the lord are required to furnish a declaration form, available with the AEO, TTD, Tirumala, expressing respect for the faith.

There is no dress code but electronic items like cell phones, cameras, lighters and torches are banned inside the temple. Smoking, consumption of alcohol/ intoxicants, and non-veg food, is prohibited in Tirumala

◆Each paid Sudarshan Ticket holder (*see 'Fast Facts'*) is entitled to two **free laddoos** after darshan. Collect a **free meal ticket** (counter, open throughout the day, near temple exit) in case you plan to partake of temple food

More to see in Tirumala

There are several must-sees in Tirumala, apart from the main temple, with respect to which the distances and directions are given here. The bathing section is cordoned off from the main body of water in the holy **Swamipushkarni Tirtha** (just south); chlorine filters purify and clean the water constantly. The **Varahaswamy Temple** (north of the Swamipushkarni Tirtha) is an ancient

Divining Tirupati

- **Lord Venkateshwara** is 'Balaji' in the North, 'Tirupati Thimmappa' in Karnataka and 'Srivari' in Andhra Pradesh. He is also Srinivasa, or where Lakshmi (Sri) resides. He is adorned with the *meru pacha*, said to be the world's largest emerald. His gold crown weighs almost 27 kilos, and is encrusted with about 28,000 diamonds. Among his exquisite pieces of jewellery are a necklace which has gold-encased tiger claws and another with an image of Lakshmi in each pendant. He also wears a necklace of tulasi beads, and another of *saligramas* mounted with gold and engraved with the Sahasranama (thousand names). His sword, the *suryakatari*, is decorated with the ten avataras. His traditional accessories, the conch and discus, and the *kavacham* (shield), are also covered with diamonds.
- There are **13 Kalyana Kattes** (places for **hair tonsuring**), performed free, or for a nominal fee of Rs 10. Hair that is thus collected is washed, dried and sorted out according to length. There is an average yield of about 800 kilos of hair per day, which is sold to the wig-making industry, earning the temple Rs 16 crores annually. Offering of hair is considered to be an act of humility and devotion to god.
- At the turn of the decade (2001-2002), the **total income of the TTD** stood at Rs 532 crores. Of this, sale of laddoos alone garnered Rs 50 crores. The temple itself employs 18,000 people. *Hundi* cash collection peaks on New Year's Day. On January 1, 2006, all previous records were broken by the collection of Rs 1.45 crores.
- A **solar cooking system** designed by the Ministry of Non-conventional Energy Sources (NCES) provides eco-friendly energy to cook approximately 30,000 meals a day.
- In 2004, the National Dairy Development Board began supplying ghee to the temple kitchen via a double-layered pipeline. The **Venkateshwara Temple needs 4,500 kilos of ghee every day**. Earlier, about 1,100 tins of ghee were transported, stocked, opened and used every day; empty containers were auctioned once in six months. There have been sporadic efforts to make the famous **Tirupati laddoos** by machine but snags have continued to keep human hands busy with making the delicious sweet.
- **Giant turbines** located on a nearby hill generate electricity for the TTD complex.
- The number of pilgrims per day averages 35,000. On special occasions, it could be over 150,000.

granite shrine dedicated to Vishnu's Varaha (boar) avatara. Traditionally, this temple is to be visited before the main shrine. The **Bedi Anjaneya Temple** (200m south) is dedicated to Hanuman, designated protector of the temple. He wears handcuffs (bedi) and is chained, so that he may not wander away from his duties. The **Venkateshwara Dhyan Mandir** ($^1/_2$ km south-east; 5 am-9 pm) is a large meditation hall with a huge portrait of Lord Venkateshwara; it's clean and quiet. The **SV Museum** ($1^1/_2$ km north-east; 8 am-8 pm; entry ticket Re 1), situated in a sprawling, well-maintained garden, has interesting exhibits of photographs, idols, representations of great personalities associated with the temple, musical instruments, arms, an ivory palanquin and wooden carvings. Attractive stone sculptures lead to the meditation hall behind the museum.

The **Sila Toranam** ($1^1/_2$ km northwest; always open) is a spectacular, natural geological formation in the form of a garland, said to be the oldest in the world at 2,500 million years. The **Chakra Tirtham** (2 km north-west, near Sila Toranam) is a waterfall marked with idols and a Sudarshana Chakra; it's reached via uneven steps and a stream. The **Gogarba Dam** (3 km north-east), which collects rain run-off, is the main source of water for Tirumala. The **Venugopala Swamy Temple** (3 km north-east; 7 am-1 pm, 2-7 pm) is a small temple with a black stone idol of Krishna. The water from the 10-m-high sacred **Akasa Ganga Tirtha Falls** (4 km north-east), reached by going down 120 steps through pretty scenery, provides the water for the daily abhishekam of Lord Venkateswara. The Skanda Purana says that a bath in the holy **Papavinasha Tirtham** (10 km north-east; 5 am-7 pm) washes away all sins; there are temples to Gangabhavani and Anjaneya near here. A man-made structure here facilitates a convenient bath; changing rooms are available. Apart from the first three, which are walking distance from the temple, all of the above sites can be reached by the **free shuttle bus**, or covered by taxi.

Festivals

Among the most important festivals is the 10-day **Brahmotsavam** celebration in October, marked by special alankarams and sevas, and chariot festivals. Many of the proceedings are telecast live on TV. **Dussehra** (Oct) and the **Teppotsava** (float festival, Mar) are also very important. In May, **Padmavathi Parinaya** (wedding) is celebrated in front of the Narayanagiri Guesthouse. **Vaikuntha Ekadashi** (Jan) is also a very auspicious day.

Alamelumangapuram/ Tiruchanur

Pilgrims to Tirupati always pay obeisance at this majestic temple to Goddess Padmavati, consort of Lord Venkateshwara, who is seen decked beautifully in silk. Tiruchanur is 4 km east of Tirupati.
♦**Timings** 5.30 am-8.30 pm; daily *annadana* from 9 am-4 pm

Srinivasamangapuram

Also known as Kalyana Venkateswara Swamy Temple, Lord Venkateshwara is seen in this impressive stone abode as a tall, life-like idol decorated beautifully with silk, jewellery and flowers. Padmavati resides in his chest. The lord and his consort are believed to have stopped here on the way to Tirumala to spend six months in Sage Agastya's ashram. The ceremonial wedding of the *utsavamurtis* is conducted daily in the Nitya Kalyana Mantapa to the north of the temple.
♦**Location** On the road to Bangalore, a 2 km deviation from the highway, 11 km from Tirupati **Timings** 5 am-8 pm

Other sites near Tirupati

Kapila Thirtha (3 km from the railway station; 5 am-9 pm; Rs 5 special darshan) is a lovely waterfall cascading down a hill. Pilgrims bathe in the tank here, and under the waterfalls. Sage Kapila is believed to have worshipped the *swayambhu* linga in the **Kapileshwara Temple** here. The reclining deity, with a measuring jar for a pillow, in the **Govindarajaswamy Temple** (1

Choose from our network of over 4000 hotels in India. Serviced apartments, budget hotels, luxury resorts, palaces, business accomodations, houseboats and more.

Hotel	Rating
Gopi Krishna	Budget
Hotel Mayura	3 ★
Fortune Kences	4 ★

MTNL/BSNL Toll Free No.
1-800-22-4878
022-4030-4878
www.travelguru.com

India's Largest Hotel Network

ANDHRA PRADESH

Tonsured devotees at Tirumala

km south of the railway station; 5 am-9 pm; special darshan Rs 5, quick darshan Rs 20) is worshipped as the elder brother of Lord Venkateshwara. According to legends, Govindarajaswamy, tired of measuring his sibling's wealth, came down to Tirupati to rest. A little ahead of here is the **Sri Venkateswara Museum** (open 8 am-8 pm; entry fee Re 1) showcasing Vaishnava temple art, and *vastras* used for dressing the lord.

WHERE TO STAY

In Tirumala
The Tirumala Tirupati Devasthanam (TTD) provides all pilgrim accommodation in Tirumala. Rents range from free to Rs 2,500 per day, including for cottages. Accommodation is provided at the **Rambagicha Guest House**, the **Varahaswamy Guest House**, the **Saptagiri Guest House**, the **Narayanagiri Guest House** and several other guest houses.

Advance reservation of accommodation at Tirumala can be made through **advance reservation** at TTD Info Centres (*see 'Fast Facts' on page 232*). Your reservation slip must be shown at the ARP (Advance Reservation Provision) Counter, Centre Reception Office, TTD, Tirumala (Tel: 0877-2263883). You can also book online at ttdsevaonline.com. If you show up without bookings, go to the Current Booking counter in the Central Reception Office at Tirumala, located next to the ARP Counter.

Devotees must mention the type of room they want at the time of advance reservation (at least 30 days ahead). Rooms, barring the VIP rooms, have basic facilities — cots, fans, attached bathrooms and toilets. Some are clean and comfortable with Western-style toilets (provided on request), and running hot water. Single pilgrims can only get dormitory accommodation.

Karnataka State Guest House (Tel: 2277238; Tariff: Rs 150-1,500), which offers basic facilities a kilometre to the south-west of the temple, is the only facility in Tirumala that is not managed by the TTD.

In Tirupati
Srinivasam Complex (Tariff: Rs 200-600, equal amount as deposit) is TTD's accommodation in Tirupati, and is located opposite the Road Transport Corporation Complex; they have AC and non-AC rooms, allotted for a 24-hr stay. Advance reservation, to be ensured 20 days ahead, can be made by sending a demand draft for Rs 600 (AC) or Rs 200 (non-AC), drawn in favour of the Executive Officer, TTD, and mailed to the Dy Executive Officer, Srinivasam Complex (Tel: 0877-2264537, 2264540-41), near RTC Bus Stand, Tirupati-517501.

Tirupati has many good hotels and budget lodges. The **Ramee Guestline Hotel** (Tel: 2280366/ 800; Tariff: Rs 1,300-2,200), 3 km south-east from the bus stand, has a bar and restaurant. **Bhima's**

HOTEL KA GURU, TRAVELGURU

HOTEL ROOM ANYWHERE IN INDIA, YOUR BUDGET.

Meet the Hotel Advisors* of Travelguru. People who know India's cities and towns in and out. They help you find the best hotel room for your budget, with the amenities you need and in the area of the city that you require.

Choose from our network of over 4000 hotels in India. Serviced apartments, budget hotels, luxury resorts, palaces, business accommodations, houseboats and more. **From Jaipur to Hyderabad, Shimla to Pune, get your hotel room instantly confirmed.**

1-800-22-4878
022-4030-4878
www.travelguru.com

India's Largest Hotel Network

*The people featured above are actual Travelguru employees

ANDHRA PRADESH

Shopping for religious souvenirs at the many stalls in Tirumala

Paradise (Tel: 2237271-74; Tariff: Rs 650-1,500) is a good hotel 1$^1/_2$ km south of the bus stand. **Hotel Mayura** (Tel: 2225251; Tariff: Rs 900-1,450), 1 km north of the bus stand, is also reasonably good, as is **Hotel Sindhuri Park** (Tel: 2256430-37; Tariff: Rs 1,080-1,980). **Hotel Grand** (Tel: 2257115; Rs 545-2,200) is opposite the noisy bus stand but the hotel itself is nice. **Sreekanth Lodge** (Tel: 2259208; Tariff: Rs 250-750) and **Suresh Residency** (Tel: 2222999; Tariff: Rs 400-800) are other budget options.

For details, see Accommodation Listings on pages 493 (Tirumala) and 494 (Tirupati)

WHERE TO EAT

In Tirumala
Basic free meals (vegetable dishes, chutney, rice, sambhar, rasam and buttermilk) are provided at the **Nitya Anna Dana Hall** (next to shopping complex). More than 25,000 pilgrims eat in this big hall every day. The four **Mayura Hotels** (Tel: 2225251) are clean and serve cheap tiffin items and meals (special banana leaf meal Rs 50). **Woodside Restaurant**, near the SV Museum, is another good option. The **Saptagiri Woodlands Restaurant** (located near the Saptagiri Guesthouse) is recommended for its hot and tasty South Indian vegetarian snacks and meals. There are a number of smaller cafés which serve basic South Indian tiffin dishes. Eat any time at the long row of cheap, roadside dhaba-style joints near the Swamipushkarni Tirtha.

TIP Prices at all restaurants in Tirumala are fixed by the TTD; ask ahead for garlic-free food

In Tirupati
The **Ramees Guestline Hotel's** (Tel: 2280366) restaurant serves both veg and non-veg food. **Balaji Woodlands**, near the bazaar, is clean and good for South Indian tiffin dishes and meals. **Bharani Restaurant** (1$^1/_2$ km east of bus station) is also a decent option for South Indian tiffin items and meals. The APTDC-operated **Punnami Restaurant** (Tel: 2289123), located in the Srinivasam Complex (Tel: 2264537) is a self-service restaurant, which is inexpensive, clean, and serves tasty food promptly. ■

Inputs by Lalitha Sridhar

A divine Kalamkari painting, an art form that Srikalahasti is justly famous for

SRIKALAHASTI
VAYU LINGAM — SHIVA AS WIND

State Andhra Pradesh
Location Srikalahasti is hemmed in by the low-lying Kailasagiri Hills and is situated on the banks of River Swarnamukhi, in Chittoor District of southern Andhra
Distance 114 km NW of Chennai **JOURNEY TIME** *By road* 4 hrs *By rail* 2½ hrs + ½ hr by road
Route NH5 to Tada via Errukancheri, Naravarikuppam, Panjetti, Puduvayal and Gummidipundi; state highway to Srikalahasti (*see route guide on page 228*)

■ BY JAYA MADHAVAN

Srikalahasti is usually a hurried halt en route to Tirupati. What irony that we breeze past like the wind from this Panchabhoota Shivasthala, one of the five magnificent temples where Shiva is propitiated as air, water, fire, earth and sky respectively. In Srikalahasti, Shiva presides as the Vayu Lingam. Like the justly famous Kalamkari paintings, which too draw attention to Srikalahasti, this temple town is rich with colours and textures, steeped in tradition and history. It is said life changes for the better for one who visits the temple of Srikalahasti. There is only one way to find out how true this is, and rushing by isn't it.

LEGENDS AND MYTHOLOGY

The name Srikalahasti is derived from *sri* meaning spider, *kala* or serpent and *hasti* or elephant, and speaks of the devotion

ANDHRA PRADESH

D RAVINDER REDDY/ RAVI PRESS PHOTO

Dwajasthamba, Srikalahastisvara Temple

→ FAST FACTS

When to go Pleasant from Nov to Feb
Tourist offices
● APTDC ❶ ❺
31/ 14 Burkit Road, T Nagar, Chennai
Tel: 044-65439987
Website: tourisminap.com
● TTDC ❶ ❺
No. 2, Wallajah Road, Chennai
Tel: 044-25367850-54
Fax: 25361385; Email: ttdc@vsnl.com
Website: tamilnadutourism.org
STD code 08578

of these three creatures to Lord Shiva. Urnanabha, son of the celestial architect Vishwakarma, was such an excellent sculptor that he would copy whatever Brahma created. Enraged, Brahma cursed him to be born as a spider but said he would be freed of the curse if he worshipped Shiva at Dakshina Kailasam. Kala, the serpent, was banished to earth because of his delay in returning from the netherworld to adorn the neck of Shiva. Hasti, Shiva's attendant, was committed to life on earth for his lack of propriety in disturbing the privacy of Shiva and Parvati. All three attained liberation when they worshipped Shiva at Dakshina Kailasam. The temple is one of the 51 Shaktipeeths, marking the spot where Goddess Sati's skull fell.

ORIENTATION

The **main bus stand** is 1 km north-east of the **Srikalahastisvara Temple**. The **railway station** is 2 km north-west of it. Autos are the quickest way to get around.
◆**Packages** TTDC (Chennai Tel: 044-25367850, see 'Fast Facts' at left) has a day trip from Chennai to Srikalahasti, which also covers Thiruttani by non-AC coach (Rs 640, without food). At least 15 persons must register and departure is according to the group's convenience
◆APTDC (Chennai Tel: 044-65439987, see 'Fast Facts' at left) arranges a night trip (6.30 pm-5 pm next day) out of Chennai to Srikalahasti and nearby places like Tirumala by AC Volvo (adults Rs 1,110; children (4-8 yrs) Rs 888, including accommodation and darshan at 5 am). Book at least 15 days in advance

THINGS TO SEE AND DO

Don't opt for the whirlwind tour. A full day will allow you to admire the frescoes and sculptures in the main temple, visit the small temples, climb the hills to catch the views and spend a quiet hour at the *tirtham* or the waterfalls.

Srikalahastisvara Temple

Adorned by three grand towers and flanked by the Durgambika, Kannappa and Kumaraswamy hills, the temple faces west, on the banks of the **River Swarnamukhi**. Despite the large crowds gathered for the morning worship, once you enter the precincts of the temple, the massive pillars, high ceiling and huge prakarams still your mind.

The sanctum contains a *kavacha* (armour) topped by a serpent's hood, beneath which lies the fragile *swayambhu* linga, shaped like an elephant's trunk. The linga has never been touched by human hands. All offerings are made to the bronze *utsavamurti*. The deity is surrounded by lamps. While the other lamps burn steadily, the lamp to the right of the deity moves constantly as if pushed by the wind in the otherwise airless *sannidhi*. The priest explains that the flickering flame is Shiva manifested as wind in the shrine. To the right of the sanctum is Sati manifested as Jalandhara (top half of a body) or as Gnana Prasoonambika, the goddess of knowledge. To the left, as one walks from the northern gopuram, is a shrine for Patala Vinayaka. The idol was found on the bed of the Swarnamukhi, 35 ft below the ground.

The Rahu Ketu Sarpadosha Nivarana Puja is considered to be efficacious for those with astrological setbacks including Sarpadosha (planets in horoscope hemmed in between Rahu and Ketu). This puja is performed daily between 6.30 am and 8.30 pm (Rs 250-500, including puja materials). The grandest festival is **Maha Shivaratri** (Feb), during which a **Brahmotsavam** is conducted for nine nights. The other important festivals are **Navaratri** and **Vinayaka Chaturthi**. On the third day from Sankranthi, the deity is taken round the hill in a procession in which the entire town joins in.

◆**Location** 2 km south-west of the bus stand **Timings** 6 am-9.30 pm (9 pm on Tue, Wed, Thu) **Temple Tel** 08578-222240, 221140

TIP Special darshan costs Rs 50. Cameras not allowed in inner prakarams

Other temples

The **Bhakta Kannappa Temple** on Kannappa Hill ($1/2$ km east of main temple) is dedicated to the legendary hunter who sacrificed his eyes for Shiva. You will also find the **Chaturmukeshvara Temple** (open 6 am-6.30 pm) to Shiva as a linga with four faces. There is a shrine here dedicated to Brahma, who is said to have worshipped Shiva there to regain his ability to create. One can drive halfway up the hill, after which there is a climb of 75 steps to the shrine. Autos charge Rs 50 for a round-trip from the main temple.

You can also visit the **Sri Subrahmanya Swamy Temple** in Vijnanagiri (1 km east of main temple; 150 steps up;

DELHI KI GURU
Deepti, Hotel Advisor at Travelguru. Well acquainted with NCR, she knows the shortest route to N.E.P.Z from Connaught Place.

Choose from our network of over 4000 hotels in India. Serviced apartments, budget hotels, luxury resorts, palaces, business accommodations, houseboats and more.

1-800-22-4878
022-4030-4878
www.travelguru.com

India's Largest Hotel Network

ANDHRA PRADESH

open 8 am-1 pm, 4-8 pm), the **Durgambika Temple** on Durgambika Hill ($1/2$ km north of main temple; 50 steps up; open 8 am-1 pm, 4-6 pm), and the **Prasanna Varadaraja Swamy Temple** (in town centre; open 6 am-9 pm).

WHILE IN SRIKALAHASTI

The **Veyilingala Kona Waterfall** is 8 km east of the main temple. It's best visited before 4 pm, after which the area becomes lonely. Nearby is the **temple of Sahasra Linga** (open 7.30 am-6 pm), a single linga etched with 1,000 miniature lingas. A round-trip by auto from the main temple costs Rs 150; it's Rs 250 for half a day.

→ GETTING THERE

Rail Nearest railhead: Renigunta Junction (26 km/ 40 mins) **Best option TO** Chennai Express (dep: Chennai Central 7 am; arr: Renigunta 9.15 am) Taxis charge Rs 400-500 return **Best option FROM** Chennai Express (dep: Renigunta 5.15 pm; arr: Perambur 6.58 pm, Chennai Central 7.35 pm)
Car Srikalahasti is a short 4-hr drive from Chennai. Drive north, exiting Chennai by the Errukancheri High Road past Vyasarpadi and Errukancheri suburbs, onto NH5 and drive till Tada via Puduvayal and Gummidipundi. Turn left onto the state highway to Srikalahasti
Bus APSRTC (Tel: 044-24792233, Mobile: 09444160990) buses leave every half hour starting 4.30 am until 9.30 pm from Koyambedu in Chennai (Rs 64). TNSETC (Tel: 044-24794709) has many services to Srikalahasti between 6 am-noon and 2-10.40 pm from Koyambedu (Rs 42)

The **Bharadwaja Tirtham** (less than $1/2$ km south of the main temple) is named after Sage Bharadwaja, who meditated here in the Treta Yuga. The adjoining garden with its view of the hills is a quiet spot for a picnic.

SHOPPING

Srikalahasti is famous for **Kalamkari**, a method of painting natural dyes on to cotton or silk with a bamboo pen. Shops in Sriram Nagar Colony and the BP Agraharam (1-$1^1/2$ km west of the temple) sell Kalamkari panels and borders. Prices range from Rs 70-150 for a 25 sq cm piece, depending on the quality of cloth.

WHERE TO STAY

The Devasthanam has a **Pilgrims Choultry** (Tel: 08578-221185; Tariff: Rs 50-400). Its **Trinetra Guest House** (Tariff: Rs 150-500) offers non-AC and AC rooms with basic facilities. **Hotel Swarna Residency** (Tel: 223065/ 67-68, 224415; Tariff: Rs 375-702), opposite the temple, is better than these two.

For more hotels and details, see Srikalahasti Accommodation Listings on page 493

WHERE TO EAT

The biggest eateries are two called **Saravana Bhavan**, opposite the temple but they are not authorised branches of the popular Chennai chain and do not match its standards. Instead, buy **prasad** at the temple and dig into the lovely *puliyore* (tamarind rice), laddoos and *murukkus*. The temple also offers hygienically prepared **free noon meals** to nearly 200 pilgrims. Tokens are handed out between 10.30 and 11 am in the corridor outside the Gnana Prasonambika Sannidhi. Food is served in the mandapam inside the temple in three batches starting at 11.30 am. On Sundays and Mondays, an additional 200 tokens are given out. ■

The intricately sculpted pillars of the Virabhadra Temple

DILIP BANERJEE

LEPAKSHI

STORIES CAST IN STONE

State Andhra Pradesh
Location This hilltop town holds a rich heritage in Anantapur District of southern Andhra, 14 km east of Hindupur, close to the Karnataka border
Distance 461 km from Chennai **JOURNEY TIME By road** 8 hrs **By rail** 5 hrs + 3 hrs by road **By air** 1 hr + 3 hrs by road
Route NH4 to Kolar via Poonamallee, Sriperumbudur, Ranipettai, Chittoor, Palmaner and Mulbagal; NH207 to Chik Ballapur via Sidlaghatta; NH7 to Kodikonda; state road to Lepakshi (*see route guide on page 228*)

■ BY MAYA JAYAPAL

Lepakshi fights its desolation with grandeur. Tales spill out of its every edifice, many so splendid that they defy imagination and belief, effortlessly transporting visitors to a world of lost honour, curses, answered and unanswered prayers.

The temple at Lepakshi was built during the reign of Achyuta Deva Raya (1530-1542) of the mighty Vijayanagara Kingdom. It's only befitting then that the huge boulders strewn around Lepakshi look similar to the ruins of another Vijayanagara gem — Hampi.

Legend has it that Lepakshi's name refers to the bird Jatayu, which was wounded while trying to rescue Sita from Ravana. Lord Rama then said with compassion: "Le Pakshi", which in Telugu means "Get up, bird".

Behind the temple's name is yet another tale about two brothers, Virupanna and Veeranna, who commissioned its construction. Virupanna, the treasurer of the kingdom, loosened his purse strings to build the temple, giving

CHENNAI WEEKEND BREAKS | 247

rise to rumours of embezzlement. The ruler eventually summoned him. Anticipating punishment, Virupanna plucked out his eyes and dashed them against the outer wall. Zealous guides now point to two red spots on the temple wall, which, they say, start weeping in the rain. The name, therefore, could also have been derived from 'lep kshi' (embalmed or painted eye).

The temple was never completed. Even today, it is believed that a blind Virupanna wanders around the temple, anguished by a dream he could not fulfill.

THINGS TO SEE AND DO

The Lepakshi Temple stands atop a granite hillock called **Kurmasaila** (Hill of the Tortoise). A relief of a tortoise adorns a wall inside the temple.

→ GETTING THERE

Air Nearest airport: HAL Airport, Bangalore (130 km/ 3 hrs), connected to Chennai by 22 daily flights from numerous airlines. Taxi to Lepakshi costs Rs 1,600
Rail Nearest railhead: Bangalore (130 km/ 3 hrs) **Best option TO** Bangalore Mail (dep: Chennai Central 11.15 pm; arr: Bangalore City 5.30 am). A taxi to Lepakshi costs Rs 1,500 **Best option FROM** Chennai Mail (dep: Bangalore City 10.45 pm; arr: Chennai Central: 4.40 am)
Car Follow NH4 (Bangalore Highway) to Kolar via Sriperumbudur, Ranipettai, Chittoor, Palmaner and Mulbagal. From Kolar, turn right on the road leading Sidlaghatta on NH207, and continue till Chik Ballapur to join NH7. Drive north and shortly after you cross the AP state border comes Kodikanda Checkpost. Turn left for Lepakshi, 15 km away

The outer *prahara* has two striking sculptures: the 7-ft **Ganesha** and the huge 18-ft tall **Nagalinga**. Canopied by a seven-hooded cobra, the linga stands on a massive uncut stone split in the centre (haphazardly cemented by conservationists). It is said that the structure was carved by a workman while waiting for his mother to bring him lunch. When she saw her son's work, she praised it and the base cracked. Local lore attributes this to the belief that a mother's praise can have an adverse impact.

The temple has three small shrines of Papaneswara, Raghunatha and Virabhadra (the main shrine). All have a common Ardha Mandapa. The Mukha Mandapa and the Natya Mandapa come next.

There's a profusion of paintings on the roofs, walls and sculptured pillars of the shrines. In the front side of the **Virabhadra shrine**, on the ceiling, is what is acknowledged as the **largest mural in Asia**. It's a huge rectangular panel, about 7 by 4 metres, with Virabhadra (Lord Shiva) at the centre. The painting has dimmed with age and neglect. Nevertheless, it gives the impression of a gigantic figure floating in the sky. At the bottom is a painting of Virupanna and his family praying.

In the centre of the brilliantly sculpted and pillared **Mukha Mandapa** is the beautiful dance hall or **Natya Mandapa**, supported by pillars bearing fine figures of divine musicians. Brahma is seen in the act of clashing his cymbals. Surya plays the *naadaswara*, Tumbura and Narada strum *tumburas* while Nataraja lifts his foot in a dance posture. The sculpture of Rambha, the celestial dancer, is so well executed that one feels her performance could start at any moment.

Next door is the **Kalyana Mandapa**, where Shiva and Parvati are said to have got married. The unfinished hall opens into the sky. Between the Kalyana Mandapa and the main shrine lies a **giant footstep**, said to be Sita's. Inside the footprint is a perennial spring.

The unusual **Lata Mandapa** (Hall of Creepers), to the western side of the Kalyana Mandapa, has 42 pillars in four parallel rows. The 96 different patterns of creepers in the hall are said to have inspired the weavers of Andhra Pradesh.

About half a kilometre away is the famous **Lepakshi Bull**, the monolith Nandi, carved out of red granite. The chain around its neck is precisely etched, down to the insignia of the Vijayanagara Kingdom: the mythical bird with an elephant in its claws, hanging as a pendant. Like the Nagalinga, the bull was carved by a workman during his leisure hours.

Warning Beware of monkeys who hang around the temple complex

→ FAST FACTS

When to go October to February when the temperatures are cool
Tourist office
● APTDC ❶ ❻
31/14 Burkit Road, T Nagar, Chennai
Tel: 044-24353373, 65439987
Mobile: 09840580577
Website: tourisminap.com
STD codes Lepakshi 08544; Hindupur 08556

WHERE TO STAY AND EAT

In Lepakshi
AP Tourism's **Punnami Guest House** (Tariff: Rs 150) is the only place to stay in Lepakshi. It's basic, has just three rooms, and is difficult to book in advance.

In Hindupur
Your best bet is to stay in Hindupur, 14 km from Lepakshi. **The Nandini Gardens Hindupur Tourism Complex** (Tel: 08556-222636; Tariff: Rs 200-450) on the outskirts of the town, on Bangalore Road, has 13 rooms of which 4 are cottages and one an AC room. Its **Nandini Garden Restaurant** serves Chinese, tandoori, Andhra and Karnataka cuisine. The privately-owned **Palla Residency** (Tel: 224959; Tariff: Rs 300-899), with its own restaurant, is a new, upmarket addition.

Alternatively, you can stay in Bangalore and do Lepakshi as a day trip. For your trip to Lepakshi, pack food and carry drinking water. There are no roadside eateries in the village, not even cold drink sellers, and absolutely no shopping.

For details, see Lepakshi Accommodation Listings on page 493 ■

JAIPUR KA GURU
Zafar, Hotel Advisor at Travelguru, knows where to head for the finest tie-n-dye bandhani sarees.

Choose from our network of over 4000 hotels in India. Serviced apartments, budget hotels, luxury resorts, palaces, business accommodations, houseboats and more.

1-800-22-4878
022-4030-4878
www.travelguru.com

India's Largest Hotel Network

View of southern Andhra's rugged Nallamali Range from Horsley Hills

HORSLEY HILLS
SUMMER SOJOURN, SARKARI STYLE

State Andhra Pradesh
Location Horsley Hills is located at 4,152 ft in the Nallamalai Range on Andhra's southwestern border with Karnataka
Distance 276 km NW of Chennai **JOURNEY TIME** *By road* 7 hrs
Route NH4 to Palmaner via Sriperumbudur, Ranipettai and Chittoor; NH219 to Madanapalle via Pungannur; state roads to Horsley Hills (*see route guide on page 228*)

■ BY ANURAG MALLICK

In an earlier avatar when Horsley Hills was not the commercial hill station it is now, it used to be an undeveloped rustic hillock. According to local legend, a pious woman called Mallamma used to live on the top of the hill where she was protected and looked after by an elephant (*yenugu* in Telugu). Word soon got around and the place was rather simplistically dubbed Yenugu Mallamma Konda (hill).

News of this also reached WD Horsley, Collector of Cuddappah District, who was desperately seeking an escape from the heat and fiery food of the Andhra plains. He came here on a hunch and was bowled over by the natural beauty of the place. In 1870, he constructed two houses and thus laid the foundation of a hill resort, which was duly named after him. The hills became his summer retreat and the sarkari trend continued with the hilltop villa becoming the summer residence of the Andhra Pradesh Governor.

HORSLEY HILLS

THINGS TO SEE AND DO

On first glance, it's easy to dismiss Horsley Hills as a touristy resort with bureaucratic bungalows that has nothing to offer except cement bunks and parks with slides. However, a closer look reveals that it's not without its interesting share of quirks. For one, it's perhaps one of the few places in India that calls a tree by name. A 150-year-old **eucalyptus tree** near Horsley Bungalow is endearingly called Kalyani.

The lush forests around Horsley Hills are ideal for nature walks, picnics and drives. The hill station has a few interesting excursions but beyond that, there's not much else. If you are looking for a place where you can just put up your feet and relax, this is it.

Horsing around

The most prominent tourist spot is **Gali Bandalu** (Windy Rock), a rocky slope that derives its name from the gusty winds that blow nearly all day. The **Eastern** and **Western** viewpoints are great places to watch the sun rise and set.

Kids can frolic in the three tiny gardens and parks here. The numerous trees and moderate temperature spell lots of **birdwatching**. A small natural **lake**, 1 km down the hill, is great for angling.

About 40 km from Horsley Hills and often confused with it is **Gurram Konda**, between Madanapalle and Raichoti. Literally 'Horse Hill', it is so named because its steep pathway was once accessible only on horseback. At the foot of the hill is a small fort called **Mahal**.

Temple and followers

The **Yenugu Mallamma Temple** here is an ancient shrine, dedicated to the pious Mallamma who was looked after by a tusker.

The indigenous Chenchu tribes involve themselves in basket-weaving

→ FAST FACTS

When to go All year round. The busy seasons are March to June and September to October
Tourist offices
● APTDC ❶
Punnami Hill Resort, Horsley Hills, Madanapalle, Tel: 279323-24
● TTDC ❶ ❻
No. 2, Wallajah Road, Chennai
Tel: 044-25367850-54
Fax: 25361385; Email: ttdc@vsnl.com
Website: tamilnadutourism.org
STD code 08571

CHENNAI WEEKEND BREAKS | 251

ANDHRA PRADESH

Soaking in the Raj-era ambience

→ GETTING THERE

Road Horsley Hills is a 276-km/ 7-hr drive from Chennai along NH4 (Bangalore Highway) to Palmaner via Sriperumbudur, Ranipettai and Chittoor. At Palmaner, turn right along NH219 to Madanapalle via Pungannur. Horsley Hills is just 27 km from here, and most of the stretch is on NH205

and collection of honey. They are renowned for their Pungannur breed of cattle with its disproportionately high yield of milk.

Rishi Valley School

A prestigious institution run by the J Krishnamurthy Foundation, Rishi Valley is noted for its alternative mode of teaching. The school is 25 km from Horsley Hills, located in a valley that was declared a bird preserve in 1991. Its wooded groves make it an excellent haunt for birdwatchers. Visitors can check out the school only during school vacations, and need permission from the principal (Tel: 08571-280044/ 582/ 622) to visit while school is on.

WHERE TO STAY AND EAT

Horsley Hills has a plethora of sarkari bungalows, government-run lodges and guesthouses like **Co-operative Society Guest House**, **Sanatorium Guest House**, **Forest Rest House**, **Rajahmundry Bungalow** and **Mount Pleasant**. The Forest Rest House has to be booked at Madanapalle (Forest Range office, Madanapalle, Tel: 08571-222436). All the rest must be booked in advance from the AP Tourism office in Chennai (*see Fast Facts on page 251*).

AP Tourism's **Punnami Hill Resort** (Tel: 08571-279323-24; Tariff: Rs 600-2,000) arranges treks, and banquets at its **Pongali Restaurant**. They also run the **Yatri Nivas** (Tel: 222436; Tariff: Rs 750). **Abhiram Resorts** (Tel: 279328; Tariff: Rs 250-350), opposite Pongali Restaurant, is a budget option. The **Forest Rest House** (Tel: 279325; Tariff: Rs 400-800) behind the bus stand offers room service and hot water. **Ganesh Lodge** (Tel: 222102; Tariff: Rs 120-300) is also behind the bus stand.

Punnami Hill Resort, Yatri Nivas and Ganesh Lodge have their own restaurants.

For details, see Horsley Hills Accommodation Listings on page 492 ∎

Its all happening out there! So come enjoy the view with Outlook Traveller Getaways: Insight Guide for
SRI LANKA, NEW ZEALAND, FINLAND, EGYPT & SWITZERLAND

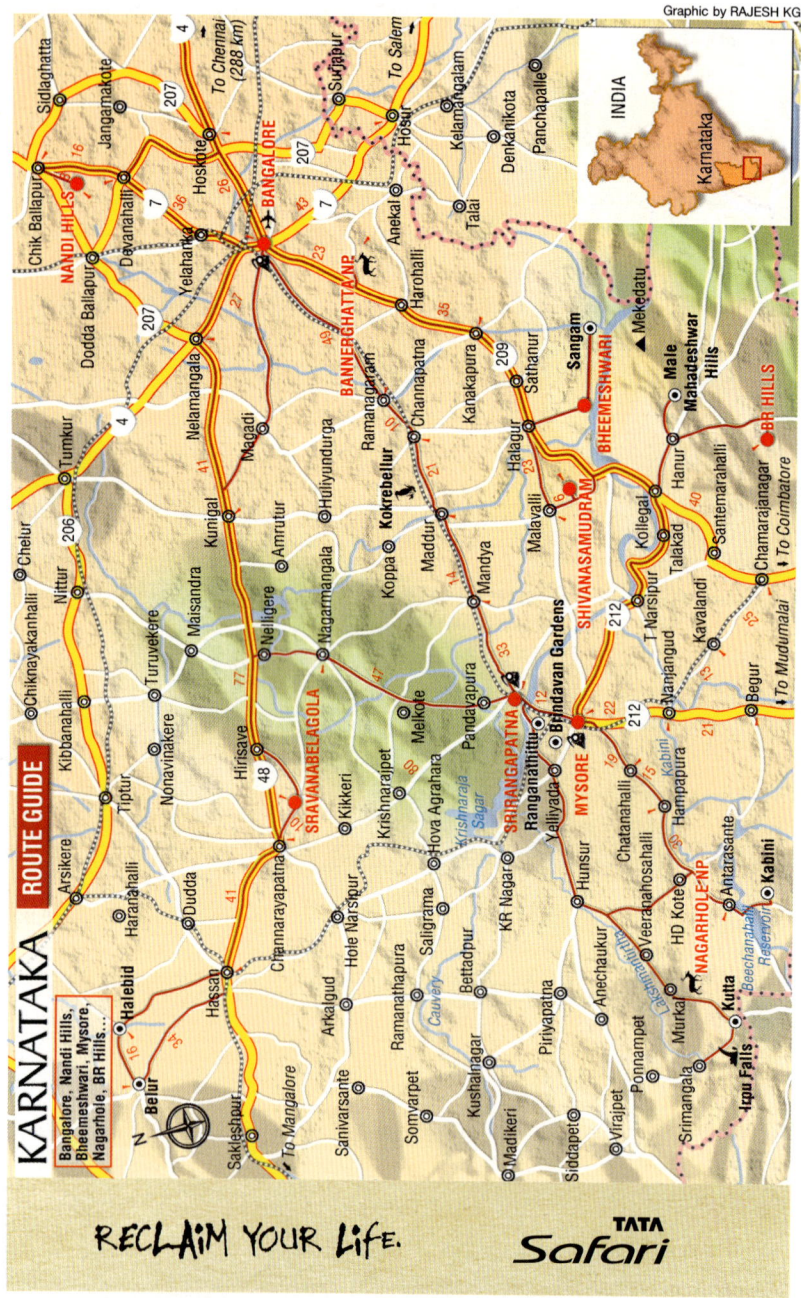

Karnataka

Feel your worries fade as you heal in Bangalore's spas... Ride a tusker in parks by the Cauvery River... All in the Tiger of Mysore's former realm

HEALING IN BANGALORE

State Karnataka
Location In South Karnataka, just 40 km from the Tamil Nadu border at Hosur
Distance 331 km W of Chennai JOURNEY TIME *By rail* 5 hrs *By air* 1 hour *By road* 7 hrs
Route NH4 to Bangalore via Poonamallee, Sriperumbudur, Ranipettai, Chittoor, Palmaner, Mulbagal, Kolar and Hoskote (*see route guides on pages 12 and 254*)

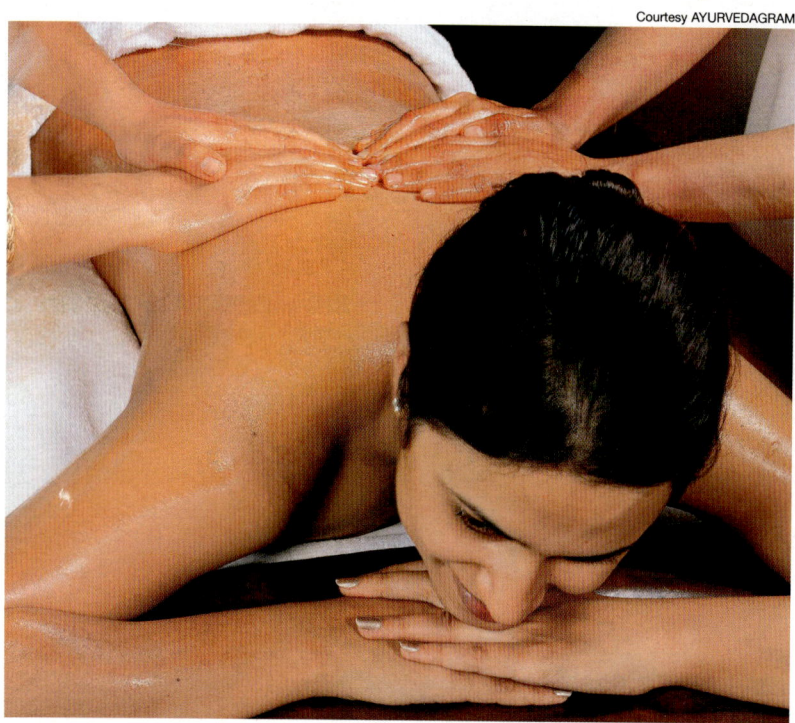

Courtesy AYURVEDAGRAM

A soothing weekend break in fast-paced Bangalore? Yes! There's much that you can do over two days here — get close to the wild at **Bannerghata** (*see page 264*), soak in the views at **Nandi Hills** (*see page 271*) or catch a mahseer at **Bheemeshwari** (*see page 274*). But the most rejuvenating breaks Bangalore offers are in the luxury spas and specialised wellness centres on the outskirts of the metropolis, which rate among the best in India. Save some weekends of the year for a Solah Shringar massage in the luxurious setting of the **Golden Palms Hotel & Spa**... Get authentic Ayurvedic treatments in the 'old Kerala' ambience of **AyurvedaGram**... or follow the Dalai Lama's path to **Soukya**, India's only complementary medicine facility, for a combination of Naturopathy, Hydrotherapy, Ayurveda and much more to help you face the next Monday feeling just a little human again.

THE GOLDEN PALMS HOTEL & SPA

Temple of Pleasure

■ BY SONIA NAZARETH

Golden Palms, built in mock Spanish hacienda style, is set on 18 acres of lush landscaped gardens in secluded countryside. Sanjay Khan, popularly known as the Bollywood 'matinee idol of yesteryear', is the chairman and managing director of this spa and super deluxe hotel. This luxury destination was built at a cost of 33 million US dollars by World Resorts Limited. Wander around a little and you'll stumble onto jogging tracks, a giant lagoon-like swimming pool, tennis and squash courts and a snooker table. The spa has an ultra-modern gymnasium made distinct by separate sections for men and women.

There's something here for everyone. For the health lover, it is the spa. For the foodie, the six restaurants and bars. For the businessman, there is a selection of boardrooms, meeting rooms and conference rooms. The business centre is well-equipped with everything from Internet to courier service, to a printer for hire. For the baby, there's the nursery and the playroom. Anxious mamas can leave their little muskrats in the safe custody of a hostess, as they lie rejuvenating in the spa. No kidding.

Here's an excerpt from the online guest book: "Our unexpected stopover in Bangalore at the Golden Palms Hotel & Spa was very pleasant. It is beautifully managed and the service is of First Grade. All of us who participated in the trip will long remember the good time and hospitality."

David Rockefeller
American Billionaire & Philanthropist
Rockefeller Center, New York

Oh well, what's good enough for a Rockefeller is good enough for us....

→ GETTING THERE

Air HAL Airport, Bangalore, connected to Chennai by 22 daily flights from numerous airlines
Rail Bangalore City Junction **Best option TO** Shatabdi Express (dep: Chennai Central 6 am; arr: Bangalore City Junction 10.50 am) **Best option FROM** Shatabdi Express (dep: Bangalore City Junction 4.25 pm; arr: Chennai Central 9.30 pm)
TIP Shatabdi doesn't run on Tuesdays; the overnight Bangalore/ Chennai mail trains are also good options
Car A longish journey for a weekend break, but do-able if you leave early. The drive to Bangalore along NH4 across southern Andhra via Ranipettai, Chittoor, Hosur and Hoskote takes $7^1/_2$ hours
Bus Private Volvo (Rs 550), AC (Rs 450) and non-AC (Rs 350) overnight services leave Chennai's Metropolitan Bus Terminus (Tel: 044-24794705) at Koyambedu between 9 and 11 pm

TREATMENTS AND TARIFFS

The entire range of international massages is on offer. For Rs 1,000 you can have a **Classic Back massage**. The 2-hr **Javanese Mandi Lulur** will cost Rs 3,500. A **Basic Scalp massage** is Rs 700 while a **Solah Shringar**, a full-body exfoliation with sandalwood and turmeric followed by an Indian head massage, costs Rs 3,200. The menu also includes: Body wraps and scrubs, Thai and Oriental therapies, Naturopathy, Reflexology, Hydrotherapy, Vichy showers, beauty treatments, Ayurvedic therapies, skin care, diet advice, Yoga, Meditation and Ayurvedic consultation. These delicious treats may be sampled on their own or as part of a package.

KARNATAKA

→ FAST FACTS

Location Amidst 18 acres of lush gardens in secluded countryside in Village Nagurur, near Hobli, 25 km north-west of Bangalore

Getting there Golden Palms is a 25-km drive from Bangalore's central MG Road. Take Tumkur Road all the way to Yeshwanthpur. Opposite the Himalaya Drug Company take a U-turn and look for signage for the turn-off on the left for Golden Palms, which is 3 km away on Golden Palms Avenue, off Tumkur Road. While the traffic may be heavy on occasion, the road leading up to Golden Palms is a smooth one. Regular taxis cost Rs 600 each way. But the resort's pick-up-and-drop service at Rs 1,200 (return) is the best option

Contact Golden Palms & Spa Resort, Golden Palms Avenue, Hobli, off Tumkur Road, Bangalore
Tel: 080-23712222; Fax: 23710033
Email: info@goldenpalmsspa.com
Website: goldenpalmsspa.com

The **packages** include **Honeymoon, Vedic Essence, Lifestyles of the Rich and Famous, Weight Management, Rejuvenation** and **Ayurvedic Day Spa**. Staffed by a team of professionals in healthcare systems such as Ayurveda, Naturopathy and Allopathy, the spa offers specialised therapeutic treatments. The **Therapeutic package** is customised depending on the ailment. The disorders covered under this package are: insomnia, diabetes, hypertension, gastric problems, bronchial asthma, arthritis (rheumatoid, gout and osteo), neurological (paralysis, Parkinson's, etc), skin disorders (eczema, psoriasis), sinusitis, computer vision syndrome and cardiovascular disorders.

A **1-day package** ranges from Rs 1,900-4,500. Included in it is a single treatment, buffet lunch, etc and ends with evening tea and cookies. For those inclined towards a longer stay, the **3N/4D Rejuvenation package** costs Rs 31,000 for a single room. The **7N/6D Therapeutic package** will set you back by Rs 99,000 for a single room. For details, log on to goldenpalmsspa.com.

Most packages include accommodation (with taxes), airport transfers, meals at the spa café, free use of steam, sauna, jacuzzi, fitness centre, swimming pool and sports centre, master health check, spa-customised treatments daily, herbal medications (if required during the course of stay), a detailed *prakruti* (individual constitution) analysis and pulse diagnosis with the Ayurvedic doctor, diet, lifestyle, Naturopathy and fitness consultation. The treatment regimen also includes customised sessions of Yoga and Pranayam. These packages could extend to 10/ 14/ 21 days, depending on the availability of accommodation and facilities.

ACCOMMODATION AT GOLDEN PALMS

The hotel has 132 deluxe rooms, 16 deluxe suites and 2 presidential suites.

BANGALORE SPAS

Photos: COURTESY GOLDEN PALMS & SPA RESORT

At Golden Palms: Relaxing at the poolside Aqua Bar by night; Healing by day (left)

Of course, luxury comes at a price. Hiring a presidential suite will set you back by Rs 27,500 per night. In comparison, the deluxe suites cost Rs 18,000 while the deluxe rooms are priced at a rate of Rs 9,800 for single occupancy and Rs 11,000 for double occupancy.

MEALS AT GOLDEN PALMS

There are six food and beverage outlets to choose from. At **Café Solaire**, feast on breads and bakes, grilled delicacies, and cold meats, desserts and seasonal fruits. For standard Chinese fare it's **Hidden Dragon**. For kebabs and biryani it's **Badshash** the open-air poolside restaurant. For fine dining and dancing Italian-ishtyle, it's **Sorrento**.

When in the mood for fruit or vegetable juice, make for the **Spa Bar**, where you can chew your way through mounds of juicy fruit, steamed vegetables and other similar fare in keeping with the instructions of the spa doctor.

On occasion make for **Aqua Bar** that churns out poolside cocktails or **Nostalgia Bar** to glug from a gourd of fine wine while watching old Hollywood and Bollywood flicks on a giant plasma television screen.

AYURVEDAGRAM HERITAGE WELLNESS CENTRE
Looking Bangalore, Talking Kerala

■ BY SONIA NAZARETH

Rated as one of the country's top spas, AyurvedaGram is an Ayurvedic village. It has 12 acres of land in Whitefield, upon which entire dismantled antique buildings and structures from around Kerala have been relocated.

Always on call is the resident Ayurvedic physician. Also on the premises are therapists, a dispensary, Yoga and Meditation centre, residential cottages and a vegetarian restaurant — all under the personalised attention of trained staff. The treatment centre has separate sections and therapists for men and women. Each section has doctors' consulting rooms, treatment rooms and steam baths. Sensitivity has been shown in the development of the project and the health care centre feels less like a hospital and more like a resort.

The visitors' book is replete with comments such as "a nice Therapeutic and Curative Experience... Excellent Ambience and Courteous staff" and "A great experience... We found it easy to

KARNATAKA

relax, reflect and rejuvenate here" (that was CK Prahlad, the management guru).

TREATMENTS AND TARIFFS

When you arrive at AyurvedaGram Heritage Wellness Centre, you undergo a detailed examination by a resident medical doctor. On the basis of this, a specific treatment package is designed for you. The ailments for which treatment is offered include spondylitis, arthritis, ulcers, rheumatism, diabetes, back problems, cholesterol and gastric disorders, obesity and depression.

♦**Standard treatment packages** include Panchakarma Detoxification, Stress Management, Weight Reduction, Yoga and Meditation, Rejuvenation, Spine and Joint Care, Lifestyle Disease Management and Old Age Care. These packages extend over 7/ 14/ 21 days, the details and prices of which are available on request.

♦**Rejuvenation and Stress Management packages** are available for the healthy. **24-hr stay tariff:** Rs 3,550 (single) and Rs 6,050 (double). This includes the complete routine from consultation with the physician to massage, Yoga, steam bath, use of gym, vegetarian cuisine, etc.

♦**Rejuvenating Ayurveda Experience:** 2N/ 2D Package costs Rs 7,050 (single), Rs 11,900 (double); 7N/ 8D Package costs Rs 47,671 (single), Rs 83,560 (double).

♦**Satvik Day Tour** from 9 am to 4.30 pm, at a charge of Rs 1,460 per person, is available for those who want to simply spend a day at the AyurvedaGram.

→ FAST FACTS

Location At Hemandanahalli, in Whitefield, a suburb of Bangalore, which is a 24 km/ 1½-hr drive from the city centre, MG Road, and 17 km from Bangalore Airport

Getting there AyurvedaGram is a 1½ hrs drive by taxi from MG Road. Drive past Marathahalli, past Brookfield towards Whitefield Town. Turn at Hope Farm Junction and go towards Chikka Thirupathi, until a road sign points you in the direction of AyurvedaGram. A taxi charges around Rs 600 each way, but the resort's pick-up-and-drop service is the best option

Contact AyurvedaGram Heritage Wellness Centre, Hemmandanahalli, Samethanahalli Post, Whitefield, Bangalore. Tel: 080-65651090-91/ 94, Mobile: 09845071990
Email: response@ayurvedagram.com
Website: ayurvedagram.com

Caution On the first day of your stay at AyurvedaGram, the Chief Physician decides the course of your treatment. A special diet-and-rest pattern is recommended. However, the option to follow this regulated lifestyle lies with you. Alcohol and non-veg food are not served nor permitted to be brought from outside

ACCOMMODATION AT AYURVEDAGRAM

Not exactly Thoreau's hut and wild nature on your doorstep, but a near imitation. **Kerala-style residential cottages** — called Nalukettus, Kovilakams, Manas and Illams — the traditional Malayalam names of live-ins made of teak and rosewood, are standard accommodation here, in an attempt to recreate the charm of old-world Kerala. Entire structures in the resort have been relocated here from that state. The steep roofs and low overhanging eaves are architectural adaptations against strong monsoon winds and copious rains of Kerala, and to add to the authentic feel of the place, coconut and peepal trees have been transplanted here.

To the existing 31 rooms, there are plans to add nine more. As for untamed

BANGALORE SPAS

Courtesy AYURVEDAGRAM

AyurvedaGram — a slice of traditional Kerala in Bangalore

nature, the closest you come to it is the pleasant sight of rabbits, pigeons and ducks that mill about the ponds and gardens, which surround your room.

The rooms are available in three categories — **Heritage Suite** (single Rs 7,875, double Rs 9,000; **Heritage** (single Rs 4,500, double Rs 5,400); and **Classique** (single Rs 3,375, double Rs 4,050). The Heritage Suite (only one) is an independent antique cottage with a verandah, living room, bedroom and attached bath with a tub. The Heritage room is a spacious double-bedded room with a garden bath facility fenced off for privacy. The Classique is a spacious room in a Nalukettu, an antique building that consists of 11 rooms and a hall. All of these open onto a common verandah. Prices given are room tariff plus taxes.

Although the room looks traditional from the outside, it is furnished with every modern amenity. I plug my laptop into a wall-socket while the television sings in the background. However, authenticity may be found in the detail — in the replica beds, the red terracotta floor tiles. What drove me up the plastered whitewashed walls was the Internet speed here, which is very slow.

MEALS AT AYURVEDAGRAM

I'm seated in the **Ootupura Restaurant**, which is built in the same architectural style as the rest of the resort. As I sit savouring my uthappam, a flock of geese wander by the pond outside. Brightly coloured fish gobble their food amid floating magenta lotuses.

The meals are strictly vegetarian but wide-ranging. From Kerala cuisine to Continental. Most of the produce is organic. A typical Kerala feast or *sadya* is making its way towards me. And soon I am surrounded with mini-dishes of sambar, rasam, olan, kaalan, pachadi, khichdi, aviyal and thoran. A medley of pickles and chutneys encircle this already pretty landscape. Almost every dish prepared in Kerala is adorned with coconut and spices like cinnamon, cardamom, ginger and cloves. I wash this meal down with the juice of a tender coconut. While this traditional multi-course meal is delicious, as is the general fare served, the Continental dishes seem less authentic. Think pasta in tomato soup.

No alcohol is served or sold. Those with specific concerns like obesity are served meals that are specially prepared according to the instructions of a doctor.

KARNATAKA

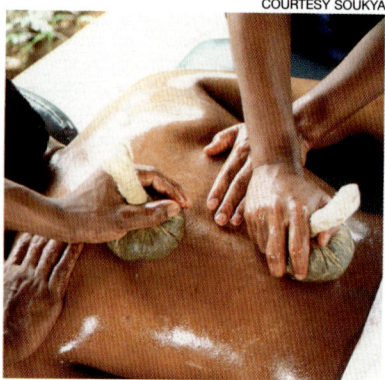

Ayurvedic kizhi treatment at Soukya

→ FAST FACTS

Location On the outskirts of Whitefield Town, east of Bangalore city, about 7 km from Hope Farm Junction on the Marathahalli Road past the International Technological Park
Getting there The route to Soukya is fairly simple — straight down Airport Road, into Whitefield, turning right at Hope Farm Junction, from where onwards there are prominent signboards. However, the traffic is very heavy up to Hope Farm Junction, and roads equally bad after that. Local taxis are available on hire in Bangalore City at the rate of Rs 350 for 4 hrs or 40 km (whichever is less), or Rs 700 for 8 hrs or 80 km
Contact Soukya, International Holistic Health Centre, Soukya Road, Samethanahalli, Whitefield Bangalore. Tel: 080-23518405-06 Mobile: 09845374400
Email: info@soukya.com
Website: soukya.com
Caution Soukya is a non-smoking, non-alcohol zone

SOUKYA: DR MATHAI'S INTERNATIONAL HOLISTIC HEALTH CENTRE
Destination Well-being
■ BY PAYAL DHAR

Soukya's USP is that it is the only **complementary medicine facility** in India, offering a fusion of advanced medical care, traditional systems of knowledge such as Ayurveda or Yoga, the relatively new medical system of Homeopathy and complementary therapies such as Acupressure, Reflexology, Hydrotherapy etc. Soukya was set up in 2002 by Dr Isaac Mathai and Suja Isaac. It is housed in a 30-acre organic farm in Whitefield, on the outskirts of Bangalore.

Apart from de-stress and rejuvenation programmes, Soukya also provides medical consultation and treatment for patients, including the treatment of degenerative conditions. There are separate areas for living, dining, treatment, consultation and administration.

In all, Soukya has a guest network from over 40 countries, and some of its well-known visitors include Archbishop Desmond Tutu, Sarah Ferguson, Duchess of York, the Dalai Lama, Mallika Sarabhai, Sting, George Harrison and Ravi Shankar.

TREATMENTS AND TARIFF

Soukya offers some **short packages**, which include deluxe accommodation, food, refreshments, use of recreational facilities, and all taxes.
- **Basic Day package** with Ayurvedic rejuvenation massage, Reflexology and Yoga costs Rs 4,900
- **Special Day package** with Hydrotherapy, hot stone massage and mud packs costs Rs 9,900
- **Gold package** (1N/2D) a combination of Ayurvedic treatments with Hydrotherapy and Reflexology costs Rs 11,500
- **Platinum package** (2N/3D) a variety of massages and treatments costs Rs 28,000

In the **longer packages**, the costs cover daily rates of treatments alone and accommodation costs are extra.

There are several **de-stress** and **rejuvenation programmes** as well, including various combinations of Ayurvedic and Naturopathic treatments, Reflexology, Acupressure, Hydrotherapy, Yoga, Meditation as well as therapies such as mud packs.

Soukya also offers medical programmes for cardiac problems, hypertension, diabetes, arthritis, asthma, de-addiction and chronic problems, but the treatment details and rates are only available after your health evaluation.

Clients are required to pay 18 per cent extra in taxes on all treatment packages.

ACCOMMODATION AT SOUKYA

Soukya sets great emphasis on sustainable and holistic living. Living here is an experience in ecologically sound concepts such as solar water heating, drip irrigation and rainwater harvesting. Near heavenly bliss is achieved by the fact that mobile phones are not permitted outside of rooms.

There are 16 accommodation spaces — 12 deluxe 'cottages' and 4 suites. Each is completely private with its own garden and a sit-out area. The suites even have open-air showers in the garden. The rooms are large, airy, comfortable and very tastefully decorated, offering every contemporary comfort.

A **deluxe room** costs Rs 7,600 per day for single occupancy and Rs 9,900 per day for double occupancy. The **suite** is Rs 24,700 per day, and the **2-bedroom presidential suite** comes at Rs 48,100 per day. Add 10 per cent extra for tax.

Rates are inclusive of food, herbal drinks, daily consultations, Yoga twice a day and recreational and swimming facilities. Treatment costs are additional.

MEALS AT SOUKYA

I remember my first day at Soukya when I was ravenously hungry after my massage but a bit worried because according to the 'Your day at Soukya' timetable, lunch was long past. But when I finally reached the dining area, a picturesque open-air pavilion with a covered roof, with wind chimes and light bamboo furniture, I was pleasantly surprised to find that the staff were expecting me. Food in Soukya is vegetarian and the menus are fixed. Most of it is grown in-house, in the organic garden, and prepared nutritiously. Lunch and dinner start with a soup and salad. This is followed by chappatis/ rice, with a dal and three kinds of delicious vegetable preparations. For dessert, there's a bowl of fruit.

Food costs are included in accommodation/ package rates. ∎

An inquisitive tiger welcomes a busload of visitors to the park
DELEKS NAMGYAL/ PHOTOINDIA

BANNERGHATTA NATIONAL PARK
LOCKING EYES WITH CATS

State Karnataka
Location Just 23 km south of Bangalore City in Bangalore (Urban) District
Distance 354 km W of Chennai **JOURNEY TIME** *By rail* 6 hrs + 45 mins by road *By air* 55 mins + 1½ hrs by road *By road* 8 hrs
Route NH4 to Bangalore via Sriperumbudur, Ranipettai, Chittoor, Palmaner, Kolar, Hosur and Hoskote; district road to Bannerghatta (*see route guide on pages 12 and 254*)

■ BY SHEILA KUMAR

It's a sight to quicken the pulse; to thrill visitors unused to the behaviour of wild animals; to amaze even the tourist skeptical of safaris that all too often resemble a visit to the zoo. A pair of lions, a regally maned male and his dignified mate, gambol beside a water source. At first, the lion worries a plastic bottle left behind by some careless visitor. Even as I start to fret that he'll ingest the plastic, he loses interest in it and starts to tug at his mate's tail instead. She puts up with it for a while and then snarls a warning. They end up in a half-hearted squabble, mock wrestling and growling just a wee bit. We watch for a while and reluctantly drive on. I wonder about the fact that the lions didn't even spare us a glance, though our van had been parked just a few feet away from them.

I am in the Bannerghatta Biological Park, Bangalore's favourite getaway. I have signed on for a Jungle Lodges Resorts (JLR) night-stay package, which includes all safaris and meals. Earlier that day, I had checked in at the JLR camp; 1½ km inside the park, past ponds filled with blooming pink lotus, huge anthills, black boulders of all sizes, and an overreaching canopy of bamboo. As one approaches the camp, spotted deer and sambar stop in their tracks to cast curious stares.

When I was in my tent, I heard the loud chatter of birds and looked out for them. And I found them in all hues... green-winged, brown-throated, sleek black, bright yellow and blue... hopping on leafy branches and flitting from tree to tree — each adding its own mellifluous tone to the bird chorus. At 3 pm, I set off for the Grand Safari with some other guests, in the safari van. The Grand Safari includes the Lion Safari, the Tiger Safari and the Bear Safari. We did the Bear Safari first. The park has 28 bears, of which we glimpsed a few. Some were fast asleep curled up against rocks, others nosed around the trees, still others were shovelling up mud. One little fellow was so alarmed by the sound of our van that he scampered behind a building and poked his head out to see if we had left. Some of these bears are animals rehabilitated from circuses.

The Lion Safari was the next highlight. In the tiger zone, we have one well-fed cat come up close to the van and sniff us. His attention wanes soon, however, as another tiger approaches the wire enclosure here and he goes off to guard his territory with a threatening roar. To add to the sound and fury, a white tiger comes up on the other side and roars lustily. It is quite something to imagine these roars reverberating across an open jungle; an awesome sound that can only be described as thrilling.

It's not our day for spotting elephants, however. We don't spot even one, in the range or anywhere else. However, on our way back to the camp, we see a young leopard saunter down a dirt path, all sleek muscle and power. The safaris, stage-managed or not, make the Bannerghatta visit fully worth the time and money.

Back at the camp, I decline the offer of a wildlife movie and bonfire. Instead, I climb into a hammock, close my eyes and relax; I listen to the wind whistle high among the treetops. After a while, I look up to see the miniscule light of a plane blinking far up, and as the night darkens, I watch the stars growing brighter, framed by leafy fronds. Suddenly, the night seems full of the distant roar of big cats.

Next morning, after my wake-up 'cuppa' tea, I head outside where KN Mahadeva ("Call me KNM"), the affable guide, is ready to take me on a 40-min walk through the Herbivore Safari grounds. Sambar, gaur, antlered deer all stop to stare at us, a little disturbed by our presence. A female sambar comes up

Graphic by SURAJ WADHWA

KARNATAKA

Marsh heron perches on a leaf

→ FAST FACTS

When to go Open all year round but you get to see the park at its greenest between mid-June and August
Tourist offfice
● DFO, Bannerghatta NP ❶
Bangalore District
Tel: 080-27828540, 27828300
Email: bannerghatta@vsnl.net
Website: bannerghatabiopark.org
STD code Bangalore 080

close to say a personal hello. We come upon a pack of magnificent gaur and KNM tells me not to lock eyes with the most magnificent specimen, Arjun. I can't help but look at him, find him looking coldly at me, and I look hurriedly away. The walk yields sights aplenty. Herons, kingfishers, jungle fowl, many a herd of antlered deer, spotted deer, chinkara ("Salman Khan's favourite animal," KNM says facetiously), barking deer, nilgai, and even rock formations. I was particularly intrigued by a woodpecker's insistent drilling at a branch.

Breakfast at the camp is puri bhaji and egg and toast, all chased down with some excellent coffee. We then head to the zoo, which is a fun ramble but quite tame after the safaris we did the evening before. We get to see many elephants at their gathering point, though. When I leave the place, it's with a heart and mind full of big cats, regal, dignified and simply magnificent.

ABOUT BANNERGHATTA NP

The Bannerghatta National Park was established in 1971. The park is made up of 10 reserve forests of the Anekal Range of the Bangalore Forest Division. Surrounded by hills dotted with ancient temples, the park lies on the Bannerghatta Road, 23 km from the town centre, in the southern precincts of Bangalore City. It is 104.27 sq km of moderate jungle and shrubland at an altitude of 3,375 ft. The terrain is interspersed with valleys, streams and scenic spots. The main parkland vegetation is dry deciduous forests and thorny scrub with patches of moist deciduous forests. It's crisscrossed by streams that fill up in the monsoons.

The wild expanse of this small but important National Park, located just beyond the Bannerghatta Biological Park (BPP), is home to wild Asiatic elephants. The two natural predators here are the leopard and the wild dog. The forests here are also home to barking deer, sambar, sloth bear, wild pig and at least 180 species of birds.

Being so close to a major metro has created its own problems for the park. With growing industrial/ urban and biotic pressures, there is increasing threat to the already fragile wildlife habitat and its residents. There is a strong need to take action to protect both the forest and the animals. Incidents of poisoning of leopards and electrocution of elephants are on the rise. The sharp increase in destructive human activities (poaching, grazing, fires, quarrying) is also affecting the park.

ORIENTATION

Tourists are not permitted to enter the core zones of Bannerghatta. Visitors have to drive on for another 5 km to the entrance to the **Bannerghatta Biological Park** (BBP), which is open to visitors. This Biological Park (adjoining the National Park) is where the Forest Department has rehabilitated lions and tigers (rescued from circuses and elsewhere) in semi-wild environs that are similar to their natural habitat. This has become an area of interest and upwards of 10 lakh visitors throng this park every year to be up close and personal to the big cats. The BBP comprises a **zoo** (a short distance from the entry gates, on the right), with many mammals, reptiles and birds. There's also a small **museum** and **auditorium** in the zoo. The **BBP Office** near the entry gate issues tickets for the zoo and safaris. The parking area lies near the entrance opposite the zoo.

There are several soft drinks vendors near the entry point and kiosks (run by KSTDC) in the zoo precincts. The **Herbivore enclosure** (housing blackbuck, bison, cheetal and sambar) is located to the right, a few kilometres past the zoo. About $1^1/_2$ km from the entry gate, close to the Herbivore enclosure, is the KSTDC run **Jungle Lodges Nature Camp**, where visitors can take up the lion and tiger safari packages (including night stays) on offer. The main safari road starts from the entry gate, veers left towards the lion and tiger enclosures past an abandoned quarry, on either side of which lie the **butterfly garden** and a park. The **bear enclosure** is near the **Rescue Centre** (which is off tourist limits).

After a zoo visit, you must return to the entry gate area to go on any of the safaris that you have opted for. The **Grand Safari** covers all four enclosures. Other options are the **Tiger and Lion safari, elephant joy ride** and a **short trek** in the Herbivore enclosure. The Forest Department runs the safaris. Jungle Lodges has its own vehicles,

KARNATAKA

which do the safaris in conjunction with the Forest Department.
♦**Zoo tickets** Weekdays Rs 30, holidays Rs 35 **Timings** 9.30 am-4.30 pm; closed Tuesdays **Grand safari** Weekdays Rs 70, holidays Rs 90 **Tiger and lion safari** Weekdays Rs 35, holidays Rs 55 **Elephant joy ride** Weekdays Rs 35, holidays Rs 45 **Short trek** Rs 55

THINGS TO SEE AND DO

Day-trippers usually ramble around the zoo, eat at one of the many food stalls outside the park gates and take the safaris in the Forest Department vans and mini-buses. One of the best options for tourists is to opt for an overnight Jungle Lodges Resort (JLR) safari package, as part of which you travel in a grilled safari van with open slots for taking photos. Lion, tiger and bear safaris are part of this package. The next morning, you can go on the Herbivore Safari (involving a 4-km short trek).

The zoo

The zoo is a sprawling area. The hippo and the incredibly still crocs are special favourites. You get to see all kinds of animals — zebra, langur, porcupines and jackals amidst a lovely canopy of mixed trees such as sandalwood, *jalari, chujjullu, neem,* tamarind and *zizyphus,* amongst others. The zoo auditorium screens 45-min films from 12.30-4 pm. There is a **museum** (entry free) in the zoo environs filled with sad displays of musty, moth-eaten stuffed animal trophies and some damaged old photographs.
♦**Film tickets** Adults Rs 5, children Rs 2 **Museum timings** 9.30 am-5.30 pm

Reptile Park

The Reptile Park has its shares of snakes, venomous and non-venomous, as well as huge monitor lizards. The aviary is full of all kinds of small and big, silent and chattering birds.

Mirza Hill

About 1 km from the entry gate is Mirza Hill (no one seems to know whom the hill is named after), popular among amateur trekkers. It's also a place where impromptu picnics are held.

Butterfly Park

Tourists can see up to 50 species of butterflies under a large glass dome in this specially recreated natural habitat, the first of its kind in India. Landscaping, running brooks of water and the multi-coloured butterflies flitting around make for a lovely experience.

→ GETTING THERE

Air Nearest airport: Bangalore Airport (40 km/ 1½ hrs), connected to Chennai by 22 daily flights by many airlines. Taxi charges Rs 1,115 to Bannerghatta
Rail Nearest railhead: Bangalore (25 km/ 45 mins) **Best option TO** Bangalore Mail (dep: Chennai Central 11.15 pm; arr: Bangalore Cantt 5 am, Bangalore City 5.30 am). Taxi to Bannerghatta costs Rs 800 for a drop **Best option FROM** Chennai Mail (dep: Bangalore City 10.45 pm, Bangalore Cantt 11 pm; arr: Chennai Central: 4.40 am)
Car A longish journey for a weekend break. It's far better to take the train. Follow NH4 to Bangalore across southern Andhra via Ranipettai, Chittoor, Hosur and Hoskote (7½ hours). Then follow the Bannerghatta Road south of Bangalore
Bus TNSETC (Rs 260) and private buses (Rs 400-570) including Volvos leave every half hour between 9.30 pm and 5 am for Bangalore from Chennai's Mofussil Bus Terminus (Tel: 044-24794705) at Koyambedu

KARNATAKA

A shy stag startled by visitors takes cover amidst thick foliage

Hajjamana Kallu

The Bannerghatta Biological Park is full of rocks and boulders of various sizes and textures. Within the park stands the **barber stone**, a naturally shaped rock that resembles the stone barbers traditionally use to sharpen their blades on. It is a mammoth rock, affording some fine views of the shrubland below. Located about 3 km from the entry gate, it is closed to the public but those staying at the Jungle Lodges Nature Camp can visit this viewpoint.

Uddigebende

This is a burial place of great antiquity, where long slabs of slate still lie about. These stone burial spots or **megaliths** are believed to be more than 3,000 years old and were used by the Irula tribesmen till a few years ago. Another legend goes that tribals, known as the Pandavas, used these ledged structures as their dwellings. The viewpoint at the spot looks down into elephant territory. It's closed to the public; you can only access it if you're staying at the Jungle Lodges Nature Camp.

WHERE TO STAY AND EAT

The Jungle Lodges **Bannerghatta Nature Camp** (Tel: 080-25597021; Tariff: Rs 650-1,400) is set $1^1/_2$ km inside the park. The 2 huts go for Rs 1,400 each per night, the Swiss tents (8 in all) for Rs 900, and a bed in the dormitory Rs 600.

The package includes accommodation, lunch, dinner and breakfast, herbivore/ lion/ tiger/ bear safari, nature walks with guide, zoo visit, forest entry fee plus taxes — a good bargain, indeed. The **Gol Ghar** is a circular open dining area, in which Jungle Lodges serves wholesome veg and non veg meals.

Just off the Bannerghatta Road, about 15 km towards Bangalore, is **Grasshopper** (Tel: 080-26593999, 26580225), a fashion store and restaurant where you get excellent Continental food. Their lemon cheesecake with grape sauce is to die for. You need to call ahead and make reservations before you land up there for a meal.

For details, see Bannerghatta Accommodation Listings on page 495 ■

Photographs by PRASHANT PANJIAR

Approaching rain clouds paint a dramatic sky over the Nandi Giri

NANDI HILLS
A BYTE-SIZED PARADISE

State Karnataka
Location The Nandi Giri, watered by the Arkavati, Pennar and Palar rivers, are just north of Doddaballapur in Kolar district
Distance 391 km W of Chennai JOURNEY TIME **By rail** 6 hrs + 2 hrs by road **By air** 55 mins + 2 hrs by road **By road** 8½ hrs
Route NH4 to Hoskote via Poonamallee, Sriperumbudur, Ranipettai, Chittoor, Palmaner, Mulbagal and Kolar; SH to Devanahalli; NH7 to Chik Ballapur; state roads to Nandi Hills via Karahalli Cross and Betta Cross (*see route guides on pages 12 and 254*)

KARNATAKA

■ BY SHEFALI VAIDYA GANESH

Nandi Hills is a craggy range squatting obstinately on the absolutely flat surrounding plains, just outside Bangalore. These are not gently rolling hills, but a giant, 2,000-foot granite monolith towering over you that seems to appear from nowhere. The effect is magical.

The hills get their name from the beautiful statue of Nandi standing guard outside the Yoganandeeshwara Temple atop the hills. Elsewhere, the peaks give birth to the rivers Arakavati, Pennar and Palar. Nandi Hills have for long attracted a loyal following among royalty and

→ **FAST FACTS**

When to go Nandi Hills are blessed with a pleasant climate all year round
Tourist office
● KSTDC ❶ ❺
Badami House, NR Square, Bangalore
Tel: 080-22275869, 22275883
Fax: 22352626; Email: kstdc@vsnl.in
Website: karnatakatourism.org
STD code 08156

KARNATAKA

Bhoganandeeshwara Temple at the base of Nandi Hills

→ GETTING THERE

Air Nearest airport: Bangalore (60 km/ 2 hrs), connected to Chennai by 22 daily flights by numerous airlines. Taxis to Nandi Hills cost Rs 1,650-2,650 return
Rail Nearest railhead: Bangalore **Best option TO** Bangalore Mail (dep: Chennai Central 11.15 pm; arr: Bangalore City 5.30 am) **Best option FROM** Chennai Mail (dep: Bangalore City 10.45 pm; arr: Chennai Central: 4.40 am)
Car A longish drive for a weekend. Rail is much more convenient. Drive till Hosur, 43 km short of Bangalore on NH4 via Ranipettai, Chittoor and Kolar. At Hosur, turn right on NH207 till Devanahalli. Then turn left and head for Karahalli Cross. From here, turn left to Betta Cross, from where you'll turn right for Nandi Hills, just 8 km away
TIP Nandi Hills vehicle entry toll: Rs 60

commoners alike. Tipu Sultan, who ruled Mysore in the late 18th century, came here to recover from the din of battle. He fortified Nandi Hills and made it his summer haven. The Brits took over Nandi Hills, looking for the salubrious climate of their homeland. Sir Mark Cubbon, former Commissioner of Bangalore, made it his official summer residence. Many bungalows the Brits built still pepper the hills. Dignitaries, including Mahatma Gandhi, Jawaharlal Nehru and Queen Elizabeth, have visited since. The point of all this name-dropping is that, with cobbled paths leading up to hills full of birdsong, Nandi Hills is a good getaway for you and your family too.

THINGS TO SEE AND DO

Reaching the top is easy as there's a good, motorable road going all the way up. If you are in need of a drastic workout, take the steep flight of 1,175 steps from the base of the hills to the top. Nandi Hills is the place where laziness can be perfected into an art form. The most strenuous activities here are long ambles along the walkways meandering along the hills.

Tipu's Drop

Tipu's Drop, a near 2,000 foot-high sheer cliff has a gory past. It is the place from where prisoners would be hurled to their death by Tipu Sultan's decree.

If you want to get the best out of Tipu's Drop, wait until the last tour bus departs with its cargo of noisy day-trippers. Then watch the dusk paint the horizon in vibrant colours. As the dusk melts, the lights of Bangalore become visible in the distance. The city sparkles beneath you like a giant rangoli decorated with diyas.

Yoganandeeshwara Temple

This temple — the abode of Shiva the ascetic — at the top of the hills was built by the Cholas. The two *dwarpalakas* guarding the entrance to the sanctum sanctorum merit quite a bit of attention. This ancient temple also has an inscription in the name of Sambhaji, son of Chhatrapati Shivaji.

Amrita Sarovar

This large tank is fed by perennial springs, and is called the lake of ambrosia! Visit it at night, when it shimmers in the moonlight. Nearby lies the *chabootara* or platform where Tipu Sultan used to pray.

Nehru Nilaya

This is the house Nehru lived in while vacationing here. It was renamed to commemorate his visit and is now a guest house belonging to the Horticulture Department (*see 'Where to Stay'* below).

◆ **Entry fee** Rs 3 **Vehicle fee** Cars Rs 60, bikes Rs 21 **Timings** 7 am to 10 pm

Bhognandeeshwara Temple

This beautiful stone temple, at the base of the Nandi Hills, dates back to the period of the Bana dynasty, but was rebuilt over the centuries by Chola, Hoysala and Vijayanagara kings. The Nandi here is massive. Locals refer to Bhoganandeeshwara as the *doddu* (big) Nandi and Yoganandeeshwara as the *chikka* (small) Nandi.

WHERE TO STAY AND EAT

Nandi Hills has only one accommodation option. **Nehru Nilaya**, the Horticultural Department Guest House (Tel: 08156-250901; Tariff: Rs 260-1,120) offers 25 rooms and has a restaurant. Book these from the office of the Director of Horticulture, Lalbagh, Bangalore (Tel: 080-26579231).

There also are seasonal places run by locals that rustle up good fare.

For details, see Nandi Hills Accommodation Listings on page 498 ∎

BANGALORE KI GURU
Richa, Hotel Advisor at Travelguru, has the best entertainment tips on the city of Baked Beans.

Choose from our network of over 4000 hotels in India. Serviced apartments, budget hotels, luxury resorts, palaces, business accommodations, houseboats and more.

1-800-22-4878
022-4030-4878
www.travelguru.com

India's Largest Hotel Network

iCONTRACT.TG.07.3248

M BALAN/ SOUTHINDIAPICTURE

Waiting for the Cauvery to throw up a catch

BHEEMESHWARI
DISCAUVERY WEEKEND

State Karnataka
Location On the banks of the mahseer-laden Cauvery, just south of Bangalore in eastern Mandya district
Distance 431 km W of Chennai JOURNEY TIME **By rail** 6 hrs + 2¼ hrs by road **By air** 55 mins + 2¼ hrs by road **By road** 10 hrs
Route NH4 to Bangalore via Poonamallee, Sriperumbudur, Ranipettai, Chittoor, Palmaner, Mulbagal, Kolar and Hoskote; NH209 to Halagur via Kanakapura and Sathanur; village road to Bheemeshwari (*see route guide on pages 12 and 254*)

■ BY ANUPAMA REDDY
AND SIRISHA DAMISETTY

The turnoff from NH209 onto the village road at Halagur, just a short way out of Bangalore, transports you to meandering roads down green mountainsides. The only traffic stops will be the rare herd of spotted deer sailing across the road. This is only a taste of what awaits you at the camps in Bheemeshwari.

A barefoot walk along the river's edge, sipping hot coffee on the verandah of your cabin overlooking the river, being woken up by monkeys jumping on your tent, are the promise here. Nature treks into the wilderness, coracle rides, kayaking, outdoor camping, amateur fishing and professional angling are the icing on the cake.

While you may catch glimpses of rare species of birds, wild elephants and sloth bears, you are sure to see the famous mahseer no matter which season you go. Sightings of the mahseer will be all around you in the form of souvenir photographs and proud accounts by the friendly staff.

THINGS TO SEE AND DO

Bheemeshwari's Cauvery Fishing Camp and two more camps at Doddamakkalli and Galibore along the Cauvery are run by Jungle Lodges as wildlife retreats and adventure resorts.

Mahseer magic

The fishing camps are an angler's paradise, with the Cauvery home to one of the finest game fish in the world — the mahseer. The peak season for professional angling is from October to mid-April. The camp allows 10 lines for the season for professionals, so book well in advance, as the camp is in high demand from anglers across the globe. There's also amateur fishing on offer, with guides to help you learn the ropes.

The Cauvery's feisty mahseer is among the largest freshwater fish to be found in the world, with some fine specimens reaching an awe-inspiring size of over 60 kg. That's why this little village in the jungles of Mandya plays host to anglers from around the world, boasting not one but three camps to meet the demand.

→ FAST FACTS

When to go The camps are open all year round. The angling season is October to mid-April
Tourist/ booking offices
● KSTDC ❶ ⓑ
Badami House, NR Square, Bangalore
Tel: 080-22275869; Fax: 22352626
Email: kstdc@vsnl.in
Website: karnatakatourism.org
● Jungle Lodges Booking Office ⓑ
Tel: 080-25584111, 25597944

The disappearance of mahseer look-alikes in Ireland and Malaysia has placed the fish firmly on the list of endangered species. Which means you don't get to take your catch home, but have to release it after photographs have been taken and congratulations received. If you catch any other fish (up to 5 pounds), you can save it for your dining table.

Even if you aren't a keen angler yourself, watching others do the hard work is quite an absorbing task. The size and immense strength of the fish makes the sport a test of patience and perseverance for even the most experienced

KARNATAKA

Colours of a wet monsoon morning at Bheemeshwari

→ GETTING THERE

Air Nearest airport: Bangalore (100 km/ 2¼ hrs), connected to Chennai by 22 daily flights by numerous airlines. A four-wheel-drive taxi to Bheemeshwari will cost between Rs 1,800 and 2,000
Rail Nearest railhead: Bangalore **Best option TO** Bangalore Mail (dep: Chennai Central 11.15 pm; arr: Bangalore City 5.30 am) **Best option FROM** Chennai Mail (dep: Bangalore City 10.45 pm; arr: Chennai Central: 4.40 am)
Road A longish drive for a weekend break. Drive the 331 km to Bangalore via Ranipettai, Chittoor and Hoskote (7½ hrs). Head south of the city to exit via Kanakapura on NH209. Follow the road via Sathanur to Halagur. Turn left onto the village road to Bheemeshwari, 16 km away. This stretch has Jungle Lodges' signboards at all the turnings

angler. Making a catch can take hours of patient waiting and skill gained over the years. But when you finally bag the mahseer, the victory tastes as sweet as its firm flesh. Which you may not eat.

Wildlife treks
These treks are conducted in three categories, easy, medium and tough, ranging from a 4- to 30-km distance. The treks take you into neighbouring hills, full of wildlife and a cornucopia of plants used in Ayurveda. You can also catch a glimpse of rural life as you pass through some of the villages, pay obeisance at the Hanuman Temple and sink your teeth into wild berries to get a 'taste' of your environs.

Quick and easy routines
Boat rides in coracles and barbecues along the river's edge are the extras here. Carry along some mosquito repellent (flammables not allowed), snacks for kids and water-resistant footwear. But leave your swimwear behind because crocs in the water and whirlpools mean swimming is a complete no-no.

KARNATAKA

Courtesy JUNGLE LODGES

The eponymous pelican at Kokrebellur

Doddamakkali and Galibore

Doddamakkali is 7 km upstream from Bheemeshwari and Galibore 16 km downstream. The former is accessible by both boat and road from Bheemeshwari. Doddamakkali is deep in the forest in a valley, ideal for adventure lovers who are willing to rough it out. Galibore, however, involves a more circuitous route by road (some of it no more than a cow path) which takes almost $1^{1}/_{4}$ hrs.

Both camps are similar to Bheemeshwari and offer similar activities. But they're on a smaller scale and there's no electricity — a luxury you will be provided with only on hot summer nights — which gives them a rustic feel. The rest of the time, make do with hurricane lamps.

WHERE TO STAY AND EAT

The **Cauvery Fishing Camp** (Tel: 08231-694248; Tariff: Rs 1,650-2,200 per person per night) in Bheemeshwari is the largest of the three run by Jungle Lodges in the area. The camp has 8 Swiss tented cottages, 2 cottages and 8 log huts. The tariff includes all meals, stay, coracle rides, angling and taxes.

TIP All you get here is beer

Galibore Fishing Camp (Tel: 694305; Tariff: Rs 1,650 per person per night), located in the forest, has 12 tented cottages (twin-sharing) with attached loos. Tariff includes stay, all meals, angling, a coracle ride, joy fishing and taxes. The camp also has its own genset.

Doddamakkalli Fishing Camp (Tel: 694348; Tariff: Rs 1,400, per person per night) is located deep in the forest. The tariff includes stay in 10 tented Swiss cottages, all meals and angling. There's no electricity here and only hurricane lanterns and torches to work with. Book well in advance at Jungle Lodges in Bangalore. You can't go to any of the camps without a booking.

AROUND BHEEMESHWARI

Sangam and Mekedatu (50 km)
Sangam, at the confluence of the Arakavati and Cauvery, is set in lush forests. Mekedatu, 5 km from Sangam, is known for its rock formations. SH86B connects Mekedatu and Sangam to Kanakapura.

The **Bush Betta Camp** (Tel: 080-41125220; Tariff: Rs 2,450 per head per day) at Mekedatu is located in a village outside the Cauvery Wildlife Division. It has two traditional village houses (8 pax). Those opting for the conservation activities programme can stay in tents in the forest. The tariff includes safaris, all meals, fishing and trekking.

Kokrebellur Pelicanry (60 km)
This little village attracts birds ranging from painted storks to cranes from all over the world. Pelicans particularly favour Kokrebellur. But do visit during peak season (October to March).

For details, see Bheemeshwari Accommodation Listings on page 495 ∎

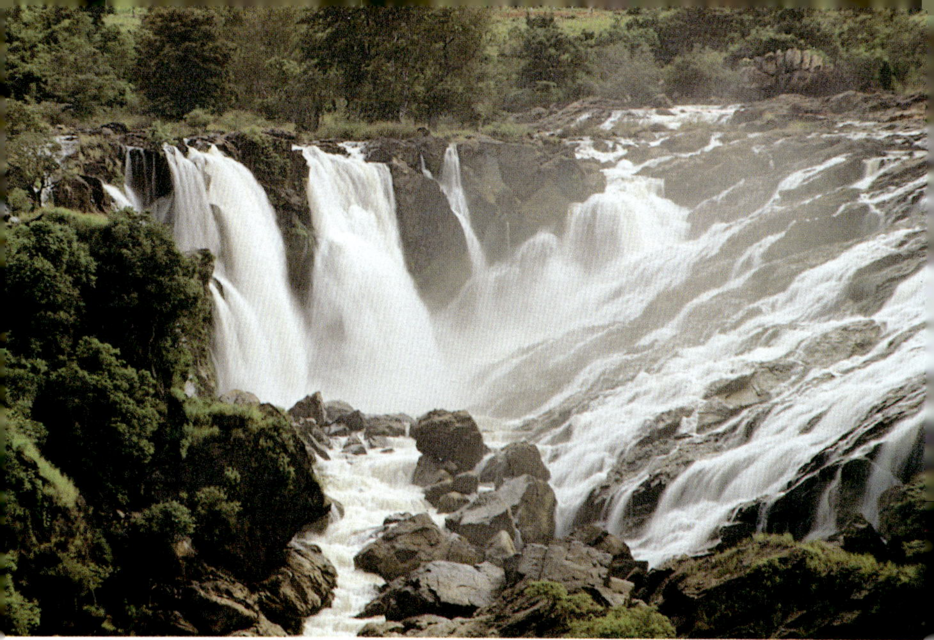

The twin falls of Shivanasamudram — Barachukki and Gaganachukki

SHIVANASAMUDRAM
THE FOREST IN YOUR BACKYARD

State Karnataka
Location Shivanasamudram, in eastern Mandya district, skirts the Cauvery Sanctuary
Distance 440 km W of Chennai **JOURNEY TIME By rail** 6 hrs + 2½ hrs by road **By air** 55 mins + 2½ hrs by road **By road** 10½ hrs
Route NH4 to Bangalore via Poonamallee, Sriperumbudur, Ranipettai, Chittoor, Palmaner, Mulbagal, Kolar and Hoskote; NH209 to Shivanasamudram via Kanakpura, Malavalli and Panditahalli (*see route guide on pages 12 and 254*)

■ BY ANISH VOHRA

Rolling foothills and green expanses, sudden bursts of flaming red amidst green, and winding, picturesque roads... this is as close to bliss in the countryside as you can get. Down the twisting district road from Malavalli, you suddenly come upon the slightly askew signpost that reads 'Georgia Sunshine Village'. The turn-off is basically a dirt track seeming to meander into pure jungle. Well, shift into first gear, adjust your seat and go for

→ **FAST FACTS**

When to go The best time to visit is in the post-monsoon months, from August till December, extending into February. The forest will be lush and the falls at their fullest
STD code 08231

KARNATAKA

Vivid colours of Manchanahalli Village, where time seems to stand still

→ GETTING THERE

Air Nearest airport: Bangalore (109 km/ 2½ hrs), connected to Chennai by 22 daily flights by numerous airlines. Taxis to Shivanasamudram will cost Rs 1,800 **Rail** Nearest railhead: Bangalore **Best option TO** Bangalore Mail (dep: Chennai Central 11.15 pm; arr: Bangalore City 5.30 am) **Best option FROM** Chennai Mail (dep: Bangalore City 10.45 pm; arr: Chennai Central: 4.40 am) **Car** A longish drive for a weekend break. Drive the 331 km to Bangalore via Ranipettai, Chittoor and Hoskote (7½ hrs). Head south of Bangalore to exit via Kanakapura on NH209. Follow the road till Malavalli, 23 km away. Continuing on NH209 turn left to Panditahalli (9 km), then left again on a district road to Hebbani (4 km). Turn right onto the dirt track for about 1½ km and you'll arrive at the turn-off to Georgia Sunshine

it... Winding, curving, bumpy and all but non-existent, the track continues through the jungle till you're sure you're lost. Then, quaint red-tiled rooftops peep through the foliage... Welcome, the forest seems to murmur.

Shivanasamudram is the domain of Mother Nature. Gentle rolling foothills seduce with their pristine freshness, the woods are virgin and the experience is sublime. These hills are home to wild boar, peacocks, partridges, elephants and even the occasional marauding panther. Bands of elephants have been known to venture as near as the village outskirts in these regions. Take that turn onto the back roads for a quiet weekend in the forest at the Georgia Sunshine Village, a few kilometres away from the roaring falls of Shivanasamudram.

THINGS TO SEE AND DO

From the Panditahalli turn-off you get to Hebbani Village; drive 5 minutes down a twisting district road and all of a sudden, the signpost saying 'Georgia Sunshine Village' jumps out of the greenery. Turn off onto a dirt track that winds through the jungle. Look out for the signpost announcing a left turn onto a small path. Look carefully, because the signpost is 20 ft above the eye-line. A couple of more turns from here and you hit Georgia Sunshine Village.

Shivanasamudram is an ideal weekend break thanks to the country home of the Hatherell family, Georgia Sunshine Village, named for your hostess, Georgia Hatherell. Anyone who is looking for nothing more than nature at its untouched best is welcome here. The place is the experience and the keyword is 'chill'.

Those in dire need of rest may grab a book, put up their feet and relax by one of the many little streams that run through the woods around Georgia Sunshine. Those who can't sit still can hare off further into the woods in search of waterfalls, wildlife or fish to catch.

Gaganachukki and Barachukki falls

The Cauvery, the lifeline of Karnataka, splits into two streams here — Barachukki and Gaganachukki. About 9 km by road from Georgia, turn left at Panditahalli and drive to Shri Vishveshwaraya Hydroelectric Plant, labelled as the 'Bluff'. From Bluff, it is a short 5-minute drive to the falls.

Beautiful cascades of water spread out over two vast hillsides will greet you. The water is being diverted to feed what was the first hydroelectric plant in Asia (built in 1902 by the maharaja of the erstwhile Mysore State).

Gaganachukki houses a fall-side **dargah** on the opposite bank, a short drive across to the other hillside. A word of caution though — in these regions, the falls represent a literal Xanadu for boisterous local revellers and their ilk. The falls are best avoided on public holidays while being quite acceptable on weekends. Don't swim here, though, it is treacherous and a number of mishaps have occurred in the past.

A couple of food stalls and a few vendors selling fresh coconut water and locally-grown gooseberries liberally spiced with red chilli powder complete the experience.

Barachukki is just beyond the Dargah, a few kilometres away. The falls here form a sylvan, deep pool. You can swim here or even catch a coracle ride (Rs 20-30). The best time to visit is August to February.

Trekking

The forests here are lush, which also means that traditional walking trails do not exist and that a trek is what it is meant to be — tough and rough. The Hatherells will organise a guide who'll chart out a route and also accompany you. Routes are customised to the energy levels of trekkers and can vary from a

KARNATAKA

simple 2-hr amble to a day-long trip, complete with food, water and supplies thrown in. Animal sightings are rare on these treks, nevertheless groups have been known to get lucky and spot fresh elephant footprints and dung! Rates are Rs 100 for a 3-hr trek for 4 people.

Fun fishing

As the name implies, this isn't meant for those serious anglers out for the aquatic kill of their lifetime. A bamboo rod is recommended. If hard-core fishermen ask for a real rod and reel, the Hatherells will gladly supply you one. Add a picnic lunch or snacks, and chill. The headwork or the check-dam on the Cauvery, which helps channelise water to the hydroelectric plant, is a great place to fish, as are a couple of rivulets and streams nearby. Evenings are a good time to fish. These waters abound in carp, murrel and a smaller variety of the valiant mahseer.

Village visits

When was the last time that you actually walked through a village that seems lost somewhere in time and space? Where you can still find farm implements made by hand and actually have a market for cow bells? The villages of Malavalli, Panditahalli, Manchanahalli, Hebbani and Shimsapura offer all this and more. Don't miss the traditional Friday markets.

The forest at night

A forest by daytime is harsh and distant, by night it becomes an enigma. A drive at night is a great way to indulge in some post-dinner thrills and spot some wildlife. Do take your car out; the Hatherells will provide a guide, on the house.

PRANAV PURUSHOTHAM

Fish a la Georgia

A simple, easy to cook and very tasty Georgia Fish Recipe

Ingredients

Half kg fish, 2 teaspoons chilli powder, 1 teaspoon each of coriander, cummin (jeera), mango (amchur) and tandoori masala powders, $1/2$ teaspoon turmeric powder, 1 teaspoon ginger-garlic paste, $1/4$ cup coriander and half of that of mint leaves to be ground into a paste, 2 tablespoons vinegar and salt to taste

Method

Mix all of the ingredients and marinate the fish in the paste for 2 to 3 hrs. Then shallow fry in just a little oil. Seer and murrel respond best to this treatment, but you can use any other fleshy fish like *bangda* (mackerel) that suits your taste.

WHERE TO STAY AND EAT

Georgia Sunshine Village (Tel: 08231-247646/783, Mobile: 09845754661; Tariff: Rs 1,596-2,156 per person per day) is the only place to be. The 4 cottages (8 rooms) retain a homely atmosphere and personalised charm. Facilities include a mini swimming pool, lounge and library. The tariff includes fun fishing, bonfires, a morning trek, all meals, tea and coffee. Bonfires can be arranged.

Meals are cooked from fresh produce. Carry your own liquor. Book well in advance online or at their Bangalore office, where you need to pay ahead.

For details, see Shivanasamudram Accommodation Listings on page 498 ∎

Rulers, mortal and divine, adorn an auto in Tipu's former capital

SRIRANGAPATNA
THE BECKONING ISLE

State Karnataka
Location Tipu Sultan's former capital is an island in the Cauvery River, 12 km from Mysore
Distance 458 km SW of Chennai JOURNEY TIME *By rail* 10 hrs *By air* 55 mins + 3 hrs by road *By road* 11 hrs
Route NH4 to Bangalore via Poonamallee, Sriperumbudur, Ranipettai, Chittoor, Palmaner, Mulbagal, Kolar and Hoskote; SH17 to Srirangapatna via Ramanagaram, Channapatna, Maddur and Mandya (*see route guide on pages 12 and 254*)

KARNATAKA

■ BY NANDINI SRINIVASAN

Many tales of valour and glory are tucked into the folds of the unassuming island town of Srirangapatna, former capital of one of the bravest sons of Karnataka. Maybe it's due to the guile of the beautiful Cauvery River that you tend to lap up every anecdote the guide narrates. You tend to believe that the legendary sword of Tipu Sultan, housed within the State treasury, is sacred and no one dare touch it.

And, if stones could speak, probably every tiny pebble on the banks of the Cauvery would make the English go red with reminiscences of Tipu's conquest over the 'Unconquerable Empire'. The lanes between the turfed outline of the Srirangapatna Fort bear touching memorials to the life of this unique king.

But if you're not too keen on going 'histerical' on a weekend and need other diversions, Srirangapatna won't let you down. The drive itself, past the golden rocks on which *Sholay* was shot and through the paddy fields of Mandya, is rewarding in itself.

It's not too difficult to find your way around within Sriranga, or to find what

KARNATAKA

you want most out of your weekend. Cross the river to enter the town. Turn right for the abode of Ranganathaswamy and Tipu's fort, left to commune with a beautiful river, the melody of whose movement you will carry in your heart for a long time to come.

THINGS TO SEE AND DO

Srirangapatna is set within and around the ruins of Tipu Sultan's fort, which encompasses most of what lies on the north bank. The fort, built during the Vijayanagara era, strengthened by the Wodeyars and then taken over by Haider and Tipu, is considered to be the second strongest in India. It cannot be viewed as a single entity, rather your interaction with it is a constant as you roam between the sights along the north bank, passing through its Bangalore, Mysore, Delhi, Water and Elephant gates. Every so often its walls will rear up in picturesque locales perfect for a photo-op, like near the aged Wellesley Bridge.

Jame Masjid

As you enter the town the minarets of the mosque beckon you. This simple yet graceful structure was built in 1787 by Tipu. The prayer hall has a row of cusped arches and a ceiling carved with grapevine designs.

Sri Ranganathaswamy Temple

The presiding deity of the holy isle of Srirangapatna elicits a very different response from his devotees. There's something about the expression on Sri Ranganathaswamy's face that's very human. A long walk through his dark, many-pillared temple leads you to his sanctum. Within lies the lord, on the back of a snake, with a most benevolent smile.

The **Lakhadweepotsava**, when one lakh lamps are lit during Makara Sakranthi is a sight to behold. Outside the temple, an ancient chariot awaits your inspection, as do a dozen stalls selling kitschy keepsakes that are worth a look. Pick up sets of Tipu Sultan post-cards... Tipu beheading Britishers, Tipu killing a tiger with his bare hands, and so on.

◆**Timings** 7.30 am-1 pm, 4-7.30 pm
Puja timings 8-9.30 am, 7-8 pm

Captain Bailey's Dungeon

A little further up the temple towards the right will take you to the place the British dreaded the most. On an elevated platform near the fort wall are the dungeons where Tipu's prisoners of war were jailed. In the underground prison you can see hooks on the walls to which the prisoners hands were chained. In the midst of the chamber lies a well-preserved cannon.

The Obelisk

A furlong down from the dungeon is a monument that marks the place where Tipu Sultan died, while trying to prevent a British soldier from pulling out his legendary sword from it's scabbard. His body lay there for two days before the locals noticed and recognised it. A commemorative obelisk, housed within a small enclosure into which you may not enter, marks the very spot where Tipu fell dead. You can't enter, but may take a photo through the railings.

→ FAST FACTS

When to go Sriranga is pleasant all through the year, but November to April is the coolest period
Tourist office
● KSTDC ❶ ❺
Hotel Mayura River View
Near PWD Rest House, Srirangapatna
Tel: 08236-217454/55, 09341022209
STD code 08236

Resting place of the legendary Tipu Sultan, tiger of Mysore

Darya Daulat Baug

This wooden palace built by Tipu in 1784, set amidst manicured lawns and flowerbeds, looks modest from the outside, and is for the most part hidden from sight by green shades. But the wealth of paintings on the walls and the intricacy of the interiors leave the visitor enthralled. Also called the Summer Palace, it was used by Tipu as an alternative to receive visitors and conduct durbars.

There is a good collection of period furniture, coins, fabulous paintings, murals and plenty of historical data of Hyder Ali and Tipu's conquests in the museum within the palace. The painting, by Robert Home, of Lord Cornwallis receiving the sons of Tipu Sultan as hostages touches the chords of your heart. One of the most impressive items on display is a world-famous portrait of Tipu by the great German neoclassical painter Johann Zoffany. Probably the closest likeness you'll ever see of the great king.

If you've carried lunch, the palace lawns are an ideal place to idle around under trees full of great big bumblebee hives and monkeys. The palace is on the road to Ganjam and Sangama.

♦**Entry fee** Rs 5, foreigners Rs 50-100
Video camera fee Rs 15 (in the garden only) **Timings** 8.30 am-5 pm
Note Still cameras can't be used within the museum, video cameras may be used with permission from the Director General, ASI, New Delhi

Gumbaz

Tipu Sultan, his father Hyder Ali, his mother, sons and other members of the royal family lie buried in this monument. The inscription in Persian on its western wall says *'from this the moon has borrowed its light'* and refers to it as the 'House of Sleep'. Tipu's favourite tiger stripes cover the walls. At the Dariya Daulat Bagh, turn left and continue along the Sangama Road till you reach a fork in the road. Here turn right towards Gumbaz and Sangama.
♦**Timings** Sunrise to sunset

Sangama

The Sangama, 3 km south of the town centre, is where the two branches of the Cauvery re-unite in joyful exuberance. A pilgrim's chamber lies in ruins just before the steps that lead down the

KARNATAKA

PRASHANT PANJIAR

Gracious host

Scores of birds home in every year on a group of islands in the Cauvery, just west of Srirangapatna. As soon as we entered the gates of **Ranganathittu Bird Sanctuary**, along a path lined with tall, thick bamboo, we were assailed by the chattering of thousands of birds. We emerged into a clearing and bumped into crowds waiting for their turn to clamber into a boat and explore the nesting grounds of Ranganathittu. We took a 'private' and jumped into the vivid blue wooden boat. Almost as soon as the boatman pulled away, we were drawn into the magic of the Cauvery.

As we glided over the river, huge flocks of bats flapped above our heads. Everywhere that a foothold could be wangled, there were birds, some even on logs floating slowly down the river. Our boatman pointed out the species to us, 'iggrate', 'daaturr', 'cuomorint', '*magar-machch*'. Not very sure we heard him correctly, we asked, '*Magar-machch*?' And sure enough, those still logs floating on the river weren't made of wood but flesh and blood. We continued our ride, totally seduced by the river and its feathered guests. It was only the mosquitoes that forced us to get up and leave. Not that we minded their company, for it was the high presence of aquatic insects that attracted the birds to Ranganathittu.

Ranganathittu is 4 km from Srirangapatna. Drive towards Mysore on SH17, take the deviation to the right (a board here says Ranganathittu) via the Paschimavahini Bridge. After a distance, take a deviation left to Ranganathittu (board present). The best time to visit is December to April.

♦ **Entry fee** Adult Rs 20, child (3-12 years) Rs 10, foreigners Rs 60 **Cameras** Still Rs 3-10, 8 mm-16 mm Rs 100, video Rs 150 **Vehicle entry** Bus Rs 100, car Rs 50, van Rs 20, two-wheeler Rs 10 **Boat ride fee** Rs 25, children Rs 10 **Timings** 8.30 am-5.30 pm

Lesley A Esteves

small ghat to the water. The tiniest of shrines marks the spot where the waters meet. The river is full of coracles taking pilgrims for a dip.

Dodda Ghosai Ghat

This bathing spot, with a **Sri Radha Madhava Temple** by the banks, is nice enough for a dip in the Cauvery, but watch out for the water level. It's not a good idea to wade too deep into the waters when the river is almost full. The temple is run by the Narasingha Chaitanya Mutt and is open to visitors only on Sundays between 6 am and 6 pm. To get there, turn right at the 200-year-old **Abbe Dubois Church** opposite Ganjam on the Sangama Road.

Pandavapura

The small town of Pandavapura has a very interesting mythological background. It is said the demon Bakasura resided here and harassed the villagers who sent him a cartful of eatables along with a person to devour everyday. That is why the place was originally called 'Hiri Yede' (*yede* means food). But when the Pandavas stopped here during their exile, Bheema slayed the demon and the

SRIRANGAPATNA

place was renamed Pandavapura. The **Pandavapura Lake** is famous for *katla* and *kuchulu* fish. Pandavapura is also home to the only temple in India that is dedicated to Ahalya. From Srirangapatna's Baburayana Koppal Circle, turn right for Pandavapura (10 km).

Karighatta

About 1 km after the Wellesley Bridge back towards Bangalore, cross the bridge over the Lokapavani River and turn right towards Bannur. Another 3 km further, you reach the 450 steps that lead up to the **Venkatramana Temple** atop Karighatta hillock. The sweet smell of jaggery being made in the huts nearby permeates the air. The temple is situated in a large compound fringed with tamarind and gooseberry trees.

WHERE TO STAY

Srirangapatna offers good options, most by the river. **Amblee Holiday Resort** (Tel: 08236-217474-75, 09845446999; Tariff: Rs 1,200-1,800) has a swimming pool and a small boating stretch along the Cauvery, peopled by ducks that surround your boat. Fishing is part of the package. The Cauvery River flows behind **Fort View Resorts** (Tel: 252577/ 777, 09945248172, 09845353751; Tariff: Rs 1,000-1,350) as well, providing a soothing view from the rooms. **Hotel Mayura River View** (Tel: 217454-55; Tariff: Rs 500-750), the KSTDC place, has a line of cottages along the riverbank and a small playground. The location is magical. The river lies a stone's throw away from your balcony. **Balaji Garden Resort** (Tel: 217355-56; Tariff: Rs 350-750) has 46 rooms, a pool and a playground.

→ GETTING THERE

Air Nearest airport: Bangalore (127 km/ $3^1/_2$ hrs), connected to Chennai by 22 daily flights by numerous airlines. Taxis to Srirangapatna cost Rs 2,200 one way
Rail Srirangapatna **Best option TO** Mysore Express (dep: Chennai Central 21.30 pm; arr: Srirangapatna 7.18 am) **Best option FROM** Chennai Express (dep: Srirangapatna 8.20 pm; arr: Chennai Central 7.20 am)
TIP Chennai Express halts for only two minutes at Srirangapatna
Car A long journey, so avoid self-drive for a weekend break. The drive to Bangalore along NH4 via Ranipettai, Chittoor, Hosur and Hoskote takes $7^1/_2$ hrs, then it's another 3 to Srirangapatna via Channapatna and Maddur

KARNATAKA

DELHI KI GURU
Deepti, Hotel Advisor at Travelguru. Well acquainted with NCR, she knows the shortest route to N.E.P.Z from Connaught Place.

Choose from our network of over 4000 hotels in India. Serviced apartments, budget hotels, luxury resorts, palaces, business accommodations, houseboats and more.

1-800-22-4878
022-4030-4878
www.travelguru.com

India's Largest Hotel Network

iCONTRACT.TG.07.3248

CHENNAI WEEKEND BREAKS | 287

KARNATAKA

Priests at the many-pillared abode of Lord Ranganathaswamy

Aquarium Amusement Theme Park Resorts (Tel: 217442; Tariff: Rs 750), popularly known as Fun Fort, has 10 rooms and 1 dorm (can accommodate 200-250 people, Rs 25 a head). Located 3 km after Srirangapatna towards Mysore, it has a water park, an amusement theme park, restaurants, and offers video games, boating and go-karting.

For more hotels and details, see Srirangapatna Accommodation Listings on page 499

WHERE TO EAT

Eat at the resorts, or at the holes-in-the-wall on the highway. The latter serve only thalis and dosas, but are fresh and safe for kids. A few bakeries in the heart of town make excellent fresh bread, biscuits, chips and cake. The food in the resorts isn't flattering enough, but they do have tables laid out near the river. The **Mayura River View** needs an overhaul of its menu, hopefully to bring in some South Indian cuisine.

AROUND SRIRANGAPATNA

Mysore (12 km)
See facing page

Mahadevapura (13 km)
Drive 8 km further up from Karighatta to this picturesque village, famous for its movie connections. Many regional movies have a couple of scenes shot here, as it provides an ideal backdrop for a rustic setting. In fact, there is also a house specially constructed for shooting. The Cauvery is particularly enticing here.

Kere Thonnur (14 km)
About 2 km ahead of Pandavapura is Kere Thonnur. Tall trees along the shores enhance the beauty of Thonnur Lake. Sail around the lake in *theppas* (coracles). The temples here date back to the 13th century when the Cholas ruled these parts. Tipu called the lake Moti Talab. On the way up, stop and get under the falls created by water cascading down from the lake. ■

Incredible !ndia

Vanakkam!

A common Tamil way of greeting everyone It means welcome, respect, adoration, worship, reverence….so you know what to expect when you come to Tamil Nadu.

Temples

Meenakshi Temple, Madurai

Tamil Nadu is blessed. You sometimes wonder, is there a temple for each of its citizens?

It is as if every big city, small town and village is known by the divine company it keeps. So in Chidambaram it is Nataraja, the cosmic dancer who rules. Madurai is home to Meenakshi. In the you-will-miss-it-if-somebody-doesn't-mention-it small town called Srivilliputhur, stands one of Tamil Nadu's tallest temples with its *gopuram* (temple tower) rising to 192 feet. Incidentally, this *gopuram* is the official symbol of the Government of Tamil Nadu. As for Kanchipuram, they have simply lost count of the number of places of worship and have taken to calling it a temple town instead. The grand conceptions, majestic *gopurams*, art, sculpture and carvings on the *gopurams* and inside the temples are all amazing and uniquely Tamil; they are living, throbbing places of spirituality with an unbroken tradition of worship that goes back to centuries. Pray that you come here sooner!

Beaches

Marina Beach, Chennai

The good news is Tamil Nadu has a 1000-km coastline. The better news is most of it is unexplored, pristine. You can thank the locals suitably for leaving it alone when you land up here. In Kanniyakumari, you will find land's end. Didn't someone say three is a crowd? Here sea is a crowd. In a unique confluence, you will find the Indian Ocean, the Bay of Bengal and the Arabian Sea meeting at Kanniyakumari. You can also visit the beautiful Tiruchendur beach temple dedicated to Lord Mururga. In a way it is a come down for him, because he usually prefers the hills! There is Vattakotai beach, near Kanniyakumari. We haven't advertised it much, because we hope you will end up doing it. Then there is Tharangambadi or Tranquebar with its Danish Fort. Tranquebar is known for its ozone-rich beach. And as you head north, towards Chennai, there is Mamallapuram. With its great beach and Shore Temple, it is a sight. It is also a site; a UNESCO World Heritage Site to be precise. Finally, there is Chennai, the state capital, itself washed by the world's second longest beach - the Marina. So, see you soon!

Brahadeeshwara Temple, Thanjavur

The big temple is one of the five UNESCO World Heritage Sites in Tamil Nadu.

Culture

Mamallapuram Dance Festival

Tamil Nadu has always been a haven of peace. If at all there is war, it is a war of words. Over which dance form is superior, which painting is better, which temple has better sculptures or which *raga* is apt for a given time in a day. On any given evening you can enjoy Bharatnatyam – the classical, extraordinarily graceful dance form that speak through eyes and *mudras* (hand gestures) to bring mythologies, stories and the emotions in them alive. An evening at a Carnatic music concert can be a sublime experience. The folk arts are full of energy, rustic humour, playfulness and many times prayers to a favourite deity. *Karagaattam* is a rhythmic dance in praise of *Mari Amman*, the goddess who showers blessings in the form of rain. Balancing a pot on their heads, the dancers give you a show that will, like the pots, remain firmly in your memory. What if you don't have any musical instrument? You do a *Kummi*. *Kummi* a joyful dance with the clapping of hands. *Oyil Kummi* is where anklet sounds come into play. *Silambattam* is Tamil Nadu's very own, original martial art form. There is, of course, more to this list, we suggest you discover them.

Waterfalls

Hogenakkal Falls

The river meanders on and once in a while it takes a spectacular break. Like the ones at Courtallam and Hogenakkal in Tamil Nadu. Dubbed the Spa of the South, Courtallam is a refreshing shower bath that combines curative powers and great natural beauty. It is said the waters run through a forest of herbs which gives them medicinal properties. Is this what they mean by water therapy? Courtallam, in fact, has nine separate waterfalls so we would not really advise a weekend visit. There are a number of good places to stay. But avoid the bathroom showers! Hogenakkal, elsewhere in Tamil Nadu, is another great place for a good body spray. In local language it means 'smoking rocks'. The fantastic white spray as the water crashes over the rocks is what gives this awe-inspiring effect of smoke and mist. Hogenakkal also enjoys the reputation of a great massage spot where masseurs give you an oil massage right amongst the rocks and water. You can say oil and water mixes quite well here. The peace of the surrounding thick forests, coracle boat rides which take you right to the point where the water hits the deck are all experiences that will make your eyes turn misty once you're back home.

Wildlife

Mundanthurai Tiger Sanctuary

There is this old jungle saying "once bitten twice smitten". Wildlife enthusiasts pine only for the forests. You just cannot satisfy them with a visit to the local zoo. There are many rules to be followed if you go to the jungle. Like not wearing a perfume (the animals can smell it miles off and it puts them off), like keeping quiet (you want to hear the tiger roar, don't you?), colourful clothes are a strict no, wear brown, dark green etc. (in any case, the animals don't wear any), no smoking please (it can start fires) and sorry no music either (why would anyone in their senses want to miss the sounds of the forests?). The reward for all this discipline can be enriching. Tamil Nadu has the Mundanthurai Project Tiger Sanctuary where you can spot the endangered lion-tailed macaque. It is found only in these parts of India. Mudhumalai with its great elephant & bison population and the Point Calimere & Vedantangal bird sanctuaries will all whet your appetite if wildlife and adventure is your game.

Sarees

Tamil Nadu has its own silk route. It begins in Kanchipuram. Some four centuries ago, there came to this small temple town a clan of weavers, who, with magical skill, wove splendid silks. Before long, their fame spread. The silk saris of Kanchipuram (*Kanchi pattu* in Tamil) are now fabled for their beauty and for their quality, which truly has no equal. The silk yarn (of the finest Karnataka mulberry silk) used in Kanchipuram is actually three silk threads twisted into one. This is interleaved with *zari* which is silk thread intertwined with silver thread and then gilded with genuine gold. Intricate traditional motifs grace the saris, making them part of the rich art heritage of Tamil Nadu. Not surprisingly, Kanchi saris can sometimes cost several thousand dollars. Each! Kanchi has a challenger in a neighbouring town called Arni, where lighter, simpler silk saris are made. Chettinad, where you will find Chettinad palaces and great food, also has a different kind of sari, Kandangi, made of cotton. So too in Salem, Rasipuram and Coimbatore. Madurai's Sungadi, fine gold bordered muslin, appear to complement its magnificent temples and the fragrant jasmines (every one who breathes will smell them). Finally, a word of appreciation for becoming grace with which the women of Tamil Nadu wear the saris.

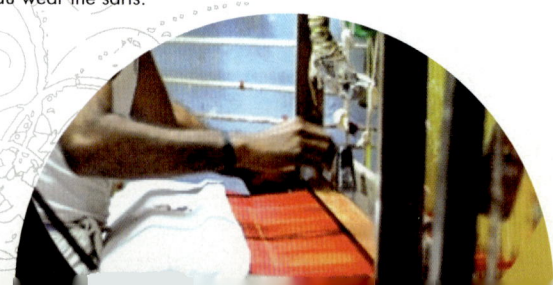

Chettinad House

A sample of how the kings lived. Some even take in lodgers and it doesn't cost a king's ransom either.

Mamallapuram

The nice sound of a chisel on rock as the sculptor cuts away;

Medical

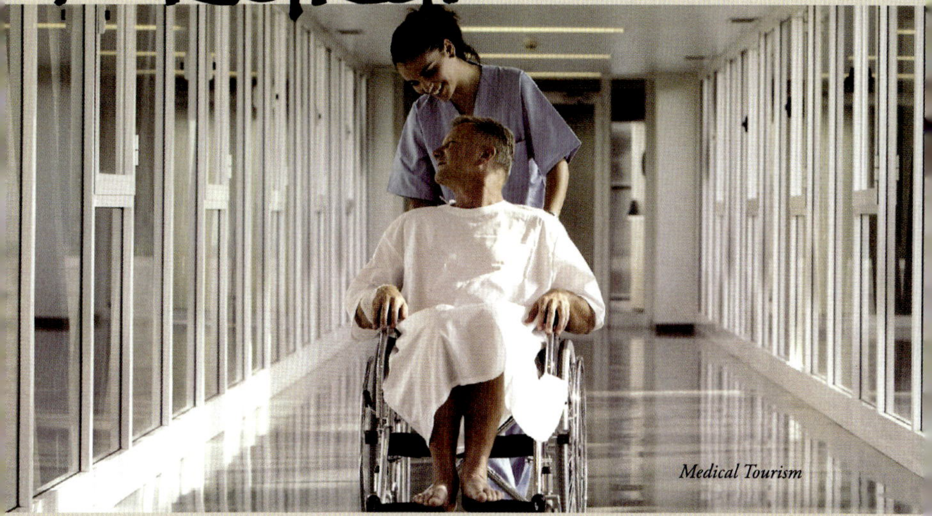

Medical Tourism

Come to Tamil Nadu even if you're not well enough to enjoy its food, heritage and culture. For the state has some of the finest medical facilities in the world, and can make you well with minimal fuss and expense. The most advanced technologies will come to your aid in Chennai's world-class hospitals. Experienced doctors and expert medical staff will take good care of you. Tamil Nadu is also the home to Sidha tradition. This ancient system of medicine uses plants and minerals to treat not just an ailment, but the whole body, for complete and long-lasting cures. Tamil Nadu also offers alternatives like Ayurveda, Unani and a healthy dose of prevention with some of the finest Yoga teachers and practitioners. And then, when you're feeling 100% fit, take in the sights and sensations of Tamil Nadu.

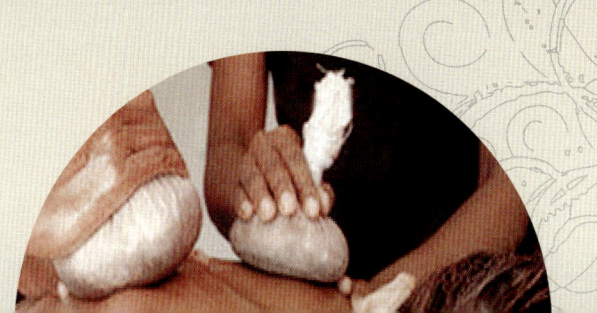

Adventure

Raindrop Boat House (Mudaleyar Kuppam)

Yes, we have great mountains that you have to climb 'because they're there'. As well as thick, uncharted forests that you can explore and get lost in. In fact, Tamil Nadu has two of the nine biospheres in India, at Udhagamandalam (Ooty) and Gulf of Mannar. We also have lovely hill stations. In Kodaikkanal, you can try the *molaga bajjis* (vicious chillies hidden in delicious batter and fried). In the carefully preserved national parks, you can enjoy nature at its rawest, wildest best. The Mudumalai Wildlife Sanctuary, for instance (if you're feeling particularly intrepid, you can say 'boo' to the placid elephants or shoot the tigers with your camera from the safety of a jeep). Off the vast coast of Chennai, take a ride on a *kattu maram*, the Tamil word for a simple but unsinkable wooden canoe that puts out to sea, with the waves submerging it completely at times. By the way, this is the word that became the modern 'catamaran'. Having worked up an appetite, try some fresh fish *kari* (the word that later became the famous 'curry') with rice. Work it all off with some paragliding or hang gliding or para jumping. Let the water toss you around at Manimutharu (Tirunelveli) and Hogenakkal (Dharmapuri), where you can go white water rafting. Cycle up and down the beautiful, steep mountain paths in the Ooty Bicycle Safari. The real adventure though, is out on the streets, where an incredible variety of experiences ambushes your senses. But we will not go into detail about all that. It would spoil the surprise.

Kanniyakumari

Saint-poet Thiruvalluvar is Tamil Nadu's wise counsel on every facet of life. This magnificent, 133 ft. statue is the Tamilians tribute to him.

Hogenakkal

An oil massage by experts in a setting that is spectacular. Call it nirvana if you like.

Food

If the sunrise has a taste, it is this. The flavour of freshly filtered Kumbakonam Degree coffee. Try to drink it the way Tamilians do, letting it cascade from a steel tumbler at shoulder height into a steel saucer at waist level, steam wraiths rising, Invigorated, let us move on to Kanchipuram, for some hot *idlis*. The next stop is Chidambaram, for some *pongal* that will let you taste heaven. Please hurry and finish, we have a mid-morning snack scheduled in Mayavaram. *Paruppu thenga*. Pulses with shredded coconut. Later, en route to Karaikudi, allow us to remind you that Tamil Nadu has one of the oldest vegetarian traditions in the world. This distinction does not mean that it cannot also have a glorious non-vegetarian cuisine. Have a long and leisurely Chettinad lunch, a cornucopia of meat and sweet (Chettinad chicken and *kozhi paniyaram* are signature dishes). Hurry to Thanjavur, for 'tiffen' - a quintessentially Tamil snack-meal that can include *pakoda, upma, dosa, laddu, pongal, uthappam, adai avial* and of course, fresh filter coffee. And yes, some *murukku* (meaning 'twist') in Manapparai. Quickly hop over to Salem for juicy mangoes, the favourite fruit of royalty. Sweet tooth still not satisfied? Try Tirunelveli *halwa*. Time for dinner and for that matter any meal, it must be Madurai. You can feast on hot *dosas, idlis* and coffee at all hours of day and night. Full? Not until you've sampled the rich variety of Tamil desserts. There is much that we have left out, for want of space. We hope your stomach is more capacious.

experience yourself.

Tamil Nadu Tourism

For details on TTDC's attractive package tours with excellent accommodation, transport facilities, please contact:
Tamil Nadu Tourism Complex, Wallajah Road, Chennai - 600 002. **INDIA.** Ph: 91-44-25383333 / 25384444. Fax: 91-44-25361385 / 25382772
E-mail: ttdc@vsnl.com, website: www.tamilnadutourism.org. For online reservations, please log on to: www.ttdconline.com
Call: **Chennai** 91-44-25389857 • **Mumbai** 91-22-24110118 • **New Delhi** 91-11-23745427 • **Kolkata** 91-33-24237432 • **Goa** 91-832-2226390

H SATISH

The sun sets on the Wodeyar capital, still steeped in old-world charm

MYSORE
SUNSET BOULEVARD

State Karnataka
Location Close to Srirangapatna, Tipu Sultan's territory at one time, sylvan Mysore has the Cauvery and Kabini rivers to its north and south respectively
Distance 470 km SW of Chennai **JOURNEY TIME** *By rail* $10^1/_2$ hrs *By road* $11^1/_2$ hrs *By air* 55 mins + 4 hrs by road
Route NH4 to Bangalore via Poonamallee, Sriperumbudur, Ranipettai, Chittoor, Palmaner, Mulbagal, Kolar and Hoskote; SH17 to Mysore via Ramanagaram, Channapatna, Maddur, Mandya and Srirangapatna (*see route guides on pages 12 and 254*)

KARNATAKA

■ BY ARCHANA RAI

To veer off State Highway 17 and pass through the arched gate to Mysore city is a symbolic act. One leaves behind the frenetic bustle and the determined post-modernist throb of Bangalore, Mysore's eastern neighbour and, in many ways, the gracious old city's upstart sibling.

Up until 1973, when Mysore State was renamed Karnataka, it was the spirit of Mysore that imbued the cultural and social life of the region. To be a cultivated person was to be Mysorean. But through the 1970s, as Bangalore strode ahead into the emerging world of technology, Mysore remained enmeshed in a time-warp of old-worldly royalty.

The Wodeyars made Mysore grand and irresistible, particularly so under the rule of Chikka Devaraja Wodeyar (1673-1704). He generously promoted art and literature, besides instituting

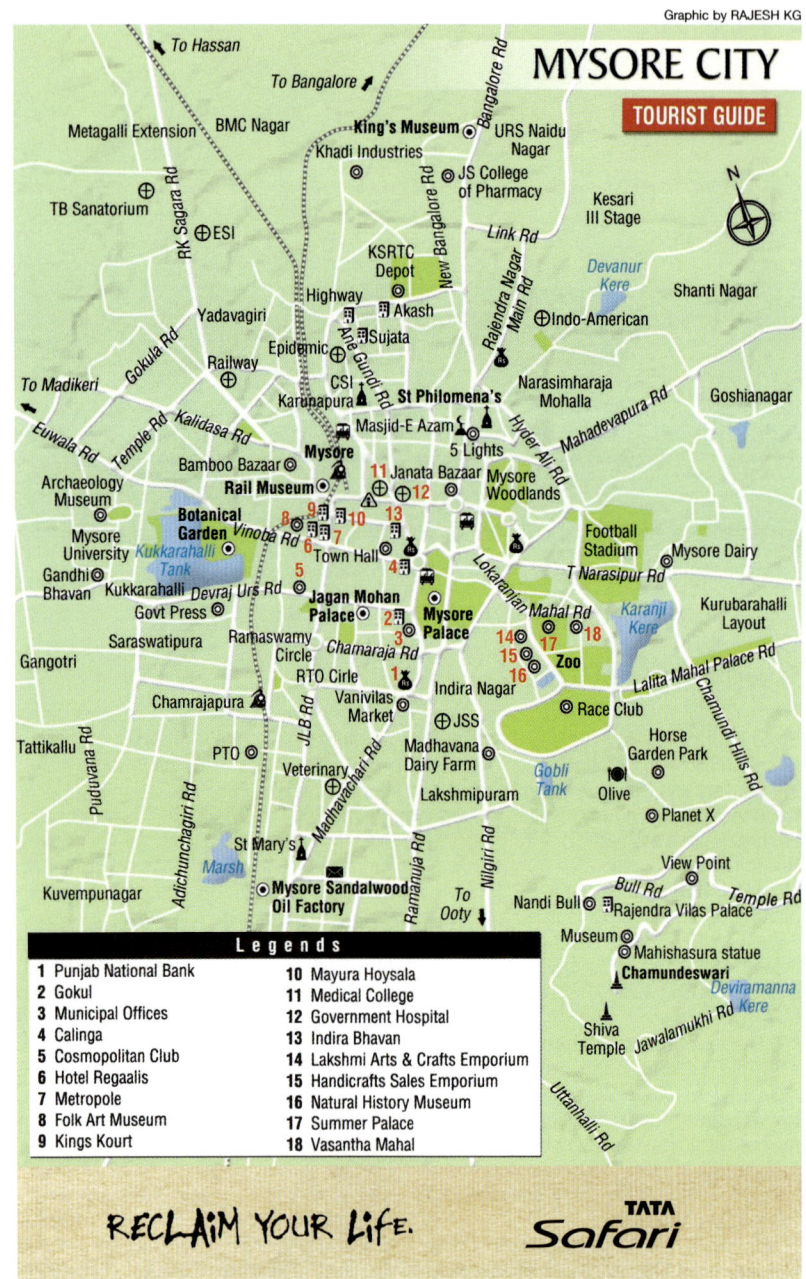

MYSORE

DINESH SHUKLA

Mysore's famous Indo-Saracenic Amba Vilas Palace, home of the Wodeyars

large-scale administrative reforms. By the late 18th century, however, the Wodeyar sway over Mysore weakened when their general, Haider Ali, rebelled to establish a capital in nearby Srirangapatna (*see page 283*). The young kingdom barely had the time to consolidate itself when the British started interfering. Haider Ali's son, Tipu Sultan, bravely took on the challenge till he was killed in the Battle of Mysore in 1799, earning the grudging admiration of his opponents, who nicknamed him the 'Tiger of Mysore'.

The Wodeyars returned to rule Mysore, subject to the British writ. Once again Mysore revived its links to art, literature, music and learning. It's a tradition that lives on till today. Like the die-hard fans of RK Narayan's *Tales from Malgudi*, who'll swear they can recognise its landmarks everywhere.

Mysore is a city that harks back to a past when the finer things in life still mattered. It's a place where time is measured in seasons and not seconds, and where a horse-drawn tonga still runs alongside an autorickshaw.

THINGS TO SEE AND DO

Mysore's glorious past does not live in its royal edifices, churches or museums. It's palpable in the unhurried yet often grand lifestyle of its people, and its literature and performing arts. Cap the experience with a Mysorean sunset. "Even today I would assert, after having visited many parts of the world, that nowhere can you witness such masterpiece sunsets as in Mysore..." wrote RK Narayan in *My Days*.

The palaces

Home to the Wodeyars, the Indo-Saracenic **Amba Vilas Palace** was built in 1912 — a fire had burnt down the old wooden residence in 1897. Designed by British architect Henry Irwin, this awesome palace is dominated by domes, turrets and colonnades. Beautifully restored and maintained, the palace is a treasure trove of art antiques and rare collectibles. In the **Marriage Pavilion** (thrown open to public only during Dasara, *see page 292*) you can view the magnificent chandeliers, cast-iron pillars

KARNATAKA

Traditional regalia for the Ayudha Puja during Dasara festivities

from Glasgow, and a Belgian glass-decorated ceiling. This is also where the jewel-studded 14th century **Golden Throne** is placed.

♦**Entry fee** Adults Rs 20, students Rs 10 **Timings** 10 am-5.30 pm, open all days **Cameras** Not allowed **Tel** 0821-2421051

Adjacent to the palace is the **Maharaja's Residence**, now a museum with a good collection of art and artefacts. Normally lit on Sundays and public holidays, the grandiose structure is a treat, especially during Dasara. Illuminated every evening, its entire panoply of 96,200 bulbs shine bright.

♦**Entry fee** Rs 20 **Timings** 10 am-5.30 pm, open all days **Cameras** Not allowed

The **Jagan Mohan Palace** houses the **Sri Jayachamarajendra Art Gallery**, with its collection of paintings by Raja Ravi Varma and Nicholas Roerich.

♦**Entry fee** Adults Rs 25, children Rs 15 **Timings** 10 am-5 pm, open all days

Located 5 km from the Amba Vilas Palace, within the sprawling campus of the University of Mysore, lies the beautiful **Jayalakshmi Vilas Palace** built in 1905. It houses one of Mysore's best landmarks, the **Folklore Museum**. With over 6,500 articles on display, this museum is considered one of the biggest of its kind in Asia.

♦**Entr fee** Adults Rs 25, children free **Timings** 10 am-5 pm, closed on public holidays **Cameras** Not allowed

The second largest palace in the city, the **Lalitha Mahal**, is a spectacular white stone building, situated at the foot of the Chamundi Hills. Built in 1913 by Krishnaraja Wodeyar IV, it served as a retreat for the maharaja's guests. The tradition continues with ITDC now running it as a 5-star hotel.

Atop the Chamundi Hills, the abandoned **royal retreat of Rajendra Vilas**' main draw is its spectacular view of Mysore and the surrounding hills.

Mysore's famous Dasara

The Mysore Dasara festivities are spread out through several locations in the city. The palace ground serves as a massive open-air venue with the lit palace providing a stunning backdrop to performances by a string of venerable names from the world of Indian classical arts. There is a moment worth witnessing every evening, when the sun sets and all 96,200 palace lights come on at once, greeted by a spontaneous gasp of awe from the assembled crowd. The performances at the palace last year included such heavyweights as Rashid Khan, Balamuralikrishna, Parveen Sultana, Vishwamohan Bhatt and Hariprasad Chaurasia.

I wrangled an entry into the palace to watch the maharaja's **Ayudha Puja** on the penultimate day of the festivities, a ceremony that is closed to the public. By the time I argued my way inside the palace gates, the puja was in full swing. The maharaja stood on a dais, decked in flowing mauve robes, with glittering necklaces coiled around his neck and an exquisite turban on his head.

A **marching band** provided romping, if somewhat incongruous, accompaniment to the rites. Camels, caparisoned elephants, palanquins and luxury cars passed before the king; to each he made an offering of flowers before motioning that they be taken away. The band trumpeted on through 'Serenade in the Night' and 'The Cariappa March', before ending with a rousing rendition of the Mysore anthem.

Also in the palace grounds was a **vintage car display**, featuring cars like the 1930 Delage D8 designed by the legendary Italian Guiseppe Figoni and the 1939 Ford V8 Van, once an ordinary postal van, now a precious relic. I walked on, admiring the 1947 MG TC, the 1955 Jaguar XK 140 and several vintage motorbikes, among them the 1956 Triumph T100 and 1942 Norton 500 Military. These vehicles would flag off the Jambu Savari on the final day.

The festival is capped by the **Vijayadashami** procession, also called the **Jambu Savari**, which follows a 4^1/$_2$-km route from the palace to the Banni Mantap grounds.

→ FAST FACTS

When to go Mysore enjoys a salubrious climate throughout the year
Tourist offices
- Dept of Tourism
Govt of Karnataka, Old Exhibition Building, Irwin Road Mysore
Tel: 0821-2422096
- KSTDC
Transport Wing, Yatri Niwas Building, JLB Road, Mysore. Tel: 2423652
Website: kstdc.nic.in
STD code 0821

Choose from our network of over 4000 hotels in India. Serviced apartments, budget hotels, luxury resorts, palaces, business accomodations, houseboats and more.

Hotel	Rating
Hotel Ginger	Budget
Pai Vista	3 ★
Royal Orchid Brindavan Garden	4 ★

MTNL/BSNL Toll Free No.
1-800-22-4878
022-4030-4878
www.travelguru.com

travel**g**uru™
India's Largest Hotel Network

KARNATAKA

Twin spires of the British-era Gothic St Philomena's Church

Exactly on time, the Karnataka chief minister made his appearance, along with the king who, wearing a white T-shirt and a white cap, was a little less extravagantly dressed than expected. Cannons boomed across the palace grounds, marking the beginning of the festivities. The vintage cars rolled out of the palace gates, greeted by a roaring, adoring public. The rest of the procession followed, the star of which was the elephant Balarama, carrying on its back the idol of the goddess Chamundi.

The range of cultural forms showcased in the procession was staggering — Dollu Kunita, giant Garudi puppets, Shaivite Veeragase dancers, Pata Kunita, Nandi Dwaja... These were interspersed with tableaus, some celebrating the wonders of Mysore, others freezing moments from the epics, still others celebrating the diversity of religions.

The festival begins nine days prior to Dasara. In 2007, it begins on October 12. During Dasara, Mysore is teeming with activity — cultural performances, melas, pujas and processions (check for details at *www.mysoredasara.com*).

Rail Museum
Located behind the railway station, this little known but impressive museum has a collection of locomotive coaches, paintings and photographs, narrating the 'Rail Story'. The prize exhibit is the **Maharaja's Saloon**, especially crafted for Wodeyar rulers in 1899.
◆**Entry** Free **Timings** 10 am-5 pm Open all days **Cameras** Free

St Philomena's Church
Mysore's only British edifice, on Ashoka Road north of the Amba Vilas Palace, is the Gothic Church built in 1931. It's an imposing deep-chocolate coloured structure with impressive stained-glass windows and twin spires that stretch 175 ft into the sky.
◆**Entry** Free **Timings** 8 am-8 pm, open all days **Cameras** Not allowed

Chamundeswari Temple
Perched atop the Chamundi Hills (1,000 ft), on the eastern edge of Mysore, sits this 11th century temple dedicated to Goddess Chamundi (Durga), family deity of the Wodeyars. You can either climb

Experience a Kings Lifestyle only at Kings Kourt
Mysore

Kings Kourt HOTEL

- Central Location - heart of the heritage city
- 50 Centrally Air-conditioned Spacious Rooms and Suites
- Mysore Memories - Multi Cuisine Restaurant
- 2 Banquet Halls
- Cocktail Circuit - lounge bar
- Business Centre
- Heritage Tours
- Fitness Center and Spa*
- Swimming Pool*
- Free Airport Transfers*

*Coming Soon

VIVEK HOTELS | Tel: +91 80 4112 2661 Mob: +91 98450 02659 / 93421 28358
email: sales@vivekhotels.com www.vivekhotels.com

the 1,000 steps to the temple or drive up winding *ghat* roads. As you approach the temple you can see the towering statue of the demon Mahishasura. Not far off is the majestic monolithic Nandi.

♦**Special darshan** Rs 10 **Timings** 7.30 am-2 pm, 3.30-6 pm and 7.30-9 pm; open all days

Sri Jayachamarajendra Zoo

Mysore boasts one of the best zoos in the country, with a large collection of rare animals like tapir, chimpanzee, giraffe, zebra and white tiger. You need at least two full hours to visit all corners of the zoo. Take the tram, which, for a nominal fee drives you through the zoo grounds.

♦**Entry fee** Adults Rs 25, children Rs 10 **Cameras** Still Rs 60, video Rs 100 **Timings** 9 am to 5 pm, Tuesdays closed

→ GETTING THERE

Air Nearest airport: Bangalore (139 km/ 4 hrs), (Tel: 080-25223344/ 1530) connected to Chennai by 22 daily flights by numerous airlines. Taxis to Mysore cost Rs 2,400-3,400

Rail Mysore Junction **Best option TO** Mysore Express (dep: Chennai Central 9.30 pm; arr: Mysore 8.05 am) **Best option FROM** Chennai Express (dep: Mysore 8.05 pm; arr: Perambur 6.34 am; Chennai Central 7.20 am)

Car A long journey, making self-drive avoidable for a weekend break. The drive to Bangalore along NH4 across southern Andhra via Ranipettai, Chittoor, Hosur and Hoskote takes $7^{1}/_{2}$ hours, then another 4 hrs to Mysore via Maddur and Srirangapatna

TIP If driving, don't forget to taste the famous *vadai* of Maddur en route

Folklore Museum

Housed in the majestic Mysore University Campus, called **Manasa Gangothri**, the museum is an excellent repository of Mysore art. A visit to the museum is incomplete without a stroll on the **Kukkarahalli Lake Bund**. It remains Mysore's favourite walking track. You might also like to do a quick 'dekko' of the similarly dying **Lingambudhi Lake**, home to many species of birds. A couple of good museums have opened recently. One is at the Wellington Lodge near the city bus station.

♦**Folklore Museum timings** 10 am to 5 pm, Sundays closed

GRS Fantasy Park

Located on 20 acres on the outskirts of Mysore, this is an aesthetically designed water amusement park. The park has a restaurant serving wholesome veg food. GRS (Tel: 0821-2582781-82) is opposite the RBI Colony, off the road to Brindavan Gardens, in Metagalli.

♦**Entry fee** Rs 225-300 **Timings** 10.30 am to 6 pm, Sundays and national holidays 10 am to 7.30 pm

Planet X

Driving back from Chamundi Hills, a deviation to the left and onto Maharana Pratap Singh Road in Nazarabad takes you to this amusement centre, famed for its go-karting track. The campus (Tel: 0821-2431043) includes a bowling alley, a video-game arcade, a restaurant and a disco at weekends.

♦**Timings** 4 to 11 pm

SHOPPING

For shopaholics, Mysore's well-planned markets are a treat. At the **Devaraj Urs Market** (off Sayyaji Rao Road), you will find Mysore's very own special fragrant jasmine and the tangy betel leaf. Also, on **Sayyaji Rao Road** is the **Cauvery Arts Emporium** (Tel: 0821-2443669; Timings: 9.30 am-7 pm), known for its

KARNATAKA

Sorting tangy betel leaves — a Mysore speciality — at Devaraj Urs Market

genuine sandalwood and ivory inlay work. If you are looking for antiques, check out **Nayanotsav**, near the zoo.

Drop by at the **Government Silk Weaving Factory** (Tel: 0821-2481803; Timings: 9.30 am-6.30 pm), on Mananthavady Road, where you can watch the famous Mysore silk saris being woven (9 am-2 pm, Sundays closed). The factory also houses a retail outlet on the premises, besides one on KR Circle. The **Government Sandal Oil Factory**, where sandal oil is extracted and used in the production of the famous Mysore Sandal Soap, is worth a visit. For permission to visit, contact the factory management (Tel: 2483651; 9 am-1 pm, 1.30-5.30 pm).

WHERE TO STAY

Mysore has plenty of hotels to choose from, but do book in advance. Top of the list in a city known for its palaces is **The Green Hotel** (Tel: 0821-2512536; Tariff: Rs 1,750-6,000), near the university campus west of the city centre. Formerly the Chittaranjan Palace, its USP is environmentally sustainable tourism.

Kadur Inn (Tel: 2402210, 2402840; Tariff: Rs 1,350-1,850), on the Mysore-Hunsur Road, is typical of the resort hotels that dot the city's outskirts.

Towards the Chamundi Hills, luxury reigns at ITDC's royal haven, the **Lalitha Mahal Palace Hotel** (Tel: 2470470-76; Tariff: Rs 5,500-30,000). The **Village Resort** (Tel: 2481310; Tariff: Rs 3,050-7,320), near the Chamundi Hills, is close to Mysore's only disco (Planet X) and go-karting track. Nearby is the **Indus Valley Ayurvedic Centre** (Tel: 2473263; Tariff: Rs 2,475-3,175) with its bouquet of Ayurvedic health packages.

Closer to the city centre is the compact and efficient **Ramanashree Hotels** (Tel: 2522202/ 65; Tariff: Rs 1,795-4,295), near the bus stand. For a more moderate budget there's the **Hotel Siddhartha** (Tel: 2522888/ 999 ; Tariff: Rs 960-1,460). For a cheaper yet comfortable stay, the traditional choice of families transiting through Mysore is **Hotel Dasaprakash Paradise** (Tel: 2410366; Tariff: Rs 950-2,750) that offers a feel of old Mysore and good food. Then there is **Hotel Mayura Hoysala**

KARNATAKA

(Tel: 2425597/ 6160 ; Tariff: Rs 800-1,300) run by KSTDC that also books sightseeing tours.

Among the cheaper options, try **Hotel Calinga** (Tel: 2431310; Tariff: Rs 300-540), near the bus stand, which has 76 rooms and a travel desk. **Hotel Ayodhya** (Tel: 2449592; Tariff: Rs 350-1,250) arranges sightseeing. All these hotels are in the city centre.

For more hotels and details, see Mysore Accommodation Listings on pages 496-498

WHAT TO EAT

Taking a tiffin break in Mysore is the most delicious thing to do. The city dishes out terrific **'set' dosas** (fluffy, soft pancakes made of beaten rice, served in sets of three), **masala dosas**, *uppittu* (commonly known as **upma**) and **rava idli**. Tasty savouries like churmuris and peanut masala also entice. But the most outstanding feature of the city is the web of bakeries set up by Mysore's Vaishnavite community, the Iyengars. Try out the vegetable bun cakes and *nipattus* at the **Iyengar Bakeries** on Devaraj Urs Road and the nearby Sayyaji Rao Road.

The sublime **Mysore rasam** is arrived at by adding a freshly ground masala of coriander seeds, dry red chilli and desiccated coconut. The crisp Mysore masala dosa is lashed on the inside with a light spread of a tangy coconut and red chilli paste. And how can anyone forget the **Mysore pak** — if ever there was a simple recipe that called for the greatest expertise, it had to be the sweetmeat that Mysore made famous. The perfect Mysore pak will melt in your mouth.

The restaurant at **Hotel Dasaprakash** is recommended for the best in South Indian thalis. **Bombay Tiffany's** high teas are great. **Nalpak** (Tel: 0821-2516602; Timings 7 am-3 pm; 4.30-9.30 pm) in VV Mohalla is the place to head for Karnataka delicacies like **akki** and **ragi roti**, and **bisi-bele-huli-anna**.

Brindavan Gardens by the Cauvery River

NAMIT ARORA/ PHOTOINDIA

AROUND MYSORE

Srirangapatna (12 km)
See page 283

Brindavan Gardens (18 km)
Mysore's *piece de resistance*, Brindavan Gardens lies to the north-west of the city, at the foot of the **Krishna Raja Sagar Dam** on the River Cauvery. It is a massive 130 ft high and 8,600 ft long. Arrayed below the dam is the terraced and well-tended garden, landscaped with fountains — one of them actually dances to music (show between 7 and 8 pm). You can go boating in one stretch of the reservoir. Great setting for a pleasant evening but it's crowded on weekends.
♦**Entry fee** Adults Rs 25, children Rs 15 **Timings** 9 am-9 pm, open all days **Cameras** Still Rs 100, video only with special permission, and with charges ■
With Ajay Krishnan on Dasara festivities

KARNATAKA

People and animals share resources near the K Gudi Camp in BR Hills

BILIGIRI RANGASWAMY HILLS
SOLACE AT LORD RANGANATHA'S FEET

State Karnataka
Location 3,375 ft above sea level between the Cauvery and Kapila rivers in Chamarajanagar District, along the easternmost borderlands of the Western Ghats
Distance 556 km SW of Chennai **JOURNEY TIME** *By rail* 10$^1/_2$ hrs + 2 hrs by road
Route NH4 to Bangalore via Poonamallee, Sriperumbudur, Ranipettai, Chittoor, Palmaner, Mulbagal, Kolar and Hoskote; NH209 to Kollegal via Kanakapura, Malavalli and Shivanasamudram; state road to BR Hills via Hanur (*see route guide on pages 12 and 254*)

■ BY SUNAAD RAGHURAM

The drive from the town of Chamarajanagar in the plains was uneventful, taking me past a string of quiet villages. The jeep then roared up the hills and soon I left behind the dirt and grime. I was but a few kilometres from the K Gudi Jungle Camp in Biligiri Rangana Betta, or BR Hills.

The birds held a divine orchestra while the emerald green trees swayed in a cadence. The air was fresh and sweet.

The only pressing engagements seemed to be a relaxed walk, hearing my inner self speak, lolling on a hammock, a repast of good food and, of course, listening to the birdsong.

As we banked a curve on the winding road, the sun glinted amidst the humongous trees and stillness mingled with silence. A few minutes later, close to a junction where a mud track goes in the direction of the historic Boodipadaga Guest House, inside a thick bush of lantana, we noticed what looked like a

BILIGIRI RANGASWAMY HILLS

mass of hazy blackness. We stopped the jeep to investigate. Suddenly, it moved. And then another one by its side. Two sloth bears! As they broke cover just a few feet in front of us and started running across the road in that typical ambling, sideways gait, it became clear that this area was teeming with wildlife.

The BR Hills Wildlife Sanctuary, also known as the Biligiri Rangaswamy Temple WLS, was formed in June 1974 close to the BR Temple precincts, with an area of 322 sq km. It was expanded further in 1987 to cover a total area of 534 sq km. The strategic location of the sanctuary provides an excellent bridge between the Western and Eastern Ghats, facilitating the exchange of the gene pool of the vast diversity of flora and fauna between them.

This wildlife corridor witnesses some of the largest numbers of wild elephants and tigers east of the Western Ghats in the central southern peninsular region. The forest is also home to gaur, sloth bear, giant flying squirrel and the endangered chousingha (four-horned antelope).

THINGS TO SEE AND DO

The two **entry points** to the sanctuary are **Yelandur** and **Chamarajanagar**, which are about 40 km apart. The whole area is covered with thick jungle, a multitude of peaks rising and falling like the ebbs and tides in an ocean of green. Whether you choose to just soak in the goodness of nature or fold your hands in silent prayer at the temple, rest assured it will recharge your frazzled batteries and rejuvenate your senses.

◆**Park entry fee** None **Vehicle fee** Rs 500 per day **Park timings** Sunrise-sunset

Biligiri Rangaswamy Temple

The deity of this temple is Ranganatha whose giant sandals evoke both amazement and piety. Legend has it that he wanders the forests after sundown, keeping vigil. And in keeping with his stature, the size of his footwear: 21 inches.

→ FAST FACTS

When to go Open all year round but Sep-Apr is the best season. During summer (Apr-mid Jun) it is a wonderful retreat from the heat of the plains
Tourist office
● Deputy Conservator of Forests
Wildlife Division, Sultan Sheriff Circle Chamarajanagar. Tel: 08226-222059
Mobile: 09448077881
STD code 08226 (Chamarajanagar)

KARNATAKA

→ **GETTING THERE**

Air Nearest airport: Bangalore (235 km/ $5^1/_2$ hrs), connected to Chennai by 22 daily flights by numerous airlines. A taxi to BR Hills from Bangalore costs Rs 2,500-3,000 approx

Rail Nearest railhead: Mysore Junction (90 km/ 2 hrs) **Best option TO** Mysore Express (dep: Chennai Central 9.30 pm; arr: Mysore 8.05 am) Taxi to BR Hills costs Rs 1,200 approx **Best option FROM** Chennai Express (dep: Mysore 8.05 pm; arr: Perambur 6.34 am; Chennai Central 7.20 am)

TIP The rail connection makes BR Hills a possible weekend break. The road journey is for longer duration vacations

Car Self-drive is not an option for a weekend break. For a longer vacation, follow NH4 to Bangalore across southern Andhra via Ranipettai, Chittoor, Hosur and Hoskote ($7^1/_2$ hrs). Take NH209 south-east of Bangalore to Chamarajanagar via Kanakapura, Malavalli, Shivanasamudram and Kollegal. The entrance to the sanctuary is about 40 km away

White socked bison at K Gudi

Said to be a few thousand years old, the temple is perched on a peak and can either be reached on foot or by vehicle. The point where the temple sits is high enough to offer panoramic views of almost the entire region. Right behind the temple is a spine-chilling 1,000-foot drop, with the depth and denseness of the jungle below visible. Iron railings have been installed for safety.

Dodda Sampige Mara

This is a mammoth champak tree deep inside the forest that is locally revered. According to the Soliga tribals, Sage Agasthya planted it some 3,000 years ago. The stream flowing nearby to where the tree stands is a sight to behold. Approach is only by jeep.

Boodipadaga

Deep inside the sanctuary is a regal hunting lodge. Now slightly derelict, it was once a famous forest residence of the erstwhile Mysore rulers. It was here that elephants were trapped by the pit method. And it was here that the scourge of the jungle, brigand Veerappan, was incarcerated for a few weeks in 1986. It was also from here that he famously escaped, then eluded capture for many years until eventually he was killed. Today it is the Forest Department Inspection Bungalow (IB).

The 8-km drive on the game road to reach the Boodipadaga IB is a treat, as you'll go past many waterholes where herds of elephants usually congregate.

K Gudi Jungle Camp

If you take the road from Chamarajanagar past Vandarbal Village at the foothills, it is 10 km to K Gudi (it can also be reached from the Yelandur side). K Gudi is short for Kyatedevaragudi, named after a jungle deity Kyateshwara, whose shrine exists in the vicinity of the decades-old hunting bungalow of the Wodeyars, the former royals of Mysore. Reaching K Gudi is quite a thrill as the

MM Hills

At 160 km from BR Hills, the hills of Male Mahadeshwara Betta are no excursion. Lord Shiva is worshipped by local tribals as Mahadeshwara. The 'Male' has nothing to do with the masculinity of the deity but is derived from 'Malay', meaning mountain. His hill-temple attracts many devotees. The devotees (called Devara Guddaru) have a unique form of prayer, where they smear their foreheads, eyebrows and necks with ash and dance with cymbals in their hands. If you are lucky, you might get to witness this magical spectacle called 'Kamsale Nritya' or 'The Dance of the Cymbals'. A good time to visit MM Hills is during Mahashivaratri.

road weaves up a steep road through dense jungle. Chances of spotting elephants and gaur are numerous, even as herds of spotted deer and the tall and stately sambar move around through the bushes. There has been many an occasion when even a panther and a tiger have been seen on this road in broad daylight.

Even if you are not fortunate enough to spot wildlife on the main road, the camp's safari into the jungle that takes you on the Ane Hadu Road into the environs of the Basavananni Kere area deep inside, should give you ample scope to explore the wild and spot animals. The journey through the jungle is bound to be full of surprises as you could find an animal standing right in the middle of the game road as you bank a curve or go up an incline. There are two tame elephants in the camp, Kyateshwara and Jayalakshmi. It is Jayalakshmi on whose sturdy back you ride into the jungle.

WHERE TO STAY AND EAT

Visitors have three options here — the tented Jungle Lodges camp at K. Gudi, a Forest Rest House and an Inspection Bungalow located deep in the sanctuary.

K Gudi Camp (Tel: 08226-296086; Tariff: Rs 1,900), the Jungle Lodges' luxury-tented accommodation is full of rustic stylishness. It has 8 permanent furnished twin-bed tents with modern toilet facilities. Three furnished ethnic huts on stilts (log huts) with attached modern toilet facilities are also available. Quaint hurricane lamps light up the night, as there is mercifully no electricity here. The **Gol Ghar** at the K Gudi Camp offers sumptuous buffet breakfast, lunch and dinner along with coffee and tea. Dinners are enjoyed around a campfire.

The **FRH** (Tel: 222059; Tariff: Rs 750) has four rooms and is run on solar power. The accommodation is pretty basic and you need to bring your own provisions, including cooking gas. The cook here can arrange for your meals. This can be booked through the office of the Deputy Conservator of Forests (*see Fast Facts on page 303*). The **Boodipadaga Inspection Bungalow** (Tel: 222059; Tariff: Rs 750), with two rooms, has similar facilities as the FRH and is also booked through the DCF's office.

For details, see BR Hills Accommodation Listings on page 496 ■

KARNATAKA

DINESH SHUKLA

A coracle ride on the quiet Cauvery River affords a closer sighting

NAGARHOLE NATIONAL PARK
THE SERPENT RIVER

State Karnataka
Location Spread over Mysore and Kodagu districts, Nagarhole is bounded by the Kabini River to the south, the Wayanad Sanctuary to its south-west and the Bandipur Tiger Reserve to its south-east
Distance 566 km SW of Chennai JOURNEY TIME *By rail* 10^1/$_2$ hrs + 2 hrs by road *By air* 55 mins + 5 hrs by road
Route NH4 to Bangalore via Sriperumbudur, Ranipettai, Chittoor, Mulbagal and Hoskote; SH17 to Srirangapatna via Maddur; bypass via Ranganathittu; SH88 to Hunsur; state roads to Nagarhole via Veeranahosahalli and Murkal (*see route guides on pages 12 and 254*)

■ BY BHARATH SUNDARAM

As soon as we drove ahead from Hunsur, the town closest to the park, a mongoose scampered across the road into the fields nearby. The trees were taller, more densely packed in, and the air became distinctly cooler. I saw circular patches of what looked like chopped grass flattened on the road: it was dry elephant dung.

As we reached the Nagarhole Park, we stopped at the forest checkpost, where the driver and the forest guard exchanged greetings. The driver cautiously asked if elephants had been sighted on the main road that day. His tension eased visibly when he received an answer in the negative. Majestic teak trees towered over us, and I became aware that but for the racket the bus was making, the forest was silent. The silence was broken every now and then by the raucous calling of a peacock, or by the cackle of the jungle fowl. Most animals seemed to have sheltered themselves from the harsh midday sun.

I wanted to stay as close as I could to the forest, so I chose one of the rest houses managed by the Forest Department within the sanctuary. The accommodation was pretty basic, but it was clean.

After freshening up, I decided to opt for a jeep ride around the forest. There's a well-defined network of roads in the forest, good for the tourist, but possibly a source of disturbance for the animals — it doesn't help that the tourists are often noisy. The Forest Department maintains 'view-lines', 10-m long areas on both sides of the roads, where shrubbery and trees are cleared so that the tourist has an unbridled view of the wildlife. These spots, usually created by burning down the plants, also attract animals — fresh grass sprouts in these areas, functioning as magnets for fauna. It helps that the terrain in Nagarhole is mostly flat; visibility is high, especially in areas where there is primarily a grassy forest floor.

I spotted a few herds of cheetal and troops of langurs as soon as we started the drive. As we turned around a particularly sharp curve, our driver brought the jeep to a halt. We heard a faint sawing noise — a mixture of a rasp and a cough, the distinct call of the leopard. Immediately, we heard the alarm calls of langurs. Holding our collective breaths and our cameras, we waited. Soon enough, a leopard and two cubs emerged onto the road. The leopard saw us, and sauntered indignantly across the road and into the jungle. The cubs lingered, curious. But they too scampered across, anxious to stay close to their mother. By now, it was half past five in the evening, and it was time to head back. On the way back, we saw a herd of elephants grazing. As the light was rapidly diminishing, our driver was not happy to see them — elephants have poor eyesight, and are known to charge at vehicles. These elephants, however, were uninterested in us.

Back in camp, after a hot bath, I enjoyed a simple but sumptuous meal. I also saw a few wildlife videos at the camp's Wildlife Interpretation Centre. The documentary being screened was about the tiger. Who knew, maybe I would get a chance to see the magnificent animal.

The next morning, we left the camp at daybreak, with hope written large on our faces. It was a beautiful misty morning, and condensation rose from the road surface like steam. We saw a herd of sambar, browsing cautiously by the side of the road. All of a sudden, they would look around frantically, and then return to the meal — as if nothing had happened before. Nearby, we heard the screech of the crested-serpent eagle. Looking closer, I saw that it held a small snake in its claws — it was breakfast-time in Nagarhole!

→ FAST FACTS

When to go Between Oct and Apr; it is usually closed in the hot season. The most comfortable time to visit in terms of climate is between Nov and Mar. It does get chilly in Jan and Feb
Wildlife/ Forest Department office
● Deputy Conservator of Forests ❶ ❻
Hunsur Wildlife Division,
Hunsur-571105, Karnataka
Tel: 08222-252041
Email: dcfwlhun@rediffmail.com
STD codes Hunsur 08222, Nagarhole 08228, Kutta 08274

KARNATAKA

Machan overlooking the Kabini River

We slowed down as we approached a waterhole: this spot was supposed to be a favourite with tigers. While waiting, I spoke to our driver Bomma, and asked him whether he had seen any tigers this month. After thinking for not less than five minutes, he told me that he had seen them everyday, except for the previous Saturday and Sunday! Bomma became impatient after waiting for sometime, and suggested that we head elsewhere, and I agreed. I was visiting in October, and there was plenty of water everywhere. Therefore, chances of seeing a tiger at a waterhole were fewer than in summer. We did, however, see a stripe-necked mongoose as we left the waterhole.

The sun's rays became stronger, and the birds more active. Woodpeckers, drongos, tree-pies and orioles were flying past in an amazing riot of colour. Suddenly, the forest became silent, and we heard the cries of a sambar. After that alarm call, other animals also started theirs — there was the whoop-whoop of the langur and the high-pitched call of the cheetal, among others. We waited with bated breath, and suddenly saw the huge head of a tiger peeping out of thick lantana bushes. The big and majestic cat gazed at us for a while, and then emitted a low snarl as it crossed the road, and disappeared from our sight.

ABOUT NAGARHOLE NP

One of the oldest National Parks in India, Nagarhole (literally, 'Serpent River') was created in 1955. Nagarhole was once maintained as an exclusive hunting preserve for the Mysore royal family. Shortly after Independence, Nagarhole was declared a National Park, and was managed by the Indian Forest Department, which also constructed rest houses and other accommodation facilities within the park. It was renamed after Rajiv Gandhi in 1992. The park limits were increased to its present-day area of 645 sq km in 1974.

Expect to see herbivores like the elephant, gaur, sambar, cheetal, muntjac (barking deer), chousingha (four-horned antelope) and wild pig. Nagarhole is also an excellent place to sight dhole, leopard, sloth bear and tiger.

ORIENTATION

The park is part of the Nilgiri Biosphere Reserve, and is very close to both the Bandipur Tiger Reserve and the Mudumalai Wildlife Sanctuary (*see page 219*). Nagarhole forms the catchment area for three rivers: Nagarhole, Lakshmana Teertha and Kabini. The altitudes vary between 600 and 900m; the highest elevation here is Masal Betta Peak (959m). The **Kabini River**, the largest of its waterways, is to the south of the park.

NAGARHOLE NATIONAL PARK

Most tourists enter the park from **Hunsur**, which is north of the park. The Forest Department has well-maintained cottages and dormitories in **Nagarhole** (to the south-west), **Sunkadkatte** (to the south-east) and **Murkal** (to the centre of the park). Private accommodation is available near Hunsur and **Kabini**. The Forest Department office at Hunsur and at the park entrance facilitate hiring of guides and jeeps, and offer mini-bus safaris and elephant rides, subject to availability. Safaris begin from the Range Office inside the park, 45 km from Hunsur via Veeranahosahalli. Even though the forest roads are well maintained, some areas require a vehicle equipped with a four-wheel drive.

♦**Park entry fee** Indians Rs 60, foreigners Rs 200 **Guide fee** Rs 200 **Cameras** Still free, handycam Rs 150, video Rs 300 **Park and safari timings** 6-8 am, 4-6 pm **Mini-bus safari fee** Rs 35 per head **Elephant ride** Rs 75 **Private jeep entry fee** Rs 750 per day

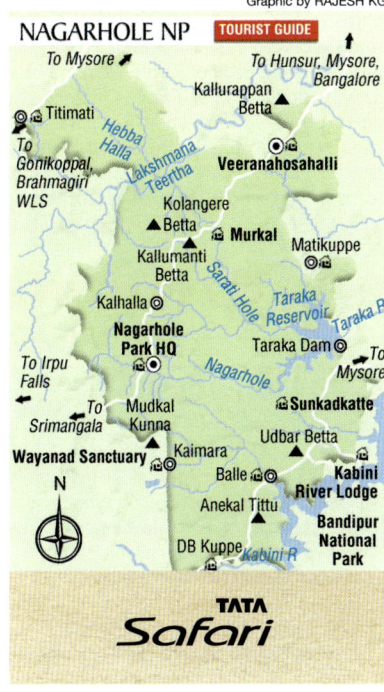

THINGS TO SEE AND DO

While Nagarhole is a known elephant habitat, most of the excitement obviously is centred on spotting a tiger. The striped king of the jungle may not oblige you with an appearance, but sightings of other animals such as deer and gaur are all but guaranteed.

Mini-bus safari

The Forest Department runs 45-minute mini-bus safaris into the park in the morning and evening. It offers no jeep safaris itself but allows private jeep safaris into the park, provided permission is granted by the Forest Department at

KARNATAKA

Hunsur (*see Fast Facts on page 307*). It is mandatory to hire a Forest Department guide (fee Rs 40) on these jeep safaris. Safaris start from the Range Office at the entry point 25 km inside the park from the Veeranahosahalli Checkpost, close to the Jungle Inn Resort. Visitors can hire jeeps at Nagarhole for a safari, for which they pay by the hour (minimum Rs 250 an hour/ 20 km). For one's own jeep, the vehicle fee is Rs 150 per hr. It's the best chance to see animals, but do remember to wear dull clothing, and avoid shouting if you wish to see wildlife without chasing them away.

Elephant joyride

Clearly not for the avid wildlife lover, the joyride comprises tourists being paraded on an elephant for 30 mins. These are subject to availability.
♦ **Elephant ride fee** Rs 75

→ GETTING THERE

Air Nearest airport: Bangalore (235 km/ 5 hrs), connected to Chennai by 22 daily flights by numerous airlines. Taxis charge Rs 2,500 approx for a drop to Nagarhole. Most resorts will arrange pick-ups at a price. There are also buses that run from Bangalore to Hunsur (Rs 150)
Rail Mysore Junction (95 km/ 2 hrs)
Best option TO Mysore Express (dep: Chennai Central 9.30 pm; arr: Mysore 8.05 am). Take a taxi (Rs 1,500 for a drop), or ask your resort for a pick-up
Best option FROM Chennai Express (dep: Mysore 8.05 pm; arr: Perambur 6.34 am; Chennai Central 7.20 am)
Car Self drive is not an option for a weekend break. For a longer vacation, follow NH4 to Bangalore across southern Andhra via Ranipettai, Chittoor, Hosur and Hoskote (7½ hrs). Catch SH17 to Srirangapatna via Maddur and Mandya. Then take the Mysore Highway Bypass via Ranganathittu onto SH88 to Hunsur. Near Hunsur bus stand take a left towards Heggadadevankote. After a short drive, you'll reach Nellorepala Junction. Take the right turn towards the Veeranahosahalli Gate of Nagarhole NP. From here head for the Murkal Gate, and approximately 20 km further is the Nagarhole Reserve Forest Office. The safaris begin from here

WHERE TO STAY AND EAT

As Nagarhole is a popular tourist destination, there are plenty of options here to suit a number of budgets. Visitors can opt for simple accommodation inside the forest, or stay in private property that's close to the jungle and offers an intimate experience of the forest. In fact, Nagarhole has become a more attractive option because of the attractive stay options it offers.

Forest Department Options

The Karnataka Forest Department has 12 cottages and three dormitories inside Nagarhole, in places such as **Sunkadkatte** and **Murkal**. The tariff varies from Rs 60 per person per night for a dormitory (Rs 120 for foreigners) to Rs 800-1,100 for a cottage (Rs 1,600-2,200 for foreigners). Cottages are charged on a twin-sharing basis. The tariffs are not inclusive of food. There are a few canteens that serve simple but sumptuous food at nominal rates. For reservations contact the Deputy Conservator of Forests (Tel: 08222-252041), Wildlife Division, Hunsur-571105.

Private Hotels

Jungle Inn (Tel: 08222-246022/ 160, Mobile: 09448271975; Tariff: Rs 2,300, US$ 110 for foreigners) is located in **Veeranahosahalli**, the northern end of

How to remember whom to call for an unforgettable holiday in the forest.

A little more than 4 hours from Bangalore nestles 1 truly luxurious resort where 1 is treated to a 5 star jungle experience. You could go on a 2 hour jungle safari (we conduct them 2 times a day), kayak on the river or go on a trek. Maybe you'll see lots of wildlife, maybe you'll see 0. Either way you'll leave with 0 regrets.

Call (080) 4115 2200 today
www.cicadaresorts.com
For reservations from Monday to Saturday call the number listed, anytime between 9.30 am and 6.00 pm.
On Sundays and public holidays please call +91 99456 02305.
Email: info@cicadaresorts.com

KARNATAKA

Irpu Falls near the Kerala border

the park. It has 4 Swiss tents, 5 double-bedded rooms and 3 dorms (two 6-bedded, one 8-bedded). The tariff includes stay, all meals and one safari and a visit to the elephant camp/trekking in the park. Its quaint thatched restaurant, Gudara, serves decent Continental and Indian food. Outdoor barbecues are arranged on request.

The **Kabini River Lodge** (Tel: 08228-264402/ 05; Tariff: Rs 2,750-3,500), run by the Jungle Lodges Resorts, is located on the southern border of the park, adjoining the Kabini backwaters. Rated by *Tatler's* of London to be one of the top five wildlife resorts in the world, the Kabini River Lodge — once the hunting lodge of the king of Mysore — is the best place to see elephants in summer, when the waters of the Kabini recede, leaving behind grass that elephants are fond of. They have rooms, tents and cottages. The buffet lunch is excellent. The tariff is inclusive of all meals, one safari into Nagarhole, a coracle ride and an elephant ride. Outdoor barbecues are arranged on request.

Cicada Kabini (Tel: 08228-264444/ 506; Tariff: Rs 7,000-25,000) is another lovely lodge set on the banks of the serene Kabini. Accommodation is in smart stone cottages. Safaris, organised by the resort and led by passionate naturalists, are always rewarding.

Homestays

The **Vana Arathi** (Tel: 08274-244228/ 888; Tariff: Rs 1,500, Rs 1,250 for vegetarians) is a homestay spread over 150 acres in **Nanchi**. You can watch game from the estate itself. Activities include estate walks, safaris to the park and boating in a fibreglass boat.

Another homestay is located about 6 km from Kutta (7 km from Nagarhole); on the road towards Srimangala, turn left at Manchally. About 2 km from there is the **Chilligiri Estate** (Tel: 08274-244265, Mobile: 09448582496; Tariff: Rs 750-850), named after a pepper plantation and the Brahmagiri Range that forms the backdrop.

For more hotels and details, see Nagarhole Accommodation Listings on page 498

AROUND NAGARHOLE

Irpu Falls (15 km)
Located at the base of the Brahmagiri Range that forms the boundary between Karnataka and Kerala, the Irpu Falls (a height of 170m) are a stunning site during the monsoon. The **Ishwara Temple** here is of considerable importance. Lord Rama is believed to have consecrated the Shivaling here. It is customary to pay your respects here before taking a dip in the Lakshmana Tirtha. A jeep ride from Nagarhole and back will cost approximately Rs 500. ■

Photographs by M BALAN/ SOUTHINDIAPICTURE

A devotee offers abhishekham at the feet of Gommatesvara

SRAVANABELAGOLA
DHAVALA SAROVARA — SAINT OF THE SILVER LAKE

State Karnataka
Location Sravanabelagola's twin hills rise out of a flat expanse in the southernmost reaches of the Deccan Plateau
Distance 486 km W of Chennai JOURNEY TIME *By rail* 10 hrs + 2½ hrs by road *By air* 55 mins + 3½ hrs by road
Route NH4 to Nelamangala via Poonamallee, Sriperumbudur, Ranipettai, Chittoor, Palmaner, Mulbagal, Kolar, Hoskote and Bangalore; NH48 to Channarayapatna via Kunigal; state highway to Sravanabelagola (*see route guides on pages 12 and 254*)

■ BY VIJAY NAMBISAN

Driving towards Sravanabelagola, even 10 km away a man-like shape becomes apparent, brooding over the flat landscape from atop the only hill on the horizon. From outside the town a gigantic bust is clearly visible, but within the town he is masked by his hill and his temple. This gentle colossus, Bahubali or Gommatesvara, has been gazing out upon the world for just over a thousand years.

Yet he is among the younger permanent residents of Sravanabelagola. Its history reaches back to the earliest days of an idea of India. The first Indian emperor, Chandragupta Maurya, made his retreat here after relinquishing his empire to his son, and undertook a fast unto death in accordance with the Jaina tradition. That was over 2,300 years ago,

KARNATAKA

Serene gaze of Gommatesvara

→ FAST FACTS

When to go October-March are the most temperate months
Tourist offices
● Tourist Information Centre ⓘ
Sravanabelagola Digambara Jain Math Institution Managing Committee
Tel: 08176-257226
● Karnataka Tourism Office ⓘ
Sravanabelagola, Tel: 257254
STD code 08176

and even Chandragupta was not the first Jain to seek refuge here.

The Jaina teaching is more a way of life than a religion. Though it admits the whole Hindu pantheon, it adores the divine in humanity. Yet Jain art abounds in classical depictions of male and female deities. The key to this apparent paradox is that humans need a figure to meditate upon, to realise the best in themselves. And surely they have it in Gommatesvara. At over 17m, his is said to be the tallest statue carved from a single rock in Asia (some say the world).

LEGENDS AND MYTHOLOGY

An inscription of about 1180 at Sravanabelagola tells the story of Bahubali. Gommata or Bahubali was a son of Adinatha, the first Tirthankara. His brother Bharata, who ruled at Ayodhya, challenged his brothers to fight for the kingdom. Bahubali defeated Bharata but returned the kingdom to him. He then stood for a whole year in the Yogic pose (Pratima Yoga), which the statue also holds. But he could not attain peace because he was standing on his brother's land. Bharata, understanding this, gave him back the kingdom, upon which he attained enlightenment.

Both local inscriptions and histories say that Bhadrabahu, a Jaina acharya and descendant of Mahavira, predicted a famine in the north and moved from Ujjain to Sravanabelagola with 12,000 disciples. He was followed by Chandragupta Maurya, who attended to the acharya in his last days and thereafter attained samadhi himself.

ORIENTATION

Sravanabelagola is centred around the *bela-kola* (white tank) that gives it its name. Sravana derives from the Sanskrit word *sramana*, meaning ascetic, and is the common appellation of Jain monks. The tank is about 150m square and best seen during the climb. It is easy to walk around the town. The stiffest challenge is the climb up the hills: over 650 steps to the top of **Vindhyagiri Hill** (to the south) and about half that to **Chandragiri Hill** (to the north). Palanquins (*dolis*) are available for the former.

THINGS TO SEE AND DO

The smaller hill, Chandragiri, has the older and richer monuments. A little lower down the hill, within an old stone wall, are 16 monuments, 13 of which are temples. All the temples are of Jain Tirthankaras. The oldest date to the 8th century CE and the oldest inscriptions to at least the 6th century CE. The larger hill, Vindhyagiri, has the statue of Bahubali at its summit with a temple around him and several smaller temples below. The statue is supposed to have been consecrated in 983 CE. The town between these hills has many Jain temples and monasteries.

It's best to rise early, in whatever season, and make the longer climb up the rock-cut steps of Vindhyagiri while the air is fresh.

Vindhyagiri

An elegant three-celled temple, 572 steps up, stands on a high terrace buttressed by slabs of rock. This is the **Odegala Basadi** and has images of the Tirthankaras Adinatha, Neminatha and Santinatha. It's another 100-odd steps to the top of the hill, and there are smaller shrines and many structures along the path. Notable is the figure of Gullakayajji, an old woman said to be Goddess Padmavati's incarnation, who inspired the sculpting of Gommatesvara. She cleaned the statue with a local fruit, a *gulla-kayi*, when Chavundaraya (*see below*) could not.

The main doorway to the basadi at the top is called **Akhanda-bagilu** because it was carved out of a single stone. Flanking the door are figures of Bahubali and his brother Bharata. Up more steps and round more turns, you come at last to the quadrangle where Gommatesvara stands. He is sculpted with all the *mahapurusha lakshana* (signs of a great man) such as long earlobes, broad shoulders and long arms. The expression of peace on his face is worth travelling a long way to see.

Chavundaraya was a scholar and writer as well as minister of the Ganga king Rachamalla. Jaina legend says that when his mother was told the story of Bahubali she vowed not to eat or drink until she had seen his famous image at Paudanapura (said to be near Purushapura or Peshawar). Chavundaraya set out with her on the long journey but near the present site Goddess Padmavati appeared to him in a dream. She said the journey was impossible just then but that Bahubali would appear at Vindhyagiri.

CHENNAI KI GURU
Prachi, Hotel Advisor at Travelguru. Has tips on Chennai which get you away from the tourist spots and help you enjoy the city like the locals.

Choose from our network of over 4000 hotels in India. Serviced apartments, budget hotels, luxury resorts, palaces, business accommodations, houseboats and more.

1-800-22-4878
022-4030-4878
www.travelguru.com

India's Largest Hotel Network

KARNATAKA

Next morning, Chavundaraya ascended Chandragiri and shot an arrow towards the bigger hill, where it hit a rock. He had the statue carved out of this monolith. It is conceived as the main figure in an imaginary temple, and set against the sky it is the epitome of the Digambara ('sky-clad') Jain ideal. The actual sculptor is unknown.

In the corridor around the quadrangle are some 30 marvellously carved figures of the Tirthankaras. Since each is represented with his own characteristic emblems, this is as good as a university course to any student of iconography in Indian art.

There is a Navakalasha Puja to Gommatesvara every Sunday at 8 am.

→ GETTING THERE

Air Nearest airport: Bangalore (155 km/ 3½ hrs), connected to Chennai by 22 daily flights. Taxis to Sravanabelagola cost Rs 2,500 (one-way)
Rail Nearest railhead: Srirangapatna (80 km/ 2 hrs) **Best option TO** Mysore Express (dep: Chennai Central 21.30 pm; arr: Srirangapatna 7.18 am). Taxi to Sravanabelagola costs Rs 1,800 approx **Best option FROM** Chennai Express (dep: Srirangapatna 8.20 pm; arr: Chennai Central 7.20 am)
Car A long drive, best avoided on a weekend journey. For longer vacations, drive to Bangalore along NH4 across southern Andhra via Ranipettai, Chittoor, Hosur and Hoskote (7½ hrs). Continue on NH4 till Nelamangala (27 km away), then turn left onto NH48 (Mangalore Highway) till Channarayapatna via Kunigal. Just short of Channarayapatna, turn left to Sravanabelagola, 10 km away

Only Jains are allowed to perform *abhisheka*. The **Mahamastakabhisheka** or ritual anointing of Gommatesvara is a grand event that takes place once in 12 years. The last one was in February 2006.
♦**Tourist Information Centre** (Tel: 08176-257226) of the SDJMIMC at the foot of Vindhyagiri is helpful with info and advice. Also try the **Karnataka Tourism Office** (Tel: 257254) next door
TIP Footwear must be left at the bottom of the hill (at Chandragiri too)

Chandragiri

To the historically minded, Chandragiri is much more interesting than the larger hill. Known as Katavapra (which connotes a fortification) or Kalvappu from ancient times, it gained sanctity from the visit of Acharya Bhadrabahu. His **cave** and that of Chandragupta higher up are redolent of an age when kings and holy men lived only for their duty, their dharma, to their followers or subjects.

There are 576 inscriptions in the rocks — the most on a single site in India. They date from the 6th to the 19th century and speak of a dozen different dynasties including the Gangas, Rashtrakutas, Chalukyas, Hoysalas, Vijayanagara and Wodeyars. Notable are the signature of Chavundaraya and the title 'Kaviratna' denoting the Kannada poet Ranna.

Inside the wall below (perhaps the 'vapra' of the old name) is a wealth of architecture. Most of the basadis are in the southern vimana style but betray half a dozen different influences.

The **Kattale-basadi** is the most elaborate. It has a passage around the sanctum, but the tower overhead is now missing. The 1.8-m figure of Adinatha is a fine piece of Hoysala art. The annexe, the **Chandragupta-basadi**, is probably the oldest basadi here. It's remarkable for its two delicate, filigreed screens of soapstone. These bear minutely carved scenes from the story of Bhadrabahu's dream and Chandragupta's abdication, and their end in Sravanabelagola.

KARNATAKA

Visitors come from across the globe to see the Chennakesava Temple at Belur

The free-standing **Kuge Brahmadeva Pillar** perhaps dates to 974 CE. It has a seated figure of Brahmadeva on top and elephants supporting the pedestal.

WHERE TO STAY AND EAT

The **SDJMIMC** (Tel: 08176-257258) has 25 guest houses and two dharamshalas on the edge of town. These have rooms with 2, 3, 4 and 5 beds, plus large unfurnished halls. The rates range from Rs 110 for an unfurnished room for four people in a dharmashala, to Rs 510. Write to the General Manager, Accommodation Section, SDJMIMC, Sravanabelagola, Hassan District-573135, Karnataka. Jains may also write to the Secretary (Tel: 257226), SDJMIMC (address as above). There is accommodation at Vindhyagiri itself, and Jaina food is available.

Hotel Raghu (Tel: 08176-257238; Tariff: Rs 200-700), facing the tank in the centre of town, is the most conveniently placed, but is very ordinary.

Hassan, the district town, offers some good alternatives. **Southern Star Hassan** (Tel: 08172-251816-17; Tariff: Rs 1,120-1,792) has 47 rooms and a restaurant, bar and travel guides. In the middle segment is **Gurudev International** (Tel: 261047, 269525-26; Tariff: Rs 550-1,026), which has a bar and five restaurants. Another option is **Sri Krishna** (Tel: 263240-43; Tariff: Rs 650-1,500), which has a veg restaurant.

Sravanabelagola is strictly vegetarian. **Hotel Raghu** is a reasonable place for refreshments, offering tiffin and thalis. There is a **Jain Dosa Palace** on the north side of the tank. Jaina food is available at the SDJMIMC-run temple hostel.

Besides the restaurants in the hotels, there are eating houses all over Hassan.

For details, see Sravanabelagola Accommodation Listings on page 499

AROUND SRAVANABELGOLA

A visitor is strongly recommended to see the Yadava temples at **Belur** (35 km from Hassan) and the **Hoysala** temples at Halebid (40 km from Hassan). ■

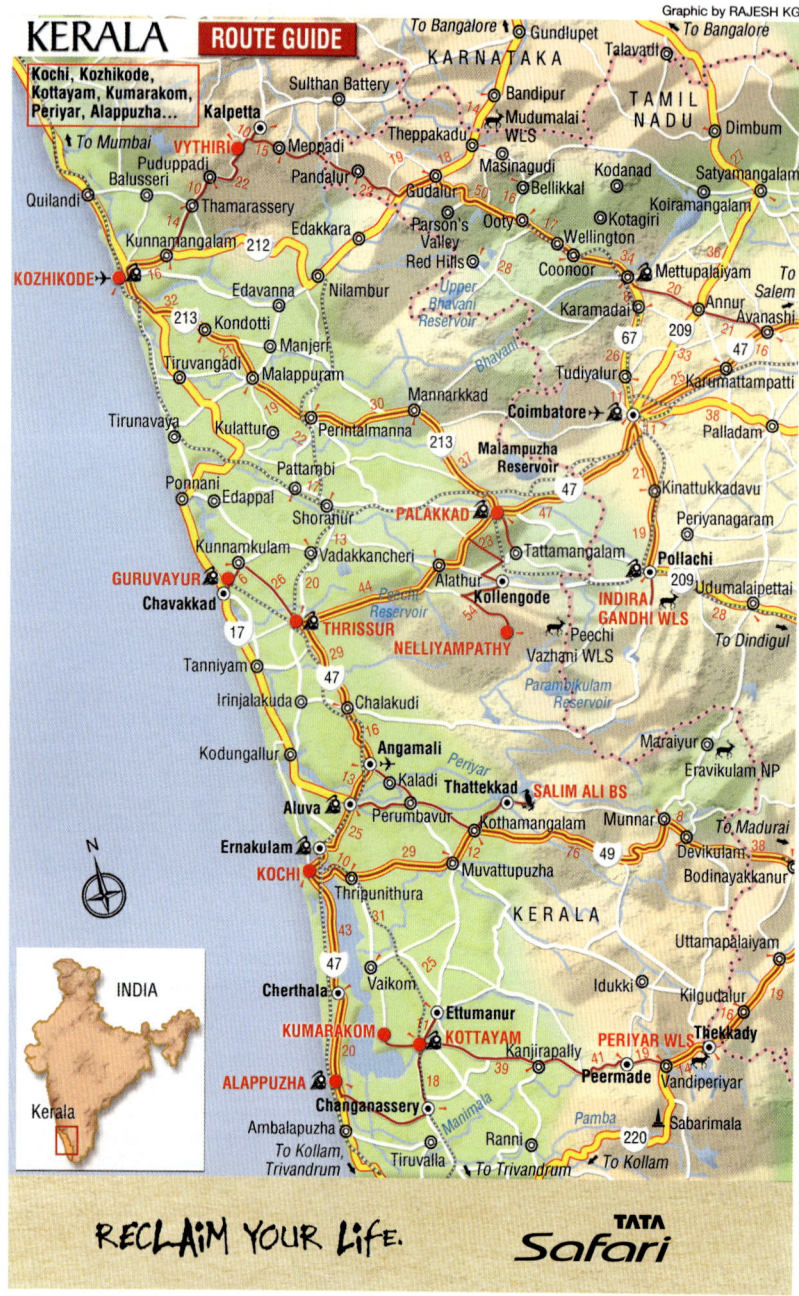

Kerala

Glorious days on fabled backwaters... Tusker spotting by Periyar Lake... Or a taste of real spice in Kochi's bazaars are all just a train ride away

SAIBAL DAS

PALAKKAD
FIELDS OF GOLD

State Kerala
Location A 32.2-km long gap in the Western Ghats, Palakkad lies 47 km to the west of Coimbatore, an expanse of plains dotted with hills
Distance 568 km SW of Chennai **JOURNEY TIME By rail** 8 hrs **By air** 55 mins + 1¼ hrs by road
Route NH45 to Ulundurpettai via Tabaram, Chengalpattu, Tindivanam, Vikravandi and Villupuram; NH68 to Salem via Tiyagai Durgam, Kallakkurichi, Talaivasal, Attur and Valappadi; NH47 to Palakkad via Bhavani, Perundurai, Avanashi and Coimbatore (*see route guides on pages 12 and 320*)

■ BY DEEPA A AND SHEILA KUMAR

The coronation is just a week away, but the king is missing. He has left no trail, he has no close family to fret about his whereabouts, and perhaps he has wandered for years with no memories of his kingdom or subjects. When they trace him, he's washing dishes in a hotel in Andhra Pradesh.

Like a forgotten feather, the story gently floats above the streets of Palakkad, nudging a solitary memory on a rain-washed afternoon, lodging itself in a grandfather's fond, once-upon-a-time narrative. Sometimes, when the power disappears with the sun on a summer evening, the story glows in the candlelight, its brightness overshadowing the debates on the weepy TV soaps, if only for a moment.

It's difficult to place these stories, to give them a date or year, in a town where the lines between the past and the present are inexplicably blurred. Even the *Palghat Gazetteer* was overwhelmed enough to be brutally honest. "It is with great pleasure and no small relief that I bring out the gazetteer," the editor sighed in the preface of the tome. "Certain circumstances caused to render the compiling of the gazetteer a time-consuming task."

There is a sneaking suspicion that Palakkad enjoys being difficult. No label fits, no description is precise. Like a town that had rather be a village, it makes way for chariots during festivals, and beams gloriously when the sunlight falls on its golden paddy fields. Like a village that wants to be a town, it adores air-conditioned restaurants and faux amusement parks, and is immensely proud of the local cable channels which cover everything from school sports to dirty streets.

There's the enticing aroma of a cuisine that's unique to Palakkad, dishes that skillfully and flavourfully blend the ingredients of Kerala with those just across the border in Tamil Nadu. There is also the tandoori chicken and the gobi manchurian that are sometimes as popular, the colas that many drink but never endorse, not if the companies are slurping water anyway. There are the mesmerising beats of the **panchavadyam**, sharing sound waves with film songs that are alternatively soulful or blissfully joyous.

Palakkad revels in defying descriptions. Even the king who went missing clearly wasn't keen on a title. A few days after the coronation, he couldn't be found, yet again.

ORIENTATION

Many sights, hotels, restaurants, shops and cab services are in the vicinity of Palakkad's arterial Sultanpet Main Road. **Tipu's Fort** is at the southern end of this road. The DTPC office is just west of the fort. The **KSRTC Bus Stand** is further west from here, opposite Hotel Green Park. **Palghat Station** is in the heart of the town, just off Shoranur Road.

THINGS TO SEE AND DO

Tipu's Fort
The fort is Palakkad's motif, rising above a hill at the end of the town, neither grand nor entirely unimpressive. It's well-preserved, and on breezy evenings, a pleasant place to walk around, especially now that it's been landscaped and hosts a **children's park**. Surprisingly, the fort wasn't built to guard the land. It's said that Haider Ali, who constructed the fort in 1766, intended it to improve communication between Palakkad and Coimbatore. In 1784, after an 11-day siege, the British stormed the fort. It later fell into the hands of the Zamorin but was recaptured by the British in 1790. Today, it is ruled by the Archaeological Survey of India (ASI). There is an open-air **auditorium** and a **museum** inside the fort.

Jain Temple, Jainmedu
This temple on the Kalpathy River is believed to have been built about 500 years ago by a Jain head, Inchanna Satur,

→ FAST FACTS

When to go September to April is best
Tourist offices
● DTPC ❶
West Fort Road, Palakkad
Tel: 0491-2538996
● Dept of Tourism ❶
Govt of Kerala, Tourism Complex, 2, Wallajah Road, Chennai
Tel: 044-25369789
● KTDC ❶❺
Tourist Reception Centre, Tourism Complex, 2, Wallajah Road, Chennai
Telefax: 044-25382639
Website: ktdc.com
STD code 0491

KERALA

The colours of piety

Agrarian Palakkad is famous for its cattle races through emerald paddies, the annual festivities of the Bhagavathy temples and the colourful Mappila Muslim *nerchas*.

The **Kalapootu Cattle Race** is held annually between December and January, under the aegis of the Cattle Race Club of India, at a time when the farmers are relatively free. About 120 pairs of cattle take part. Palakkad is the only place where cart races are also conducted. The races draw a crowd of almost 50,000 every year.

Chitoor Kongan Pada celebrates devi as protector. It is held on the first Wednesday after the new moon in the month of Kumbham (February-March). There are Kummatti performances, or mock preparations for war following which the participants enact the war. A specially chosen women conducts the puja. In the evenings, *vellichappads* (oracles) dance like dervishes.

People from four neighbouring villages participate in the **Manappullikaavu Vela** at the 1,200-year-old Manappullikaavu Bhagavathy Temple. It honours the deity in her Van Durga, Bhadrakali incarnation with a *raktapushpanjali*, elaborate devi pujas and fireworks. The festival is held in Vrischikam (November-December) and Kumbham (February-March) month.

Also in Kumbham, the **Chenakathur Vela** is held near Ottapalam. There are 41 days of pooja, 17 days of *tholpaavakoothu* (puppetry shows), Kathakali performances and 16 elaborate horse effigies on display.

The **Ottappalam Nercha**, held in the month of Makaram, commemorates the death of saint Uthaman Auliya. In a grand procession, offerings of rice and coconuts are brought to the Ottappalam mosque.

The famous **Nenmara-Vellangi Vela** invokes the blessings of Nellikulangara Bhagavathy on the 20th day of Meenam (March-April) every year. Kummatti, Karivela and Andivela folk rituals are performed. Five villages take part in this festival, which includes a fireworks display.

The famous **Kalpathy Ratholsavam** is held in Thulam (October-November). Even as it starts at the Vishwanathaswamy Temple at Kalpathy, it is simultaneously celebrated in Chathapurma and new Kalpathy, all on the banks of the Kalpathy Puzha.

for the Jain sage Chandranathaswamy. The granite walls are devoid of decoration. An idol of Chandranathan occupies the first division of the temple, Vijayalakshmi and Jwalamohini the second, Rishabha Nathan the third, and Parswa Nathan and Padmavathi the fourth. An air of austerity marks this place. Lit lamps flank the main statue. Palakkad was once home to a community of 400 Jain families, but their numbers have diminished.

♦**Location** On the south bank of the Kalpathy River in Jainmedu, just beyond the Chunnambuthara area, 3 km from the centre of Palakkad **Timings** 7-10.30 am, 5-7 pm

TIP Alert the caretakers who live within the compound to let you inside

Vadakkanthara Temple

The Vadakkanthara deity, Bhagvathy, is an incarnation of Kannagi, the heroine of the Tamil epic *Silappadhikaram*. One long-lasting tradition here is the fireworks that are set off at 6 pm sharp in the temple compound; locals have been known to set their clocks by this sound.

♦**Location** En route to Jainmedu **Timings** 5-11.30 am, 4.30-7.30 pm **Main festival** Valiya Vela every three years (next in 2009)

Manapullikaavu

The devi is the main idol here and it is one of the two major temples in Palakkad, the other being the Vadakkan-thara shrine. The Manapullikaavu idol is *swayambu* and can be found to one side of the *sreekovil*. The main idol in the sanctum is a later installation.

♦**Location** East Yakkara **Timings** 6-10.30 am (till 11.30 am on Sundays, Tuesdays and Fridays), 5-7 pm **Main festival** Vela Pratishta Festival in May

Kalpathy Agrahara and Vishwanathaswamy Temple

For a small structure, the Vishwanatha-swamy or Shiva Temple has an imposing *kodimaram* or flagpole, reaching for the skies. It is from this flagpost that the temple banner flies during the **Kalpathy Ther**, a chariot festival (usually held in November) in which all the temples in the area participate (*see The colours of piety on facing page*). Traffic comes to a halt as Kalpathy decks up for the festival with characteristic aplomb.

The Shiva Temple is a low quad-rangular building on the banks of the Kalpathy River, dating back to 1425. It has been built as a replica of the Kashi Temple at Varanasi. Apart from the temple, one reason to visit the place is to experience the way of life of an old Palakkad agraharam (*see page 326*).

♦**Location** On the southern bank of the Kalpathy River, on the road to Mannarkad and Kozhikode **Timings** 5-11.30 am, 5-7.30 pm

An astrologer uses cowries to divine the future in a Palakkad temple

Kumarapuram Temple

The Kumarapuram Temple, accessed via the Kumarapuram agraharam on the banks of the Bharatapuzha, used to be a major centre of Vedic learning. The presiding deity at the temple is Prasanna Venkatachalapathy, flanked by his consorts, Alamelu and Mangalambal. The rituals performed here are similar to those at Tirumala (*see page 231*), and it is believed that the two deities, Venkateswara in Andhra, and Venkatachalapathy here, have equal powers.

♦**Location** Near Kalpathy Bridge **Timings** 6-10.30 am, 5-7 pm

Emoor Bhagvathy Temple

The temple is located in Kallekullangara, 8 km from Palakkad, after Olavakkode. Legend has it that the Goddess Bhagavathy agreed to appear before a holy man, but instead of keeping it a secret, the man disclosed it to others in his excitement. When the goddess emerged from the temple, she found many people had gathered, and disappeared. It's believed that devotees saw only her upraised hand, and this is what is worshipped at the temple. In the mornings, the deity is worshipped as Saraswati, in the noon as Lakshmi and in the evening as Durga. The main festival here is Navrathri.

Visit a gramam

Legend traces the setting up of Palakkad's agraharams or gramams to a remarkably romantic story. It's said that a prince of the royal dynasty of Kochi fell in love with an adivasi girl, and was ostracised for his relationship with an 'outcast'. The prince decided to settle down in the area and set up the Palakkad royal dynasty. The Namboodiri Brahmins in the region, who wanted no part in officiating the ceremonies of an ex-communicated prince, left the area. The Palakkad kings sought the help of Brahmins living on the other side of the gap, and they graciously agreed. Tamil Brahmins thus settled down in Palakkad and the areas where they lived grew into gramams.

Take a stroll down Kalpathy, Kumarapuram, Ramanathapuram or Chokkanathapuram to soak in the ambience of a gramam. **Ramanathapuram** has three shrines, dedicated to Vishnu, Shiva and Ganesh. The 30-35 families who still live here have preserved their way of life. Vedas and shastras are orally passed down from one generation to the other.

OLAPPAMANNA MANA

A Special Unique Heritage Home Stay Hours, You Remember For Years.

At A Glance

Really, centuries old heritage home and not a newly constructed model. Enjoy a vacation to get recharged yourselves. Infotainments not available anywhere else, at nominal extra costs. Stay here and go to see places like Silent Valley, Kanjirapuzha Dam, Kerala Kalamandalam etc. Located in a 20 acre eco-friendly atmosphere. Tourists traveling from North to South or South to North of Kerala have to deviate just 30 km only from main National High Way..

Contact : Mr.O.N.Damodaran
Olappamanna Mana, Vellinezhi (PO),
Dist:- Palakkad,Kerala, Pincode:- 679504
Ph: 91 466 2285383/2285797/ 91 09847764532
olappamannadamodaran@gmail.com (preffered),
damodaran@olappamannamana.com
www.olappamannamana.com

SHOPPING

Palakkad's **Valiya Angadi** (big bazaar), is full of shops stocking traditional bell metal ware, peacock *villakus, thooku* or hanging *villakus, nilavillakus,* utensils such as *kindi, lota, mondha* and *ashtamangalyam* sets. There is an **antique warehouse** without a name located just opposite the Nurani Saneeswaran Temple, which is a treasure trove of bric-a-brac, *objets d'art* and furniture from *illams, manas* and Chettinad palaces. **Mannadiar Handicrafts** in Valiya Angadi is another shop where you can procure reasonably priced Kerala souvenirs.

Nedungadi's Saree Paradise (Tel: 0491-2532117/ 3117) on Court Road and **Maharaja Silks** (Tel: 2538786) on Sultanpet's Main Road stock a good range of *neriyathu mundu* sets and Travancore saris in cream and gold.

Palakkad is reported to have the highest number of jewellery shops in Kerala after Thrissur. You can check out the latest gold designs in **New Mannadiar** (Tel: 2500861, 09349618721) at Market Road, **Pavizham** (Tel: 2503292/ 4292) on GB Road, and **Alukka's** (Tel: 2525842) in PV Towers on TB Road.

WHERE TO STAY

Palakkad has a few decent hotels, but some of the nicest among them are situated outside town. **Sri Chakra International** (Tel: 0491-2570901-06; Tariff: Rs 800-2,100), at Krishna Gardens in Chandranagar, is among the best, with 49 rooms, a pool, bar, restaurant, coffee shop, an ayurvedic centre and a health club. Their Rice Bowl Restaurant serves good Kerala seafood and more. They also offer tours around Palakkad, including to the **peacock sanctuary** at Mayiladumpara.

Hotel Indraprastha (Tel: 2534641-47; Tariff: Rs 750-2,050), near the fort on English Church Road, is also good, with a separate veg-only coffee shop that looks like a *koothambalam* with disco lighting. **Hotel KPM International** (Tel: 2534601-05), also near the fort on the Press Club Road, is walking distance from most places. **Kanoos East Fort Resort** (Tel: 2532507, 2526935; Tariff: Rs 330-690) at Fort Maidan is a good hotel with 24 rooms and a travel desk.

Other hotels include **The Fort Palace Hotel** (Tel: 2534621; Tariff: 385-1,380), which has 18 rooms on West Fort Road. **Hotel Gazala** (Tel: 2546581-84; Tariff: Rs 300-1,700) is Palakkad's nicest mid-range option, though located on the main

→ GETTING THERE

Air Nearest airport: Coimbatore 60 km/ 1¼ hrs), connected to Chennai by 10 daily flights by Paramount Airlines, Indian, Air Deccan, Jet Airways and Kingfisher Airlines. Taxi to Palakkad costs Rs 1,000
Rail Palakkad Station **Best option TO** Alleppey Express (dep: Chennai Central 9.15 pm; arr: Palakkad 5.20 am) **Best option FROM** Chennai Express (dep: Palakkad 9.05 pm; arr: Chennai Central 6.05 am)
TIP Mangalore Mail (going) and Chennai Mail (return) are also excellent options for a weekend break
Car This long drive across the breadth of Tamil Nadu from Chennai, till the crest of the Western Ghats, cannot be attempted on a weekend break. Stick to the excellent train connections for a weekender. For longer vacations, follow NH45 to Ulundurpettai via Tindivanam and Villupuram. Turn right onto NH68 to Salem via Talaivasal and Attur. At Salem, join NH47 till Palakkad via Bhavani, Avanashi and Coimbatore

Here, the indulgence of a palace
meets the austerity of an ashram.

Kalari Kovilakom, like Ayurveda, is a way of life. Totally binding, yet absolutely liberating. Extremely demanding, yet wonderfully fulfilling. Wake up call before the sun's up. Warm water to drink. Meditation. Yoga. Ayurvedic regimens based on your physician's recommendation. Time to awaken your senses. Time to read. Time to think. Time to do nothing. All in an out-of-this-world ambience that is not disturbed by the telephone or the television. Backed by a head-on-shoulders - feet-on-ground policy that does not permit wine, tobacco and shoes. It is total surrender to nature and the healing power of Ayurveda. And to the pleasures of a palatial suite, a sensational vegetarian cuisine and never-ending stories of a rich past.

KALARI KOVILAKOM
VENGUNAD
The Palace For Ayurveda
| a cgh earth experience |

Central Reservations: Casino Building Cochin Kerala India Phone: +91-484-3011711 Fax: 2668001
Email: contact@cghearth.com   www.cghearth.com

KERALA

An elephant is all decked up for a Bhagavathy temple's annual festivities

market road, near the Head Post-Office. It has 30 rooms, a café, an ayurvedic spa and a travel desk.

Outside Palakkad
On the Chittoor Road, 16 km from Palakkad in Kodumbu, is the plush **Kairali Ayurvedic Health Resort** (Tel: 04923-222553/ 623; Tariff: Rs 2,500-10,000), spread across more than 50 acres of landscaped gardens. Kairali's amenities include a fully-equipped health centre, yoga, meditation and astrology. Kairali offers 3- to 21-day ayurveda packages.

In Kootanad on the Pattambi Road is **Rajah Healthy Acres** (Tel: 0466-2371744; Tariff: Rs 1,140-7,200), a 180-acre rubber plantation with the ayurvedic treatment centre housed in an old wooden manor house. The highlights here, apart from the very highly specialised nature cures, are the herbal garden, mineral outdoor spa baths, and the cottages panelled with fragrant vetiver and neem. Treatments range from three to 28 days.

A first hand experience of the Palakkad way of life can be had at **Kandath Tharavad** (Tel: 04922-284124, 09349904124; Tariff: Rs 6,000-10,000), the ancestral homestead of the Bhagavaldas clan in Thenkurussi Village. This house, dating back to more than 200 years, is built in the *ettukattu* style.

To stay in one of Kerala's best-preserved heritage Namboodiri illams, book yourself into the venerable **Olappamanna Mana** (Tel: 0466-2285383; Tariff: Rs 4,500), in Vazhukappara, just 2 km off the road to Shoranur.

For more hotels and details, see Palakkad Accommodation Listings on pages 508-509

WHERE TO EAT

For the gourmand, Palakkad has many culinary delights to offer on a steel thali: masala vadas, bondas, *kozhukattas*, sugary *unniappams*, spicy *bajjis* and the like. Some tea stalls on the outskirts of town serve the Ramasseri idli, a flat steamed delicacy that bears little resemblance to the common or garden idli as we know it, but tastes differently delicious.

> Very often, on remote islands
> we stumble across ourselves.

And that's exactly what happened to us. Which is why when we started creating a holiday environment on the Bangaram Island of Lakshadweep, we hired nature as our chief architect. An architect who believed in the beauty of minimalism and the immaculate game plan of life on earth. The virgin coral reefs, the  turquoise blue lagoons, the silver beaches and the lush green coconut palms inspired us to preserve the bounty of this island, hitherto untouched by man. Here sailfishes, yellow fins, travellys, wahoos, record size barracudas and turtles reigned supreme. So we blended in our hotel - and every little detail about it - quietly and unobtrusively with the landscape of the island. Which is why there's more to this experience. Like the magic of discovering yourself over and over again. As the castaway, as the wise old fisherman, as the incurable romantic, as the dolphin or perhaps the seagull...

Central Reservations: Casino Building Cochin Kerala India Phone: +91-484-3011711 Fax: 2668001
Email: contact@cghearth.com www.cghearth.com

KERALA

Fresh Kerala toddy by any other spelling is just as cool

Ashok Bhavan (Tel: 2546380), on GB Road in Sultanpet is the best place to tuck into steaming hot breakfasts. The **Noorjehan Hotel** (Tel: 2522717, 2515668) on GB Road is the one place where anyone who craves a bite of something meaty rushes to. It does some great non-veg biryanis, *pathiris* and mutton curries. Other restaurants serving very decent fare include **Curry House** at VH Road and **Hitec Plaza** (Tel: 2510740), opposite the KSRTC Bus Stand on Shoranur Road. Smaller eateries include **Magik Oven** (Tel: 2504781) and **KR Bakes**, located just ahead of Tipu's Fort.

AROUND PALAKKAD

Malampuzha (14 km)

This popular picnic spot derives its name from the Malampuzha River, a tributary of the Bharatapuzha. Clamber up onto the ropeway — said to be the first of its kind in South India. The **ropeway** gives you a clear view of the Malampuzha Gardens nestled below the ghats, from a height of 60 ft. The 20-minute ride in the sky will thrill your kids.

◆**Entry fee** Rs 5, vehicle entrance over dam Rs 2 **Ropeway fee** Rs 31 **Timings** 10 am-12.30 pm, 2-7 pm **Tel** 2815129

The **Rose Garden** is reputed to have over a hundred varieties. The **Snake Park** houses several rare species of snakes, like the Forsten's cat snake, the brown vine snake and, of course, the king cobra. Also in the park are some varieties of water snakes, crocodiles and the American green iguana.

◆**Entry fee** Rs 5 **Timings** 8 am-5 pm

Malampuzha's **Fantasy Park** offers a menu of 20 rides.

◆**Entry fee** Adults Rs 25, children Rs 20 **Timings** 8 am-8 pm

You can also hire rowboats, pedal-boats, water scooters and motorboats to take you around the Malampuzha Reservoir. Ask for these at KTDC's **Garden House** (Tel: 0491-2815217; Tariff: Rs 450-900), Malampuzha's best hotel, right near the gardens with a restaurant and beer parlour. **Hotel Tripenta** (Tel: 2815210/ 20; Tariff: Rs 650-1,650) nearby offers Ayurvedic massages.

For details, see Palakkad Accommodation Listings on pages 508-509 ■

Inputs by KG Kumar

EXPERIENCE BLISS...

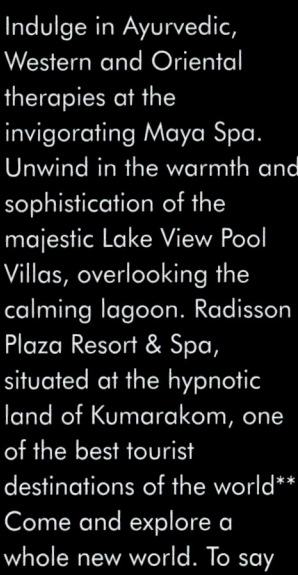

Indulge in Ayurvedic, Western and Oriental therapies at the invigorating Maya Spa. Unwind in the warmth and sophistication of the majestic Lake View Pool Villas, overlooking the calming lagoon. Radisson Plaza Resort & Spa, situated at the hypnotic land of Kumarakom, one of the best tourist destinations of the world** Come and explore a whole new world. To say

For Personalised offers*
contact our reservation centre
*Condition apply. Subject to availability

Radisson Plaza Resorts & Spa Kumarakom:
Karottukayal, Kumarakom, Kottayam,
Kerala 686 563, India
E-mail:sales@radissonkumarakom.com
www.radisson.com/kumarakomin

To book, call direct on:
Kumarakom +91 481 252 7290
Mumbai +91 22 6452 5555/2605 2923-27
Delhi +91 11 2341 7177-78 or
Call us on toll free 1800 1800 333

** (National Geographic).

RADISSON PLAZA RESORT & SPA KUMARAKOM
KERALA, INDIA

Chennai • Delhi • Dhaka • Goa • Jalandhar • Kathmandu • Khajuraho
Kumarakom • Noida • Raichak (Kolkata) • Shimla • Varanasi

Gardens of organic tea paint the slopes of Nelliyampathy a vivid green

NELLIYAMPATHY
BERRY BEAUTIFUL

State Kerala
Location Nelliyampathy is perched at a height of 4,600 ft above sea level in the Western Ghats, a 1½ hr drive 54 km south of Palakkad
Distance 622 km SW of Chennai JOURNEY TIME **By rail** 8 hrs + 1½ hrs by road **By air** 55 mins + 3 hrs by road
Route NH45 to Ulundurpettai via Tambaram, Chengalpattu, Tindivanam, Vikravandi and Viluppuram; NH68 to Salem via Tiyagai Durgam, Talaivasal, Attur and Valappadi; NH47 to Palakkad via Bhavani, Perundurai, Avanashi and Coimbatore; district roads to Nelliyampathy via Nenmara and Pothundy Dam (*see route guides on pages 12 and 320*)

■ BY SHEILA KUMAR

It takes 23 hair-pin bends to drive up to Nelliyampathy. But that's not the dizzying part of this story. At 4,600 ft above sea level, Nelliyampathy can be described as a tiny hill station. And how inadequate that is. For this little gem of the Sahyadri Range had its foothills lined richly with coffee, tea and orange plantations. There too were the sparse swamps of *nelli* (Malayalam for gooseberry) trees that are said to have given Nelliyampathy its name.

As the road continued its determined ascent, tantalising flashes of the Pothundy Reservoir below impelled us to stop and take pictures. Meanwhile, the dense and verdant forest languorously unveiled itself. Look out for elephants, bison, langur and deer — we surprised a huge sambar, which stood transfixed in the glare of our headlights. In retrospect, I think I was feeling light-headed simply with the sheer bliss.

THINGS TO SEE AND DO

Ridges of varying heights and the deep valleys scooped out between make up the Nelliyampathy Range. The highest peak is Nellikota, or **Padagiri**, at 5,200 ft above sea level. The other lofty peaks are Vellachimudi, Valiyavana, Mayanmudi and Vela Vanchan. The road up from the Pothundy Dam runs through the hill station and beyond. Paths lead off it into the forests, filled with very valuable teak of extraordinary height and girth.

A view to die for
Spending time at Nelliyampathy is all about soaking in the hills, spotting wildlife or savouring the beautiful panorama from vantage points like **Kesavan Para** (11 km from Nelliyampathy) and Seethargundu.

Seethargundu, 8 km from Nelliyampathy, is believed to be the place where Lord Rama's consort Sita took rest on her journey back from Sri Lanka. Today, a tall, gnarled tree marks the spot. Nearby, a small **Devi Temple** atop the adjacent Kollengode Hill beckons the faithful. In between lie orange plantations where one can pick up bottles of extra sweet squash or other Nelliyampathy specials like coffee, tea and guava preserve.

→ FAST FACTS

When to go Nelliyampathy is cool all year round, but do avoid the hill station in the truly ferocious monsoon months of June, July and August. February to May can get warm, but evenings are always pleasant
STD code 04923

Trekking tracks
Seethargundu, Palakapandy, Kesavan Para and Kara Para are all connected with trekking paths. Wear appropriate clothing and footwear (the scrub can be thorny). Arm yourself with drinking water and, preferably, hire a local guide recommended by your hotel.

Bird and animal watching
The Nelliyampathy Hills are known to be the habitat of the Malabar hornbill, the Indian woodpecker, red jungle fowl, all kinds of parrots and owls, as well as the chubby Malabar squirrel, among other wildlife. A good pair of binoculars and

BANGALORE KI GURU
Richa, Hotel Advisor at Travelguru, has the best entertainment tips on the city of Baked Beans.

Choose from our network of over 4000 hotels in India. Serviced apartments, budget hotels, luxury resorts, palaces, business accommodations, houseboats and more.

1-800-22-4878
022-4030-4878
www.travelguru.com

India's Largest Hotel Network

KERALA

Ripening Nelliyampathy oranges

→ GETTING THERE

Air Nearest airport: Coimbatore (114 km/ 3½ hrs), connected to Chennai by 10 daily flights by Paramount Airlines, Indian, Air Deccan, Jet Airways and Kingfisher Airlines. Cab fare to Nelliyampathy is Rs 2,500 approx
Rail Nearest railhead: Palakkad Station (54 km/ 1½ hrs) **Best option TO** Alleppey Express (dep: Chennai Central 9.15 pm; arr: Palakkad 5.20 am) Taxi to Nelliyampathy costs Rs 1,000.
Best option FROM Chennai Express (dep: Palakkad 9.05 pm; arr: Chennai Central 6.05 am)
Car This long drive cannot be attempted on a weekend break. Stick to the excellent train connections. For longer vacations, follow NH45 to Ulundurpettai via Tindivanam and Villupuram. Turn right onto NH68 to Salem via Talaivasal and Attur. At Salem, join NH47 till Palakkad via Bhavani, Avanashi and Coimbatore. From Palakkad, take the district roads south via Koduvayur and Palavur to Nenmara and Nelliyampathy

abundant reserves of patience will reward visitors with some special sightings.

Maampara Peak
While Nelliyampathy does have a few peaks affording awesome views, **Raja's Cliff** at Maampara is absolutely breathtaking, both figuratively and literally. A bald knoll 5,249 ft above sea level, Maampara is accessed by a jungle path, bone-jarringly rocky and steep. At times, the jeep ride can seem almost a vertical one. The view from the top is amazing, literally redefining the word 'panoramic', with the reservoir and rivers gleaming like sashes of silver far below.

On a clear day, you can see the Chaliyar, Meenkara and Aliyar dams sparkling below. Besides this, Pollachi and Coimbatore can be glimpsed on one side, Palakkad to another and below lies the pastoral hamlet of Kollengode. Near Maampara, the **Victoria Church**, an abandoned relic of the Raj, sits in solitude atop a rock. The summit lies directly in line with the Palghat Gap, thanks to which the breeze here is a full-blown gale!

Pothundy Reservoir
Just before Nelliyampathy and past Nenmara Village lies the Pothundy Reservoir, surrounded by a landscaped garden — an ideal picnic spot. Two flights of steps off the road and you are in another world, facing the cool and calm waters of the reservoir — surrounded by hills crowned by fat wreaths of clouds. It's fed by the Manchady, Kalchandy and Challa tributaries of the Bharatapuzha. In turn, the reservoir feeds the Gayathri River at the dam site… water, water everywhere and what a sight to drink in!
♦**Timings** 10 am-5 pm **Tel** 04923-244224/ 32

WHERE TO STAY AND EAT

Sleepy Nelliyampathy has four good options. The **Whistling Thrush Bungalow** (Mobile: 09447144921; Tariff: Rs

KERALA

Green gardens surround a colonial-era homestay in Poothundu

4,500) is in Poothundu, a short drive further up the Nelliyampathy Road, accessed through a plantation. Green gardens surround this colonial bungalow. Many quiet walks lead from here.

Greenland Resort (Tel: 04923-246245/ 66; Tariff: Rs 600-1,500) is set in an estate surrounded by forests. It offers 20 rooms, a restaurant and a playground for kids. Non-guests may eat here on advance notice. **ITL Resorts** (Tel: 246357/ 464; Tariff: Rs 750-1,750) in Kaikatty has 6 rooms and a 6-bedded dorm, and a restaurant. Outdoor games and trekking in the forested hills is possible. Non-guests are welcome at the restaurant here.

Apart from the hotels, there are no established eateries in Nelliyampathy.

For details, see Nelliyampathy Accommodation Listings on page 508

AROUND NELLIYAMPATHY

Kollengode (45 km)
The picturesque hamlet of Kollengode seems to have been caught in a time warp, a slice of tradition that has been, is and, in all probability, will remain just so. Kollengode was the birthplace of the poet **P Kunhiraman Nair** and his poorly preserved **memorial** (open 10 am-5 pm) stands opposite the Raja's High School. **Vishnu Temple** (open 5-11 am, 5-8 pm) at Kaachamkurissi, at one corner of Kollengode, is a popular shrine. The village comes alive when the temple celebrates the **Arat Festival** in May.

Kollengode is now home to high-end tourism, with the old Kollengode Palace now a swanky ayurvedic resort. The **Kollengode Palace Ayurvedic Resort** (Tel: 04923-263155/ 922-25; Package tariff: Rs 2,31,000 for 14 days per person) of the CGH Earth group offers 18 olde worlde rooms. They offer top quality Ayurvedic treatments running from 3 to 28 days in one of the most scenic places possible — green-gold fields of paddy nestled in the midst of moody blue ghats scoured by needle-thin waterfalls. The hotel endorses an Ayurvedic lifestyle in its most substantive and authentic form. Get here from Nelliyampathy via Pothundy, Nenmara and Elavenchery. ■

DISCOVER THE WONDERS OF INDIA
with Outlook Traveller Getaways

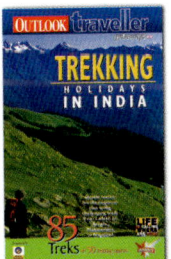
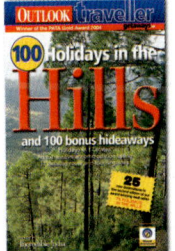
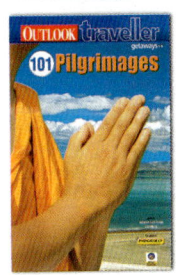

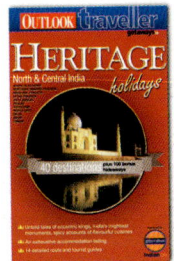
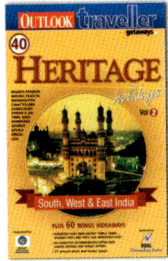

Life's an incredible journey

Elephants gather before the Vadkkunathan Temple for the famous Thrissur Pooram

THRISSUR

VADAKKUNNATHAN — LORD OF THE NORTH

State Kerala
Location The cultural capital of Kerala lies in the centre of the state, in the flatlands between the coast and the hills of the Peechi Reserve Forest rising to its east
Distance 635 km SW of Chennai **JOURNEY TIME By rail** 9 hrs **By air** 1 hr + $1\frac{1}{4}$ hrs by road
Route NH45 to Ulundurpettai via Tambaram, Chengalpattu, Tindivanam, Vikravandi and Viluppuram; NH68 to Salem via Tiyagai Durgam, Kallakkurichi, Talaivasal, Attur and Valappadi; NH47 to Thrissur via Bhavani, Perundurai, Avanashi, Coimbatore, Palakkad and Alathur (*see route guides on pages 12 and 320*)

■ BY LATHA ANANTHARAMAN AND SHEILA KUMAR

This is Kerala's culture capital, full of academies of literature and arts, a town so content with its past that modernity is still something to be gaped at. Shaktan Thampuran, the king who transformed Thrissur into a cultural treasure trove, would have approved. After all, it was a simple life that the man who broke the hold of feudal chieftains over the kingdom believed in. Three centuries after his time, the town that saw the rule of the Portuguese, the Dutch and the British continues to be true to Thampuran's ideology. And it's the ordinary that makes Thrissur so extraordinary even today.

This is the land of Shiva, Thiru-Shiva-Perur, and the town is centred on the temple to Vadakkunnathan or the Lord of the North. The clearing in front of the temple, called Thekkinkadu because it used to be a teak forest, is the site of the popular Thrissur Pooram (*see page 342*).

Surrounded by a bustling city, Vadakkunnathan remains aloof from the noise of the multitudes. Though his works are everywhere, he himself is invisible.

Equally invisible is Shakthan Thampuran. He restored temples that were damaged during the invasions of Haider Ali and Tipu Sultan and ruled over an age of prosperity. But nowhere in the town, not even in his palace, can you find a statue or painting of him.

LEGENDS AND MYTHOLOGY

Legend says that when Parasurama reclaimed the land of Kerala from the sea, he wanted to establish a worshipful community here. He asked Shiva and his family to descend from Kailasa to bless the inhabitants of this new land. They did come down, riding the bull Rishabha, and landed under a peepal tree. From that tree, Parasurama invoked Shiva to the location of the present sanctum of Vadakkunnathan and installed a Shiva lingam. He then installed the Vaishnavite emanation nearby and the united power as Shankaranarayana in the middle of the two. The Vadakkunnathan Temple is therefore considered to be the very first temple of Kerala. Parasurama is said to have anointed the lingam with ghee, a practice that continues to this day. The lingam is now invisible under an enormous mound of ghee, which miraculously does not become rancid and is not invaded by insects.

THINGS TO SEE AND DO

The Vadakkunnathan Temple and the 64-acre field on which it stands form the centre of the town. The road circling it is called the **Swaraj Round** or simply the Round and the location of most hotels, restaurants, and shops is given with reference to the Round. Autos are the easiest way to get around.

Two days in Thrissur give you ample time to see the sights mentioned here.

Vadakkunnathan Temple

In this vast compound, the orthodox follow an elaborate pattern of circumambulation, described on a board on the **koothambalam**. About 20 yards outside the gate is the **moolasthanam** or the place at which the deity originally manifested itself. Just inside the gate is a triangular stone labelled **Kali**. Believers say this stone grows imperceptibly, and that when it reaches the height of the gopuram, it will split in two and herald the end of the Kalyug. Located clockwise around the outer prakaram are shrines to Gosalakrishnan, Rishabha, Parasurama (represented by a stone lamp), Simhodara (Shiva's celestial attendant), Sastha and Adi Sankara.

Adi Sankara has a special relationship with this temple. He was born in answer to his parents' prayers to Vadakkunnathan and is said to have established the temple's rituals. Some accounts say he attained samadhi here. The **Sankara Samadhi** on the western side of the prakaram, marked by a conch and discus,

→ FAST FACTS

When to go The festivals are in Aug-Apr, and cool weather lasts till October
Tourist offices
● DTPC ❶ ❺
Vyjayanti Building, East Nada, Guruvayur
Tel: 0487-2550400
● Dept of Tourism ❶
Govt of Kerala, Tourism Complex, 2, Wallajah Road, Chennai
Tel: 044-25369789
● KTDC ❶ ❺
Tourist Reception Centre, Tourism Complex, 2, Wallajah Road
Chennai. Telefax: 044-25382639
Website: ktdc.com
STD code 0487

KERALA

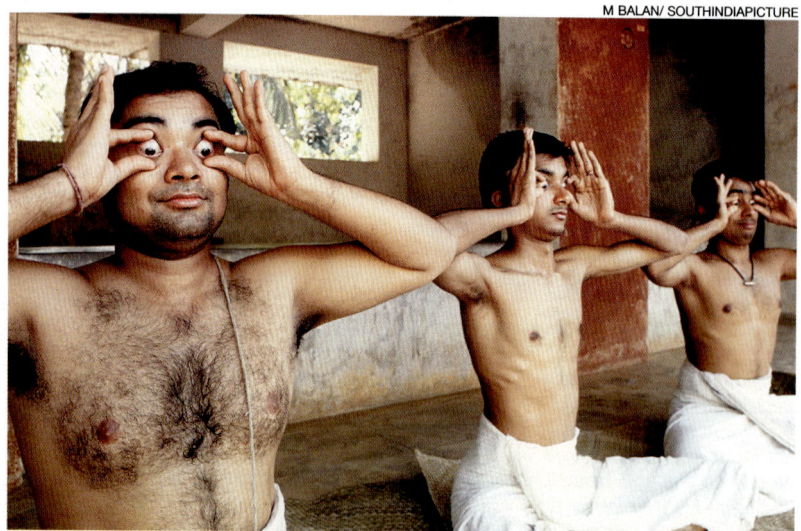

Students learn Kathakali moves in the cultural capital of Kerala

is far older than the Sankara shrine, which was built in the 1980s, but it is a simple memorial, not a tomb.

The **pooram**, the most famous event in Thrissur, is celebrated over two days in the Malayalam month of Mesha (April-May). It features processions of elephants and musicians bringing the deities of several temples to the field in front of the Vadakkunnathan Temple. The climax is the elephant line-up (15 from each temple) on the Round accompanied by the famous *panchavadyam* orchestra. In the evenings there is music and fireworks.

In the *koothambalam*, just inside the west gate, **Chakyarkoothu** is performed from Krishna Jayanti to Mahanavami (for 40 days starting late Aug), followed by **Koodiyattam** for 7-14 days.
◆**Timings** 4.30-10 am, 5.30-8.30 pm **Devaswom Tel** 0487-2426040
TIP All temples mentioned here have a dress code. To enter the inner courtyard, men must wear dhotis and bare their upper bodies. Women may enter in saris or salwar kameez, not in Western dresses. Cell phones have to be switched off

Paramekavu Bhagavathy Temple
The mother goddess, consort of Shiva, is said to have manifested herself first inside the premises of the Vadakkunnathan Temple, but was later shifted to the present shrine. She is considered a manifestation of Bhadrakali. The idol is larger than life and fills the sanctum.
◆**Location** 200m east of main temple **Timings** 4.30-10.30 am, 5-8.30 pm

Thiruvambady Krishna Temple
The temple was built 300 years ago and renovated by Shaktan Thampuran two centuries ago. A shrine to Bhagavathy stands to the left of the main sanctum.
◆**Location** On Shoranur Road, a 15-min walk (or Rs 8 auto ride) north of the main temple **Timings** 5-11 am, 5-8.30 pm **Website** thiruvambadytemple.com

Shakthan Thampuran Palace
Also known as Palace Thoppu, the grounds holding the imposing palace and lovely gardens house the tombs of three nobles, including that of Shakthan Thampuran, the greatest ruler of the

Kochi dynasty. The palace is a classic example of the simple and spartan lifestyle of Kerala's rulers. With loads of woodwork sans embellishments, the palace in no way reflects the power that rested with its owners. There are several halls, including a resplendent musical hall where art forms were staged.

♦**Location** Near the North Bus Stand and the Municipal Stadium **Palace timings** 10 am-1 pm, 2-4.30 pm, Mondays closed **Entry fee** Adults Rs 6, children Rs 4 **Tel** 2323631

Also within the palace grounds is the **Archaeological Museum**, which houses a melange of artifacts. Wooden models of the grand old *ambalams* (temples), burial pots and Harappan shards are part of the exceptional collection. The **Heritage Garden** here is very well maintained, with a *sarppakaavu* (snake shrine), a tank and a Shiva temple within its precincts.

♦**Entry fee for museum and garden** Adults Rs 10, children Rs 5 **Timings** 9.30 am-5 pm; Mondays and national holidays closed **Tel** 0487-2323631

Zoo

This is a run-of-the-mill specimen, but with some special surprises thrown in... a set of healthy hippos, some very pink flamingoes, tigers, camels and the sweet mithun of the North-Eastern hills. In the **Snake Park**, you'll find king cobras, kraits, vipers and rat snakes.

♦**Location** On Palace Road in Chembukkavu **Entry fee** Adults Rs 6, children Rs 4 **Cameras** Still Rs 10, video Rs 20 **Timings** 9 am-5.15 pm

Within the zoo compound is the **Natural History Museum** with some dusty specimens under equally dusty glass cases. But just beyond is the far more interesting **Art Museum**, which holds a fine collection of wood carvings, metal sculptures and ancient jewellery. A magnificent silver snake god is a beauty. **TIP** No cameras allowed inside

♦**Timings** 10 am-5 pm; Zoo entrance tickets hold for the museums too

Marthoma Mariam Big Church

In Thrissur, they call this the Valiya Palli, or big church, but because of its age and not its size. This is the oldest church in these parts and the headquarters of the Chaldean Syrian Church (Church of the East) in India, dating back to when Shakthan Thampuran settled 64 Syrian Christians in Thrissur around the end of the 18th century. Interestingly, parts of the main Mass are still held in Syriac, the old language; they follow old rites and have no idols or pictorial representations of Christ inside the chapel, only the Cross. Huge glass chandeliers and coloured glass balls hang from the ceiling and the wood used here came from the once lush teak forests surrounding the Vadakkunathan Temple.

KERALA

◆**Location** Opposite the Police Club on High Road **Service timings** Weekdays 7-8 am, 4.30-5 pm, Sundays 7.30-9.30 am **Main Festival** Koodash Etta Festival on the last Sunday of October, or first Sunday of November **Tel** 2421731

Dolores Basilica

This Roman Catholic Church, called Puthen Palli, was built in 1875. The steeple, at 140 ft, stands out clear and white, and can be seen from almost anywhere in town. The chapel has no less than 15 altars.
◆**Location** Near Jubilee Medical College **Service timings** 6 and 7.30 am, 5.30 pm, Sundays 10 am as well **Tel** 2420906

→ GETTING THERE

Air Nearest airport: Cochin International Airport, Nedumbassery (63 km/ 1¹/₄ hrs), connected to Chennai by six daily flights by Paramount Airways, Kingfisher Airlines, Jet Airways and Air Deccan. Pre-paid taxi to Thrissur costs Rs 700
Rail Thrissur Station **Best option TO** Trivandrum Mail (dep: Chennai Central 8 pm; arr: Thrissur 5.05 am) **Best option FROM** Chennai Express (dep: Thrissur 7.10 pm; arr: Chennai Central 6.05 am)
TIP Chennai Mail is also a good option on the return
Car This long drive across the breadth of Tamil Nadu and Kerala from Chennai cannot be attempted on a weekend break. Stick to the excellent train connections for a weekender. For longer vacations, follow NH45 to Ulundurpettai via Tindivanam and Viluppuram. Turn right onto NH68 to Salem via Talaivasal and Attur. At Salem, join NH47 till Thrissur via Bhavani, Avanashi, Coimbatore, Palakkad and Alathur

SHOPPING

Bell metal is special to the region and is found in shops on Round South and Round West as well as on Kuruppam Road. Visit the **Nadavaramba Krishna & Son** store (Tel: 2421040/ 852, 2426470) on Kuruppam Road for the best bell metal *villakus* and *ashtamangalyam* sets.

Also visit **Mangalore Music Stores** on Round South, where you can pick up musical instruments such as *chenda*, *edakkal* and *kombu*. MO Road, which leads off Round South, is thick with jewellery shops. Reputedly, Thrissur has the most number of **jewellery stores** in all of Kerala. Brilliant **silk saris** are also available in major stores like **Silk City** (Tel: 2322648) in City Centre and **Kalyan Silks** (Tel: 2331363, 2320356) on Round North. Every clothing store will have Travancore mundu sets with gold borders for Rs 500 upwards.

WHERE TO STAY

Thrissur has a large number of hotels across all budgets. The most centrally located accommodation is available at **Hotel Elite International** (Tel: 0487-2421033-43; Tariff: Rs 391-2,300) on Chembottil Lane, off Round South. They have friendly service, a multi-cuisine restaurant, a bar, a garden, and a children's park. A budget option just across the road is **Gurukripa Lodge** (Tel: 2421895; Tariff: Rs 150-320), a family place with cosy rooms opening into a courtyard. It serves breakfast and has some retro charm but could be cleaner.

Luciya Palace (Tel: 2424731; Tariff: Rs 475-1,450), on Marar Road, has airy rooms with a good view. **Hotel Sea Fort** (Tel: 2424067; Tariff: Rs 220-1,035), earlier called Alukkas Tourist Home, on RS Road, is a decent budget option.

Close to the South Bus Stand, KSRTC Bus Stand and the railway station is **Sidhartha Regency** (Tel: 2424773; Tariff: Rs 750-1,400), which has a bar,

KERALA

River terns take flight in Thrissur's Peechi-Vazhani Sanctuary

pool, gym and multi-cuisine restaurant. Near the North Bus Stand, on Palace Road, KTDC runs **Yatri Niwas** (Tel: 2332333; Tariff: Rs 400-600).

For more hotels and details, see Thrissur Accommodation Listings on pages 511-512

WHERE TO EAT

Pathan's is the best-known vegetarian meals place, but there are less crowded and neater veg eateries all over the Round, including **Hotel Bharath** (Chembottil Lane), which has decent enough food. Further down is the veg/non-veg **Hotel Saffron**, which has a pretty AC restaurant upstairs serving good Chinese and Indian food.

Kerala seafood is the speciality at **Calcutta** (Tel: 0487-2420838, 2441430; noon-10 pm) on Kuruppam Road. Tiffin and biryani are best at **Jaya** (Tel: 2427751; 6 am-midnight), also on Kuruppam Road. Veg Kerala thalis can be had at **Ambady Restaurant** (Tel: 2335770; 8.30 am-10.30 pm) on Railway Station Road. **Café Casino** is famous for its karimeen pollichathu and chicken varatha curry.

Thrissur has two branches of **Indian Coffee House** — one on Round South (Tel: 2421794) and the other near North Bus Stand (Tel: 2331749).

AROUND THRISSUR

Arattupuzha (16 km)
The **Dharmasastha Temple** here is set on the banks of a river that came to be called Arattupuzha because at one time more than a hundred deities were being immersed at this point (the ceremonial immersion of idols is called *arattu*). The idol, seated and carrying a vessel of nectar in the right hand, represents Sastha or Master of the Shastras. Legend says it was installed by Sage Vasishta, guru of Rama, over 3,000 years ago.

This is the site of the real pooram, the nine-day **Arattupuzha Pooram** (Mar-Apr), said to be a 1,600-year-old tradition. Nearly 80 elephants line up and there are fireworks and various types of melam or orchestral music.
♦**Location** Head south on SH22 **Timings** 5-11 am, 5-8 pm
TIP Men must remove their shirts before entering the inner prakaram ■

An off-duty temple elephant gets a bath at the Punathoor Kotta Elephant Camp

GURUVAYUR
BHOOLOKA VAIKUNTHAM — VISHNU'S ABODE ON EARTH

State Kerala
Location Coastal Guruvayur, bordered by dense greenery, is 32 km west of Thrissur
Distance 667 km SW of Chennai **JOURNEY TIME** *By rail* 9 hrs + 3/4 hr by road *By air* 1 hr + 2 hrs by road
Route NH45 to Ulundurpettai via Chengalpattu, Tindivanam, Vikravandi and Viluppuram; NH68 to Salem via Tiyagai Durgam, Kallakkurichi, Talaivasal, Attur and Valappadi; NH47 to Thrissur via Bhavani, Perundurai, Avanashi, Coimbatore, Palakkad and Alathur; state highway to Guruvayur (*see route guides on pages 12 and 320*)

■ BY LATHA ANANTHARAMAN

Guruvayur is a small town in Thrissur District not far from the sea. There is no sea breeze, the sand has long been hidden under paving stones, and we can't hear the roar of the ocean. All eyes, ears and hearts are drawn inwards, to what is for many of us the centre of the universe. Life here revolves around the Sri Krishna or Guruvayurappan Temple.

The small idol, made of black bismuth stone, represents Mahavishnu carrying his conch, discus, lotus and mace. The pujas conducted here are said to have been laid down by Adi Sankara. They are performed by celibate priests who, for the duration of their tenure (six months at a time), do not leave the premises. Much of this worship is carried out behind closed doors, and the silence and mystery enhances the effect of the sudden, radiant glimpses of the deity.

KERALA

The temple is crowded nearly all year round and is a favourite stop on the way to Sabarimala. All this makes a good darshan quite an achievement, but the long, hot wait is forgotten in one timeless moment that leaves everyone with beaming faces.

LEGENDS AND MYTHOLOGY

The diminutive idol of Vishnu is said to have been worshipped by Krishna himself and is associated with the end of his life. When Dwarka was flooded at the end of the Dwaparayuga, Krishna handed the idol to the gods Guru and Vayu for safekeeping. As they searched for the best place for the idol, they met Parasurama, who brought them to the Rudratirtha Lake, where Shiva sat in meditation. Shiva told them to install the idol on that spot already consecrated by his presence and considerately moved to the other side of the lake, where the Mammiyur (Mahima-ur) Shiva Temple now stands.

Although the idol is believed to be ancient, the Sri Krishna shrine and temple are only about 500 years old. Legend says a Pandyan king was told that he would die of snakebite and went to pray to Guruvayurappan. When the appointed time of his death passed without incident and he questioned the astrologer, he was shown the snakebite on his foot and told that he had survived because of his absorption in the lord. In gratitude he built the temple and endowed it with funds.

ORIENTATION

The **Guruvayurappan Temple** is the focal point of Guruvayur. It is surrounded by an inner ring road and an outer ring road. Four roads or *nadas* radiate from the north, east, south and west of the temple. The temple is about a 10-min walk from the **Government Bus Stand** to the north-west as well as the **Private Bus Stand** to the south-east. The **railway station** is 3 km away, north-east of the temple. Most of the shops, restaurants and hotels are within walking distance of the temple. Autos charge Rs 20 even for a short ride.

THINGS TO SEE AND DO

Most tourists and pilgrims spend just the morning at the Guruvayurappan Temple and move on to their next destination, but this usually allows only for one darshan after a long wait in a queue. If you stay overnight you can get the less crowded afternoon or evening darshan, visit some of the nearby temples, watch the spectacular night procession, see a Krishnattam performance, and catch one of the early morning pujas.

Guruvayurappan Temple

Sometimes there is a queue just to reach the main east entrance, but don't let that distract you from the opportunity for a pre-darshan. Tiptoe as you cross the first threshold and you will see the oil lamp

→ FAST FACTS

When to go Between June and October
Tourist offices
● DTPC 🛈 🅑
Vyjayanti Building, East Nada, Guruvayur
Tel: 0487-2550400
● Dept of Tourism 🛈
Govt of Kerala, Tourism Complex, 2, Wallajah Road, Chennai
Tel: 044-25369789
● KTDC 🛈 🅑
Tourist Reception Centre, Tourism Complex, 2, Wallajah Road
Chennai. Telefax: 044-25382639
Website: ktdc.com
STD code 0487

of the inner sanctum and a fairly clear if distant vision of Guruvayurappan, especially if he has been coated in sandal paste. The entrance area is shaded by a lofty porch and dominated by the gold-covered flagstaff and a large granite altar stone dedicated to Guru and Vayu. Near the flagstaff is a dish of bright red *manjaadi* (*Adenanthera pavonina*) and *kunni-kuru* (*Abrus precatorius*) seeds, which devotees take in their hands and drop back three times to rid themselves of skin ailments. As you go around the outer prakaram there is a **shrine to Ayyappa** on the south side and a roofless **Durga shrine** in the north-east corner (which legend says dates from before the Mahavishnu idol, when the area was a forest). Here devotees stop and face north-west to salute Mammiyur Shiva.

At the threshold to the inner sanctum is your second chance for pre-darshan before the crowd carries you forward to the sanctum itself. Once you have reached the inner sanctum, don't rush out again but stop to see the **murals on the sanctum walls**.

In the inner and outer prakarams, there are *balikallu* or small round altars set into the floor. These represent Indra, Agni, Ganapathy, Yama and other guardian deities of the temple and are to be treated as carefully as the idols. Circumambulate outside these altars, not inside them. As you come out of the north exit after darshan, you can get sandal paste prasadam at a counter against the far north wall.

The *utsavam* idol is taken on elephants in a procession or *siveli* around the temple three times a day, and various kinds of instruments are played. The night procession starts just after the sanctum closes and is the grandest. By the time it ends, the temple is fully illuminated (this is called the **chuttuvilakku**). The oil lamps attached in a grid all over the walls of the inner prakaram are lit up so that the walls shimmer with tiny flames, and the many-tiered lamps

Krishna idols for sale on East Nada

flanking the main entrance are also lit. It is a beautiful sight.

Many devotees offer *thulabharam* or their own weight in a wide range of items useful to the temple, such as bananas, ghee, jaggery, paddy, coconuts, or even coir rope, to keep a promise made by them or on their behalf.

An episode of **Krishnattam**, a cycle of eight verse dramas about the life of Krishna, is performed almost every night after *siveli*, at the northern part of the outer prakaram. The dramas are patterned after Jayadeva's *Gita Govinda* and were composed in the mid-17th century by Manaveda, a Zamorin, especially to be performed at this temple.

The temple celebrates its *utsavam* or **annual festival** in the month of

KERALA

View of the 16th century Guruvayurappan Temple's sanctum sanctorum

Meenam (Feb-Mar), starting with an **elephant race**. **Chakyarkoothu** is performed in the koothambalam in the south-east corner of the outer prakaram.

The 12-day **Chembai Music Festival** of classical music, named for the illustrious Carnatic singer and composer Chembai Vaidyanatha Bhagavatar (1896-1974) and patterned after the Thyagaraja Aradhanai at Thiruvaiyaru (*see page 110*), takes place in Nov-Dec, during the Ekadasi Festival. About 2,000 Carnatic musicians usually attend.

◆**Timings** 3-11.30 am, 4.30-9 pm **Temple Tel** 0487-2556335 **Devaswom** 2556672 **Website** guruvayurdevaswom.org

TIP Only Hindus are allowed into the temple. The dress code is strict. Men must wear dhotis and not wear shirts; saris or ankle-length skirts for women

Mammiyur Mahadevan Temple

This is the spot to which Shiva moved after offering his own place to Guruvayurappan. For that gracious act he is known as Mahima. In the sanctum Parvati is also considered to be next to Shiva, though invisible. There are also shrines to Vishnu, Ganesha, Subramania and Ayyappa, lavished with recently painted murals, among which the images of Mohini are outstanding. During Navaratri a shrine to Saraswati, the Navaratri Mandapam, is open, and the temple hosts a **Carnatic Music Festival** featuring almost 600 musicians. The dress code is the same as for the Guruvayurappan Temple.

◆**Location** 1 km north-west of the Guruvayurappan Temple **Timings** 4.45 am-12.30 pm and 4.45-8.30 pm

Parthasarathy Temple

This temple has an idol that is said to have been installed by Adi Sankara, for whom there is a shrine in the compound. The sanctum has wheels and horses added to resemble a chariot. The nearby **Venkitachalapathy Temple** has a shrine to Saint Ramanujan, just outside.

◆**Location** Near the railway station, 2 km northeast from the Guruvayurappan

Temple **Timings** 4.30 am-12.30 pm and 4.30-8.30 pm (both temples)

Palayur Church

Of great importance to Christians is the church at Palayur, believed to have been founded by St Thomas the Apostle at the place where he converted India's first Christians. St Thomas reached Kodungallur, not far from Palayur, in 52 CE. The Palayur Church is therefore 2,000 years old, the oldest of Kerala's 'seven-and-a-half churches' founded by St Thomas. It is a stark, austere church with a silver statue of St Thomas on the roof and charming stone *villakus*. A novena and mass in honour of St Thomas are held each Tuesday.

◆**Timings** 9-11 am, 4-6 pm

More to see

The famous **elephant camp** at **Punnathoorkotta** is located on the grounds of the old Guruvayur Palace. Nearly 70 elephants, donated by devotees including Tamil Nadu's former chief minister Jayalalitha, live here. The grounds are well shaded, and both children and grown-ups are fascinated by the sight of what elephants get up to when they're off duty. Those on temple duty are bathed daily, the others twice a week.

◆**Location** 2 km north of the Guruvayurappan Temple **Entry fee** Rs 5 **Timings** 8 am-5 pm

The **Devaswom Museum** just off the East Nada houses a large collection of unusual offerings to Guruvayurappan, including toy planes, models of houses, flutes, elephant teeth, and even a rifle.

◆**Location** Just off East Nada **Timings** 8 am-8 pm, Mon-Sat

WHERE TO STAY

The town is full of hotels and lodges, but except in the off-season (mid-Sep to mid-Oct), do book ahead. Lone travellers, especially women, are treated with suspicion unless they have reservations. The East Nada is brightly lit and is the best location for those who will be walking in the wee hours after Krishnattam or for Nirmalya Darshan.

Among the many hotels at the higher end are **Rugmini Regency** (Tel: 0487-2551873; Tariff: Rs 635-1,035), which is very near the temple, and the grander **Krishna Inn** (Tel: 2550777; Tariff: Rs 1,300-3,500). Both have multi-cuisine restaurants and do online bookings.

Hotel Sopanam Heritage (Tel: 2555244/ 542; Tariff: Rs 800-1,850) is a deluxe 4-star located on East Nada, very close to the temple. The hotel offers a speciality veg restaurant, swimming pool with a poolside coffee shop, car rental and sightseeing tours.

Sri Gokulam Vanamala (Tel: 2555503; Tariff: Rs 690-1,500) is on

Choose from our network of over 4000 hotels in India. Serviced apartments, budget hotels, luxury resorts, palaces, business accomodations, houseboats and more.

Hotel	Rating
Veeramani	3 ★
Vanamala Kusumam	3 ★
Fort Gate	3 ★

MTNL/BSNL Toll Free No.
1-800-22-4878
022-4030-4878
www.travelguru.com

travel**guru**™
India's Largest Hotel Network

South Nada. It has a veg restaurant, a travel desk and cable TV. One of the best options in Guruvayur. **Hotel Prarthana Inn** (Tel: 2557755; Tariff: Rs 520-1,450), near the Private Bus Stand on East Nada is a distant third behind Sopanam and Vanamala. It doesn't have a restaurant, but offers meals through room service (24 hrs). **Bhasuri Inn** (Tel: 2558855; Tariff: Rs 450-1,400) on East Nada, is among the best mid-range options, with two restaurants, a travel desk and 24-hr room service. **Rvee's Hotel Regency** (Tel: 255444; Tariff: Rs 450-1,600) near Balakrishna Theatre on East Nada has 36 rooms, a travel desk, 24-hr room service and an Internet café.

The **Devaswom** (Tel: 2556335) runs four facilities (Rs 175-700), all located south and east of the east gate. To book rooms, send a demand draft or money order to the Administrator, Guruvayur Devaswom, Guruvayur-680101.

The KTDC runs **Mangalya** (Tel: 2554061; Tariff: Rs 604) on East Nada with six-bed family rooms. There is also **Anjanam** (Tel: 2552048; Tariff: Rs 175-375) on West Nada, and **Nandanam** (Tel: 2556266; Tariff: 300-600), near the railway station.

For details, see Guruvayur Accommodation Listings on pages 500-501

GETTING THERE

Air Nearest airport: Nedumbassery Airport at Kochi (77 km/ 2 hrs), connected to Chennai by six daily flights by Paramount Airways, Kingfisher Airlines, Jet Airways and Air Deccan. Prepaid taxi to Guruvayur costs about Rs 1,130

Rail Guruvayur Station, but the Madras-Guruvayur Express is not a convenient connection. Thrissur Station (32 km/ $^3/_4$ hr; Tel: 0487-2424148) is much better connected for a weekend break **Best option TO** Trivandrum Mail (dep: Chennai Central 8 pm; arr: Thrissur 5.05 am). Taxi to Guruvayur costs Rs 400 approx **Best option FROM** Chennai Express (dep: Thrissur 7.10 pm; arr: Chennai Central 6.05 am)

Car This long drive cannot be attempted on a weekend break. Stick to the excellent train connections. For long vacations, follow NH45 to Ulundurpettai via Tindivanam. Turn right onto NH68 to Salem via Talaivasal and Attur. Join NH47 till Thrissur via Bhavani, Avanashi, Coimbatore, Palakkad and Alathur. From Thrissur, head north to Kunnamkulam and turn left to Guruvayur

WHERE TO EAT

There are a large number of eateries towards the east and south of the temple. Early birds can get breakfast from 4 am at **Ramakrishna Lunch Home**, the nearest eatery, or from 5 am at **Indian Coffee House** (closed Tuesdays) or from 6 am at the clean and friendly **Annapoorna Vegetarian Restaurant**. All of them are on the East Nada, as are **Saravana Bhavan** and the livelier **Hotel Nandini** (Tel: 0487-2556509), two other clean places. All of these serve South Indian meals, with Kerala specialities such as avial and olan, on banana leaf and tiffins all day. For North Indian and Continental food as well as South Indian, try the restaurants at **Rugmini Regency**, **Krishna Inn** and **Sopanam Heritage**, although you will not get breakfast before 7 am.

The temple itself feeds thousands of people a free prasadam meal daily. At night, a more limited number are fed. The meals are Kerala-style, rice-based and substantial. They often include payasam, and during festivals such as Onam and Vishu (Malayalam New Year), there is an especially elaborate meal. ■

For once, drifting aimlessly can be extraordinarily enriching.

Spice Coast Cruises takes you on a journey through the heartland of Kerala in a houseboat. A journey that bares the indescribable beauty, the very soul of Kerala. Our Kettuvallams (barges of yore converted into houseboats) echo our philosophy of life - only natural and local materials are used for the interiors - coir matted decks and canopies made of split bamboo and palm fronds. This simplicity is also reflected in the meals that our cook serves you on board our houseboats, which on a typical day would include among other divine dishes, the famed Karimeen and freshwater prawns. To help you experience the beauty of the backwaters in all its totality, our Kettuvallams come with extra awnings. Which not only give you the best of the breeze, but also enable you to get a better view of the unique water world of simple joys and pleasant surprises that slowly unfold before you.

Spice Coast Cruises
a c g h e a r t h e x p e r i e n c e

Central Reservations: Casino Building   Cochin   Kerala   India   Phone: +91-484-3011711   Fax: 2668001
Email: contact@cghearth.com   www.cghearth.com

Boat rides are very promising for wildlife sightings

Photographs by M BALAN/ SOUTHINDIAPICTURE

PERIYAR TIGER RESERVE
OF BIG CATS AND WILD DOGS

State Kerala
Location Thekkady, through which one enters the Periyar Tiger Reserve, lies in the Cardamom Hills in Idukki District in south-east Kerala, contiguous to the Kalakad-Mundanthurai Tiger Reserve in Tamil Nadu
Distance 553 km SW of Chennai JOURNEY TIME **By rail** 12 hrs + 2 hrs by road **By air** 1 hr + 4 hrs by road
Route NH45 to Theni via Chengalpattu, Tindivanam, Viluppuram, Ulundurpettai, Veppur, Trichy, Manapparai, Vadamadurai, Dindigul and Vattalakundu; NH220 to Thekkady via Uttamapalaiyam and Kilgudalur (*see route guides on pages 12 and 320*)

■ BY SHANTHI RADHAKRISHNAN

Periyar was silent at twilight, bereft of tourists, when a troupe of Nilgiri langur decided to break the quiet. They swung on the branches above, keeping a bunch of cooing doves company. A hunting party of birds, after a great deal of argument, agreed to make peace and turn in for the night.

A golden glow spread across the lake and a hush fell around us again. Suddenly, the sharp call of a barking deer broke the silence, and a Nilgiri langur joined in. There was a great deal of commotion on the other side, clearly visible from our perch on the boat landing by the lake. Obviously, a predator was around. Was it a tiger?

We had just been on a boat ride, during the course of which we had been lucky enough to glimpse many of nature's wonders: elephants and gaur, cormorants drying their wings, freshwater tortoises sunning on stumps jutting out of the water, and once, even a playful otter swimming sleekly and diving after fish. We were all set to enjoy the sounds and silences of the forest at dusk, when the uproar, from one side of the lake, made us hopeful that we would see the lord of the jungle, the tiger, in all its frightening beauty. As we sat with our eyes peeled, into our view came a frightened and gasping sambar fawn, closely followed by a pack of wild dogs. The last rays of the sun seemed to set the rusty red coat of the dogs on fire. They had obviously managed to separate a fawn from a herd of sambar. In desperation, the hapless fawn ran into the waters of the lake to escape its attackers. But cornered by the most ruthlessly efficient predator in Indian forests, the fawn did not seem to have even a fighting chance. As they always do, the dhole chased the animal till it became exhausted and then went in for the kill.

It wasn't a pleasant scene, and yet we watched the high drama enacted before us in horrified fascination, till the dark curtains of the night fell over the gory scene. We were silent as we made our way back to the secure confines of the hotel lobby.

More excitement, tinged with danger, was in store for us. We were to go on a night walk, called Jungle Patrol or Night Patrol, through the forest. Not so long ago, all one could do in Thekkady was to view wildlife from the relative safety of a boat deck. Nowadays, there's the added thrill of the night walk, which makes the forest experience even more intimate.

We started at around 7 pm, and the atmosphere was unnerving at first. A few in the group began to guffaw and speak in high decibels, probably to overcome their nervousness. The guide urged us to keep quiet and our silence was amply rewarded. In the diffused starlight, our shadows danced and merged with that of the foliage looming around us. A loud flap of wings caused us to virtually jump out of our skin. The wind sighed and carried the faint fragrance of flowers that blossom in the night. Something small scurried across our path. A civet cat, whispered the guide. A while later we saw bright, shiny red spots — we had come eye-to-eye with a nightjar that had frozen in its tracks thanks to the beams from our torch.

Half in anticipation and half in dread, we wondered what we would do

Choose from our network of over 4000 hotels in India. Serviced apartments, budget hotels, luxury resorts, palaces, business accomodations, houseboats and more.

Hotel	Rating
Wildernest	Budget
Silver Crust	3 ★
Wild Corridor	5 ★

MTNL/BSNL Toll Free No.
1-800-22-4878
022-4030-4878
www.travelguru.com

travelguru™
India's Largest Hotel Network

The person featured above is an actual Travelguru employee

KERALA

if we came across a tiger. Putting our worries to rest, the guide told us in a hushed voice that most animals disappear upon hearing the faintest of noises from humans. Soon after, we saw pairs of green eyes turned inquisitively towards our torchlight — it was a small herd of sambar watching us. At the end of the trek, we returned pleasantly exhausted to our rooms at the Aranya Nivas where a nice long hot shower and a sumptuous meal rounded off with fresh fruits awaited us. And then it was time to sleep, perchance to dream, of more adventures in the wild.

ABOUT PERIYAR

Situated in the Idukki District of South Kerala, the Periyar Wildlife Sanctuary, also known as Thekkady, is the oldest and largest of the protected areas. The Mulla Periyar Irrigation Dam, constructed in 1895, was considered an engineering marvel at that time. But the dam inundated a large tract of forestland and created a 26 sq km long lake, which is today the main watering hole of the reserve. The stark stumps of rotting, forlorn trees that seem to hold up their arms in despair are now home to a number of birds, including cormorants and darters.

The name Thekkady comes from *thekku* or teak trees while Periyar is named after Periyar, or the Big River. Tropical evergreen and deciduous forests, bamboos, reed banks and savannahs are spread over the 777 sq km of hills, valleys, plains and waterlogged areas that make up the reserve. The story goes that when the son of Lord Wellington downed a mighty tusker at Periyar in the 1930s, the erstwhile king of Travancore, Sree Chithira Thirunal Balarama Varma, was so saddened that he immediately extended protection to the denizens of the forest.

Graphic by SURAJ WADHWA

Prudent Networks
Your Travel Companion

Gaze with wonder eyed-admiration as the king of the jungle yawns while lazing on jungle greens, see birds soar high up in the sky as they display their colorfully painted wings and beaks as you explore and enjoy India Wildlife Tours with Prudent Networks Pvt. Ltd.

Experience a fusion of glorious sensations of adventure, wild joy, beauty and freedom as you set out game watching deep into the forests of India with India Wildlife Tours. Revel in wild India Heritage Tours as you explore Ranthambhore Fort ruins within dense Ranthambhore forest thickets on Rajasthan Tours with Prudent Networks' India Wildlife Tours.

Laze on a coir houseboat as it floats on sparkling backwaters; see cormorants fly overhead and spot flitting silver fishes as you gaze into transparent green backwaters on Kerala Tours and India Luxury Tours with Prudent Networks. Laze on a coir houseboat as it floats on sparkling backwaters; see cormorants fly overhead and spot flitting silver fishes as you gaze into transparent green backwaters on Kerala Tours and India Luxury Tours with Prudent Networks.

Prudent Networks
Suite - 218, Ansals Majestic Tower,
Vikaspuri, New Delhi - 110018, India
Telephone Nos: +91-11-41586840 / 41586940
Mobile No: +91-9811203268
Fax No: +91-11-41586740
E-Mail: info@prudentnetworks.com

KERALA

A bonnet macaque sticks to the rules

→ FAST FACTS

When to go Sep-Mar is the best time, when you can enjoy greenery without the accompanying rains
Tourist offices
● Deputy Director (Project Tiger), Periyar Tiger Reserve, Thekkady
Tel: 04869-222027, 222284
● Eco-tourism Centre
Ambady Junction, Kumily
Tel: 04869-224571
TIP For plantation and tea factory tours, nature walks, Periyar Tiger Trail border trekking, bamboo rafting
● Dept of Tourism, Govt of Kerala Tourism Complex, Wallajah Road Chennai. Tel: 044-25369789
● KTDC Tourist Reception Centre TTDC Complex, 2, Wallajah Road Chennai. Telefax: 044-25382639
Website: ktdc.com
STD code 04869

By 1950, the area had gained the status of a wildlife sanctuary and twenty-eight years later, it was brought under Project Tiger. The core area of the sanctuary was designated as a National Park in 1982 and, in 2004, the Periyar Foundation was formed, under the aegis of which the park administration and the locals got together to strengthen conservation efforts. In fact, the Periyar model is considered so remarkably successful that other National Parks are urged to follow it.

ORIENTATION

The Kottayam-Thekkady Road ends at **Kumily** on the Kerala-Tamil Nadu border. There is only one entry point to the Periyar Tiger Reserve, through the small village of **Thekkady**, 4 km from Kumily. You can either reach it by bus or autorickshaw, both of which ply between the two villages.

The starting point of the reserve is the **boathouse**, roughly 2 km from the entry gate. This distance can be either covered on foot or in a vehicle. All treks, boat rides and walks begin from this point. Near the boathouse is the **Eco-tourism Centre**, where you can sign up for trekking as well as other activities in the centre. The **Pamba River** flows on the western side of the reserve. The best way of seeing the reserve is by taking a boat ride on the man-made **Periyar Lake**.

All vehicular traffic within the sanctuary comes to a standstill from 6 pm to 6 am and unless accompanied by a guide, it would be unsafe to wander around after nightfall. However, it is extremely pleasant to take a stroll in the daytime, when there's a good chance of spotting many birds, the Malabar giant squirrel and the Nilgiri langur.

♦**Park entry fee** Indians Rs 25, foreigners Rs 300 **Cameras** Still Rs 25, video Rs 200 **Vehicle entry fee** Rs 50 **Timings** 6 am-6 pm

KERALA

The magnificent, highly endangered Malabar giant squirrel

TIP Binoculars are available on hire but are generally in a very poor condition. So take your own along

THINGS TO SEE AND DO

There are several eco-tourism programmes in the Periyar Tiger Reserve, which include trekking, night trekking, camping and bamboo rafting. All of these present exciting opportunities to see animals and birds up, close and personal. Contact the Eco-tourism Centre (Tel: 04869-224572) at Ambady Junction, Kumily, for signing up for these programmes. All these are very popular and booked months in advance, so make your reservations well ahead.

Boating

The best way to view wildlife is from the boat on the **Mulla Periyar Lake**. The reservoir today is a valuable eco-system in its own right, with a number of creeks, promontories and small islets serving as habitats for wildlife. The hills around the lake provide food for elephants, gaur and sambar. Wildlife sightings, especially those of herds of elephants, are quite frequent when you take the boat ride.

The boats that ply here are run by either the Forest Department or the Kerala Tourism Development Corporation (KTDC). Since the number of boat trips and the timings are inflexible, it's best to book one's seat well in advance. The boat jetty is near the Wildlife Information Centre.

♦**KTDC boating fee** Upper deck Rs 110, lower deck Rs 55 **Forest Department boating fee** Rs 40 **Timings** 9.30 am, 11.30 am, 2 pm, 4 pm

Serious wildlife photographers have the option of hiring a small two-seater at the cost of Rs 350 per trip; the small boat facilitates a quieter and closer approach to animals and to the banks of the lake.

Walk in the wild

One of the eco-tourism programmes is the nature walk, covering 4-5 km on different routes and lasting 3 hrs. It

Taste....
the Spices in the Tranquility of Kerala

WE OFFER:
AYURVEDA • HILL STATION TOURS • HONEYMOON PACKAGES • TEA BUNGALOW STAYS
MICE • ECO TOURISM PACKAGES • ADVENTURE TOURS

GSR TOURS
Great Southern Revelation Tours Pvt. Ltd.

Your Holiday Maker

86, TOOTING HIGH STREET, LONDON, SW17ORN
Tel: 004420 86820969, Fax: 004420 87673462
E-mail: gsrlon@gmail.com

BMRA 2A, BALAKRISHNA MENON ROAD,
EDAPPALLY, COCHIN - 680 024, KERALA, INDIA.
T : 0091   999   5436009
     0091   989   5889708
     0091   938   7162761
gsrtours@gmail.com
www.gsrtours.com

P.O. BOX - 25152, MUSAFA ROAD, ABUDHABI, UAE
Tel: 00971 25525061, Mob: 00971 506169150
E-mail: gsruae@gmail.com

INDIA   UAE   UK

provides tourists an excellent opportunity to spot birds and butterflies, and occasionally, large animals. The charges are Rs 100 per person, and there can be a maximum number of five persons in each group. The walks are held at 7 am and 2 pm. A trained tribal guide accompanies each group and helps tourists identify the flora and fauna.

Jungle patrol
There is regular patrolling of the fringe areas of the forest, and this programme allows your participation. Thereby, the patrol, an effort to conserve the forest, doubles as a tourism venture; the tourist too gets a chance to help in the conservation effort. The 3-hr-long night trek can be undertaken in one of several slots: 7-10 pm, 10 pm-1 am and 1-4 am. Each slot has eight visitors, moving in two separate teams. An armed forest guard accompanies each group. The charges are Rs 500 per person.

Bullock cart discoveries
This half-day package gives the visitor the novel experience of travelling in a covered bullock cart to the farmlands of a village adjacent to the reserve. A maximum of nine persons can take the trip at a time, at the rate of Rs 500 per person; there has to be a minimum payment of Rs 1,000 (meaning, at least two people have to avail of the package). The trip starts at 6 am and ends at around 2.30 pm.

Bamboo rafting
This full-day programme involves trekking through different habitats, while the rafting itself lasts 3 hrs. It starts at the boat landing at 8 am; the guides take you inside the forest for a trek and then back to your raft to sail back in the evening. The programme gets over by 5 pm. The charges are Rs 1,000 per person, inclusive of food and entrance fee; there has to be a minimum of two persons, with a maximum of 20 persons per day. The programme presents an excellent opportunity to spot wildlife.

Tribal heritage tour
Besides a tour through the village where Mannans — one of the oldest communities to inhabit the dense forests of the area — live, visitors get a glimpse of tribal culture thanks to a visit to the **Tribal Heritage Museum**. On display are fishing gear and hunting traps, medicinal plants, vessels, furniture and cereals. Rituals and ceremonies of the Mannans are represented through models and paintings.

→ GETTING THERE

Air Nearest airport: Cochin International Airport, Nedumbassery (204 km/ 4 hrs; Tel: 0484-2610115), connected to Chennai by six daily flights by Paramount Airways, Kingfisher Airlines, Jet Airways and Air Deccan. Pre-paid taxi to Thekkady costs Rs 2,840
Rail Nearest railhead: Kottayam Station (113 km/ 2 hrs; Tel: 0481-2562933, 2563535) **Best option TO** Trivandrum Mail (dep: Chennai Central 8 pm; arr: Kottayam 8.05 am). Taxi to Thekkady costs Rs 1,271 **Best option FROM** Chennai Mail (dep: Kottayam 5.35 pm; arr: Avadi 6.09 am, Perambur 6.24 am, Chennai Central 7 am)
Car This long drive across the breadth of Tamil Nadu cannot be attempted on a weekend break. Stick to the excellent train connections. For longer vacations, follow NH45 past Chengalpattu, Tindivanam, Viluppuram, Ulundurpettai, Trichy, Manapparai, Dindigul and Vattalakundu to Theni. Follow NH220 south over the Western Ghats to Thekkady via Uttamapalaiyam and Kilgudalur

WELCOME HOME TO
PERIYAR RESERVE BUNGLOW

Next time when you plan a homely holiday choose
Kerala Homestays for Holidays.
We offer our Kerala Tour Packages networked
through our quality Homestays which will be a private
and personalised experiance.
We at stayhomz have a network of over thirty homes
warmly welcoming travelers from world over to
stay in plantation bungalows, backwater homes and
restored heritage properties functioning as homestays
spread across the entire span of this tiny strip of land.

STAY HOMZ , KP IX 340/A, Pottamkulam Buildings, Kootickal, Mundakkayam
Kottayam District, Kerala - 686 514, South India
Ph: 91+4828 284310 [Off], 91+4828 284154 [Res]. M: 9447084310. Fax: 91+4828 284154
mail@stayhomz.com | www.stayhomz.com

KERALA

Edappalayam Forest Inspection Bungalow within the reserve forest

◆**Museum timings** 9 am-5 pm **Entry** Free **Tour charges** Rs 100 per person **Tour timings** 8 am-noon, 2-4 pm

Jungle story
This involves an overnight stay at a cottage for two at **Kokkara**, an hour's walk from the forest check-post. Check-in is at 4 pm and check-out at 7 am the following morning. At Rs 2,000 for two persons, the payment is inclusive of the entrance fee, trekking and dinner. The stay at the inn gives you a chance to enjoy the beauty of the jungle at night. Facilities are available for just two persons per night.

Bamboo grove
This is an eco-friendly area with accommodation for visitors in eight huts made exclusively with natural materials such as bamboo and grass. An ideal milieu for nature sensitisation camps, there are facilities for lectures, discussions, audio-visual presentations and field visits. The charge is Rs 2,000 for one cottage and the rate is inclusive of food for two, boating, trekking and entrance fees.

Border hiking
This is a full-day hard trek oriented towards conservation, starting at 8 am and ending at 5 pm. The trekking trail passes through altitudes of 900-1,300m, offering the tourist several beautiful views. Sightings of gaur and elephants are also not uncommon on this route. A maximum number of 10 persons are taken in two groups each day. The charge of Rs 750 per person covers the entrance fee and refreshments. Two guides and an armed forest guard accompany the tourists.

Periyar tiger trail
This includes two programmes (1N/2D and 2N/3D) that only the medically fit and those in the 15-65 age-group can take part in. Conducted by poachers-turned-protectors, the programme covers between 20 and 35 km, depending on the route chosen. Armed guards accompany the groups, which consist of five visitors

Vijaya Corporate

It's not everyday that you have a pool in your drawing room.

If it does for a holiday, it has to be a great holiday. Our **Pool studio*** is altogether a rare experience. The garden suite where you have a charming exclusive private garden all for you, is another memorable experience. And the honeymoon suite will take you out of the world on your honeymoon. It's not everyday that you have beautiful, rare experiences, is it?

*The only 3 pool studios in South India are at The Elephant Court.

Thekkady P.O., Idukki District, Kerala, India 685 536
Tel.: +91 4869 224696/97/98 Fax: +91 4869 224238
email: info@theelephantcourt.com
For reservations: +91 484 4024440, +91 484 4024441
Fax: +91 484 2205369
email: reservations@theelephantcourt.com
www.theelephantcourt.com
A venture of Vijaya Hospitality and Resorts Ltd.

THE ELEPHANT COURT
The life in wildlife

KERALA

Skilled Munnar adivasi fishermen show off the day's catch

and five guides; simple vegetarian fare is prepared en route and accommodation is in tents. The charges are Rs 3,000 per person (a minimum of Rs 5,000 has to be paid for the programme to be organised) for the 1N/2D trek and Rs 5,000 per person for the 2N/3D trek (a minimum of Rs 7,500 has to be paid for this programme). The best part about the programme is not only the fact that the route passes through hills and valleys, giving you a good chance to encounter wildlife, but you also get to hear exciting stories from the former poachers.

Mangaladevi Temple

Located 12 km from Thekkady, at the reserve's northern boundary, are the ruins of a stone temple. The deity is Mangaladevi or Kannagi, the protagonist of the Tamil epic *Silapaddikaram*, who legendarily burnt down Madurai (*see page 151*). The view from this spot is striking. On the full moon day of April-May (*Chithra Pournami*), pilgrims congregate in this temple.

Spice plantation visits

The Kerala Tourism Information Centre (Tel: 04869-222620) located near the main reserve entrance gate at Kumily organises 4-hr tours to spice plantations. Visitors are also taken to the **Connemara Tea Factory**, 15 km outside the sanctuary, and to flower gardens. The tours are offered twice a day, departing at 10 am and 2.30 pm. Those who take the morning tour can witness processing techniques at a tea factory.
♦**Tour fee** Rs 350 **Timings** 10 am-5 pm

WHERE TO STAY AND EAT

Thekkady has a wide range of stay options, ranging from luxurious to basic hotels. Many of them have packages, so do check these out. All the hotels offer meals and non-guests can eat at most without advance notice.

Inside the forest
KTDC's **Aranya Nivas** (Tel: 04869-222023; Tariff: Rs 4,518-7,105) is a good

See the spice plantations tucked away between the misty mountains. Or the lush waterfalls humming continuously amongst the trekking trails. Hear the sound of silence as you rejuvenate with a relaxing massage among dense foliage. Taste God's own offerings at our restaurant as you savour sumptuously on the delectable cuisine of Kerala. Smell the aroma of nature across the long, lazy walks in our spice plantations. Touch the beauty of life at Shalimar Spice Garden.

Shalimar Spice Garden

HEIGHTEN YOUR SENSES.

10 VILLAS
10 STANDARD ROOMS
2 RESTAUTANTS – FALLING LEAVES & HIBISCUS
AYUVEDA CENTER
INFINITY POOL
2 LOUNGES
8 ACRES OF SPICE PLANTATIONS
1 ACRE OF ORGANIC FARMS

anantara
Hospitality Pvt. Ltd
www.anantara.in

Shalimar Spice Garden
Murikkady P.O. Idukki Dist., Kerala - 685 535, INDIA
Tel : +91 4869 222 132 / 223 022
Email: Shalimar@anantara.in (Central reservations)
Hotel: Shalimar_resort@vsnl.com

For Reservations contact:
Bangalore: 540, 16th Main Road, 3rd Block, Koramangala, Bangalore 560034, India.
Tel: +91 080 41306352, 41306357. Fax: +91 080 41306357.
Email: bangalore.sales@anantara.in
Mumbai: +91 9820625606. Email: bombay.sales@anantara.in

KERALA

Safely perched on a watch tower in Periyar Tiger Reserve, out of wildlife's reach

option for birdwatchers, as it's right inside the forest. It has a restaurant and pool. KTDC's **Lake Palace** (Tel: 222024; Tariff: Rs 9,000, with meals) has a spartan exterior that's well contrasted with its lovely interiors. The hotel, with just 6 suites, can be approached only by boat, as a result of which guests have to be back by dusk — boats do not ply after sunset.

KTDC's **Periyar House** (Tel: 222026/546; Tariff: Rs 1,250-2,500) is located midway between the main entrance and the boathouse. It organises boating, trekking and plantation visits, and has a restaurant. It also has a children's park.

Outside the forest

High-end options abound near the forest. **Taj Garden Retreat** (Tel: 222401; Tariff: Rs 3,800-6,500) is close to the main gate and has cottages with a rural ambience. The CGH Earth Group's **Spice Village** (Tel: 222315-16; Tariff: Rs 8,000-11,200) is located in a spice garden near the forest. **Muthoot Cardamom Country** (Tel: 224501-03; Tariff: Rs 5,500-8,000) has a café, a gym, a pool and a massage centre, while **Saj Jungle Village** (Tel: 223363; Tariff: Rs 5,000-10,000) on Mangaladevi Road has a restaurant and a pool. **Hotel Tree Top** (Tel: 223286-87; Tariff: Rs 2,500-7,500) has 8 cottages, 12 deluxe rooms and a 4-bedroom bungalow.

Bamboo Grove Lodge (Tel: 224571; Tariff: Rs 2,000), adjacent to the forest, has 10 well-equipped cottages and offers Keralite food. They also organise boating, rafting and trekking.

Mid-range options include **Hotel Kumily Gate** (Tel: 222500; Tariff: Rs 900-1,900), which offers views of the Periyar Dam, and has a restaurant. **Hotel Lake Queen** (Tel: 222084-86; Tariff: Rs 600-1,400) at Thekkady Junction has 51 rooms, two restaurants and a café. **Michael's Inn** (Tel: 222355-56; Tariff: Rs 1,300-2,500) nearby offers 26 rooms and a restaurant. **Hotel Ambadi** (Tel: 222193-95; Tariff: Rs 1,150-1,600) is a comfortable hotel with a nice restaurant.

Enlightenment, they say, is like the lifting of the gentle mist; here it is laced with the fragrance of the hills.

Set unobtrusively in the Periyar wilderness on the lofty Western Ghats, Spice Village exudes the spirit and ethos of this reservoir of nature. Here nature controls the temperature. Nature's songs will be the only piped music you hear. Nature will be the only television you watch... Spice Village at Thekkady is a quiet extension of the rainforests around, almost as though an integral part of nature's design. Modelled after the dwellings of the local tribal inhabitants, all the cottages, are built with split bamboo and elephant grass. This raw presence of nature can be felt throughout our hotel - which, more than a statement of style, was a necessity, considering the fragile ecosystem around.

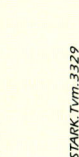

Spice Village
a cgh earth experience

Central Reservations: Casino Building Cochin Kerala India Phone: +91-484-3011711 Fax: 2668001
Email: contact@cghearth.com   www.cghearth.com

KERALA

Otters get cosy with each other on the banks of Mullaperiyar Lake

The Wildernest (Tel: 224030; Tariff: Rs 2,300-3,650) has 10 rooms and offers TV, hot and cold running water and a writing desk in each room.

The Wildside Villa (Mobile: 094474 33096; Tariff: Rs 875-1,500) on Amalambika Convent Road has accommodation in a treehouse, as well as 6 rooms. **Mickey Cottage** (Tel: 223196, Mobile: 09447284160 [Murali]; Tariff: Rs 350-750) offers 5 budget rooms. **TAS Cottage** (Tel: 223396; Tariff: Rs 500) in Labbakandam has 2 rooms and a kitchen.

For more hotels and details, see Periyar Accommodation Listings on pages 509-511

AROUND PERIYAR

Gavi (18 km)
A scenic place 18 km from Thekkady, this area comes under the management of the Kerala Forest Development Corporation (KFDC). The **Green Mansions** retreat is located in this place, and you can go trekking, canoeing, angling or birdwatching here. Accommodation comprises open-air tents or treetop houses. The KFDC and the eco-development committee, with members of the indigenous community and forest officials, run two programmes here. One involves staying at an eco-lodge, and the other includes a day-trip to the areas around.

Peermade (39 km)
Unspoiled and verdant, the rolling hills of Peermade, located 39 km away, were named after the 13th century Sufi saint, Peer Mohammed. A global traveller and a friend of the Travancore royal family, Peer Mohammed settled in Kuttikanam in Peermade and was buried at the foot of the Peeru Hills. His tomb itself is small and unassuming.

A more popular reason for visiting this spot is the breathtaking view of the hills of Idukki and Sabarimala, set against blue skies. The slopes of Peermade abound in practically every conceivable type of plantation. Sprawling tea estates cover much of the land, but cardamom, rubber, vanilla and coffee plantations are also aplenty. ∎

A shoal of Kottayam's favoured ducks on the Vembanad backwaters

PRASHANT PANJIAR

KOTTAYAM
LAND OF FIRSTS

State Kerala
Location In Kottayam District of south-central Kerala, sandwiched between the backwaters to the west and the plantations at the foothills of the Ghats to the east
Distance 666 km SW of Chennai **JOURNEY TIME By rail** 12 hrs **By air** 1 hr + 2 hrs by road
Route NH45 to Theni via Chengalpattu, Tindivanam, Viluppuram, Ulundurpettai, Veppur, Trichy, Manapparai, Vadamadurai, Dindigul and Vattalakundu; NH220 to Vandiperiyar via Uttamapalaiyam, Kilgudalur and Thekkady; SH to Kottayam via Peermade, Kanjirapally and Pambadi (*see route guides on pages 12 and 320*)

■ BY DIVYA ANAND

When the sun furtively steps out of the clouds on a monsoon day, a lazy glow envelops the fields of Kottayam. Rain-kissed fields preen and pose for the stray sunbeam, and coconut palms sway in the soft breeze. Blue waters cut across this swathe of emerald green, and the sparkling colours make you wonder if Earth has snatched a fistful of rainbow from the sky. The god of all things big and small, it's clear, is always in a magnanimous mood in Kottayam.

That should explain the poetry in its palm-fringed backwaters, the musings that crimson sunsets invoke even in the most hardened of politicians. But there is no flashy celebration of beauty here, no boisterous acknowledgements. The days continue to weave themselves around the routine: the aroma of a spicy duck roast, the ergonomics of the ubiquitous rubber plantations, the stern black and white letters of freshly printed newspapers.

KOTTAYAM

Perhaps Kottayam prefers its hard-earned credentials a bit more than the natural radiance it's been blessed with. It cherishes the rubber and spice plantations that have made it a commercial centre, and is fittingly proud of the fact that it was the first town in India to achieve 100 per cent literacy. It's the heart of Kerala's publishing industry, and is now hoping to add an 'ecocity' tag to its many labels. It's also a true melting pot of varied cultural and religious influences. And somewhere tucked in between is the town that Arundhati Roy put up on the world map, mostly somnolent, but always bursting with colours.

ORIENTATION

The railway track follows the course of the **Meenachil River** into Kottayam. You step out of the station at the northern end of town. The city lies between you and the Kodoor River to the south, whose backwaters lead into **Vembanad Lake**. A short walk south from the station and you are on the arterial **Shastri Road**, which leads west to **Seematti Circle** at the heart of Kottayam, centred on the Thirunakkara Temple. A short distance from the circle is **Baker's Junction**, an important landmark. Running parallel to Shastri Road is the **KK (Kottayam-Kumily) Road**. MC (SH1) and TB roads lead south from Seematti Circle to the **Kodimatha Boat Jetty** on the Kodoor River, where operators offer boats for backwater tours. Shops, restaurants, hotels and sights line all four roads. Take the KK Road east to get to Cheriapally, Valiapally and the **Thazathangady Juma Masjid**.

Kottayam has two **bus stands**, but the best way to move around town is by autorickshaw, even if meters are purely ornamental. Taxis are aplenty.

THINGS TO SEE AND DO

Kottayam may be known for its backwaters and houseboats, but its religious monuments and heritage structures are a must-see.

Thirunakkara Mahadeva Temple

A huge banyan tree rustles in salutation, right at the entrance. An edifice of immense grace and beauty, there is nothing ostentatious about this temple. All is subtle, simple and spacious.

With two praharams, a spacious *koothambalam* and an *anathottil*, the **Thirunakkara Temple**, built by a Thekkumkur Raja, is appropriately hailed as the archetype of traditional Kerala temple architecture. The temple is more than 500 years old and the chief deity is Shiva. The highlight is of course the low roofed stage or the *koothambalam*. With carved wooden bay windows on all four sides, the dances are visible even from the outside. Further to its right stands the *anathottil* or the elephant stable, a

→ FAST FACTS

When to go October to February. Though Kottayam is beautiful during Kerala's renowned monsoon (June to September), you may not be able to do a backwater cruise

Tourist offices
- Dist. Tourism Promotion Council
  Boat Jetty, Kodimatha, Kottayam
  Telefax: 0481-2560479
- Tourist Information Counter
  Dept of Tourism, Govt of Kerala,
  Nattakom, Government Guest House,
  Kottayam. Tel: 0481-2342303
- KTDC
  Tourist Reception Centre, Govt of Kerala, TTDC Complex, 2, Wallajah Road, Chennai. Tel: 044-25382639
  Website: ktdc.com

STD code 0481

KERALA

Thazathangadi Juma Masjid, one of the oldest mosques in India

slanting roof supported by six pillars, where the temple tusker is tethered. Subsidiary shrines of Ganesha, Ayyapa and Muruga are located inside the outer praharam. The most striking feature of most temples in Kerala is the silence, broken only during puja times by the panchavadyam (an ensemble orchestra). The sprawling temple grounds or the Thirunakkara Maidanam has witnessed many a historic event and is a good place to while away lazy evenings.

♦**Cameras** Still Rs 50, video Rs 100 **Timings** 4-11 am, 5-8 pm **Main festival** Painguni Utsavam on March 15 **Tel** 0481-2583898

TIP Photography is not allowed inside

St Mary's Knanaya Church, Valiapally

Not very far from the temple, atop a small hill and nursed by the Meenachil, stands the ancient St Mary's Knanaya Church, known as Valiapally. It was built in 1550 by the descendants of Syrian Knanaya Christians who migrated to India in 345 CE, on land gifted by a Hindu chieftain. The church has two granite **Persian crosses**, each carved out of a single slab of stone dating back to the 4th and 7th centuries CE. Both bear inscriptions in the Pahalavi language, once the official language of the Sassanid dynasty of Persia. The crosses apparently were brought here from an older church in Kodungalloor. The altar and ceiling are exquisitely carved, decorated with vegetable dye paintings depicting scenes from the Bible. But nothing beats the baptismal font, set into an alcove in the thick church walls, more than a metre in diameter.

♦**Timings** 8 am-8 pm **Main feast** St George's Feast on April 24 **Tel** 2563324

St Mary's Orthodox Church, Cheriapally

A short distance from the Valiapally stands the **Cheriapally**, or small church, which is neither small nor typically church-like. A synchronous blend of temple and Portuguese architecture, St Mary's Orthodox Church was built and consecrated by the Portuguese in 1579, with the patronage of the local raja.

The large brick outer walls, the huge hanging lamp in the hall and the granite pillars are reminiscent of temples in

Kerala, while the vegetable dye paintings on the altar walls and ceiling, depicting the life of Christ, are signature Portuguese and are as old as the church itself. Sadly, heritage conservation was not a factor in renovation: the paintings on the lower half of the altar wall have been ruthlessly whitewashed.

The porch with granite pillars and carved wooden ceilings, the tiled roof, the baptism basin hewn out of a single stone and the bay windows add to the uniqueness of the church.

♦**Timings** 7.30 am-12.30 pm, 7.30 am-6 pm (Saturdays) **Festival** January 15 **Tel** 0481-2566744

Thazathangadi Juma Masjid (2 km)

Also in the vicinity, on the banks of the Meenachil, stands this beautiful double-storeyed traditional structure made of teak. The Thazathangadi Juma Masjid is one of the oldest mosques in India, believed to be more than 1,000 years old. On first glance, you may be forgiven for mistaking it for a temple or a raja's palace, for this mosque has a *nalukettu* (square inner courtyard), exquisitely carved wooden gabled roof, a traditional bathing area and latticed windows. A marvellous amalgamation of architecture to absorb.

♦**Location** In Thazathangadi, 4 km away from Kottayam **Timings** 7 am-6 pm **Tel** 0481-2584610

TIP Women are not allowed inside

Backwater escapes

The Kottayam experience won't be complete unless you test the waters of the Vembanad Lake. Several operators at the boat jetty in Kodimatha offer tours around the lake. A few we recommend are **Dolphin Boat Services** (Tel: 0481-2584352, 09846095400), and **Cruise & Cruise Boat Service** (Tel: 2363805, 09846096494). Typical charges for day-long boat rides are Rs 225-300, inclusive of lunch. The best option would be to go on a day-long package tour with stopovers at a manmade island called R-Block (2 hrs), Kumarakom Bird Sanctuary (30 mins) and Pathiramanal Island (1 hr), that falls en route to Alleppey (2 hrs).

TIP Time indicates speedboat journey to each place

SHOPPING

Clothes and jewellery are the chief draws in Kottayam. **KK Road** buzzes with jewellery shops and sari showrooms. If you are looking for Travancore saris and dress material, try **Kasavukada** (Tel: 0481-2566840) in Arafa Towers, west of Thirunakkara Temple. Peep into any of the jewellery shops like **Allapatt** (Tel: 2567850), **Alukka's** (Tel: 2300611/ 13) and **Bhima**, if not to buy then just to give yourself an idea of the Malayali's love for the yellow metal. Other places

Choose from our network of over 4000 hotels in India. Serviced apartments, budget hotels, luxury resorts, palaces, business accomodations, houseboats and more.

Hotel	Rating
Chamundi Hill Palace	Budget
Pearl Regency	3 ★
The Windsor Castle	3 ★

MTNL/BSNL Toll Free No.
1-800-22-4878
022-4030-4878
www.travelguru.com

India's Largest Hotel Network

KERALA

to visit are **Seemati** (Tel: 2563396) on MG Road; they have a special showroom called Temple of Silk; **Narmada** (Tel: 2564583), **Parthas** (Tel: 2563796) and **Pulimmootil Silk House** (Tel: 2563295), on MG Road are also excellent places to pick up typical gold-bordered, cream-coloured Kerala saris.

If you are a collector of antique items, a small shop tucked away on the highway in Kodimatha is just the right stop. Its modest setting hides a wealth of artefacts from all over Kerala. Pick up old lamps, Chinese pickle jars and lamp shades.

WHERE TO STAY

There are plenty of hotels to choose from in Kottayam, though most prefer to make Kumarakom their base. There are many stay options available within town and afar by the Vembanad.

Akkara House (Tel: 0481-2516951; Tariff: Rs 2,750-3,750) is a homestay in a traditional Syrian Christian mansion set on a few acres by the Meenachil River, a few kilometres away from Kottayam. You will need a boat to get to your room here. Akarra Home has three spacious rooms, overlooking the central courtyard, which has steps leading down to the river. You can take cruises upriver to Aymenem, visit a rubber plantation and Kumarakom, and dine on traditional Syrian Christian cuisine.

Also outside Kottayam is **Serenity** (Tel: 2456353; Tariff: Rs 9,807), a private villa hotel at Kanam Estate, surrounded by rubber estates and spice gardens. Set in a 1920s-built estate bungalow, Serenity offers a regal plantation experience, with private verandahs for each room, and a gorgeous swimming pool.

The Windsor Castle (Tel: 2363637-38; Tariff: Rs 3,000-4,500) on the banks of Vembanad Lake has rooms done in modern and traditional style. The Lake Village, as the traditional complex is called, has lake-facing rooms designed like traditional Kerala *illam* and *tharavadu* homes. Boating, fishing and Ayurveda are added pluses.

Vembanad Lake Resort (Tel: 2361633, 2360866; Tariff: Rs 500), next door to Windsor, has cottages facing the waters. Their restaurant Chakara serves fresh catch from the lake. Houseboat and speedboat cruises are also organised by the resort.

Prime location and great food are two major pluses if you choose **Anjali**

→ GETTING THERE

Air Nearest airport: Cochin International Airport, Nedumbassery (91 km/ 2 hrs; Tel: 0484-2610115), connected to Chennai by six daily flights by Paramount Airways, Kingfisher Airlines, Jet Airways and Air Deccan. Pre-paid taxi to Kottayam is Rs 1,500

Rail Kottayam Station (Tel: 0481-2562933, 2563535) **Best option TO** Trivandrum Mail (dep: Chennai Central 8 pm; arr: Kottayam 8.05 am **Best option FROM** Chennai Mail (dep: Kottayam 5.35 pm; arr: Avadi 6.09 am, Perambur 6.24 am, Chennai Central 7 am)

TIP Alleppey Express is also a good option to Kottayam

Car This long drive across the breadth of Tamil Nadu and Kerala from the east coast to the west cannot be attempted on a weekend break. Stick to the excellent train connections. For longer vacations, follow NH45 past Chengalpattu, Tindivanam, Viluppuram, Ulundurpettai, Trichy, Manapparai, Dindigul and Vattalkundu to Theni. Follow NH220 south over the ghats to Vandiperiyar via Uttamapalaiyam, Kilgudalur and Thekkady. Continue west along the state highway to Kottayam via Peermade, Kanjirapally and Pambadi

Park (Tel: 2563661; Tariff: Rs 700-1,250) on KK Road. All the major shops, the market and the Thirunakkara temple are a few paces away. **Pearl Regency** (Tel: 2561123-25; Tariff: Rs 1,200-4,500) in TB Junction is a fairly new hotel of the luxury kind and one of the best. Apart from suites, executive and standard rooms they also have apartments, all classy and comfortable. **Homestead Hotel** (Tel: 2560467, 2562346; Tariff: Rs 317-1,438) is bang in the heart of the town, opposite the Malayala Manorama office. Clean rooms and the adjoining restaurants serving great North Indian and South Indian food makes it perfect for the budget traveller. **Hotel Aida** (Tel: 2560467; Tariff: Rs 350-1,300), an old Kottayam establishment on MC Road with a rooftop restaurant and bar, offers quality service. **Paradise Resorts** (Tel: 2524983/ 721; Tariff: Rs 3,250) near the Nazareth Church has the Oottupura Restaurant and a travel desk.

For more hotels and details, see Kottayam Accommodation Listings on page 505

WHERE TO EAT

Kottayam's Syrian Christian connections have endowed a distinct flavour to its cuisine as well. Churuttu, Kozhalappam, Meen Mappas, vella appam, Kodampulli meen curry are signature Kottayam. Spices and kodumpulli (fish tamarind) are the chief ingredients and if you are not inclined towards spicy food, do caution the chefs in advance. **Karumpumkala** (Tel: 2434864) the oldest family-run restaurant on the Changannassery-Kottayam route is famous for its seafood specialities served hot and spicy, the way the locals like it. Tiger prawns, crabs and oysters are also a good choice. Try the deadly combo of kappa (tapioca) and karimeen (pearlspot) washed down with kallu (toddy) at **Vyshali Restaurant** (Tel: 2360486) in Manipuzha or their special-fried frog legs for the adventurous. You can pick up savouries like *churuttu* and *kozhalappam* from **Anne's Bakery** at Bakery Junction and their famous wheat halwa. **Best Bakery** (Tel: 2561604), opposite the Collectorate is another place to buy Syrian Christian snacks.

The restaurant at **Anjali Hotel** (Tel: 2563661) on KK Road serves Chinese and Kerala items. Their karimeen mappas, avial and other local delicacies are as good as home made. **Meenachil Restaurant** in the Homestead Hotel (Tel: 2560467) on KK Road and its sister concern **Thali** in the same complex offers decent North and South Indian fare (Tel: 2560467). The

Kottayam's specialities: Meen mapas with idiappam and meen korma (below)

Race Blind for The Best Adventures
…..Talking about your Holidays at Kerala

WE OFFER:

- Yachting
- Gliding
- River Rafting
- Rock Climbing
- Kayaking
- Wildlife Trekking
- Cliff Camps
- Tree House Stays

GSR TOURS
Great Southern Revelation Tours Pvt. Ltd.

Your Holiday Maker

86, TOOTING HIGH STREET, LONDON, SW17ORN
Tel: 004420 86820969, Fax: 004420 87673462
E-mail: gsrlon@gmail.com

BMRA 2A, BALAKRISHNA MENON ROAD,
EDAPPALLY, COCHIN - 680 024, KERALA, INDIA.
T: 0091 999 5436009
0091 989 5889708
0091 938 7162761
gsrtours@gmail.com
www.gsrtours.com

P.O. BOX - 25152, MUSAFA ROAD, ABUDHABI, UAE
Tel: 00971 25525061, Mob: 00971 506169150
E-mail: gsruae@gmail.com

INDIA — UAE — UK

KERALA

The old and new faces of Kottayam — a town rich for discoveries

Vembanad Lake Resort's (Tel: 2361633) **Chakara Restaurant** serves Continental, Indian and North Indian cuisine, the treat being the fresh catch from the Vembanad cooked the Kottayam way.

AROUND KOTTAYAM

Mannanam (11 km N)
A drive up the Mannanam hillock is worth the effort just for the breathtaking view of Kottayam. Besides being associated with the Blessed Father Chavara (credited with miracle cures), Mannanam is the seat of the first seminary of the Malabar Church (1833), the first Catholic Sanskrit School in Kerala (1846), the first printing press (the CMS Press started by Rev Benjamin Bailey in 1846) in Kerala, the first Catholic English School (1846), and the first daily newspaper in Malayalam, the *Deepika* (1887).

The 19th century **St Joseph's Church** in Mannanam has been renovated many times, but it retains its original altar, adorned with gold filigree work and paintings said to have been executed by Tamilian artists. To the right of the church is the old Sanskrit school, now a small **museum** showcasing a printing press and church memorabilia. The most brilliant repertory of church history is preserved at the **Chavara Art Museum** nearby. Take the Medical College Road out of Kottayam for Mannanam.
♦**Timings** 6 am-7.30 pm **Tel** 2598350

Ettumanur (12 km N)
The **Shiva Temple** here is the most important of the three big Shiva temples in Kottayam District. An inscription at the base of the main shrine says the repairs and consecration ceremony were held in 1545. The gopuram has mural paintings, most of which are hidden under layers of whitewash. Look out for the big brass lamp facing the shrine. Its central shrine is circular in shape and surmounted by a conical roof. The shrine is adorned with **intricate woodwork** depicting scenes from Hindu mythology.
♦**Location** On Vaikom Road **Timings** 5 am-noon and 5-8 pm **Cameras** Still Rs 50, video Rs 100 **Tel** 0481-2537675

Nature holds forth the secret
of life in her hands, knowing that
only the wise will reach out.

Coconut Lagoon, beside the fertile banks of the breathtakingly beautiful Vembanad Lake in Kumarakom, celebrates the simple joys of life. Here, in the midst of the backwaters and the never-ending lake, stands a tile-and-timber mansion, a typical traditional Kerala tharavad, painstakingly transplanted and restored. An architectural marvel, this homestead exudes the charm of the Kerala life of yore. And transports one back in time to a world of peace and contentment.

Coconut Lagoon
a cgh earth experience

STARK.Tvm.3328

Central Reservations: Casino Building Cochin Kerala India Phone: +91-484-3011711 Fax: 2668001
Email: contact@cghearth.com **www.cghearth.com**

KERALA

The unique roofless sreekovil of the 800-year-old Saraswati Temple, Panachikkad

Panachikkad Temple (13 km S)
En route to Changanassery, ensconced within a grove of greenery, lies a temple dedicated to Saraswati, the goddess of knowledge. The deity here is housed in a sunken tank-like structure, open to the sky, surrounded by a rare species of creepers and a pond that is fed by tiny channels of perennial springs. The old idol is hidden behind a maze of leaves. The shrine is believed to be more than 800 years old. Adjoining this is another wooded grove that hides an unusual idol of Yakshi. A temple dedicated to Vishnu, said to date to the 1st century CE, is also situated within this unusual setting.
♦**Puja timings** 5.30-10.30 am, 5-7.30 pm **Tel** 2330670

Changanassery (18 km S)
The name Changanassery goes back to the 12th century, when a Thekkumkur raja, Udaya Mathanda Varma, built a temple, a church and a mosque equidistant from each other, to hear the sound of the *shanghu* (conch), the *natham* (chime of the church bells) and the *sseri* (muezzin's call) every morning. The rituals and festivals of the temple, church and mosque are still inter-linked. The three houses of worship are all within walking distance of each other.

The **Kavil Bhagwati Temple** with its gopuram and gold-plated flagstaff, venerates Goddess Kali. The idol, adorned with gold jewellery and shimmering in the nebulous light of oil lamps, is a glorious sight.
♦**Entry** Free **Timings** 5-10 am, 5-8 pm

At the **St Mary's Metropolitan Cathedral**, look for the beautiful green and gold altar and an old traditional hanging lamp. The cathedral welcomes annual processions from the mosque and the temple.
♦**Timings** 5.30 am-8 pm **Tel** 2420048

The **Pazhayapalli Mosque** completes the perfect picture of religious amity. Sadly, nothing much is left of the old structure except a maqbara.
♦**Timings** 5.30 am-8.30 pm **Tel** 2421786
TIP Only men may enter ■

KERALA

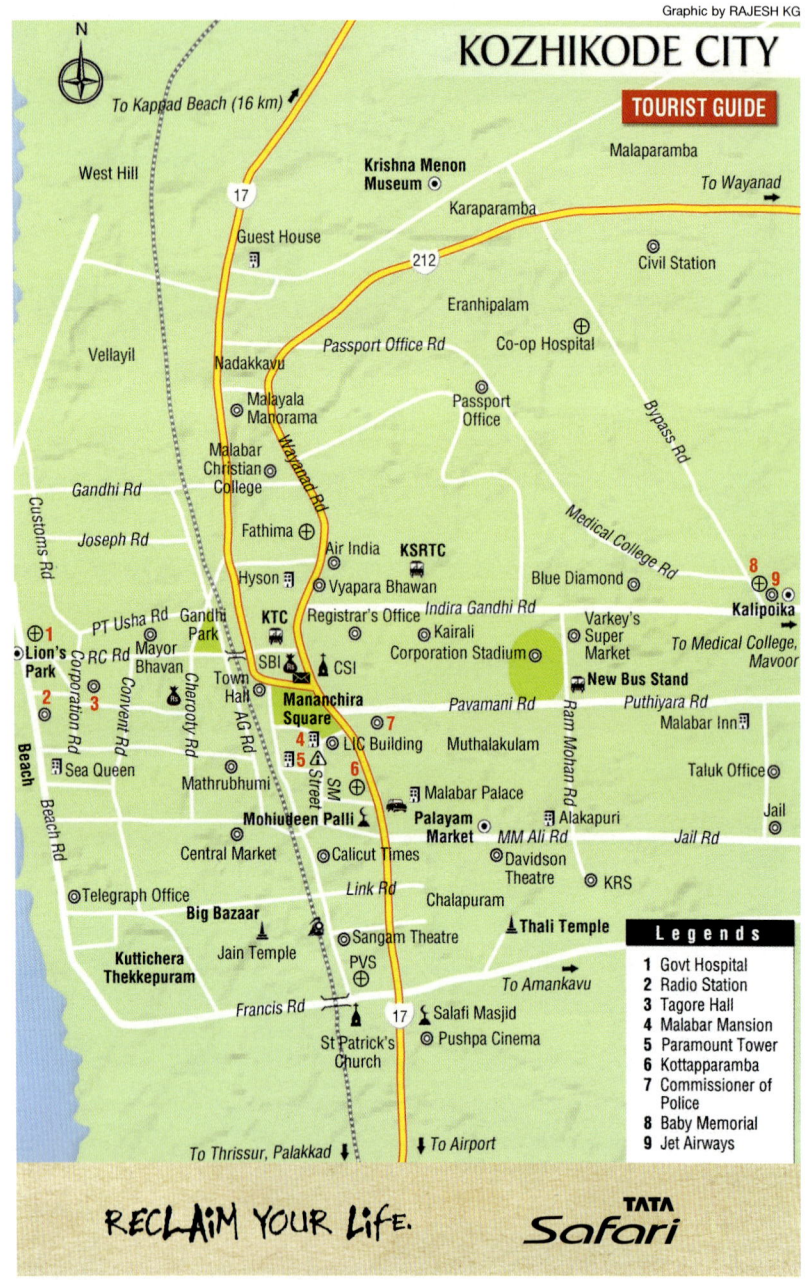

Historic Kappad Beach, where the Portuguese first landed in India

KOZHIKODE
HARBOUR OF HONESTY

State Kerala
Location The greatest port of Malabar is on the southern Malabar Coast, between the backwaters of Kallai and Beypore rivers
Distance 707 km SW of Chennai JOURNEY TIME *By rail* 11½ hrs *By air* 1 hr + ¾ hr by road
Route NH45 to Ulundurpettai via Tambaram, Chengalpattu, Tindivanam, Vikravandi and Viluppuram; NH68 to Salem via Tiyagai Durgam, Kallakkurichi, Talaivasal, Attur and Valappadi; NH47 to Palakkad via Bhavani, Perundurai, Avanashi and Coimbatore; NH213 to Kozhikode via Mannarkkad and Malappuram (*see route guides on pages 12 and 320*)

■ BY NP HAFIZ MOHAMAD

Once upon a time, two Arab princes from Muskeeyat (possibly today's Muscat) set out in search of a place to establish trade links. At each port where the royal yacht moored, they left behind three jars of date pickle for safekeeping, saying they would collect it on their way back. On their return, a few months later, they went back to each port to reclaim what they had left behind. The jars were full of date pickle, but sans the gold coins the princes had hid in one of the three.

Eventually, they reached a most remote port where they had dropped in earlier. Here, they were surprised to find their three jars intact and the gold coins untouched. Impressed by the honesty of the inhabitants, the Arab princes dropped anchor. That port, which came to be known across the seas as the Harbour of Honesty, was Kozhikode.

KERALA

Is the story myth or fact? Perhaps you would ponder over it before you visit the lovely city, before you trip over the aroma of sweetmeats in Mithai Theruvu, or spot the playful dolphins in the sea off Dolphin Point. But once here, it's impossible to dwell too much on sieving fact from fiction. For, there are a thousand flavours to relish, not the least the delectable Kozhikodan halwa, as many heady fragrances to inhale, and memories to savour over time, perhaps in another place, another year.

Here, the whiff of history is too powerful to ignore, and in fact, it would be rather unwise to discount it. After all, it's only in Kozhikode that the beach will pull back to reveal a tale about Vasco da Gama's famous voyage from Lisbon. He reached Kappad in 1498, and his meeting with the Samuthiri (Zamorins, the rulers of Kozhikode) is something that film dialogues are made of. Gama was surprised to discover that the unquestionably rich king was a simple man, dressed only in a *mundu* and shawl. The explorer, resplendent in his admiral attire, is said to have exclaimed: "Is this the famous Zamorin, the ruler of a great land?"

It's likely that you'll marvel along similar lines while walking around today's Kozhikode. There are the shopping complexes and the gigantic hoardings of movies that seek to move you to tears, and gleaming concrete houses congenially sharing breathing space with red-roofed old homes. There is very little to suggest that this land was once a major trading centre, that the scent of its spices drew people from across the globe, including the chroniclers of that time — Al-Barooni, Abdur Razaq, Ibn Batuta. Their records say that in the 'Kulifa' or 'Kalikoot' of yore, as many as 200 yachts could be found moored in the harbour at one time.

Over time, all that changed. The Samuthiri fell out with the Portuguese, prompting a violent sea battle in which the latter sided with the Kochi king. Then came the Dutch, the French and the British, all of whom fought over the prize catch that was Kozhikode.

Thankfully, the only invaders now are those hoping to catch a glimpse of Kozhikode's past, and they do find it, even if it's juxtaposed against the sometimes chaotic present. The ancient bridge standing next to the sea defines today's Kozhikode remarkably well. There it stands, dilapidated, somewhat forlorn, not a brick harking back to its past as a welcoming motif for tired seafarers. There are no dazzling yachts moored in the harbour, but glancing at the pretty fishing boats bobbing in the waves, it's impossible to imagine that something is missing.

→ FAST FACTS

When to go September to February is the best time. Kozhikode is battered by the monsoon rains, but this is the time for treatments at the excellent Ayurveda centres. A visit during Ramzan will be an unforgettable experience for a foodie

Tourist offices
- Dist. Tourism Promotion Council ❶ ⓑ
Mananchira Square
Kozhikode Tel: 0495-2720012
- Dist. Tourism Promotion Council ❶ ⓑ
Tourist Information Counters
Kozhikode Railway StationTel: 0495-2702606; Karipur Airport
Tel: 0483-2712762
- Dept of Tourism, Govt of Kerala ❶ ⓑ
Tourism Complex, Wallajah Road,
Chennai. Tel: 044-25369789
- KTDC Tourist Reception Centre ❶ ⓑ
TTDC Complex, 2, Wallajah Road
Chennai. Telefax: 044-25382639
Website: ktdc.com
STD code 0495

KOZHIKODE

Prayer time at the Jama'atpalli Mosque near Mananchira Square

ORIENTATION

The city was built with the Samuthiri's residence and fort as its central point. The Manavikraman Chira, built by the Samuthiri, is now known as the **Mananchira Square** and the city grew around it. Most of its attractions, such as the **Mishkaal Mosque** and the **Thali Temple**, are to be found near the square. Remnants of the old trading centre are in the **Palayam Market**, the **Mithai Theruvu** (literally, Sweet Meat Street), and in the markets adjacent to the Thali Temple. Kozhikode's southern boundary is the Kallai River. The hills of Wayanad loom on the eastern horizon. All the rivers that flow through Kozhikode, the Korapuzha, Kallar and Ferokepuzha, spring from these hills.

THINGS TO SEE AND DO

Mananchira Square

Located in the heart of the city, this square wraps around **Mananchira Tank**, which was originally the private bath of the Samuthiris. Along with two adjoining gardens, it makes a pretty picture. The **Commonwealth Trust Factory** (Comtrust), the **Town Hall** and the **Public Library** were set up around the tank later.

The **Lalitha Kala Academy Hall** hosts many art exhibitions by artists from Kozhikode. The **CSI Church**, the renovated **Pattalam Mosque** and the 500-year-old **Commonwealth Spinning Mill** are just some of the other important landmarks that dot the square. **Kuttichera**, an old Mapilla settlement where the **Mishkaal Mosque** is located, is nearby.

Visit the **Kuttichera Tank**, considered sacred by both Muslims and Hindus, as well as the 14th century mosque, **Jama'atpalli**, which is said to have the largest floor area of all the mosques in Kerala. Also nearby is **Mucchandipalli**, the oldest mosque in Kozhikode, built on land donated by the Samuthiri Raja in the 13th century. Don't miss its lovely ceiling.

KERALA

Kozhikode Beach, with its Lion's Park and marine aquarium, offers lots of timepass

Sweet Meat Street

This street, the famous Mithai Theruvu, which got its name from a sweet that Calicut is famous for, starts from Mananchira Square. Available in popular colours of red, yellow, green and black, this sweet is the Kozhikodan halwa. Kozhikodan's amazing fried and roasted banana chips are also available here.

The Palayam Market

Once occupied by the armed forces of the Samuthiris, the Palayam Market is today a very busy place, with crowds thronging the local bus stand and the vegetable market. Nearby is the **Mohiudeen Mosque**, which is the only mosque in Kerala with a closed circuit TV to enable the Imam to preach to the entire congregation, spread out over different storeys of the mosque, at the same time.

Valiya Angadi

In the 'big bazaar', located between the beach and the town, you can get a taste of the age-old fish trade of Kozhikode. The whole place is usually a picture of chaos and confusion with hand-pulled carts, trucks, lorries and vehicles of all shapes and dimensions vying with each other for docking place to load and unload tonnes of fish. Here, wholesale trading of fresh, salted and preserved fish is conducted as it has been for centuries.

Thali Temple

A temple built by the Samuthiris, this was the venue for the famous **Revathi Pattathanam** function, in which exponents of various arts exhibited their talents in front of the Samuthiri. The temple is still a thriving place of worship (only Hindus are allowed inside). Adjoining the temple is the old *kovilakam* of the Samuthiris, which is now the Samuthiri School.

♦**Timings** 5-11 am, 5-8.30 pm **Main festival** 8-day Utsavam from April 13-20

Valayanad Devi Temple

This hilltop Parvati temple was built by the Samuthiris. The Mankavu and Thiruvannoor *kovilakams* nearby reflect the architecture of that period, with a central courtyard and heavy woodwork.

♦**Location** In Govindapuram, 3 km from Calicut on the Mankavu Road **Timings** 5 am-10 pm, 4-8 pm

Kozhikode Beach

A walk along Kozhikode Beach, with the sea breeze in your face, is a special experience. Try the seafood delicacies such as *kallumakaya* (mussels) available on the beach at numerous stalls. There's a **Lion's Park** with a play area for children. Stand at the tip of the old bridge over the breaking waves, and one may even spot a dolphin or two far out in the sea (this is also called Dolphin Point). There's a **marine aquarium** nearby.

◆**Park timings** 4-8 pm **Aquarium entry fee** Adults Rs 5, children Rs 3 **Timings** 8 am-8 pm

Regional Science Centre

Kozhikode has a **planetarium**, and a **science park**, both in the same complex. Huge working models of bisects are among the nearly 50 exhibits at the science park that are a great hit with kids. The **aquarium** is also popular. The complex also boasts a **3D-theatre**.

◆**Location** Opp New Mofussil Bus Stand on Indira Gandhi (Mavoor) Road **Entry fee** Rs 5 **Timings** 10.30 am-6.30 pm **Planetarium show fee** Rs 15 **Planetarium show timings** Noon, 2, 4 and 6 pm **3D show timings** 11 am, 1, 3 and 5 pm **Tel** 2770571

Pazhassi Raja Museum

The Pazhassi Raja Museum exhibits wall paintings, antique handicrafts, old coins, models of temples, megalithic dolmonoid cysts and *kodakallu* (umbrella stones). Some paintings of the extremely talented artist Ravi Varma are displayed at the **VK Krishna Menon Art Gallery** nearby.

◆**Location** East Hill, 6 km from Kozhikode **Entry fee** Adults Rs 10, children Rs 5 **Cameras** Still Rs 25, video Rs 200 **Timings** 9 am-4.30 pm **Tel** 2384382

TIP Pictures can only be taken from outside and not in the gallery or museum

Kirtads

The Kerala Institute of Research and Development of Scheduled Tribes and Castes is an adivasi study centre situated in Chevayur, $9^1/_2$ km from Kozhikode. There is a **library** dedicated to literature on adivasis here and a **museum**.

◆**Location** Chevayur is on NH212 towards Kalpetta. Kirtads is $1^1/_2$ km from Chevayur **Timings** 10.15 am-5.30 pm, public holidays, Sundays and second Saturdays closed **Tel** 2357329, 2356805

CVN Kalari Sangam

Kerala's ancient martial art form Kalaripayattu has close links with Kozhikode. Apart from the Kalari centres here, the brave hero of the *Vadakkan Veera Gatha* (Folktales of the North), Thacholi Othenan, is said to have been born in Vadakara (45 km from Kozhikode). CVN Kalari Sangam (Tel: 04950-

Choose from our network of over 4000 hotels in India. Serviced apartments, budget hotels, luxury resorts, palaces, business accommodations, houseboats and more.

1-800-22-4878
022-4030-4878
www.travelguru.com

India's Largest Hotel Network

2769114), which has a legendary position because of the remarkable Kalari fighters who have come out of its portals, arranges special demonstrations on request. The centre is in Nadakkavu.
♦**Timings** 6-9 pm and 4.30-7.30 pm for martial art classes and demonstrations **Treatment timings** 7.30 am-1 pm

Kallai

Originating from the Western Ghats and ending in the Arabian Sea, the River Kallai is famous for its timber business, and many sawmills are to be found on its banks. Often, you will spot logs tied together like rafts meandering on the river, sent down from the forests of Nilambur in the Western Ghats of neighbouring Mallapuram District. This economical transport option is the main reason for the flourishing timber trade. Visit it just to stand on the bridge across the Kallai, and to enjoy the panoramic view of the river meeting the Arabian Sea. Sunsets are particularly beautiful.

Kappad Beach

A moss-covered monument marks Vasco da Gama's arrival here on May 18, 1498. It was here that da Gama's envoy was astonished to be addressed in Castilian by a man from Seville, who had become a Kozhikodan Muslim. What were the Portuguese doing here, enquired he. And the envoy famously replied: "We seek Christians and spices."

The legendary beach is a nice picnic spot, 16 km from the city.

Elathur

This place is north of Kappad, located where the Korapuzha River meets the Arabian Sea. You can hire a country boat for a ride on the river. Shellfish and *kallumakaya* are abundant on the rocks jutting out to the sea.
♦**Location** 20 km from Kozhikode, just north of Kappad

GETTING THERE

Air Nearest airport: Karipur Airport (26 km/ $^3/_4$ hr; Tel: 0483-2711314), connected to Chennai by a daily Indian Airlines flight. Pre-paid taxi into Kozhikode costs Rs 350 from the airport
Rail Kozhikode Station **Best option TO** Mangalore Mail (dep: Chennai Central 8.15 pm; arr: Kozhikode 7.45 am) **Best option FROM** Chennai Mail (dep: Kozhikode 5.30 pm; arr: Chennai Central 5.25)
Car A drive across the southern peninsula from Chennai to Kozhikode is beautiful but cannot be attempted on a weekend break. Stick to the excellent train connections for a weekender. For longer vacations, follow NH45 to Ulundurpettai via Tindivanam and Viluppuram. Turn right onto NH68 to Salem via Talaivasal and Attur. At Salem, join NH47 till Palakkad via Bhavani, Avanashi and Coimbatore. Take NH213 across the Palghat Gap to Kozhikode via Mannarkkad and Malappuram

SHOPPING

The very sweet **Kozhikodan halwa**, seasoned with dry fruits and prepared in pure coconut oil, is a much sought after speciality that visitors must carry home. Another speciality is the Kozhikode **banana chips**. Most bakeries stock it, but if you scout around town, you can find many small carts dishing these out straight from the pan.

Visit the **spice market** at Court Road, and the **Chembotti Theruvu** to shop for bell metal artefacts. **Models of urus**, or yachts made of teak, can be bought at Beypore (*see 'Urus of Beypore' on page 392*). Kozhikode was once famous for its **muslin** and **handloom** cloth. Today, you can pick up, among

Get Lost
Where No one's Gonna Know.

www.fringeford.com
email: bookings@fringeford.com
Bangalore: +91 9880086411
Hyderabad: +91 9848159009

KERALA

SAIBAL DAS

Urus of Beypore

For centuries, the coastal town of Beypore has been a famous shipbuilding centre. Its *uru*, the country craft built by traditional shipbuilders known as Khalasis, still has a huge market and continues to attract Middle Eastern buyers from across the Arabian Sea.

You can reach Beypore by taxi or bus from Kozhikode. If you were to get off at the last bus stop, you'd walk past skeletons of huge boats, and junk shops selling rusted, ancient anchors, until you reach the harbour at the mouth of the Chaliyar River. There, under thatched roofs, are large boats (some 65m long and 700 tonnes in weight) being worked on, often by wizened old Khalasis. Amazingly, almost all the work, including rolling the huge beams into place, is done manually. It often takes 50 Khalasis over a year to carve and shape an *uru* out of teak and jackfruit timber. It's then towed to a West Asian port such as Dubai, where it is fitted with a diesel engine.

There's not much activity during the monsoons or when business is dull, so check at your hotel if boat building is happening before you set out for Beypore. Still, you can be sure to catch the town's toy boat maker, who puts little ships of the most intricate designs into bottles. Model boats can also be bought from the **Kairali Emporium** (Tel: 2723753) in Kozhikode. Those made from teak can cost up to Rs 15,000; those from coconut Rs 500.

KG Kumar

other things, traditional cream-and-gold *mundus*.

WHERE TO STAY

Hotel accommodation is available across budgets in Kozhikode. At the upper end is the **Taj Residency** (Tel: 0495-2765354; Tariff: Rs 3,100-6,500), facing the beach on PT Usha Road, with a highly reputed Ayurvedic centre. **Malabar Palace** (Tel: 2721511-17; Tariff: Rs 1,350-3,250) and **Hyson Heritage** (Tel: 2766423; Tariff: Rs 475-3,000) are other high-end hotels providing excellent accommodation and great food. **Fortune Hotel** (Tel: 2768888; Tariff: Rs 1,980-2,970) is another good hotel, which has a Kerala restaurant. Located on the beach is the **Renaissance Cochin Kappad Beach Resort** (Tel: 0496-2688777/ 9192-93; Tariff: Rs 2,000-2,200), with a swimming pool, restaurant, Ayurvedic centre, and a playing area for kids.

An excellent option for genuine Ayurvedic treatment is **Harivihar** (Tel: 2765865; Tariff: Rs 3,560-5,000), a hotel set in the 150-year-old ancestral home of the Kadanathu royal family, now owned by Dr C Kumar and Dr Neeta. Set in a large garden in Bilathikulam, a quiet corner of town, Harivihar offers a range of treatments. There are also evening performances of Kathakali and other dances to be enjoyed.

The **Victorian Beach Heritage Inn** (Tel: 2762055-56; Tariff: Rs 1,700) on Beach Road is a historic hotel. It was built in 1890 as a burra sahib watering hole. Fifty years later, it was converted into a hotel, and has hosted Somerset Maugham, Chester Bowles, Zakir Hussain and Jawaharlal Nehru among others.

Close to Beypore Beach is the **Tasara Centre for Creative Weaving** (Tel: 2414233/ 832; Tariff: Rs 2,500-3,500), which offers weaving, dyeing and printings courses apart from accommodation. Their Weaver Bird Package for 4 days and 3 nights inclusive of

Kerala's best kept secret is now ★★★★★

Winner of 32nd Trade Leaders Club International award Madrid, Spain

KADAVU RESORT & AYURVEDA CENTRE

N.H 17 Calicut By-Pass Road, P.O. Feroke College
Calicut - 673 632, Kerala, India
Tel: +91 483 2830023, 027, 570
Fax: +91 483 2830575
E-mail: sales@kadavuresorts.com
Website: www.kadavuresorts.com
www.kadavuayurvedaresort.com

KERALA

Interiors of a traditional Malabar Muslim house in Kuttichera

meals, costs Rs 9,000. You can learn weaving, printing and dyeing at this centre, set up by the Vadakkiniyedath family in 1979 to preserve this lesser-known craft heritage of Beypore.

Reliable mid-range options include **Asma Tower** (Tel: 2723560; Tariff: Rs 375-1,035) on Mavoor Road, **Calicut Tower** (Tel: 2723202; Tariff: Rs 375-1,035) in the Markaz Complex on Indira Gandhi Road, **Hotel Maharani** (Tel: 2723101; Tariff: Rs 400-1,700) and **Hotel Alkapuri** (Tel: 2723451-54; Tariff: Rs 150-1,000). Kerala Tourism's **Malabar Mansion** (Tel: 27223911; Tariff: Rs 275-385) is situated in the centre of the city, and has great accommodation and food.

Kadavu Resorts (Tel: 0483-2830570/023; Tariff: Rs 4,000-6,900) is beautifully located by the green banks of the Chaliyar River, 19 km south of Kozhikode. It boasts a Green Leaf-certified Ayurveda centre.

For more hotels and details, see Kozhikode Accommodation Listings on pages 505-506

WHERE TO EAT

Of all the regional cuisines of India, perhaps the mention of the cuisine of the Malabar Coast excites the maximum palates, and with good reason. Even as Calicut Port contributed the wealth of Kerala spices to the world, traders from the far seas left their own indelible influences on Kozhikodan kitchens. The Arab influence is particularly of note.

Kozhikode offers a variety of cuisines, from the simple vegetarian to the meat-heavy, spicy dishes. And you just have to try *kallumakaya porichathu* (mussels fry, had with rice) and *pathal* (a ring-shaped rice *pathiri*).

The **Taj Residency** (Tel: 0495-2765354) has a multi-cuisine restaurant. The **Hyson Heritage** (Tel: 2766423) offers special dishes such as *neriya pathiri*, tissue paper-like rice chappatis and all types of biryanis. **Fortune Hotel** (Tel: 2768888) has a restaurant called **Tharavad**, which offers many Keralite dishes such as *kanji* (rice-soup), *kappa varuthathu* (tapioca

fried), *meen molakittathu* (a hot fish curry), and a splendid Kerala meal for lunch with more than 18 dishes served on a banana leaf.

Don't neglect to taste Malabar biryani in Malabar, for this is the only region in Kerala that serves biryani during Onam. In almost all non-vegetarian restaurants in Kozhikode, you will get Kozhikodan chicken or mutton biryani, which is very different from the North Indian or Hyderabadi biryani. A place where you can enjoy a proper Malabar-style chicken or mutton biryani, and beef curry with Malabar *porotta*, is **Sagar Hotel**, near the KSRTC Bus Stand. Sagar's new **branch**, a little further down the road, is more spacious and comfortable. **Bombay Hotel** (Tel: 2366730; 7 am-midnight), near St Joseph's Boys High School, and **Hotel Alkapuri** (Tel: 2723451-54) are old establishments famous for their biryani and chicken fry.

But to really enjoy Kozhikodan-style food, one has to go to **Zain's**, a restaurant run by a Kuttichera Muslim lady. Here you will get *puttu* with local fish stew, or wheat *pathiri*, a Kuttichera special, served with *kozhi nirthiporichathu*, a chicken fry with egg or *kada* (a small bird) fry. Kuttichira ghee rice is famous, best had with a mellow beef stew prepared in coconut milk. The sweet meats of the Muslims of Kozhikode are legendary. These include *chattippathiri, mutta marichathu, muttappathiri, muttamala, mutta surkka* — all prepared with eggs. Kozhikodan *pazham nirachathu* (banana fry with coconut) and sweet coconut samosa or *bayakkada* (made of banana) are also available in Zain's.

Rahmath Hotel on KP Kesava Menon Road is famous for its *beef varattiyathu* with *porotta*. **Paragon Restaurant** (Tel: 2761020; 9 am-11.30 pm) near Head Post Office is the best choice for fish, especially fried prawns or prawn curry accompanied by *vellapam*. For tiffin, try **Woodlands Restaurant** on Kallai Road, **Dakshin the Veg** (Tel: 2722648) on Indira Gandhi Road, near the KSRTC Bus Stand, and **Vasantha Bhavan** on Court Road.

Parippu vadas near Mananchira Square

PRASHANT PANJIAR

AROUND KOZHIKODE

Thikkodi Light House and Payyoli Beach (30 km)
The lighthouse remains a guiding beacon for many a seafarer. From Kappad itself, you can see the lighthouse silhouetted against the eastern skyline. With prior permission (Tel: 0496-2691064), you can climb up the winding stairs, for a breathtaking view of the Arabian Sea.

Payyoli Beach, just north of Thikkodi, is synonymous with PT Usha, India's most famous sprint queen, who hails from this tiny town. The beach has seen her perfect her sport. Payyoli also shot to international fame because of the conservation endeavours initiated to protect marine turtles here. ■

A journey of a thousand miles begins with a single step.

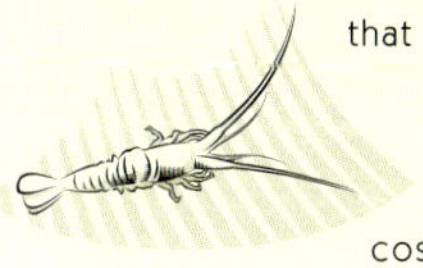

Casino Hotel is where we started our journey - one that took us to discovering ourselves and the world anew. This is where we learnt many of the lessons that guide us today. And perfected many of the experiences that we offer today. Situated in the Willingdon Island of Cochin, the hotel captures the essence of Cochin which is at once cosmopolitan and traditional. And our hotel enables you to travel gracefully between these two worlds - right from the moment you are greeted into the hotel with a traditional welcome - complete with garlands and aarti. This is in fact, our unique way of introducing you to the little surprises that await you. Especially the richness of simple, natural, yet elegant interiors of this hotel, that carry **tradition and modernity** with elan. You'll experience this duality of space and time even in our restaurants and in the fare that is dished out. Which is perhaps why an experience in Casino is so exotic, yet so familiar.

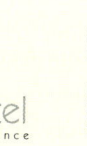

Casino Hotel
a cgh earth experience

Central Reservations: Casino Building Cochin Kerala India Phone: +91-484-3011711 Fax: 2668001
Email: contact@cghearth.com www.cghearth.com

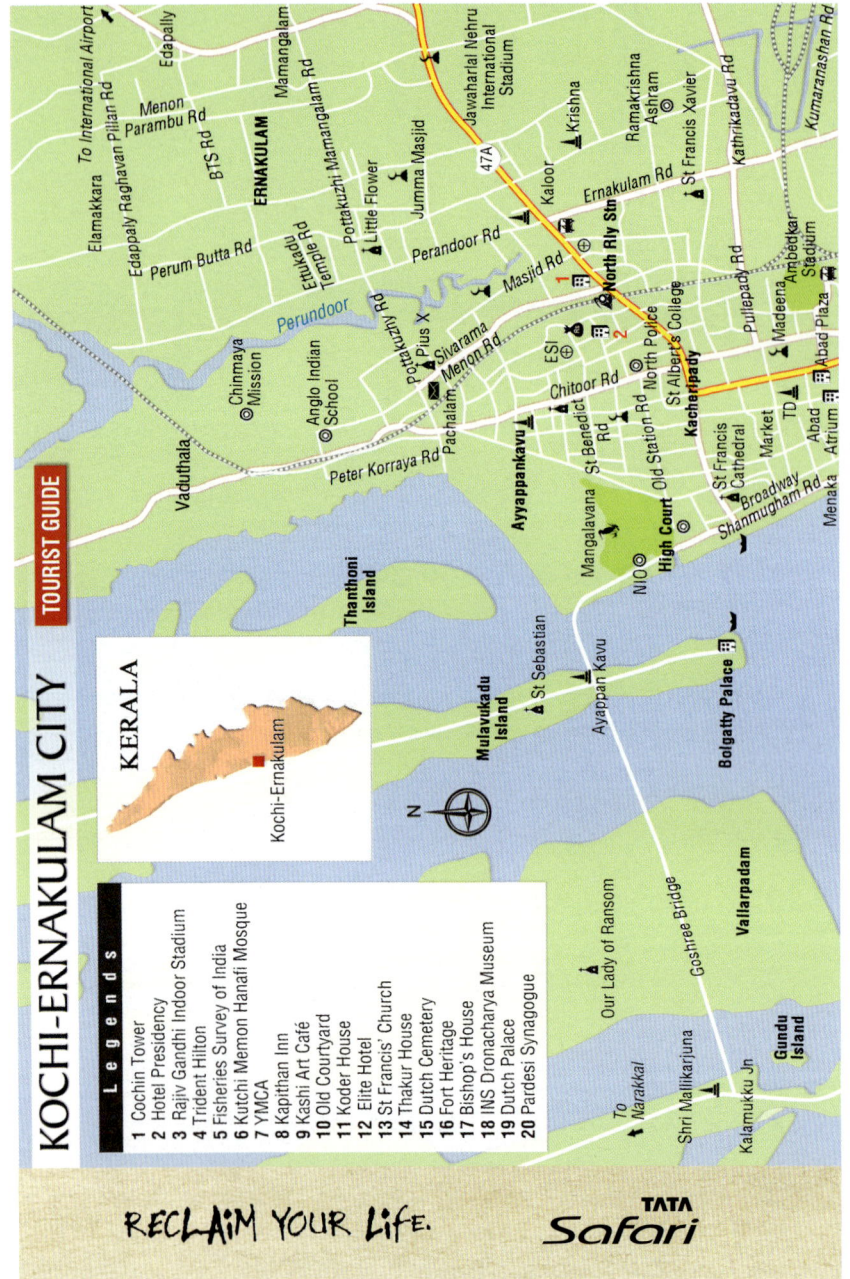

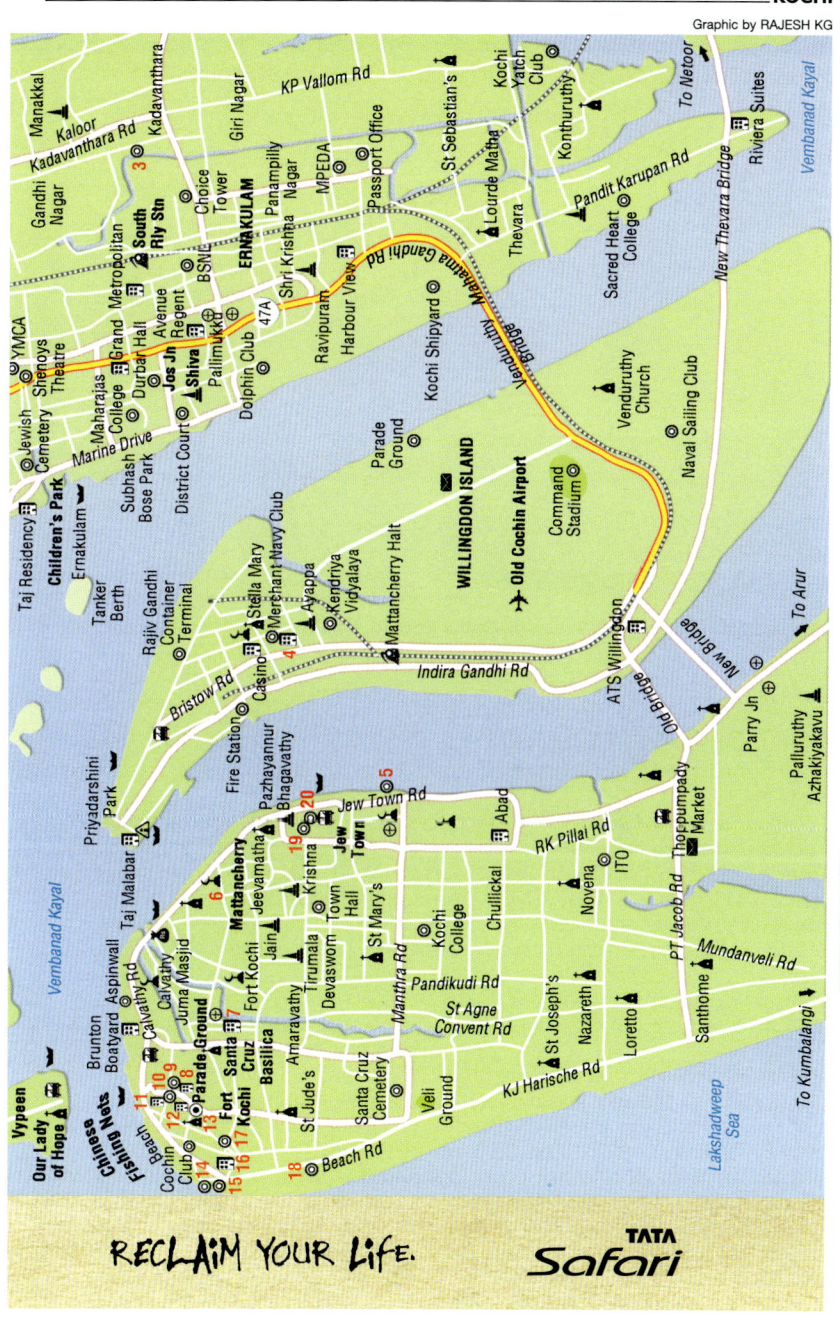

Chinese fishing nets near Vasco da Gama Square, Fort Kochi

KOCHI
PORT OF MANY COLOURS

State Kerala
Location The port of Kochi on the Lakshadweep Sea in Central Kerala, encompasses Fort Kochi and Mattancherry, a few islands in Vembanad Lake and Ernakulam on the mainland
Distance 663 km SW of Chennai **JOURNEY TIME By rail** $10^1/_2$ hrs **By air** 1 hr + $^3/_4$ hr by road
Route NH45 to Theni via Chengalpattu, Tindivanam, Ulundurpettai, Veppur, Trichy, Manapparai, Dindigul and Vattalakundu; NH49 to Kochi via Bodinayakkanur, Devikulam, Munnar, Kothamangalam and Thripunithura (*see route guides on pages 12 and 320*)

■ BY ANIL NAIR AND AMBIKA MENON

Seasoned travellers would agree that landing in the old Kochi airport's tabletop aircraft-carrier-like island-runway always used to feel like a precursor to the excitement of being in Kerala's most cosmopolitan city. That used to be quite a while ago. The civilian airport is now on the outskirts of mainland urbania but it must be said Kochi still welcomes visitors with traditional warmth and contemporary gumption. Constructed with the sloping roof typical of traditional Kerala homes, the new terminal has become an apt metaphor to the city that lies beyond — a self-assured juxtaposition of both the past and the present. The beautiful highway to bustling Ernakulam confirms this enjoyable contradiction.

Till recently, Kochi was Cochin, and only half as frenetic. It was a lagoon that made Kochi a cherished destination as far back as the early-16th century and it is the same lagoon that makes Kochi one of the nation's busiest ports now.

Once upon a time what we see today was little more than a fishing hamlet. It was an eponymous flood that transformed Kochi's destiny by turning it into a natural harbour. The rich aroma of spices and sandalwood drew the Europeans here and they soon wrested the profitable spice trade from Arab merchants. Political ambition propelled business. Soon enough, the Portuguese, the first Europeans to land in Kochi, were even appointing the Thampuran, the Raja of Cochin. The crown could only be had with the blessings of Lisbon and later, thanks to the Dutch invaders, of Holland. The Portuguese and the Dutch eventually had to make way for the British East India Company, which effected supreme control through colonisation. It is to Kochi's credit that the city welcomed, endured, survived and eventually, triumphed over all those who were lured by these undoubtedly bewitching shores. Four centuries ago, Niccolo dei Conti advised fellow-Florentines to make their money in Canton but spend it in Kochi. In today's Kochi, you can do both.

The other defining element in assimilating this city is the symbiotic relationship between land and water that one witnesses here. The best way to discover it is to take a cruise along the *kayal* from Ernakulam to Perumbalam and back, which should take about two hours. Cast off at sunrise and the silence, unbroken but for bird caw, resembles the world at the beginning of time.

The Vembanad *kayal* is home to thousands of fisherfolk. You can see them gliding along in their graceful canoes, wide nets trailing. In the shallows, they can be seen beating the water with palm-leaf switches and then gathering the stunned fish by the armfuls. On the return leg, proceed to the harbour mouth to just wet your keel in the ocean. Between Fort Kochi and Vypeen, the gentle breeze tousles the surface of the water, hinting at what lies beyond.

ORIENTATION

The particular geography of India's most beautiful port affords every traveller a dramatic first approach to Fort Kochi. Driving in from the airport down the Alleppey-Trivandrum highway, you

→ FAST FACTS

When to go Any time of the year
Tourist offices
● Dist Tourism Promotion Council
Old Collectorate Building, Park Avenue Road, Ernakulam. Tel: 0484-2367334
TIP Info Counter for Ernakulam District
● Tourist Information Counter
Department of Tourism, Government of Kerala, Government Guest House, near St Theresa's College, Shanmugham Road, Ernakulam. Tel: 2360502
● Tourist Information Counter
Kochi International Airport, Angamaly Tel: 2610115, ext 2105
● KTDC Tourist Reception Centre
Shanmugham Road, Ernakulam
Tel: 2353234; Fax: 2382199
Email: ktdccok@sancharnet.in
● India Tourism
Government of India Tourist Office, Willingdon Island. Telefax: 2668352
All-India tourist helpline: 1913
● Dept of Tourism, Govt of Kerala
Tourism Complex, 2, Wallajah Road, Chennai. Tel: 044-25369789
● KTDC Tourist Reception Centre
TTDC Complex, 2, Wallajah Road Chennai. Telefax: 044-25382639
Website: ktdc.com
STD code 0484

emerge in busy **Ernakulam**, Kochi's modern counterpart on the Kerala mainland. Massive container ships signal the bridge to **Willingdon Island**, from where you catch the first glimpse of the calm **Vembanad** *kayal* and the first scent of salt in the air. Across the length of the island and down another bridge, you see the palm-shrouded coast of Mattancherry. The peace of the *kayal* is gone now, as the waters move with urgency to their meeting with the **Lakshadweep Sea**. The aroma of salt grows stronger, till it permeates the air of the town beyond the bridge, competing with the aromas emerging from the bakeries of **Thoppumpady Bazaar**, and disappearing briefly in the packed spice markets of **Mattancherry**. Nothing can compete with the aroma of pepper. When the salt gets a decidedly fishy tang, and the streets all of a sudden grow calm, you have reached **Fort Kochi**, where time seems to have stopped.

The pace of life varies from layer to layer in the most-visited destination in Kerala. Transport options between these layers are aplenty. **Ferries** are a cheap way to travel, with some great views thrown in. Ernakulam's **Main Jetty** (for Vypeen, Willingdon Island, Fort Kochi and Vallarpadom) is next to the Children's Park, off Foreshore Road. Another jetty in Ernakulam is near the **High Court** (for Bolgatty) on Shanmugham Road. The **KSRTC Bus Stand** is behind Hotel Luciya, midway between **Ernakulam North** and **Ernakulam South railway stations**.

Two **bridges** built in colonial times link Ernakulam to Mattancherry and Fort Kochi. Bridges of more recent vintage connect Ernakulam to Bolgatty and Vypeen, and to the elegant **bypasses** that ring Greater Kochi all the way to the **international airport**, 26 km away.

Taxis are aplenty, charging Rs 900 per day approx. **Autos** are handy for negotiating the back streets. You can rent a **bicycle** for the quieter districts of Fort Kochi and Mattancherry. Distances in Fort Kochi are short.

GETTING THERE

Air Cochin International Airport, Nedumbassery (34 km/ 3/4 hr, Tel: 0484-2610115), connected to Chennai by six daily flights by Paramount Airways, Kingfisher Airlines, Jet Airways and Air Deccan. Pre-paid taxi to Kochi is Rs 466
Rail Ernakulam North and Ernakulam Town stations, 2-km apart **Best option TO** Trivandrum Mail (dep: Chennai Central 8 pm; arr: Ernakulam Town 6.45 am **Best option FROM** Chennai Mail (dep: Ernakulam Town 7.15 pm; arr: Avadi 6.09 am, Perambur 6.24 am, Chennai Central 7 am)
TIP Alleppey Express and Chennai Express are also good options
Car This long drive across the breadth of Tamil Nadu and Kerala from the east coast to the west should not be attempted on a weekend break. Stick to the excellent train connections. For longer vacations, follow NH45 past Chengalpattu, Tindivanam, Viluppuram, Ulundurpettai, Trichy, Manapparai, Dindigul and Vattalakundu to Theni. Follow NH49 over the Western Ghats to Munnar via Devikulam, then down to Ernakulam via Kothamangalam and Muvattupuzha

THINGS TO SEE AND DO

The richest sightseeing is in the heritage quarter of Fort Kochi and Mattancherry. Spend the evenings, after the monuments close for the day, in the shops and cafés of Ernakulam. Be sure to take a ride in a Kochi ferry, or a longer boat ride from Ernakulam's main jetty to islands in the backwaters like Kothad to the north or Kumbalangi to the south.

There is history at every step on the streets of Fort Kochi

IN FORT KOCHI AND MATTANCHERRY

Fort Kochi has preserved its history well and presents a vivid panorama of a time when traders and warriors landed on her shores. On your first day, it will be difficult to absorb the beauty of Fort Kochi. On my first day I was all but overwhelmed. There is history at every second step here, a homestay in a renovated colonial era villa at every third, and punctuating these are dozens of elegant restaurants and cafés. The distance between the interesting, ancient and famous places in Fort Kochi is short. You can comfortably get everywhere by foot, which is the best way to experience this quarter.

TIP Get yourself a copy of Kerala Tourism's Fort Kochi pamphlet, which has a walking tour map of Fort Kochi and conducted island cruise schedules

The Fort Kochi Bus Stand, on the waterfront, is a good place to get your bearings. All the major sights are in the vicinity. Calvathy Road, on which you stand, curves south all the way around Fort Kochi, past the Chinese fishing nets, Vasco Da Gama Square, the Dutch Cemetery and Fort Kochi Beach. A turn into any of the lanes running south off Calvathy Road takes you into the heart of Fort Kochi. A walking tour must include Koder House, Vasco House, Bastion Bungalow, Bishop's House and Thakur House. Do the inside half from say, 8 to 11 am and the outer half skirting the waterfront from 4-6 pm.

TIP KTDC's **Fort Tour** (Rs 100 per person; 9 am-12.30 pm, 2-5.30 pm; Tel: 0484-2353234) covers prominent structures of the fort such as the Pardesi Synagogue and St Francis' Church

St Francis' Church

The Portuguese traveller and merchant, Pedro Alvarez Cabral, dropped anchor at Kochi in 1500, accompanied by Franciscan and Dominican friars and Jesuit missionaries. Vasco da Gama followed in 1502. He died in 1524 and was interred in St Francis' Church. It's the oldest

European church in India, and its name and form changed with every new coloniser who claimed the land as his own.

In 1503, the church was a wooden chapel of St Bartholomew, built by Franciscan friars. It was rebuilt in stone and re-dedicated to St Anthony in 1516. Restored by the Dutch, it served the Lutherans. In 1795, the British converted it to an Anglican church and gave it its present name.

Conflicting claims assign the church variously to St Francis of Assisi and to St Francis Xavier, who visited Kochi in 1542. Now under the Church of South India, it shelters the original grave of Vasco da Gama. His remains, though, were exhumed and removed to Lisbon.

Of particular interest here are the early 16th century palm leaf deeds of the Thampuran, granting Portuguese *nadhuvazhi* — middle-rung feudal lords — status and rights, and the **Doop Book**, a register of baptisms and marriages, maintained by Catholics till they were replaced by Lutherans.

♦**Entry** Free **Timings** 9.30 am-1 pm, 2-5 pm; Mass on Sundays

TIP Only still cameras, not video, are allowed inside

The Dutch Cemetery

As you emerge from the church, to the left is the Parade Ground, where successive European soldiers conducted drills. Past the ground and down the road is the Dutch Cemetery, where the first grave was laid in 1724. The old tombstones here provide glimpses of Kochi's Dutch past.

TIP Request the caretaker of St Francis Church to have the gates of the Dutch Cemetery opened for you

A 10-min walk towards the beach from the cemetery is the only surviving fortification of the Portuguese — the **Fort Immanuel**. The town grew within the confines of the fort, which was built in 1503 and rebuilt in 1538. The fort was dynamited by the British in 1806. There's not much to see here and the beach is unswimmable, so make the effort only if you have plenty of time.

House hunt

Fort Kochi is dotted with old colonial-style houses, still in good condition. A lovely mansion to gape at is the **Thakur House**, a private property made famous as the home of the protagonists in Ismail Merchant's *Cotton Mary*. Built by the Dutch as a club, the house stands overlooking the sea and is said to have underground passages. To get a good idea of its architectural style, view it from the headland behind the Dutch Cemetery. The gate to the house falls on the road to the cemetery.

Returning to the Parade Ground and continuing down Tower House Road, on your right is a striking bungalow built in 1695 by the Dutch East India Company. Known as **David Hall**, its most famous occupant was Hendrik Adrian van

Church where Vasco da Gama was buried

NAMIT ARORA/ PHOTOINDIA

KOCHI

Tourists take a break between sightseeing at Jew Street, Mattancherry

Rheede, the Dutch Governor of Kochi from 1673 to 1677. Samuel Koder, a Jewish businessman, later bought the house, lending it its present name, **Koder House**, now fabulously restored and run as a heritage hotel.

Walk down the lane, called **Rose Lane**, to the left of Koder House, to get an idea of its architecture. A wooden bridge spanning the lane connects two sections of the house. You'll also see **The Old Courtyard**, once a part of Koder House, also now a heritage hotel.

Next to it is yet another heritage hotel, the **Old Harbour Hotel**. Built over the ruins of a Portuguese hospice in 1808, Old Harbour Hotel acquired the character of a British inn. Once a boat club, it later belonged to Carritt Moran, a tea brokerage company). **Ballard Bungalow** nearby is another heritage home that is now a hotel. At the crossroads stands the old **Pierce Leslie Bungalow**, the erstwhile office of the coffee merchants.

Bastion House is further south of Koder House, next to the Parade Ground. Built in 1667 to guard the harbour, it commands a panoramic view of the sea. Believed to have tunnels, it is now the sub-collector's residence. It stands on the Stomberg Bastion of the old fort, which once supported cannons.

Malabar House, at the southern end of Parade Ground, has a striking Dutch Colonial façade. It was the residence of the Grindlays Bank manager during the British era. The building has been remodelled and converted into a heritage hotel.

From here, turn right and come to the waterfront on Pathalam Road. At the corner of Elphinstone Road is the **Bishop's House**. Its location on a hillock, overlooking the Parade Ground, and its imposing Gothic arches proclaim the eminence of its earlier occupants. Built in 1506 on the Groningen Bastion of Fort Immanuel, the Dutch Governor Van Goens occupied it in 1663. The Diocese of Kochi eventually acquired it for Bishop Dom Jos Ferreira, whose control extended over Sri Lanka, Burma and Malaya. Within its premises is the **Indo-Portuguese Museum**, housing some of the earliest artefacts of the Catholic community of Kerala.

♦**Entry fee** Indians Rs 10, foreigners Rs 25 **Timings** 10.30 am-12.30 pm, 2.30-5 pm; Mondays closed

The Dutch force, considerably smaller than the Portuguese, found it impossible to service the fort and reduced it to a third, taking care, however, to retain the main buildings. To the Dutch goes the credit of Fort Kochi's town plan. Many surviving warehouses, with wide, buttressed walls, are distinctly Dutch.

The emblem of the Dutch East India Company, VOC, is carved on a large wooden gate, called the **VOC Gate**, built in 1740. The gate, on the far crescent of the Parade Ground, watches over the entrance to **Studer Hall**, which once housed Dutch offices.

Walk past the VOC Gate, step in if you like, and venture behind St Francis' Church. You'll get a completely different perspective from this angle and at the crossroads, you'll see two of the three surviving Portuguese residences.

Diagonally opposite, to the right, is **Vasco House**, one of the oldest surviving Portuguese bungalows, believed to have been the home of Vasco da Gama. If you look from the road, only the typical Portuguese staircase is evident through the mullioned windows and balconies. Diagonally to the left is a well-maintained private bungalow from the same era. Turn right at Vasco House and at the next crossroads, turn right again, onto Peter Celli Street. It's the only lane in the Fort Kochi area that houses a third of the old Portuguese colonial residences.

Santa Cruz Basilica

On the right side of Bastion Street stands Santa Cruz Basilica. Built as a church by the Portuguese, Pope Paul IV elevated it to a cathedral in 1558. The British demolished it in 1795 when they seized Fort Kochi. In 1887, a new church was built on the vacant site, commissioned by Bishop Dom Gomez Ferreira. Its Gothic façade with soaring spires is imposing and its interiors are even more impressive. Beautiful paintings on the ceiling recall the Sistine Chapel. In 1984, Pope John Paul II proclaimed it a Basilica. Following the Dutch conquest of Kochi in 1663, most places of worship were turned into warehouses. But this cathedral was spared, the puritanical streak of the Calvinists reined in by the obvious beauty of the church's stained glass and the life-like caryatids watching over the quaint confessional boxes.

♦**Timings** 9 am-1 pm, 3-5 pm **Mass timings** Daily 6 and 7 am and 6 pm (all Malayalam), Saturdays 6 pm (English), Sundays 4.30 pm (English) **Tel** 2215799 **Website** santacruzbasilica.org

Princess Street

In this back street, a few steps from the Basilica and one of the oldest in Fort Kochi, the buildings are all in colonial style, with their peeling pastel, bronze stucco walls and flowerpot-laden windowsills. Starting at the northern end is the now abandoned **Koder Warehouse**, followed by a line of

Princess Street, Fort Kochi

PRASHANT PANJIAR

The Portuguese Santa Cruz Basilica on Bastion Street, Fort Kochi

homestays and boutiques, all set in colonial-era villas. Fort Kochi finds renewal in harmless pastimes, even if it means nothing more than to see and be seen, as on **Loafer's Corner** at Princess Street's southern end.

The Chinese connection

Proof of Chinese influence in Kerala is the huge cantilevered *cheenavalas* or Chinese fishing nets, hung from teakwood and bamboo poles. These can be seen off **Vasco da Gama Square**.

Kublai Khan's traders introduced these nets to the local fisherfolk sometime between 1350 and 1450 AD. Ma Huan, a diplomat accompanying Chinese admiral Cheng Ho (1371-1433), provided the first historical reference to Kochi. He wrote, "The fishermen are tourist-friendly and will happily let you join them. Stalls serve fresh delicious seafood and tender coconuts and a spectacular view of the sunset."

Today, too, you can sample delicious seafood at the 'You buy, I cook' stalls near the Chinese fishing nets.

Mattancherry

Places of worship nestle together in Fort Kochi. Standing peacefully between a synagogue and a church, the **Calvathy Jamaath Mosque** on Calvathy Road, along the waterfront, blends effortlessly with the landscape. Built by Arab traders, it favours the Kerala style of architecture and it's worth going there for the view from the outside, even though visitors are not welcome inside.

Another must-see is **Mattancherry Palace** (1555), gifted by the Portuguese to the Thampuran as a conciliatory gesture after their governor looted Palluruthi Temple in 1542. After the Dutch defeated the Portuguese in the Battle of Mattancherry in 1662, the palace was renovated in Burgher style. Visit it for the incredibly intricate and beautiful murals that adorn the walls. The themes have been picked up from the epics and the murals have been executed in vegetable and mineral dyes. The temple of the tutelary devi of the Kochi Rajas stands in the courtyard.

◆**Entry fee** Rs 2 **Timings** 10 am-5 pm, Fridays closed **Cameras** Not allowed

KERALA

The Jews, who arrived as traders during Solomon's reign, preserved their uniqueness, unlike the Arabs who adopted Indian traditions or the Chinese who left these shores. Only four Jewish families remain in Kochi today, but an enduring motif of their contribution is the **Pardesi Synagogue**. Built in 1567, it was partially destroyed in 1664 when the Portuguese ransacked Jew Town (*see below*). The Dutch rebuilt the synagogue. Its Belgian chandeliers reflect the unique flooring, consisting of hand-painted Cantonese willow pattern tiles, a memorial to the Chinese-Jewish trade. No two tiles have the same design.

The Old Testament scrolls here are believed to be the oldest in the world, as are the stone tablets with Mosaic Laws and Hebrew inscriptions. Of historical interest are the copper plates executed by the Thampuran of Kochi (1565-1601), bestowing land, rights and other powers equivalent to that of *naduvazhis* to Jews.

The **clock tower** built in 1760 has recently been renovated. Three clock faces, one in Hebrew, another in Malayalam and the third with Roman numerals, have been uncovered. It is believed that the fourth, now covered with bricks, was in Arabic.

◆**Entry fee** Rs 2 **Timings** 10 am-1 pm, 3-4 pm; Saturdays and Jewish holidays closed

TIP Only still cameras, and not video, are allowed inside

In the Jewish settlement of Mattancherry, the area around the synagogue (Jew Town) is filled with antique shops and spice trading, though the trade is now handled by the Gujaratis. The **International Pepper Exchange** is close to the synagogue.

IN ERNAKULAM

John Kenneth Galbraith, Kennedy's ambassador to India, famously compared Ernakulam to San Francisco's Oakland. New generation banks and bourses, bars and eateries, boutiques and garment retailers on Ernkulam's arterial **MG Road** reek of contemporary chic.

Many of **Broadway's** buildings retain their sloping roofs and inverted V elevations. Pharmacies rest cheek-by-jowl with plate glass merchants and vegetable wholesalers. There is nothing a shopper can't get here. Fronting Broadway is what was once the city's pride — the

Bolghatty — the oldest existing Dutch palace outside the Netherlands

M BALAN/ SOUTHINDIAPICTURE

KOCHI

Interiors of the 16th century Pardesi Synagogue in Jew Town, Mattancherry

'seventy feet' road — and, beyond it, the backwater. And where the old jetty was all strangled in kelp and faded fish rope, there is now the **Marine Drive promenade**. From here, you can watch the Ernakulam-Vypeen ferry make its slow passage across the *kayal*.

The **Shiva Temple** in Ernakulam is an oasis of calm. The lingam here is said to have been worshipped by Arjuna. Just to the north of the srikovil is a shrine without an idol, representing Shiva as Kirathamoorthy, or forest hermit.

The annual **Ernakulam Utsava** in January is spread over eight days. On the seventh day is **Pakalpooram**, when the deity is taken out in a procession with caparisoned elephants and the Panchavadyam orchestra. It culminates with the famous **Pandimelam** — a percussion extravaganza — and fireworks.

◆**Location** Fore Shore Road **Timings** 3.30-11.30 am, 4-8 pm **Tel** 0484 -2369804 **TIP** Men must not wear lungis and must bare their upper bodies. Mobiles must be switched off inside the temple

ON THE ISLANDS

Along with a few smaller uninhabited islands in its vicinity, Willingdon Island was created artificially by the British with dredged up silt. Together, these islands tether the lagoon to its current channel so that it doesn't seek a shortcut to the sea and turn the city into a swamp.

Willingdon Island

The last trespassers of this land, the British, have also left their mark in the city. They made Kochi their own after reaching an 'understanding' with the Kochi ruler Shakthan Thampuran in 1767. The old offices and warehouses at Willingdon Island reflect the Industrial Revolution of Britain and its ensuing prosperity. Though it continues to be a trading centre and port, the Indian Navy's Southern Naval Command occupies pride of place on the eastern coast of Willingdon Island, with the Cochin Shipyard conveniently just across the water in Ernakulam. The port and Port Trust are on the western shore

KERALA

Jew Town in Mattancherry is the best place to buy antiques and spices

of Willingdon Island, as are wharves and warehouses. Offices of trading companies, many retaining their original names, line the roads.

Bolgatty Palace

Follow narrow village roads down to the tip of Mulavukadu Island to the fabulous Bolgatty Palace. This is the oldest existing Dutch palace outside the Netherlands, built in 1744 by a Dutch trader, later the British Resident's manor and today a Kerala Tourism hotel. The approach by ferry to Bolgatty from the High Court Jetty in Ernakulam affords a panorama that takes in Ernakulam, Willingdon Island, Mattancherry and Vypeen. Have lunch at the Pearl Spot Restaurant here, and take a stroll on the lawns facing the lagoon. Or play a game of golf. Non-members are charged Rs 200 per person for 2 hours.

Vypeen

Vypeen is a long finger pointed into the water — 24 km long and 2.5 km wide — the sea and backwater on either side. The lighthouse at **Ochanthuruthu** offers a panoramic view of Kochi. There is also the **Church of Our Lady of Hope** near the Vypeen jetty, an important pilgrim centre. But most people come to Vypeen to splash around on **Cherai Beach**.

♦**Lighthouse fee** Adults Rs 5, children Rs 3 **Timings** 3-5 pm **Tel** 2205720

SHOPPING

To savour the flavour of Kochi's ancient spice trade, get to the wholesale markets in Mattancherry, where you can also pick up quaint antique items, spices, coffee and tea besides the usual souvenir bric-a-brac. Try **Malabar Spices Shop** or **RK Spices** in Mattancherry for black pepper, dry ginger, red chilli and galangal root. Look out for furniture shops that produce a variety of rosewood reclining chairs and tables and ship these anywhere in the world.

MG Road in Ernakulam is where the chic branded shops are located. This is the place to shop for gold. **AKP Metals &**

Alloys (Tel: 2361298) on Broadway has bronze and bell metal *urlis* for Rs 430 upwards, per kg. For mundus head to Church Landings Street, where **Balaramapuram Hand Weaves**, **Ramachandran** and **Kasavukada** (Tel: 2372395), opposite each other, stock every kind of mundu. Another excellent place for mundus and traditional cream and gold Travancore saris is **Kalyan Silks** (Tel: 4081111). Handicrafts at **Kairali** (Tel: 2354507) on MG Road include items made from cane, reeds, natural fibres, rosewood, sandalwood and cedar. The **KTDC Complex** on Shanmugham Road also has handicrafts.

WHERE TO STAY

In Fort Kochi

Ranging from heritage homes to luxury suites, most of these options in the heart of Kochi's heritage zone offer atmosphere and character in large doses. **Malabar House** (Tel: 0484-2216666; Tariff: Rs 6,500-9,500) is an excellent hotel. The handsome 18th-century mansion offers a rich aesthetic experience, outstanding cross-cultural food and efficient, very warm service. **Trinity** (Tel: 2216669; Tariff: Rs 6,500-17,870) has just three suites, on the first floor of the building that was once the headquarters of the Dutch East India Company. It is run as an extension of Malabar House (meals, massages and other services are at the latter, a 2-min walk away).

Koder House (Tel: 2218486; Tariff: Rs 8,147-13,580) is possibly the most striking building in Fort Kochi. The beautiful red-washed structure is set just off the beach. The three-storey hotel features only six suites, each with a very large bedroom, dressing area and bathroom. The hotel also features a restaurant that serves Kerala-Jewish food, the pricey Serena Spa, as well as a tiny pool in the back courtyard.

The Old Harbour Hotel (Tel: 2218006, 09847029000; Tariff: Rs 6,440-12,880; www.oldharbourhotel.com) is in the plot next to Koder House, and has 13 rooms set around the garden or with views of the sea.

Princess Street is among Fort Kochi's most beautiful, with quite a few family-run home stays. The most elegant of these is **The Old Courtyard** (Tel: 2215035/ 6302; Tariff: Rs 2,250-4,600), set in a well-looked-after mansion, with just eight rooms decorated with antique colonial furniture, such as four-poster beds with mosquito net frames and mirrors in odd places.

The CGH Earth Groups' legendary **Brunton Boatyard** (Tel: 0484-2215461-65; Tariff: Rs 12,100-17,000) is built famously on a former boatyard, near the Chinese fishing nets. Its whitewashed walls, sloping tile roof and terracotta

KERALA

Preparing for a kathakali performance in a Fort Kochi hotel

floors with a giant rain tree in front blend with the old town's casual spirit.

Ballard Bungalow (Tel: 2215854; Tariff: Rs 1,200-2,800), set in a heritage Dutch colonial mansion near Port Boat Jetty on Ballard Road, is owned and run by the Cochin Diocese. The mansion holds seven rooms, a restaurant and a very helpful travel desk.

Set in another heritage Dutch mansion is **Fort Heritage** (Tel: 2215333; Tariff: Rs 2,842-4,930) on Napier Street. **Fort House** (Tel: 2217103; Tariff: Rs 1,200-2,800) is near the Customs House.

In Ernakulam

The **International Hotel** (Tel: 2380401/ 2091; Tariff: Rs 1,200-3,500) is in the city centre, but off the main artery. It has class and an old-world charm.

Best Western The Avenue Regent (Tel: 2377977; Tariff: Rs 3,000-7,500) on MG Road is an excellent option with 54 rooms, a restaurant and bar, a cake shop and travel desk. **Grand Hotel** (Tel: 2382061; Tariff: Rs 1,450-1,700) located on MG Road has 39 rooms and offers sightseeing. **Hotel Abad Atrium** (Tel: 2381122, 2384374; Tariff: Rs 2,500-4,500) also on MG Road, has 52 rooms, a swimming pool, health club and Ayurvedic rejuvenation centre.

Gaanam Hotel (Tel: 2377202; Tariff: Rs 650-1,300) on Chittoor Road offers 37 rooms, sightseeing and boat cruises. **Hotel Cochin Tower** (Tel: 2401910; Tariff: Rs 600-2,500) at Lisie Junction has 45 rooms and a multi-cuisine restaurant. **Alapatt Regency** (Tel: 2344413; Tariff: Rs 750-1,250) at Palarivattam has a multi-cuisine restaurant and bar. **The Renaissance Cochin** (Tel: 2344463-64, 2345316; Tariff: Rs 2,400-3,000) is among the best hotels in the city, with 47 rooms, speciality restaurants, a swimming pool, gym, sauna, Jacuzzi and Ayurvedic massages. **The Metropolitan** (Tel: 2375412; Tariff: Rs 1,250-2,550) near South Railway Station has 39 rooms and a multi-cuisine restaurant.

On Willingdon Island

Taj Malabar (Tel: 2668010/ 292; Tariff: Rs 5,500-14,000) is a 5-star deluxe hotel.

LIVE THE LEGEND

WELCOME TO KODER HOUSE

KODER HOUSE is a three-storey heritage boutique hotel opposite the beach at Fort Kochi, Kerala, India. Until recently, it belonged to the most illustrious Cochin Jewish family, the Koders. This House had been a host to Presidents, Prime Ministers, Viceroys, Ambassadors and prominent dignitaries. This dwelling also finds a prominent place on INTACH's list of heritage sites, and a visit to Fort Kochi is considered to be incomplete without a visit to this historic monument.

FACILITIES: There are six 800 Sqft. sheer luxury suites, and each is grand with a huge bedroom, sitting room and bathroom with Jacuzzi. And services are equally select. The Multicuisine Restaurant overlooks a Plunge Pool. The world renowned Serena Wellness Spa offers rejuvenation to guests. Personal valet for each room. Plus of course, there is a Business Centre, Library, Bridge and services like Foreign exchange, Electronic safe, Internet data Port and Cable TV in each room, Doctor-on-call and Laundry.

Koder House, Tower Road, Fort Cochin, Cochin - 682 001, Kerala, India,
Tel: +91 484 2218485, Fax : 2217988, e-mail : koderhouse@gmail.com,
koderhouse@sify.com, www.koderhouse.com

KERALA

View of the Fort Kochi shore from the approaching Ernakulam ferry

Its heritage suites look out on to the lagoon. The spacious, manicured lawns front the backwater.

The CGH Earth Group's flagship, **Casino Hotel** (Tel: 2668421; Tariff Rs 4,200-5,200) offers unmatched views of the harbour, fabulous dining and Ayurvedic treatments. The bar even has cocktails based on homegrown Kerala liquor and ayurvedic health drinks.

The Trident (Tel: 2669595; Tariff: Rs Rs 6,500-10,000) is housed in an elegant low rise building with the traditional Kochi sloping terracotta tile roof on Bristow Road. It has 96 rooms, a beauty salon, swimming pool and gift shop.

On Bolgatty Island
KTDC's **Bolgatty Palace** (Tel: 2750003; Tariff: 3,500-7,500; *see page 410*) is a 5-min drive from Ernakulam and set in exquisite surrounds. You'll see it from the ferries to Kochi and Willingdon Island. Ayurvedic treatments and excellent Kerala cuisine are on offer. You play golf here, even if you aren't a guest.

On Vypeen Island
Stay near Cherai Beach on Vypeen Island in **Cherai Beach Resort** (Tel: 2481818; Tariff: Rs 900-4,500), which has 30 cottages, Ayurvedic treatments and Ootupura Restaurant.

For more hotels and details, see Kochi Accommodation Listings on pages 502-504

WHERE TO EAT

In Fort Kochi/ Mattancherry
Fort Kochi's restaurants are a living record of the rich history of this port. There is no better starting point than The Brunton Boatyard's **History Restaurant** (Tel: 2215461, 2215557). Its storybook menu tells of the history of Kochi, and offers dishes carefully collected from families in Fort Kochi. For a taste of Kochi's Jewish past, sample chuttulli meen, fish cooked in green masala. Thahinya rubyan is an Arabian dish of tiger prawns. The Gujarati traders of Mattancherry too are

Kerala is God's own country, Welcome to His permanent address

 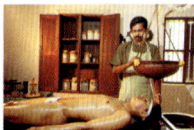  

- Best beach of Kerala ■ Resorts surrounded by backwaters ■ Coconut Lagoons ■ Multi-Cuisine Restaurant ■ Ayurveda spa ■ 42 Independent garden villas ■ A/C Conference halls
- Floating & Open air restaurants ■ Eco friendly-Pollution free locale-adjacent to the city and airport.

BEACH & BACK WATERS

CHERAI BEACH RESORTS
COCHIN KERALA INDIA

Vypin Island, Kochi, Kerala, India - 683 514, Ph: +91 - 484 - 2416949, 2481818, 3297651, 3253101, Fax: +91 - 484 - 2417333, Mobile: 98472 31400.
E-mail: enquiry@cheraibeachresorts.com   www.cheraibeachresorts.com

KERALA

The freshest seafood can be sampled at the 'You Buy, I Cook' stalls in Fort Kochi

immortalised here with a tasty mixed vegetable undhiyo.

When I visited the **Menorah Restaurant** in the boutique Koder House Hotel (Tel: 2218485), one of their popular Indo-Jewish food festivals was underway, and here the chutulli was even better than The History's version. There was also a stuffed chicken in Jewish gravy, beef kothiporichathu marinated in Jewish spices, and elaggal, a red beef curry.

A few steps from Koder House are the famous **'You Buy, I Cook'** stalls that cook fish caught from the Chinese fishing nets. You can choose from sole, lady fish, mullet, pomfret, king fish, tiger prawns, blue scampi, lobster, white king prawns, calamari, crab, oysters, mussels. The cook at **Café Del Mar** stall (Tel: 9895614200, 9249777847) is particularly accomplished.

The restaurant in **The Old Courtyard Hotel** (Tel: 2216302, 2215305) on Princess Street has a few good Portuguese dishes like baked mussels and beef salpicao. They also do regional Kerala specialities and a very satisfying Continental breakfast.

Near the Bishop's Palace, is a family-run restaurant called **Addy's 1776** (near Bishop's House and Britto School, Fort Kochi, Tel: 2215977, 09847745491), set in the covered backyard, where Kathakali performances or local bands entertain diners. They serve a delicious fish roasted in banana leaf.

Euro-Mallu fusion seafood is the speciality at the restaurant at **Malabar House** (Tel: 2216666). The best choice on the menu is the fabulous, famous Malabar House seafood platter. There's a good selection of Continental food too. Leave room for their excellent desserts.

The Teapot (Tel: 2218035) on Peter Celli Street has plenty of character, with hundreds of ageing kettles as decoration, tea chests for tables and impressive Vasco da Gama ashtrays. Sip peppermint-flavoured Nilgiri's brew or try the excellent planter's breakfast.

Kashi Art Café (Tel: 2215769; kashiartcafe.com) on Burgher Street, set in another old Portuguese villa in the

lane parallel to Princess Street, is an oasis of quiet with an art gallery in front. An inner courtyard has *balcaos* running all the way round, and tables on the side. The café has a freshly set menu everyday.

The fame of the aromatic Kayee's mutton biryanis with date chutney served at **Rahmathulla Hotel** (Tel: 2226080, 2354321; Ernakulam Branch: Kayee's Hotel, Durbar Hall Road) on New Road in Mattancherry has traveled well beyond Kerala. Try the spicy curry of soft cooked mutton with pathiri, and Kayee's special Kochi fish and prawn biryanis.

In Ernakulam
The **Grand Pavilion Restaurant** of the Grand Hotel (Tel: 2382061), next to Wood's Manor on MG Road, is famous for its karimeen dishes and variety of regional Kerala specialities, like karimeen polichathu of Kuttanad, wrapped in banana leaves and steamed.

Fry's Village Restaurant (Tel: 2353983, 5587333), at the southern end of Chittoor Road, has been serving the most authentic Kerala dishes in Ernakulam for two decades. Opt for the Kerala fish and veg thalis for lunch. They have a good range of Malabar biryanis and a rare range of porottas including Malabar, wheat, Ceylon and kothu porotta.

Karimeen from the Vembanad kayal

SAIBAL DAS

So famous are the **Pai Brother's** (Tel: 2374879) for the 36 dosa varieties they serve that they have the honour of a street named for them. Tuck into a crisp poddy onion bullseye or duck egg masala or a thattil kutty dosa. It takes more time to decide what you'll eat than it takes the brothers to make it.

Old-timer **Four Foods Restaurant** (Tel: 2351026) on Shanmugham Road serves separate menus for lunch and dinner. At lunch time, sample the mini Travancore oonu, a simple veg thali. Four Foods is more promising by night, when they offer traditional Syrian dishes of Kuttanad, like karimeen polichathu.

Ernakulam's famous **Ceylon Bake House** (Tel: 2376275) on MG Road is the place to buy savoury and sweet banana chips, bitter gourd, tapioca and jackfruit chips and stacks of luridly coloured Kozhikode halwa. **KR Bakes** (Ernakulam Tel: 4050033), 'serving with love since 1963' at several branches across Kochi, is also good for these edible souvenirs.

A peep into **toddy shops** is recommended. Try the ones at Nettoor on the Ernakulam-Island Bypass and Mullapanthal near Thripunithura. There is the staple kappa kari, which is fish and tapioca, and puttu (rice cakes steamed in bamboo) with beef roast. You can also choose from fresh catch or try out more exotic items like rabbit and toad meat.

On Willingdon Island
The speciality seafood **Fort Cochin** restaurant in Casino Hotel (Tel: 2668421) offers the same rich choices as the 'You buy, I cook' stalls in Fort Kochi. The **Rice Boat Restaurant** moored to the side of the Taj Malabar (Tel: 2666811, 266801; dinner only) is shaped like the jackwood kettuvalloms that ply the *kayal*, on which the restaurant appears to float. If you look up from your tart prawn curry, you may get to see a massive ship glide past not far from your table. ∎

Inputs by Latha Anantharaman and Lesley A Esteves

Cochin's No.1 choice for an authentic vegetarian experience

The convenience of city living

- Spacious, well-furnished rooms / suites (AC & non-AC)
- Four fully equipped conference halls
- Subhiksha AC restaurant serving North Indian & South Indian delicacies
- Kempu - The coffee shop
- Business centre
- Sweet centre & book shop
- Ample parking space.

The charmed life of a countryside

- Lakeside cottages (AC & non-AC)
- AC restaurant
- Fully equipped conference halls
- Full-fledged business centre
- Coffee shop
- Board room
- Parking for 150 cars
- Palm-fringed waterfront
- Lake with boating facilities
- Ayurvedic treatment centre

Bharat hotel
Durbar Hall Road, Cochin 682 016
Tel: 0484 2353501, 3295090. Fax: 2370502
Email: bthekm@vsnl.com

SAROVARAM
NH 47 Bypass, Maradu, Cochin.
Tel: 0484 2305519, 3295155. Fax: 2304494
Email: sarovaram@satyam.net.in

www.bharathotel.com

KERALA

ATUL LOKE

A dream honeymoon in a 'floating hotel' on Vembanad Lake at Kumarakom

KUMARAKOM
LANGUID DAYS ON VEMBANAD LAKE

State Kerala
Location Where the Meenachil River meets the Vembanad backwaters in south-central Kerala, 16 km from Kottayam
Distance 682 km SW of Chennai JOURNEY TIME *By rail* 12 hrs + $^1/_2$ hr by road *By air* 1 hr + 2 hrs by road
Route NH45 to Theni via Chengalpattu, Tindivanam, Viluppuram, Ulundurpettai, Veppur, Trichy, Manapparai, Vadamadurai, Dindigul and Vattalakundu; NH220 to Vandiperiyar via Uttamapalaiyam, Kilgudalur and Thekkady; KK Road to Kottayam via Peermade, Kanjirapally and Pambadi; SH to Kumarakom (*see route guides on pages 12 and 320*)

■ BY KG KUMAR

When former Prime Minister Atal Behari Vajpayee chose to holiday here in 2000, he surprised the nation with his *Musings from Kumarakom*, saying time was ripe "to resolve problems of the past" and "move towards a better future". Kumarakom, on the banks of Vembanad Lake, has that effect on people. Of course, it doesn't hurt to have a special way with words, but Kumarakom does provide oodles of inspiration.

This placid resort village on the Kuttanad backwaters drags the muse out of even the most poetically challenged. So pack your quill and head for what are arguably the most beautiful acres along the Kuttanad backwaters, to palm-

KUMARAKOM

fringed canals, clumps of coir retting in water, a fishing boat returning with the day's catch, a boat laden with pots and pans making the rounds to shoppers in waterfront houses...

ORIENTATION

Make no bones about it, Kumarakom is a 'resort' destination. This tiny village on the edge of Vembanad Lake was practically unknown till one Henry Baker purchased land from the erstwhile Raja of Travancore to build himself a grand home. When the last of the Bakers left India, Taj Hotels stepped in to turn it into a fancy resort, changing the fortunes of the once-quiet fishing hamlet. Kumarakom today is a maze of modern resorts and heritage home stays spilling over the island's bank.

The road from Kottayam ends at Kumarakom's jetty, right near Market Junction and the Bay Island Driftwood Museum. The Bird Sanctuary is north of the jetty, where the Meenachil River meets Vembanad Lake.

THINGS TO SEE AND DO

The Vembanad backwaters have to be experienced slowly, leisurely and languidly. The best way to do it is to hire a kettuvallom, the traditional rice boat-turned-houseboat. These floating hotels range from tiny canoes to houseboats capped by elaborate superstructures of bamboo and rosewood, panelled with mats of screwpine. KTDC (Tel: 0481-2525861/ 64) offers motorboat (Rs 550 per hr), and pontoon boat (Rs 1,500 per hr) rides. There are scores of private operators too, at the boat jetty. Take the waterways past paddy and coconut

→ FAST FACTS

When to go
October to February. You may not be able to do a backwater cruise during the monsoon (June to September)
Tourist offices
● Dist. Tourism Promotion Council ❶❺
Boat Jetty, Kodimatha, Kottayam
Telefax: 0481-2560479
● Tourist Information Counter ❶
Dept of Tourism, Govt of Kerala, Nattakom, Government Guest House, Kottayam. Tel: 2342303
● KTDC ❶❺
Tourist Reception Centre, Govt of Kerala, TTDC Complex, 2, Wallajah Road, Chennai. Tel: 044-25382639
Website: ktdc.com
STD code 0481

Choose from our network of over 4000 hotels in India. Serviced apartments, budget hotels, luxury resorts, palaces, business accomodations, houseboats and more.

Hotel	Rating
Lake Palace	Budget
Backwater Retreat	3 ★
Radisson Plaza	5 ★

MTNL/BSNL Toll Free No.
1−800−22−4878
022-4030-4878
www.travelguru.com

The person featured above is an actual Travelguru employee

KERALA

A darter admires the view in the Kumarakom Bird Sanctuary

groves, mangroves, along freshwater canals and rivers that debouch into Vembanad Lake. Pathiramanal Island, a 10-acre isle an hour's ride from the bird sanctuary, is an ideal midway point for a backwater picnic in the company of birds. The island has an interesting tale of creation attached to it. Apparently, it was born after a young Brahmin boy dived into the Vembanad Lake, slicing its waters into two halves. Maybe it's a metaphor for a belief (not entirely incorrect) that the landmass here was once under the sea. A cruise along the Vembanad Lake is the best way to get a feel of the place. From Kumarakom to Pathiramanal is one hour by boat. Around Onam, the Vembanad waters come alive with the **Kumarakom Arpookara Vanitha Jalmela** and the **Kavanthikara Boat Race**. It's also possible to fish in these waters. Some of the resorts also offer water-skiing and windsailing.

Bird Sanctuary

The Kumarakom Bird Sanctuary is spread across 14 acres on the eastern banks of the Vembanad Lake. It's best to visit the sanctuary on foot by a 1_-km long walking track, where you are likely to spot heron, darters, storks, teals and common egrets. Or take a boat ride, which brings you closer to waders like waterfowl and ducks, and some fliers like parrots, larks and flycatchers. Between November and February the sanctuary turns into a transit lounge for migratory birds.

♦**Entry fee** Indians Rs 5, foreigners Rs 45 **Guide fee** Rs 100-200 **Timings** 6 am-6.30 pm

Bay Island Driftwood Museum

As you drive in from Kottayam or get off your houseboat at the Kumarakom Jetty, a distinctive building with its pillared verandah and sloping tiled roof at Market Junction invites inspection. This unique museum displays 'the art of the sea' — chiselled driftwood gathered from the beaches of the Andaman and Nicobar Islands in the Bay of Bengal, hence the name. The driftwood pieces were chiselled by curator Raji Punnoose, a

Holiday in an exotic villa afloat on a calm, picturesque lake.

Pristine Island is an eco-friendly backwater resort located near Cochin, on the western side of the Vembanadu Lake. The first of its kind in Kerala, Pristine Island Resort is set in a beautiful island situated in the middle of the "Kaithapuzha Lake, an extension of the Vembanadu Lake. Merely 20 km away from Kochi, Pristine Isle, as the name symbolizes is truly pure and unspoilt. The unique beauty and ambience of the property make it the only one of its kind in the entire tourist map of Kerala.

Pristine Island

Pristine Isle Resort Pvt. Ltd.
Kovilakom, Kodamthuruth, Kuthiathode P.O, Cherthala,
Alappuzha Tel: 0478-2561900, 2561716
E-mail: mail@pristineisle.in
Web: www.pristineisle.in

City Office : Sai Nivas, Chilavannur Road, Kadavanthra,
Kochi-682 020. Tel: 0484 2318848, Fax: 0484 2318847

KERALA

retired teacher, into shapes that vary from a crocodile found off Port Blair's Wandoor Beach to a sculpture of Netaji Subhash Chandra Bose addressing an audience from wood collected off Mayabunder Beach in Middle Andaman. You can also purchase some sculptures here.

→ GETTING THERE

Air Nearest airport: Cochin International Airport, Nedumbassery (106 km/ 2 hrs; Tel: 0484-2610115), connected to Chennai by six daily flights by Paramount Airways, Kingfisher Airlines, Jet Airways and Air Deccan. Pre-paid taxi to Kumarakom is Rs 1,270
Rail Nearest railhead: Kottayam (Tel: 0481-2562933; 15 km/ $1/2$ hr) **Best option TO** Trivandrum Mail (dep: Chennai Central 8 pm; arr: Kottayam 8.05 am). A taxi to Kumarakom costs Rs 250-300 **Best option FROM** Chennai Mail (dep: Kottayam 5.35 pm; arr: Avadi 6.09 am, Perambur 6.24 am, Chennai Central 7 am)
TIP Alleppey Express (going) is also a good option
Car This long drive across the breadth of Tamil Nadu and Kerala from the east coast to the west cannot be attempted on a weekend break. Stick to the excellent train connections. For longer vacations, follow NH45 past Chengalpattu, Tindivanam, Viluppuram, Ulundurpettai, Trichy, Manapparai, Dindigul and Vattalakundu to Theni. Follow NH220 south over the Western Ghats to Vandiperiyar via Uttamapalaiyam, Kilgudalur and Thekkady. Continue west along the Kerala state highway to Kottayam via Peermade and Kanjirapally. Kumarakom is a 15-km drive further west of Kottayam

♦**Entry fee** Rs 50 **Timings** 10 am-5 pm, Sundays 11 am-5 pm, Mondays closed **Tel** 2517530 **Website** www.bay-island-museum.com
TIP If informed in advance, museum will be opened for groups on Mondays

WHERE TO STAY AND EAT

Kumarakom has some of the most beautiful and expensive resorts in Kerala, and a few inexpensive home stays.

Baker's Bungalow, home to four generations of the eponymous family of missionaries, is in the best traditions of the Raj. An inspired location, at the head of a lagoon set back from the lake, the bungalow owes nothing whatever to local architectural traditions, and everything to the architecture of the British in India. If Kumarakom has been catapulted onto the tourism map of the elite, it's probably all because of the Bakers. After all, Kumarakom is but one of the many fishing villages in Kerala, pleasant but hardly exceptional. When the last of the Baker family moved back to England, and sold the house, Kumarakom patently lacked the fine climate of Munnar, elsewhere in Kerala. It even lacked fresh water, supplies of which had to be painstakingly fetched by bullock-cart. The Taj Group, into whose hands the property eventually fell, created the **Taj Garden Retreat** (Tel: 0481-2524377, 2525711; Tariff: Rs 9,900-19,400), a resort worthy of visiting Prime Ministers. Cottages stud the side of the lagoon, an Ayurvedic centre and swimming pool lie directly opposite Baker's Bungalow. The Vembanad Lake stretches into the distant horizon on one side, and narrow canals typical of the backwaters exist on the other. The resort boats the Baker's Restaurant and Sunset Bar, a swimming pool, gym, Ayurvedic treatments and a souvenir shop and offers boating and water sports, sightseeing, cruises on the backwaters and fishing.

An Oasis On The Vembanad

The Backwater Resort is a full-service spanking new resort at Kumarakom hugging the shores of the Lake Vembanad. Spread across 3 acres the ambiance here is typically Keralan yet complimented with every modern convenience. Swaying coconut palms cast cool shadows over the twin storied dwelling units each with four double rooms all of which offer stunning views of the backwaters and let in the cool fragrant breeze that endlessly caress the shore of the Lake Vembanad. *The Waves* is our multi-specialty restaurant that offers a variety of delectable fare from around the world including authentic Gujarati, Maharashtrian, Continental, Kolapuri cuisines as well as traditional Keralan delicacies. The vegetarian fare is cooked in a separate kitchen to ensure its purity and flavour.

The Backwater Resort
Kumarakom South, Kerala, India.
Tel:+91- 481- 2525388, 09387077707, 09895078044
Fax: 0481-2525388
thebackwater@gmail.com
reservation@thebackwater.co.in
www.thebackwater.co.in

KERALA

Most of the resorts in Kumarakom lie on the Vembanad Lake shores

The CGH Earth Group's **Coconut Lagoon** (Tel: 2524373/ 4491/ 5834; Tariff: Rs 12,000-19,350) is possibly the most beloved of all of Kerala's luxury resorts. It's everyone's favourite, from snooty young couples to boisterous Gujarati families to bleeding-heart tree-hugging types — and it's large-hearted enough to accommodate all happily (okay, everyone who can afford the tariffs). Like the Kumarakom Lake Resort, it mixes up the accommodation, offering heritage cottages as well as sleek contemporary villas, the latter set bang on the shores of the Vembanad Lake. The hotel offers stay in heritage mansions and bungalows, once traditional *tharavadus* brought here from different parts of Kerala and carefully reassembled. Coconut Lagoon offers a pool, rice boat cruises, country boat rides and Ayurvedic treatments. The food is outstanding and the service warm.

The **Kumarakom Lake Resort** (Tel: 2524900, 2524501; Tariff: Rs 11,500-55,000) is a fabulously polished pie of a resort that understands well the needs of the luxury traveller. There's a wide range of accommodation -- from 'heritage villas with private pools' to 'meandering pool villas' (each villa opens out onto a river-like pool), 'heritage lake view villas' and so on. But even if you plump for a heritage villa, you'll get it sanitised: old wooden walls but no musty smell, red oxide floor perhaps but not a crack in sight, open-air baths but no curious creepy-crawlies... The resort has an ayurvedic centre and offers backwater cruises, bicycles, cooking classes, fishing, a gift shop, health club, sight-seeing, speed boats, swimming pool with jacuzzi and water sports.

Kumarakom's newest luxury property is the 18-acre five-star deluxe **Radisson Plaza** (Tel: 2527272; Tariff: Rs 47,500-57,500), right on the shores of the lake. The resort offers plush villas with private pool, cottages and deluxe rooms in a tranquil landscaped setting. A number of specialised treatments, including the popular Dead sea water therapies, are available at its in-house Ayurveda spa.

Backwater Ripples (Tel: 2523300/ 3600; Tariff: Rs 6,800-11,400) has 34

EXPERIENCE BLISS...

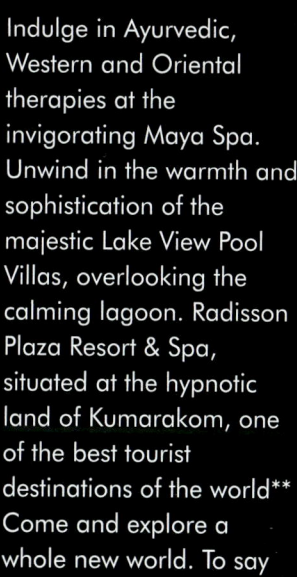

Indulge in Ayurvedic, Western and Oriental therapies at the invigorating Maya Spa. Unwind in the warmth and sophistication of the majestic Lake View Pool Villas, overlooking the calming lagoon. Radisson Plaza Resort & Spa, situated at the hypnotic land of Kumarakom, one of the best tourist destinations of the world** Come and explore a whole new world. To say

For Personalised offers*
contact our reservation centre
*Condition apply. Subject to availability

Radisson Plaza Resorts & Spa Kumarakom:
Karottukayal, Kumarakom, Kottayam,
Kerala 686 563, India
E-mail:sales@radissonkumarakom.com
www.radisson.com/kumarakomin

To book, call direct on:
Kumarakom +91 481 252 7290
Mumbai +91 22 6452 5555/2605 2923-27
Delhi +91 11 2341 7177-78 or
Call us on toll free 1800 1800 333

** (National Geographic).

PLAZA
RESORT & SPA KUMARAKOM
KERALA, INDIA

Chennai • Delhi • Dhaka • Goa • Jalandhar • Kathmandu • Khajuraho
Kumarakom • Noida • Raichak (Kolkata) • Shimla • Varanasi

KERALA

cottages and rooms spread over seven acres on the lake shore, the Cordon Bleu restaurant, a swimming pool, water sports and the Vedasparsh Ayurvedic Spa. The resort also offers stay in the middle of Vembanad Lake on Arayannam, their eco-friendly houseboat with two bedrooms with attached bathrooms, two upper decks and a loft.

The Abad Group's **Whispering Palms** (Tel: 2523824; Tariff: Rs 6,500-12,000), sprawls along the Vembanad banks in Konchumada, with 53 rooms in 42 cottages. The pool fronts the lake, and water scooters, water skating and banana boat rides on the lake are offered. Plus there's an Ayurveda centre and health club and a multi-cuisine restaurant.

Kerala Tourism's **Waterscapes** (Tel: 2525861/ 64; Tariff: Rs 5,000-9,000) has 40 rooms facing Vembanad Lake. Apart from offering a pool, an Ayurveda centre, boating, birdwatching at the sanctuary and angling, the staff will take you to Pathiramanal Island, and to watch toddy-tapping in paddy fields.

Illikkalam Lake Resort's (Tel: 2524234, 2525651; Tariff: Rs 2,100-4,000) cottages are situated in acres of greenery and fruit trees, 10 metres from the banks of Vembanad Lake. The resort also offers houseboat accommodation. At **Golden Waters** (Tel: 2525826-27; Tariff: Rs 6,500-7,500), an intricate lacework of canals intersects the 17-acre waterfront property. There are 28 quaint cottages, all constructed on the banks of the canals, each accessible by boat or by foot over cobbled pathways and rustic bridges. The cottages are set across 13 small islands.

Tharavadu Heritage Home (Tel: 2525230, 2523632; Tariff: Rs 850-1,200) connected to the Bay Island Driftwood Museum is among the nicest traditional homes here. **GK's River View Home Stay** (Tel: 2597527; Tariff: Rs 1,300) is on the banks of the Meenachil River in Pulikkuttyserry. It offers five rooms, Ayurveda, boating, taxis and sightseeing. **Philipkutty's Farm** (Tel: 09895075130) is in Vechoor, north of Kumarakom, with three waterfront villas.

You can dine at any of the hotels here, including the homestays, with prior notice. Dine on delicious Kuttanad food at different spots of the Vembanad Lake shore. Grilled lobster, karimeen polichathu and creamy prawn curry is on offer at Kumarakom Lake Resort's **Vembanad Seafood Bar**. The resort also offers the **Ettukettu** and **Thattukada** restaurants. The speciality at Coconut Lagoon's **Tharavadu** and **Fort Kochi** restaurants is also seafood. Waterscapes has **Pearlspot Restaurant**, offering excellent karimeen and duck dishes.

For details, see Kumarakom Accommodation Listings on pages 506-508 ■

Kumarakom offers Kuttanad delicacies such as karimeen porichathu (below)

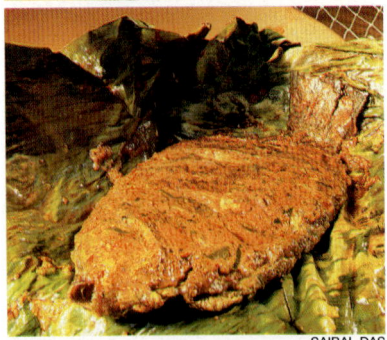

SAIBAL DAS

Prudent Networks
Your Travel Companion

Enclosed with water from the three sides, India – a destination full of adventure and excitement, is home of some world-renowned beaches. Come and discover the emerald beauty of Kerala beaches, vibrant lifestyle of beaches of Goa or the simple charm of Andaman and Nicobar beaches, beach vacations in India add more glitters to this fantastic land of culture. Enjoy the beauty of sea, sun, and sand or just have finest seafood culinary experience, India beaches offer you all that you desire.

Laze on a coir houseboat as it floats on sparkling backwaters; see cormorants fly overhead and spot flitting silver fishes as you gaze into transparent green backwaters on Kerala Tours and India Luxury Tours with Prudent Networks.

Set foot on divine greens and see a deep green paradise i.e. - Kerala on Kerala Tours with Prudent Networks Pvt. Ltd. Tour temple towns, fishing hamlets, enchanting beach country and romantic hill splendor on Kerala Tours and experience the refreshing effects of ayurveda, natural oils and glorious green Kerala cures.

Prudent Networks
Suite - 218, Ansals Majestic Tower,
Vikaspuri, New Delhi - 110018, India
E-Mail: info@prudentnetworks.com

Telephone Nos: +91-11-41586840 / 41586940
Mobile No: +91-9811203268
Fax No: +91-11-41586740

KERALA

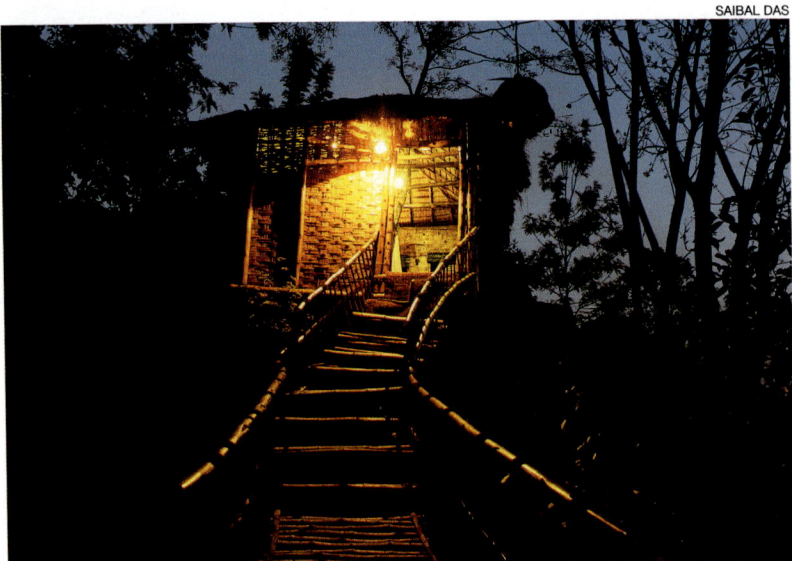

SAIBAL DAS

An eco resort in a picturesque setting in Vythiri's rainforests

VYTHIRI
LUXURY ON THE ROCKS

State Kerala
Location Tucked into the Wayanad Hills in north Kerala, above Kozhikode
Distance 741 km SW of Chennai **JOURNEY TIME By rail** $11^{1}/_{2}$ hrs + $1^{1}/_{2}$ hrs by road **By air** 1 hr + 2 hrs by road
Route NH45 to Ulundurpettai via Tambaram, Chengalpattu, Tindivanam, Vikravandi and Viluppuram; NH68 to Salem via Tiyagai Durgam, Kallakkurichi, Talaivasal, Attur and Valappadi; NH47 to Avanashi via Perundurai; SH to Mettupalaiyam via Annur; NH67 to Gudalur via Coonoor and Ooty; ghat road to Vythiri via Devala, Pandalur, Meppadi and Chundale (*see route guides on pages 12 and 320*)

■ BY SUGATA SRINIVASARAJU

A cup of tea at a roadside teashop, just before we entered Kalpetta, was a grand initiation to what lay ahead on the road for us. There couldn't have been a more refreshing welcome to Wayanad than this tea that was filled with the aroma of freshly crushed cardamom and pungent traces of ginger.

We had been wondering what to expect from Vythiri and Wayanad. Wouldn't it be similar to the other towns, tucked into the valleys of the Western Ghats? There are the similar hills, the gorges and ravines that look so alike, the mist that wraps you, the wildflowers and bouquets of thorns that invariably make a tryst with your urban skin. What else could you find, besides this, in Wayanad? As it turned out, we found a great deal.

There are very few places that simultaneously offer a holistic experience of wilderness and education, combined with the comfort of a modern holiday. Wayanad is a confluence where the needs of the body, mind and soul are met. You can trek both mountains and streams, and bathe under waterfalls balancing yourself on sharp rocks. You can simply lie down and dream as big as the sky's expanse, with the symphony of wild calls in the background. Or you could turn philosophical and measure death with dry leaves. If you are enterprising, you can speak to plantation owners who trade coffee, tea, spices, vanilla and exotic oils. And while you are at it, you can talk to plantation workers about the aesthetics of the red flags that dot the lush green terraces of manicured tea hills. You can listen to scary legends by the campfire and accidentally pick up lessons in history. By way of just desserts, there is sumptuous Malabar food to indulge in. These myriad experiences come together as one perfect package in Wayanad.

ORIENTATION

Vythiri is an unassuming little town. All the places that a tourist might like to visit are within a 40-km radius of the town. If you do not engage your own vehicle, you may have to depend on the local rickshaws and old-style Willys jeeps. It is difficult to put in a kind word for them! If you have a modest budget and want to make the best use of your time, then the strategic location to stay would be in nearby Kalpetta, the district headquarters. It is a livelier place.

THINGS TO SEE AND DO

Suchipara and Kanthampara Falls
The best way to begin your trip to Wayanad is by visiting the waterfalls here. The travel and trek to the falls is a perfect summary of Wayanad. Suchipara is the most attractive of them all. It is about 22 km from Kalpetta and you have to take a serpentine road through the tea gardens to reach it. 'Suchi' in the local language literally means needle and it is reflective of the rocks that the water falls on. You will have to walk a kilometre and a half from the motorable road before you reach the falls. At places en route the terrain runs deep and untamed — a shoe with a good grip is an absolute necessity. The three-tongued waterfalls are almost hidden in the dense

→ FAST FACTS

When to go Obviously, it rains for a good part of the year in the rainforests of Wayanad. May to September are real wet months. It never gets too cold

Tourist offices
● Dist. Tourism Promotion Council ❶ ❻
Pookote Lake, Vythiri PO; Tel: 04936-255207; Website: dtpcwayanad.com
TIP For hotel reservations in Wayanad, boating, horse riding, children's park and aquarium visits
● Dist. Tourism Promotion Council ❶ ❻
Collectorate Office, Civil Station
Kalpetta North PO
Tel: 04936-202134; Fax: 203347
TIP For trekking, camping, adventure tours, guided tours, forest walks, wildlife trekking tours and hotel reservations
● Tourist Information Counter ❶
Dept of Tourism, Govt of Kerala;
address as above; Tel: 04936-204441
● KTDC ❶ ❻
Tourism Complex, 2, Wallajah Road
Chennai. Telefax: 044-25382639
Website: ktdc.com
STD code 04936

equatorial forest. The algae on the sharp-edged rocks at ground zero makes them very slippery. But if you perch yourself at a distance, it is quite a treat to watch the endless ferocity of water. Suchipara is also known as **Sentinel Rockfall**. Kanthampara Falls are on the adjacent side of the rocky area of Suchipara. At a particular point from Suchipara the Kanthampara Falls are visible as a much thinner stream of jumping water. To avoid exhaustion from a steep climb back, try out a couple of amlas (gooseberries), marinated in a special salty syrup that makeshift shops on the route offer — it rejuvenates you instantly.

Meenmutty Falls

Meenmutty is about 29 km from Kalpetta, off the Ooty Road. This again demands a 2-km forest trek, which is less exhausting than the Suchipara path, but equally fulfilling. Locals have a tendency to praise this waterfall excessively, which drops from 985 ft and has a triple-decker effect. This spot is certainly more serene.

Lakkidi

This is a place for good photo opportunities, about 5 km from Vythiri and 17 km from Kalpetta. The gateway of Wayanad offers a breathtaking valley-view. It is one of the highest points in the district at 2,300 ft. The serpentine flow of the road that is literally chiselled out of the **Thamarassery Ghat** below will surely tempt your camera. **Greeshmam Resorts**, located a few paces away, is also a fine vantage point to view the valley. A note of caution about the valley view area — monkeys come here in hordes!

Pookote Lake

It's ideal to visit Pookote Lake as you head back to Vythiri from Lakkidi. It is 3 km from the valley view and nearly a kilometre from Vythiri. A motorable road off the main road leads you up to the entrance of the lake. We went there for a break and it was crowded with hundreds of holidaying families. We had to wait for quite a while for our turn to go boating. Meanwhile, we discovered a walkway around the lake, which was a welcome relief from the melee. The aquarium in the lake complex is eminently avoidable.

♦**Location** In Thalipuzha, 4 km from Vythiri **Timings** 9 am-5 pm **Boating fee** Pedal boat Rs 30-50, rowboat Rs 50,

→ GETTING THERE

Air Nearest airport: Karipur International Airport, Kozhikode (88 km/ 2 hrs, Tel: 0483-2711314), connected to Chennai by a daily Indian Airlines flight. Pre-paid taxi to Vythiri costs Rs 1,289
Rail Nearest railhead: Calicut (62 km/ 1½ hrs) **Best option TO** Mangalore Mail (dep: Chennai Central 8.15 pm; arr: Calicut 7.45 am). Taxi to Vythiri costs Rs 1,150 **Best option FROM** Chennai Mail (dep: Calicut 5.30 pm; arr: Chennai Central 5.25 am)
Car A drive across the southern peninsula and over the ghats from Chennai to Vythiri cannot be attempted on a weekend break. Stick to the excellent train connections for a weekender. For longer vacations, follow NH45 to Ulundurpettai via Chengalpattu, Tindivanam and Viluppuram. Turn right on NH68 to Salem via Tiyagai Durgam, Kallakkurichi, Talaivasal, Attur and Valappad. Follow NH47 to Avanashi via Perundurai, then turn right on the state highway to Mettupalaiyam via Annur and follow NH67 as it curves up to Gudalur via Ooty and Coonoor. At Gudalur, turn left to Nadangi, then right to Chundale via Pandalur and Meppadi. Turn left to Vythiri

Mists lingering around Chembra Peak, sentinel of the Wayanad region

kayaking Rs 100 **Horse cart rides** Rs 60 **Aquarium entry fee** Adults Rs 2, children Re 1 **Tel** 04936-255207

While you are at Pookote Lake, a visit to the **Uruvu Eco Shop** is a must, to check out products made out of two dozen varieties of bamboo by adivasis and women of the area. We fell in love with the bamboo shirt hangers and wine bottle covers. They also sell gift packets of spices, pickles and forest honey. If this shop interests you then you should visit their factory (Tel: 04936-326896), 26 km away en route to Suchipara Falls. You will find them experimenting with some new products and design.
♦**Timings** 9 am-7 pm

Karalad Lake

There is greater quiet at this 7-acre lake because it is less publicised, although facilities for angling and boating are in place. The trek to this lake can also be exciting. It is about 16 km from Kalpetta and in a completely different direction from Pookote.
♦**Location** In Thariode, further north from Pookote Lake, 8 km from Vythiri **Timings** 9 am-6 pm **Boating fee** Pedal boat Rs 50 (30 min)

Chembra Peak

Your steadfast fellow traveller in the entire 40-50 km you will travel in and around Vythiri is the looming Chembra Peak. It is the tallest summit in the region at 6,890 ft above sea level. It is almost a keeper of Vythiri's conscience. To get to the top of this peak is a whole day affair and one should preferably start early. Four hours is what the local people say they need to get to the summit from the base camp, but for the uninitiated city-bred climber, it could take an hour more. More than half-way up the peak, at about 4,921 ft, a crystal clear lake temporarily erases the exhaustion of the climb. Chembra is such an obsession that some people come to Wayanad just to scale the Chembra and return after doing nothing else. The District Tourism Promotion Council organises treks to the peak. A guide (Rs 500) accompanies groups of up to 10 people up the peak. DTPC also organises wildlife treks. A one-day trek costs Rs 250 and includes food. The 2-day package with food and sleeping bag-tented accommodation comes for Rs 1,000. They take just 10 people at a time.

You can also go trekking on your own with a guide from DTPC, which

KERALA

DINESH SHUKLA

Fresh produce in the bazaar at Kalpetta, the district headquarters

arranges permits from the Forest Department. They also make camping equipment available (tents Rs 400 per night and sleeping bag Rs 50).

WHERE TO STAY

There are a number of places that you can choose in and around Vythiri depending on how comfortable your wallet feels. At the top-end is undoubtedly the **Vythiri Resorts** (Tel: 04936-255366-67; Tariff: Rs 3,500-5,500), $3^1/_2$ km from the main road. The approach to the resort is rugged and unpaved, enhancing the feel of the jungle. It is spread across 150 acres in the middle of thick rainforests. It has a natural swimming pool and a hanging bridge that seems to imitate the gentle swing in your moods. It even has its own trekking routes within its grounds. Staying in this resort could itself be a complete holiday. Since it has now become a retreat for big corporates, you need to check availability of accommodation well in advance.

Jungle Park Resorts (Mobile: 09947282801; Tariff: Rs 3,000-10,000) on Finster Hills offers Ayurvedic treatments, hammocks, trekking, birdwatching, elephant safaris, horse rides, trekking to villages and sightseeing tours to the Wayanad Wildlife Sanctuary, Pazhassi Raja's tomb, Kuravadweep, Pakshipathalam, Edakkal Caves, Tusharagiri, Chembra Peak, Meenmutty Falls, Pookote Lake and the Thirunelly Temple.

The cottages and tree huts of **Stream Valley Cottages** (Tel: 202787, 255860, 09447933860; Tariff: Rs 2,500-3,000) are very inviting.

Wynberg Resorts (Tel: 247823, 09447300371; Tariff: Rs 1,800-4,000) is set in the picturesque surroundings of the Kuzhivayal Estate at Thrikkaipetta, 6 km from Vythiri towards Kalpetta. Wynberg offers 5 cottages, 2 stilt houses, a tree house and 2 Swiss tents plus many games and excursions.

In Lakkidi, the beautiful **Rain Country Resorts** (Tel: 329798-99; Tariff: Rs 2,700-3,900) has a natural pool in its front garden, perfect for lazy swims.

Set amidst hills, this hotel incorporates the beauty of its setting into its design. The eight comfy cottages have elegantly appointed bathrooms lit with natural light. Apart from lots of games, they also arrange fishing and sightseeing around Wayanad. The sprawling **Greeshmam Resorts** (Tel: 255355/ 716; Tariff: Rs 1,300-1,750) here, overlooks the valley. The resort offers treks and horse-riding.

Nearby Kalpetta has some pretty decent and affordable hotels. **Green Gates** (Tel: 04936-202001-04; Tariff: Rs 2,000-3,500) is the first among a line of these hotels in Kalpetta. Green Gates offers both rooms and cottages. **Hotel Haritagiri** (Tel: 202673; Tariff: Rs 990-2,900), 2 km from Green Gates, is where you will find a bar besides accommodation. A huge outdoor play area is under construction. Next in the line would be **The Woodlands** (Tel: 202547, 203677; Tariff: Rs 950-2,250) with 32 rooms, restaurants, Ayurvedic massage, a travel desk and shopping arcade.

Royal Palm Holiday Home (Tel: 206096, 09447143124; Tariff: Rs 1,700-5,000) has 6 rooms and 2 cottages, a restaurant, a swimming pool, an Ayurvedic treatment centre, a beauty parlour, trekking, boating and outdoor games.

For more hotels and details, see Vythiri Accommodation Listings on pages 512-513

WHERE TO EAT

Most hotels and resorts have a multi-cuisine kitchen. But if you want to try out something that is authentically Malabar then, in Kalpetta, the best place to go would be **Hotel Pankaj** attached to the PPS Tourist Home (Tel: 04936-203731-32) on Pinangode Road. **Haritagiri** offers decent quality Malabar food, but the food at **Green Gates** is just about okay. The **New Form Restaurant** (Tel: 202892) here offers a fairly wide range. There is Kerala fare as well as Chinese, Continental and North Indian meals. Its speciality is Malabar-style biryani. **Kalpetta Restaurant**, near the bus stand on the Kozhikode Road, is from the famous 'meals only' category of Kerala restaurants. They close as early as 8.30 pm. Hotel Harithagiri's **Kuruva Restaurant** serves traditional Malabar food, plus Mughlai, tandoori and Chinese dishes.

Rain Country serves authentic Kerala cuisine, made with veggies from their kitchen garden. The seafood here is excellent. If you're not staying at **Vythiri Resort**, be sure to book a table at their restaurant for at least one meal, served on a banana leaf. Try their famed Malabar chicken curry or Mangalorean fish curry with fluffy *appams*, followed by *payasam*.
TIP The only two bars that have a family ambience are at Haritagiri and PPS ■

KERALA

A black-headed oriole waits patiently for an early worm

SALIM ALI BIRD SANCTUARY
FEATHERED HAVEN

State Kerala
Location In Thattekkad in Ernakulam District, spread over 25.16 sq km in the foothills of the Western Ghats, including part of the Bhoothathankettu Dam on the Periyar River
Distance 631 km SW of Chennai JOURNEY TIME *By rail* 10 hrs + 1^1/$_4$ hrs by road *By air* 1 hr + 1^1/$_2$ hrs by road
Route NH45 to Theni via Chengalpattu, Tindivanam, Viluppuram, Ulundurpettai, Veppur, Trichy, Manapparai, Vadamadurai, Dinidigul and Vattalakundu; NH49 to Kothamangalam via Bodinayakkanur, Devikulam and Munnar; state roads to Keerampara; ferry to Thattekkad (*see route guides on pages 12 and 320*)

■ BY SANJEEV VARMA

As I drive to the end of a newly constructed bridge across the moss green Periyar River on my two-wheeler, Thattekkad stands as lovely and as inviting as ever on the opposite bank. To the east, the 1,716-foot high Njayapilli, the highest point in Thattekkad, cuts a dark silhouette against an early morning sky. I've virtually lost count of the number of times I've frequented this pristine terrain; and each time, I experience something new, or discover an interesting tale to treasure.

After completing the formalities at the sanctuary gate at Shivakshetrapadi, we disappear into the forest, accompanied by a friendly local guide. Suddenly, a flock of egrets takes flight, painting dapples of pure white against the verdant canvas. As always, giant squirrels raise their staccato alarm calls from the high trees, warning other denizens of our intrusion.

Crunching fallen leaves underfoot, we walk briskly, following our energetic guide who suddenly makes a detour to the right, cutting through a delicate trekking path towards the river. Here we chance upon the ruins of an ancient Shiva temple, with nothing more than stones strewn all around. Now comes our big surprise. Our guide points to a tree just beside us, and straining my eyes, I see the shadowy outline of a bird, sleeping lengthwise on a branch. The mottled, greyish-brown plumage is perfect camouflage, blending with the branches, and only its slightly hooked bill is conspicuous. My heart skips a beat. Before I can say anything, our guide gently whispers, "Ceylon frogmouth." We are all elated, for this is a rare species of bird, difficult to spot, and we feel privileged to see one.

The forest canopy suddenly comes to life as a shrieking flock of rose-ringed parakeets fly across the blue sky. Three pairs of Malabar grey hornbills, flapping loudly from tree to tree, add their raucous cries to the symphony. By mid-afternoon, the birds are at their chirping best.

As we walk in the forest, I think of how this landscape undergoes a dramatic change in the rains. Wild flowers spring up in a profusion of colours and the undergrowth bustles with fresh life. Of course, it is the drier spells, which paint the forests an earthy brown, that are ideal for birdwatching. As the trees are leafless, spotting birds is much easier. But whatever the season, I know I will be coming back for more.

→ FAST FACTS

When to go Thattekkad can be visited any time of the year, except in the monsoons (Jul-Aug), as things can get really soggy. Best sightings are in Nov-Jan, during the winter migration of several exotic species

Tourist offices
- Assistant Wildlife Warden, Thattekkad Bird Sanctuary, Njayappilli PO, Thattekkad-686691. Tel: 0485-2588302
- KTDC Tourist Reception Centre ❶ TTDC Complex, 2, Wallajah Road Chennai. Telefax: 044-25382639 Website: ktdc.com
- Dept of Tourism, Govt of Kerala ❶❺ Tourism Complex, Wallajah Road, Chennai. Tel: 044-25369789

STD code 0485

MUMBAI KA GURU
Hari, Hotel Advisor at Travelguru was born and raised in Mumbai. Use his tips and you will fully enjoy the city that never sleeps.

Choose from our network of over 4000 hotels in India. Serviced apartments, budget hotels, luxury resorts, palaces, business accommodations, houseboats and more.

1-800-22-4878
022-4030-4878
www.travelguru.com

India's Largest Hotel Network

iCONTRACT.TG.07.3248

KERALA

ABOUT SALIM ALI BIRD SANCTUARY

Way back in the 1930s, the late Dr Salim Ali described Thattekkad as "the richest bird habitat in peninsular India, comparable only with the eastern Himalayas". A sanctuary was established here in 1983. A number of animals are also found in the sanctuary, and these range from snakes and elephants to giant squirrels and flying lizards. As many as 300 species of birds are said to be found here.

The undulating terrain is covered by tropical evergreen and semi-evergreen forests, and grasslands. Teak, rosewood, jungle jack, red sandalwood, *Lagerstroemia microcarpa* and *Terminalia paniculata* abound, along with the huge Tetrameles nudiflora — locally known as *cheeni*. The latter's lightweight wood is used in the matchstick and plywood industries. Another find here is the rare *telli*, whose aromatic sap is used as incense.

ORIENTATION

The Salim Ali Bird Sanctuary lies across the **Periyar River**, at one end of the **Thattekkad Bridge**. The entrance gate is 50m to the left, as is the counter where you pay your fee for entry and guide services (compulsory). The guides here have immense knowledge of the forests, can take you through less explored trekking paths, and are the best bet to help you out in case of emergencies. As soon as you enter the sanctuary gate, at Sivakshetrapadi, steps to the right lead down to the **Animal Rehabilitation Centre**. Opposite the centre, steps lead up to the **Deer Park**. The **Taxidermic Museum** is adjacent to the park.

Vehicles are not allowed inside the sanctuary. You can park your vehicles either outside (in which case, safety cannot be guaranteed) or right inside the entry gate (vehicle entry fees apply). The sanctuary is intercepted by the Old

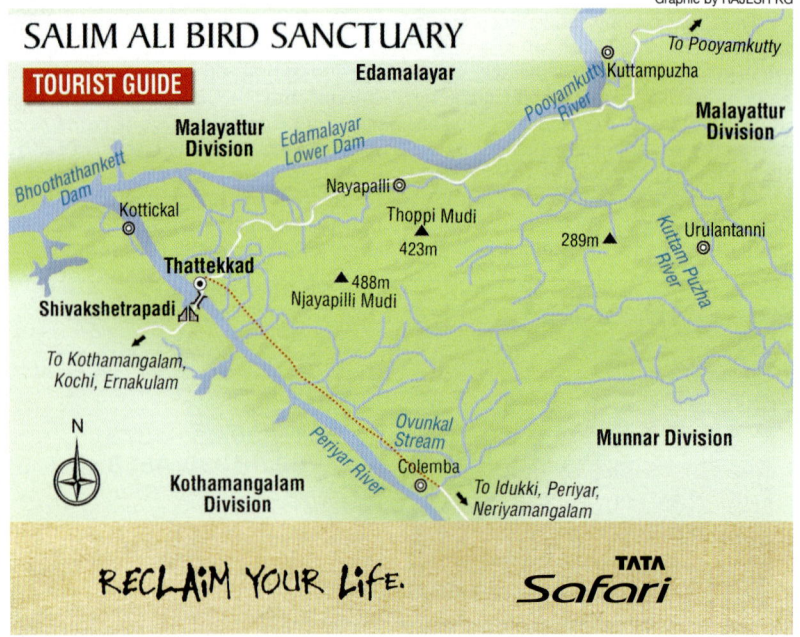

Graphic by RAJESH KG

Take a Wilderness Break

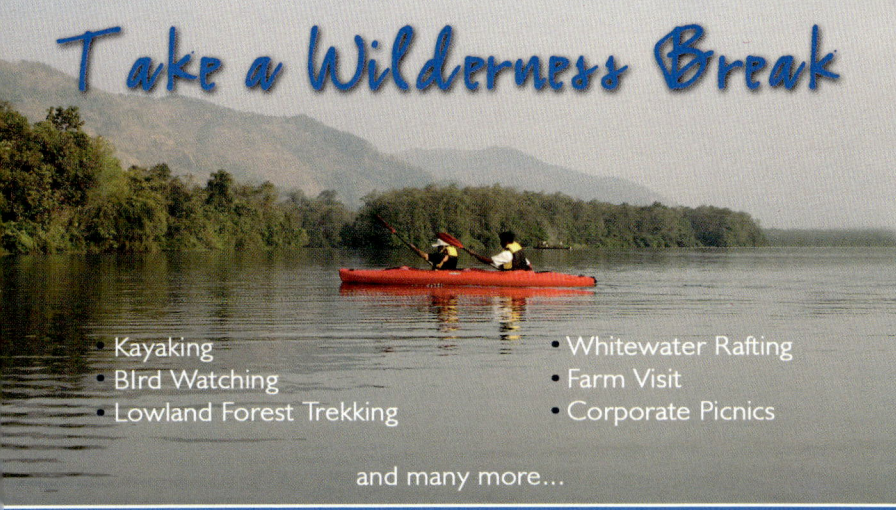

- Kayaking
- Bird Watching
- Lowland Forest Trekking
- Whitewater Rafting
- Farm Visit
- Corporate Picnics

and many more...

The Hornbill Camp
Thattekkad

KALYPSO
eco lodges & camps

G 340, Panampilly Nagar, Kochi- 682036.
Tel: +91-484-2092280 Fax: +91-484-2312627
Email: info@thehornbillcamp.com
www.thehornbillcamp.com
www.kalypsoadventures.com

KERALA

Munnar Road, and to its east lies 22 sq km of the forest. The Forest Inspection Bungalow is to the eastern side, and is close to the road. **Inchathotty Village** is to the eastern side of the sanctuary; there are two seasonal streams of **Ovunkal** (to the eastern side) and **Kolambay** (which is the sanctuary's easternmost boundary).

♦**Sanctuary entry fee** Indians Rs 10, foreigners Rs 100 **Vehicle entry fee** Light vehicles Rs 25, heavy vehicles Rs 150 **Cameras** Still Rs 25, video Rs 150 **Sanctuary timings** 6 am-6 pm

TIP There are no fixed charges for guides, members of the local Eco-Development Committee, which works for the forest's conservation. So do pay them generously

GETTING THERE

Air Nearest airport: Kochi International Airport, Nedumbassery (49 km/ 1½ hrs), connected to Chennai by six daily flights by Paramount Airways, Kingfisher Airlines, Jet Airways and Air Deccan. Taxi to Thattekkad is Rs 800 approx
Rail Nearest railhead: Aluva (Alwaye, 55 km/ 1¼ hrs) **Best option TO** Trivandrum Mail (dep: Chennai Central 8 pm; arr: Aluva 6.07 am) Taxi to Thattekkad is Rs 800 **Best option FROM** Chennai Mail (dep: Aluva 7.35 pm; arr: Avadi 6.09 am, Perambur 6.24 am, Chennai Central 7 am)
Car This long drive across the breadth of Tamil Nadu and Kerala cannot be attempted on a weekend break. Stick to the excellent train connections. For longer vacations, follow NH45 past Chengalpattu, Tindivanam, Viluppuram, Ulundurpettai, Trichy, Manapparai, Dindigul and Vattalkundu to Theni. Follow NH49 over the Western Ghats to Kothamangalam via Devikulam and Munnar. From Kothamangalam, drive 7 km down the Poyamkutty Road to Keerampara, then another 6 km to the ferry (people Re 1, vehicles Rs 40) to Thattekkad. On the opposite bank, the Poyamkutty Road continues right. To your left is Shivakshetrapadi, the entrance gate to Thattekkad, 50 m away

THINGS TO SEE AND DO

There is no denying the beauty of the forest, where there's a wealth of wildlife. Perhaps the most amazing thing about it is the opportunity it offers for discovery, and rediscovery too. For instance, the peninsular bay owl, considered extinct in these parts, has been spotted again. An exciting find has been that of tiger pugmarks — the lord of the jungle is practically unheard of in Thattekkad. Remember to carry a pair of binoculars. There could be leeches too, so carry salt.

Rich mammalian habitat

Thattekkad is noted for its small mammalian population. Elephants are seasonal migrants, often found at **Inchathotty**, a village on the sanctuary's eastern periphery. Elephants also frequent the two seasonal streams of **Ovunkal** and, further east, **Kolambay**. When we approached Ovunkal, telltale signs of these regal behemoths were everywhere. The overpowering smell of fresh dung and urine, trees stripped of their bark, broken bamboo shoots and signs of mud play were enough to pump our adrenalin. But locals warn visitors to follow the scent of the elephants with caution, as elephant charges are common in these parts. The powerful pachyderms share the forests with other mammals including sambar, barking deer and bonnet macaques. The trees are also home to another arboreal creature, the magnificent Travancore flying squirrel — nocturnal creatures whose loud, plaintive calls bring alive the night.

Opens Early. Shuts Late.

In&Out Convenience Stores from Bharat Petroleum.
Now shop and do much more while you fuel.

**Groceries • ATM • Money Transfer • Music • Beverages • Chocolates
• Ice-creams • Snacks • Ready-to-eat • Frozen Foods**

The Papillon story

If you love painted beauties, check out places where the sunlight never hits the ground, often close to the little rivulets that lead off from the **Periyar River**. Here you are sure to find a variety of extremely colourful butterflies with equally exotic names. Malabar rose, Southern or Western Ghats birdwing, lime butterfly, Malabar banded swallowtail, red Helen, Buddha peacock, Paris peacock, Tamil catseye, blue mormon, and the Malabar raven are just a few of the commonly sighted species.

Kochi-based Kalypso Adventures (Kochi Tel: 0484-6583573, 2092280, 09447031032) offers an overnight **Lowland Forest Tour** ex-Kochi through Thattekkad geared for butterfly spotting. Sign on because **Thattekkad** is a prime site. They also offer 7-day butterfly-spotting tours through Kerala which also take you to Top Slip and Mudumalai in Tamil Nadu.

Photos: SATYAN MEPAYUR

Watch where you step

The forests are also full of snakes. We saw a vine snake camouflaged against a little bush beside our path, with only its flickering tongue betraying its presence. Indian rock pythons and king cobras are to be found in the dense evergreens close to the streams, while the spectacled cobra, the Russell's viper, and the bad-tempered saw-scaled viper prefer the deciduous forests.

Bhoothathankettu and Edamalayar

From Kothamangalam, a 15-km/ 20-min ride on the Kothamangalam-Edamalayar route takes you to this popular picnic spot. The dam, its reservoir and a children's park are big attractions here. Another picturesque option is the Edamalayar Lower Dam, 12 km further in from Bhoothathankettu. At sunset, the eerie silence of the surrounding jungles is often shattered by the loud booming sounds of boisterous Nilgiri langurs.

More to do

Visit the **Animal Rehabilitation Centre**, where wounded or stray animals are fed and cared for, until they are ready to be released back into the wild.

Opposite the centre is the **Deer Park**, which has sambar — the largest Indian cervid — and beautiful cheetal in open-air enclosures. The **Taxidermic Museum** showcases the rich variety of Thattekkad's denizens. Amongst birds, the powerful crested hawk eagle, the gorgeous paradise flycatcher, and the tropic bird deserve mention. But the *piece de resistance* is undoubtedly an 8-foot long king cobra.

♦**Timings** 8 am-6 pm for all

WHERE TO STAY

There are two good options at Thattekkad, both confusingly named Hornbill. The privately run **Hornbill Camp** (Kochi Tel: 0484-6583573, 2092280, 094470 31032; Tariff: Rs 3,000), located outside

> History feigns sleep,
> eager to be woken up
> to tell a hundred stories.

To touch the soul of any destination, you need to go back in time. To relive its rich history and vibrant culture. Which is why, stepping into Brunton Boatyard in Fort Cochin is like stepping into the distillery of history. The hotel imbibes the many influences that have made Fort Cochin what it is today and takes you back in time to the eventful past of the centuries old boatyard of Geo Brunton and Sons. Here, people who kept coming from time immemorial left their legacy. Here, diverse cultures united to create an enchanting harmony. Which takes you back in time to relive the glory of yore. From the enormous Indo-Portuguese punkahs in the lobby, to the ancient anchor in the green courtyard, every little detail here has a story to tell. With all of the hotel's 22 rooms overlooking the Arabian Sea in the foreground, through which sailed many a trading vessel of yore, it is easy to drift into another time, another space.

Brunton Boatyard
a cgh earth experience

Central Reservations: Casino Building Cochin Kerala India Phone: +91-484-3011711 Fax: 2668001
Email: contact@cghearth.com www.cghearth.com

KERALA

Locals and visitors take the ferry across the great Periyar River to Thattekkad

the sanctuary, is for serious birders. The cottage tents have sit-outs and en suite, open-to-the-sky bathrooms. There is no electricity here, but the camp has solar-powered lights at night.

TIP Hornbill Camp closes in the monsoon months of June to August

The Forest Department's **Hornbill Inspection Bungalow** (Tel: 0485-2588302, 09477697620; Tariff: Indians Rs 300-600 per room, foreigners US$ 20) is on the opposite bank. Offering an even more intimate tête-à-tête with the forest is the Forest Department's three-storey **watchtower** (Indians Rs 600 for 24 hrs, foreigners US$ 20). Its strategic location in the forest gives you a perfect opportunity to spot animals and birds. Accommodation is on the top floor. Its kitchen offers good meals. The government-run **dormitory** (Tel: 0485-2588302, 09447697620), 300m from the entrance, has 50 beds (Rs 80 a bed, Rs 2,000 for the entire dorm). Food is available on request.

TIP Be sure to book well in advance

In Anakkayam, 8 km from Thattekkad via Kuttampuzha, is the lovely **Periyar River Lodge** (Tel: 0485-2588315, 094477 07173, Kochi Tel: 0484-2207173; Tariff: Rs 3,200), located right on the riverbank. The 75-year-old teakwood house is a traditional *nalukettu*. Settle into a charu *kasera* (armchair) and watch the Periyar glide by. Apart from offering bird-watching tours to Thattekkad, boat tours at Bhoothathankett Dam and half-day tours to the Peendimedu Falls, the lodge also organises rides in *kettuvallams*, country boats, rafts and canoes, bike tours and fishing expeditions.

Jose George's **Plantation Home Stay** (Tel: 0485-2570717, 09388620399; Tariff: Rs 5,625-7,200) at his sprawling Mundackal Estate, on NH49 at Pindimana near Kothamangalam, is another superb option outside Thattekkad. It offers birdwatching accompanied by an experienced ornithologist, houseboat stays, cycling, hiking, Syrian Christian cooking classes and plantation tours.

Also 8 km from the sanctuary at Palamattom is the **Birds Lagoon Village Resort** (Tel: 09447025123; 0485-2572444; Tariff: Rs 2,000-3,500), which has a swimming pool and an Ayurvedic centre, and offers boating facilities.

For details, see Thattekkad Accommodation Listings on page 511 ∎

Photographs by PRASHANT PANJIAR

A kettuvallom pulls in to Alappuzha

ALAPPUZHA
LIFE IN SLOW MOTION

State Kerala
Location Sandwiched between the Arabian Sea and the Punnamada backwaters on Kerala's southern coast, 71 km S of Kochi
Distance 711 km SW of Chennai **JOURNEY TIME** **By rail** 13½ hrs **By air** 1 hr + 2 hrs by road
Route NH45 to Theni via Chengalpattu, Tindivanam, Viluppuram, Ulundurpettai, Veppur, Trichy, Manapparai, Vadamadurai, Dindigul and Vattalakundu; NH220 to Vandiperiyar via Uttamapalaiyam, Kilgudalur and Thekkady; SH to Kottayam via Peermade, Kanjirapally and Pambadi; SH11 to Alappuzha via Chennamkary
Alternative Route Follow route to Kochi (*see page 400*), then take NH47 to Alappuzha via Arur and Cherthala (*see route guides on pages 12 and 320*)

KERALA

■ BY SUSAN VISVANATHAN

There is a quay in Alappuzha, a storm-battered relic that stares at the sea rather forlornly, a reminder of all that this small and lovely town was once upon a time. A few years ago, you could walk some distance out to the Arabian Sea, on the wooden boards of the quay, and see the blue waters through the gaps. The waves would then tell you a story, of the resplendent Venice of the East that was once the entry town to Kerala, much before Kochi (*see page 400*) became the harbour of choice.

CHENNAI WEEKEND BREAKS | 445

KERALA

It's difficult to imagine that Alappuzha misses its past, for, though commerce flourishes here, it's startlingly untouched by modernity. When a rice mill came up in 1980, it called for a major celebration. And when a railway track was laid in the early nineties, it was considered an astounding event! Everything about this town reinforces that old world feeling - the colonial era government houses, grand and graceful despite the years, the canals, green and coated with weeds, filled with boats carrying hay or bananas.

The sea, Alappuzha's enduring motif, remains beautiful and dangerous in equal measure, often lashing angrily as it did during the tsunami of December 2004, or quietly lapping against the pure white sands, its waters bountiful with catch for the fisherfolk. The Malayali writer Thakazhi Sivasankaran Pillai immortalised the contradiction in his award-winning novel *Chemmeen*; the sea that blesses can also take everything away. But, it's impossible to call the sea moody while walking on the beach on a winter afternoon, the white lighthouse standing tall against the clear blue skies.

The canals throw up another study in contrasts. Boatmen row past the weeds with amazing grace even as traffic hurtles above their heads on modern bridges with names such as Iron Bridge, Stone Bridge or even a Palace Bridge! As vehicles whiz past, the canal reflects a myriad colours in the tiny space that the water hyacinth has not-so-generously left for the sunlight to seep in — that of the water lily, of a bird's wings, or the brilliant hues of the tropical sky. These are the interior canals, where tourists aren't given the luxury of enjoying boat rides. But in August, during Onam, another canal resounding with the hurrays of the Nehru Trophy boat race — one of the most celebrated events in Kerala — more than make up.

For all its small town appearance, Alappuzha has an impressive history. The port was built by Raja Kesava Das, the dewan of Travancore, in the 18th century. An enduring contribution came from the Darraigh Smaile and Company, whose founder James Darraigh, an Irish man, introduced the coir industry to the town. The story about how they brought technicians "Bannerjee and Mukherjee" from Bengal to teach locals the art of spinning yarn from coir now enjoys a legendary status here. Today, rubber plantations may be more important than coir factories, but the tradition continues: among the fisherfolk, you'll find the women working on coir and magically moulding it into ropes or mats. Many a tale has been spun around this yarn, and like the story of Alappuzha itself, each tale is to be relished and remembered.

→ FAST FACTS

When to go Post-monsoon, Oct to May
Tourist offices
● Dist Tourism Promotion Council 🛈 🌐
Boat Jetty Road, Alappuzha
Tel: 0477-2251796; Fax: 2251720
Email: alp-dtpcalpy@sancharnet.in
Website: alappuzhatourism.com
TIP For hotel reservations, daily backwater cruises, 'Round the Venice of the East on Foot' tours, houseboat and car rental
● Tourist Information Office 🛈
Department of Tourism, Government of Kerala, near boat jetty. Tel: 2260722
● Dept of Tourism, Govt of Kerala 🛈 🌐
Tourism Complex, Wallajah Road, Chennai. Tel: 044-25369789
● KTDC Tourist Reception Centre 🛈 🌐
TTDC Complex, 2, Wallajah Road
Chennai. Telefax: 044-25382639
Website: ktdc.com
STD code 0477

ALAPPUZHA

Bhagawathy Temple in the Kokanastha Brahmin enclave of Mullackal

ORIENTATION

There are at least six navigable canals in the town. The **Vadai Canal North Bank** (VCNB) and **South Bank** (VCSB) roads, and **Commercial Canal North Bank** (CCNB) and **South Bank** (CCSB) roads run parallel to each other across the city. In the East, these canals open to the **Punnamada Kayal** (backwaters), thereby connecting the city to the mesh of backwater trails, which were once abuzz with traders and travellers. Follow the VCNB and VCSB roads to Alleppey's **Boat Jetty** on the Punnamada backwaters, crowded with numerous houseboat and backwaters operators. On the western side, the canals end near the pier on **Alleppey Beach**. Traffic hurtles over the canals along Alleppey's Iron, Stone and Palace bridges. These inner canals are not open to tourists, but you can stand on the edges of the traffic and watch the flight of birds, the occasional water lilies and the brilliant hues of tropical sky reflected sometimes in the water, where the weeds allow a space of burnished water. The names of the bridges convey an older gentler time, when there was very little traffic, and like the disused pier, the bridges were designed for pedestrians.

The **railway station** is in south-west Alappuzha, near the District Hospital.

THINGS TO SEE AND DO

Alleppey's allure is the backwaters. Begin with a cruise from the Boat Jetty, then stroll back into town past the canals covered with mauve hyacinths. While the town's natural beauty is awe-inspiring, look for the heritage structures too: the tales they tell are truly remarkable. Much of the architecture in Alappuzha, particularly of government offices is colonial, and it has survived the years and the continuous use very well.

Alappuzha has witnessed many a nationalist and social reform movement, and its remnants — such as the Punnapra-Vayalar martyr's column — dot the region. The Punnapra-Vayalar agitation is considered by some as a landmark revolt by workers against authoritarian landlords, and movements such as these have shaped Alappuzha.

Alleppey Beach

Alappuzha was once the busiest coast south of Mumbai, and its canals and backwaters helped in the passage of cargo — be it tea, rubber or other produce from the hills — to the sea. The lighthouse and the pier helped the boats ferry across, facilitating trade in their own way. Today, the 1,000-ft long pier, built in 1862 by Captain Hugh Crawford, is a mere skeleton of its past. The bricks have mostly fallen apart or been washed away by the sea and it's risky to walk on it. Yet it exudes an unmistakable colonial air. Entry to the lighthouse is restricted.

There are several entertainment facilities on this beach (Vijaya Beach), including a children's park run by the District Tourism Promotion Council (DTPC), which is quite nice if you discount the garish swings. There are also boating facilities.

♦**Park entry fee** Adults Rs 5, children Rs 3 **Timings** 4-7 pm

Backwaters

This is a must-do on your Alleppey holiday. A backwater cruise on the Punnamada Kayal takes you along canals past scenic islands (*see below*), offering sublime views of coconut and paddy fields, Chinese fishing nets and toddy tappers at work. Boats can be hired from the Tourist Boat Jetty near the bus station. You can also ask DTPC for a private cruise (Fee: Rs 200 per hour for a group of 10 and Rs 350 for a group of 20; Timings: 8 am to 7 pm) at the jetty behind the DTPC office. KSRTC boats cruise the backwaters too, up to the villages all around. Options include an Alleppey-Kollam 8-hr daily cruise, Alleppey-Kottayam (Fee: Rs 1,500 for 10 persons; $2^1/_2$ hrs). Longer options include entire holidays spent aboard your own houseboat.

The Punnamada Kayal is the starting point for the annual boat races in Alappuzha. This is where the Nehru Boat Race, the biggest snake boat race in the state, is held during the second Saturday of August. Watching the snake boats competing with each other is an awesome sight. There are boats in all sizes, some with as many as a hundred rowers and several cheerleaders!

TIP *See 'Boat races' on page 456*

R and QST Block islands

Alappuzha's beauty is not merely in its backwaters, but in the manmade islands that you will find amidst the waters. These islands are hedged by mud walls, a

→ GETTING THERE

Air Nearest airport: Kochi International Airport, Nedumbassery (90 km/ 2 hrs). A pre-paid taxi to Alappuzha will cost Rs 1,000 approx

Rail Alleppey Station (Tel: 0477-2253865) **Best option TO** Alleppey Express (dep: Chennai Central 9.15 pm; arr: Alleppey 10.50 am) **Best option FROM** Chennai Express (dep: Alleppey 4.10 pm; arr: Avadi 5.03 am, Perambur 5.13 am, Chennai Central 6.05 am)

Car This long drive across the breadth of Tamil Nadu and Kerala from the east coast to the west should not be attempted on a weekend break. Stick to the excellent train connections. For longer vacations, follow NH45 past Chengalpattu, Tindivanam, Viluppuram, Ulundurpettai, Trichy, Manapparai, Dindigul and Vattalakundu to Theni. Follow NH220 south over the Western Ghats to Vandiperiyar via Uttamapalaiyam, Kilgudalur and Thekkady. Then take the KK Road to Kottayam via Kanjirapally. At Kottayam, the MC Road goes south towards Changanassery, 18 km away, from where you turn right on to SH11 to Alleppey, 27 km away

ALAPPUZHA

Swimming in one of the many canals that run through Alappuzha

haven for migratory birds, with paddy fields inundated with water through the year. These fields stand below sea level. **R Block** is especially famous for the fresh toddy served to guests. Drop in and hang around in the toddy shop till the next boat comes! Try the delicious dishes at the shop, such as crabs, clams, prawns and a variety of fish that are endemic to the backwaters. And if you are keen on taking a dip, the islands are the best bet. Kerala State Water Transport Department (Tel: 0477-2252510; Timings: 10 am-5 pm) offers cruises to R Block.

◆**Passenger boat capacity** 100 people **Cruise fee** Rs 7 **Duration** $1^{1}/_{2}$ hrs **Timings** 7.30, 9.30 and 11.30 am, 2.30 and 5.30 pm **Speedboat capacity** 3 people **Cruise fee** Rs 650 per hour **Motorboat capacity** 15 people **Cruise fee** Rs 280 per hour

TIP *See pages 450-451 for a listing of private backwater operators in Alappuzha*

Mullackal

The Alappuzha Town is built around a Konkani Brahmin settlement known as Mullackal, and it is in this settlement

KERALA

HOTEL KA GURU RECOMMENDS IN
ALLEPPEY

Choose from our network of over 4000 hotels in India. Serviced apartments, budget hotels, luxury resorts, palaces, business accomodations, houseboats and more.

Hotel	Rating
Arcadia Regency	Budget
Pagoda Resort	3 ★
House Boat (Grandeur)	Gold Class

MTNL/BSNL Toll Free No.
1-800-22-4878
022-4030-4878
www.travelguru.com

travelguru™
India's Largest Hotel Network

The person featured above is an actual Travelguru employee

Backwater tour operators

Alleppey Tourism Development Co-operative Society
Contact G Raghu **Address** A-837, Komala Road, Alappuzha **Tel** 0477-2243462 **Fax** 2231145 **Email** info@atdcalleppey.com **Website** atdcalleppey.com **Services** Runs the Coir Village Lake Resort in Trikkunapuzha, houseboat, motorboat and speedboat service across the entire backwaters of south Kerala, day cruises, 2-5 day Backwater Magic packages starting at Rs 9,000 per couple, including 2 nights in Coir Village Resort and one night in a houseboat

Aqua Holidays Tours & Travels
Contact Das **Location** Opp Boat Jetty **Address** 14 Municipal Shopping Complex Building, Alappuzha **Tel** 2261209 **Fax** 2261861 **Email** aquaholidays@sancharnet.in **Services** AC and non-AC houseboats, speedboat, motorboat and day cruise services for Alappuzha, Kumarakom and Thottappaly, packages and houseboat tours starting at Rs 5,500 per couple per night
TIP Kochi Agent: Intersight Tel: 0484-2316637

Bharath Tourist Service Society
Contact Tom **Address** Raiban Complex, near Boat Jetty, Alappuzha **Telefax** 2262262, 2264860 **Mobile** 09447304376 **Email** info@btsstourism.com **Website** btsstourism.com **Services** Houseboat, motorboat and day cruises in Alappuzha and Kumarakom, 3-5 day packages starting at Rs 4,000, houseboat tours at Rs 4,500 per couple per night

Blue Lagoon Tourist Services
Contact Hanson **Address** Kiosk No. 4, VCSB Road, Alappuzha **Tel** 2260103/ 4103 **Mobile** 09847075975 **Fax** 2237103 **Email** alleppeytour@vsnl.com, bluelagoon@sancharnet.in **Website** alleptour.com **Services** Associated with Royal Park, Coconut County, Marari Beach, Punnamada Lake Resort and Lake Palace hotels among others in Alleppey, houseboat and motorboat services for Kochi, Kollam, Kumarakom and Kottayam, 2-5 day honeymoon packages starting at Rs 5,000 and houseboat tours at Rs 4,000 per couple per night

Bon Voyage Backwater
Contact Sushil Kumar **Address** Raiban Shopping Complex, Boat Jetty, Alappuzha **Tel** 2245576, 2261079 **Mobile** 09847310105 **Email** bonvoyage@sancharnet.in **Website** bonvoyagebackwater.com **Services** Associated with Alleppey Beach Resort, houseboat, motorboat, speedboat, day cruises across the entire southern backwaters, 5D packages, honeymoon package starting at Rs 4,000 per couple per night, special Whole Backwater Package for Rs 30,000

Coco Planet Tours & Travels
Contact Switen George **Location** Near Nehru Trophy Finishing Point **Address** Thatampally Post, Alappuzha **Tel** 0477-3223505, 2239904 **Mobile** 09847325026 **Fax** 2239903 **Email** kerala_houseboats@yahoo.com **Website** beautifulkerala.com **Services** Houseboat, motorboat and day cruises from Alleppey to Kochi and Kumarakom, 5-7 day Kerala packages starting at Rs 20,000, houseboat tours at Rs 4,000 per couple per night

District Tourism Promotion Council
Contact Kala **Location** Near Bus Stand, opp Canara Bank **Address** Boat Jetty Road, Alappuzha **Tel** 2251796 **Fax** 2251720 **Email** dtpcaipy_dptpcaipy@sancharnet.in **Website** alappuzhatourism.com **Services** Houseboats from Alleppey to Kumarakom (Rs 6,000), houseboats at Rs 4,500 for 2 adults and 2 children with meals, motorboats at Rs 200 per hour for 15 people, daytime motorboat backwater cruise (10.30 am-6.30 pm), arrangement of boat pass from Amritapuri Ashram by 4 pm, houseboat packages

Marvel Cruise
Address Akkarakkalam House, Mullackal, Alappuzha **Tel** 2264341 **Mobile** 09947235684 **Email** marvelcruise@sancharnet.in **Website** marvelcruise.com **Services** Houseboat and

ALAPPUZHA

V MUTHURAMAN

A traditionally built 'floating hotel' awaits custom on the Punnamada Kayal

day cruise services, authentic Kerala food prepared on board, village walks with guide, fishing from the houseboat, packages start at Rs 5,000-7,500

My Dream Cruise & Tours
Contact Hasheem **Location** Near Komala Hotel, Zilla Court Ward, Alappuzha **Tel** 3290365 **Mobile** 09846075978 **Email** mydream@india.com **Website** mydreamindia.com **Services** Houseboats, day cruises, motorboats, canoes, 2-week Kerala package including backwaters starts at Rs 45,000 per couple

Pooja Tours and Travels
Contact Ratheesh **Address** Above Bata Showroom, Mullackal, Alappuzha **Tel** 2239886-87 **Fax** 2238857 **Email** poojatours@spectrum.net.in **Website** poojatours.com **Services** Operate two houseboats

Pulickattil Tour Links
Contact Devasia **Address** Boat Jetty, Alappuzha **Telefax** 2251877 **Mobile** 09847051877 **Email** pulikatiltours@yahoo.com

Services Houseboat, motorboat, speedboat and day cruises in Alleppey, Alleppey backwater 3 day packages starting at Rs 4,000 per couple per night, among other packages

River and Country Tours
Contact Tommy Joseph **Location** Opp Boat Jetty **Address** No. 13, Municipal Library, Shopping Complex, Zila Court Ward, Alappuzha **Tel** 2243581 **Mobile** 09846045386 **Fax** 2245386 **Email** rivercountry@asianetindia.com **Website** riverandcountry.com **Services** Houseboats, motorboats and speedboats across the entire southern backwaters, day cruises, backwater packages

Soma Houseboats
Contact Pramesh **Address** Nehru Trophy Boat Race Finishing Point, Thathampally PO, Alappuzha **Telefax** 2264112 **Mobile** 09447686870 **Email** somatheeram@vsnl.com **Website** somahouseboats.com **Services** Cruises from Allepey all over the southern backwaters (Rs 2,000-6,000 per night, inclusive of meals)

KERALA

Kites wave goodbye as crowds watch the sun set off Alleppey Beach

that the Bhagavathy Temple can be found. The main deity at the temple is Goddess Bhagavathy, though there are also installations of *navavigrahangal* or the nine planets. The settlement specialises in the trade of making sweets. A temple to Mariamman, the twin sister to the Mullackal Bhagavathy, is a kilometre away from Mullackal.

The main festival at the temple is Chirappu, held in December, when all of Alappuzha decks up with festoons and flags. A fair, with vessels and several items on display and sale, is also organised during this time.

♦**Timings** 5-11 am, 5-8 pm **Main festival** 10-day Mullackal Chirappu in late December

SHOPPING

Shopping is always exhilarating in Alappuzha, for it is not what one buys here that is important, but the joyous feeling of being part of a throng of people who obviously love shopping! The streets, say near the Mullackal shopping junction, are filled with the scent of lime and jasmine and sandalwood and spices (vendors selling cloves, pepper and lime sit every half a metre on the busy road). This is where people of the district come to when they need to shop for weddings, so there is always an air of urgency and jubilation here. In winter, crowds of Sabarimala devotees spill into the town, and the streets are filled with vendors. Then, you can pick up everything from sharp knives, combs, games, toys and clothes to incense, wood carvings and heavy metal utensils.

Alappuzha has known a thriving pepper and spice trade, not to mention a paper trade. Some of the oldest and best stationers in Kerala, such as the **PA George Company** (Tel: 2251475) are from this town. Also famous is a "gold, silver and diamond street", where you will find at least 30 shops, **Bhima** (Tel: 2251288, 2251691) being the most famous, selling carefully crafted jewellery. There are also shops selling fine muslin, bronze items and copper ware.

Experience
the excellence

Lake Palace
A LUXURY BACKWATER RESORT

Phone: 91-477-2239701 - 4 & 2230001 - 6
Fax: 91-477-2239705
E-mail: info@lakepalaceresort.com
Website: www.lakepalaceresort.com

Thirumala Ward, Chungam, Alleppey, Kerala, India

KERALA

The best places to try spicy Kuttanad food in Alappuzha are its famous toddy shops

Popy's (Tel: 2251425) and **St George**, the best known umbrella brands in Kerala, are based here, and there are many others who mend and sell umbrellas of equally good quality.

There is a lovely **Khadi Gandhi Store** on the main street, where you get cheap fabric of excellent quality, possibly like the ones the Romans were enamoured of 2,000 years ago. **Seemati** (Tel: 2251774), in one of the side streets, has a good selection of fine, gold-bordered saris, sold at rates much cheaper than in other towns in Kerala.

WHERE TO STAY

You will find a cluster of hotels on NH47, about 2 km from the centre of town, offering high end and middle-end accommodation. These are all well-connected to the town by taxi, bus or autorickshaw.

The **Marari Beach Resort** (Tel: 0477-2863801-09; Tariff: Rs 12,800-19,250) sprawls across 25 acres, off the soft sandy beach at the fishing village of Maraikulam, just north of Alappuzha. The 52 cottages are separated from the sea by a windbreak of coconut palms. Relaxing oil and herbal massages, and longer-term authentic Ayurvedic treatments are offered, as are open-air yoga classes. Fresh karimeen, prawns and lobsters are served at Fort Cochin, the resort's speciality seafood restaurant.

Marari Beach Home (Tel: 2243535 Mobile: 09447132836; Tariff: Rs 3,500-4,370) is another resort in serene environs on Mararikulam Beach.

Anamika The Villa is a 100-year-old Syrian Christian *tharavad* in the heart of Alleppey. The heritage home has been painstakingly renovated. The hotel arranges kettuvallom cruises, speed, motor and paddle boats, visits to a coir-making village and cultural evenings, with Kathakali or Mohiniattam performances.

Gowri Residence (Tel: 2236371/ 471, Mobile: 09847055371; Tariff: Rs 500-1,000), just outside Alleppey near the Udupi Sree Krishna Temple in Thondankulangara, is another tharavad thrown open to travellers. They offer backwater tours and Ayurvedic massage.

Loll by the lakeside. Take a dip by the tree-cocooned pool. Take a walk on the pathways that border the village. And soak in a way of life that you will wish you could have for a lifetime.

Makes you wonder why getaways can't be for a lifetime.

Punnamada, Alleppey, Kerala, India, Tel: 91 477 2233690, Fax: 91 477 2233694
Mail: mail@punnamada.com, www.punnamada.com

KERALA

Boat races

Imagine 20-odd bedecked ram-snouted battle wagons with high flaring tails, spectators packed on the palm shaded banks, a breath held back in tense expectation — and then as the starter's flag is brought down — a mighty roar that tears out of a thousand throats!

The oldest boat race in Kerala, the **Champakulam Boat Race** commemorates the journey of the Lord Krishna idol from Kurichi to the temple of Sri Krishna at Ambalapuzha. The three-day event, held in the Moolam Day of the Malayalam month of Midhunam (June-July) includes a water pageant and a boat race (held on the third day of the festivities).

Probably the holiest of all, the **Aranmula Boat Race** is said to take its name from 'Aru' (six) and 'mula' (bamboo) alluding to a bamboo raft on which the Sri Parthasarthy Temple idol is said to have been brought to the temple at Aranmula. Held in the month of Chingam (Sept) the highlight of the pageant are the 26 boats that recreate the journey and the traditional songs that accompany it.

The **Payippad Boat Race** held on the lake by the same name celebrates the installation of the idol found in Payippad Lake

At the Nehru Trophy Boat Race

at the 16th century Subramanya Swamy Temple in Haripad. The journey from the lake to the temple is celebrated with a boat race held every year on the third day of Onam.

On 22 December 1952, India's first Prime Minister Jawaharlal Nehru was invited for a boat ride from Kottayam to Alleppey. Nehru took the ride and on the way witnessed a nine-boat race at Punnamada Lake. The event excited him so much that he jumped into the boat that won the race. Originally known as the Punnamada Boat Race the event was renamed **Nehru Trophy Boat Race** after Nehru's death.

Raheem Residency (Tel: 2230767/ 9767; Tariff: Rs 5,000-6,000), 'a gift from the past for the present', is a heritage home located on Alleppey Beach. The six spacious rooms are furnished with traditional items made of teak, and there's a two-bedroom independent unit in a separate courtyard, refurbished from old outhouses used to store coconuts. Raheem Residency arranges traditional wedding services complete with flowers, drummers, elephants, the wedding feast and witnesses, if necessary, for guests of all religious denominations, followed by honeymoon in their Honeymoon Suite.

Alleppey Beach Resort (Tel: 2260125, 2263408; Tariff: Rs 1,500- 3,000) has 8 rooms off Alleppey Beach. One of the better options, with private access to the beach, and houseboat and motorboat cruises on the backwaters.

The Prince Hotel (Tel: 2243752-56; Tariff: Rs 1,250-2,500), on Cherthala Road, has a poolside restaurant, with regular evening music shows. They serve local cuisine, although the Continental cuisine is the safest and best bet. The handicraft shop here sells ethnically embroidered clothes as well as some exquisitely carved silver jewellery. Budget options include the **KTDC Motel Aaram** (Tel: 2244460/ 760; Tariff: Rs 350-1,100), on Kalappura, and the **Government Guest House** (Tel: 2246503; Tariff: Rs

The beach shares her treasures with just a few; for the others there's just the sun, sand and sea.

We've understood that you can see a destination, you can touch a destination and you can live a destination. Evolved travellers like you seek **living, breathing impressions**. For you, a beach has much more to offer than the sun, sand and surf. The magic of the sea lies in the lives of the fisher folk. In their songs, in their hopes, their fears, their simple joys. Which is why here, in Marari Beach, in quaint Alleppey, we have ensured that your experience encompasses the people that lend life to them. We believe that a holiday comes alive only when the hotel breathes the life of the community around it - be it the flavour of the fish curry as only boatmen can serve, the rhythm in the song of the fisher folk as they haul in their catch or the amazing simplicity in the way they thatch their roof with palm fronds. A string of magical experiences is yours to savour.

Marari Beach
a cgh earth experience

Central Reservations: Casino Building Cochin Kerala India Phone: +91-484-3011711 Fax: 2668001
Email: contact@cghearth.com   www.cghearth.com

KERALA

Malabar porottas at a chai kada near Gujarathi Street in Alappuzha

220-440), near Prince hotel on NH47. The KTDC hotel has a restaurant.

The Coir Board's guesthouse **Padipura Residence** (Tel: 2244978, 2245001; Tariff: Rs 600-1,200) near the District Court offers six double rooms and meals on request.

Many visitors to Alleppey opt for its unique stay offer — in a kettuvallom (houseboat) on the backwaters. Houseboats are run by both private operators and the state tourism department (*see 'Backwaters Operators' on pages 450-451 to book your stay*).

For more hotels and details, see Alappuzha Accommodation Listings on page 499

WHERE TO EAT

Alappuzha's proximity to the sea, and the many canals that crisscross it, have ensured that the area is famous for seafood delicacies in particular, and fish in general. There are other food items too that you just have to try, such as the appams and the stew at Hotel Green Corner in Pazhayangadi. Hotel Aaryas (Tel: 0477-3290389) near the medical college, serves excellent vegetarian food. Gujarathi Street near the beach has good hotels specialising in North Indian food. The Mullackal area has good vegetarian fare, made in the Udupi style.

For the true local experience, you have to taste kappa (tapioca) and karimeen pollichathu, pearlspot fish (a backwater fish) baked over coals, covered in banana leaves, or karimeen curry. Tapioca is a staple diet of the region, apart from rice, and is cut into slices, boiled and usually eaten along with fish curry. Konchu (brackish water prawns) pollichathu and varal fry are also equally delicious.

For a truly memorable eating-out experience, drop in at the toddy shop at the R-Block Island, where apart from konchu and karimeen, all the delicacies are freshly caught from the water, cooked and served. You won't complain that the food takes time to be served, because you get to relish some toddy in the meanwhile.

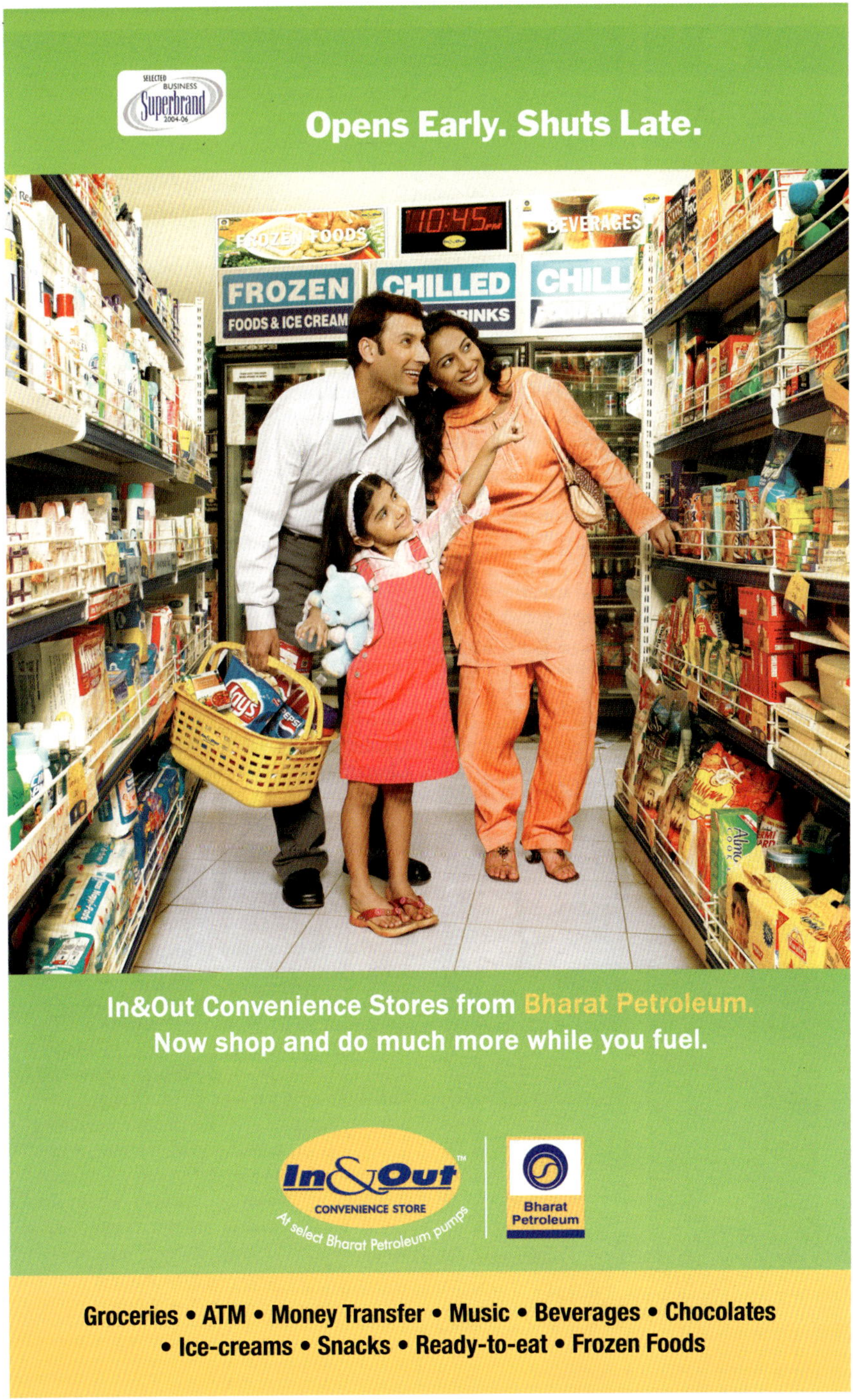

Opens Early. Shuts Late.

In&Out Convenience Stores from Bharat Petroleum.
Now shop and do much more while you fuel.

Groceries • ATM • Money Transfer • Music • Beverages • Chocolates
• Ice-creams • Snacks • Ready-to-eat • Frozen Foods

KERALA

The **Kalpakavadi Inn** (Tel: 0479-2492239), at Kannalippalam near the Thottapalli Spillway, has fine food and delectable toddy. The inn is surrounded by a coconut grove, set next to a backwater, and it has cottages where you can sit and relax while fresh fish caught from the lake is prepared.

In Alappuzha Town, the **KTDC Motel Aaram** (Tel: 2244460; Tariff: Rs 350-1,100) on NH47 serves lunch, with karimeen fry and vegetables done in local style. They also have a buffet meal. **Prince Hotel** (Tel: 2243752-56) serves a fine dish of grilled prawns in Continental style.

Excellent bakeries are to be found opposite the small temples in the main street, and their fruit cake has a rich brown heavy Christmasy quality, all round the year. You will find clusters of bakeries near the jetty and in the Mullackal Ward.

AROUND ALLEPPEY

Arthunkal (22 km)
The **Saint Andrew's Church** at Arthunkal, built by the Portuguese in 1591, reflects the Hindu influence on the Jesuit missionaries who supervised its construction. Both Christian and Hindu devotees flock to this pilgrim spot. The Arthunkal Perunnal, a famous feast celebrated here, is dedicated to St Sebastian. On the way back, stop at Chennaveli, where an old man called Sasiettan runs a toddy shop that serves excellent toddy and food.

Cherthala (20 km)
To the north of Alappuzha lies Cherthala, where you will get to see the traditional way of manufacturing coir — it's a noted coir weaving centre in Kerala. While driving from Alappuzha, before Cherthala, you will come across a diversion to **Ex Era Weaves**, where spinning is done finely with thread from coconut fibre. It's closed on Sunday.

North of Cherthala Town is a very ancient Bhagavathy Temple, famous for its annual festival. About 2 km away is Vayalar, where the Punnapra-Vayalar revolt took place. During the revolt in 1946, workers (organised and led by Communists) rose against authoritarian landlords in the area. The Travancore State Police were deployed to crush the uprising, and though they managed to brutally suppress the revolt, the workers' struggle soon acquired the dimension of something of a legend. Even today, some consider it as an important agitation towards the setting up of democratic rule in Kerala. Today, there is a Martyrs' Memorial here, where you will still find coconut palms bearing bullet marks. ■

Inputs by KV Cybil

Stone bridge across Vadai Canal

Specials

Catch the Mountain Railway and trek in the Nilgiri Hills... Take a hike in serene Kodai... Or stay out of the way as the bulls run wild in Alanganallur

Days in the forest

Following a forgotten mountain trail in the Western Ghats

■ BY SANJIV VALSAN

Sharing an abandoned bungalow with a wild bison for the night was turning out to be a rather workable arrangement. He kept to himself, occupying the room he was used to, and I, something of an uninvited guest, generally stayed in mine, trying not to stir the situation. It was a cold night, but I think we both slept easy in our forest rest house at Vandarvu.

"There's a 'fison in there," Jawahar, my guide, had remarked, waving a torch around. He was something of an add-on himself, having joined me the previous day at Berijam Lake in the middle of my trek. This was at the insistence of a hospitable, yet overly anxious man at the Berijam Forest Office whom they all called 'Sir', and whose luxuriant grey moustache had cringed in anguish upon my insistence in broken Tamil that I would trek alone from Kodaikanal to Top Station, near Munnar, in spite of the recent sighting of a wild elephant in the area who had given birth to a calf, and was likely to charge at anyone in her path.

Turning back wasn't an option. I had already finished a quarter of the four-day trek after an unusual amount of planning. The original idea had been to trek on the Old Kodaikanal-Munnar Road, part of an old British-built interstate highway. It was the highest motorable road in

India south of the Himalayas, but the stretch between Kodi and Munnar is now a reserved forest area and closed to vehicles.

I needed a written trekking permission letter from the Range Officer at Munnar, who readily agreed, provided the District Forest Officer at Kodaikanal too gave me an authorising letter. Four faxes down, it was becoming clear that the permission was not forthcoming. I could either take another route, or choose to trek through reams of fax.

And thus another route was born. After consulting a few local trekking agents, I decided to trek from Mannavanur, near Kodaikanal, to Berijam, a high-altitude lake known for its abundant wildlife and sheer size; take the old jungle road up to a point close to the Kerala border, and from there, walk along another route that was still in Tamil Nadu and trek across to the Kerala side from Klaverai Village, which was outside any reserved forest. The Kodaikanal DFO was friendly, efficient and keen on promoting nature tourism, and processed my trekking order in under an hour.

The walk to Berijam Lake through an unused forest road lined with pine, wattle and eucalyptus set the mood, and I was feeling invincible by the time I reached the waterfront and the range office at sundown. In the two days I spent at Berijam, 'Sir' took something of a liking to me, and, at his insistence, I agreed to walk till the border of the RF area with a guide. We managed to find Jawahar(lal) to accompany me, since he lived in one of the villages near the forest and knew the area well.

There had been a bit of a mix-up with my booking because a local MP had arrived and occupied the room I was supposed to be in, and I ended up bunking with two forest officers, who were a good source of trekking information. One of my new roommates invited me to join a group he was taking on a day trek, along with Pallanisamy, another forest officer and an old hand. The plan was to trek through the Mathiketan Shola.

Our shola walk traversed a patch of grassland. But the only animal we got to see for a brief flash was a sambar, which disappeared upon hearing the group's chatter. By this time, a man in our group, having been bitten by a leech, had already become hysterical, cussing disbelievingly in horror. Leech-dominated comments lingered for a bit. It was at this point that Pallanisamy began to let forth his random tidbits of jungle trivia bordering on the bizarre, such as "Leeches' favourite blood groups are O+ and AB."

**Picturesque short-cut to market;
View from the Berijam trail** (left)

Photographs by SANJIV VALSAN

Indian wild bison, or gaur, are a common sight at Berijam Lake. On my arrival at the Berijam Forest Rest House, the canteen keeper called me to the backyard and pointed a torch out for me, and there it was, some eight feet away — an unbelievably huge black bovine in white socks, nearly seven feet tall with horns the size of sickles, and munching on our canteen leftovers. It was inexplicably strange how the supposedly dangerous beast looked vulnerable, embarrassed even, caught in the torchlight eating canteen waste.

Having been acquainted with the gentle ways of this potentially moody beast, it was with only the slightest hesitation that two days later I found myself sharing an abandoned Forest Department Rest House with a gaur. He was next door, and used a separate entrance. Over the years of the house's disuse, plants had grown out of many corners, colonising all the toilets; it didn't seem that unreasonable that animals should follow suit. Our gaur, having spent the night, probably left very early in the morning. Apart from a Giant Malabar Squirrel that once ran across the trail that afternoon, this would be my last encounter with an unusual wild animal on the trek.

Up to a point, the route from Berijam to Vandarvu followed the old Kodaikanal-Munnar Ghat Road, built by the British in the early 20th century, and now left to the elements, stripped of tar and traffic. The old milestones, however, are still in place, indicating distances to Munnar, Kodaikanal, Madurai and Cochin, as are the bridges that traverse the many gurgling freshwater streams on the way and the old British Highway Department Bungalow at Vandarvu.

Most of the hike passes through natural and man-made forests till Vandarvu. The views really begin to open up on the way to Klaverai, a charming little village in the clouds. At Klaverai I parted ways with my companions.

On any given day there are people crossing the state border from Klaverai to Kovilur on foot, as no roads connect the two villages. The initial stretch of the walk was both easy and scenic; with a near panoramic view of the range. The

→ FAST FACTS

When to go The pleasant summer makes April-May best to do the trek
Trek itinerary
Day 1: Kodaikanal-Mannavanur Village by bus, jeep or taxi. Walk from Mannavanur to Berijam Lake
Day 2: Berijam Lake-Marian Shola-Kathrikai Odai-Vandarvu. Halt at Forest Rest House at Vandarvu
Day 3: Vandarvu-Klaverai. Rudimentary but reasonably clean accommodation available at Klaverai for Rs 40-150 a day
Day 4: Klaverai-Kovilur, then catch a bus to Munnar. Cross the state border to reach Kovilur village, where buses leave for Munnar and Ernakulam, via Top Station
Special permission This must be taken from the District Forest Officer (Tel: 04542-241287). For more information see www.dindigul.nic.in/KodaiTrek.htm.
Where to stay
For options in Kodi: *see page 174*
Along the trek: Book early to stay at the forest rest houses. The one at Berijam charges a nominal rate and meals are available. The ones at Marian Shola, Kathrikai Odai and Vandarvu are usually unoccupied and you can stay for free

Family-run tea shop at Klaverai Village, just short of the Kerala state border

trail meandered through some shaded forest paths and terraced fields, with flowers and butterflies all around; it later ran uphill, where a few original shola forests, wiped out in all but a few patches, contrasted with the eucalyptus plantations.

I proceeded downhill. The light soon began to cone down from the dense clouds to spotlight the mountainscape. Colourful songbirds appeared from nowhere, unafraid.

At Kovilur, people played card games, some sat on their porches, which along with many of the houses, were mostly built on elevated platforms. I could hear adivasi *chenda* percussion music. The source turned out to be a church, also perched high up on a constructed platform and accessible through a ladder-like staircase.

I was tempted to climb it. But I had a bus to catch to Munnar, as I was constantly reminded by a number of villagers.

"Run!" some of them insisted, but I was in no shape to, with my heavy backpack and four days of walking behind me. I watched the 5 pm bus leaving, by now at least 500m away, when a dozen men whistled out to the bus in unison, loud enough to make the driver stop. Hopeful once again, I began to walk as briskly as possible in long strides, tired as I was. The driver, apparently losing patience, began to drive away again, and to my utter amazement, my new comrades once again whistled him to a halt. Now I really had to run, backpack, dangling cameras, utterly breathless and even half wanting to miss the bus and stay here longer. Other travels beckoned on the west coast, and I needed to pass Munnar anyway. But wait, it turned out that this bus was going all the way to Kochi. Should I or shouldn't I? I decide not to decide. No more planning for now, just enjoy the sunset. ∎

PRASHANT PANJIAR

Treks in the Nilgiris

Walking the Blue Mountains through shola forests and plantations

■ BY ALLEN MENDONCA

The Nilgiris, also known as the Blue Mountains, constitute India's oldest mountain ranges and are located at the junction of the Western and Eastern Ghats, 8,200-8,500 ft above sea level. They stretch slightly into Kerala and Karnataka and are best suited for novice trekkers.

The hill stations of Ooty, Kotagiri and Coonoor offer ideal bases for interesting treks into the mountains where dense shola forests blend perfectly with tea estates, orange groves, coffee plantations, rolling meadows, bubbling brooks, tumbling waterfalls and crystal clear lakes.

OOTY-MUKURTHI LAKE TREK

TIME	3-4 DAYS
LEVEL	EASY
IDEAL SEASON	JUN TO FEB
LOCATION	WEST SOUTH-WEST OF OOTY

Day One
OOTY-PORTHIMUND
TIME 6-8 HOURS
LEVEL MODERATE

SHORT TREKS IN THE NILGIRI

The town of Ooty is bisected by the state highway. So to begin the trek, you have to head towards the highway and then follow it westwards. After 3 km, look for a sign on the left that says **Parson's Peak**. Turn onto the dirt track winding upwards and west. Soon you'll be trekking across the upper reaches of the Nilgiris and meadows. After 8 km, you'll be on top of Parson's Peak overlooking the grassy knoll of **Parson's Valley**. The mountain slopes gently towards the west. If you want to avoid the long slog, you could even take a bus from Ooty to the base of Parson's Peak and walk onwards from here.

From the peak, you'll be able to spot the tiny hamlet of **Porthimund**, with its red-tiled houses nestling in the mountains. But to get there, you have to first descend into the valley. Right after the summer rains in April-May, it's a spectacular sight to behold, for wild flowers of various hues carpet the valley as far as the eye can see. It takes about 3-4 hrs to get to Porthimund, where you can take a tea/ coffee break. Camp overnight here, but carry your own provisions.

Day Two
PORTHIMUND-MUKURTHI LAKE
TIME 2 HOURS
LEVEL EASY

From Porthimund, head 5 km west towards the Mukurthi Lake and dam. The walk takes you through eucalyptus plantations, coffee estates and a few small hamlets. It's a superb experience walking through this pristine area and breathing the crisp mountain air. Although the lake is on the fringe of the Mukurthi National Park and one is tempted to explore the jungles, getting permission for entry is near impossible. This is because the wildlife authorities want to preserve the pristine environment, quite like in Kerala's Silent Valley National Park. But don't fret, there's plenty of pleasure to be had by the lake. Hire a boat or go fishing.

You can camp overnight at the dilapidated **Electricity Department Bungalow**, but only with permission from the Superintendent Engineer, Generation Circle, Kunda (Tel: 0423-2509225, 09443048001). Or stay at the **Nilgiris Wildlife and Environment Association Bungalow** (Tel: 0423-2447167 for bookings). Both are on the south side of the lake.

Day 3
MUKURTHI LAKE-PORTHIMUND AND BEYOND
TIME 2 HOURS
LEVEL EASY

Return the same way to Porthimund, from where you can either get a taxi or bus back to **Ooty** or drive northwest to **Pykara Falls** and the **Pykara Lake**. You can have lunch at one of the lakeside eateries and then catch a bus or taxi back. Or drive another 20 km north over undulating terrain to the **Mudumalai National Park**.

The park is home to the tiger, bison, elephant, wild boar and other fauna (the endangered Nilgiri tahr

Trekkers can spot the Nilgiri Tahr; A trail through pine forests (left)

E HANUMANTHA RAO/ WILDERFILE

lives in the upper reaches of the hills). There is an elephant safari every hour or so from the elephant camp at **Theppakadu** on the outskirts of the park. You can stay overnight at the **Theppakadu Log Hut** and **Theppakadu Sylvan Lodge** (for bookings contact Wildlife Warden Ooty, Tel: 0423-2444098; or DFO Kotagiri, Tel: 0423-2526235) and catch a bus or mini van, which ply regularly to Ooty.

Getting There and Out

From **Porthimund to Ooty**, get picked up by a pre-arranged taxi (1 hr/ Rs 1,100) from Ooty. Bus services are unreliable. From **Porthimund to Pykara Lake**, arrange taxi pick-up (1 hr/ Rs 1,100). There is no bus service on this route. **Pykara to Ooty** by taxi is 1 hr, 20 mins/ Rs 650. **Pykara to Mudumalai Wildlife Sanctuary**, on the direct route via Talakunda (40 km), is 2 hrs by Sumo (Rs 1,300). No shared jeeps and buses are available on this route. **Mudumalai to Ooty** is 1½ hrs by jeep (Rs 500-600). Buses for Ooty are available from Masinagudi Town, 5 km from Theppakadu, the entrance gate of Mudumalai Sanctuary.

Toda temple

SRIKANTH KOLARI

OOTY-RED HILLS TREK

TIME	4-5 DAYS
LEVEL	EASY
IDEAL SEASON	OCT TO MAY
LOCATION	SOUTH OF OOTY

Day One

OOTY-EMERALD
DISTANCE 12 KM **TIME** 4 HOURS
LEVEL EASY

Pack provisions, tents and water and head south-west from Ooty on the **Muthorai Road**, and walk over meadows and hillocks parallel to the road towards **Red Hills**. After 8 km, you'll pass the villages of **Muthorai** and **Pallada**, and a little later, **Ithalar**. From here you'll have to trek across wide meadows keeping south till you reach the town of **Emerald** with its lovely lake. This is in fact the 'Lake District' with a total of eight lakes. Pitch your tent anywhere along the shore of the lake.

Day Two

EMERALD-AVALANCHE
DISTANCE 12 KM **TIME** 4 HOURS
LEVEL EASY

Head south for 12 km until you come across the **Avalanche Dam** and the **Avalanche Village** (named after a massive landslide in 1823). The village, home to the Toda tribe, is surrounded by forests of silver oak, pine, cypress and rhododendrons. There are also magnolias and orchids and a trout stream. Find a suitable spot and camp overnight.

Days Three to Five

Retrace your way back to **Ooty** via **Parson's Valley**, or head to **Red Hills**. Head northwards along the lake on the Red Hills Road for 7 km, to the **Red Hills Nature Resort**, where you can stay overnight. The next day, hike 14 km to Parson's Valley, and on the fifth day walk back to Ooty.

SHORT TREKS IN THE NILGIRI

VIJAY KUTTY/ INDIAPICTURE

Pristine Pykara Lake is one among many reservoirs dotting the Blue Hills

DAY HIKES AROUND KOTAGIRI

KOTAGIRI-KODANAD
DISTANCE 20 KM **TIME** 6-8 HOURS
LEVEL MODERATE

Kotagiri, at a height of 6,540 ft, is the heart of the tea-growing area, east of Ooty. From Kotagiri head north east of the town on the vast stretches of meadow parallel to the road to reach **Kodanad**, 20 km away. The place offers picture-postcard views of tea estates and the **Moyar River** in the valley below. If you wish to stay the night, there is the **Kodanad Forest Rest House** (for bookings contact DFO Nilgiris North Division, Tel: 0423-2443968). Or retrace your way back to Kotagiri or Ooty.

KOTAGIRI-ST CATHERINE FALLS
DISTANCE 8 KM **TIME** 2-3 HOURS
LEVEL EASY

Musically called Geddhehaada Halla, meaning 'foothill valley river' in the vernacular, this magnificent 250-ft double-cascaded waterfall is the second highest in the district. From Kotagiri, you'll need to take the Mettupalayam Road branching off at Aravenu and walk 8 km till the falls. Either return to Kotagiri or to Ooty.

→ **FAST FACTS**

When to trek All year round
Tourist offices
● Wildlife Warden
Mount Stuart Hill
Udhagamandalam (Ooty)-643001
Tel: 0423-2444098
● Department of Tourism
Govt of Tamil Nadu, Wenlock Road, Ooty. Tel: 0423-2443977
● TTDC
No. 2, Wallajah Road, Chennai
Tel: 044-25367850-54
Website: tamilnadutourism.org

KOTAGIRI-LONGWOOD SHOLA
DISTANCE 3 KM **TIME** 1 HOUR

Between August and September and then again in early December, the birder and wildlife enthusiast alike can head to Kotagiri. Just 3 km from here is the beautiful 20-hectare **Longwood Shola Forest**, a lush, wild tract. Take written permission from the DFO, Nilgiri North Division, Mt Stuart Hill, Ooty-643001, before taking the road to **Milidhane**, which branches a short while later to Longwood. Explore the sholas with a guide or the forest guard who will check your papers at the entrance. Longwood also has a **Forest Rest House** (for bookings contact Nilgiris DFO; *see page 489*). Also contact the **Nilgiris Wildlife and Environment Association** for more information (Tel: 0423-2447167).

Getting there and out
From **Ooty to Kotagiri**, it's 36 km/ 1½ hrs by taxi (Rs 500) or 2 hrs by bus (Rs 8). Buses run every 45 mins from Ooty. From **Kotagiri to Kodanad**, get picked up at Kodanad by pre-arranged taxi (16 km/ ½ hr/ Rs 500) from Kotagiri. **Kotagiri to St Catherine Falls** via Kattapettu is 20 km/ 1 hr by jeep (Rs 400). **St Catherine Falls to Ooty** is 56 km/ 2½ hrs by jeep (Rs 800-1,000). Return the same way to Ooty from Kotagiri.

Dolphin's Nose near Coonoor

D VINOD/ AGP PHOTOBANK

COONOOR-THE DROOG TREK

TIME	5-7 HOURS
LEVEL	EASY
DISTANCE	18 km
IDEAL SEASON	APR TO JUN, SEP TO OCT
LOCATION	SOUTH-EAST OF OOTY

Like in Ooty, the state road cuts through the middle of Coonoor. Head south-east on this state road to **Lamb's Rock** 9 km away. The rock, on a precipice, overlooks the **Coimbatore plains**. Past this is **Lady Canning's Seat**, named after the Viceroy's wife.

Keep to the road and after 3 km you'll spot **Dolphin's Nose**, a greyish black rock remotely resembling a dolphin's snout and overlooking the valley. Take a break and retrace your steps. Five kilometres before Coonoor, you'll spot a detour to **Mettupalaiyam Road**, due south-east. **Law's Falls** are located at the junction of the Coonoor and Katteri streams, about 20 mins from Mettupalaiyam Road.

From here head east to **The Droog**, a ruined 16th century fort believed to have been used by Tipu Sultan. There are a number of springs holding promise of healing properties, the most famous being **Maan Sunai** (Deer Spring). You can see the state highway in the north. Trek down 2 km and take a bus to **Coonoor** as there are no hotels or guest houses close by.

Getting there and out
From **Ooty to Coonoor**, it's about 17 km/ 45 mins by taxi (Rs 350) or 1 hr, 10 mins by bus (Rs 7). Take the same route back.

For details on the destinations Ooty, Coonoor, Parson's Valley, Red Hills, Kotagiri and Mudumalai, see 'The Nilgiris' Section from pages 184-226 ■

Jallikattu, Alanganallur

■ BY ROHINI MOHAN

As I look in horror at a guy sharpening his bull's horn with obvious delight, I'm reassured by my man Friday (every tourist within 10 inches of a rampant bull must have one) that all the exit restrictions are placed in such a way that a clueless stroller doesn't get in the way of a bull running wild in the village. "There are no rules in this game, you see," he says, "the bull can be anywhere, and it can think anyone is the bull-tamer."

So this is what India's own bullfight is about: a thousand mad bulls, more than 10,000 people packed in the backyard of a small village temple, and no rules. One by one, bulls are let loose into an arena full of unarmed bullfighters. It used to be a one-man-to-one-bull game, and even today only one man can tame each animal. Not kill, just hang on to the hump for 50m in the crowd as the bull bucks and twists to throw him off. But in people's drunken blind bravery, the bulls don't have it easy. Their tails are bitten, eyes poked, their stomachs prodded with sticks. But after watching for a while, I realise that the bulls are the ones that are less physically hurt than the hundreds that lie in the hospital for weeks after this day. They — the bulls and the tamers — are reared and trained for just that. Safe? No. Increasingly attracting tourists? Yes.

This bull taming, *jallikattu*, is a centuries-old tradition in Alanganallur, in rural Madurai District. A toothless old man with a thigh full of proud scars tells me it all started when small pox affected the village ages ago. People prayed for a cure, and offered this game as "blood sacrifice". So if even a year goes by without a drop of blood smearing the village earth, he says the local goddess will make sure an epidemic hits the village. "Of course, these days, there's no small pox," he adds, "so maybe cholera will come." So abidingly every year, on January 16, *jallikattu* brings out the wild. ■

Keeping the faith

A little village in the Cauvery Delta comes alive with drama in real life

■ BY LALITHA SRIDHAR

Where is **Melattur**? Tucked away in Tamil Nadu's verdant Cauvery Delta, it is just 18 km from Thanjavur (*see page 98*). Drive past Thiruvaiyaru, onwards to Papanasam and Thirukarukavur. After miles of emerald fields and snaking canals, suddenly, there is Melattur. If you are visiting during the Bhagavad Mela Natya Natakam Festival, the organisers will be happy to help you get there. On Narasimha Jayanti, sometime between mid-April and mid-May, Melattur welcomes visitors with unmatched hospitality.

The **Bhagavad Mela Natya Natakam Utsavam** (festival) is not a commercial enterprise and blatant tourism is discouraged. A result of the Bhakti Movement, the festival is Tamil Nadu's oldest link to Sanskrit street theatre. For a whole week, all-night plays are performed by an amateur, all-male cast on the path that leads up to the local temple. From being a sleepy rural hamlet, Melattur transforms itself into a teeming venue for unique performances. Everyone is host for whoever needs a roof. The kitchen is a community affair and no one goes hungry.

Melattur is also a Tamil village steeped in Telugu history. The Bhagavad Mela Natya Natakams were written by Brahmin scholars who migrated to Thanjavur during the Bahmani Sultan invasion of Telengana. The then king here, Achutappa Naik, was a renowned patron of the arts. It was his support that helped the legendary Venkatramana Sastri create a unique temple art, rendered in classical music and dance, rich with bhakti traditions that drew heavily from the Bhagavad Puranas. He wrote several plays in Sanskrit and Telugu, his native tongue. The Natya Natakams (literally, dance dramas) eventually fell into disuse and were lost to posterity. Ten out of the original 12 plays were restored by the single-minded dedication of one man — S. Natarajan, sometimes simply referred to as Melattur

Natarajan — great-great grandson of the eponymous AVS.

Natarajan, whose grandfather sold their ancestral land to attempt a revival, traced the original texts, some of them in tattered palm leaf, and sequenced them into renditions that could be enacted. He also brought in a modern element of professionalism by training amateur actors in the basics of classical dance, investing in simple stage props and technology like sound systems.

Nevertheless, the spirit of the Melattur Bhagavad Mela remains unchanged. There are no rehearsals. All performances are extempore. Those who are engaged in sustaining this tradition have different careers, almost all are employed away from Melattur and some are abroad; most have ancestral links to the village but they congregate at Melattur only for the annual festival. Nobody is paid for performing here. Natarajan, now 61 and awarded the Sangeet Natak Akademi award in 2004, has worked all his life in Dubai. It is his life's savings that have kept the Melattur Bhagavad Mela going. He is also the only performer to have acted here for 57 continuous years.

The first night's performance is always *Prahlada Charitram*. This play can only be performed here in Melattur, in front of the temple whose presiding deity is the fourth avatar of Vishnu, Lord Narasimha. Essentially, the artistes are presenting the play for the temple deities. The night begins with a *nadaswaram* recital and soon thereafter, vocal music fills the charged atmosphere. The standard is pure Carnatic but it involves a *pundareegam* (the invocation), a *konnangi* (buffoon) act interspersed with innocent clowning, the *thodaimangalam* (a synopsis of the entire play), and the entrance of Pillaiyaru (Ganesha, who blesses the entire proceedings) — these are ritual beginnings for all plays. With that sort of warm-up, there begins the story of Prahlada.

It is a story we all know and it is a story that can be told in five minutes. At the Melattur Bhagavad Mela, it is more than a story. It is an experience. Seven-and-a-half hours of a night that seems to be rushing by and standing still at the same time. The night revels in Prahlada's devotion, in the energetic ancillary cast of demons and disciples, and finally, in the arrival of Lord Narasimha himself. It is believed that he who plays Narasimha becomes Narasimha.

For information, contact Sri Lakshmi Narasimha Jayanti Bhagavad Mela Natya Nataka Sangam, 63-64, South Street, Melattur-614301, Thanjavur District, Tamil Nadu or email bhagavatamela@excite.com ■

Vocal performance and Prahlada Charitram (left) **at the Melattur Mela**

Photographs by G SIVAPERUMAL

Photographs by SAIBAL DAS

Nilgiri Mountain Railway

The old Nilgiri Mountain Railway hasn't run out of steam

■ BY ALDE BARAN

Never has any train been so grumbled about. Every passenger is whining: about the train's snail's pace, about the non-cushioned seats, about the absence of a restroom on board.

Right from the indignant voices at the ticket counter to the tiffs about unreserved seat occupation, it's one continuous groan.

"Q please," the little piece of white cardboard in the Mettupalaiyam station says weakly in blue ballpoint ink, and people rush to line up in front of it. A German lady doesn't quite grasp the idea, and decides to follow the stationmaster around, a wad of rupees scrunched in her hand. But each time she flashes a hopeful beam at him, she is shown the "Q", where her more worldly-wise partner stands already. Others who hadn't thought of booking their tickets in advance stand in jump-train readiness, clutching their bags and babies.

Amid all the chaos, a sharp, long whistle from the distance gets the queue straightened. The blue train chugs into Mettupalaiyam station, and its arrival is downright dramatic, what with it emerging from behind steam and smoke, and coming to a halt with a tired hiss. This 'toy train' has all of five coaches, but as first-timers look nervously around for aid, porters, canteenwallahs and railway employees of various ranks dish out much-sought advice and well-deserved slaps on the wrist. I am steered into the Second Class reserved coach by a couple of cops. Judging by their shock when I leave my seat after depositing my bag there, I am not to leave my place till the TTE arrives.

When he does, he awards two seconds per head to the passengers revelling in the benefit of their forethought, before going on to the unreserved coaches, where I suspect he has more fun.

The First Class coach is the only one blessed with cushions. But luxurious sitting is hardly a requirement in a train that, instead of just showing you breathtaking scenes, physically takes people through them. Each halt station on the route is sightseeing heaven, which makes every single person step down to ogle at brooks, waterfalls, and tea estates, or buy weak chai that must be had for its nose-warming steam.

The broad-gauge rail system of the Nilgiri Passenger, also called the Nilgiri Mountain Railway (NMR), is the steepest in Asia (gradient 1:12.5) and covers the longest distance, 46 km, compared to other mountain railways in India (Darjeeling and Shimla). Connecting Mettupalaiyam (1,070 ft) and Ooty/ Udhagamandalam (7,230 ft) in the Nilgiri Hills, the NMR takes me so deep into the mountains that I can judge the sheer drop, discover varying tastes of mint tea in every station, count the tea-leaf pickers, and smile at kids waving at the train.

The recurrent whistles of the steam engine when it stops at quaint military towns seem to come right out of colonial times. The NMR used to be the vehicle for the British in India to get away from the sweltering heat of the plains. Its first section was only halfway up the hills from Mettupalaiyam (MTP), up to the cantonment area of Coonoor (CNR). Since it was extraordinarily steep between Kallar (the second stop after MTP) and CNR, the train was run by a unique rack and pinion system designed by a Mr Riggenback, the Swiss inventor of the Rigi System of Mountain Railways in 1876.

Rack bars with teeth-like grooves were laid in between the two conventional rails to form a sort of ladder up which the engine climbed and pushed the train. Powered by coal and steam, the NMR, till today, takes a serpentine course through sloping hills, manoeuvring curves as sharp as 18 degrees.

Started in 1882, the NMR project was completed in 1899 by the Nilgiri Railway Company with Riggenback's help. The train is now just another line owned by the Railways, and to get more mileage out of its track record, they extended the line another 27 km to Ooty, the 'queen of hill stations' in South India.

→ FAST FACTS

Timings The NMR 'toy train' leaves Mettupalaiyam every day at 7.10 am and takes nearly 5 hrs to do the journey uphill to Ooty (arrives 12 pm). It does the return run in under 4 hrs, leaving Ooty at 3 pm and arriving at Mettupalaiyam at 6.35 pm. The train covers a distance of 46 km, travelling through 208 curves, 16 tunnels and 250 bridges

Tickets First Class reservation: Rs 142; Second Class reservation: Rs 27. You can book the entire train for a private tour going from Ooty to Runnymede and back, covering Lovedale, Ketti, Aruvankadu, Wellington, and Coonoor in between. It costs Rs 500 per person and the price is revised every season, inclusive of food and sightseeing

The NMR makes only one trip up and down everyday, taking 5 hours uphill (Mettupalaiyam-Ooty), and four hours down (Ooty-Mettupalaiyam). And except for the special train that runs in the peak season from April to June, there is only a single train. Also, the steam engine operates just for the first section — 19 km from MTP to CNR.

I'm informed that uphill traffic is very little, and that most takers for the NMR are tourists. The locals, apparently, have seen enough of the foliage, and like to get about faster.

Extensive rice fields surround the 7-km stretch between MTP and Kallar, and all that fresh cool air takes me by surprise. When I mention it to the TTE, he smiles and asks me if I would accommodate some more people in my coupe, so "they can also enjoy the fresh air". Since Kallar is what is called an operational stop, there are many ticketless line workers hopping on at MTP, claiming to be close relatives of the country's railway minister. But they come with their own version of

A fistful of flowers at Wellington

the train's magic, and jump off at Kallar anyway. After that, those left on the train are passengers who'll stay on till Ooty. By the time the next (and most scenic) stop, Runnymede, arrives, faces start to get familiar, smiles are exchanged, biscuits passed around, and honeymooning couples identified.

Most people on the NMR seem to have hopped on assuming it would be just another train journey. But the small 30-seater coaches, detachable windows and wooden seats confuse them. Most of all, they cannot understand why the train must dawdle so. The average speed is supposed to be 13 kmph, and there are brakesmen sitting in little balconies in front of each coach, manually maintaining this pace. Over 13 kmph could apparently cause broken teeth on the rack with too much friction, and less than 13 kmph could cause the train to simply slide backwards down the hill. Of course, as soon as this is explained to us impatient passengers, we think it better for everybody if we just shook off the restless city attitude, and enjoyed the trip.

When Coonoor Station comes, it is abuzz with activity. The steam engine must be removed and the train attached to a YMD4 diesel engine. The diesel engine made an appearance on the NMR only in 1993 — to supplement the ageing steam loco fleet. However, the YMD4 class of diesels can only work the relatively flat incline from Coonoor to Ooty, and the rack section is still in the hands of the capable steam locos.

The NMR stops in Coonoor for almost 15 minutes and I do some looking around, while curling cold fingers around a cup of blissfully warm mint tea. In the Coonoor Loco Shed stand five steam engines, of which only three are in working

NILGIRI MOUNTAIN RAILWAY

The NMR follows a serpentine course through sloping hills

condition. And those oldies, too, require a refill of water at almost every station now. It's fascinating to look at the whole process of water and coal replenishing, and routine nuts-and-bolts checks at every stop, handled by unimpressed railway employees who offer matter-of-fact explanations to tourists.

The camaraderie between the tourists gets stronger with each collective howl filling every one of the 16 tunnels the train passes through. After Coonoor, most stops are very brief, just long enough to take a picture and grab a vada and beverage. The rest of the journey is now a blur of terrace gardens, streams, and craggy, grim-looking 'blue mountains'. There are now halts at little towns with seemingly one-dimensional identities. So, Wellington is a military town with one of the best officers' training colleges in the world; Ketti is the world's widest valley and has a needle industry; Aruvankadu houses the Cordite factory; Lovedale is almost synonymous with the Lawrence School. It isn't possible to take a walk in these towns during the journey, of course. (Later, though, I rent a bike to hit all the towns by road. To ride parallel to the NMR, seeing waving people and hearing their howls ring from inside tunnels is worth it in the cold rain.)

Rain, from inside the Nilgiri Mountain Railway, has to be the most uplifting sight ever. Some people keep their windows open and stick their tongue out. I choose to keep my window closed and watch it shudder as the rain hits it. When we finally arrive at Ooty, people disembark, but stick around for a few minutes more.

Yes, they look like they're checking their luggage. But maybe another cup of mint tea will warm them enough to admit that they're actually gazing affectionately at the toy train that gave them a journey that was, strangely, not about the destination at all. ∎

SPECIALS

CHENNAI WEEKEND BREAKS | 477

INFORMATION

TRAVEL HELPLINES

A ready reckoner to some useful numbers in Chennai, Coimbatore, Madurai, Trichurapalli, Bangalore, Kochi and Kozhikode for your weekend travel planning

■ AIR

CHENNAI STD 044
AIRPORT INFORMATION

ANNA INTERNATIONAL AIRPORT
Trisulam, Chennai
Tel: 22560551
Airport Manager Tel: 22560501
Pre-paid Taxi Tel: 22561903
Airport Police Tel: 22564282/ 4102
Airport Computer Room
(Announcement Desk)
Tel: 22564271
KAMARAJ-MEENAMBAKKAM DOMESTIC TERMINAL I
Airport Manager Tel: 22560501
ANNA INTERNATIONAL AIRPORT TERMINAL II
Arr Tel: 22564214 **Dep** Tel: 22564661

CHENNAI AIRLINE OFFICES

TIP All the Chennai Airport offices of the following airlines are located within the Kamaraj-Meenambakkam Domestic Terminal, Anna International Airport, Trisulam, Chennai

AIR DECCAN
● **Airport Office** Tel: 22561880
Res/ Arr/ Dep Enquiry Mobile: 09840377008
● **City Office**
47, Deshbandhu Plaza, Whites Road, Chennai
Tel: 42033209, 32978596, 32980801
Mobile: 09382340130; Fax: 28585008
Email: geetha.haribbu@airdeccan.net
Website: flyairdeccan.net
Flights to Bangalore, Coimbatore, Kochi, Madurai, Trichy
Office hours Mon to Sat 9 am-6 pm

AIR INDIA EXPRESS
● **Airport Office** Tel: 22561747; Fax: 22561706
Tele Check-in Tel: 22561065, 22560747
(Business Class only)
Reservations Toll Free: 1800 22 7722
Arr/ Dep Enquiry Tel: 22560747
● **City Office**
19, Marshall's Road, Egmore, Chennai

Tel: 28578152-53/ 59/ 8165/ 67
Fax: 28555055
Email: maacity@airindiaexpress.in
Website: airindiaexpress.in
Flights to Trichy

INDIAN
● **Airport Office** Tel: 22560011
Tele Check-in Toll Free: 18001801407
Reservations Toll Free: 18001801404
Arr/ Dep Enquiry Toll Free: 18001801407
● **City Office**
19, Marshall's Road, Egmore, Chennai
Tel: 23453300, 23453355; Fax: 28555208
Email: indian@indian-airlines.com
Website: indian-airlines.nic.in
Office hours Mon to Sat 9.30 am-5.30 pm
Toll Free 18001801407
Flights to Bangalore, Coimbatore, Kochi, Madurai, Trichy, Tirupati

INDIGO AIRLINES
● **Airport Office** Tel: 22560286-87
Res/ Arr/ Dep Enquiry Toll Free: 18001803838; Mobile: 09910383838
● **City Office**
144/145, Malavika Centre, Kodambakkam High Road, Nungambakkam, Chennai
Tel: 65272272/ 62; Fax: 28269151
Email: maa.indigo@interglobe.com
Website: goindigo.in
Office hours Mon to Sat 9 am-5.30 pm
Flights to Bangalore

JET AIRWAYS
● **Airport Office** Tel: 39893333
Tele Check-in Tel: 39893333
Res/ Arr/ Dep Enquiry Tel: 39893333
● **City Office**
Thapar House, 43/44 Montieth Road, Chennai
Tel: 39893333; Fax: 28555109
Email: maaresv@jetairways.com
Website: jetairways.com
Office hours Mon to Sat 9 am-8 pm
Flights to Bangalore, Coimbatore, Kochi, Madurai, Trichy, Tirupati

TRANSPORT DIRECTORY

KINGFISHER AIRLINES
- **Airport Office** Tel: 22561827/ 29
Fax: 22561830
Res/ Arr/ Dep Enquiry Toll Free: 18001800101
- **City Office**
124, Bhagiratha Residency, Marshall's Road Egmore, Chennai
Tel: 28584366-67; Fax: 28584407
Email: salesmaa@flykingfisher.com
Website: flykingisher.com
Office hours Mon to Sat 9.30 am-6 pm
Toll Free 18001800101, 18002333131, 18002333535
Flights to Bangalore, Coimbatore, Kochi, Madurai, Trichy

PARAMOUNT AIRWAYS
- **Airport Office** Tel: 22561667-70
Reservations Toll Free: 18001801234
Arr/ Dep Enquiry Tel: 22561667-70
- **City Office**
Alexander Square, 34-35, Sardar Patel Road Guindy. Tel: 43909090; Fax: 42328157
Email: feedback@paramountairways.com
Website: paramountairways.com
Office hours Mon to Sat 9.30 am-7 pm
Flights to Bangalore, Coimbatore, Kochi, Madurai

SPICEJET
- **Airport Office** Mobile: 09871803333
Email: marketing@spicejet.com, custrelations@spicejet.com
Website: spicejet.com
Res/ Arr/ Dep Enquiry Toll Free: 18001803333; Mobile: 09871803333
- **Corporate Office** 0124-3913939
Office hours 24 x 7
Flights to Bangalore

BANGALORE STD 080
AIRPORT INFORMATION
BANGALORE INTERNATIONAL AIRPORT
Location HAL, Bangalore. Tel: 25223344/ 8011
Airport Manager Tel: 25221530
KSTDC Pre-paid Taxi Tel: 25220501
Airport Police Tel: 22942544
Airport Computer Room (Announcement Desk) Tel: 65960815
DOMESTIC/ INTERNATIONAL TERMINAL
Airport Manager Tel: 25221530

COIMBATORE STD 0422
AIRPORT INFORMATION
PEELAMEDU AIRPORT
Location Civil Aerodrome PO, Airport Road Coimbatore. Tel: 2591905
Airport Director Tel: 2592155
Pre-paid Taxi Tel: 09363142543
Airport Police Tel: 2580804, 2570200
Airport Computer Room (Announcement Desk) Tel: 2592155
DOMESTIC/ INTERNATIONAL TERMINAL
Airport Terminal Manager Tel: 2591905

KOCHI STD 0484
AIRPORT INFORMATION
COCHIN INTERNATIONAL AIRPORT
Nedumbassery, Kochi. Tel: 2610115
Airport Director Tel: 2610006
Airport Terminal Manager Tel: 2610033
Pre-paid Taxi Tel: 2610115 ext 2107 (Domestic); ext 2242 (International)
Airport Police Tel: 2610115 ext 2117
Airport Computer Room (Announcement Desk) Tel: 2610115 ext 2232
DOMESTIC TERMINAL
Airport Manager Tel: 2610115 ext 2110
INTERNATIONAL TERMINAL
Airport Manager Tel: 2610115 ext 2221

KOZHIKODE STD 0483
KARIPUR INTERNATIONAL AIRPORT
Location Karipur, Malappuram District, 26 km south of Kozhikode
Airport Exchange Tel: 2711314
Airport Director Tel: 2712630; Fax: 2711406
Airport Terminal Manager Tel: 2710517
Pre-paid Taxi Tel: 09846493848
DOMESTIC TERMINAL
Airport Manager Tel: 2710517 ext 490
Mobile: 09895009038
INTERNATIONAL TERMINAL
Tel: 2710517 ext 491

MADURAI STD 0452
AIRPORT INFORMATION
MADURAI AIRPORT
Location Perungudi, Arupukottai Road Madurai. Tel: 2690717
Airport Controller Tel: 2690717
Approved Car Rental Service
Mobile: 09894911448

INFORMATION

Airport Police Tel: 2690474
Airport Computer Room (Announcement Desk) **Call concerned airlines** Indian Tel: 2690333, 2690433; Jet Air Tel: 2690771-74; Air Deccan Tel: 2690034; Paramount Airways Tel: 2690605-08; Kingfisher Toll Free: 18001800101
DOMESTIC TERMINAL
Airport Terminal Manager Tel: 2690692

TRICHURAPALLI STD 0431
AIRPORT INFORMATION

TRICHY AIRPORT
Location Pudukottai Highway Road Trichurapalli. Tel: 2340551
Airport Director Tel: 2341810
Airport Enquiry Tel: 2340554
AAI Approved Call Taxi Tel: 2233011/ 022
Airport Police Tel: 2340863
Airport Announcement Desk Tel: 2340554
DOMESTIC/ INTERNATIONAL TERMINAL
Airport Director Tel: 2341810

■ RAIL
CHENNAI STD 044
ENQUIRIES

Chennai City Railway Station General Enquiry (computerised)
Arr/ Dep Tel: 132
PNR Status/ Berth Availability Tel: 131
Toll Free 131, 1361 (computerised, English); 1363 (Tamil)

TICKET RESERVATION CENTRES

Chennai Central Station Tel: 131, 1361, 25353816/ 3218/ 0586
Egmore Station Tel: 28194579
Annanagar Station Tel: 26631188
Mylapore Station Tel: 24954252
Saidapet Station Tel: 24329970

STATION MANAGERS

Chennai Central Station Tel: 25350586
Egmore Station Tel: 28194533
Perambur Station Tel: 25512736
Avadi Station Tel: 26555408
Tambaram Station Tel: 22390101
Mambalam Station Tel: 24344951

SECURITY

IGP Railway Police (Chennai Central) Tel: 28261415/ 718, 26223727®

Railway Police Control Room Chennai Central Station Tel: 25355077
Railway Police Control Room Egmore Station Tel: 28190382/ 2026
Railway Protection Force Chennai Central Station Tel: 25352414
Railway Protection Force Egmore Station Tel: 25324450; Mobile: 09444226322

■ ROADWAYS
CHENNAI STD 044

TAMIL NADU STATE EXPRESS TRANSPORT CORPORATION
Address Chennai Metropolitan Bus Terminus (CMBT), Koyambedu
Arr/ Dep Enquiry Tel: 24794705/ 09
Buses going to Tamil Nadu, Karnataka, Kerala, Andhra Pradesh
Police Station (SETC Bus Stand) Tel: 100

OMNI BUS ASSOCIATION
(for private bus operators)
Address Behind CMBT Bus Terminal Koyambedu Market, Chennai
Arr/ Dep Enquiry Tel: 24799500
Mobile: 09840794924, 09444015729
Buses going to Tamil Nadu, Pondicherry Karnataka, Andhra Pradesh

ANDHRA PRADESH STATE ROAD CORPORATION
Address Chennai Metropolitan Bus Terminus Koyambedu Market
Arr/ Dep Enquiry Tel: 24792233
Manager Mobile: 09444160990
Buses going to Andhra Pradesh

AUTOMOBILE ASSOCIATION OF SOUTHERN INDIA

CHENNAI
Address AASI Centre, No. 187, Anna Salai
Tel 044-28521162/ 4061 **Fax** 28511548 **Email** aasi40@hotmail.com **Website** aasindia.in

BANGALORE
Address AASI, India Garage Building, No. 63, St Marks Road **Tel** 080-25597960, 25587701

COIMBATORE
Address AASI, India House, 1246 Trichy Road **Tel** 0422-2302994

TRANSPORT DIRECTORY

KOCHI
Address AASI, No. 9, 39/3396, Ravipuram Road, Ernakulam **Tel** 0484-2357361

KOZHIKODE
Address AASI, TF, Parapurath Shopping Complex, East Nadakavu, Eranchipalam PO **Tel** 0495-2369766

MADURAI
Address AASI, Raaj Sesh Mahal, No. 16 Bharathi Ula Road, Race Course **Tel** 0452-2528158

OOTY
Address AASI, C/o M/s Simpson & Co Ltd Garden Road **Tel** 0423-2442223

TIRUCHIRAPALLI
Address AASI, 2-C, Promenade Road Cantonment **Tel** 0431-2460102

CHENNAI CAR RENTAL SERVICES

Angel Travels Anna Nagar
Tel: 044-42693928, 30527097

Bala Tourist Service Kodambakkam High Road, Nungambakkam
Tel: 28224545; Mobile: 09841033444

Blue Star Travels 2nd Street, Royapettah
Tel: 28350968/ 679

Harringtan Cabs Sputank Road, Chetpet
Tel: 28361206/ 665; Mobile: 09841062382

Sam Tours & Travels T-Nagar
Tel: 28340661/ 2103

Raj Travels Pantheon Road, Egmore
Tel: 42022891; Mobile: 09840128289

Sai Cabs Raju Naicker Street, West Mambalam; Tel: 42122143-44
Mobile: 09381030918

Southern Travels Opp Chennai Central Railway Station, Near Mount Road
Tel: 25385253, 25364864
Mobile: 09841040906

Swastik Travels Ashok Nagar
Tel: 24742933/ 44; Mobile: 09841585573

VKB Travels Mylapore
Tel: 24990889, 42030889
Mobile: 09444034113

VM Motors Tours & Travels Wallajah Road Chepauk; Tel: 42157200; Mobile: 09443351797

TOURIST OFFICES

INFORMATION ⓘ BOOKING ⓑ

STATE TOURISM OFFICES

TAMIL NADU

Tamil Nadu Tourism Development Corporation (TTDC)
Website: tamilnadutourism.org

TTDC ⓘⓑ
Tourist Complex
No. 2 Wallajah Road
Chennai-600002
Tel: 044-25367850-54
Fax: 25361385
Email: ttdc@vsnl.com
Website: ttdc.com

Dept of Tourism, Govt of Tamil Nadu ⓘ
Address as for TTDC
Tel: 044-25367850-54

ANDHRA PRADESH

Andhra Pradesh Tourism Development Corporation (APTDC)
Website: tourisminap.com

APTDC ⓘⓑ
31/14 Burkit Road
T Nagar, Chennai-600017
Tel: 044-24353373, 65439987
Fax: 24353373
Website: aptourism.in

KERALA

Kerala Tourism Development Corporation (KTDC)
Website: ktdc.com

KTDC Tourist Information Centre ⓘⓑ

Address as for TTDC
Telefax: 044-25382639

Department of Tourism Government of Kerala ⓘ
Address as for TTDC
Tel: 044-25369789
Website: keralatourism.org

PONDICHERRY

Pondicherry Tourism Development Corporation (PTDC)
Website: tourism.pon.nic.in

PTDC Tourism Information Centre ⓘ
Address as for TTDC
Tel: 044-2330532
Email: tourismpondy@sify.com
Website: pondicherry.com

INFORMATION

MILES TO GO BEFORE YOU REACH

The destination is closer than you think, or further than you imagined.

Destination	*Distance	By road	By rail	By air
TAMIL NADU				
MAHABALIPURAM	58 km	✓1½ hrs		
KANCHIPURAM	75 km	✓1½ hrs		
VEDANTHANGAL	86 km	✓1¾ hrs		
THIRUVANNAMALAI	198 km	✓4½ hrs		
CHIDAMBARAM	226 km	✓5 hrs		
YELAGIRI HILLS	253 km	✓5 hrs	3 hrs + ¾ hr	
TRANQUEBAR	279 km	✓6 hrs		
KUMBAKONAM	303 km	7½ hrs	✓9 hrs	
NAGAPATTINAM	308 km	7½ hrs	✓9 hrs	
TIRUCHIRAPALLI	327 km	8 hrs	✓7 hrs	50 mins
THANJAVUR	339 km	8 hrs	✓7½ hrs	50 mins + 1½ hrs
YERCAUD	350 km	6½ hrs	✓7 hrs + 1 hr	
HOGENAKKAL FALLS	355 km	✓8 hrs		
CHETTINAD	444 km	8½ hrs	✓8½ hrs + 2 hrs	1 hr + 2 hrs
KAMARAJAR VALLEY	447 km	8½ hrs	✓7 hrs + ¾ hr	1 hr + 2½ hrs
MADURAI	461 km	8½ hrs	✓8½ hrs	1 hr
PALANI	479 km		✓7 hrs + 1½ hrs	1 hr + 3 hrs
KODAIKANAL	521 km		✓7½ hrs + 2½ hrs	1 hr + 3½ hrs
INDIRA GANDHI WLS	597 km		✓8 hrs + 2 hrs	55 mins + 2 hrs
PONDICHERRY				
PONDICHERRY	162 km	✓3 hrs		
THE NILGIRIS				
COONOOR	571 km		✓9¼ hrs + 1 hr	55 mins + 2 hrs
OOTY	588 km		✓9¼ hrs + 1½ hrs	55 mins + 2½ hrs
RED HILLS	600 km		✓9¼ hrs + 2½ hrs	55 mins + 3½ hrs
BELLIKKAL	604 km		✓9¼ hrs + 2 hrs	55 mins + 3 hrs
PARSON'S VALLEY	607 km		✓9¼ hrs + 2 hrs	55 mins + 3 hrs
MUDUMALAI WLS	661 km		✓9¼ hrs + 3 hrs	55 mins + 4 hrs

* Approximate distance from Chennai   + Additional time by road from the nearest railhead/ airport

ACCESS AT A GLANCE

HOURS TO GO BEFORE YOU SLEEP

Here's a reckoner to distances and travel time from Chennai

Destination	*Distance	By road	By rail	By air
ANDHRA PRADESH				
SRIKALAHASTI	114 km	✓4 hrs	✓2 hrs + 1/2 hr	
TIRUMALA	174 km	✓3 1/2 hrs	2 hrs + 20 mins	
HORSLEY HILLS	276 km	✓7 hrs		
LEPAKSHI	461 km	8 hrs	✓5 hrs + 3 hrs	
KARNATAKA				
BANGALORE	331 km	7 hrs	✓5 hrs	1 hr
BANNERGHATTA NP	354 km	8 hrs	✓6 hrs + 3/4 hr	55 mins + 1 1/2 hrs
NANDI HILLS	391 km	8 1/2 hrs	✓6 hrs + 2 hrs	55 mins + 2 hrs
BHEEMESHWARI	431 km	10 hrs	✓6 hrs + 2 1/4 hrs	55 mins + 2 1/4 hrs
SHIVANASAMUDRAM	440 km	10 1/2 hrs	✓6 hrs + 2 1/2 hrs	55 mins + 2 1/2 hrs
SRIRANGAPATNA	458 km	11 hrs	✓10 hrs	55 mins + 3 hrs
MYSORE	470 km	11 1/2 hrs	✓10 1/2 hrs	55 mins + 4 hrs
SRAVANABELAGOLA	486 km		✓10 hrs + 2 1/2 hrs	55 mins + 3 1/2 hrs
BR HILLS	556 km		✓10 1/2 hrs + 2 hrs	
NAGARHOLE NP	566 km		✓10 1/2 hrs + 2 hrs	55 mins + 5 hrs
KERALA				
PERIYAR TR	553 km		✓12 hrs + 2 hrs	1 hr + 4 hrs
PALAKKAD	568 km		✓8 hrs	55 mins + 1 1/4 hrs
NELLIYAMPATHY	622 km		✓8 hrs + 1 1/2 hrs	55 mins + 3 hrs
SALIM ALI BS	631 km		✓10 hrs + 1 1/4 hrs	1 hr + 1 1/2 hrs
THRISSUR	635 km		✓9 hrs	1 hr + 1 1/4 hrs
KOCHI	663 km		✓10 1/2 hrs	1 hr + 3/4 hr
KOTTAYAM	666 km		✓12 hrs	1 hr + 2 hrs
GURUVAYUR	667 km		✓9 hrs + 3/4 hr	1 hr + 2 hrs
KUMARAKOM	682 km		✓12 hrs + 1/2 hr	1 hr + 2 hrs
KOZHIKODE	707 km		✓11 1/2 hrs	1 hr + 3/4 hr
ALAPPUZHA	711 km		✓13 1/2 hrs	1 hr + 2 hrs
VYTHIRI	741 km		✓11 1/2 hrs + 1 1/2 hrs	1 hr + 2 hrs

✓ *Recommended option (taking into account the time, budget, connectivity and mobility options at destinations)*

INFORMATION

INFORMATION

TRAINS TO EACH DESTINATION

To make the most of your short weekend, you need a train that's fast and convenient. Here are our picks for the best

Destination	Train Name	Station/ Departure	Arrival (nearest station)
ALAPPUZHA	6041 Alleppey Express	MAS 21.15	Alleppey 10.50
BANGALORE	2007 Shatabdi Express	MAS 6.00	Bangalore City Junction 10.50
BANNERGHATTA	2657 Bangalore Mail	MAS 23.15	Bangalore City Junction 5.30
BELLIKKAL	2671 Nilagiri Express	MAS 21.00	Mettupalaiyam 6.15
BHEEMESHWARI	2657 Bangalore Mail	MAS 23.15	Bangalore City Junction 5.30
BR HILLS	6222 Mysore Express	MAS 21.30	Mysore Junction 8.05
CHETTINAD	2637 Pandian Express	MS 21.30 TBM 21.55	Madurai Junction 6.15
COONOOR	2671 Nilagiri Express	MAS 21.00	Mettupalaiyam 6.15
GURUVAYUR	2623 Trivandrum Mail	MAS 20.00	Thrissur 5.00
INDIRA GANDHI WLS	2671 Nilagiri Express	MAS 21.00	Coimbatore Junction 5.00
KAMARAJAR VALLEY	2637 Pandian Express	MS 21.30 TBM 21.55	Dindigul Junction 4.30
KOCHI	2623 Trivandrum Mail	MAS 20.00	Ernakulam Town 6.40
KODAIKANAL	2637 Pandian Express	MS 21.30 TBM 21.55	Kodaikanal Road 5.06
KOTTAYAM	2623 Trivandrum Mail	MAS 20.00	Kottayam 7.55
KOZHIKODE	2601 Mangalore Mail	MAS 20.15	Kozhikode 7.45
KUMARAKOM	2623 Trivandrum Mail	MAS 20.00	Kottayam 7.55
KUMBAKONAM	6177 Rockfort Express	MS 22.30 MBM 22.40 TBM 23.00	Kumbakonam 7.30
LEPAKSHI	2657 Bangalore Mail	MAS 23.15	Bangalore City Junction 5.30
MADURAI	2637 Pandian Express	MS 21.30 TBM 21.55	Madurai Junction 6.15
MUDUMALAI	2671 Nilagiri Express	MAS 21.00	Mettupalaiyam 6.15
MYSORE	6222 Mysore Express	MAS 21.30	Mysore Junction 8.05
NAGARHOLE	6222 Mysore Express	MAS 21.30	Mysore Junction 8.05
NANDI HILLS	2657 Bangalore Mail	MAS 23.15	Bangalore City Junction 5.30

TRAIN RECKONER TO
BEST SUITED FOR A WEEKEND BREAK
options to each destination, with departure timings from all Chennai stations the train halts at on the way out

Destination	Train Name	Station/ Departure	Arrival (nearest station)
NELLIYAMPATHY	6041 Alleppey Express	**MAS** 21.15	Palakkad 5.20
OOTY	2671 Nilagiri Express	**MAS** 21.00	Mettupalaiyam 6.15
PALAKKAD	6041 Alleppey Express	**MAS** 21.15	Palakkad 5.20
PALANI	2637 Pandian Express	**MS** 21.30 **TBM** 21.55	Dindigul Junction 4.30
PARSON'S VALLEY	2671 Nilagiri Express	**MAS** 21.00	Mettupalaiyam 6.15
PERIYAR TR	2623 Trivandrum Mail	**MAS** 20.00	Kottayam 7.55
RED HILLS	2671 Nilagiri Express	**MAS** 21.00	Mettupalaiyam 6.15
SALIM ALI BS	2623 Trivandrum Mail	**MAS** 20.00	Aluva 6.02
SHIVANASAMUDRAM	2657 Bangalore Mail	**MAS** 23.15	Bangalore City Junction 5.30
SRAVANABELAGOLA	6222 Mysore Express	**MAS** 21.30	Srirangapatna 7.18
SRIKALAHASTI	2164 Chennai Express	**MAS** 7.00	Renigunta Junction 9.15
SRIRANGAPATNA	6222 Mysore Express	**MAS** 21.30	Srirangapatna 7.18
THANJAVUR	6177 Rockfort Express	**MS** 22.30 **MBM** 22.40 **TBM** 23.00	Thanjavur 6.15
THRISSUR	2623 Trivandrum Mail	**MAS** 20.00	Thrissur 5.00
TIRUCHIRAPALLI	6177 Rockfort Express	**MS** 22.30 **MBM** 22.40 **TBM** 23.00	Tiruchirapalli 5.15
TIRUMALA	7651 Kacheguda Express	**MS** 17.00	Renigunta Junction 20.00
VYTHIRI	2601 Mangalore Mail	**MAS** 20.15	Kozhikode 7.45
YELAGIRI HILLS	2675 Kovai Express	**MAS** 6.15	Jolarpettai 9.08
YERCAUD	6669 Yercaud Express	**MAS** 22.30 **PER** 22.45	Salem Junction 5.10

LEGEND: MAS CHENNAI CENTRAL **MS** CHENNAI EGMORE **MBM** MAMBALAM **PER** PERAMBUR **TBM** TAMBARAM

THE BEST TRAINS?
These train options have been chosen on the basis of arrival time at destinations which optimise time for a weekend break. For instance, while there are faster trains between Chennai and Renigunta, the Kacheguda Express is best suited for an early morning darshan. In case you choose to visit Tirumala for a longer period than a weekend break, then the Chennai Express, which takes just over 2 hours to Renigunta, would indeed be a better option.

INFORMATION

TRAINS TO EACH DESTINATION

Here are our picks for the best options from each destination back to Chennai,

Destination	Train Name	Station/ Departure	Arrival (nearest station)
ALAPPUZHA	6042 Chennai Express	Alleppey 16.10	AVD 5.03 PER 5.13 MAS 6.05
BANGALORE	2008 Shatabdi Express	Bangalore City Junction 16.25	MAS 21.30
BANNERGHATA	2658 Chennai Mail	Bangalore City Junction 22.45	PER 3.54 MAS 4.40
BELLIKKAL	2672 Nilagiri Express	Mettupalaiyam 19.45	PER 4.24 MAS 5.10
BHEEMESHWARI	2658 Chennai Mail	Bangalore City Junction 22.45	PER 3.54 MAS 4.40
BR HILLS	6221 Mysore Express	Mysore Junction 20.15	PER 6.34 MAS 7.20
CHETTINAD	2638 Pandian Express	Madurai Junction 20.45	TBM 4.54 MBM 5.14 MS 5.45
COONOOR	2672 Nilagiri Express	Mettupalaiyam 19.45	PER 4.24 MAS 5.10
GURUVAYUR	6042 Chennai Express	Thrissur 19.10	AVD 5.03 PER 5.13 MAS 6.05
INDIRA GANDHI WLS	2672 Nilagiri Express	Coimbatore Junction 20.55	PER 4.24 MAS 5.10
KAMARAJAR VALLEY	2632 Nellai Express	Dindigul Junction 22.15	TBM 5.19 MBM 5.34 MS 6.10
KOCHI	2624 Chennai Mail	Ernakulam Town 19.15	AVD 6.09 PER 6.24 MAS 7.00
KODAIKANAL	2638 Pandian Express	Kodaikanal Road 21.25	TBM 4.54 MBM 5.14 MS 5.45
KOTTAYAM	2624 Chennai Mail	Kottayam 17.35	AVD 6.09 PER 6.24 MAS 7.00
KOZHIKODE	2602 Chennai Mail	Kozhikode 17.30	PER 4.39 MAS 5.25
KUMARAKOM	2624 Chennai Mail	Kottayam 17.35	AVD 6.09 PER 6.24 MAS 7.00
KUMBAKONAM	6178 Rockfort Express	Kumbakonam 19.30	TBM 4.16 MBM 4.34 MS 5.15
LEPAKSHI	2658 Chennai Mail	Bangalore City Junction 22.45	PER 3.54 MAS 4.40
MADURAI	2638 Pandian Express	Madurai Junction 20.45	TBM 4.54 MBM 5.14 MS 5.45
MUDUMALAI	2672 Nilagiri Express	Mettupalaiyam 19.45	PER 4.24 MAS 5.10
MYSORE	6221 Mysore Express	Mysore Junction 20.15	PER 6.34 MAS 7.20
NAGARHOLE	6221 Mysore Express	Mysore Junction 20.15	PER 6.34 MAS 7.20
NANDI HILLS	2658 Chennai Mail	Bangalore City Junction 22.45	PER 3.54 MAS 4.40

TRAIN RECKONER FROM

BEST SUITED FOR A WEEKEND BREAK
with arrival timings at all Chennai stations the train halts at on the way in

Destination	Train Name	Station/ Departure	Arrival (nearest station)
NELLIYAMPATHY	6042 Chennai Express	Palakkad 21.05	AVD 5.03 PER 5.13 MAS 6.05
OOTY	2672 Nilagiri Express	Mettupalaiyam 19.45	PER 4.24 MAS 5.10
PALAKKAD	6042 Chennai Express	Palakkad 21.05	AVD 5.03 PER 5.13 MAS 6.05
PALANI	2632 Nellai Express	Dindigul Junction 22.15	TBM 5.19 MBM 5.34 MS 6.10
PARSON'S VALLEY	2672 Nilagiri Express	Mettupalaiyam 19.45	PER 4.24 MAS 5.10
PERIYAR TR	2624 Chennai Mail	Kottayam 17.35	AVD 6.09 PER 6.24 MAS 7.00
RED HILLS	2672 Nilagiri Express	Mettupalaiyam 19.45	PER 4.24 MAS 5.10
SALIM ALI BS	2624 Chennai Mail	Aluva 19.35	AVD 6.09 PER 6.24 MAS 7.00
SHIVANASAMUDRAM	2658 Chennai Mail	Bangalore City Junction 22.45	PER 3.54 MAS 4.40
SRAVANABELGOLA	6221 Mysore Express	Srirangapatna 20.30	PER 6.34 MAS 7.20
SRIKALAHASTI	2163 Chennai Express	Renigunta Junction 17.15	PER 18.58 MAS 19.35
SRIRANGAPATNA	6221 Mysore Express	Srirangapatna 20.30	PER 6.34 MAS 7.20
THANJAVUR	6178 Rockfort Express	Thanjavur 20.30	TBM 4.16 MBM 4.34 MS 5.15
THRISSUR	6042 Chennai Express	Thrissur 19.10	AVD 5.03 PER 5.13 MAS 6.05
TIRUCHIRAPALLI	6178 Rockfort Express	Tiruchirapalli 22.00	TBM 4.16 MBM 4.34 MS 5.15
TIRUMALA	2163 Chennai Express	Renigunta Junction 17.15	PER 18.58 MAS 19.35
VYTHIRI	2602 Chennai Mail	Kozhikode 17.30	PER 4.39 MAS 5.25
YELAGIRI HILLS	2676 Kovai Express	Jolarpettai 18.13	MAS 21.20
YERCAUD	6670 Yercaud Express	Salem Junction 22.00	PER 3.44 MAS 4.30

LEGEND: AVD AVADI **MAS** CHENNAI CENTRAL **MS** CHENNAI EGMORE **MBM** MAMBALAM **PER** PERAMBUR **TBM** TAMBARAM

THE BEST TRAINS?

These train options have been chosen on the basis of arrival time at Chennai which are optimal for getting back to your routine. For instance, while there are faster trains between Chennai and Kochi, the Chennai Mail leaves Ernakulam at night and arrives in Chennai early next morning, well in time for school and office. In case you choose to visit Kochi for a longer period than a weekend break, then the Trivandrum-Chennai Express is an even faster option, though it arrives much later, at 9.45 am

INFORMATION

TRAVEL AGENTS

All these agents provide hotel, rail and air bookings and car rental. Most will book bus tickets. Only the special services they offer, apart from these basic ones, are listed

IN TAMIL NADU

CHENNAI STD 044

ADYAR TRAVEL BUREAU
Location Near Adyar Signal **Address** 81, First Main Road, Gandhi Nagar, Adyar **Tel** 24411485/ 51195 **Fax** 24917490 **Email** atb@adyar travel.com **Website** adyar travel.com **Special Services** Transport in Kerala, houseboat cruises **Popular Package** 3N/4D Munnar-Kumarakom, Rs 13,500-25,000 per couple **Timings** 9.30 am-6.30 pm

AIRSILAND TOURISM
Location Near Temple Tower **Address** NS House, 475/31, A2, Anna Salai, Nandanam **Tel** 24349883 **Mobile** 09840859317 **Email** airis landtourism@yahoo.co.in **Special Services** Temple tour packages **Popular Package** Mahabalipuram-Pondicherry day tour at Rs 300-400 per person **Timings** 24 hrs

AKSHAYA INDIA TOURS AND TRAVEL
Location Near ICICI Bank ATM **Address** A-1/3, Kushkumar Road, Nungambakkam **Tel** 28224188/ 99 **Mobile** 09444393594 **Email** tours@akshayaindia.com **Website** akshayaindia.com **Special Services** Day tours in Tamil Nadu, village, cultural tours around Chennai **Popular Packages** Balaji Darshan at Rs 4,500 per couple; Mahabalipuram-Pondicherry beach tour at Rs 5,000 per couple **Timings** 9.30 am-5.30 pm

CHARU TRAVELS
Location Opp Nakida Hotel **Address** 5, 1st Main Road, Kasturibai Nagar, Adyar **Tel** 42187198 **Email** charutravels@airtelbroad band.in **Special Services** Day tours in and around Chennai **Popular Package** 5-8 days Pilgrimage Package at Rs 10,000 per person **Timings** 9.30 am-5.30 pm

DESTINATION ASIA
Location Near Waves Textile Store **Address** 114/5, 5-Star Apts, Padikuppam Road, Anna Nagar West **Tel** 65911342 **Mobile** 09840431168 **Travel Services** Car rentals **Special Services** Customised packages for South India **Popular Packages** 2N/ 3D packages to Munnar, Ernakulam, Kodaikanal, Mysore and Ooty at Rs 1, 000 per person per destination **Timings** 9.30 am-5.30 pm

MADURA TRAVEL SERVICE
Location Opp Egmore Station **Address** 11/3, Gandhi Irwin Road **Tel** 28192002/ 2970 **Mobile** 09841078674-75 **Email** india@maduratravel.com **Website** maduratravel.com **Special Services** Chennai city tours, day tours around Tamil Nadu **Popular Package** 3N/ 4D Kerala Package at Rs 5,000 per person **Timings** 24 hrs

PARVEEN TRAVELS
Location Opp Roxy Theatre **Address** 24, Mookathal Street, Purusawalkam **Tel** 26421158, 26424348 **Email** parveen travels@md2.vsnl.net.in **Website** parveentravels.com **Special Services** Tamil Nadu sightseeing **Popular Packages** Kodaikanal at Rs 3,600 per person; Rameshwaram-Madurai at Rs 2,200 per person **Timings** 24 hrs

PEGASUS TRAVELS & TOURS
Location Near Don Bosco School **Address** FF, Elcanso Building, 10, Casa Major Road **Tel** 28192883, 42054036 **Mobile** 09444024399 **Email** pttinbound@vsnl.net **Website** pegasustravels.com **Special Services** Day tours to Pondicherry, Mahabalipuram; 3-14 day package tours to Ooty, Madurai, Kanyakumari **Popular Package** 3N/ 4D Kerala Package at Rs 7,500 per person **Timings** 9.30 am-6 pm

SARATHY TRAVELS
Location Near Hotel Park Sheraton **Address** 19 Hegde Apts, 7th Main Road, RA Puram **Tel** 42112221 **Mobile** 09444443223 **Email** rshan muka@yahoo.co.in **Special Services** Temple tours **Popular Package** 2N/ 3D Navagraha Temples Tour at Rs 10,000 per couple **Timings** 9 am-6 pm

SOUTH TOURISM
Location Near Saravana Bhavan **Address** No. 1, Z

TRAVEL AGENTS

Block, 19th Street, Anna Nagar **Tel** 42179092 **Mobile** 09444001117 **Email** praveen@wttw.in **Website** southtourism.in **Special Services** Wildlife, Ayurveda, yoga and meditation tours, temple tours **Popular Package** 7N/ 8D Chennai-Madurai Pilgrimage Package at Rs 26,000 per person **Timings** 10 am-6 pm

TRAVEL AIR

Location Near Anand Theatre Circle **Address** 16, Arati Chambers, 189, Mount Road **Tel** 28521623/ 5012 **Fax** 28524610 **Email** traveller@travellerindia.com **Website** travellerindia.com **Popular Package** 2N/ 3D Kerala Package (with 1 night on houseboat) at Rs 15,000 per couple **Timings** 10.30 am-6.30 pm

WELCOME TOURS & TRAVELS

Location Opp Spencer Plaza **Address** 150, Mount Road **Tel** 28460614 **Fax** 28461645 **Email** agmesh@vsnl.com **Website** allindiatours.com **Special Services** Customised tours around Tamil Nadu **Popular Package** 4N/ 5D Munnar-Periyar-Alleppey at Rs 16,000 per person **Timings** 24 hrs

COIMBATORE STD 0422
PEARLS TOURS & TRAVELS

Location Near Karuparayan Temple **Address** 19/ ID, SP Kumarasamy Gounder Street, Sanganoor Main Road, Sanganoor **Tel** 2331605 **Mobile** 09842226662, 09840075806 **Website** pearlsindiatour.com **Special Services** Tailormade packages anywhere in India **Timings** 9 am-7 pm

KODAIKANAL STD 04542
TRAVEL IN

Location Opp Bus Stand **Address** JC Complex, Kodaikanal **Tel** 240880 **Mobile** 0994941627, 09842172072 **Email** kodaitravelin@rediffmail.com **Special Services** Group deals, tailormade packages in South India **Popular package** 4N/ 5D Kodai-Munnar-Thekkady Rs 4,000 per person, 3N/ 4D Mudumalai-Rameshwaram-Kanyakumari, at Rs 2,500 per person **Timings** 9.30 am-7 pm

MADURAI STD 0452
SRI MURUGAN TRAVEL AGENCY

Location Near Rani Furniture **Address** 10, North Aavani Moola Street **Tel** 2622561, 2624168 **Mobile** 09443062256 **Email** murugan_travel@yahoo.co.in **Special Services** Kerala tours, day packages and pilgrimage tours in South India **Timings** 9 am-9 pm

SURYA TOURS & TRAVELS

Location In Hotel Sulochana Palace **Address** 56/96, West Perumal Maistry Street **Tel** 4373158 **Mobile** 09894376717 **Fax** 2349669 **Email** ksurya2005@eth.net **Special Services** Kerala taxi tours, day packages and pilgrimage tours in South India **Popular Package** 6D/ 5N Thekkady-Munnar-Kochi-Chennai at Rs 5,200 per person **Timings** 9 am-9 pm

OOTY STD 0423
PIO TOURS AND GUIDES

Location Opp Ganesh Theatre **Address** Balaji Complex, Walsham Road **Tel** 2450665 **Mobile** 09443345258 **Email** cjohn14@rediffmail.com **Special Services** Packages for South India, hotel and rail bookings **Popular Package** Ooty-Coonoor city day tour at Rs 1,000 per couple **Timings** 10 am-8 pm

PRICOL TRAVELS

Location Near Higginbotham's **Address** Supermarket Building, Commercial Road **Tel** 2442604, 2444912 **Email** mbtravel@dataone.in **Special Services** Packages for South India **Timings** 9 am-5.30 pm

TRICHY STD 0431
SOUTH TOURISM

Location Beside Kollidakarai **Address** No. 5, Annai Avenue, Vasant Nagar Extn, Kollidakarai, Srirangam **Tel** 2433372, 2437183, 2432874 **Fax** 2432874 **Email** tours@southtourism.in **Website** southtourism.in **Special Services** Customised tours around South India **Popular Package** 5N/ 6D Kerala Package at Rs 27,000 per couple **Timings** 9.30 am-8.30 pm

INDIAN TRAVEL SERVICE

Location Near Srirangam Temple **Address** 33, Chandranagar, Srirangam **Tel** 2435219 Telefax 2430832 **Website** tourism-southindia.com **Special Services** Transport in Kerala **Popular Package** 1N/ 2D Houseboat Package at Rs 6,000 per couple **Timings** 10 am-7 pm

IN KERALA

ALAPPUZHA STD 0477
ALLEPPEY ONLINE TOUR OPERATORS

Location Next to Lord Krishna

INFORMATION

Bank **Address** Vijaya Complex, Jetty Road **Tel** 0478-2582235 **Mobile** 09846243894 **Email** alleppeyonline@yahoo.com **Website** keralaatitsbest.com **Special Services** Kerala packages, health tours **Popular Package** 5N/ 6D 'A Little of Everything' Package at Rs 15,500 per couple **Timings** 9 am-6 pm

BON VOYAGE BACKWATER

Location Near jetty **Address** Raiban Shopping Complex, Boat Jetty **Tel** 2261079 **Email** bonvoyage@sancharnet.in **Website** bonvoyageback water.com **Special Services** Houseboat, motorboat, speedboat, day cruises **Popular Package** Backwater Package at Rs 26,000 per couple **Timings** 9 am-6 pm

COCO PLANET TOURS AND TRAVELS

Location Near Nehru Trophy Race Finishing Point **Address** Thatampally Post, Alleppey **Tel** 2239903-04 **Mobile** 09847325026 **Email** kerala_houseboats@yahoo.com **Website** beautifulkerala.com **Special Services** Houseboats, eco-friendly Kerala tours **Popular Package** 2N/ 3D Kerala Package at Rs 10,800 per couple **Timings** 24 hrs

MARVEL CRUISE

Location Near the jetty **Address** Akkarakkalam House, Mullakkal, Alleppey **Tel** 2264341 **Mobile** 09947235684 **Email** cruise@marveltour.net **Website** marveltour.net **Special Services** Day cruise, village walks with guide, fishing on houseboat **Popular** **Package** 2N/ 3D Cruise Package at Rs 11,978-17,424 per couple **Timings** 9 am-6 pm

MY DREAM CRUISE & TOURS

Location Near Komala Hotel **Address** Zilla Court Ward **Tel** 3090365 **Mobile** 09846075978 **Email** mydream@india.com **Website** mydreamindia.com **Special Services** Houseboats, backwaters **Popular Package** Day cruise at Rs 3,500 per couple **Timings** 9.30 am-6 pm

KOTTAYAM STD 0481

CRUISE AND CRUISE TOURS AND TRAVELS

Location Opp Kodimatha Jetty **Address** AKM Building, GF, Kodimatha **Tel** 2363805 **Mobile** 09846042805 **Email** pradeepmathew98460@yahoo.co.in **Special Services** Backwater houseboat tours **Popular Package** Kochi 1N/ 2D at Rs 1,300 per couple **Timings** 24 hrs

DOLPHIN TOURIST BOAT SERVICE

Location Near jetty **Address** Korattiyil Building, Boat Jetty Road, Kodimatha **Tel** 2584352 **Mobile** 09846095400 **Email** info@dolphinboatservice.com **Website** dolphinboatservice.com **Special Services** Houseboat cruise **Popular Package** Houseboat stay at Rs 5,000 per couple per day **Timings** 8 am-6.30 pm

MALAYA WORLD TOURS

Location Near KSRTC Bus Stand **Address** Shangrila Plaza, TB Road **Tel** 2565903/ 13 **Mobile** 09447145894 **Fax** 2563503 **Email** malayas@asianetindia.com **Special Services** Houseboats **Popular Package** Kuttanadan Holiday Package at Rs 28,000 per couple **Timings** 9.30 am-5.30 pm

KOZHIKODE STD 0495

AKBAR TRAVELS OF INDIA

Location Near Transport Bus Stand **Address** 60401 CD Kashkand Chambers, Bank Road **Tel** 2360802, 2765734, 2766596 **Mobile** 09846470600 **Fax** 2368662 **Email** calicut@akbartravels.co.in **Website** akbartravelsofindia.com **Special Services** Houseboats, Kerala tours **Popular Package** Kerala Package at Rs 12,000 **Timings** 9.30 am-6.30 pm

NAVEEN TRAVELS

Location Next to Hotel Hyson Heritage **Address** Kashand Chambers, Bank Road **Tel** 3292864 **Telefax** 2765895 **Email** sprabhu@hotmail.com **Special Services** Houseboat trips, wildlife packages **Popular Package** 2N/ 3D Wayanad Package at Rs 16,000 per couple **Timings** 9.30 am-5.30 pm

KOCHI STD 0484

EBENEZER HOLIDAY

Location Near Sai Service **Address** GF, Mohammad Haji Building, NH-17, Edapally **Tel** 2802808 **Mobile** 09846057535 **Email** dreamholidays@sify.com **Website** paradisekerala.com **Special Services** Houseboats **Popular Package** Munnar-Thekkady-Kochi at Rs 4,500-30,000 per couple **Timings** 9 am-5.30 pm

EXCEL INDIA TOURS

Location Near Ambalakadu Jetty **Address** 10/130, Nettoor **Tel** 2701580 **Mobile**

TRAVEL AGENTS

09447070158 **Email** info@excelindiatours.com **Website** excelindiatours.com **Special Services** Houseboats **Popular Package** 7D/ 6N backwater, beaches, pilgrimage and trekking package starting Rs 70,000 per person

KALYPSO ADVENTURES
Location Opp Avenue Centre Hotel **Address** G340, Panampilly Nagar **Tel** 6583573 **Mobile** 09447031032 **Telefax** 2312627 **Email** info@kalypso adventures.com **Website** kaypsoadventures.com **Special Services** White-water rafting on Periyar River, home stays, village and adventure tours **Popular Package** 7N/ 8D Western Ghats Endemic Bird Tour at Rs 31,000 per person **Timings** 9 am-5 pm

PIONEER TRAVELS
Location Opp Nima Cold Storage **Address** Pioneer House, 5th Cross Road, Willingdon Island **Tel** 2666148 **Fax** 2668490 **Email** pioneer@pner.com **Website** pioneer travels.com **Special Services** Budget-friendly customised tours **Popular Package** Houseboat Package at Rs 4,500-12, 000 per couple **Timings** 9.30 am-5.30 pm

WILD KERALA TOUR COMPANY
Location Near Kashi Art Gallery **Address** 6/480, KVA Building, Bazaar Road, Mattancherry **Tel** 3299520 **Mobile** 09846162157 **Email** mail@wildkeralatours.com **Website** wildkeralatours.com **Special Services** Eco-tourism, wildlife **Popular Package** 2N/ 3D Chinnar Wildlife Sanctuary at Rs 11,000 per couple **Timings** 9.30 am-5.30 pm

PALAKKAD STD 0491
ITL TOURS
Location Opp Town Railway Station **Address** First Floor, Moopar Complex, RS Road **Tel** 2536784 **Fax** 2539022 **Email** pgt_itl@sancharnet.in **Website** itlservice.net **Special Services** Wildlife tours **Popular Package** 2N/ 3D Thekkady Package at Rs 5,000 per couple **Timings** 9.30 am-8 pm

THRISSUR STD 0487
JOSEY TOURS AND TRAVELS
Address Uthaya Building, St Thomas College Road **Tel** 2444467 **Mobile** 09846035222 **Fax** 2423016 **Email** josey tourskerala.com **Special Services** Spice tour of Thekkady, historical Cochin and mountains of Munnar tours, camping in South India **Timings** 9 am-7.30 pm

IN KARNATAKA

BANGALORE STD 080
HAMMOCK LEISURE TRAVELS
Address 314/1, Vijay Kiran Building, First Floor, 7th Cross, Domlur Layout **Tel** 25352877/ 7963 **Fax** 25354222 **Email** hammock@ vsnl.net **Special Services** Transport in Kerala, houseboat cruises, tailormade packages **Timings** 9.30 am-6.30 pm

CLIPPER HOLIDAYS
Location Next to Outlook Office **Address** Suite 406, Regency Enclave, 4, Magrath Road (off Brigade Road) **Tel** 25599032/ 034 **Fax** 25599833 **Email** clipperblr@airtelbroad band.in **Website** clipperholi days.co.in **Special Services** Wildlife, treks, tribal and meditation tours, temple tours and holiday packages in South India **Timings** 9.30 am-7 pm

ORAKLE TOURS & TRAVELS
Address No. 104, Mariyappa Building, Kalasipalyam Main Road **Tel** 32984118, 26700132, **Mobile** 09448230450 **Email** orakletravels@gmail.com **Website** orakletravels. theindiancenter.com **Special Services** Hill tours, holiday packages in Kerala and South India **Timings** 24 hrs

MYSORE STD 0821
AIRES TOURS & TRAVELS
Location Near Mahajana College Grounds **Address** 68, Hospital Road, Jayalakshi-puram **Tel** 2513572 **Mobile** 09448053572 **Email** shanthi aruna@rediffmail.com **Special Services** Hotel bookings in Karnataka, Nagarhole, Mudumalai, Bandipur, backwaters, wildlife, temple tours **Popular Package** Bandipur Wildlife Sanctuary at Rs 2,000 per person per night **Timings** 9 am-6 pm

SKYWAY INTERNATIONAL TRAVELS
Location Next to Blue Dart Courier Service **Address** No. 370/4, JLB Road **Tel** 2444444, 2426642 **Fax** 2439762 **Email** skyway@vsnl.com **Website** skywaytour.com **Special Services** South India tours **Popular Package** 6N/ 7D Discover South India Package at Rs 17,500 per person **Timings** 9 am-6 pm

ACCOMMODATION LISTINGS

LEGEND

- **FF** First Floor
- **FRH** Forest Rest House
- **Opp** Opposite
- **PO** Post
- **SF** Second Floor
- **TE** Taxes extra

Accommodation type? Spot these flags
HERITAGE **HIGH-END**
TTDC **KSTDC**

Special Hotel needs? Spot these flags
BIRDWATCHING **TREKKING**
AYURVEDA **SPA** **YOGA**

METRO RESERVATIONS

To book any TTDC, APTDC, PTDC or KTDC hotel in Chennai, see the Tourist Offices listing on page 481

HOTELS EASY ACCESS

ALAPPUZHA	499	KOZHIKODE	505	RED HILLS	524
BANGALORE	495	KUMARAKOM	506	SHIVANASAMUDRUM	498
BANNERGHATTA	495	KUMBAKONAM	519	SRAVANABELGOLA	499
BELLIKKAL	514	LEPAKSHI	493	SRIKALAHASTI	493
BHEEMESHWARI	495	MADURAI	519	SRIRANGAPATNA	499
BR HILLS	496	MAHABALIPURAM	520	SWAMIMALAI	524
CHETTINAD	514	MUDUMALAI	521	THANJAVUR	524
CHIDAMBARAM	515	MYSORE	496	THATTEKKAD	511
COONOOR	515	NAGAPATTINAM	522	THIRUVANNAMALAI	525
GURUVAYUR	500	NAGARHOLE NP	498	THRISSUR	511
HOGENAKKAL	516	NANDI HILLS	498	TIRUCHIRAPALLI	526
HORSLEY HILLS	492	NELLIYAMPATHY	508	TIRUMALA	493
INDIRA GANDHI WLS	516	OOTY	522	TIRUPATI	494
KAMARAJAR VALLEY	516	PALAKKAD	508	TRANQUEBAR	526
KANCHIPURAM	517	PALANI HILLS	524	VEDANTHANGAL	527
KOCHI	502	PARSON'S VALLEY	524	VYTHIRI	512
KODAIKANAL	517	PERIYAR TR	509	YELAGIRI HILLS	527
KOTTAYAM	505	PONDICHERRY	513	YERCAUD	527

ANDHRA PRADESH

HORSLEY HILLS STD 08571

Abhinam Resorts
Location Opp Pongali Restaurant **Tel** 279328 **Rooms** 10 **Tariff** Rs 250-350 **Facilities** Car rental, hot water, room service

Forest Rest House
Location Behind bus stand **Tel** 279325 **Rooms** 6 **Tariff** Rs 400-800 **Facilities** Cook, hot water, room service **Madanapalle Reservations** Forest Range Office **Tel** 08571-222436

Holiday Homes
Location Next to Punnami Hill Resort **Tel** 279307 **Mobile** 09440671253, 09440273724 **Rooms** 15 **Tariff** Rs 500-1,000 **Facilities** Restaurant, attached bath, hot water, massage centre, travel desk, room service

Punnami Hill Resort **APTDC**
Location Hilltop **Tel** 279323-24 **Rooms** 48 **Tariff** Rs 600-2,000; TE **Credit Cards** Visa, Master **Facilities** Restaurant, bar, swimming pool, Ayurvedic massage, kids' play area, trekking, room service **Chennai Reservations** See page 481

Yatri Niwas
Location Hilltop **Tel** 279323-24 **Rooms** 8 **Tariff** Rs 1,260; TE

TIP Unless specified, credit cards are not accepted at hotels

Disclaimer Only a representative listing of hotels in each area has been given. The facilities listed may not be exhaustive. Tariff indicates the approx range (lowest to highest) of the rates prevailing at the time of going to press. The listings given here should not be construed as recommendations by the publisher

HOTELS

Credit Cards Visa, Master **Facilities** Attached bath, room service

LEPAKSHI STD 08556

Hotel Ajanta
Location Opp RTC Bus Stand **Address** Penukonda Road, Hindupur **Tel** 222156, 224977 **Rooms** 60 **Tariff** Rs 90-600 **Facilities** Restaurant, bar, car rental, laundry, room service

Hotel Garudadri
Location Near Govt Hospital and Private Bus Stand **Address** Penukonda Road, Hindupur **Tel** 220808 **Rooms** 28 **Tariff** Rs 100-200 **Facilities** Travel desk, laundry, attached bath, room service

Hotel Palla Residency
Location Near Station **Address** Railway Station Road, Hindupur **Tel** 224869/ 959, 228759 **Rooms** 33 **Tariff** Rs 300-899 **Facilities** Veg restaurant, laundry, attached bath, car rental, room service

Nandini Gardens
Location Near bus stand **Address** Prashant Nagar, Bangaloro Road, Hindupur **Tel** 222636 **Mobile** 09908052385 **Rooms** 20 **Tariff** Rs 250-450 **Facilities** Bar, travel desk, attached bath, room service

SRIKALAHASTI STD 08578

Hotel Swarna Residency
Location Opp Srikalahastisvara Temple **Address** Car Street **Tel** 223065-68 **Mobile** 09393608337 **Rooms** 25 **Tariff** Rs 375-700 **Facilities** Restaurant, attached bath, hot water, room service

Shiva Sadan Pilgrim's Choultry
Address Srikalahastisvara Temple premises **Tel** 222240 (Temple Office) **Rooms** 74 **Tariff** Rs 50-400 **Facilities** Attached bath, hot water

Trinetra Guest House
Address Srikalahastisvara Temple premises **Tel** 221185 **Rooms** 50 **Tariff** Rs 50-400 **Facilities** Attached bath, hot water

TIRUMALA STD 0877

Tirumala Tirupati Devasthanam
Accommodation Rooms and cottages, at Rambagicha, Varahaswamy, Saptagiri, Narayanagiri, Sri Padmavati and other guest houses. Rooms are clean and comfortable with Western-style toilets (provided on request), and running hot water. Single pilgrims can only get dormitory accommodation **Tariff** ranges from Rs 100-2,500 per day

Advance reservation of accommodation at Tirumala can be made in three ways:
- Advance reservation at TTD Info Centre, T Nagar, Chennai. Tel: 044-42129498, 28573835; Reservation fee: Rs 100; reservation slip to be shown at the ARP (Advance Reservation Provision) Counter, Central Reception Office (CRO), TTD, Tirumala (Tel: 0877-2263883).
- Sending a Demand Draft (DD)/ Money Order (MO) of Rs 100 to the Asst Executive Officer (Reception), TTD, Tirumala-517504; confirmation slip sent by post to be shown at the ARP Counter.
- Book accommodation online at ttdsevaonline.com; receipt and identity proof to be shown at the Internet Counter in Sri Padmavathi Guest House, Tirumala.

Current booking At CRO, next to the ARP Counter at Tirumala. Free choultries and paid accommodation (Tariff: Rs 50-200) available for a 24-hr stay.

Karnataka State Guest House
Location Next to temple **Address** Karnataka State Charity, Tirumala **Tel** 2277238, 2277426 **Rooms** 86 **Tariff** Rs 500-1,500 **Facilities** Restaurant, attached bath, room service

ACCOMMODATION LISTINGS

TIRUPATI STD 0877

AP Tourism Guest House
APTDC
Address Srinivasam Amenities Complex, Tirumala-Bypass Road **Tel** 2280611, 2289123 **Rooms** 140 **Tariff** Rs 400-1,155 **Credit Cards** Visa, Master **Facilities** Multi-cuisine restaurant, travel desk, car rental, room service **Chennai Reservations** See page 481

Bhimas Deluxe Hotel
Location Near Tirupati East Railway Station **Address** 34-38 Car Street **Tel** 2225521, 6669199 **Website** thirupathibhimashotels.com **Rooms** 69 **Tariff** Rs 950-1,050 **TE Credit Cards** Visa, Master **Facilities** Restaurant, laundry, travel desk, room service

Hotel Bhima's
Location Near Tirupati East Railway Station **Address** 42-G, Car Street **Tel** 2225744, 6669300 **Rooms** 70 **Tariff** Rs 325-650 **Facilities** Veg restaurant, laundry, attached bath, hot water, travel desk, car rental, room service

Hotel Bhima's Paradise
Location Opp Ramanuja Circle **Address** 33-37, Renigunta Road **Tel** 2237271-72 **Fax** 2237277 **Rooms** 89 **Tariff** Rs 650-1,500; TE **Credit Cards** Visa, Master **Facilities** Veg restaurant, travel desk, laundry, room service

Hotel Bliss MID-RANGE
Location Near Ramanuja Circle **Address** Renigunta Road **Tel** 2237770-73 **Fax** 2237774 **Website** blisstirupati.com **Rooms** 92 **Tariff** Rs 1,100-4,200; TE **Credit Cards** Visa, Master **Facilities** Restaurants, bar, travel desk, kids' park, shopping arcade, laundry, room service

Hotel Kalyan Residency
Location Near Railway Station **Address** 177, TP Area **Tel** 2259780-89 **Fax** 2259757 **Website** kalyanresidency.com **Rooms** 54 **Tariff** Rs 1,095-1,995; TE **Credit Cards** Visa, Master **Facilities** Multi-cuisine restaurant, travel desk, laundry, room service

Hotel Mayura
Location Opp Tirupati Main Bus Stand **Address** No. 209, Town Planning Area **Tel** 2225251/ 925 **Fax** 2225911 **Email** mayura@nettlinx.com **Rooms** 65 **Tariff** Rs 900-1,450; TE **Credit Cards** Visa, Master **Facilities** Multi-cuisine restaurant, travel desk, laundry, room service

Hotel PLR Grand MID-RANGE
Location Next to APSRTC Central Bus Stand **Address** Near Sandhya Theatre **Tel** 2257115 **Website** hotelplrgrand.com **Rooms** 100 **Tariff** Rs 545-2,200; TE **Credit Cards** Visa, Master **Facilities** Multi-cuisine restaurant, travel desk, laundry, room service

Hotel Ramee Guestline
Location Beginning of the road to Tirumala **Address** 14/ 37, Karakambadi Road, PO Akkarampalli **Tel** 2280366/ 800, 2281708 **Fax** 2281774 **Website** ramee-group.com **Rooms** 114 **Tariff** Rs 1,300-2,200; TE **Credit Cards** Visa, Master **Facilities** Multi-cuisine restaurant, café, bar, travel desk, swimming pool, health club, laundry, room service

Hotel Sindhuri Park MID-RANGE
Location Near Tirupati Railway Station **Address** 14-2-118/119, TP Area **Tel** 2256430-37 **Fax** 2256438 **Website** hotelsindhuri.com **Rooms** 54 **Tariff** Rs 1,080-1,980; **TE Credit Cards** Visa, Master **Facilities** Multi-cuisine restaurant, travel desk, laundry, room service

Sri Padmavati Guest House
Location Opp SV University, near bus stand **Address** Chittoor Road **Tel** 2264510-11 **Rooms** 36 **Tariff** Rs 400-1,000 **Facilities** Canteen (food on prior notice), attached bath, hot water

The Bhimas Residency
Location Near Railway Station overbridge **Address** Renigunta Road **Tel** 2237371-72 **Website** thirupathibhimashotels.com **Rooms** 77 **Tariff** Rs 1,520-3,260; TE **Credit Cards** Visa, Master **Facilities** Restaurant, café, travel desk, laundry, room service

TTD Alipiri Guest House
Location On road to Tirumala **Address** Alipiri Road **Tel** 2264502 **Rooms** 42 **Tariff** Rs 100 **Facilities** Attached bath, hot water

TTD Guest House
Location Opp APSRTC Bus Stand **Address** Srinivasam Amenities Complex, Tirumala-Bypass Road **Rooms** 410 **Tariff** Rs 200-600 **Facilities** Restaurant, attached bath, hot water **Reservations** Deputy Executive Officer, Srinivasam Amenities Complex, TTD, Tirupati **Tel** 0877-2264537/ 40-41

TTD Sri Govindaraja Swamy Choultry and TTD Sri Kodandarama Swamy Choultry
Location Behind Tirupati Railway Station **Tel** 2264501 (Central Reception/ Asst Executive Officer); 2264503 **Rooms** 246 and 220 **Tariff** Free at former; Rs 50 at latter **Facilities** Attached bath
TIP No advance booking

HOTELS

KARNATAKA

BANNERGHATTA NP

Banerghatta Nature Camp
Address Bannerghatta National Park **Rooms** 2 log huts, 8 Swiss tents, 1 dorm **Tariff** Log huts Rs 1,400, Swiss tents Rs 900, dorm (32 beds) Rs 600 (all per person per night); includes stay, meals, jeep safari, visit to the National Park, forest entry fees and taxes **Bangalore Reservations** SF, Shrungar Shopping Centre, MG Road **Tel** 080-25597021/ 24-25

BANGALORE SPAS STD 080

AyurvedaGram Heritage Wellness Centre AYURVEDA
Location 7 km from Hope Farm Junction **Address** Hemmandanahalli, Samephamahalli Post, Whitefield **Tel** 65651090-91/ 94 **Mobile** 09845071990 **Website** ayurvedagram.com **Rooms** 31 **Tariff** Rs 3,375-9,000 **Credit Cards** Visa, Master **Facilities** Restaurant, health club, herbal garden, Ayurveda, panchakarma, Kerala therapies, yoga, meditation, jogging track, Internet

Institute of Naturopathy and Yogic Sciences
Location Opp Jindal Aluminium Factory **Address** Jindal Nagar, Tumkur Road **Tel** 23717777 **Website** inysonline.org **Rooms** 140, 26 dorms **Tariff** Rs 300-6,000, dorm Rs 300-500 **Credit Cards** Visa, Master **Facilities** Diet centre, swimming pool, health centre, naturopathy, yoga, psychologist counselling, acupuncture, hydrotherapy, library, Internet, beauty parlour, washing machine, walking track, reflexology, sky cycling ground

Soukya International Holistic Health Centre AYURVEDA
Address Soukya Road, Samethanahalli, Whitefield **Tel** 25318405-06, 7945001-02 **Mobile** 09845374400 **Website** soukya.com **Rooms** 12 cottages, 4 suites **Tariff** Rs 7,600-48,100 **Credit Cards** Visa, Master **Facilities** Open air restaurant, swimming pool, yoga, homeopathy, naturopathy, Ayurveda, panchakarma, medical treatments, gift shop, 30 acre organic farm, therapy centre, beauty treatments, jogging track, biking track, reflexology, games, open air showers

The Golden Palms Hotel & Spa
Location Outskirts of Bangalore **Address** Golden Palms Avenue, Hobli, Tumkur Road **Tel** 23712222 **Fax** 23710033 **Website** goldenpalmsspa.com **Rooms** 132, suites 16, 2 Presidential suites **Tariff** Rs 11,000-27,500 **Credit Cards** AmEx, Visa, Master **Facilities** Restaurants, bar, swimming pool, health club, jogging track, games, cosmetic surgery clinic, spa, dental treatment studio

BHEEMESHWARI STD 08231

Bush Betta ANGLING
Location On the Cauvery River **Address** Cauvery Angling Camp, Mekkedatu **Tel** 080-41125220-01 **Email** bushbetta@vsnl.com **Rooms** 12 cottages **Tariff** Rs 2,350 per person **Credit Cards** NA **Facilities** Dining hall, river crossing, safaris with Cauvery Wildlife Division, rock climbing, angling, campfires

Cauvery Fishing Camp ANGLING
Location Riverside **Address** PO Byadarahalli, Halgur Hobli, Malavalli Taluk **Tel** 694248 **Mobile** 09449599779 **Website** junglelodges.com **Rooms** 8 log huts, 8 Swiss tents, 2 cottages **Tariff** Rs 1,650-2,200 per person per night **Facilities** Buffet meals, coracle rides, joy fishing, guided trekking and elephant rides **Bangalore Reservations** SF,

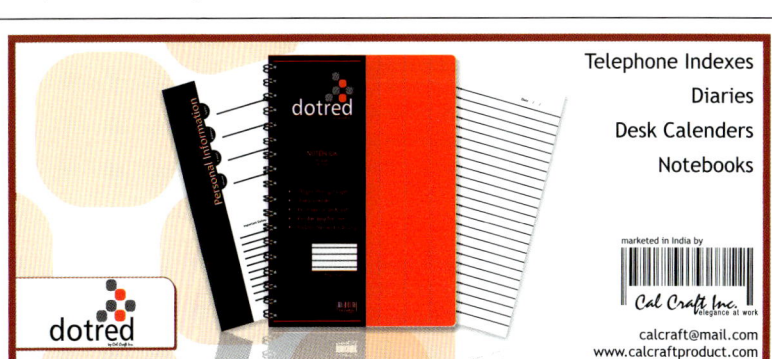

ACCOMMODATION LISTINGS

Shrungar Shopping Centre, MG Road **Tel** 080-25597021/ 24-25

Doddamakkali Fishing and Nature Camp `ANGLING`

Location Riverside **Address** PO Byadarhalli, Halgur Hobli, Malavalli Taluk **Tel** 694348 **Mobile** 09449599779 **Website** junglelodges.com **Rooms** 10 tented cottages **Tariff** Rs 1,400 per person per night **Facilities and Bangalore Reservations** See Cauvery Fishing Camp above

Galibore Fishing and Nature Camp `ANGLING`

Location Riverside **Address** Uyamballi Post, Sangam, Kanakapura Taluk **Tel** 694305 **Mobile** 09449599779 **Email** galibore@junglelodges.com **Website** junglelodges.com **Rooms** 12 tented cottages **Tariff** Rs 1,650 per person per night **Facilities and Bangalore Reservations** See Cauvery Fishing Camp above

---

BR HILLS STD 08226

Boodipagada Inspection Bungalow

Address Inside the sanctuary **Rooms** 2 **Tariff** Rs 750 **Facilities** Caretaker prepares meals, attached bath **Reservations** Deputy Conservator of Forests, Wildlife Division, Sultan Sheriff Circle, Chamarajanagar **Tel** 08226-222059 **Mobile** 09448077881

FRH

Address Inside the sanctuary **Rooms** 4 **Tariff** Rs 750 **Facilities and Reservations** See Boodipadaga IB above

K Gudi Wilderness Camp

Location In the forest **Address** Kyatha Devaraya Gudi, BR Hills **Tel** 296086 **Mobile** 09449599779 **Website** junglelodges.com **Rooms** 3 log huts, 8 tented cottages **Tariff** Rs 1,900 per person per night **Credit Cards** Visa, Master **Facilities** Elephant rides, jeep safari **Bangalore Reservations** 2F, Shrungar Shopping Centre, MG Road **Tel** 080-25597021/ 24-25

MYSORE STD 0821

Bombay Tiffanys `BUDGET`

Location Behind Chamundeswari Talkies **Address** 313, Sayyaji Rao Road Cross **Tel** 2435255-57 **Fax** 2433105 **Email** bombaytiffanys@yahoo.co.in **Rooms** 60 **Tariff** Rs 390-950 **Credit Cards** Visa, Master **Facilities** Travel desk, sightseeing, laundry, room service

Hotel Darshan Palace `MID-RANGE`

Location Opp Regency Theatre **Address** Lokranjan Mahal Road, Nazarbad **Tel** 2520794 **Fax** 2564083 **Rooms** 30 **Tariff** Rs 500-1,400; TE **Credit Cards** Visa, Master **Facilities** Hot water, laundry, room service

Hotel Dasaprakash Paradise `MID-RANGE`

Location Near Akashvani **Address** 104, Vivekananda Road, Yadavagiri **Tel** 2410366, 2515655 **Fax** 2514400 **Email** hotelparadise@airbroadband.in **Rooms** 90 **Tariff** Rs 825-1,750; TE **Credit Cards** AmEx, Visa, Master **Facilities** Multi-cuisine restaurant, bar, travel desk, laundry, lockers, room service

Hotel Govardhan `BUDGET`

Address Sri Harsha Road **Tel** 2417832, 2431960, 2429402 **Fax** 2420998 **Rooms** 60 **Tariff** Rs 150-900 **Facilities** Restaurant, travel desk, room service

Hotel Mayura Hoysala `KSTDC`

Location Near Railway Station **Address** 2, JLB Road **Tel** 2425597, 2425349 **Rooms** 17 **Tariff** Rs 650-1,000; TE **Credit Cards** Visa, Master **Facilities** Multi-cuisine restaurant, bar, laundry, room service **Chennai Reservations** See page 481

Hotel Mayura Yatrinivas `KSTDC`

Location Near Railway Station **Address** Jhansi Laxmi Bai Road **Tel** 2423492 **Rooms** 21, dorm 1 (16-20 bedded) **Tariff** Rs 300-800, dorm bed Rs 75 **Facilities** Restaurant, laundry **Chennai Reservations** See page 481

Hotel Nalapad Residency

Location Near Bannimantap Extn **Address** Dr Nelson Mandela Road **Tel** 2491117 **Website** nalapad.com **Rooms** 40 **Tariff** Rs 1,200-3,600; TE **Facilities** Restaurant, café, health club, travel desk, laundry, room service

Hotel Ramanashree

Location Near Mysore Palace **Address** 43/ A, Hardinge Circle **Tel** 2522202/ 65 **Fax** 2565781 **Website** ramanashree.com **Rooms** 66 **Tariff** Rs 1,795-4,295; TE **Credit Cards** AmEx, Visa, Master **Facilities** Multi-cuisine restaurant, laundry, lockers, travel desk, room service

Hotel Regaalis Quality `HIGH-END`

Location Central **Address** 13/ 14, Vinoba Road **Tel** 2426426, 2427427 **Fax** 2421689 **Website** ushashriramhotels.com **Rooms** 108 **Tariff** Rs 6,200-12,320; TE **Credit Cards** AmEx, Visa, Master **Facilities** Multi-cuisine restaurant, bar, beauty parlour, health club, swimming pool, forex, room service

HOTELS

Hotel Roopa MID-RANGE
Location Next to Hotel Ramanashree **Address** 2724/ C, Bangalore-Nilgiri Road **Tel** 2440044/ 3770 **Fax** 2443775 **Website** hotelroopa.com **Rooms** 52 **Tariff** Rs 900-2,500; TE **Credit Cards** Visa, Master **Facilities** Multi-cuisine restaurant, travel desk, laundry

Hotel The Roost BUDGET
Location Near Bajaj Auto Showroom **Address** Hinkal Village, Hunsur Road **Tel** 2410077 **Rooms** 12 **Tariff** Rs 810-1,026 **Credit Cards** Visa, Master **Facilities** Restaurant, bar, attached bath, room service

Indus Valley Ayurvedic Centre AYURVEDA
Location Opp Lalitha Mahal Palace Hotel **Address** Talavane Farm, Lalithadripura **Tel** 2473263/ 266/ 437 **Fax** 2473590 **Website** ayurindus.com **Rooms** 24 **Tariff** Rs 1,760-3,175; TE **Credit Cards** Visa, Master **Facilities** Restaurant, Ayurvedic massages, therapies and beauty treatments, yoga

Kadur Inn MID-RANGE
Location 2 km from BMH Hospital, near Ring Road **Address** Hunsur Road, near Hinkal Village **Tel** 2402210/ 840-41 **Fax** 2402209 **Email** kadur limited@yahoo.com **Rooms** 28 **Tariff** Rs 900-1,550; TE **Credit Cards** AmEx, Visa, Master **Facilities** Restaurant, bar, health club, games, room service

Kings Kourt Hotel MID-RANGE
Location Near Metropole Circle **Address** Jhansi Lakshmi Bai Road **Tel** 2421142 **Fax** 2422384 **Website** vivekhotels.com **Rooms** 51 **Tariff** Rs 1,800-4,000; TE **Credit Cards** AmEx, Visa, Master **Facilities** Multi-cuisine restaurant, laundry, Internet, travel desk, room service

Lalitha Mahal Palace Hotel HERITAGE
Address Lalithadripura **Tel** 2470268/ 470/ 476 **Fax** 2470555 **Website** lalithamahalpalace.com **Rooms** 54 **Tariff** Rs 5,000-30,000; TE **Credit Cards** AmEx, Visa, Master **Facilities** Multi-cuisine restaurant, beauty parlour, health club, games, library, travel desk, shopping arcade, locker, room service

Maurya Palace BUDGET
Location Opp Palace **Address** Sri Harsha Road **Tel** 2435847, 2435912/ 913 **Fax** 2429304 **Email** sangroup_hotel@yahoo.com **Rooms** 27 **Tariff** Rs 625-1,195; TE **Credit Cards** Visa, Master **Facilities** Multi-cuisine restaurant, bar, travel desk laundry, room service

Maurya Residency BUDGET
Location Next to Maurya Palace **Address** Sri Harsha Road **Tel** 2523375-76 **Fax** 2429304 **Email** sangroup_hotel@yahoo.com **Rooms** 24 **Tariff** Rs 785-1,195; TE **Credit Cards** Visa, Master **Facilities** Restaurant, travel desk, laundry, room service

Mayura Cauvery KSTDC
Location Inside Brindavan Gardens **Address** 18 km from Mysore **Tel** 08236-215876 **Rooms** 15 **Tariff** Rs 350 **Facilities** Restaurant, laundry **Chennai Reservations** See page 481

Royal Orchid Metropole
Location Opp King's Court Hotel **Address** 5, Jhansi Lakshmi Bai Road **Tel** 4255566 **Fax** 4255555 **Website** royalorchidhotels.com **Rooms** 30 **Tariff** Rs 4,000-7,000; TE **Credit Cards** AmEx, Visa, Master **Facilities** Restaurant, bar, café, swimming pool, fitness centre, travel desk, room service

Button Notebook

Telephone Indexes
Diaries
Desk Calenders
Notebooks

marketed in India by
Cal Craft Inc.
elegance at work
calcraft@mail.com
www.calcraftproduct.com

INFORMATION

ACCOMMODATION LISTINGS

The Green Hotel ECO-TOURISM
Location Next to BM Hospital on Hunsur Road **Address** 2270, Vinoba Road, Jayalakshmipuram **Tel** 2512536, 4255000 **Fax** 2516139 **Website** greenhotelindia.com **Rooms** 30 **Tariff** Rs 1,750-6,000; TE **Credit Cards** Visa, Master **Facilities** Restaurant, bar, Ayurvedic massage, travel desk, library, room service

The Viceroy MID-RANGE
Location Opp Mysore Palace **Address** 355/ 1A, Rajendra Enterprises, Sri Harsha Road **Tel** 2428001, 2434687 **Fax** 2433391 **Website** theviceroygroup.com **Rooms** 30 **Tariff** Rs 1,175-2,800; TE **Credit Cards** Visa, Master **Facilities** Multi-cuisine restaurant, travel desk, car rental, laundry, room service

The Village Resort HIGH-END SWIMMING POOL AYURVEDA
Location Outskirts of Mysore **Address** 106 Nanjangud Road **Tel** 2481310/ 766 **Telefax** 2481441 **Website** thevillagemysore.com **Rooms** 22 **Tariff** Rs 2,500-6,000; TE **Credit Cards** Visa, Master **Facilities** Multi-cuisine restaurant, swimming pool, health club, tennis court, cricket nets, table tennis

The Windflower Spa And Resorts HIGH-END SPA SWIMMING POOL
Location Behind Mysore Race Course **Address** Maharana Pratap Road, Nazarbad **Tel** 2522500 **Fax** 2522400 **Website** thewindflower.com **Rooms** 39 **Tariff** Rs 3,600-9,000 **Credit Cards** AmEx, Visa, Master **Facilities** Restaurant, bar, lounge, swimming pool, health club, spa, yoga, games, sightseeing, cycling, trekking, room service

NAGARHOLE NP STD 08274
Cicada Kabini ADVENTURE SWIMMING POOL WELLNESS
Location Adjacent to Kabini River Lodge **Address** Survey No. 60/ 1, Nishana, Karapura Village, Antarasante Hobli **Tel** 08228-264444/ 506, 263655 **Mobile** 09945602305 **Fax** 264507 **Website** cicadaresorts.com **Rooms** 19 cottages, 1 villa **Tariff** Rs 7,000-25,000; TE **Credit Cards** Visa, Master **Facilities** Restaurant, swimming pool, health club, safari vehicles, western holistic therapies, laundry, room service

Chilligeri Estate HOME STAY
Location In plantations, 3 km from Irpu Falls **Address** PO No. 167, Chilligeri Estate, Manchalli Village, Kutta **Tel** 244265 **Mobile** 09448582496 **Rooms** 4 **Tariff** Rs 750 (with meals) **Facilities** Home-cooked meals, laundry, sightseeing trips, trekking

Jungle Inn
Address 19th km, Hunsur-Nagarhole Road, Veeranahosahalli **Tel** 08222-246022/ 160 **Mobile** 09448271975 **Website** jungleinnnagarhole.com **Rooms** 6, Swiss tents 6, dorms 4 **Tariff** Rs 1,900-2,300 **Facilities** Multi-cuisine restaurant, coracle rides, safaris, trekking, wildlife films

Kabini River Lodge
Location Riverside **Address** Karapura, PO Nissana Belthur **Tel** 264402-03 **Fax** 264405 **Website** junglelodges.com **Rooms** 14, cottages 10, tented cottages 6 **Tariff** Rs 2,750-3,500 **Facilities** Restaurant, safaris, coracle rides **Bangalore Reservations** SF, Shrungar Shopping Complex, MG Road, Bangalore **Tel** 080-25597021/ 24-25 **Fax** 25586163

Kings Sanctuary SWIMMING POOL
Address Veeranahosahalli **Tel** 246444 **Mobile** 09845005659 **Fax** 246332 **Website** vivekhotels.com **Rooms** 24 suites **Tariff** Rs 8,500 **Credit Cards** Visa, Master **Facilities** Restaurant, swimming pool, health club, safaris, bird watching, games

Nagarhole Guest House
Location Inside NP **Address** Regional Forest Office, Nagarhole NP **Tel** 244221 **Rooms** 4 cottages, 2 dorms **Tariff** Rs 750, dorm bed Rs 50 **Facilities** Food on request, attached bath, hot water **Hunsur Reservations** DCF, Wildlife Division, Hunsur **Tel** 08222-252041 **Mysore Reservations** Field Director, Project Tiger, Aranya Bhavan, Ashokapuram **Tel** 0821-2480901 **Email** fdptrm@sancharnet.in

Vana Arathi Guesthouse HOME STAY
Location Amidst coffee plantations, touching the NP **Address** Nanchi Estate, PB No. 17, Kutta **Tel** 244228/ 888 **Rooms** 2 **Tariff** Rs 1,250-1,500 **Facilities** Home cooked meals, car rental, hot water

NANDI HILLS STD 08156
Nehru Nilaya
Address Horticulture Department Guest House **Tel** 250901 **Rooms** 25 **Tariff** Rs 260-1,120 **Facilities** Restaurant, hot water, room service **Bangalore Reservations** Director of Horticulture, Lalbagh **Tel** 080-26579231

SHIVANASAMUDRAM STD 08231
Georgia Sunshine Village SWIMMING POOL
Location On Shimshapura Road

HOTELS

Address PO Hebbani, Malavalli Taluk **Tel** 247646, 247783 **Mobile** 09845754661 **Website** georgia sunshine.com **Rooms** 8 **Tariff** Rs 1,596-2,156 **Facilities** Dining room, swimming pool, fun fishing, games room, lounge, library **Bangalore Reservations** Flat 01, Shobha Diamond, 23/ 1, Aga Abbas Ali Road, Ulsoor **Tel** 080-25590660, 41135824

SRAVANABELAGOLA STD 08176
Gurudev International
Address BM Road **Tel** 269525/ 1051-52 **Telefax** 269528 **Rooms** 30 **Tariff** Rs 550-1,026; TE **Credit Cards** Visa, Master, Diners **Facilities** Restaurants, bar, travel desk, laundry, room service, TV

Hotel Sri Krishna
Location Opp BSNL **Address** BM Road **Tel** 263240-43 **Fax** 233904 **Rooms** 49, suites 2 **Tariff** Rs 650-1,500; TE **Credit Cards** Visa, Master **Facilities** Restaurant, travel desk, room service, TV

Raghu Hotel
Location Near bus stand **Address** Kalyani Road **Tel** 257238 **Mobile** 09844068852 **Rooms** 20 **Tariff** Rs 200-700 **Facilities** Restaurant, guides, laundry, car rental, room service

Southern Star Hassan
Address BM Road **Tel** 251816/17 **Fax** 268916 **Website** usha shriramhotels.com **Rooms** 47 **Tariff** Rs 1,120-1,972; TE **Credit Cards** Visa, Master **Facilities** Restaurant, travel desk, guides, Ayurvedic massage, gym, library, laundry, room service

SRIRANGAPATNA STD 08236
Amblee Holiday Resort
MID-RANGE

Location Overlooking Cauvery River **Tel** 217474 **Telefax** 217475 **Mobile** 09845446999 **Rooms** 33 **Tariff** Rs 1,200-1,800; TE **Credit Cards** Visa, Master **Facilities** Multi-cuisine restaurant, bar, games, pool, playground, boating, fishing, car rental, room service

Balaji Garden Resort **BUDGET**
Location Next to bus stand **Address** Mysore-Bangalore Road **Tel** 217355-56 **Rooms** 46 **Tariff** Rs 350-750 **Facilities** Restaurant, laundry, playground, car rental, room service

Fort View Resorts **MID-RANGE**
Location Fort village **Address** Mysore-Bangalore Road **Tel** 252577 **Mobile** 09845353751 **Fax** 253877 **Website** fortview resorts.com **Rooms** 12 **Tariff** Rs 1,000-1,350; TE **Facilities** Restaurant, bonfire, fishing, laundry, travel desk, hot water

Hotel Mayura River View
KSTDC **BUDGET**

Location Next to Cauvery River **Tel** 217454-55 **Mobile** 09341022209 **Rooms** 12 cottages **Tariff** Rs 500-750 **Facilities** Restaurant, bar, fishing, laundry, games, car rental, room service **Chennai Reservations** See page 481

KERALA

ALAPPUZHA STD 0477
Alleppey Beach Resort
MID-RANGE

Location Near Railway Station **Address** Beach Road **Tel** 2263408, 2260125 **Website** thealleppeybeachresorts.com **Rooms** 8 **Tariff** Rs 1,500-2,990; TE **Credit Cards** AmEx, Visa, Master **Facilities** Multi-cuisine restaurant, private beach, house boat, motor boat, backwater cruise, massage, room service

Alleppey Prince Hotel
MID-RANGE

Location Near Railway Station **Address** Alleppey-Sherthalai Road, NH47 **Tel** 2243752-56 **Fax**

Telephone Indexes
Diaries
Desk Calenders
Notebooks

marketed in India by

Cal Craft Inc.
elegance at work
calcraft@mail.com
www.calcraftproduct.com

ACCOMMODATION LISTINGS

2243758 **Website** alleppeyprincehotel.com **Rooms** 36 **Tariff** Rs 1,250-2,500; TE **Credit Cards** AmEx, Visa, Master **Facilities** Restaurants, bar, swimming pool, travel desk, houseboats, backwater trips, shopping arcade, safe, laundry, room service

Gowri Heritage Home BUDGET
Location Near Udupi Sree Krishna Temple **Address** Thondankulangara, Avalookkunnu PO **Tel** 2236371/ 471 **Mobile** 09847055371 **Website** gowriresidence.com **Rooms** 10, 1 dorm (10 bedded) **Tariff** Rs 500-1,000, dorm Rs 600 **Facilities** Restaurant, backwater cruise, transfers, sightseeing, car and bike rental, travel desk, Internet

Hotel Royale Park MID-RANGE
Location Near backwaters **Address** Near KSRTC Bus Stand, YMCA Road **Tel** 2237828, 2238728 **Fax** 2264828 **Website** hotelroyalepark.com **Rooms** 28 **Tariff** Rs 700-2,400; TE **Credit Cards** Visa, Master **Facilities** Multi-cuisine restaurant, bar, café, travel desk, bookshop, laundry, boating, backwater cruises, room service

Keraleeyam AYURVEDA
Location Near Snake Boat Race starting point **Address** Thatampally PO **Tel** 2231468, 2236950 **Mobile** 09847050711 **Fax** 2251068 **Website** keraleeyam.com **Rooms** 14 **Tariff** Rs 1,425-2,280 **Credit Cards** Visa, Master **Facilities** Meals, Ayurvedic centre, hot water, attached bath, travel desk, boating, backwater cruises

KTDC Motel Yatri Niwas KTDC
Location 4 km from Alappuzha Beach **Address** Kalappura **Tel** 2244460/ 760 **Website** ktdc.com **Rooms** 17 **Tariff** Rs 350-1,100; TE **Facilities** Multi-cuisine restaurant, beer parlour, Ayurvedic massage, travel desk, laundry, attached bath, boating, backwater cruises, room service **Chennai Reservations** See page 481

Lake Palace HIGH-END SWIMMING POOL AYURVEDA
Location On an island, near Boat Race finishing point **Address** Thirumala Ward, Chungam PO **Tel** 2239701-04, 2230001-06 **Mobile** 09447645707 **Fax** 2239705 **Website** lakepalaceresort.com **Rooms** 38 cottages **Tariff** Rs 4,500-6,500; TE **Credit Cards** AmEx, Visa, Master **Facilities** Multi-cuisine restaurant, café, swimming pool, Ayurvedic centre, health club, kids' playground, laundry, minibar, travel desk, boating, backwater cruises

Marari Beach Resort SWIMMING POOL AYURVEDA
Location Near the beach **Address** North SL Puram, Mararikulam **Tel** 2863801-09 **Fax** 2863810 **Website** cghearth.com **Rooms** 62 **Tariff** Rs 12,800-19,250 (with meals); TE **Credit Cards** Visa, Master **Facilities** Restaurants, bar, beach restaurant, beach bar, Ayurvedic centre, swimming pool, tennis, yoga, games, cycling tours, travel desk, souvenir shop, laundry, sightseeing, boating, backwater cruises

Pagoda Resorts AYURVEDA SWIMMING POOL
Location Near KSRTC Bus Stand **Address** Near Kallupalam, Chungam PO **Tel** 2252549-50, 3091301 **Telefax** 2251697 **Website** pagodaresorts.com **Rooms** 12 cottages **Tariff** Rs 1,500-3,700; TE **Credit Cards** AmEx, Visa, Master **Facilities** Restaurant, swimming pool, health club, Ayurvedic centre, travel desk, Internet, fridge, boating and houseboat cruises arranged, room service

Privacy SWIMMING POOL
Location Sanctuary Bay **Address** TP111/ 185, Kannankara PO, Thaneermukkom **Tel** 2582794 **Website** malabarhouse.com **Rooms** 3 **Tariff** Rs 6,500-17,870 **Credit Cards** Visa, Master **Facilities** Meals, swimming pool, boating, village walks

Raheem Residency AYURVEDA
Location Near Alleppey Beach **Address** Beach Road **Tel** 2230767/ 9767 **Website** raheemresidency.com **Rooms** 7 **Tariff** Rs 5,000-6,000; TE **Credit Cards** Visa, Master **Facilities** Restaurant, swimming pool, Ayurvedic centre, travel desk, boating, backwater cruises

GURUVAYUR STD 0487

Anjanam KTDC
Location Near the temple **Address** West Nada **Tel** 2552048 **Rooms** 4 dorms **Tariff** Rs 175-375 **Facilities** Restaurant, attached bath, hot water **Chennai Reservations** See page 481

Bhasuri Inn MID-RANGE
Location Opp Municipal Bus Stand **Address** East Nada **Tel** 2558855-88 **Fax** 2550999 **Website** bhasuriinn.com **Rooms** 70 **Tariff** Rs 450-1,400; TE **Credit Cards** Visa, Master **Facilities** Veg restaurant, café, travel desk, car rental, attached bath, laundry room service

Govindam Residency BUDGET
Location Near temple **Address**

HOTELS

West Nada **Tel** 2552540/ 42 **Rooms** 15 **Tariff** Rs 350-700 **Facilities** Meals, attached bath

Hotel Elite
Location Walking distance from temple **Address** East Nada **Tel** 2555216/ 6215 **Fax** 2555218 **Website** eliteguruvayur.in **Rooms** 85 **Tariff** Rs 550-1,600; TE **Credit Cards** Visa, Master **Facilities** Veg restaurant, car rental, travel desk, laundry, attached bath, room service

Hotel Fort Gate
Location Near the Elephant Sanctuary **Address** Kottappady **Telefax** 2556950/ 0326-27 **Mobile** 09447991836 **Email** hotelfortgate@gmail.com **Rooms** 11 **Tariff** Rs 800-1,500; TE **Credit Cards** Visa, Master **Facilities** Restaurant, bar, travel desk, laundry, room service

Hotel Krishna Inn MID-RANGE
Location Opp private bus stand **Address** East Nada **Tel** 2550777-84 **Fax** 2554169 **Website** krishnainn.com **Rooms** 51 **Tariff** Rs 1,300-3,500; TE **Credit Cards** Visa, Master **Facilities** Multi-cuisine restaurant, car rental, café, safe, room service

Hotel Prarthana Inn MID-RANGE
Location Opposite Private Bus Stand, East Nada **Tel** 2557755/ 66/ 77 **Fax** 2557766 **Website** prarthanainn.com **Rooms** 15 **Tariff** Rs 520-1,450; TE **Facilities** Veg restaurant, car rental, laundry, room service

Hotel Remanika Regency
Location Near the temple **Address** East Nada **Tel** 2555647/ 8297 **Email** remanika@remanikaregency.com **Rooms** 22 **Tariff** Rs 341-1,552; TE **Facilities** Restaurant, travel assistance, laundry, room service

Hotel Rugmini Regency
Location Near the temple **Address** East Nada **Tel** 2551873-74 **Fax** 2551872 **Website** rugminiregency.com **Rooms** 40 **Tariff** Rs 635-1,035 **Credit Cards** AmEx, Visa, Master **Facilities** Restaurant, travel desk, temple darshan and puja arrangements, laundry, room service

Hotel Sopanam Heritage MID-RANGE
Location Opp Pvt Bus Stand **Address** East Nada **Tel** 2555244/ 542 **Fax** 2556753 **Website** sopanamguruvayoor.com **Rooms** 63, suites 6 **Tariff** Rs 800-1,850; TE **Credit Cards** Visa, Master **Facilities** Three restaurants, travel desk, free pick up from and drop off at the temple at any time, car rental, laundry, room service

Hotel Sri Gokulam Vanamalaa
Location Near Guruvayur Temple **Address** South Nada **Tel** 2555503-4/ 213-14, 2556702 **Fax** 2555504 **Website** gokulamvanamaalaa.com **Rooms** 30 **Tariff** Rs 690-1,500; TE **Credit Cards** AmEx, Visa, Master **Facilities** Multi-cuisine restaurant, travel desk, laundry, room service

Mangalya Tourist Home KTDC
Location Near the temple **Address** Vaijayanthi Building, East Nada **Tel** 2554061 **Mobile** 09446072954 **Rooms** 6 (6 beds per room) **Tariff** Rs 604 **Facilities** Veg restaurant, attached bath, car rental, travel desk **Chennai Reservations** See page 481

Mayura Residency MID-RANGE
Location 2 km from temple **Address** West Nada **Tel** 2553608/ 7174, 2555174/ 8707 **Fax** 2553174 **Website** mayuraresidency.com **Rooms** 65 **Tariff** Rs 550-2,500; TE **Credit Cards** Visa, Master **Facilities** Multi-

Telephone Indexes
Diaries
Desk Calenders
Notebooks

marketed in India by
Cal Craft Inc.
calcraft@mail.com
www.calcraftproduct.com

ACCOMMODATION LISTINGS

cuisine restaurant, travel desk, laundry, room service

Rvee's Hotel Regency
Location Near Railway Station **Address** Opp Balakrishna Theatre, East Nada **Tel** 2552222/ 4444/ 7777 **Email** rveesregency@hotmail.com **Rooms** 36 **Tariff** Rs 450-1,600; TE **Facilities** Multi-cuisine restaurant, Internet, travel desk, laundry, room service

RVK Residency
Address East Nada **Tel** 2553555 **Fax** 2554655 **Rooms** 40 **Tariff** Rs 350-950 **Facilities** Car rental, attached bath, room service

Vyshakh International
Location Near Temple Pond **Address** East Nada **Tel** 2554674-75, 2550964 **Website** vyshakh.com **Rooms** 30 **Tariff** Rs 400-1,800; TE **Credit Cards** Visa, Master **Facilities** Veg restaurant, café, travel desk, car rental, laundry, room service

KOCHI STD 0484
IN FORT KOCHI
Ballard Bungalow `HERITAGE`
Location Near Cochin Port Boat Jetty **Address** Ballard Road **Tel** 2215854 **Fax** 2215620 **Website** cochinballard.com **Rooms** 5, suites 2 **Tariff** Rs 1,200-2,800; TE **Credit Cards** Visa, Master **Facilities** Breakfast, Internet, travel assistance, room service

Brunton Boatyard `HERITAGE`
Location Near Chinese Fishing Nets **Address** Calvethy Road **Tel** 2215461-65 **Fax** 2215562 **Website** cghearth.com **Rooms** 26 **Tariff** Rs 12,100-17,000; TE **Credit Cards** Visa, Master **Facilities** Restaurants, café, billiards table, sea-facing rooms, swimming pool, travel desk

Delight Tourist Resort
Location Near Fort Kochi Beach **Address** Parade Ground, Post Office Road **Tel** 2217658 **Fax** 2216301 **Website** delightful homestay.com **Rooms** 6 **Tariff** Rs 500-1,800; TE **Credit Cards** Visa, Master **Facilities** Ayurvedic massage, backwater-facing roof garden, travel desk, Internet, phone, laundry

Fort Heritage `HERITAGE`
Location Near Fort Kochi Beach **Address** 1/ 283 Napier Street, Elphinstone Road **Telefax** 2215333/ 455, 2216901 **Website** fortheritage.com **Rooms** 12, suites 3 **Tariff** Rs 2,842-4,930 **Credit Cards** Visa, Master **Facilities** Restaurant, Ayurvedic centre, car rental, houseboats, Internet, laundry, sightseeing

Fort House
Location Near Mattancherry Customs House **Address** 2/ 6A Calvathy Road **Tel** 2217103 **Website** hotelforthouse.com **Rooms** 17 **Tariff** Rs 1,200-2,800 **Credit Cards** AmEx, Visa, Master **Facilities** Restaurants, café, Ayurvedic massage centre, book shop, travel desk, laundry

Koder House `SPA`
Location Opp Children's Park **Address** Tower Road **Tel** 2218485-86 **Fax** 2217988 **Website** koderhouse.com **Rooms** 6 **Tariff** Rs 8,147-13,580 **Credit Cards** Visa, Master **Facilities** Restaurant, spa, jacuzzi, plunge pool, forex, safe, Internet, laundry

Malabar House `AYURVEDA`
Location Facing St Francis Church **Address** 1/ 268, Parade Road **Tel** 2216666 **Fax** 2217777 **Website** malabarhouse.com **Rooms** 17 **Tariff** Rs 6,500-9,500; TE **Credit Cards** Visa, Master **Facilities** Restaurant, cultural performances, swimming pool, Ayurvedic Kalari spa, travel desk, room service

The Old Courtyard `HERITAGE`
Location Near the beach **Address** Princess Street **Tel** 2216302/ 5035 **Website** oldcourtyard.com **Rooms** 8 **Tariff** Rs 2,250-4,600; TE **Credit Cards** Visa, Master **Facilities** Restaurant, classical performances, day tours, travel desk, room service

Trinity
Location Opp Parade Ground **Address** 1/ 658 Ridsdale Road **Tel** 2216669 **Website** malabar house.com **Rooms** 3 **Tariff** Rs 6,500-17,870 **Credit Cards** Visa, Master **Facilities** Breakfast, open air bathrooms, swimming pool, laundry, travel assistance

IN ERNAKULAM
Bharat Hotel `AYURVEDA`
Location Near Shiva Temple and Indian Airlines office **Address** Gandhi Square, Darbar Hall Road **Tel** 2353501/ 735 **Fax** 2370502 **Website** bharat hotel.com **Rooms** 91 **Tariff** Rs 700-2,200; TE **Credit Cards** AmEx, Visa, Master **Facilities** Restaurant, Ayurveda centre, boating, laundry, travel desk

Gaanam Hotel `MID-RANGE`
Location Near Ernakulam South Station **Address** Chittoor Road **Tel** 2377202/ 5408/ 6123 **Fax** 2375261 **Email** gaanam@md3.vsnl.net.in **Rooms** 40 **Tariff** Rs 650-1,300; TE **Credit Cards** AmEx, Visa, Master **Facilities** Restaurant, boat cruises, laundry, sightseeing, travel desk

HOTELS

Grand Hotel MID-RANGE
Location Near Ernakulam South Railway Station **Address** MG Road **Tel** 2382061 **Fax** 2382066 **Website** grandhotelkerala.com **Rooms** 39 **Tariff** Rs 1,450-1,700; TE **Credit Cards** AmEx, Visa, Master **Facilities** Multi-cuisine restaurant, bar, beauty parlour, Internet, sightseeing, travel desk

Hotel Abad Atrium AYURVEDA
Location 2 km from Railway Station **Address** MG Road **Tel** 2381122, 2384374 **Fax** 2370729, 2384383 **Website** abadhotels.com **Rooms** 52 **Tariff** Rs 2,500-4,500; TE **Credit Cards** AmEx, Visa, Master **Facilities** Multi-cuisine restaurant, Ayurvedic rejuvenation centre, health club, swimming pool, laundry, travel desk, room service

Hotel Excellency
Location Behind Hotel Avenue Regent **Address** Jose Junction, Nettipadam Road, PB No. 1748 **Tel** 2378251-58 **Fax** 2378259 **Website** hotelexcellency.com **Rooms** 68 **Tariff** Rs 900-1,050; TE **Credit Cards** AmEx, Visa, Master **Facilities** Multi-cuisine restaurant, laundry, sightseeing, travel desk, room service

Hotel Luciya
Location Near KSRTC Bus Stand **Address** Stadium Road **Tel** 2381177/ 2471, 3043177 **Email** hotelluciya@sancharnet.in **Rooms** 107 **Tariff** Rs 150-950 **Facilities** Restaurant, bar, laundry, sightseeing, travel desk, room service, attached bath

Hotel Presidency
Location Near Ernakulam North Railway Station **Address** Paramara Road **Tel** 2394040/300 **Fax** 2393222 **Website** presidencyhotel.com **Rooms** 109 **Tariff** Rs 2,000-2,975; TE **Credit Cards** AmEx, Visa, Master **Facilities** Multi-cuisine restaurant, café, sightseeing, travel desk, room service

Hotel Woodlands
Location Central **Address** MG Road **Tel** 2382052, 2368900 **Fax** 2382080 **Email** woodland1@vsnl.com **Rooms** 65 **Tariff** Rs 633-1,898; TE **Credit Cards** Visa, Master **Facilities** Restaurant, laundry, sightseeing, travel desk, room service

Mermaid Hotel AYURVEDA SWIMMING POOL
Location Riverbank **Address** Mermaid Complex, Kaniampuzha Road, Vyttila **Tel** 2307999, 2307806-09 **Fax** 2307804-05 **Website** milmermaid.com **Rooms** 52, apartments 30 **Tariff** Rs 2,530-4,600; TE **Credit Cards** AmEx, Visa, Master **Facilities** Multi-cuisine restaurants, bar, health club, laundry, Ayurvedic health centre, private boat jetty, swimming pool, sightseeing, car rental, travel desk, room service

Paulson Park Hotel
Location Near South Railway Station **Address** Carrier Station Road **Tel** 2378240-49 **Fax** 2375072 **Website** paulsonparkhotel.com **Rooms** 52 **Tariff** Rs 495-1,800; TE **Credit Cards** Visa, Master **Facilities** Restaurants, laundry, Internet, travel arranged, room service, attached bath

Sealord Hotel
Location Central **Address** Shanmugham Road **Tel** 2382472-73 **Fax** 3042543 **Website** sealordhotels.com **Rooms** 35 **Tariff** Rs 900-1,900; TE **Credit Cards** AmEx, Visa, Master **Facilities** Restaurants, travel desk, sightseeing, room service

Taj Residency HIGH-END SWIMMING POOL
Location Marine Drive **Address**

Telephone Indexes
Diaries
Desk Calendars
Notebooks

marketed in India by
Cal Craft Inc.
calcraft@mail.com
www.calcraftproduct.com

INFORMATION

ACCOMMODATION LISTINGS

Shanmugham Road **Tel** 2371471 **Fax** 2371481 **Website** tajhotels.com **Rooms** 108 **Tariff** Rs 4,500-7,500; TE **Credit Cards** AmEx, Visa, Master **Facilities** Restaurants, café, swimming pool, health club, Ayurvedic massage, travel desk, car rental, room service

The Avenue Center Hotel
AYURVEDA

Location Near Malayalam Manorama Office **Address** Panampilly Avenue, Panampilly Nagar **Tel** 2315301-02 **Fax** 2315304 **Website** avenuecenter.com **Rooms** 20 **Tariff** Rs 1,700-3,000; TE **Credit Cards** AmEx, Visa, Master **Facilities** Multi-cuisine restaurant, laundry, travel desk, room service

The Avenue Regent
AYURVEDA

Location Near Ernakulam South Railway Station **Address** 39/2026, MG Road **Tel** 2377977, 2388688, 3013333-34 **Fax** 2375329 **Website** avenueregent.com **Rooms** 53 **Tariff** Rs 3,000-7,500; TE **Credit Cards** AmEx, Visa, Master **Facilities** Multi-cuisine restaurant, lounge bar, café, travel desk, forex, IDD, Internet, health club, Wi-Fi, Ayurvedic centre, sightseeing

The International Hotel
AYURVEDA

Location Between MG and Chittoor roads **Address** 3563, MG Road **Tel** 2380401/ 2091 **Fax** 2373929 **Website** theinternationalhotel.com **Rooms** 60 **Tariff** Rs 1,200-3,500; TE **Credit Card** AmEx, Visa, Master **Facilities** Multi-cuisine restaurant, bar, café, Ayurveda centre, beauty parlour, laundry, travel desk, room service

The Metropolitan MID-RANGE

Location Central **Address** Near South Railway Station **Tel** 2375412/ 6931 **Fax** 2375227 **Website** metropolitancochin.com **Rooms** 39 **Tariff** Rs 1,250-2,550; TE **Credit Cards** AmEx, Visa, Master **Facilities** Multi-cuisine restaurant, bar, café, laundry, travel desk, room service

The Renaissance Cochin
AYURVEDA

Location Near Ernakulam North Railway Station **Address** PB No. 2310, Palarivattom **Tel** 2344463-64, 2345316, 3292056, 3290270 **Fax** 2331561 **Website** renaissancecochin.com **Rooms** 47 **Tariff** Rs 2,400-3,000; TE **Credit Cards** Visa, Master **Facilities** Multi-cuisine restaurants, Ayurvedic rejuvenation massage, swimming pool, health club, jacuzzi, pastry shop, laundry, travel desk, room service

The Woods Manor MID-RANGE
AYURVEDA **SWIMMING POOL**

Location Near railway station **Address** Woodlands Junction, MG Road **Tel** 2382055-59 **Fax** 2382080 **Website** thewoodsmanor.com **Rooms** 57 **Tariff** Rs 1,770-3,400; TE **Credit Cards** AmEx, Visa, Master **Facilities** Multi-cuisine restaurant, swimming pool, Ayurveda centre, Internet, travel desk, laundry

ON WILLINGDON ISLAND
ATS Willingdon

Location Near Old and New bridges to Fort Kochi **Tel** 2667282/ 643-49, **Fax** 2667043 **Website** atshotels.com **Rooms** 22 **Tariff** Rs 750-1,750; TE **Credit Cards** Visa, Master, **Facilities** Multi-cuisine restaurant, bar, forex, sightseeing, travel desk, room service

Casino Hotel AYURVEDA

Location Near Trident Hotel and old dockyard **Tel** 2668421 **Fax** 2668001 **Website** cghearth.com **Rooms** 67 **Tariff** Rs 4,200-5,200; TE **Credit Cards** AmEx, Visa, Master **Facilities** Multi-cuisine restaurant, bar, laundry, Ayurvedic centre, forex, swimming pool, travel desk, room service

Taj Malabar HIGH-END SPA

Location Adjacent to Cochin Port Trust **Tel** 2668010/ 292, 2666811 **Fax** 2668297 **Website** tajhotels.com **Rooms** 96 **Tariff** Rs 5,500-14,000; TE **Credit Cards** AmEx, Visa, Master, Diners **Facilities** Multi-cuisine restaurants, bars, spa, Ayurveda centre, health club, swimming pool, travel desk, Internet, laundry, minibar, room service

The Trident Hilton AYURVEDA

Address Bristow Road **Tel** 2669595 **Fax** 2669393 **Website** trident-hilton.com **Rooms** 85 **Tariff** Rs 6,500-10,000; TE **Credit Cards** AmEx, Visa, Master **Facilities** Multi-cuisine restaurant, bar, beauty salon, swimming pool, Ayurveda centre, bookshop, Wi-Fi, Internet, room service, travel desk, room service

ON BOLGHATTY ISLAND
Bolgatty Palace KTDC
HERITAGE

Location Facing harbour **Address** PO Mulavukadu **Tel** 2750003/ 500/ 600 **Fax** 2750457 **Website** ktdc.com **Rooms** 26 **Tariff** Rs 3,500-7,500; TE **Credit Cards** Visa, Master **Facilities** Restaurant, beer parlour, travel desk, Ayurvedic massage centre, laundry, kids' playground, sightseeing, room service **Chennai Reservations** See page 481

HOTELS

KOTTAYAM STD 0481

Akkara House HOME STAY
Location 5 km from railway station, near Shiva Temple **Address** Mariyataruth PO **Tel** 2516951 **Rooms** 4 **Tariff** Rs 2,750-3,750 **Facilities** Home-cooked meals, attached bath

Cherian Ashram Ayurvedic Resort AYURVEDA
Location 7 km from Railway Station **Address** KK Road, Ayrattunada **Tel** 2371334/ 964 **Fax** 2372871 **Website** cherianashram.com **Rooms** 18, cottages 2, dorm 1 **Tariff** Rs 450-750, dorm Rs 200 **Facilities** Holistic treatment, yoga, meditation, organic fruits therapy, airport transfers, sightseeing, home-cooked meals, Internet

Homestead Hotel
Location Central **Address** KK Road **Tel** 2560467, 2562346 **Fax** 2560740 **Rooms** 39 **Tariff** Rs 317-1,438 **Credit Cards** Visa, Master **Facilities** Restaurants, car rental, laundry, hot water, attached bath, room service

Hotel Aida
Location Near KSRTC bus stand **Address** Aida Junction, MC Road **Tel** 2568391-98, 2568400-01 **Fax** 2568399 **Website** hotelaidakerala.com **Rooms** 35 **Tariff** Rs 350-1,300 **Credit Cards** Visa, Master **Facilities** Restaurants, bar, laundry, Internet, car rental, room service

Pearl Regency
Location Near Hotel Aida **Address** TB Junction, MC Road **Tel** 2561123-25 **Website** pearlregencyktm.com **Rooms** 25 **Tariff** Rs 1,200-4,500 **Credit Cards** Visa, Master **Facilities** Restaurant, laundry, fridge, room service

Serenity
Address Kanam Estate **Tel** 2456353 **Fax** 2457063 **Website** malabarhouse.com **Rooms** 5 **Tariff** Rs 9,807 **Credit Cards** Visa, Master **Facilities** Restaurant, swimming pool, taxi, laundry, room service

The Windsor Castle HIGH-END AYURVEDA SWIMMING POOL
Location Lake-facing **Address** Kodimatha **Tel** 2363637, 2363638/ 40 **Fax** 2363738 **Website** thewindsorcastle.net **Rooms** 40, 17 cottages **Tariff** Rs 3,000-4,500; TE **Credit Cards** AmEx, Visa, Master **Facilities** Restaurants, bar, swimming pools, Ayurvedic massage, beauty parlour, boating, car rental, forex, safe, cake shop, gift shop, laundry, room service

Vembanad Lake Resort
Address Kodimatha **Tel** 2360866, 2361633 **Fax** 2363259 **Email** ktm_vembanad@sanchar.net.in **Rooms** 10 cottages **Tariff** Rs 500 **Credit Cards** Visa, Master **Facilities** Restaurants, bar, ice cream parlour, house/motorboat rides, laundry, travel desk, car rental, room service

KOZHIKODE STD 0495

Alkapuri Guest House
Location Near railway station **Address** MM Ali Road **Tel** 2723451-54, 2720218 **Telefax** 2720219 **Email** alakapurihotels@yahoo.com **Rooms** 38 **Tariff** Rs 150-1,000; TE **Credit Cards** AmEx, Visa, Master **Facilities** Restaurant, laundry, car rental

Beach Heritage Inn
Address Beach Road **Tel** 2762055-56 **Website** beachheritage.com **Rooms** 6 **Tariff** Rs 1,700 **Credit Cards** Visa, Master **Facilities** Restaurant, laundry, forex, room service

Calicut Tower
Location Near railway station

ACCOMMODATION LISTINGS

Address Markaz Complex, IG Road **Tel** 2723202 **Fax** 2720702 **Rooms** 90 **Tariff** Rs 410-1,500; TE **Credit Cards** Visa, Master **Facilities** Restaurant, laundry, travel desk, room service

Fortune Hotel `SWIMMING POOL`
Location 3 km from Kozhikode **Address** Kannur Road **Tel** 2768888 **Fax** 2768111 **Website** fortunekozhikode.com **Rooms** 63 **Tariff** Rs 1,980-2,970; TE **Credit Cards** AmEx, Visa, Master **Facilities** Multi-cuisine restaurant, bar, travel desk, safe, swimming pool, health club, massage, room service

Harivihar `AYURVEDA`
Location Near Bilabhikulam Temple **Tel** 2765865 **Mobile** 09847072203 **Fax** 2762747 **Website** harivihar.com **Rooms** 8 **Tariff** Rs 3,560-5,000 **Facilities** Meals, Ayurvedic treatment, travel desk, Internet

Hotel Victorian Beach Heritage
Location On the beach, near Gujarathi Hall **Address** Beach Road **Tel** 2762055-57 **Fax** 2365363 **Website** beachheritage.com **Rooms** 10 **Tariff** Rs 1,200-1,400; TE **Credit Cards** Visa, Master, Diners **Facilities** Restaurant, laundry, sightseeing, travel desk, lockers, room service

Hotel Maharani `BUDGET`
Location Near Pughiyara Junction **Address** Taluk Road **Tel** 2723101-07 **Telefax** 2723108 **Website** hotelmaharani.com **Rooms** 44 **Tariff** Rs 400-1,700; TE **Credit Cards** Visa, Master **Facilities** Multi-cuisine restaurant, laundry, travel desk

Hotel Sasthapuri `BUDGET`
Location Near railway station **Address** MM Ali Road, Palayam **Tel** 2723281-82/ 85 **Fax** 2721543 **Website** sasthapuri.com **Rooms** 62 **Tariff** Rs 200-1,000; TE **Credit Cards** AmEx, Visa, Master **Facilities** Multi-cuisine restaurant, bar, health club, laundry, car rental, room service

Hyson Heritage
Location Near railway station **Address** PB 114, Bank Road **Tel** 2766423/ 726 **Fax** 2766518 **Website** hysonheritage.com **Rooms** 88 **Tariff** Rs 475-3,000; TE **Credit Cards** AmEx, Visa, Master **Facilities** Restaurant, café, room service, Internet

Kadavu Resorts
Location On the banks of River Chaliyar **Address** NH17, Calicut Bypass Road, PO Feroke **Tel** 0483-2830023/ 027/ 570 **Fax** 2830575 **Website** kadavuresorts.com **Rooms** 84 **Tariff** Rs 4,000-6,900; TE **Credit Cards** AmEx, Visa, Master **Facilities** Restaurants, bar, café, Ayurveda, yoga, health club, beauty parlour, boating, swimming pool, games, travel desk, forex, library, curio shop, cultural programmes

Malabar Mansion `KTDC`
Location Near LIC Office **Address** SM Street, Mananchira **Tel** 2722391 **Fax** 2721221 **Website** ktdc.com **Rooms** 11 **Tariff** 275-385 **Facilities** Restaurant, beer parlour, laundry, travel desk, room service **Chennai Reservations** See page 481

Malabar Palace `MID-RANGE`
Location Near railway station **Address** Manuelson Junction, Govt Hospital Road **Tel** 2721511-17 **Fax** 2721794 **Website** malabarpalacecalicut.com **Rooms** 52 **Tariff** Rs 1,350-3,200; TE **Credit Cards** AmEx, Visa, Master **Facilities** Restaurant, bar, café, laundry, sightseeing, travel desk, room service

Taj Residency `HIGH-END` `AYURVEDA` `SWIMMING POOL`
Address On PT Usha Road **Tel** 2765354 **Fax** 2766448 **Website** tajhotels.com **Rooms** 70, suites 4 **Tariff** Rs 3,100-6,500; TE **Credit Cards** Visa, Master **Facilities** Restaurant, bar, café, swimming pool, Ayurveda centre, health club, book shop, souvenir shop, car rental, room service

The Renaissance Cochin Kappad Beach Resort `AYURVEDA` `SWIMMING POOL`
Location On the beach **Address** PO Chemancheri, Toovapara, Kappad **Tel** 0496-2688777/ 9192-93 **Fax** 2689194 **Website** renaissancekappadbeach.com **Rooms** 16 **Tariff** Rs 2,000-2,200; TE **Credit Cards** AmEx, Visa, Master **Facilities** Restaurant, café, swimming pool, health club, Ayurveda centre, laundry, sightseeing, room service

---

KUMARAKOM STD 0481

Abad Whispering Palms `HIGH-END` `AYURVEDA`
Location Banks of Vembanad Lake **Address** New Nazareth Road, Konchumada **Tel** 2523824/ 51 **Fax** 2523819 **Website** abadhotels.com **Rooms** 53 **Tariff** Rs 6,500-12,000; TE **Credit Cards** AmEx, Visa, Master **Facilities** Multi-cuisine restaurant, Ayurvedic rejuvenation centre, swimming pool, health club, games, boating, travel desk

Backwater Ripples `HIGH-END` `SWIMMING POOL` `AYURVEDA`
Location Banks of Vembanad Lake **Tel** 2523300/ 600 **Website**

HOTELS

backwaterripples.com **Rooms** 34 **Tariff** Rs 6,800-11,400; TE **Credit Cards** Visa, Master **Facilities** Multi-cuisine restaurant, swimming pool, Ayurveda spa, health club, sunset cruise, houseboats, boating, cultural programes, bookshop, travel desk, room service

Coconut Lagoon AYURVEDA
Location Next to the lake **Tel** 2524491/ 373 **Fax** 2524495 **Website** cghearth.com **Rooms** 50 **Tariff** Rs 12,000-19,350; TE **Credit Cards** AmEx, Visa, Master **Facilities** Multi-cuisine restaurants, Ayurveda centre, backwater cruises, swimming pool, boating, laundry, travel desk, room service

GK's River View HOME STAY
Location Next to the backwaters **Address** Thekke Kariyil House **Tel** 2597527 **Mobile** 094471 97527 **Website** gkhomestay-kumarakom.com **Rooms** 5 **Tariff** Rs 1,300 **Facilities** Home-cooked meals, boating, canoeing, backwater cruises, Ayurvedic massage, taxis, sightseeing

Golden Waters AYURVEDA
Location Backwaters **Tel** 2525826-27/ 638 **Fax** 2524961 **Website** goldenwaters.com **Rooms** 28 cottages **Tariff** Rs 6,500-7,500; TE **Credit Cards** Visa, Master **Facilities** Multi-cuisine restaurant, Ayurveda treatments, travel desk, boating, swimming pool, games, canoe ride, laundry, room service

Illikkalam Lake Resort
Location Banks of Vembanad Lake **Tel** 2524234, 2523282 **Website** illikkalamlakeresort.com **Rooms** 14 **Tariff** Rs 2,100-4,000; TE **Credit Cards** Visa, Master **Facilities** Restaurant, travel desk, boating, Ayurveda, backwater cruises, room service

Kumarakom Lake Resort HIGH-END AYURVEDA
Location Bank of Vembanad Lake **Tel** 2524900/ 5431/ 4430 **Fax** 2524987 **Website** klresort.com **Rooms** 51 **Tariff** Rs 11,500-55,000; TE **Credit Cards** AmEx, Visa, Master **Facilities** Restaurants, Ayurveda centre, swimming pool, backwater cruises, health club, bicycles, fishing, gift shop, houseboats, games, laundry, sightseeing, water sports, speed boats, travel desk

Lakshmi Hotel and Resorts
Location Near lake **Address** Kavanattinkara **Tel** 2523312-13 **Fax** 2523315 **Website** lakshmi resorts.com **Rooms** 8 **Tariff** Rs 2,300 **Credit Cards** Visa, Master **Facilities** Restaurant, beer parlour, Ayurvedic massage on request, boating, car rental, travel arranged, Internet, laundry, attached bath, room service

Radisson Plaza AYURVEDA SPA SWIMMING POOL
Location Banks of Vembanad Lake **Address** V-235, A1-A54, Karattukayal **Tel** 2527272 **Website** radisson.com/kumara komin **Rooms** 10 pool villas **Tariff** Rs 47,500-57,500; TE **Credit Cards** AmEx, Visa, Master **Facilities** Restaurants, café, western spa, Ayurvedic spa, travel desk, backwaters cruises, swimming pool, recreation room

Taj Garden Retreat AYURVEDA
Address 1/ 404, Kumarakom **Tel** 2524377, 2525711-16 **Fax** 2524371 **Website** tajhotels.com **Rooms** 33 **Tariff** Rs 9,900-19,400 **Credit Cards** AmEx, Visa, Master **Facilities** Baker's dining room, Sunset bar, swimming pool, health club, Ayurvedic treatment, souvenir and book shop, boating, activity hut, water sports, sightseeing,

ACCOMMODATION LISTINGS

backwater cruises, fishing, laundry, house boats

Waterscapes KTDC
Location Facing Vembanad backwaters **Address** Kavanattinkara **Tel** 2525861/ 64 **Fax** 2525862 **Website** ktdc.com **Rooms** 40 **Tariff** Rs 5,000-9,000; TE **Credit Cards** Amex, Visa, Master **Facilities** Restaurant, Ayurveda centre, swimming pool, health club, travel desk, angling, boating, bird watching, laundry, room service **Chennai Reservations** See page 481

NELLIYAMPATHY STD 04923

Green Acres Farmhouse and Resort BUDGET
Location 6 km from Nelliyampathy **Address** Palagapandy Estate, Seethargundu PO **Tel** 246245-46/ 66 **Rooms** 21 **Tariff** Rs 600-1,500; TE **Facilities** Multi-cuisine restaurant, playground, car rental, room service

ITL Resort BUDGET
Location Hill-facing **Address** Kaikatty **Tel** 246464-65, 246357 **Rooms** 6, dorms 2 **Tariff** Rs 750-1,750; TE **Facilities** Multi-cuisine restaurant, games, travel desk, trekking, sightseeing

Spring Valley Holiday Home
Location Near a tea estate **Address** Pulayanpara **Tel** 246202 **Mobile** 09447673305 **Rooms** 5 **Tariff** Rs 500-600 **Facilities** Trekking, sightseeing arranged, room service

The Whistling Thrush Bungalow
Location Amidst multi-crop plantation **Address** Poothundu Estate, PO Padagiri **Mobile** 09447144921 **Website** unusual places.info **Rooms** 3 **Tariff** Rs 4,500; TE **Credit Cards** Visa, Master **Facilities** Home cooked meals, plantation tours, TV lounge

PALAKKAD STD 0491

Champion Regency KTDC
Address Near Fantasy Park, Malampuzha **Tel** 2815217 **Rooms** 24 **Tariff** Rs 450-900 **Facilities** Restaurant, car rental, laundry, attached bath **Chennai Reservations** See page 481

Fort Palace Hotel BUDGET
Location Near Fort Maidan **Address** West Fort Road **Tel** 2534621-25 **Fax** 2534625 **Email** fortpalacehotel@rediffmail.com **Rooms** 18 **Tariff** Rs 385-1,380; TE **Credit Cards** Visa, Master, Diners **Facilities** Restaurant, bar, travel desk, laundry, room service, attached bath

Garden House KTDC
Location Near Malampuzha Dam **Address** Malampuzha Road **Tel** 2815191/ 217 **Website** ktdc.com **Rooms** 17 **Tariff** Rs 450-900 **Facilities** Restaurant, beer bar, travel desk, room service, attached bath **Chennai Reservations** See page 481

Hotel Gazala BUDGET
Location Central **Address** Near Head Post Office **Tel** 2546581 **Fax** 2546585 **Email** hotel gazala@hotmail.com **Rooms** 30 **Tariff** Rs 300-1,700; TE **Credit Cards** AmEx, Visa, Master **Facilities** Restaurant, travel desk, station transfers, room service

Hotel Indraprastha MID-RANGE
Location Near KSRTC Bus Stand and Fort **Address** English Church Road **Tel** 2534641-47 **Fax** 2539531 **Website** hotelindraprastha.com **Rooms** 30 **Tariff** Rs 750-2,050; TE **Credit Cards** Visa, Master **Facilities** Restaurant, bar, laundry, book shop, Internet, safe, travel desk

Hotel Kairali Towers
Location Opp Indira Gandhi Stadium **Address** Coimbatore Road **Tel** 2547174-77 **Email** hotelkairali.towers@rediffmail.com **Rooms** 20 **Tariff** Rs 350-900 **Credit Cards** AmEx, Visa, Master **Facilities** Restaurant, bar, laundry, room service, attached bath, hot water, TV

Hotel KPM International
Location Near Tipu's Fort **Address** Press Club Road **Tel** 2534601-05 **Fax** 2537833 **Website** kpmresidency.com **Rooms** 47 **Tariff** Rs 150-1,000 **Facilities** Restaurant, laundry, room service, TV

Kairali Ayurvedic Resort HIGH-END AYURVEDA
Location Near Palakkad Railway Station **Address** Kodumbu, Olassery PO **Tel** 04923-222553/ 623, 224402-04 **Fax** 222732 **Website** kairali.com **Rooms** 30 cottages **Tariff** Rs 2,500-10,000 **Credit Cards** AmEx, Visa, Master **Facilities** Restaurant, swimming pool, Ayurvedic centre, yoga, recreation centre, herbal garden

Kandath Tharavadu HERITAGE HOME STAY
Address Thenkurussi **Tel** 04922-284124 **Mobile** 09349904124 **Website** tharavad.info **Rooms** 6 **Tariff** Rs 6,000-10,000 **Facilities** Authentic Kerala meals, trekking at Nelliyampathy, visits to Parambikkulam, Siruvani Lake, Guruvayur, sightseeing, yoga, meditation, Ayurveda, cycling

Marhaba Residency
Location Near District Hospital **Address** 11/ 385, Robinson Road

HOTELS

Tel 2534946 **Telefax** 2525262 **Rooms** 32 **Tariff** Rs 450-1,600; TE **Credit Cards** AmEx, Visa, Master **Facilities** Multi-cuisine restaurant, laundry, travel desk, car rental, room service

Rajah Healthy Acres
Location Perumanoor, Chalissery **Tel** 0466-2371741-43 **Fax** 2371744 **Website** ayurvedic hospital.com, ayurveda-in.com **Rooms** 22 cottages **Tariff** Rs 1,140-7,200 **Credit Cards** AmEx, Visa, Master **Facilities** Restaurant, kitchenettes, sightseeing, Ayurvedic treatments

Sri Chakra International **SWIMMING POOL**
Location On NH47 Coimbatore Road, near bus stand **Address** Krishnagarden, PO Chandranagar **Tel** 2570901-06 **Fax** 2570906 **Website** hotelsri chakra.com **Rooms** 65 **Tariff** Rs 800-2,100; TE **Credit Cards** AmEx, Visa, Master **Facilities** Multi-cuisine restaurant, bar, swimming pool, health club, laundry, locker, travel desk

Tripenta Hotel **HIGH-END** **AYURVEDA**
Location 8 km from Palakkad Railway Station **Address** Opp Rock Garden, Malampuzha **Tel** 2815210/ 220/ 526 **Fax** 2815930 **Website** tripenta.com **Rooms** 26 **Tariff** Rs 650-1,650; TE **Facilities** Restaurant, Ayurvedic massage, yoga, travel desk, badminton, kids' park

PERIYAR TR STD 04869
Aranya Nivas **KTDC**
Location In the forest **Address** Kumily **Tel** 222023, 222779, 222283, 321930 **Fax** 222282 **Website** ktdc.com **Rooms** 30 **Tariff** Rs 4,518-7,105 **Credit Cards** Visa, Master **Facilities** Multi-cuisine restaurant, beer parlour, swimming pool, Ayurvedic massage, safe, boating, bamboo rafting, trekking, safari, elephant ride and plantation visits, transportation, laundry, room service **Chennai Reservations** See page 481

Bamboo Grove Lodge
Location Adjacent to Reserve **Address** Eco Tourism Information Centre, Ambadi Junction **Tel** 224571 **Website** bamboogrove lodge.com **Rooms** 10 cottages **Tariff** Rs 2,000 per cottage **Facilities** Vegetarian food, laundry, boating, rafting, trekking, safari, elephant rides

Hotel Ambadi **BUDGET**
Location 1 km from Kumily **Address** Thekkady PO **Tel** 222193-95, 222011 **Fax** 222192 **Website** hotelambadi.com **Rooms** 43 **Tariff** Rs 1,150-1,600; TE **Credit Cards** Visa, Master **Facilities** Multi-cuisine restaurant, travel desk, boating, rafting, trekking, safari, elephant rides and plantation visits

Hotel Kumily Gate **TREKKING**
Location Lake-facing **Address** Thekkady, Kumily PO **Tel** 222279 **Telefax** 222500 **Rooms** 15 **Tariff** Rs 900-1,900; TE **Facilities** Multi-cuisine restaurant, bar, travel desk, boating, rafting, trekking, safari, elephant rides, plantation tours, room service

Hotel Lake Queen
Address Kumily PO, Thekkady Jn **Tel** 222084-86 **Fax** 222187 **Website** lakequeen.com **Rooms** 51 **Tariff** Rs 600-1,400; TE **Credit Cards** Visa, Master **Facilities** Restaurants, car rental, travel desk, boating, rafting, trekking, plantation visits, safaris, elephant rides, room service

Hotel Tree Top **MID-RANGE**
Location 1 km from Thekkady **Address** Kumily **Tel** 223286-87,

ACCOMMODATION LISTINGS

223127 **Fax** 223894 **Website** hoteltreetop.com **Rooms** 8 cottages, 12 deluxe rooms, 14-room bungalow **Tariff** Rs 2,500-7,500; TE **Credit Cards** AmEx, Visa, Master **Facilities** Multi-cuisine restaurant, travel desk, Ayurveda, car rental, games, kids' park, video game arcade, baby sitting, library, safe, boating, bamboo rafting, trekking, safaris, elephant rides, plantation tours, room service

Lake Palace
Location Near Periyar Lake **Address** Thekkady **Tel** 222024, 321930, 222023, 222779 **Mobile** 0989541861 **Fax** 222282 **Website** ktdc.com **Rooms** 6 **Tariff** Rs 9,000 (with meals) **Credit Cards** AmEx, Visa, Master **Facilities** Multi-cuisine restaurant only for residents, travel desk, boating, trekking, rafting, safaris, elephant rides and plantation tours, library, laundry, room service **Chennai Reservation** See page 481

Michael's Inn `MID-RANGE`
Location Thekkady Junction **Tel** 222355-56 **Fax** 222355 **Website** michaelsinnthekkady.com **Rooms** 26 **Tariff** Rs 1,300-2,500; TE **Credit Cards** AmEx, Visa, Master **Facilities** Multi-cuisine restaurant, travel desk, boating, rafting, trekking, safari, elephant rides, plantation tours, laundry

Muthoot Cardamom County
Location 3.5 km from sanctuary **Address** Thekkady Road **Tel** 224501-03 **Fax** 222807 **Website** muthoothotels.com **Rooms** 44 **Tariff** Rs 5,500-8,000; TE **Credit Cards** AmEx, Visa, Master **Facilities** Multi-cuisine restaurant, candlelight dinner and campfire on request, café, swimming pool, health club, Ayurvedic massage centre, Internet, activity centre, gift shop, boating, trekking, safari, elephant rides, plantation tours

Periyar House `KTDC`
Location Inside the sanctuary **Tel** 222026/ 447/ 546 **Fax** 222526 **Website** ktdc.com **Rooms** 44 **Tariff** Rs 1,250-2,500; TE **Credit Cards** Visa, Master **Facilities** Multi-cuisine restaurant, beer parlour, Ayurvedic massage arranged, boating, rafting, trekking, plantation visits, safaris and elephant rides **Chennai Reservations** See page 481

Saj Jungle Village `HIGH-END`
Location Near the reserve **Address** Mangaladevi Road, Thekkady **Tel** 223363/ 73 **Mobile** 09446570644 **Fax** 224512 **Website** sajhotels.com **Rooms** 35 **Tariff** Rs 5,000-10,000; TE **Credit Cards** Visa, Master **Facilities** Multi-cuisine restaurant, swimming pool, Ayurveda centre, travel desk, health club, trekking, boating

Shalimar Spice Garden Resort `AYURVEDIC SPA`
Location 6 km from the reserve **Address** Murikkadi Post **Tel** 222132/ 3232 **Fax** 223022 **Website** shalimarkerala.net **Rooms** 10, cottages 5 **Tariff** Rs 3,920-12,600; TE **Credit Cards** Visa, Master **Facilities** Multi-cuisine restaurant, café, mini bar, swimming pool, Ayurvedic spa, massage centre, yoga, Internet, travel desk, boating, rafting, trekking, plantation tours, safaris and elephant rides, room service

Silver Crest `SWIMMING POOL`
Location 100 yards from NH220 **Address** Thekkady Road, Kumily **Tel** 222481-83 **Website** sealord hotels.com **Rooms** 30 **Tariff** Rs 2,800-3,600; TE **Credit Cards** Visa, Master **Facilities** Restaurant, swimming pool, room service

Spice Village
Location Near the forest **Address** Thekkady Road **Tel** 222315-16 **Fax** 222317 **Website** cghearth.com **Rooms** 52 cottages **Tariff** Rs 8,000-11,200; TE **Credit Cards** AmEx, Visa, Master **Facilities** Restaurants, bar, swimming pool, Ayurvedic centre, games, travel desk, plantation tours, boating, rafting, trekking, safaris, elephant rides

Taj Garden Retreat `AYURVEDA`
Location 4 km from Periyar Lake **Address** Amalambika Road, Thekkady **Tel** 222273, 222401 **Fax** 222106 **Website** tajhotels.com **Rooms** 32 cottages **Tariff** Rs 3,800-6,500; TE **Credit Cards** AmEx, Visa, Master **Facilities** Multi-cuisine restaurant, bar, Ayurveda centre, games, swimming pool, travel desk, boating, trekking, safaris, elephant rides, plantation and tea factory tours

The Wildernest `TREKKING`
Address Thekkady Road **Tel** 224030, 211471 **Mobile** 09895661192 **Website** wildernest-kerala.com **Rooms** 10 **Tariff** Rs 2,300-3,650 **Credit Cards** Visa, Master **Facilities** Café, travel desk, boating, rafting, trekking, safaris, elephant rides, plantation tours, laundry, attached bath

Wildside Villa `HOME STAY`
Location Near Taj Garden Retreat **Address** Amalambika Convent Road, Thekkady Post **Tel** 223163 **Mobile**

HOTELS

09846123202, 09447433096 **Fax** 222766 **Website** thekkady.com **Rooms** 6 **Tariff** Rs 875-1,500; TE **Facilities** Breakfast, sightseeing, car rental, travel desk, boating, rafting, trekking, safaris, elephant rides, plantation tours, laundry, room service

THATTEKKAD STD 0485
Birds Lagoon Village Resort
SWIMMING POOL

Location 8 km from Salim Ali Bird Sanctuary **Address** Palamattam Post, Cheekkod, Kothamangalam **Tel** 2572444, 2822982 **Mobile** 09447025123 **Website** birdslagoon.com **Rooms** 13 **Tariff** Rs 2,000-3,000; TE **Credit Cards** AmEx, Visa, Master **Facilities** Multi-cuisine restaurant, Ayurvedic massage, swimming pool, travel desk, boating arranged, trekking, bird-watching, safaris, sightseeing

Dormitory
Address Salim Ali Bird Sanctuary **Rooms** 1 dorm (50-bedded) **Tariff** Rs 2,000; TE **Facilities** Food on request, available, trekking with guide **Kothamangalam Reservations** Assistant Wildlife Warden, Salim Ali Bird Sanctuary, Njayappally PO, Kothamangalam **Tel** 2588302 **Mobile** 09447697620 **Contact** K Vijayakumaran Nair

Hornbill Camp
Location Near the ferry **Address** Thattekkad **Website** thehornbill camp.com **Rooms** 6 tented cottages **Tariff** Rs 2,800 **Facilities** Attached bath, sit-outs, birding tour with guide, kayaking, spice plantation tours **Kochi Reservations** Kalypso Eco Lodges and Camps, G307, Panampilly Nagar **Tel** 0484-2092280/6583573 **Mobile** 09447031032 **Fax** 2310324

Hornbill Inspection Bungalow
Location On Poyamkutty Road **Address** Salim Ali Bird Sanctuary **Rooms** 2 **Tariff** Rs 600 per room **Facilities** Food on request, cook available, trekking arranged with guide, attached bath, hot water **Kothamangalam Reservations** See Dormitory at left

Mundackal **HOME STAY**
Location 12 km from sanctuary **Address** Mundackal Estate, Pindimana, Kothamangalam **Tel** 2570717 **Mobile** 09388620399 **Website** mundackalhomestay.com **Rooms** 5 **Tariff** Rs 5,625-7,200 **Credit Cards** Visa, Master **Facilities** Cooking classes, plantation visits, bird watching, trips to Kodanadu Elephant Camp, Bhoothathankettu Dam and Salim Ali Bird Sanctuary

Periyar River Lodge
Location On the Periyar River, 8 km from sanctuary **Address** Anakayam, Kuttampuzha PO, Kothamangalam **Tel** 0485-2207173, 2588315 **Mobile** 09447707173 **Website** periyar riverlodge.com **Rooms** 2 **Tariff** Rs 2,700-3,200; TE **Facilities** Caretaker, home-cooked Kerala cuisine meals, trekking, day tours, bird watching, house boating, jeep safari to near by water fall, fishing, bamboo rafting, library

THRISSUR STD 0487
Casino Hotel **AYURVEDA**
Location Near Railway Station **Address** TB Road **Tel** 2424699 **Mobile** 09847804119 **Fax** 2442037 **Website** casinotels.com **Rooms** 47 **Tariff** Rs 900-1,500; TE **Credit Cards** Visa, Master **Facilities** Multi-cuisine restaurant, bar, Ayurvedic massage, travel desk, beauty parlour, bakery, room service

Elite International **MID-RANGE**
Address Chembottil Lane,

ACCOMMODATION LISTINGS

Round South **Tel** 2421836-39, 2421033-43 **Fax** 2442057 **Website** hoteleliteinternational.com **Rooms** 82 **Tariff** Rs 391-2,300 **Credit Cards** AmEx, Visa, Master **Facilities** Multi-cuisine restaurant, bar, laundry, travel desk, room service

Hotel Cee Pee Towers
Location Near KSRTC Bus stand **Address** Post Office Road **Tel** 2444666-70 **Fax** 2444677 **Website** hotelceepeetower.com **Rooms** 36 **Tariff** Rs 400-1,250; TE **Credit Cards** AmEx, Visa, Master **Facilities** Restaurants, café, laundry, attached bath, travel desk, room service

Hotel Manappuram
Address Kurruppam Road **Tel** 2440115/ 933 **Fax** 2427692 **Email** manotels@gmail.com **Rooms** 46 **Tariff** Rs 325-1,500; TE **Credit Cards** Visa, Master **Facilities** Restaurant, beauty parlour, laundry, safe, attached bath, travel desk, room service

Hotel Pearl Regency `MID-RANGE`
Location Near the railway station **Address** Warriam Lane **Tel** 2446661-65 **Fax** 2446663 **Rooms** 36 **Tariff** Rs 400-1,500; TE **Credit Cards** Visa, Master **Facilities** Restaurants, travel desk, laundry, room service

Hotel Sea Fort
Location Near railway station **Address** RS Road **Tel** 2424067/ 196/ 818 **Fax** 2442003 **Rooms** 70 **Tariff** Rs 220-1,035 **Credit Cards** Visa, Master **Facilities** Restaurant, bar, attached bath, car rental, room service

Luciya Palace `MID-RANGE`
Location Near Vadakkunathan Temple **Address** Marar Road **Tel** 2424469/ 731 **Fax** 2427290 **Email** luciyapalace@hotmail.com **Rooms** 36 **Tariff** Rs 475-1,450; TE **Credit Cards** AmEx, Visa, Master **Facilities** Garden restaurant, bar, travel desk, forex, safe, laundry, room service

Sidhartha Regency `MID-RANGE`
Location Near railway station **Tel** 2424773-76 **Fax** 2425116 **Website** hotelsidhartharegency.com **Rooms** 30 **Tariff** Rs 750-1,400; TE **Credit Cards** AmEx, Visa, Master **Facilities** Restaurant, bar, swimming pool, health club, travel desk, room service

Trichur Towers `MID-RANGE`
Location 1 km from railway station **Address** TB Road **Tel** 2425918 **Fax** 2425390 **Website** hoteltrichurtower.com **Rooms** 25 **Tariff** Rs 950-3,900; TE **Credit Cards** Visa, Master **Facilities** Multi-cuisine restaurant, bar, café, health club, safe, travel desk, handicraft shop nearby, laundry, library, room service

Yatri Niwas `KTDC`
Location Opp Indoor Stadium **Address** Palace Road **Tel** 2332122/ 2333 **Fax** 2332122 **Website** ktdc.com **Rooms** 14 **Tariff** Rs 400-600 **Facilities** Restaurant, beer parlour, travel desk, room service **Chennai Reservations** See page 481

VYTHIRI STD 04936

Greeshmam Resorts `TREKKING`
Location Near Oriental School of Hotel Management **Address** 3/ 142, Valley View, Lakkidi **Tel** 255355 **Mobile** 09447853839 **Email** greeshmamresorts@eth.net **Rooms** 4 **Tariff** Rs 1,300-1,750; TE **Credit Cards** Visa, Master **Facilities** Restaurant, Ayurveda centre, sightseeing, trekking, horse riding, room service

Jungle Park Resorts `HIGH-END` `AYURVEDA` `TREKKING`
Location In Finster Hills, 2 km after Vythiri **Address** Lakkidi PO **Mobile** 09947282801 **Website** jungleparkresorts.com **Rooms** 21 **Tariff** Rs 3,000-10,000; TE **Facilities** Restaurant, Ayurvedic massage, travel desk, sightseeing, trekking, lockers

Rain Country Resorts `MID-RANGE`
Location Hill-facing **Address** Lakkidi PO **Tel** 329798-99 **Mobile** 09447004369 **Fax** 205306 **Website** raincountryresort.com **Rooms** 16 **Tariff** Rs 2,700-3,900 **Facilities** Restaurant, natural pool, trekking, sightseeing, games, fishing

Stream Valley Cottages `MID-RANGE`
Location 200 m east of Thalipuzha **Tel** 202787, 255860 **Mobile** 09447933860, 09847502787 **Website** streamvalleycottages.com **Rooms** 11 cottages, 1 tree house **Tariff** 2,500-3,000 **Facilities** Food on request, travel desk, car rental, attached bath, room service

Vythri Resort `SPA`
Location Near Pookote Lake **Address** Lakkidi PO **Tel** 255366-67 **Mobile** 09447055367 **Fax** 255368 **Website** vythriresort.com **Rooms** 37 **Tariff** Rs 3,500-5,500 **Credit Cards** AmEx, Visa, Master **Facilities** Restaurant, café, swimming pool, health club, spa, Ayurvedic spa, steam room, games, lockers

Wynberg Resorts
Address Kuzhivayal Estate,

HOTELS

Thrikkaipetta PO **Tel** 247823, 320630 **Mobile** 09447300371 **Website** wynberg.in **Rooms** 2 villas, 1 tree house, 1 eco tree house, 1 luxury tent, 6 eco cottages **Tariff** Rs 1,800-4,000 **Facilities** Food Kourt restaurant, travel desk, games, lockers, Internet, laundry, room service, TV **Chennai Reservations** Dr Vanchi Swaran **Address** 993, H-Block, 11th Main Road, Anna Nagar **Mobile** 09941244392

PONDICHERRY

PONDICHERRY STD 0413

Adishakti
Location Between Pondicherry and Auroville **Address** Adwaitam, 8 Appavou Nagar, Vazhakulam **Tel** 2622287/ 402 **Website** adishaktitheatrearts.org **Rooms** 7 **Tariff** Rs 1,300-1,500 **Facilities** Buffet meals, theatre, residence packages, treatments, martial arts lessons, kalaripayattu performances and cultural events, massages, yoga

Anandha Inn AYURVEDA
Location Central **Address** 154, SV Patel Road **Tel** 2330711-19 **Fax** 2331241 **Rooms** 70 **Tariff** Rs 1,850-3,900 **Credit Cards** AmEx, Visa, Master, Diners **Facilities** Multi-cuisine restaurant, bar, pastry shop, swimming pool, health club, Ayurvedic massage, spa, beauty parlour, travel desk, room service

Ashram Park Guest House
Location On the beach **Address** 1, Goubert Avenue **Tel** 2233644 **Website** sriaurobindoashram.org **Rooms** 85 **Tariff** Rs 400-1,000 **Facilities** Restaurant, reading room, meditation room, garden, bicycle and scooter rental

Coloniale Heritage
Location Near the beach **Address** 64, Rue Roman Rolland **Tel** 2224720/ 4200334 **Website** colonialeheritage.com **Rooms** 6 **Tariff** Rs 2,000-3,000 **Facilities** Laundry, attached bath for some rooms, room service

Hotel Annamalai International
Address 479, Kamaraj Salai **Tel** 2247001-14 **Fax** 2247015 **Website** hotelannamalai.com **Rooms** 70 **Tariff** Rs 1,750-3,600; TE **Credit Cards** AmEx, Visa, Master **Facilities** Restaurants, pool on roof, travel desk, laundry, room service

Hotel de L'Orient HERITAGE
Location Central **Address** 17, Rue Romain Rolland **Tel** 2343067-68, 2343074 **Fax** 2227829 **Website** neemrana hotels.com **Rooms** 10 **Tariff** Rs 2,000-5,000; TE **Credit Cards** AmEx, Visa, Master **Facilities** Restaurant, bar, gift shop, sightseeing, travel desk, laundry, room service

Hotel de Pondicherry
Location Near the beach **Address** 38, Rue Dumas **Tel** 2227409 **Fax** 2277410 **Email** hoteldepondicherry@yahoo.co.in **Rooms** 10 **Tariff** Rs 1,500-2,800; TE **Credit Cards** AmEx, Visa, Master **Facilities** Multi-cuisine restaurant, laundry, travel desk, sightseeing, room service

Hotel Kailash Beach Resort
Location On the beach **Address** Sudalai Street, Poornankuppam Village, Ariyankuppam Commune **Tel** 2619700-03 **Fax** 2619704 **Website** kailashbeachhotel.com **Rooms** 36 **Tariff** Rs 2,300-3,600; TE **Credit Cards** AmEx, Master, Visa **Facilities** Multi-cuisine restaurant, bar, swimming pool, massage, bookshop, games, laundry, travel desk, room service

Hotel Mass
Location Adjacent to new bus

ACCOMMODATION LISTINGS

stand **Address** Maraimalai Adigal Salai **Tel** 2204001-11, 4207001 **Fax** 4207012 **Website** hotelmass.com **Rooms** 78 **Tariff** Rs 1,500-5,000; TE **Credit Cards** AmEx, Visa, Master, Diners **Facilities** Restaurants, bar, swimming pool, health club, beauty parlour, Internet, travel desk, laundry, room service

Hotel Pondicherry Ashok Beach Resort
Location Near Pondicherry University, 12 km before Pondy **Address** East Coast Road, Kalapet Beach **Tel** 2655160-63 **Mobile** 09443226479 **Fax** 2655140 **Website** ashokresort.com **Rooms** 21 **Tariff** Rs 2,800-3,200 **Facilities** Restaurant, bar, laundry, Internet, car rental, travel desk, room service

Hotel Qualithe
Location Near the beach **Address** Labourdonnais Street **Tel** 2334325 **Email** rajarathnam8@engineer.com **Rooms** 7 **Tariff** Rs 200-1,000 **Credit Cards** AmEx, Visa, Master **Facilities** Restaurants, bar, roof garden, travel desk, room service

Hotel Satsanga
Location French Colony, near Old Law College **Address** 30-32, Labourdonnais Street **Tel** 2225867 **Mobile** 09894022457 **Rooms** 10 **Tariff** Rs 750-2,000 **Credit Cards** AmEx, Visa, Master **Facilities** Multi-cuisine restaurant, travel desk, car rental

Hotel Surguru
Address 104, SV Patel Road **Tel** 2227290, 2339022 **Fax** 2334377 **Website** hotelsurguru.com **Rooms** 57 **Tariff** Rs 790-1,200; TE **Credit Cards** Visa, Master **Facilities** Multi-cuisine restaurant, Internet, travel desk, laundry, room service

Rendezvous Inn `HERITAGE`
Location Corner of Rue Suffren **Address** 30, Rue Suffren **Tel** 2227677 2339132, 2330238 **Rooms** 6 **Tariff** Rs 5,500 **Credit Cards** AmEx, Visa, Master **Facilities** Restaurant, jacuzzi, coffee-maker, room service

St James Court Beach Resort
Location Near the beach **Address** Chinna Kalapet, Opp Pondicherry Engineering College **Tel** 2655275/76/174 **Website** stjamescourtbeachresort.com **Rooms** 10 **Tariff** Rs 1,250-2,500 **Credit Cards** AmEx, Visa, Master **Facilities** Multi-cuisine restaurant, bar, laundry, travel arranged, attached bath, hot water, room service

The Dune Village `AYURVEDA`
Location On the beach **Address** Pudhukuppam, Keelputhupet **Tel** 2655751 **Mobile** 09345706709 **Website** thedune.in **Rooms** 42 **Tariff** Rs 3,300-9,750 **Credit Cards** Visa, Master **Facilities** Restaurants, swimming pool, Ayurveda centre, spa, yoga, meditation, health club, beach games, DVD library, room service

The Promenade `AYURVEDA`
Location Situated beside the old lighthouse and opp the Gandhi statue **Address** 23, Goubert Avenue **Tel** 2227750 **Fax** 2227141 **Website** sarovarhotels.com **Rooms** 35 **Tariff** Rs 3,250-7,500 **Credit Cards** AmEx, Visa, Master, Diners **Facilities** Restaurants, bar, swimming pool, health club, Ayurvedic massage, reflexology, travel desk, car rental, bike rental, sightseeing, room service

Villa Helena
Location Opp PWD office **Address** No. 13, LBS Street **Tel** 2226789 **Email** villahelena@satyam.net.in **Rooms** 4 **Tariff** Rs 2,000-2,500 **Facilities** Breakfast, attached bath, hot water

TAMIL NADU

BELLIKKAL STD 0423

Silver Stones Estate
Location Near Kalhatty Falls **Address** Bellikkal, Hulhatti Village **Rooms** 2, dorm 1 (6 beds) **Tariff** Rs 1,250 **Facilities** Home cooked meals, sightseeing, trekking, pick-up from Coonoor, hot water **Coonoor Reservations** 65, Woodcote Estate, Mount Pleasant **Tel** 0423-2206762, 2230357 **Mobile** 09486635445 **Email** panalalchordia@yahoo.com

CHETTINAD STD 04565

Chettinadu Mansion `HIGH-END`
Location Behind Raja Palace **Address** 11 AR Street, Sarma House, Kanadukathan **Tel** 273080 **Mobile** 09443495598 **Website** chettinadumansion.com **Rooms** 11 **Tariff** Rs 4,000-6,000 **Facilities** Restaurant, travel desk, laundry, attached bath, hot water, room service

Hotel Golden Singar `BUDGET`
Location Near new bus stand **Address** 100 Ft Road, Near Periyar Statue, Karaikkudi **Tel** 235521-23 **Rooms** 38 **Tariff** Rs 410-715 **Facilities** Restaurant, bar, car rental, puja arrangements, library, laundry **Chennai Reservations** No. 2, 4th Cross, Sterling Road **Tel** 044-28271419

Hotel Malar `BUDGET`
Location 2 km from railway station **Address** 159, Madurai

HOTELS

Main Road, Karaikudi **Tel** 239601-05 **Mobile** 09443123771 **Rooms** 36 **Tariff** Rs 425-750; TE **Credit Cards** AmEx, Visa, Master **Facilities** Restaurants, bar, puja arrangements, travel desk, laundry, room service

Hotel Subhalakshmi Palace
Location 1 km from bus stand **Address** No 1, Church First Street, TT Nagar, Karaikkudi **Tel** 235200/ 02 **Email** kkthsp@sancharnet.in **Rooms** 48 **Tariff** Rs 447-2,700 **Credit Cards** AmEx, Visa, Master **Facilities** Restaurant, bar, puja arrangements, travel desk, room service

The Bangala
Location Outskirts of Karaikkudi **Address** Devakottai Road, Senjai **Tel** 220221, 250221 **Website** thebangala.com **Rooms** 12 **Tariff** Rs 3,200; TE **Facilities** Home cooked meals, sightseeing, handicrafts shop, Internet, laundry, TV, room service **Chennai Reservations** 118 Santhome High Road **Tel** 044-24642985, 24934851

CHIDAMBARAM STD 04144
Hotel Akshaya BUDGET
Location Near Nagarajar Temple **Address** No 17/ 18, East Car Street **Tel** 220191-92 **Fax** 222592 **Website** hotelakshaya.com **Rooms** 27 **Tariff** Rs 350-850 **Credit Cards** AmEx, Visa, Master **Facilities** Restaurant, puja arrangements, travel desk, attached bath, room service

Hotel Ritz
Location Near Nagarajar Temple **Address** No 2, VGP Street **Tel** 223312-14 **Fax** 221098 **Rooms** 21 **Tariff** Rs 263-1,632 **Credit Cards** AmEx, Visa, Master **Facilities** Restaurant, puja arrangements, travel desk, attached bath, room service

Hotel Saradharam
Location Near Nagarajar Temple **Address** No. 19, VGP Street **Tel** 221336-40 **Mobile** 09842389678 **Fax** 222656 **Email** hsr_cdm@tanjorenet.in **Rooms** 43 **Tariff** Rs 499-1,800; TE **Credit Cards** AmEx, Visa, Master **Facilities** Restaurants, bar, travel desk, car rental, puja arrangements, laundry, room service

COONOOR STD 0423
Coral Gable Holiday Home
Location Near bus stand **Address** Club Road, Upper Coonoor **Tel** 2232561 **Rooms** 6 **Tariff** Rs 800 **Facilities** Travel arrangement, attached bath, hot water, laundry, room service

Hotel Blue Hills BUDGET
Location On a hill **Address** Mount Road **Tel** 2230174/ 892 **Mobile** 09443003175 **Rooms** 30 **Tariff** Rs 800-1,200; TE **Facilities** Restaurant, laundry, travel desk, room service

Riga Residency MID-RANGE
Location Next to Staff College **Address** Appleby Road, PO Wellington **Tel** 2234401/ 05 **Fax** 2200333 **Website** therigaresidency.com **Rooms** 27 **Tariff** Rs 1,500-1,800 **Credit Cards** AmEx, Master, Visa **Facilities** Multi-cuisine restaurant, bar, travel desk, laundry, room service

Salvation Army Guest House
Location Near Sims Park **Address** Christian Retreat Centre, 15-18 Orange Grove Road **Tel** 2230242 **Mobile** 09443897150 **Rooms** 18 **Tariff** Rs 350-1,200; TE **Facilities** Cook available, laundry, attached bath, hot water, travel desk, tennis and badminton courts

Taj Garden Retreat AYURVEDA
Location Overlooking hills **Address** Church Road **Tel**

INFORMATION

ACCOMMODATION LISTINGS

2230021/ 42, 2230208 **Fax** 2232775 **Website** tajhotels.com **Rooms** 32 **Tariff** Rs 5,500-7,500; TE **Credit Cards** AmEx, Visa, Master **Facilities** Multi-cuisine restaurant, bar, gym, games, volleyball, cricket, Ayurveda centre, travel desk, laundry, transfers, room service

The Tryst HOME STAY
Location In a tea estate **Address** Carolina Tea Estate, PO Box 6 **Telefax** 2207057 **Email** drrao@trystindia.com **Website** trystindia.com **Rooms** 6, cottage 1 (10 people) **Tariff** Rs 3,500-3,900, cottage Rs 9,000 **Facilities** Multi-cuisine restaurant, health club, billiards room, gym, library, Ayurvedic massage, driver's accommodation, laundry, Internet, attached bath, hot water, room service

Velan Hotel
Location City centre **Address** Ritz Road, Bedford **Tel** 2230084/ 484 **Fax** 2230606 **Rooms** 20 **Tariff** Rs 1,600-2,500; TE **Credit Cards** AmEx, Visa, Master **Facilities** Multi-cuisine restaurant, bar, laundry, travel desk, kids' play area, room service

Vivek Tourist Home
Location Near Upasi **Address** Figure of Eight Road **Tel** 2231292 **Mobile** 09894239227 **Website** hotelvivek.com **Rooms** 60, dorms 2 **Tariff** 400-900, dorms Rs 112 per head **Facilities** Multi-cuisine restaurant, travel desk, laundry, attached bath, hot water

Wallwood Garden HERITAGE
Location In the heart of Upper Coonoor **Address** Blair Athol, Kotagiri Road **Tel** 2230584 **Website** neemranahotels.com

Rooms 8 **Tariff** Rs 1,500-2,250; TE **Credit Cards** Visa, Master **Facilities** Restaurant, sightseeing, travel desk, room service

HOGENAKKAL STD 04342
Hotel Tamil Nadu TTDC
Location Address Pennagaram, via Hogenakkal **Tel** 256447 **Fax** 256448 **Rooms** 30 **Tariff** Rs 420-660 **Facilities** Travel assistance, laundry, attached bath, hot water, room service **Chennai reservations** See page 481

INDIRA GANDHI WLS STD 04253
Ambuli Illam
Location In Top Slip **Address** Top Slip **Rooms** 4 **Tariff** Rs 300 **Facilities** Canteen, cook, attached bath, hot water **Pollachi Reservations** Wildlife Warden, Indira Gandhi Wildlife Sanctuary, 365/ 1, Meenakarai Road **Tel** 04259-225356

Banyan Tree HOME STAY
Location Foothills of the sanctuary **Address** C/o Mr V M Prabhu, Gounder Farm, Sethumada **Tel** 244490 **Mobile** 09486037669 **Rooms** 4 suites **Tariff** Rs 4,300 **Facilities** Sightseeing, trekking, attached bath, hot water, TV **Coimbatore Reservations Tel** 0422-2573329

Bison Lodge
Location In Top Slip **Address** Top Slip **Rooms** 4 **Tariff** Rs 250 **Facilities** Canteen, attached bath, hot water **Pollachi Reservations** See Ambuli Illam above

Bison Valley Lodge
Location Near Parambikulam Dam **Address** Wildlife Warden, PO Thoonakkadavu **Tel** 277201 (Range Officer), 277250 (booking office) **Website** keralaforest.org **Rooms** 3 **Tariff** Rs 150 per

person **Facilities** Food arranged from nearby eateries, trekking, boating, attached bath **Annapady Reservations** Wildlife Warden, PO Thoonakkadavu, Annapady **Tel** 04253-277250

Chital Lodge
Location In Top Slip **Rooms** 2 **Tariff** Rs 300 **Facilities** Canteen, cook, attached bath **Pollachi Reservations** See Ambuli Illam alongside

Forest Rest House FRH
Locations Foothills of Top Slip **Address** PO Sethumada **Rooms** 2 **Tariff** Rs 250 **Facilities** Caretaker can prepare food, attached bath, hot water **Pollachi Reservations** See Ambuli Illam alongside

Hornbill Rest House
Location In Top Slip **Address** Top Slip **Rooms** 2 **Tariff** Rs 250 **Facilities** Canteen, hot water **Pollachi Reservations** See Ambuli Illam alongside

KAMARAJAR VALLEY STD 0451
Cardamom House HOME STAY
Location Lakeview **Address** Athoor Village **Tel** 2556765-66 **Mobile** 09360691793 **Fax** 2556766 **Website** cardamomhouse.com **Rooms** 6 **Tariff** Rs 3,600-4,400 **Facilities** Home cooked meals, sightseeing, car rental, bird watching, yoga, meditation, laundry, attached bath, room service

Double Dutch Resorts
Location Lakeside **Address** Holland House, Athoor Village **Tel** 2556763 **Website** travel.to/doubledutchresort **Rooms** 4 **Tariff** Rs 1,100-2,260 **Facilities** Home cooked meals, sightseeing, trekking

HOTELS

Lakeside Guest House
Location Lakeview **Address** Athoor, Dindigul **Tel** 3298132 **Website** southindiatours.net **Rooms** 5, cottages 6 **Tariff** Rs 1,500 **Facilities** Home cooked meals, travel desk, laundry, attached bath, room service

KANCHIPURAM STD 044
GRT Regency
Address 487, Gandhi Road **Tel** 27225250 **Fax** 27224263 **Website** grthotels.com **Rooms** 35 **Tariff** Rs 1,250-2,250; TE **Credit Cards** Visa, Master **Facilities** Multi-cuisine restaurant, bar, travel desk, laundry, TV, room service

Heritage Inn
Location Opp Taluk Office **Address** No. 49A, Sheikhpet, Nadu Street **Tel** 27227780/ 817 **Rooms** 27 **Tariff** Rs 490-800 **Facilities** Multi-cuisine restaurant, car rental, laundry, attached bath, hot water, room service

Hotel Jaybala International
Address 504 Gandhi Road **Tel** 27224348/ 4453 **Rooms** 33 **Tariff** Rs 150-1,090 **Credit Cards** Visa, Master **Facilities** Veg restaurant, car rental, laundry, TV, room service

Hotel Tamil Nadu `TTDC`
Location Opp Old Railway Station **Address** Kamatchi Amman Sannathi Street **Tel** 27222553-54 **Fax** 27222552 **Rooms** 20 **Tariff** Rs 350-550 **Facilities** Restaurant, bar, attached bath, hot water, car rental, room service **Chennai Reservations** See page 481

MM Hotels `BUDGET`
Location Near railway station **Address** 65/ 66, Nellukkara Street **Tel** 27227250-54 **Mobile** 09443265025 **Website** mmhotels.com **Rooms** 48 **Tariff** Rs 550-1,100; TE **Credit Cards** Visa, Master **Facilities** Restaurant, car rental, laundry, attached bath, hot water, room service

KODAIKANAL STD 04542
Green Acres
Location Near the lake **Address** Lake Road **Tel** 242384/ 3813 **Rooms** 35 **Tariff** Rs 1,350-4,990; TE **Facilities** Restaurant, games, kids' play area, laundry, travel desk, room service

Greenlands Youth Hostel
Location Near TV Tower **Address** Coaker's Walk, St Mary's Road **Tel** 240899, 241099 **Mobile** 09842316517 **Rooms** 15, dorms 6 **Tariff** Rs 800-1,600, dorm Rs 175 **Facilities** Canteen, laundry, attached bath, room service

Hill Country Holiday Resort `MID-RANGE` `AYURVEDIC SPA`
Location Valley view **Address** Pallangi Road, Attuvampati, PO Arakal **Tel** 240953-54/ 58 **Fax** 240947 **Website** hillcountryholidays.com **Rooms** 57 cottages **Tariff** Rs 2,500-3,900; TE **Credit Cards** Visa, Master **Facilities** Restaurant, games, snooker, Ayurveda spa, car rental, sightseeing, travel desk, room service

Hilltop Towers `MID-RANGE`
Location Opp Kodai International School **Address** Club Road **Tel** 240413, 242254, 242253 **Fax** 240415 **Website** indiamart.com/hilltoptowers **Rooms** 26 **Tariff** Rs 1,200-1,500; TE **Credit Cards** AmEx, Visa, Master **Facilities** Restaurants, bakery, laundry, sightseeing, car rental, room service

Hotel Astoria `MID-RANGE`
Location Near main bus stand **Address** Anna Salai **Tel** 240524/ 26 **Rooms** 27 **Tariff** Rs 950-1,200; TE **Credit Cards** AmEx, Visa, Master **Facilities** Restau-

ACCOMMODATION LISTINGS

rant, travel desk, laundry, attached bath, room service

Hotel Bala MID-RANGE
Location Opp bus stand **Address** 11/ 49, Woodwill Road **Tel** 243070-71 **Telefax** 241252 **Website** balacares.com **Rooms** 57 **Tariff** Rs 800-1,300; TE **Credit Cards** AmEx, Visa, Master **Facilities** Multi-cuisine restaurant, sightseeing, car rental, station transfers, travel desk

Hotel Grand Palace MID-RANGE
Location Near Telephone Exchange **Address** Convent Road **Tel** 242288, 243388 **Fax** 245199 **Website** hotelgrandpalace.com **Rooms** 41 **Tariff** Rs 1,550-3,350; TE **Credit Cards** Visa, Master **Facilities** Restaurant, travel desk, room service

Hotel Kodai International
Location Near the lake **Address** 17/328, Laws Ghat Road **Tel** 245190-94 **Website** kodaiinternational.com **Rooms** 70 **Tariff** Rs 2,399-4,999; TE **Credit Cards** Visa, Master **Facilities** Multi-cuisine restaurant, health club, bar, park, Ayurvedic massage, yoga, laundry

Hotel Mount View AYURVEDA
Location Near Zion School **Address** Laws Ghat Road **Tel** 241978/ 241988 **Fax** 240788 **Website** kodaimountview.com **Rooms** 28 **Tariff** Rs 1,200-3,600; TE **Facilities** Multi-cuisine restaurant, Ayurvedic massage, Internet, laundry, travel desk, sightseeing, room service

Hotel Woody's
Location Near bus stand **Address** 4/ 17/ 70, Convent Road **Tel** 240774, 242753, 244111 **Rooms** 12 **Tariff** Rs 2,250-6,600; TE **Credit Cards** Visa, Master **Facilities** Restaurant, laundry, travel desk, attached bath, room service

JS Heritage Resort MID-RANGE
Location Opp Chettiar Park **Tel** 245118 **Fax** 240693 **Website** jsheritage.com **Rooms** 16 cottages **Tariff** Rs 1,900-2,200; TE **Credit Cards** AmEx, Visa, Master **Facilities** Restaurant, bar, health club, travel desk, laundry, kids' park, room service

Kodai Resort Hotel MID-RANGE
Location Near Central Bus Stand **Address** Coaker's Walk **Tel** 242107, 240632-33 **Mobile** 09443389233 **Fax** 242108 **Website** kodairesorthotel.com **Rooms** 50 **Tariff** Rs 1,750-2,900; TE **Credit Cards** AmEx, Visa, Master **Facilities** Restaurant, travel desk, lockers, laundry, kids' park, games, room service

Lilly's Valley Resort MID-RANGE
Location Near bus stand **Address** 17/ 178, Sivanandi Road **Tel** 240558, 244307 **Fax** 241558 **Website** lillysvalley.com **Rooms** 20 cottages **Tariff** Rs 1,125-2,250; TE **Facilities** Multi-cuisine restaurant, travel desk, laundry, room service

Royal Hotels MID-RANGE
Location Near Zion School **Address** Laws Ghat Road **Tel** 240986-87 **Mobile** 09486459644 **Website** kodairoyalhotels.com **Rooms** 25 **Tariff** Rs 1,350-1,750; TE **Facilities** Restaurant, travel desk, laundry, attached bath, hot water, room service

Sterling Resorts MID-RANGE
Location Near the lake **Address** PB No. 44, Gymkhana Road **Tel** 242380-81 **Telefax** 241065 **Website** sterlingresorts.in **Rooms** 104 **Tariff** Rs 2,100-3,000; TE **Credit Cards** Visa, Master **Facilities** Restaurant, health club, travel desk, disco, games, room service

Strawberry Park MID-RANGE
Location Near bus stand **Address** Anna Salai **Tel** 242340-41 **Rooms** 20 **Tariff** Rs 1,200-1,400; TE **Credit Cards** Visa, Master **Facilities** Restaurant, travel desk, room service

Summer Migrations
Location On a hill **Address** Lourdupuram, Vilpatty Village, Naidupuram **Tel** 241943/ 53/ 55 **Fax** 2241963 **Website** thesummermigrations.com **Rooms** 30 **Tariff** Rs 2,500-4,500; TE **Facilities** Multi-cuisine restaurant, lounge bar, travel desk, sightseeing, room service

The Carlton AYURVEDIC SPA
Location Near the Lake **Address** Lake Road **Tel** 240056/ 71 **Fax** 241170 **Website** krahejahospitality.com **Rooms** 91 **Tariff** Rs 6,500 **Credit Cards** AmEx, Visa, Master **Facilities** Multi-cuisine restaurant, bar, café, Ayurvedic spa, golf (8 holes), travel desk, beauty parlour, health club, laundry, room service

Valley View Inn
Location Central **Address** 8/59, Post Office Road **Tel** 240181/ 84 **Mobile** 09442289763 **Fax** 240189 **Email** hotelvalleyviewinnkodai@sanchar.in **Rooms** 39 **Tariff** Rs 1,590; TE **Credit Cards** Visa, Master **Facilities** Restaurant, travel desk, laundry, room service

Villa Retreat MID-RANGE
Address Near Coaker's Walk **Telefax** 240940 **Website** villa

HOTELS

retreat.com **Rooms** 11 **Tariff** Rs 1,300-2,500; TE **Credit Cards** Visa, Master **Facilities** Restaurant, travel desk, room service

KUMBAKONAM STD 0435
Hotel Adithya
Address 48, Thanjavur Main Road **Tel** 2421794-95 **Email** hotathi_kmb@sancharnet.in **Rooms** 23 **Tariff** Rs 472-800 **Facilities** Restaurant, travel desk, puja arrangements, laundry, room service

Hotel Green Park
Location Near railway station **Address** No. 10, Laxmi Vilas Street **Tel** 2402852-53, 2403912-14 **Fax** 2421956 **Rooms** 33 **Tariff** Rs 582-1,500; TE **Credit Cards** Visa, Master **Facilities** Restaurants, travel desk, puja arrangements, laundry, room service

Hotel Rayas
Location Near railway station **Address** 18, Head Post Office Road **Tel** 2423170-72, 2430323, 2420323, 2432032, 2422545 **Mobile** 09842923170 **Fax** 2422479 **Email** hotelrayas@yahoo.co.in **Rooms** 54 **Tariff** Rs 500-1,750; TE **Credit Cards** AmEx, Visa, Master **Facilities** Restaurant, bar, puja

arrangements, travel desk, laundry, room service

Kasi International
Location Near Gandhi Park **Address** Town High School Road, Near Kasi Theatre **Tel** 2431055/ 255/ 779/ 749/ 739 **Mobile** 09443363187 **Fax** 2430934 **Rooms** 33 **Tariff** Rs 400-800; TE **Credit Cards** AmEx, Visa, Master **Facilities** Restaurant, laundry, room service

Paradise Resort
Address 3/ 1216 Tanjore Main Road, Ammapet, Darasuram **Tel** 2416469, 3291354 **Mobile** 09344301354 **Website** paradiseresortindia.com **Rooms** 20 **Tariff** Rs 2,450; TE **Facilities** Restaurant, travel desk, room service

MADURAI STD 0452
Fortune Pandiyan Hotel
HIGH-END **SWIMMING POOL**
Location Opp Old University **Address** Race Course, Azhagar Kovil Main Road **Tel** 2537090, 4356789 **Fax** 2533424 **Website** fortuneparkhotels.com **Rooms** 57 **Tariff** Rs 2,500-7,500; TE **Credit Cards** Visa, Master **Facilities** Multi-cuisine restaurant, bar, swimming pool, travel desk, puja arrangements,

laundry, room service **Chennai Reservations** 13, Cathedral Road **Tel** 044-28114800/ 4900

GRT Regency
Location 2 km from temple **Address** 38, Madakulam Road, Palanganatham Signal Junction **Tel** 2371155 **Website** grtregency.com **Rooms** 57 **Tariff** Rs 2,250-2,750; TE **Credit Cards** Visa, Master **Facilities** Multi-cuisine restaurant, swimming pool, health club, bar, Ayurvedic massage centre, travel desk, laundry, room service

Hotel Chentoor
Location Opp Railway Station **Address** 106, West Perumal Maistri Street **Tel** 2350490, 3042222 **Fax** 3012765 **Email** chentoor01@sancharnet.in **Rooms** 45 **Tariff** Rs 605-1,100 **Credit Cards** Visa, Master **Facilities** Multi-cuisine restaurant, bar, travel desk, laundry, room service

Hotel Germanus **MID-RANGE**
Location 7 km from Meenakshi Temple **Address** 28, Bypass Road, Arasaradi **Tel** 4356999, 2382001 **Fax** 2381478 **Website** hotelgermanus.com **Rooms** 85 **Tariff** Rs 2,000-4,500; TE **Credit**

ACCOMMODATION LISTINGS

Cards AmEx, Visa, Master **Facilities** Restaurant, café, bar, travel desk, Ayurvedic massage, laundry, room service **Chennai Reservations** G-12, GF, Prince Arcade No. 22A, Cathedral Road **Tel** 044-42149032 **Mobile** 09382138226

Hotel Park Plaza
Location Near Station **Address** 114/ 115, West Perumal Maistri Street **Tel** 3011111-21 **Fax** 3011122 **Website** hotelparkpla za.net **Rooms** 56 **Tariff** Rs 1,200-1,700; TE **Facilities** Restaurants, bar, travel desk, TV, room service

Hotel Royal Court
Location Opp Railway Station **Address** No 4, West Veli Street **Tel** 4356666 **Fax** 4373333 **Website** royalcourtindia.com **Rooms** 69 **Tariff** Rs 2,300-5,000; TE **Credit Cards** Visa, Master **Facilities** Restaurants, health club, travel desk, transfers

Hotel Sangam
Location Outskirts **Address** Azhagar Kovil Road **Tel** 2537531-37 **Fax** 2537530 **Website** hotelsangam.com **Rooms** 50 **Tariff** Rs 2,400-6,500; TE **Credit Cards** Visa, Master **Facilities** Restaurants, bar, swimming pool, travel desk, sightseeing, chess, room service

Hotel Tamil Nadu 1 `TTDC`
Location Near the temple **Address** 7B, West Veli Street **Tel** 2337471-75 **Rooms** 43 **Tariff** Rs 250-850 **Credit Cards** Visa, Master **Facilities** Restaurant, bar, laundry, attached bath, hot water, room service **Chennai Reservations** See page 481

Hotel Tamil Nadu 2 `TTDC`
Location Outskirts **Address** Azhagar Kovil Road **Tel** 2537461 **Telefax** 2533203 **Rooms** 50 **Tariff** Rs 325-1,250; TE **Credit Cards** Visa, Master **Facilities** Restaurant, bar, travel desk, laundry, attached bath, hot water, room service **Chennai Reservations** See page 481

Taj Garden Retreat `HIGH-END`
Location 7 km from railway station **Address** No. 40, TPK Road, Pasumalai **Tel** 2371601-10 **Fax** 2371636 **Website** tajhotels.com **Rooms** 63 **Tariff** Rs 3,700-5,800; TE **Credit Cards** Visa, Master **Facilities** Restaurants, bar, travel desk, sightseeing, swimming pool, fitness centre, business centre, jogging track, palm reading, Ayurvedic massage, laundry, room service

The Madurai Residency
Location Near railway station **Address** 14-15, West Marret Street **Tel** 2343140, 4380000 **Fax** 2341360 **Website** maduraire sidency.com **Rooms** 75 **Tariff** Rs 850-1,850; TE **Credit Cards** Visa, Master **Facilities** Restaurants, bar, travel desk, laundry, attached bath, room service

---

MAHABALIPURAM STD 044

Fortune Chariot Beach Resort
Location Behind Five Rathas **Tel** 27443002/ 05 **Fax** 27425050 **Website** fortunehotels.in **Rooms** 34, cottages 36 **Tariff** Rs 6,000-15,000; TE **Credit Cards** Visa, Master **Facilities** Multi-cuisine restaurant, swimming pool, health club, billiards, beach games, travel desk, laundry

GRT Temple Bay and Beach Resort `HIGH-END`
Location Next to beach **Address** Kovalam Road **Tel** 27443636 **Fax** 27443838 **Website** grthotels.com **Rooms** 72 **Tariff** Rs 6,000-12,000; TE **Credit Cards** AmEx, Visa, Master **Facilities** Restaurant, Ayurvedic massage, health club, travel desk

Hotel Golden Sun and Beach Resort `SWIMMING POOL`
Location Near the beach **Address** 59, Kovalam Road **Tel** 27442245-46 **Fax** 27442900 **Website** hotelgoldensun.com **Rooms** 58 **Tariff** Rs 1,300-2,800; TE **Credit Cards** AmEx, Visa, Master **Facilities** Restaurant, bar, swimming pool, sauna, Ayurvedic massage, travel desk, games, room service

Hotel Mamalla Heritage
Location Central **Address** No. 104, East Raja Street **Tel** 27442060/ 260/ 360 **Fax** 27442160 **Website** hotelmamalla heritage.com **Rooms** 38 **Tariff** Rs 1,050-1,500; TE **Credit Cards** AmEx, Visa, Master **Facilities** Restaurant, laundry, travel desk, room service

Hotel Tamil Nadu `TTDC`
Location Sea-facing **Address** Beach Resort Complex **Tel** 27442361-63 **Rooms** 34 **Tariff** Rs 1,350; TE **Facilities** Restaurant, bar, swimming pool, travel desk, room service **Chennai Reservations** See page 481

Ideal Beach Resort `AYURVEDA`
Location Beach side **Address** Devaneri Village **Tel** 27442240/ 3299/ 3599/ 3899 **Telefax** 27442243 **Website** resortsindia.com **Rooms** 45 **Tariff** Rs 1,850-6,000; TE **Credit Cards** Visa, Master **Facilities** Restaurant, bar, swimming pool, Ayurvedic massage, car rental, travel desk, games, Wi-Fi, tennis court, beauty parlour

HOTELS

Mamalla Beach Resort
Location Near the beach, on the ECR **Address** 108, Kovalam Road **Tel** 27442375/ 475 **Website** mamallaresort.com **Rooms** 35 **Tariff** Rs 1,045-1,750; TE **Credit Cards** AmEx, Visa, Master **Facilities** Restaurant, swimming pool, travel desk, room service

Quality Inn MGM Beach Resort
Location Near the beach **Address** 1/ 74, East Coast Road, Muttukadu **Tel** 27472435 **Fax** 27472408 **Rooms** 76 **Tariff** Rs 3,495-6,495; TE **Credit Cards** AmEx, Visa, Master **Facilities** Restaurant, swimming pool, jacuzzi, steam, Ayurvedic spa, private beach, health club, games, gift shop, room service

Sterling Mahabalipuram Beach Resort `SWIMMING POOL`
Location Next to Shore Temple **Address** Shore Temple Road **Tel** 27442287/ 3914-15 **Website** sterlingmahabalipuram.net **Rooms** 26, suites 2 **Tariff** Rs 2,200-5,000; TE **Credit Cards** AmEx, Visa, Master **Facilities** Restaurant, swimming pool, Ayurvedic centre, travel desk, room service **Chennai Reservations** 56, 4th Street, Abhiramapuram, Alwarpet **Tel** 044-24998121

Tina Blue View Lodge
Location Near the beach **Address** 34, Othavadai Street **Tel** 27442319 **Rooms** 15 **Tariff** Rs 200-500 **Facilities** Restaurant, Ayurvedic massage, sightseeing, camping, car rental

---

MUDUMALAI STD 0423

Abhayaranyan Forest Rest House `FRH`
Location Near Theppakadu **Address** PO Abhayaranyan **Rooms** 2 **Tariff** Rs 330 **Facilities** Caretaker can arrange food, hot water **Ooty Reservations** Wildlife Warden, Mt Stewart Hill, Ooty **Tel** 0423-2444098

Abhayaranyan Annexe `FRH`
Location Near Theppakadu **Address** PO Abhayaranyan **Rooms** 2 **Tariff** Rs 180 **Facilities and Ooty Reservations** See Abhayaranyan FRH above

Bamboo Banks Farm `TREKKING`
Location Foothills of Nilgiri **Address** PO Masinagudi **Tel** 2526211 **Mobile** 09443205371 **Website** bamboobanks.in **Rooms** 5 cottages **Tariff** Rs 1,125-2,000 **Credit Cards** Visa, Master **Facilities** Dining hall, safari, trekking, laundry, attached bath, hot water, room service

Forest Rest House `FRH`
Address Masinagudi PO **Rooms** 3 **Tariff** Rs 180 **Facilities and Ooty Reservations** See Abhayaranyan FRH alongside

Green Park Resorts `TREKKING`
Location Nilgiri foothills, 7 km from Mudumalai WLS **Address** Singara Road, PO Masinagudi **Tel** 2526486 **Mobile** 09443174641 **Website** greenparkmudumalai.com **Rooms** 16 **Tariff** Rs 1,000-2,500; TE **Credit Cards** AmEx, Visa, Master **Facilities** Restaurant, bar, trekking, birdwatching, night safari, elephant safari, laundry, campfire, room service

Jungle Hut `TREKKING`
Location Nilgiri foothills **Address** Bokkapuram, PO Masinagudi **Tel** 2526240/ 463 **Website** junglehut.in **Rooms** 12 **Tariff** Rs 2,387-4,700 **Credit Cards** Visa, Master **Facilities** Home-cooked meals, trekking, camping, pool, sanctuary tours, elephant rides, safaris, bonfire

Jungle Retreat `TREKKING`
Location Nilgiri foothills **Address** Bokkapuram, PO Masinagudi **Tel** 2526469-70 **Website** jungleretreat.com **Rooms** 9, tree houses 2,

ACCOMMODATION LISTINGS

bamboo huts 3, dorms 3 **Tariff** Rs 420-3,938; TE **Credit Cards** Visa, Master **Facilities** Restaurant, buffet meals, trekking, jeep safaris, elephant rides, plantation visits, games, laundry

New Mountainia Rest House
Location Near the sanctuary **Address** Bokkapuram, PO Masinagudi, Nilgiris **Tel** 2526247/ 267 **Rooms** 10 **Tariff** Rs 1,000-3,500 **Facilities** Restaurant, laundry, tours, trekking, camping, night ride, camp fire, safaris, laundry, room service

Peacock Dormitory `FRH`
Address PO Kargudi **Rooms** 3 dorms **Tariff** Rs 35 **Facilities and Ooty Reservations** See Abhayaranyan FRH on page 521

Sylvan Lodge `FRH`
Location Near Moyar River **Address** PO Theppakadu **Rooms** 4 **Tariff** Rs 330 **Facilities and Ooty Reservations** See Abhayaranyan FRH on page 521

The Cuckoo `FRH`
Address PO Kargudi **Rooms** 1 **Tariff** Rs 180 **Facilities and Ooty Reservations** See Abhayaranyan FRH on page 521

The Monarch Safari Park
Address Bokkapuram, PO Masinagudi **Tel** 2526250/ 343 **Fax** 2526326 **Website** hojoindia.com **Rooms** 24 **Tariff** Rs 1,100-2,000; TE **Credit Cards** Visa, Master **Facilities** Restaurant, games, safaris, trekking, room service

Theppakadu Log House `FRH`
Location Near Moyar River **Address** PO Theppakadu **Rooms** 3 **Tariff** Rs 330-560 **Facilities** Caretaker can arrange food, attached bath, hot water

Ooty Reservations See Abhayaranyan FRH on page 521

Wild Canopy Reserve
Address Bokkapuram, PO Masinagudi **Telefax** 2526034 **Mobile** 09443280658 **Website** wildcanopyreserve.com **Rooms** 2, tree houses 4, tents 6 **Tariff** Rs 1,500-10,000; TE **Credit Cards** Visa, Master **Facilities** Restaurant, safari, bird watching, camping, laundry, room service

NAGAPATTINAM STD 04365

Golden Sand Lodge
Location Opp Railway Station **Address** 14, Nethaji Road **Tel** 242432 **Rooms** 23 **Tariff** Rs 150-700 **Facilities** Laundry, attached bath, room service

Hotel Sea Horse
Location Near bus stand **Address** Public Office Road, Kadambadi **Tel** 247686, 247047 **Fax** 248345 **Rooms** 19 **Tariff** Rs 175-800 **Facilities** Restaurant, travel desk, laundry, attached bath, room service

Hotel Subham Park
Location Near Collectors' Office **Address** Nagore Road **Tel** 251000 **Mobile** 09842442588 **Rooms** 9 **Tariff** Rs 450-690 **Facilities** Restaurant, travel desk, laundry, room service

Hotel Tamizhagam
Location On the beach **Address** 10, Thoni Thurai Road **Tel** 221010 **Mobile** 09442081752 **Rooms** 18, suites 2 **Tariff** Rs 450-1,200; TE **Facilities** Restaurants, travel desk, laundry, attached bath, room service

Hotel VPN
Location Opp railway station **Address** 46 Nethaji Road **Tel** 240678 **Rooms** 33 **Tariff** Rs 250-950 **Facilities** Food from outside, travel desk, laundry, attached bath, room service

OOTY STD 0423

Fernhills Palace
Address Fernhill PO, Fernhill **Tel** 2443912, 2443915 **Fax** 2443097 **Website** fernhills palace.com **Rooms** suites 19 **Tariff** Rs 8,500-20,000; TE **Credit Cards** Visa, Master **Facilities** Restaurant, travel desk, jacuzzi, Internet, attached bath, room service

Holiday Inn Gem Park
Location Next to Collector's Office **Address** Sheddon Road **Tel** 2441761-62/ 42955 **Fax** 2444302 **Website** holiday-inn.com **Rooms** 95 **Tariff** Rs 6,000-20,000; TE **Credit Cards** Master, Visa **Facilities** Restaurants, bar, travel desk, swimming pool, disco, health club, beauty parlour, travel desk, Ayurveda centre, games

Hotel Blue Hill International
Address State Bank Road **Tel** 2444466/ 638 **Rooms** 88 **Tariff** Rs 550-1,500; TE **Facilities** Restaurant, bar, laundry, room service

Hotel Khems `MID-RANGE`
Location Near main bus stand **Address** Off Ettienes Road, near Alankar Theatre **Tel** 2441635-36/ 4188 **Fax** 2442461 **Website** hotel khems.com **Rooms** 44 **Tariff** Rs 900-1,500; TE **Credit Cards** Visa, Master **Facilities** Restaurant, travel desk, laundry, room service

Hotel Lakeview `MID-RANGE`
Location Near bus stand **Address** West Lake Road **Tel** 2443580-82/ 0978, 2440983 **Fax**

HOTELS

2443579 **Website** lakeview.com **Rooms** 114 cottages **Tariff** Rs 1,200-1,500; TE Credit Card AmEx, Visa, Master **Facilities** Multi-cuisine restaurant, laundry, travel desk, gift shop, horse riding, room service

Hotel Mayura Sudarshan KSTDC
Location Inside horticultural garden **Address** Fernhill **Tel** 2443828 **Website** kstdc.nic.in **Rooms** 9 **Tariff** Rs 450-650 **Facilities** Multi-cuisine restaurant, car rental, attached bath, hot water, room service **Chennai Reservations** See page 481

Hotel Nahar Nilgiris
Location City centre **Address** 52 A, Charring Cross **Tel** 2442173/ 3685/ 5797-98 **Fax** 2452253 **Website** naharhotels.com **Rooms** 87 **Tariff** Rs 2,250-3,750; TE **Credit Cards** Visa, Master **Facilities** Restaurant, café, laundry, travel desk, room service

Hotel Regency Villa
Location Inside Fernhill Palace **Address** PO Fernhill **Tel** 2443098 **Fax** 2443097 **Rooms** 19 **Tariff** Rs 1,900-2,200; TE **Credit Cards** Visa, Master **Facilities** Restaurant, laundry, fireplace, room service

Hotel Sinclairs TREKKING
Location Overlooking Nilgiris **Address** Gorishola Road **Tel** 2441376-80 **Fax** 2444229 **Website** sinclairshotels.com **Rooms** 88 **Tariff** Rs 2,000-3,480 **Credit Cards** AmEx, Visa, Master **Facilities** Restaurant, bar, games, health club, trekking, gift shop, travel desk, room service

Hotel Tamil Nadu TTDC
Location Near bus stand **Address** Charring Cross Road **Tel** 2444370-77 **Fax** 2444369 **Rooms** 64 **Tariff** Rs 825-1,425; TE **Credit Cards** Visa, Master **Facilities** Restaurant, bar, laundry, travel desk, room service **Chennai Reservations** See page 481

Hotel Villa Park
Location Near main bus stand **Address** 29/ 49, Backey Road, Ettiennes Road **Tel** 2442434-35 **Fax** 2224777 **Rooms** 106 **Tariff** Rs 1,200-2,800; TE **Credit Cards** Visa, Master **Facilities** Restaurant, laundry, room service

Howard Johnson The Monarch
Location Near Collectorate Road **Address** Off Havelock Road **Tel** 2444408/ 18/ 20 **Website** hojoindia.com **Rooms** 60 **Tariff** Rs 2,500-5,000; TE **Credit Cards** Visa, Master **Facilities** Multi-cuisine restaurant, bar, disco, swimming pool, health club, private theatre, conference hall, room service

King's Cliff
Location Opp Hotel Willow Hill **Address** Havelock Road **Tel** 2452888-89 **Mobile** 09443052890 **Fax** 2444697 **Email** holiday@littlearth.in **Website** littlearth.in **Rooms** 9 **Tariff** Rs 975-2,275 (with breakfast); TE **Credit Cards** Visa, Master **Facilities** Multi-cuisine restaurant, travel desk, Internet, sightseeing, laundry, fishing, trekking, horse riding, fireplace, hot water, room service,

Ooty Gate MID-RANGE
Location Near Charring Cross **Address** Coonoor Road **Tel** 2441623/ 45 **Rooms** 85 **Tariff** Rs 790-1,750; TE **Credit Cards** AmEx, Visa, Master **Facilities** Multi-cuisine restaurant, laundry, travel desk, lockers, attached bath, hot water, room service

Reflections Guest House
Location Between lake and bus

ACCOMMODATION LISTINGS

stand **Address** North Lake Road **Tel** 2443834/ 5800 **Email** reflectionsin@yahoo.co.in **Rooms** 12 **Tariff** Rs 600-800 **Facilities** Dining room, meals on order, travel arranged, laundry, attached bath, hot water

Savoy Hotel `AYURVEDA`
Location On Mysore Road **Address** 77, Sylks Road **Tel** 2444142-147 **Fax** 2443318 **Website** tajhotels.com **Rooms** 40 **Tariff** Rs 5,500-10,800; TE **Credit Cards** Visa, Master **Facilities** Restaurant, bar, Ayurvedic massage, travel desk, games, pony ride, room service

Sherlock `MID-RANGE`
Location Before Fortune Retreat Hotel **Address** Tiger Hill Road, Upper Thalayatimund **Tel** 2440094/ 1641 **Mobile** 09443052890 **Website** littlearth.in **Rooms** 9 **Tariff** Rs 1,375-1,975; TE **Credit Cards** Visa, Master **Facilities** Restaurant, garden, fireplace, TV

Sterling Holiday Resort
Location Near the lake **Address** PO No. 73, Kundan House Road, Fern Hill **Tel** 2441073-74 **Fax** 2445890 **Website** sterlingfernhill.com **Rooms** 177 **Tariff** Rs 2,500-5,000; TE **Credit Cards** Visa, Master **Facilities** Restaurant, laundry, health club, gift shop, games, lawn tennis, grocery shop, travel desk, trekking

The Willow Hill
Location Hill top **Address** 58/ 1, Havelock Road **Tel** 2444037, 2444758 **Website** willowhill.in **Rooms** 10 **Tariff** Rs 900-1,700; TE **Credit Cards** AmEx, Visa, Master **Facilities** Restaurant, laundry, travel desk, kid's garden, games, room service

---

PALANI HILLS STD 04545

Bison Wells Jungle Lodge
Location In the forest **Tel** 04542-240566 **Website** wilderness-explorer.in **Rooms** 1 cottage **Tariff** Rs 1,500 **Facilities** Home cooked meals, attached bath, hiking, jungle trails, bird watching **Chennai Reservations** Dreamcatcher Holidays, 5, Smith Road **Tel** 044-28511304/ 22653

Hotel Tamil Nadu `TTDC`
Location Opp Winch Station **Address** West Giri Station **Tel** 241156 **Website** tamilnadutourism.org **Rooms** 7 **Tariff** Rs 275-495 **Facilities** Restaurant, car rental, laundry, attached bath, room service **Chennai Reservations** See page 481

New Tirupur Lodge
Location Near bus stand **Address** Adivanam **Tel** 242303, 245303-05 **Email** ntl@md4.vsnl.net.in **Rooms** 88 **Tariff** Rs 200-1,100; TE **Facilities** Restaurant, car rental, guide for temple, attached bath, room service

---

PARSON'S VALLEY

Hodgson's Camp `CAMP`
Location In Parson Valley **Address** Parson Valley **Website** getoffurass.com **Rooms** Cottages 2, dorm 1 **Tariff** Rs 950 per person (with meals) **Facilities** Attached bath, hot water, guide, sightseeing trips to Western Catchment area, Mukurti reserve forest, Ooty transfers **Bangalore Reservations Tel** 080-26722750 **Mobile** 09845442224

RED HILLS STD 0423

Red Hill Nature Resort
Location Top of a hill **Address** Emerald, Nilgiris **Tel** 2595755 **Mobile** 09842259554 **Website** indianjungle.com **Rooms** 8 **Tariff** Rs 4,000 **Facilities** Restaurant, laundry, bonfire, children's park, open-air theatre, games, sightseeing, room service, TV

SWAMIMALAI STD 0435

Sterling Swamimalai
Location 2 km from the temple **Address** PO Baburajapuram, Thimmakudy Village **Tel** 2480044/ 385/ 406 **Fax** 2481705 **Website** sterlingswamimalai.net **Rooms** 28 **Tariff** Rs 2,250-3,938 **Credit Cards** Visa, Master **Facilities** Restaurant, travel desk, Ayurvedic centre, swimming pool, puja arrangements, TV

THANJAVUR STD 04362

Hotel Gnanam
Location Close to the temples, near Old Bus Stand **Address** Anna Salai, Market Road **Tel** 278501-08 **Fax** 235536 **Website** hotelgnanam.com **Rooms** 40 **Tariff** Rs 900-2,250; TE **Credit Cards** Visa, Master **Facilities** Restaurants, bar, car rental, laundry, room service

Hotel Oriental Towers
Location Near railway station **Address** 2889, Srinivasan Pillai Road **Tel** 230724/ 730, 231467 **Fax** 230770 **Website** hotelorientaltowers.com **Rooms** 163 **Tariff** Rs 600-3,000; TE **Credit Cards** AmEx, Visa, Master **Facilities** Restaurants, pub, swimming pool, forex, shopping arcade, health club, beauty salon, lockers, room service

Hotel Parisutham `AYURVEDA`
Location Near Irwin Bridge **Address** 55 GA, Canal Road **Tel** 231801, 231844 **Fax** 230318 **Website** hotelparisutham.com **Rooms** 50 **Tariff** Rs 4,500-6,500; TE **Credit Cards** AmEx, Visa,

HOTELS

Master **Facilities** Multi-cuisine restaurant, bar, barbeque lawn, swimming pool, Ayurvedic massage centre, souvenir shop, travel desk, Internet, lockers

Hotel Sangam
Location Close to the temples **Address** Tiruchy Road **Tel** 239451-56 **Fax** 236695 **Website** hotelsangam.com **Rooms** 54 **Tariff** Rs 2,100-4,600; TE **Credit Cards** AmEx, Visa, Master **Facilities** Restaurant, bar, swimming pool, souvenir shop, open air lawn, travel desk, laundry, room service

Hotel Tamil Nadu TTDC
Location Near railway station **Address** Gandhiji Road **Tel** 231325/ 421 **Website** tamilnadutourism.org **Rooms** 32 **Tariff** Rs 300-1,000; TE **Credit Cards** AmEx, Visa, Master **Facilities** Restaurant, bar, travel desk, lockers, laundry, room service **Chennai Reservation** See page 481

Hotel Temple Towers
Location Near railway station **Address** 20/ 1A, SM Road **Tel** 276333-34/ 37 **Fax** 270014 **Rooms** 22 **Tariff** Rs 450-1,000; TE **Credit Cards** AmEx, Visa,

Master **Facilities** Restaurant, bar, health club, beauty parlour, kids' playground, billiards, temple tours, attached bath, laundry, room service

Ideal River View Resort
Location On the banks of Vennar River, facing the river **Address** Palli Agraharam **Tel** 250533/ 633/ 833/ 933 **Fax** 251113 **Website** resortsindia.com **Rooms** 30 cottages **Tariff** Rs 2,600-3,500; TE **Credit Cards** AmEx, Visa, Master **Facilities** Multi-cuisine restaurants, bar, riverside summer house huts, swimming pool, indoor recreation centre, forex, sightseeing, garden, Ayurvedic massages, mini golf course, travel desk, lockers **Chennai Reservations** No 3, 2nd Street, Dr Tivumurthy Nagar, Nungambakkam **Tel** 044-28215232, 28237583

THIRUVANNAMALAI STD 04175
Arunai Anantha
Location 3 km from temple **Address** Chengam Road, NH66, Aanaipiradaan Village **Tel** 237275/ 8726 **Fax** 238728 **Email** hotelarunaianantha@ yahoo.co.in **Rooms** 13 **Tariff** Rs 1,250-2,750; TE **Credit Cards** AmEx, Visa,

Master **Facilities** Restaurant, swimming pool, puja arrangements, car rental, TV

Hotel Arunachala
Location Near the temple **Address** No 5, Vada Sannidhi Street **Tel** 228300/ 400/ 488 **Rooms** 41 **Tariff** Rs 250-900 **Facilities** Restaurant, car rental, puja arrangements, laundry, attached bath, room service

Hotel Ganesh International
Location Near Gandhi Statue **Address** 111A, Big Street **Tel** 226701-02 **Fax** 227887 **Rooms** 23 **Tariff** Rs 125-900 **Credit Cards** Visa, Master **Facilities** Restaurant, travel desk, laundry, room service

Hotel Ramakrishna
Location Near the bus stand **Address** 34F, Polur Road **Tel** 250005-06, 320055 **Fax** 250008 **Email** hotelramakrishna1998@ yahoo.co.in **Rooms** 60 **Tariff** Rs 231-880 **Credit Cards** Visa, Master **Facilities** Restaurant, car rental, room service

Hotel Trishul
Location 2 mins walk from temple **Address** No 6, Kanakarayar Mudali Street **Tel** 222219/

ACCOMMODATION LISTINGS

225500 **Telefax** 225549 **Email** trishulhotel@yahoo.co.in **Rooms** 16 **Tariff** Rs 450-1,500; TE **Credit Cards** Visa, Master **Facilities** Restaurant, bar, puja arrangements, travel desk, laundry, room service

Seshadri Swamigal Ashram
Location Next to Ramanashram **Address** Chengam Road **Tel** 236999 **Rooms** 72 **Donation** Rs 150 **Facilities** Canteen, attached bath, hot water

TIRUCHIRAPALLI STD 0431
Breeze Residency
Location Near Central Bus Stand **Address** 3/14, MacDonald's Road **Tel** 2414414 **Mobile** 09443746399 **Fax** 2461451 **Email** jenneys@satyam.net.in **Rooms** 82 **Tariff** Rs 750-3,500; TE **Credit Cards** AmEx, Visa, Master, Diners **Facilities** Restaurant, cafe', bar, travel desk, swimming pool, beauty parlour, massage centre

Hotel Annamalai
Location Opp Central Bus Stand **Address** No. 11, MacDonalds Road, Cantonment **Tel** 2412881-84 **Mobile** 09486676957 **Rooms** 33 **Tariff** Rs 575-1,200; TE **Credit cards** AmEx, Visa, Master **Facilities** Restaurant, travel desk, laundry, room service

Hotel Chitra
Location Near Chhatram Bus Stand, opp Hotel Mayas **Address** 63/1, Chintamani **Tel** 2711086-89 **Telefax** 2711090 **Rooms** 95 **Tariff** Rs 425-1,200; TE **Credit Cards** Visa, Master **Facilities** Restaurant, bar, travel desk, laundry, room service

Hotel Femina
Location Near Central Bus Stand **Address** 109, Williams Road, Cantonment **Tel** 2414274/501 **Rooms** 163 **Tariff** Rs 650-2,500; TE **Credit Cards** Visa, Master **Facilities** Restaurants, travel desk, health club, swimming pool, laundry, room service

Hotel Gajapriya
Location Opp Central Bus Stand **Address** 5 & 6, Royal Road **Tel** 2414411 **Fax** 2466456 **Rooms** 66 **Tariff** Rs 315-2,250 **Credit Cards** Visa, Master **Facilities** Restaurant, bar, travel desk, laundry, room service

Hotel Kanchana Towers
Location Near Central Bus Stand **Address** 50, Williams Road, Cantonment **Tel** 4200002-03 **Mobile** 09443700028 **Fax** 4200004 **Website** hotelkanchanatowers.com **Rooms** 40 **Tariff** Rs 420-990 **Credit cards** AmEx, Visa, Master **Facilities** Restaurant, travel desk, room service

Hotel Mayas
Address Karur Bypass Road, Chintamani **Tel** 2705712 **Fax** 2705711 **Website** hotelmayas.com **Rooms** 57 **Tariff** Rs 500-1,700; TE **Credit Cards** Visa, Master **Facilities** Restaurant, bar, travel desk, room service

Hotel Ramyas
Address 13-D/2, Williams Road **Tel** 2414646/747 **Mobile** 09842414541 **Fax** 2414852 **Website** ramyas.com **Rooms** 109 **Tariff** Rs 450-2,100; TE **Credit Cards** AmEx, Visa, Master **Facilities** Multi-cuisine restaurant, bar, travel desk, laundry, room service

Hotel Royal Southern
Location Near airport **Address** Race Course Road, Khajamalai **Tel** 2421303-08 **Fax** 2420573 **Rooms** 79 **Tariff** Rs 1,800-3,000; TE **Credit Cards** AmEx, Visa, Master **Facilities** Multi-cuisine restaurant, travel desk, swimming pool, massage, gift shop, laundry, room service **Chennai Reservations Tel** 044-24746811 **Mobile** 09884403200

Hotel Sangam
Location 1 km from Central Bus Stand **Address** Collector's Office Road **Tel** 2414480/700 **Fax** 2415779 **Website** hotelsangam.com **Rooms** 54 **Tariff** Rs 2,400-5,500; TE **Credit Cards** Visa, Master **Facilities** Restaurant, bar, café, travel desk, health club, swimming pool, room service

Hotel Tamil Nadu TTDC
Address MacDonald's Road **Tel** 2414346-48, 2414471-72 **Fax** 2415725 **Rooms** 44 **Tariff** Rs 325-850 **Facilities** Restaurant, bar, travel desk, laundry, room service **Chennai Reservations** See page 481

TRANQUEBAR STD 04364
The Bungalow on the Beach
Location Beachside **Address** 24 King Street **Tel** 288065, 289034-36 **Mobile** 09884456380 **Fax** 289038 **Website** neemranahotels.com **Rooms** 8 **Tariff** Rs 4,000-5,000; TE **Credit Cards** AmEx, Visa, Master **Facilities** Open-air restaurant, verandahs for the rooms, boating facilities, laundry, sightseeing

Hotel Tamil Nadu
Address 24 King Street **Tel** 288065, 289034-36 **Mobile** 09884456380 **Fax** 289038 **Rooms** 5, dorms 2 **Tariff** Rs 600, dorm Rs 150 **Credit Cards** AmEx, Visa, Master **Facilities** laundry, attached bath

HOTELS

VEDANTHANGAL BIRD SANCTUARY STD 044
Forest Rest House FRH
Location 1 km from the park **Address** Kodiakkarai **Tel** 27500006 **Rooms** 4 **Tariff** Rs 300-400 **Facilities** Lodging, caretaker can make food, guides **Chennai Reservations** Wildlife Warden, Vedanthangal DMS Compound No. 256, Annasalai, Teynampet **Tel** 044-24321471

YELAGIRI HILLS STD 04179
Hotel Hills
Location Opp lake **Tel** 245301-03 **Fax** 245304 **Rooms** 32 **Tariff** Rs 1,000-3,000; TE **Facilities** Restaurant, laundry, bonfire, kids' park, open-air theatre, games, sightseeing

Hotel Nigress
Location Hill-facing **Tel** 245264 **Mobile** 09442357714 **Rooms** 6 cottages **Tariff** Rs 850-950 **Facilities** Restaurant, sightseeing, kids' park, room service

Hotel Yelagiri
Location Near boathouse **Address** Athanavur **Tel** 245236 **Rooms** 20 **Tariff** Rs 500-600 **Facilities** Restaurant, car rental, sightseeing, attached bath, hot water, room service

Zeenat's Taj Garden Resort
Location Hill view **Address** Kottayur Village **Tel** 245231, 245445 **Rooms** 25 **Tariff** Rs 900-1,800; TE **Facilities** Restaurant, games, trekking, laundry, attached bath, room service

YERCAUD STD 04281
Green Fort Inn
Location Near bus stand **Address** First Estate, Pagoda Point Road **Tel** 222767 **Rooms** 8 cottages **Tariff** Rs 600 **Facilities** Restaurant, car rental, room service

Hotel Select
Location Opp bus stand **Tel** 222525 **Rooms** 17 **Tariff** Rs 300-500 **Facilities** Laundry, attached bath, hot water, room service

Hotel Shevaroys
Address Hospital Road **Tel** 222288/ 383-86 **Fax** 222387 **Rooms** 59 **Tariff** Rs 625-2,025; TE **Credit Cards** AmEx, Visa, Master **Facilities** Restaurant, bar, health club, ice-cream parlour, play area, Salem transfers, travel desk, room service

Hotel Shoba
Location Near bus stand **Tel** 222409 **Rooms** 20, dorms 2 **Tariff** Rs 250-400, dorms Rs 900 **Facilities** Restaurant, car rental, room service

Hotel Silver Holiday Cottages
Address Lake Point **Tel** 222656, 222541 **Rooms** 23 **Tariff** Rs 400-600 **Facilities** Restaurant, car rental, laundry, room service

Hotel Tamil Nadu TTDC
Address Ondikkadai **Tel** 223334-36, 222273 **Fax** 222745 **Rooms** 35 **Tariff** Rs 300-700 **Facilities** Multi-cuisine restaurant, bar, laundry, boating, car rental, kids' play area, room service **Chennai Reservations** See page 481

House of Peace
Location Near bus stand **Address** Ram Road **Tel** 222262/ 401 **Rooms** 20, dorms 4 **Tariff** Rs 175-350 **Facilities** Dining room, prayer hall, garden, car rental

Sterling Days Inn Resort
Location Near UHF **Address** PB 11, Lady's Seat **Tel** 222700/ 06/ 08 **Fax** 222537 **Website** sterlingresorts.org **Rooms** 65 **Tariff** Rs 1,750-2,700; TE **Credit Cards** AmEx, Visa, Master **Facilities** Restaurant, games, mini library, disco, bonfire, sightseeing, travel desk

ABOUT THE AUTHORS

allen mendonca is a Bangalore-based journalist, who has crusaded for over two decades for the preservation of lakes, tanks, parks and open spaces of his beloved city. He is the recipient of over a dozen awards for journalistic excellence

ambika menon has been involved with environmental and ecological issues. As the first girl in Doon School, she feels she is extremely well-placed to address gender issues. Currently she is an activist involved in sustainable development, peace and gender issues

anil nair is a journalist who has worked with various publications in Mumbai and Chennai, including rediff.com, *The Sunday Observer* and *Gentleman.* He is currently based in Kochi

anish vohra has been involved in advertising copy writing and journalism. From 1998 onwards he has written on Indian history and culture, edited content for the web and managed web-based projects

from copywriting to travel writing and a rock band to a radio station, **anurag mallick** is a nomad at heart and writer by choice. Currently based in Delhi, Anurag is also part of the Mahseer Conservation Society

bharath sundaram works as a research associate at the Ashoka Trust for Research in Ecology and the Environment, Bangalore, and is studying forest fires and invasive species

a journalist for the past 15 years, **charu soni** has worked previously with *The Statesman, The Hindustan Times* and *Tehelka.* She has also written extensively on travel and socio-cultural issues for *Outlook Traveller*, Outlook Traveller Getaways and *City Limits*

dbn murthy, based in Bangalore, is the author of 10 books and numerous articles and trekked in the Himalaya

deepa kandaswamy is a freelance writer, engineer and political analyst. Her articles have been published in six continents; the credits include ABC News, Middle East Policy, *Christian Science Monitor*, *Ms.*, *Khaleej Times*, *Data Quest* and *The Hindu*. She was nominated for the UN Media Award in 2003

janaki venkataraman is a Chennai-based freelance writer. She enjoys visiting temples in the Cauvery Delta not only because they have a therapeutic effect on her but also because of the amazing amount of historical and social information they yield

jaya madhavan is a poet and children's novelist. She loves travelling by road and exploring ancient temples. Jaya and her musician husband particularly love singing in temples for the deity

when **kg kumar** is not struggling out of the couch to shift the refrigerator from the path of the television, he can be seen pottering around pot-holed roads on his vintage Royal Enfield Bullet. In the unlikely event that it splutters to a halt, he gets down and shoots off a piece or two for sundry magazines and newspapers

latha anantharaman is a writer, editor and translator based in Palakkad. Till she started travelling for our books, her spiritual activities consisted of watching birds and digging in the garden, but the Guruvayurappan Temple has always held a special place in her life

malvika onial is a researcher in conservation science at the University of Cambridge. She has a keen interest in birds, and enjoys travelling and trekking

maya jayapal moved house 14 times in an unconscious preparation to become an accidental historian, traveller, writer and lay counsellor

nandini srinivasan was a regular contributor to the *Mysore Note Book* column of the Bangalore edition of the *Indian Express*. Which explains her enthusiasm for her city and the number of exclamation marks in her Mysore copy (which we had to delete!)

ABOUT THE AUTHORS

np hafiz mohamad writes and does illustrations for Malayalam periodicals. He has published short story collections and books for children. He has received four state-level literary awards, including the Kerala Sahithya Academy Award for children's literature. He is also the Honorary Editor of *Varthamanam*, a Malayalam daily

payal dhar is an author of children's fiction, and a freelance writer, copy editor and sometimes web designer, based in Bangalore

ponni arasu is originally from Chennai. She works on various issues relating to human rights and social change. And co-writes a legal column for *Marie Claire*

sanjeev verma, based in Kochi, works in a city-based travel and business information magazine. He has also contributed to the various publications of *The Times of India*

raman kumar is a Dehra Dun-based ecologist who focusses on bird communities in Rajasthan and Uttarakhand. He has been associated with the Wildlife Institute of India and the Forest Research Institute, Dehra Dun

shefali vaidya ganesh, a content developer in Mumbai, likes to describe herself as a writer, traveller and a dreamer

someday, **sheila kumar** will go see places just for the sheer pleasure of seeing places. Meanwhile, she hits the road, sunscreen in her handbag, and notebook and pen close at hand

shobha warrier is a journalist who covers Chennai for rediff.com. A creative writer in Malayalam, her stories have been translated into English, Kannada and Telugu

sonia nazareth is back from her Masters in Anthropology of Media from SOAS, London. Now she can be found brandishing pen and camera when she's not lecturing at St Xavier's College, Mumbai

sudha g tilak worked as a journalist with leading Indian publications for more than a decade in Chennai. She now resides in Delhi, but her heart still beats for Madras

sugata srinivasaraju is a journalist who has travelled across India and Europe passionately recording the death of mother tongues. He is currently with *Outlook* in Bangalore

sumathi chandru enjoys travelling, particularly to spiritual destinations, and writing about lesser known facts on temple history and mythology. She lives in Chennai

sunaad raghuram is very fond of the Kabini jungle and it was this love that took him to the forests there, where he researched for his book *Veerappan: The Untold Story*

dr susan visvanathan is associate professor of Sociology at JNU, New Delhi. Her book *Christians of Kerala* is in its fourth reprint. Travelling for her means "going home" and she plans these trips in such a way that she gets to see a lot of India and the world

vaishna roy used to be a hardworking business journalist with *Business Today, Outlook Money*, etc. She quit the tough routine and settled down in Chennai to sometimes do travel writing, copy editing, story-telling and, hold your breath, a walk-on role in a true-blue Kollywood fillim

vidya and **navin sigamany** live and work the corporate grind in Chennai, travelling whenever possible, wherever possible, usually on shoestring budgets. The beauty of nature and ancient architecture are particular addictions

vijay nambisan has written and worked for various journals. Besides his published poems *Gemini* (1992), his books are *Bihar is in the Eye of the Beholder* (2000) and *Language as an Ethic* (2003), all in Penguin India

vimala murthy, based in Bangalore, has several articles to her credit

vivek narayanan moves between Chennai and Delhi, where he writes and works in the public sector

INFORMATION

GO THERE FOR ...

ADVENTURE

Bheemeshwari, mahseer fishing	275
Coonoor, trekking	187
Horsley Hills, birdwatching	251
Indira Gandhi WLS, trekking	182
Kamarajar Valley, trekking	127
Kodaikanal, trekking	171
Nelliyampathy, birdwatching	335
Ooty, angling, trekking	195
Parson's Valley, trekking	216, 217
Periyar TR, river rafting	362
Vythiri, Chembra Peak trek	433
Yelagiri Hills, Swamimalai Hill trek	54

BACKWATERS

Alappuzha, cruise	448
Chidambaram, Pitchavaram	61
Kottayam, Vembanad Lake	375
Kochi, Vembanad Lake	400
Kumarakom, Vembanad Lake	420

BEACHES

Alappuzha, Alleppey Beach	448
Kochi, Cherai Beach	410
Kozhikode	389, 390, 396
Pondicherry	33
Tranquebar	66

FAIRS/FESTIVALS

Alappuzha, Snake Boat Race	456
Chidambaram, Natayanjali Festival	61
Guruvayur, Chembai Music Festival, Carnatic Music Festival	350
Kochi, Ernakulam Utsava	409
Kumbakonam, Float Festival, Mahamaham Festival	70, 71, 72
Madurai, Chithirai Thiruvizha, Vaikasi Utsavam, Oonjal, Aavani Moolam, Theppotsavam	157
Mahabalipuram, Dance Festival	17
Mysore, Dasara	292
Nagapattinam, Pooram Festival, Adibhakta Nayanar Festival	113
Ooty, Summer Festival Flower Show	194
Palakkad, Cattle races	324
Sravanabelagola, Mahamastakabhisheka	316
Srirangam, Vaikunta Ekadashi	85
Swamimalai, Brahmotsavam, Skanda Sashti Festival, Thyy Poosam Festival	78
Thanjavur, Thyagaraja Aradhanai	110
Tiruchirapalli, Temple Car Festival	83

FOOD

Alappuzha, toddy shops	458
Chettinad, Chettinad cuisine	136, 140
Kanchipuram, Kanchipuram idli	23
Kochi, pan-Kerala cuisine	414
Kottayam, toddy shops, bakeries	378
Kozhikode, halwa, chips	390
Kumbakonam, degree coffee	73
Mysore, dosas, Mysore pak	300
Palakkad, tiffin, Ramasseri idli	330
Pondicherry, French cuisine	42

HERITAGE

Chettinad, mansions	133
Darasuram, Airavateeswara Temple	76
Gangaikondacholapuram, Brihadeesvara Temple	78
Kochi	400
Kozhikode	385
Lepakshi	247
Mahabalipuram	14
Mysore, palaces	291
Ooty, Raj-era buildings	194
Palakkad, Tipu's Fort	323
Pondicherry, French colonial heritage	32
Srirangapatna, fort	283
Thanjavur	99
Tranquebar, Danish fort and church	64

HILL STATIONS

Biligiri Rangaswamy Hills	302
Coonoor	186
Horsley Hills	250
Kodaikanal	169
Nandi Hills	271
Nelliyampathy	334
Ooty	192
Parson's Valley	215
Shivanasamudram	279
Yelagiri Hills	52
Yercaud	120

GO THERE FOR...

LAKES

Bellikkal, Bellikkal Lake	209
Kamarajar Valley, Kamarajar Lake	126
Kodaikanal, Kodi Lake	172, 176
Kumarakom, Vembanad Lake	420
Ooty, Ooty Lake	194
Periyar TR, Mulla Periyar Lake	360
Red Hills, Emerald, Avalanche, Upper Bhavani	210
Parson's Valley	215
Vythiri, Pookote and Karalad lakes	432
Yelagiri Hills, Punganoor Lake	53
Yercaud, Big Lake, Small Lake	121

PILGRIMAGES

Chidambaram, Nataraja Temple	57
Chettinad, Pillaiyarpatti, Avudayarkovil	138, 140
Guruvayur, Guruvayurappan, Parthasarathy, Mammiyur Mahadevan	347, 350
Kanchipuram, Kamakshi Amman	21
Kodaikanal, Kurinji Andavar Temple	171
Kottayam, Thirunakkara Temple St Mary's Knanaya Church, St Mary's Orthodox Church, Thazathangadi Juma Masjid	373, 374, 375
Kumbakonam, Adi Kumbeswarar, Kasi Viswanathar, Sarangapani, Nachiar Kovil	71, 72, 75
Madurai, Meenakshi Amman	155
Mysore, Chamundeswari	294
Nagapattinam, Kayarohanaswamy, Vailankanni Church, Nagore Dargah	113, 114, 115
Palani, Thiruavinankudi Temple	145, 147
Sravanabelagola	313
Srikalahasti, Srikalahastiswara	243
Srirangapatna, Sri Ranganathaswamy Temple	284
Swamimalai, Swaminatha Swamy Temple	76
Thanjavur, Brihadeesvara, Bangaru Kamakshi Amman	101, 103
Thanjavur, Schwartz Church	104
Thiruvannamalai, Arunachaleswara	46
Thiruvaiyaru, Panchanatheesvarar	108
Tiruchirapalli, Malaikottai	82
Srirangam, Ranganathaswamy, Jambukeswarar	84, 86
Tirumala	231

SHOPPING

Chettinad, antiques	139
Kanchipuram, Kanchipuram saris	25
Kochi, spices	410
Kodaikanal, chocolates	172
Madurai, Sungudi cotton saris	158
Mysore, sandalwood, silk	298
Ooty, home made chocolates, flavoured fudges, tea	196
Pondicherry, candles, handmade paper, incense, pottery	38
Srikalahasti, Kalamkari work	246
Thanjavur, paintings	104

WATERFALLS

IGWLS, Aliyar Monkey Falls	183
Bellikkal, Kalhatti Falls	208
Coonoor, Catherine Falls	188
Hogenakkal Falls	94
Kodaikanal, Bear Shola Falls, Silver Cascade	171
Mudumalai WLS, Moyar Falls	224
Nagarhole NP, Irpu Falls	312
Shivanasamudram, Gaganachukki and Barachukki Falls	281
Srikalahasti, Veyilingala Kona Waterfall	246
Vythiri, Suchipara and Kanthampara Falls	431
Yelagiri Hills, Jalagamparai Waterfalls	56
Yercaud, Killiyur Falls	121

WELLNESS

Bangalore, Ayurveda, holistic healing, spa	256
Kotagiri, Ayurveda	190
Palakkad, Ayurveda	330
Pondicherry, Meditation	32

WILDLIFE

Bannerghatta NP	264
Biligiri Rangaswamy Hills	303
Indira Gandhi WLS	178
Mudumalai WLS	219
Nagarhole NP	306
Periyar TR	354
Vedanthangal Bird Sanctuary	28
Karikili Bird Sanctuary	31
Salim Ali Bird Sanctuary	436
Srirangapatna, Ranganathittu	286

INFORMATION

A

Aarupadai Veedus 148
Abbe Dubois Church,
  Srirangapatna 286
Adi Kumbeswarar Temple,
  Kumbakonam 71
Adibhakta Nayanar Festival,
  Nagapattinam 113
Adikesava Perumal Temple,
  Sriperumbudur 27
Adil Shahis of Bijapur 54
Adinatha 314, 316
Adisesha 233
Adivaraha Cave, Mahabalipuram 16
Agasthya, Sage 145, 239, 304
agraharam 78
Airavateeswara Temple, Darasuram .. 76
Aiyanar Temples **98**
Akasa Ganga Tirtha, Tirumala 239
Akasharaja 233
Akhanda-bagilu 315
Akuni Village, Nilgiris 207
Al Barooni 386
Alamelumangapuram Temple,
  Tirumala 239
Alanganallur **164, 471**
ALAPPUZHA, Alleppey 375, **445**
Ali, Dr Salim 438
Aliyar Monkey Falls **183**
Aliyar River 180, 181
Alkondesar, Thiruvaiyaru 108
Amaravathy River 180, 181
Amba Vilas Palace, Mysore 291
AMM Nattukottai, Pallathur 135
Amrita Sarovar, Nandi Hills 273
ananda thandavam dance 58
anathottil, Kottayam 373
Andaman and Nicobar Islands 422
Anna Park, Yercaud 121
Annamalai WLS 180
annapakshi, mythical bird 25
Anthony, St 404
Arabian Sea 390, 396, 445
Arakavati River 278
Aranmula Boat Race, Alappuzha 456
Arasalar River 70
Arat Festival, Kollengode 338
Arattupuzha **346**
Arc, Joan of 34
Archaeological Museum, Thrissur .. 343
Archaeological Survey of India 65, 76
Arikamedu **35, 44**
Ariyankuppam River 44
Arjuna 166
Arjuna's Penance, Mahabalipuram ... 15
Arokia Madha, Vailankanni 116
Art Gallery, Thanjavur 103
Art Museum, Thrissur 343
Arthunkal **460**
Arunachala Hill, Thiruvannamalai 46
Arunachaleswara Temple,
  Thiruvannamalai 47

Arunagirinathar, Saint 47
Arupalakshmi, Goddess 22
Aruvankadu, Nilgiris 477
Aryabhatta Gopuram, Srirangam 85
Ashram Press, Pondicherry 33
Ashta Lingam, Thiruvannamalai 48
Ashta Shakti Mandapam, Madurai .. 155
ASI Museum, Thanjavur 102
Assisi, St Francis of 404
Athangudi, Chettinad 134
Athmanathaswamy Temple,
  Avudayarkovil 140
Athoor Village, Kamarajar Valley 128
Attivaradar 25
Aurobindo Ashram, Pondicherry 33
Auroville **44**
Avalanche Lake, Nilgiris .. 196, 212, 468
Avudayarkovil **140**
Ayodhya 82, 314
Ayudhya Puja, Mysore 293
Ayyappa Shrine, Guruvayur 349
Ayyi Mandapam, Pondicherry 36
Azhagar Kovil **166**

B

B Agraharam 98
Bahubali 313
Bailey, Rev Benjamin 380
Baker's Junction, Kottayam 373
Balaji, Lord 231, 238
Balarama 294
Ballard Bungalow, Fort Kochi 405
Bambar Falls, Kodaikanal 171
Bana dynasty 273
Bandipur National Park,
  Karnataka .. 207, 219, 222, 306, 308
BANGALORE **256**
Bangaru Kamakshi Amman Temple,
  Thanjavur 103
**BANNERGHATTA
  NATIONAL PARK** **264**
Banni Mantap, Mysore 293
Barachukki Falls,
  Shivanasamudram 281
Bartholomew, St 404
Basilica Shrine, Vailankanni 115, 116
Bastion House, Fort Kochi 405
Bathing Falls, Hogenakkal 95
Batuta, Ibn 386
Bay of Bengal 422
Bear Shola Falls, Kodaikanal 171
Bear's Cave, Yercaud 121
BELLIKKAL **206**
Beri-Jam Lake **176**, 462
Beypore, Kozhikode 392
Bhadrabahu, Acharya 314, 316
Bhagavad Mela Natya Natakam
  Festival, Melattur 472
Bhagavathy Temple:
  Alappuzha 452
  Cherthala 460
  Palakkad 324

Bhakta Kannappa Temple,
  Srikalahasti 245
Bhakti movement 69
Bharadwaja Tirtham, Srikalahasti ... 246
Bharata 314
bharatanatyam 17
Bharathi Park, Pondicherry 35
Bhasyakara Chaitrotsavam 27
Bhavishyottara Purana 232
Bheema 286
BHEEMESHWARI **274**
Bhogar, Siddhar 146, 148
Bhognandeeshwara Temple,
  Nandi Hills 273
Bhonsle, Chattrapathy Babaji
  Rajah 104
Bhoothathankettu **442**
Bhrigu, Sage 232
Big Lake, Yercaud 121
BILIGIRI RANGASWAMY HILLS .. **302**
Bird Sanctuary, Kumarakom 422
Bishop House, Fort Kochi 405
Bison Valley, Nilgiris 207
boat races, Alappuzha 456
Bolgatty Palace, Kochi 410
Bombay Shola, Ooty 196
Boodipadaga, BR Hills 302, 304
Bose, Netaji Subhash Chandra 424
Botanical Garden, Yercaud 122
boules 40
Brahma Peetham, Chidambaram 59
Brahma Purana 233
Brahma Temple, Thirupattur 92
Brahmahatti 75
Brahmaloka 232
Brahmanayaki 92
Brahmapuri 87
Brahmin 472
Brahmotsavam Festival:
  Srikalahasti 245
  Sriperumbudur 27
  Swamimalai 78
Brihadeeswara Temple,
  Thanjavur 76, 101
Brihan Nayagi, Goddess 102
Brindavan Gardens **300**
British, The 21, 32, 34, 87, 122,
  .... 170, 210, 284, 291, 386
British East India Company 401
Bryant Park, Kodaikanal 170
Bryant Park, Ooty 196
Burghers 407
Butterfly Park, Bannerghatta NP 267

C

Cabral, Pedro Alvarez 403
Cairn Hills Shola, Nilgiris 196
Calvathy Jamaath Mosque,
  Mattancherry 407
Calvinists 406
Canagrayan, Pierre, *dubash* 38
Cantonese 408

INDEX

Captain Bailey's Dungeon,
Srirangapatna 284
Capuchin Tower, Pondicherry 34
Cariappa March, Mysore 293
Carnatic music 110
Carnatic War 87
Cattle Race, Palakkad 324
Cauvery Fishing Camp,
Bheemeshwari 274
Cauvery River 70, 73, 76, 82, 84, 86,
............95, 99, 101, 108, 117, 121, 275,
........281, 283, 286, 288, 289, 300, 472
Chakra Tirtham, Tirumala 238
Chakyarkoothu 342, 350
Chaldean Syrian Church, Thrissur ..343
Chaliyar River 392
Chamarajanagar 302
Champakulam Boat Race 456
Chamundi Hills, Mysore ..292, 294, 296
chandai 139
Chandikeshwarar, Lord 84
Chandra Pushkarni Tirth,
Srirangam 85
Chandragiri Hill,
Sravanabelagola 315, 316
Chandragupta-basadi,
Sravanabelagola 316
Chandrakanda Perumal 23
Chandranathaswamy, Jain sage 325
Chandrayan Durg, Gingee 51
Changanassery **382**
Chaturmukeshvara Temple,
Srikalahasti 245
Chavara Art Museum, Mannanam ..380
Chavundaraya 315
Chembai Festival, Guruvayur 350
Chembotti Theruvu, Kozhikode 390
Chembra Peak 433
Chemmeen 446
Chenakathur Vela, Palakkad 324
Chenchu tribe, Horsley Hills 251
Chennakesava Temple, Belur 318
Cherai Beach, Kochi 410
Cheriapally, Kottayam 374
Cherthala **460**
Chettiar, Alagappa 136
Chettiars 133, 134
CHETTINAD **132**
Chidambara Rahasyam 60
CHIDAMBARAM **57**
Chinese Fishing Nets:
Alleppey 448
Fort Kochi 403, 407
Chinnar WLS, Kerala 181
Chirappu Festival, Alappuzha 452
Chitharai Thiruvizha, Madurai 157
Chithirai Pournami Festival,
Azhagar Kovil 166
Chitoor Kongan Pada, Palakkad 324
Chola Ganga Tank,
Gangaikondacholapuram 78
Chola palaces, Kumbakonam 71

Chola rulers 21, 24, 71, 82,
........................100, 113, 273, 288
Chola Temple, Tirukkadaiyur 67
Chola, King Kochenkannan 87
Chola, King Muchukunda 117
Chola, King Rajendra 78
Chola, King Vikrama 58
Chola, King Rajaraja 101
Cholai Malai Temple 166
Christian IV, King 65
Christians 390
Church of Our Lady of Angels,
Karaikal 69
Church of Our Lady of Hope,
Kochi 410
Church of South India, Kochi 404
Church of the Immaculate
Conception, Pondicherry 34
Church of Zion, Tranquebar 67
Clive, Robert 88, 122
Clock Tower, Mattancherry 408
Cluny Centre, Pondicherry 34
Coaker's Walk, Kodaikanal 170
Cochin Shipyard, Kochi 409
cochonnet 40
Cockburn, MD 122
Coimbatore 470
Colombo 116
Conti, Niccolo Dei 401
COONOOR **186**, 195, 204,
.... 211, 466, 476
coracles 276
Cordite Factory, Aruvankadu 477
Cornwallis, Lord 285
Coromandel Coast 65
Cotton Mary 404
Crawford, Captain Hugh 448
Crocodile Park, Hogenakkal 97
CSI Church, Kozhikode 387
Cubbon, Sir Mark 272
Custom House, Pondicherry 33
CVN Kalari Sangam, Kozhikode 389

D

Dakshin Kailash 84
Dakshinamurthy 84
Dalai Lama 262
dandayutham 76
Danish 64, 104
Danish Governor's House,
Tranquebar 66
Dansborg Fort, Tranquebar 66
Darasuram **76**
Darraigh, James 446
Darya Daulat Baug, Srirangapatna ..285
Dasara Festival, Mysore 291
Dasaratha lingam 87
David Hall, Fort Kochi 404
Defence Services Staff College,
Wellington 188
degree coffee, Kumbakonam 73
Devakottai **138**

Devaraja Perumal 24
Devasena, Goddess 148
Devaswom Museum, Guruvayur 351
Devi Mahatmiyam 59
Devil's Kitchen, Kodaikanal 171
Dhanawantri, doctor of the gods 25
Dhandayuthapani Swamy Temple,
Palani 146, 148
Dharmasamvardhini, Goddess 108
Dharmasastha Temple,
Arattupuzha 346
Digambara 316
Dikshitars, Chidambaram 60
Divya Desams 24, 87, 113
Dodda Betta Peak, Nilgiris 190, 195
Dodda Ghosai Ghat,
Srirangapatna 286
Dodda Sampige Mara, BR Hills 304
Doddamakkalli 274, 278
Dolores Basilica, Thrissur 344
Dolphin's Nose:
Kodaikanal 170
Nilgiris 187, 470
Draupadi 16
Dravidian 14, 21
Droog Fort, Nilgiris 187, 470
Dubai 392
Dupleix, Joseph Francois 34
Durga Shrine, Guruvayur 349
Durga, Goddess 16
Durgambika Temple, Srikalahasti 246
Dutch 386, 401, 408
Dutch Cemetery, Fort Kochi 403, 404
Dutch East India Company 404, 406

E

East Coast Road 14
Eastern Ghats 120, 195, 466
Ecole Francaise d'Extreme Orient,
Pondicherry 34
Eco-Tourism Centre, Periyar ...358, 360
Edamalayar Lower Dam **442**
Ekambranathar Temple,
Kanchipuram 23
Elephant Camp, IGWLS 182
Elephant Hill, Kanchipuram 24
Elephant Race, Guruvayur 350
Elizabeth, Queen 272
Elk Hill, Nilgiris 193
Emerald Lake, Nilgiris 210, 212, 217
Emoor Bhagvathy, Palakkad 326
Eravikulam NP, Kerala 181, 182
Ernakulam 408
Erumbeswarar Temple,
Thiruverumbur 84
Ethiraja Nadavalli, Sriperumbudur 27
Ettumanur **380**

F

Fairy Falls, Kodaikanal 171
Ferreira, Bishop Dom Gomez 406
Ferreira, Bishop Dom Jos 405

INFORMATION

Figoni, Guiseppe 293
Float Festival, Kumbakonam 71
Folklore Museum, Mysore 292, 296
Fort Immanuel, Fort Kochi 404, 405
Fort Kochi 402, 403
Fort St George, Chennai.................122
Franciscan friars 403, 404
French 32, 87, 386
French Consulate General,
 Pondicherry 33
French Quarter, Pondicherry.............33

G

Gadothgajan, Yelagiri Hills 53
Gaganachukki Falls,
 Shivanasamudram 281
Galbraith, John Kenneth 408
Gali Bandalu, Horsley Hills 251
Galibore 274, 278
Gama, Vasco da 386, 390,
 ....403, 404, 406
Ganapati Homam, Chettinad 139
Gandhi Museum, Madurai 158
Gandhi, Mahatama 272
Gandhi, Rajiv 27, 308
Ganga King Rachamalla 315
Ganga River..15
Gangaikondacholapuram......**76, 78**
Garuda..235
Garudi Puppets, Mysore 294
Gavi **370**
Gayatri Mandapam,
 Kamakshi Amman Temple 22
Gayatri Mantra 22, 25
Ghafur, Malik 84
Ghosh, Sri Aurobindo 35
Giedde, Admiral Ove 65
Gingee Fort **51, 114**
Glasgow 292
Glen Falls, Kodaikanal 171
Gnana Prasoonambika,
 Srikalahasti 245
Gogarba Dam, Tirumala 238
Golf Course, Wellington 188
Gomatesvara, Sravanabelagola 313
Government Sandal Oil Factory,
 Mysore 298
Government Sheep Farm, Ooty 196
Government Silk Factory, Mysore ..298
Government Silk Farm, Yelagiri 54
Govindraja Perumal Temple,
 Chidambaram 60
Gramam, Palakkad 326
Grand Anaicut Canal..........................90
Grass Hill National Park 180, 181
Groningen Bastion, Fort Kochi 405
GRS Fantasy Park, Mysore 296
Gumbaz, Srirangapatna 285
Guna Caves, Kodaikanal 171
Gurram Konda..................................**251**
GURUVAYUR **347**
Gymkhana Club, Ooty 196

H

Haider Ali, Hyder Ali 285, 291
Hajjamana Kallu,
 Bannerghatta NP 270
halwa, Kozhikodan 386, 390
Hampi, Karnataka 96, 247
Hastagiri, Kanchipuram......................24
Hebrew inscriptions 408
Hema Pushkarni tank,
 Kumbakonam 72
Heritage Garden, Thrissur................343
Higginbotham's, Ooty 194
Ho, Cheng 407
HOGENAKKAL FALLS **94**
Holy Trinity Church, Ooty 195
Home, Robert 285
HORSLEY HILLS **250**
House of Sleep, Srirangapatna 285
Hoysala art 316
Huan, Ma 407
Hulhatti Village, Nilgiris 207

I

Idli, Kanchipuram 23
Idumban 145
Ilayathangudi, Chettinad 138
Iluppaikkudi, Chettinad 138
Inchathotty Village, Salim Ali BS......440
INDIRA GANDHI
 WILDLIFE SANCTUARY **178**
Indo-Portuguese Museum,
 Fort Kochi 405
Integral Yoga 35
International Pepper Exchange,
 Mattancherry 408
Iranikovil, Chettinad 138
Irpu Falls **312**
Irwin, Henry 291
Ishwara Temple, Irpu Falls 312
Ithalar, Nilgiris 210

J

Jadayupureeswar Temple,
 TR Pattinam 69
Jaganmohan Palace, Mysore 292
Jaimini, Sage 58
Jaina, Acharya..................................314
Jalagampari Waterfalls.....................323
Jalagamparai Waterfalls..................**56**
Jalagandeeswarar Temple, Vellore 54
Jalandhara, Srikalahasti 245
Jallikattu bull fight 164, 471
Jama'atpulli Mosque, Kozhikode 387
Jambukeswarar Temple,
 Thiruvanaikkaval 86
Janaka 87
Jatayu 69, 247
Javadhi Hills 52
Jayalakshmi Vilas Palace, Mysore ..292
Jerusalem Church, Tranquebar 67
Jesuit missionaries 403, 460
Jesus Christ......................................375

Jew Town, Mattancherry..................408
John Paul II, Pope.............................406
Jolarpettai 52, 56
Jurahareswarar shrine,
 Kumbakonam 71

K

Kabini River......................289, 306, 308
Kadambarai Reservoir 180
Kailasagiri Hills 243
Kailasanatha Temple,
 Kanchipuram 24
Kailash 145
Kalamkari paintings,
 Srikalahasti 243, 246
Kalapootu Cattle Race, Palakkad....324
Kalaripayattu 81, 389, 390
Kalhatti Falls, Nilgiris 206, 208
Kali, Goddess 382
Kaliyuga 71, 341
Kallai River.......................................390
Kallalar Stream 125
Kalpathy Agrahara, Palakkad ..324, 325
Kalpetta, Wayanad 430
Kalvappu 316
Kalvar, god..22
Kalyana Kattes, Tirumala 238
Kalyana Mahal, Gingee Fort 51
Kamakshi Amman Temple,
 Kanchipuram 22
Kamakshi, Goddess 103
Kamala Khanni Ammal shrine,
 Gingee Fort...................................51
Kamalalayam Tank, Thiruvarur 118
Kamalavati 86
KAMARAJAR VALLEY **124**, 126
Kambathadi Mandapam, Madurai ..156
Kanadukathan, Chettinad 135
Kanakasabhai, Chidambaram 59
Kanchanamala, Queen 154
Kanchi Kamakoti Peetham,
 Kanchipuram 22, 73
Kanchi Kudil Museum,
 Kanchipuram 26
KANCHIPURAM **21**, 73, 103
Kandal Church, Ooty 195
Kannagi 366
Kannappa Nils 245
Kanthampara Falls, Wayanad.........431
Kappad Beach, Kozhikode......386, 390
Karaikal...**69**
Karaikkudi, Chettinad 132, 138
Karalad Lake, Thariode...................433
Karian Shola, IGWLS 180
Karighatta, Srirangapatna 287
Karikili Bird Sanctuary **31**
Karnataka 289, 466
Karpaga Vinayakar Temple,
 Chettinad 138
Karthigai Deepam, Thiruvannamalai...48
Karthigai Festival, Swamimalai 78
Karuvurar, Saint 102

INDEX

Kasi Viswanathar Temple,
  Kumbakonam 72
Katavapra 316
Kathakali 17
Kattale-basadi, Sravanabelagola 316
kattumarams 112
kavadi 145
Kavanthikkara Boat Race,
  Vembanad Backwaters 422
Kavil Bhagwati Temple,
  Changanassery 382
Kaviratna 316
Kavunji Village, Kodaikanal 171
Kayarohanaswamy Temple,
  Nagapattinam 113
Kerala 312, 375, 387, 466
Kere Thonnur **288**
Kesavan Para, Nelliyampathy 335
Ketty Valley, Nilgiris..........193, 195, 477
Khalasis 392
Khan, Ebrahim 114
Khan, Kublai 407
Khan, Sanjay 257
Kilikoondu Mandapam, Madurai 156
Killiyur Falls, Yercaud 121
Klaveri Village 463, 464
KOCHI..**400**
Kochi rajas 401, 407
KODAIKANAL **169**, 172, 196, 462
Kodanad Estate, Kotagiri 190
Koder House, Fort Kochi 405
Koder, Samuel 405
Kodi Lake 171, 172
Kodimatha, Kottayam 373, 376
Kodoor River 373
Kokrebellur Pelicanry **278**
Kolhapur 233
Kollata Vizha Festival, Madurai 157
Kollengode **338**
Kollidam River 82, 112
Komalavalli Thayar, goddess 72
Kone, Ananda 51
Kongensgade, Tranquebar 66
Konkanastha Brahmin......................449
Kopperunjingan, King 61
Korapuzha River 390
Kotagiri **190**, 466, 469
kottans, Karaikuddi 135, 139
KOTTAYAM.........................**372**, 456
Kovilur 464
KOZHIKODE................................**385**
Krishna Mandapam,
  Mahabalipuram 16
Krishna Raja Sagar Dam, Mysore ..300
Krishna, Nanditha 233
Krishnagiri Hill, Gingee 51
Krishnamurthy, J 252
Krishna's Butterball,
  Mahabalipuram 16
Krishnattam,
  Guruvayurappan Temple 349
Kuchipudi 17

Kudamurutti River 108
Kukkarahalli Lake Bund, Mysore 296
Kulam, Peer 115
Kulasekara Pandyan, King 154, 156
KUMARAKOM **420**
Kumarakom Arpookara Vanitha
  Jalmela, Kumarakom 422
Kumarapuram Temple, Palakkad 326
Kumaraswamy Hills.........................245
KUMBAKONAM **70**
Kura Tirtham, Kumbakonam..............71
Kuriakose, Benny 135
Kurinji Andavar Temple,
  Kodaikanal 171
kurinji flowers 122, 171, 208
Kurmasaila.....................................248
Kuru Mund, Parson's Valley 217
Kuthus, Saeeda Fathima.................114
Kuttanad 420
Kuttichera, Kozhikode....................387
Kuttikanam 370
Kyatedevaragudi 304

L

Lady Canning's Seat, Nilgiris 470
Lady's Seat, Yercaud 121
Lady's Tank, Vailankanni 115
Lakhadweepotsava,
  Srirangapatna 284
Lakkidi 432
Lakshadweep Sea...........................402
Lakshmana Teertha River 308, 312
Lalitha Mahal Palace, Mysore 292
Lamb's Rock, Nilgiris 187, 470
Lawrence School, Lovedale 477
Law's Falls, Nilgiris 188, 470
Legislative Assembly, Pondicherry ...36
LEPAKSHI....................................**247**
Lighthouse, Karaikal 69
Lighthouse, Pondicherry 33
Lingambudhi Lake, Mysore 296
Lion Safari, Bannerghatta NP 265
Lion's Park, Kozhikode 389
Loafer's Corner, Fort Kochi.............407
Lokapavani River............................287
Longwood Shola, Nilgiris 190, 470
Lovedale, Nilgiris 477

M

M.Rm.Rm.House,
  Kanadukathan 135, 139
Maampara Peak 336
Maanika Vinayakar Temple,
  Tiruchirapalli 83
Macau 116
Madha Kulam, Vailankanni 115
Madhil 87
Madhurapuri 154
MADURAI **151**, 366
Maha Shivaratri, Chidambaram 61
MAHABALIPURAM **14**, 24
Mahabharata 166

Mahadevapura............................**288**
Mahal, Horsley Hills 251
Mahalakshmi, Goddess 72
Mahalingeswarar, Thiruvidaimarudur..75
Mahamaham Tank,
  Kumbakonam....................70, 71, 72
Mahamastakabhisheka,
  Sravanabelagola.........................316
Mahavira 314
Mahendran Raja Prakaram,
  Srirangam 85
Mahishasura 296
Mahishasuramardini Cave Temple,
  Mahabalipuram 16
mahseer...275
Malabar Church, Mannanam 380
Malabar House, Fort Kochi.............405
Malaikottai, Tiruchirapalli 82, 83
Malampuzha...............................**332**
Malavalli...282
Male Mahadeshwara Betta **305**
Mamara Guhai, Thiruvannamalai 50
Mammallapuram 14
Mammiyur Mahadevan Temple,
  Guruvayur 350
Manakula Vinayakar Temple,
  Pondicherry 35
Mananchira Square, Kozhikode 387
Manappullikaavu Bhagavathy Temple,
  Palakkad 324
Manasa Gangothri, Mysore 296
Mangaladevi Temple, Periyar TR 366
Mangalambigai, Goddess..................71
Mangani Festival, Karaikal 69
Mangayarkarasi Mandapam,
  Madurai 155
Manikapur 114
Manikkavachagar, Avudayarkovil 142
Mannanam..................................**300**
Mannavunar, Kodaikanal 171, 463
Maratha rulers 71, 100
Mariamman Temple, Thanjavur 103
Mariamman Theppakulam,
  Madurai 158
Mariamman, Goddess 96, 452
Marine Drive, Ernakulam.................409
Markandaya......................................68
Marthoma Mariam Big Church,
  Thrissur 343
Martyr's Memorial, Cherthala 460
Masilamani Nathar Temple,
  Tranquebar 67
Masinagudi 224
Mastan Syed Dawood Dargah,
  Karaikal 69
Mathiketan Shola 463
Matrimandir, Auroville 44
Mattancherry, Kochi 403, 407
Maurya, Emperor Chandragupta 313
Mayabunder Beach,
  Middle Andaman 424
Mayanmudi Peak 335

INFORMATION

INFORMATION

Medicinal Plant Conservation Area,
    IGWLS 180
Meenachil River.................................373
Meenakshi Amman Temple,
    Madurai...153
Meenakshi Kalyanam Chittirai
    Thiruvizha,Thiruparamkundram ..158
Meenakshi Naickan Mandapam,
    Madurai...155
Meenmutty Falls, Wayanad 432
Meeran Sahib Abdul Qadir Shahul
    Hamid Badshah 114
Mekedatu **278**
Melagiri Hills **98**
Melattur 472
Merchant, Ismail 404
Mettupalaiyam 474
Mettur Dam **98**, 121
Mirza Hill, Bannerghatta NP 268
Mishkaal Mosque, Kozhikode 387
Mission House, Arikamedu 44
Mithai Theruvu, Kozhikode 388
Mohideen, AR Syed Haja 114
Mohiudeen Mosque, Kozhikode......388
Montfort School, Yercaud 122
Moran, Carritt 405
Moti Talab Lake 288
Mount Govardhan 16
Mount Kailash 154
Moyar River 190, 207, 220, 224
Mucchandipalli Mosque,
    Kozhikode.....................................387
Mudali Pillai Mandapam,
    Madurai...155
Mudaliar, Kadanthai 155
Mudi Mund, Parson's Valley 217
**MUDUMALAI WILDLIFE
    SANCTUARY** ..207, 211, **219**, 308, 467
Mukhadwara, Tirumala 235
Mukkombu, Tiruchirapalli 90
Mukkuruni Vinayakar..................59, 156
Mukurthi Amman Temple 217
Mukurthi Lake, Nilgiris 216, 467
Mukurthi National Park 215, 467
Mulavakadu Island, Kochi................410
Mulla Periyar Lake 356, 360
Mullackal, Alappuzha 449, 452
mundus 392
Munnar 462
Murugan Temple, Jalagamparai 56
Murugan, Lord 53, 108, 158
Musical pillars, Pallathur 135
Muthiah, S 135
Muthuswamy Dikshitar's home,
    Thiruvarur 119
Muthuthandava, poet 58
MYSORE **289**, 304, 308

N

Nachiar Kovil **75**
nadaswaram 71, 473
Nadu Thittu, Vailankanni 116
naduvazhis 408
Nagadasapattinam **98**
Naganathaswamy, Thiruvarur 119
NAGAPATTINAM **112**
Nagara Kovil, Chettinad 138
Nagarathars, Chettinad....................133
**NAGARHOLE
    NATIONAL PARK** 222, **306**
Nagas 166
Nagore Dargah 114
Naik, Achutappa 114, 472
Nair, P Kunhiraman 338
Nakkerar, Sangam poet 148
Nallamalai Range 250
nalukettu 375
Namboodiri Brahmins, Palakkad 326
Nandi............................102, 108, 296
Nandi Dwaja, Mysore 294
NANDI HILLS **271**
Narada, Sage 145, 232
Narasimha Jayanti...........................472
Narasimha, Lord 473
Narasimhavarman II 24
Narasingha Chaitanya Mutt,
    Srirangapatna 286
Narayan, RK 291
Nataraja Sannidhi, Madurai 156
Nataraja Temple,
    Chidambaram 57, 58
Natesan, America 136
Natharsha Dargah,
    Tiruchirapalli 81, 88
Natharvalli, Baba 88
nattukottais 133, 138
Natural History Museum, Thrissur ..343
Natya Mandapa, Lepakshi 248
Natyanjali Festival, Chidambaram 61
Navagraha sthalas 102
Navalar, Gulam Qadir 114
Navaratri, Kanchipuram 22
Nayak Kings 21, 71, 76, 100, 113
Nayak, King Raghunatha 65
Nayanmars 142
Nayanotsav, Mysore 298
Neelayadakshi, Goddess 113
Nehru Trophy Boat Race 448, 456
Nehru, Jawaharlal 272, 456
Nellikota Peak 335
NELLIYAMPATHY **334**
Nellukadai Mariamman Temple,
    Nagapattinam...............................114
Nemam, Chettinad 138
Nenmara-Vellangi Vela, Palakkad ...324
Netherlands 410
Nilathunda, God 23
Nilgiri Biosphere
    Reserve 210, 222, 308
Nilgiri Hills........182, 196, 206, 215, 220
Nilgiri Mountain Railway 474
Nilgiri tahr 182, 217
Nilgiris Wildlife and Environment
    Association, Ooty................196, 470

Ninth Mile, Ooty 196
Nitya Pradosham, Thiruvarur 119
Njayapilli 436
Noopurangangai, Azhagar Kovil 166
Norton Bungalow, Yercaud 121
Notre Dame de Lourdes Church,
    Villianur 38
Notre Dame des Anges Church,
    Pondicherry 34

O

Observatory, Kodaikanal 170
Ochanthuruthu Lighthouse, Kochi ..410
Odegala Basadi, Sravanabelagola ...315
Old Harbour Hotel, Fort Kochi 405
Old Testament scrolls 408
Oonjal Mandapam:
    Avudayarkovil 142
    Madurai..156
OOTY **192**, 216, 266
Orchidarium, Yercaud 122
Our Lady of Health, Vailankanni 116
Our Lady of Lourdes Cathedral,
    Tiruchirapalli 88

P

Padagiri 335
Padmavati, Goddess 239
Paes, Domingo 96
Pagoda Point, Yercaud 121
Pahalavi..374
Pakalpooram, Ernakulam 409
Palace Museum, Thanjavur 104
Palada, Nilgiris.................................210
Palaeolithic Era 88
PALAKKAD **322**
PALANI 127, **144**, 196
Palayam Market, Kozhikode 388
Palayur Church 351
Palghat Gap 180
Pallathur, Chettinad.........................135
Pallava dynasty 14, 21, 82
Palluruthi Temple, Mattancherry......407
Pamba River 170, 358
Panachikkad Temple......................**382**
Pancha Ratham,
    Mahabalipuram 15, 16
Pancha Tirtham, Kanchipuram 22
Panchabhoota Shivasthala:
    Chidambaram 57
    Srikalahasti 81
    Thiruvannaikaval 46
    Thiruvannamalai 243
Panchanatheesvarar Temple,
    Thiruvaiyaru 108
panchavadyam 323
Pandavapura, Srirangapatna 286
Pandavas 16, 270, 286
Pandimelam, Ernakulam 409
Panditahalli 281
Pandya rulers 75, 133
Pandya Temple, Tranquebar 67

INDEX

Pandyan, King Malayadwaja 154
Pandyan, Maravarma Kulasekara......67
Pandyanadu 145
panther 280
Papavinasha Tirtham, Tirumala 239
Parambikulam WLS 180
Paramekavu Bhagavathy Temple,
  Thrissur 342
Parasurama 341
Pardesi Synagogue, Mattancherry ..408
parisals, Hogenakkal Falls 96
PARSON'S VALLEY...............**215**, 467
Parthasarathy Temple, Guruvayur ..350
Paschimavahini Bridge,
  Srirangapatna 286
Patala Lingam Sannidhi,
  Thiruvannamalai 48
Patanjali, Sage 58, 81, 92
Pathiramanal Island 375, 422
Pattalam Mosque, Kozhikode 387
Payippad Boat Race, Alappuzha 456
Payyoli Beach **396**
Pazhamudircholai **148**, 164
Pazhassi Raja Museum,
  Kozhikode....................................389
Pazhayapalli Mosque,
  Changanassery 382
Peer Mohammed, Sufi Saint...........370
Peermade **370**
Peeru Hills 370
pelicans 278
Periya 101
Periya Minor's veedu, Devakottai ...138
Periya Nayaki Amman Temple,
  Palani 150
Periyar Foundation, Periyar TR........358
Periyar River 436, 442
PERIYAR TIGER RESERVE **354**
Periyayaudayar Temple, Palani.......149
Persian..285
Persian Crosses 374
Perumal Peak, Kodi Hills 172
Perumal, King Cheraman 146
petanque, Pondicherry 40
Pierce Leslie Bungalow,
  Fort Kochi 405
Pillai, Thakazhi Sivasankaran 446
Pillaiyarpatti Kovil, Chettinad 138
Pillar Rocks, Kodaikanal 171
Pitchavaram Backwaters **61**
Planetarium, Kozhikode 389
Podhigai Hill 145
Pollachi 180
PONDICHERRY **32**, 69
Pookote Lake 432
Poombarai Village, Kodaikanal 171
Pooram Festival:
  Arattupuzha 346
  Nagapattinam 113
  Thrissur 342
Portamarai Kulam,
  Sarangapani Temple.....................72

Porthi Mund Lake 212, 217, 467
Portuguese........................96, 116, 374,
  ....386, 390, 401
Pothundy Reservoir.........................334
Pottramarai Kulam Tank, Madurai ..156
Prahlada Charitram 473
Princess Street, Fort Kochi.............406
Printing Press, Tranquebar 67
Public Library, Kozhikode 387
Pudukottai, Chettinad 133
Puliyar 58
Punganoor Lake, Yelagiri Hills 53
Punnamada Kayal, Alleppey....448, 456
Punnathoorkotta, Guruvayur 351
Punnoose, Raji 422
punugu 71, 84
Puranas 71, 76, 156
Putridankonda Peruman 119
Pykara Lake..........................**204**, 467

R

R Block, Alleppey 449
Radha Madhava Temple,
  Srirangapatna 286
Rail Museum, Mysore 294
Raj Niwas, Pondicherry 34, 35
Raja, Samuthiri 387
Rajaraja II, King 76
Rajaraja Museum, Thanjavur 103
Raja's Cliff, Nelliyampathy 336
Rajendra Vilas Palace, Mysore 292
Rajgiri Hill, Gingee............................51
Rakayi Amman Temple,
  Azhagar Kovil 166
Ramana Ashram, Thiruvannamalai....47
Ramana Maharishi 46
Ramanuja, Sri 27
Ramanujacharya, Sri................85, 234
Ramanujan, Srinivasa 70
Ramayana 69
Rameswaram 75
Ranga Vimana, Srirangam 82
Ranganathaswamy Temple:
  Srirangam 84
  Srirangapatna 284
Ranganathittu Bird Sanctuary **286**
Rangapillai, Ananda 33, 38
Ratnam, Mani 96
Ravana 82, 247
Raya, Achyuta Deva 247
Razaq, Abdur 386
RED HILLS **210**, 468
Revathi Pattathanam, Kozhikode 388
Rheede, Hendrik Adrian Van...........404
Rishi Valley School 252
Rockefeller, David 257
Rockfort, Tiruchirapalli 82
Roerich, Nicholas 292
Roja 96
Romain Rolland Library,
  Pondicherry 35
Roman amphorae 44

Ropeway, Malampuzha...................332
Rose Garden, Ooty 194
Rose Lane, Fort Kochi 405
Rue du Bazar, Pondicherry 34
Rue Dumas, Pondicherry 34
Rue Romain Rolland, Pondicherry 34
Rue Surcouf, Pondicherry................34
Runavimochanar, Thiruvarur 119
Russell's Viper 442

S

Sadayandi Cave Temple,
  Kamarajar Valley..........................127
Sahasra Linga Temple,
  Srikalahasti 246
Sahyadri Range...............................334
SALIM ALI BIRD SANCTUARY **436**
Samuthiri rulers, Kozhikode 386
Sangam..**278**
Sangam Age 156
Sangama Shrine, Srirangapatna......285
Sani Bhagvan, Nagapattinam..........113
Saniswarar, Lord 84
Sankara Jayanthi, Kanchipuram.......22
Sankara Mutt, Kanchipuram.............24
Sankara Samadhi, Thrissur.............341
Sankara, Adi 22, 24, 86, 341, 347
Santa Cruz Basilica, Fort Kochi 406
Santhana Ganapathy 22
Saptagiri Range...............................233
Sarabhai, Mallika 262
Sarabhoji II 104
Sarangapani Temple,
  Kumbakonam 72
Saraswati Mahal, Thanjavur 103
Saraswati, Paramacharya
  Sri Chandrasekhara 24
Saravana Poigai Temple, Palani 149
Saravanapoigai Tank,
  Thiruparamkundram.....................157
Sarkarai Padithurai Ghat,
  Kumbakonam 73
Sassanid Dynasty 374
Sastri, Venkatramana 472
Sattanur Dam..................................**51**
Satur, Inchanna 323
Schwartz Church, Thanjavur...........103
Schwartz, Rev Christian Fredriech ..104
Sebastian, St 460
Seethargundu, Nelliyampathy.........335
Selva Mansion, Pondicherry 33
Sentinel Rockfalls, Wayanad 432
Seraikar Mandapam, Madurai 155
Seshadri Swamigal Ashram,
  Thiruvannamalai 50
Sethumadai 181
Seville 390
Shakthan Thampuran Palace,
  Thrissur 342
Shaktigiri Hill 145
Shaktipeeths 244
Shankar, Ravi 262

INFORMATION

Shanmugha River 147, 149
Sharajah Madi, Thanjavur 104
Shembaganur Museum,
  Kodaikanal 172
Shevaroy Hills 120
Shimsapura 282
Shiva Gangai Tirtham,
  Thiruvannamalai 47
Shiva Kanchi, Kanchipuram 22
Shiva Purana 47
Shiva Temple:
  Ernakulam 408
  Ettumanur 380
  Thattekkad 437
  Thirukaikundram 18
Shiva, Lord 68, 244
Shivagangai Tirtham, Kanchipuram ..23
Shivakshetrapadi, Salim Ali BS 436
Shivalingams 102
SHIVANASAMUDRAM **279**
Shola forests 196, 283
Sholayar Reservoir 180
Shore Temple, Mahabalipuram 15
Shyama Shastri's home,
  Thiruvarur 119
Sigur Plateau, Nilgiris 206, 224
Sila Toranam, Tirumala 238
Silappadhikaram 154, 325, 366
Silk Farm, Yercaud 121
Silver Cascade Falls, Kodaikanal ...171
Sim's Park, Coonoor 187
Singar, Azhagiya 24
Sistine Chapel, Vatican 406
Sita 87
Sivaganga 133
Sivaganga Fort, Thanjavur 101
Sivagiri Hill 145
Skanda Sashti, Swamimalai 78
Skandashramam, Thiruvannamalai ..46
Small Lake, Yercaud 121
Snake Park, Thrissur 343
Soliga tribals, BR Hills 304
Solomon 408
Soorakkudi, Chettinad 138
Soundararaja Perumal Temple,
  Nagapattinam 113
Soundarya Lakshmi, goddess 22
sphatika lingam 59
SRAVANABELAGOLA **313**
Sri Aurobindo Ashram,
  Pondicherry 32, 34, 35
Sri Aurobindo International Centre
  for Education, Auroville 35
Sri Jayachamarajendra Art Galley,
  Mysore 292
Sri Jayachamarajendra Zoo,
  Mysore 296
SRIKALAHASTI **243**
Srinivasa Ramanujan House,
  Kumbakonam 73
Srinivasamangapuram Temple,
  Tirumala 239

Sriperumbudur.................................27
Srirangam 47, 81, 84
SRIRANGAPATNA **283**, 291, 300
St Andrew's Church, Arthunkal........460
St Andrew's Church, Orlypet,
  Pondicherry 38
St Catherine Falls, Nilgiris...............469
St Francis' Church, Fort Kochi 403
St George Church, Wellington 188
St John's Church, Tiruchirapalli 88
St Joseph's Church, Mannanam 380
St Mary's Knanaya Church,
  Kottayam 374
St Mary's Metropolitan Cathedral,
  Changanassery 382
St Mary's Orthodox Church,
  Kottayam 374
St Philomena's Church, Mysore 294
St Stephen's Church, Ooty 195
St Thomas Church, Ooty 195
Sthala Shayana Perumal,
  Mahabalipuram...............................15
Stomberg Bastion, Fort Kochi 405
Stone Dam, Tiruchirapalli 90
Stone Mound, Parson's Valley 217
Studer Hall, Fort Kochi 406
Subhadeva 86
Subrahmanya Swamy Temple,
  Srikalahasti 245
Subrahmanya, Lord 48
Suchipara Waterfalls, Wayanad 431
Sullivan, John 194
Sultan, Bahmani 472
Summer Palace, Srirangapatna 285
Sundareshwarar, Lord 154, 156
Sundarvalli Thayar..........................166
Surya Pushkarni tank,
  Thiruvaiyaru 110
Swamigal, Seshadri 48
Swamimalai **76**
Swamimalai Hill, Yelagiris 54
Swaminatha Swamy Temple,
  Swamimalai 76
Swamipushkarni Tirtha,
  Tirumala 233, 237
Swaraj Round, Thrissur..................341
Swarnamukhi River................243, 245
Syrian Knanaya Christians 374

T

Tamil Quarter, Pondicherry 33, 36
Tanjore 71
Tapas Kamakshi, Kanchipuram 22
Tarangambadi 65
Taxidermic Museum,
  Salim Ali BS 438, 442
Telengana 472
Temple Car Festival, Tiruchirapalli ...83
Thakur House, Fort Kochi..............404
Thali Temple, Kozhikode................388
Thamarassery Ghat........................432
Thampuran, Shakthan 340, 343, 409

THANJAVUR 78, **99**, 134, 472
Thattekkad, Salim Ali BS 436
Thayar Sannidhi, Srirangam 85
Thayumanavar Temple,
  Tiruchirapalli 83
Thazathangady Juma Masjid,
  Kottayam 373, 375
The Grange, Yercaud 122
The Mother 35
The Obelisk, Srirangapatna 284
The Old Courtyard, Fort Kochi 405
Thekkady 356
Thekkumkur Raja 373, 382
Theppakadu Elephant Camp,
  Mudumalai 223, 468
Theppotsavam, Madurai 119, 157
Thikkodi Light House **396**
Thillai Kali Amman Temple,
  Chidambaram 61
Thillai Mandapam, Avudayarkovil 142
Thillai Temple, Chidambaram 57
Thiru Kalyanam 86
Thiruavinankudi Temple,
  Palani 145, 147
Thiruchendur 148
Thirukaikundram **18**
Thirukalyana Mandapam, Madurai..155
Thirumalai Nayak Palace, Madurai..158
Thirumanjana Veedhi, Thiruvaiyaru...110
Thirumurthi Reservoir 180
Thirumurugatrupadai......................148
Thirunakkara Maidanam, Kottayam 374
Thiruparamkundram...............148, **157**
Thirupattur **92**
Thiruppugazh 48
Thiruthani 148
Thiruvaiyaru................................**108**
Thiruvambady Krishna Temple,
  Thrissur 342
Thiruvanaikkaval, Srirangam...........86
THIRUVANNAMALAI **46**
Thiruvarur **117**
Thiruvidaimarudur.........................**75**
Tholkappiar 234
Thomas, St 351
Thoppumpady Bazaar, Kochi 402
Thousand Pillar Hall and Museum,
  Madurai.......................................155
Thousand Pillar Hall, Srirangam 85
Thousand Pillared Hall,
  Kanchipuram 23
THRISSUR **340**
Thyagaraja Aradhanai Festival,
  Thiruvaiyaru 110
Thyagaraja Mandapam,
  Avudayarkovil 140
Thyagaraja, Sri 110, 118, 119
Thyagarajaswamy Temple,
  Thiruvarur 117, 118
Thyy Poosam, Swamimalai..............78
tiger 178, 308
Tiger Cave, Mahabalipuram 16

INDEX

Tipu Sultan ....187, 272, 283, ...285, 288, 289, 291
Tipu's Drop, Nandi Hills 273
Tipu's Fort, Palakkad 323
Tirthankara 314, 316
TIRUCHIRAPALLI **81**
TIRUMALA **231**
Tirumanjanam, Chidambaram 61
Tirumurthi Cave Temple,
   Mahabalipuram...............................16
TIRUPATI **231**, 238
Tirupattur 56
Tiruvoodal, Thiruvannamalai 48
Toda tribe, Nilgiris 212
Todaramallu 236
Tolkappiyam 48
Top Slip, IGWLS 179, 181
Top Station 462
Town Hall:
   Kozhikode....................................387
   Pondicherry 33
TRANQUEBAR................................**64**
Travancore 356, 370, 446
Tribal Heritage Museum,
   Periyar TR...................................362
Trichy Museum, Tiruchirapalli 88
Trout Hatchery, Ooty...............196, 212
tsunami, 2004 ....15, 113
Tutu, Archbishop Desmond 262

U

Uchchi Pillaiyar Kovil,
   Tiruchirapalli 83
Uddigebende, Bannerghatta NP 270
Udhagamandalam 192, 475
Udumalpet Taluk 180
Ulaganatha Temple,
   Mahabalipuram...............................16
Ulandi Range, IGWLS 181
Ulubi 166
UNESCO World Heritage sites:
   Darasuram 76
   Gangaikondacholapuram..............78
   Mahabalipuram.............................14
   Thanjavur 102
Union Church, Ooty 194
Upper Aliyar River 180
Upper Bhavani Lake, Nilgiris ..211, 212
urus 392
Uruva Eco Shop, Pookote Lake 433
Usha, PT 396
Uthamar Kovil 87
Uttamalai 96
Uttarayana, Thiruvannamalai 48

V

Vaathiya Mandapam, Palani 149
Vadakara, Kozhikode 389
Vadakkan Veera Gatha 389
Vadakkanthara Temple, Palakkad....325
Vadakkunnathan Temple, Thrissur ..341
Vadavar River 108

Vaigai River 154, 158, 172
Vaikasi Utsavam, Madurai 157
Vaikuntha..232
Vaikuntha Ekadashi, Srirangam 85
Vaikunthadwaras, Tirumala.............235
Vailankanni Church **115**
Vairavan Kovil, Chettinad 138
Vairavar Temple, Pallathur...............135
Vajpayee, Atal Behari 420
Vajra Tirtham, Swamimalai 76
Valaikaappu Mandapam,
   Thiruvannamalai 47
Valayanad Devi Temple,
   Kozhikode 388
Valiapally, Kottayam 374
Valiya Angadi, Kozhikode 388
Valiyavana Peak 335
Vallabha Ganapati, Madurai 155
Valparai 180
Van Goens, Governor 405
Vandarvu 462, 464
Vanmeeganathar, Thiruvarur....118, 119
Varadarajaswamy 235
Varahaswamy Temple, Tirumala......237
Varanasi 75
Vardaraja Perumal Temple,
   Kanchipuram 23, 24
Vardaraja Perumal Temple,
   Pondicherry 36
Vardaraja Temple, Srikalahasti 246
Varma Kalai, martial art.....................81
Varma, Chithira
   Thirunal Balarama 356
Varma, Raja Ravi 292
Varma, Udya Mathanda 382
Varman I, Narasimha........................14
Vasantha Mandapam,
   Kanchipuram 22
Vasco Da Gama Square,
   Fort Kochi............................403, 407
Vasco House, Fort Kochi 406
Veda...23
VEDANTHANGAL
BIRD SANCTUARY **28**
Vedapureswarar Temple,
   Pondicherry 36
Veeragase dancers 294
Veeranahoasahalli 310
Vegavathi River, Kanchipuram 21, 23
Vekkaliamman Temple, Woraiyur 88
Vela Vanchan Peak 335
Velangudi, Chettinad 138
Vellachimudi Peak 335
vellichappads 324
Velvan Temple, Yelagiri Hills 53
Vembanad Lake 373, 402, 421
Venkatadri Hill, Tirumala 231, 233
Venkateswara Temple,
   Tirumala 231, 235
Venkatramana Temple, Karighatta ..287
Venkitachalapathy Temple,
   Guruvayur 350

Vennar River 108
Verma, Mahendra King 83
Vettar River 108
Vibhishana 82
Vijayadashmi, Mysore 293
Vijayanagar Kings.....................21, 54, ...150, 247, 284
Vinayaka Chaturthi, Srikalahasti 245
Vinayaka, Lord 84, 108
Vindhyagiri Hill, Sravanbelagola 315
Virbhadra Shrine, Lepakshi.............248
Virupaksha Cave, Thiruvannamalai ..50
Virupanna 247
Visharoopa Darshanam Puja,
   Srirangam 84
Vishishtadwaita 27
Vishnu Temple, Kollengode 338
Vishnu, Lord 113
Vishwanathaswamy Temple,
   Palakkad 325
VK Krishna Menon Art Gallery,
   Kozhikode..................................389
Vyaghrapuri 58
Vypeen, Kochi 410
VYTHIRI **430**

W

Wandoor Beach, Port Blair 424
War Memorial, Pondicherry 33
Wayanad 222, 306, 430
Wellesley Bridge,
   Srirangapatna......................284, 287
Wellington, Nilgiris 188, 195, 477
Wenlock Downs, Ooty 195
Western Catchment Area Reserve
   Forest, Nilgiris 212, 215, 217
Western Ghats ....182, 195, ...222, 430, 466
Willingdon Island, Kochi 402, 409
Wodeyar, Chikka Devaraja 289
Wodeyar, Krishnaraja IV 292
Wodeyars 284, 289, 294, 304

X

Xavier, St Francis 404

Y

Yakshi 382
yazhis..17, 24
YELAGIRI HILLS **52**
Yenugu Mallamma Konda,
   Horsley Hills 250
YERCAUD....................................**120**
Yoga sutras 81
Yogambigai shrine, Avudayarkovil ..142
Yoganandeeshwara Temple,
   Nandi Hills 271, 273

Z

Ziegenbalg, Bartolomeus 67
Zoffany, Johann..............................285
Zoo, Bannerghatta NP 268

OTHER TITLES FROM OUTLOOK TRAVELLER GETAWAYS

   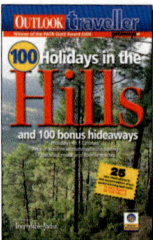

52 Weekend Breaks from Delhi
ISBN 81-901724-4-1
512 pages

52 Weekend Breaks from Mumbai
ISBN 81-901724-3-3
480 pages

52 Weekend Breaks from Bangalore
ISBN 81-901724-2-5
512 pages

100 Holidays in the Hills
ISBN 81-901724-6-8
544 pages

Kerala with Lakshadweep State Guide
ISBN 81-89449-01-X
720 pages

64 Wildlife Holidays in India
ISBN 81-89449-02-8
720 pages

101 Pilgrimages
ISBN 81-89449-03-6
1,088 pages

Rajasthan State Guide
ISBN 81-89449-05-2
512 pages

INTERNATIONAL TITLES FROM OUTLOOK TRAVELLER

  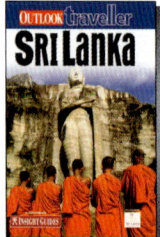 

In association with Insight Guides
Fourth Edition
368 pages

In association with Insight Guides
Seventh Edition
400 pages

In association with Insight Guides
Fifth Edition
304 pages

In association with Insight Guides
Fifth Edition
356 pages

Heritage Holidays in
North & Central India
ISBN 81-901724-5-X
544 pages

Heritage Holidays in
South, West & East India
ISBN 81-901724-8-4
576 pages

Goa State Guide
ISBN 81-901724-9-2
544 pages

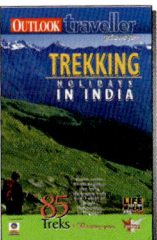

Trekking Holidays
in India
ISBN 81-89449-00-1
576 pages

Uttarakhand State
Guide
ISBN 81-89449-06-0
528 pages

HIMACHAL STATE GUIDE

Coming Soon!

WELLNESS HOLIDAYS IN INDIA

Coming Soon!

BEACH HOLIDAYS IN INDIA

Coming Soon!

Introducing CITY GUIDES

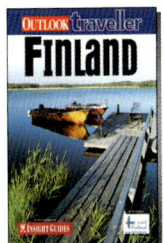

In association with
Insight Guides
Third Edition
328 pages

In association with
Insight Guides
Fifth Edition
376 pages

Delhi and NCR City Guide
ISBN 81-89449-04-4
528 pages

PHOTO CREDITS

Back Cover
At Nagapattinam Beach GANESHMUTHU

Inside the book

ATUL LOKE
SECTION OPENER Page 321 Backwater village near Alleppey

DELEKS NAMGYAL/ PHOTOINDIA
CONTENTS Page 5 Tiger greets visitors at the Bannerghatta National Park

GANESHMUTHU
CONTENTS Page 5 Building castles at the Nagapattinam Beach
SECTION OPENER Page 229 Devotional CDs at a shop near Sri Govindarajaswami Temple, Tirupati

LOKESH ABROL
SECTION OPENER Page 185 Tea gardens in the Nilgiri Hills

M BALAN/ SOUTHINDIAPICTURE
SECTION OPENER Page 13 Terracotta mural on the wall of a resort in Swamimalai

PRASHANT PANJIAR
CONTENTS Page 5 Bathing in an Alappuzha canal
Page 7 Sheepish looks at Kodaikanal

RAKESH SAHAI/ AGP PHOTOBANK
CONTENTS Page 6 Krishna's Butter Ball at Mahabalipuram

SAIBAL DAS
CONTENTS Page 4 Bath time at the Punathoor Kotta elephant sanctuary
Page 6 Tamilian household

V MUTHURAMAN
CONTENTS Page 4 The golden dome of the Nataraj Temple, Chidambaram
Page 7 Cable car ride at the Malampuzha Gardens; Going bananas at Guruvayur

VIVEK R SINHA/ WILDERFILE
SECTION OPENER Page 255 Tiger poses for the camera

WRIJU/ PHOTOINDIA
SECTION OPENER Page 461 Nilgiri Mountain Railway train moves towards Ooty

---

ACKNOWLEDGEMENTS

Outlook Traveller Getaways would like to thank the tourism officers of Tamil Nadu, Pondicherry, Andhra Pradesh, Karnataka and Kerala, Conservators of Forests and Wildlife Wardens of Tamil Nadu, Karnataka and Kerala, Lalitha Sridhar, Krishna Prasad, Latha Anantharaman, Mitali Saran, Sonia Shukla, Ashok Panda (INTACH, Pondicherry), E Saravanan of Wildlife District Office, Ooty, Raj Kumar and Ponni Arasu in Bangalore, Sibi Arasu in Chennai

WEEKEND BREAKS FROM CHENNAI

Outlook traveller

FEEDBACK FORM

We need your valuable suggestions to help us improve our guide and make it more user friendly. Mail this form to enable us to send you free updates on special packages, events and new destinations

PERSONAL INFORMATION

(BLOCK LETTERS PLEASE)

Name (Mr/ Ms) ....

Address ....

....

....

PIN Code ....

Tel. ....

Email ....

Age .... Gender: Male ☐ Female ☐

Occupation ....

Organisation ....

Single/ Married ....

No. of Children/ Ages ....

TRAVEL HISTORY

1. **How often do you take a vacation?**
   - Every 1-2 months ☐
   - Every 3-6 months ☐
   - Every 6-12 months ☐
   - Others (please specify) ☐
   ....

2. **How long was your last vacation?**
   - Weekend ☐
   - 1-2 weeks ☐
   - 2-4 weeks ☐
   - Others (please specify) ☐
   ....

3. **Where did you stay?**
   - Hotels/ Resorts ☐
   - Govt accommodation ☐
   - Friends/ Relatives ☐

4. **How much did you spend on your vacation?**
   - Less than Rs 5,000 ☐
   - Rs 5,000-Rs 10,000 ☐
   - Rs 10,000-Rs 20,000 ☐
   - Rs 20,000 and above ☐

5. **Your idea of a holiday?**
   - Adventure ☐
   - Leisure ☐
   - Pilgrimage ☐
   - Wildlife ☐
   - Others (please specify) ☐
   ....

6. **Do you refer to a guide during your travels?**
   Yes ☐ No ☐
   If yes, please specify ....

ABOUT US

1. **Where did you hear about this book?**
   - Advertising in the Outlook Group magazines ☐
   - Bookshop/ newsagent ☐
   - www.outlooktraveller.com ☐
   - Others (please specify) ☐
   ....

2. **Rate us**
   Excellent (E) Good (G) Fair (F) Average (A)
   - Content ☐   Design ☐
   - Destinations ☐   Facts ☐
   - Route guides ☐   Photographs ☐

YOUR RECOMMENDATIONS

I recommend for inclusion/ exclusion

Name of accommodation/ restaurant/ sights/ place
....
....

Address ....
....

Tel. ....

Reason ....
....
....

Make as many recommendations as you like. Attach with this form and drop it in the mail.

Mail to

The Editor
Outlook Traveller Getaways
AB-10, Safdarjung Enclave
New Delhi-110029